HISTORICAL MOMENTS

Changing Interpretations of America's Past

VOLUME **2**
Second Edition

The Civil War Through the 20th Century

Jim R. McClellan
Northern Virginia Community College

Dushkin/McGraw-Hill
A Division of The McGraw-Hill Companies

Book Team

Vice President and Publisher *Jeffrey L. Hahn*
List Manager *Theodore Knight*
Developmental Editor *Ava Suntoke*
Production Manager *Brenda S. Filley*
Director of Technology *Jonathan Stowe*
Designer *Charles Vitelli*
Typesetting Supervisor *Juliana Arbo*
Permissions Editor *Rose Gleich*
Proofreading Editors *Elizabeth Stevens, Diane Barker*
Copier Coordinator *Larry Killian*

Dushkin/McGraw-Hill

A Division of The McGraw-Hill Companies

Cover © 2000 PhotoDisc, Inc.
Cover Design *Thomas Goddard*

The credit section for this book begins on page 535 and is considered an extension of the copyright page.

Library of Congress Catalog Card Number 99-74550

ISBN 0-07-228383-1

Printed in the United States of America

2 3 4 5 6 7 8 9 10 FGR/FGR 0 5 4 3 2 1

http://www.mhhe.com

Preface

Two cars collide at an intersection surrounded by pedestrians. The sounds of the crash turn every head instantly. Shattering glass and pieces of metal fly off in every direction. Horns blare. A hubcap rolls across the road and comes to rest against the curb. A moment later, the whole incident is a part of history. Twenty witnesses see the accident, and it would seem an easy matter to piece together the story of what happened. Yet the twenty witnesses give twenty different accounts of what they think happened.

The truth about the past, whether of a minor matter or a matter of earth-shaking importance, is not easy to discover; yet the search for the truth is the goal of academic pursuit.

It is certain that the accident in question will in some way affect those directly involved. It may affect them enough to alter the course of the rest of their lives or only inconvenience them for a few days. If the public takes note at all, it may be in the form of a few words buried deep inside the next day's newspaper.

But it is also possible that the incident could affect the course of history. Seemingly insignificant events often do. Perhaps the accident delays a senator on the way to a crucial vote and the result is a change in the direction of government. Or, maybe the crash leads to the development of some automobile safety feature that subsequently saves the lives of thousands. Or maybe the accident takes the life of someone society finds irreplaceable.

The general public may be instantly aware that the accident has produced a turning point in history. Just as likely, years may pass before the importance of the event is recognized. Or, perhaps, its significance will never be fully understood. Succeeding generations will search for the truth. They will try to discover what happened, but the truth will most likely remain, like other forms of beauty, in the eyes of the beholder.

This work of two volumes attempts to present moments from the American past that in some way altered the course of history. It views these moments first through the eyes of those who lived them and then through the views of succeeding generations observing the moment from ever more distant vantage points over the passage of time. Each generation rewrites history. It has no choice but to do so. It finds itself at a place along the continuum of time different from that of its predecessors and must understand how it got there. It searches the records of the past to explain its present. Consequently, though what has passed cannot be changed, interpretations of what has passed are forever changing.

Each chapter in the book approaches its examination of a moment in history in a similar manner. Following an introduction to the event is a section entitled *First Impressions*. Here the event is described in the words of those who participated in it or through the commentary of contemporary observers. From the writings and speeches of participants, journalists, political leaders, scholars, and others, as well as from an examination of primary documents, a firsthand view of the event may be secured within the context of its times.

The next section is called *Second Thoughts*. It presents the ongoing effort to make sense of the past from a new vantage point. Some of the scholars represented in this section look at the past with the biases of their time; others seek to challenge those biases by drawing on the lessons of the past. All seek to make sense in their own time of the events that have led to their present.

The third section of each chapter is entitled *Questioning the Past*. A chapter might be conceived of as a seminar. Around the conference table sit scholars of the past and students of the present. After the topic is introduced with the words of those who lived it, scholars of succeeding generations offer their interpretations of the historical moment under review. Students of the present then continue the search for the meaning of the moment.

The moments chosen for inclusion in this book were selected because they in some way affected a large segment of the American people. Their impact may have been political, social, cultural, economic, diplomatic, psychological, or even a combination of these. No claim is made that the events studied in the chapters that follow constitute a complete listing of all the moments that have shaped the direction of American history. Indeed, every single moment finds the American people acting and reacting in ways that shape their course through history.

 New to this edition are Web sites that offer valuable resources to bring history to life. Look for them through the chapters. An annotated list of Web site addresses appears on page xxv.

The second edition has also benefited from the reviews of several scholars, whose suggestions merit the mention of their names here:

Lex Adler Sonoma State University

Martha Bonte Clinton Community College

Lillian Taiz California State University, Los Angeles

This work has also been enriched by the editing skills of Ava Suntoke of Dushkin/McGraw-Hill and by research assistance from Sylvia J. Rortvedt, librarian at the Alexandria Campus of Northern Virginia Community College, who was always quick to locate documents I could not. My wife, Catherine Lee Burwell, fortunately shares my interest in history and offered crucial support and encouragement to carry me through the necessary task of revision of the book.

Four chapters were added to Volume 2 for the second edition. One of the new chapters deals with questions arising from the effort to unite the country after the Civil War. A second looks at an aspect of American policy toward Latin America during the cold war. It focuses on the long civil war in Guatemala and the American role in that conflict. The environmental threats posed by the twentieth century are considered in a chapter on the Alaska oil spill of 1989. A chapter on the impeachment of President Clinton has also been included. In addition, new material has been added to chapters carried over from the first edition.

The final chapter—the one that would have pulled all history together into a unified and simple truth, revealed that the fundamental laws of physics, math, law, economics, nature, and cosmetology are integrated and obvious, and decoded the mysteries of life and VCR programming—was regrettably lost in the auto accident.

Jim R. McClellan

To my father-in-law Clayton Lee Burwell
and my friend and mentor Benjamin Spock—
both used their nine decades among us to make
the world a little better than they found it

About the Author

A native of Texas, Jim McClellan has served since 1975 on the faculty of Northern Virginia Community College, one of the nation's two largest community colleges. A professor of history, he teaches a wide variety of courses, most frequently American history and Native American history. He has also joined with colleagues to lead a number of seminars abroad, including field expeditions to the Maya lands of Mexico and Central America.

Dr. McClellan's previous publications and writing activities include articles on politics, book reviews, and a variety of scholarly pieces. *Historical Moments* was developed in his classroom in a continuing effort to challenge his students to think critically about historical events.

In 1997, the University of Texas at Arlington presented Professor McClellan with its Distinguished Alumni Award, the highest honor the university bestows on its graduates. He was also the recipient of the 1993–1994 Outstanding Distance Educator Award, presented by the College of the Air Tele-Consortium, for his history lectures broadcast over television in the Northern Virginia area.

Professor McClellan's many outside interests include the outdoors, travel, and community service. He is Commissioner of Human Rights and former chairman of the Alexandria Human Rights Commission. He currently serves as president of the Virginia Association of Human Rights Commissioners and has been a director of a school for adults with special needs and a child care center. He paddles his kayak on the Potomac daily, enjoys playing football and basketball, and fondly remembers dunking a basketball during halftime in front of 15,000 spectators at a Bulls game—from an exceptionally tall unicycle. In 1998, he won two silver and one bronze medals for sprint kayaking at the World Masters Games.

Contents in Brief

Contents

1 *Civil War*   **1**

1. *Diary of Gideon Welles,* Secretary of the Navy . . *1* / 2. *Alexandria Gazette and Virginia Advertiser* . . *3* / 3. Diary of Mary Boykin Chesnut, wife of General Beauregard's aide-de-camp, James Chesnut . . *5* / 4. *Alexandria Gazette and Virginia Advertiser* . . *5* / 5. Jefferson Davis's message to the Confederate Congress . . *6* / 6. President Abraham Lincoln's Special Session message . . *8* / 7. Henry Wilson, Radical Republican, speech to the United States Senate, May 1, 1862 . . *10* / 8. Clement L. Vallandigham, Democratic congressman for Ohio, "Speech on the War and Its Conduct," January 14, 1863 . . *11* / 9. Edward Pollard, editor of the *Richmond Examiner, The Lost Cause: A New Southern History of the War of the Confederates,* 1866 . . *12* / 10. Alexander H. Stephens, former vice president of the Confederacy, *A Constitutional View of the Late War between the States,* 1868 . . *13* / 11. Vice President Henry Wilson, a radical Republican, *The History of the Rise and Fall of Slavepower in America,* 1877 . . *13* / 12. James Ford Rhodes, *Lectures on the American Civil War,* 1913 . . *14* / 13. Charles and Mary Beard, *The Rise of American Civilization,* 1933 . . *14* / 14. Allan Nevins, *The Emergence of Lincoln,* 1950 . . *14* / 15. David Donald, *Lincoln Reconsidered,* 1961 . . *15* / 16. Eugene Genovese, *The Political Economy of Slavery,* 1967 . . *16* / 17. Howard Zinn, *A People's History of the United States,* 1980 . . *16*

2 *One Nation, Indivisible*   **18**

1. Correspondence between General U.S. Grant, United States Army, and General Robert E. Lee, commanding the Army of Northern Virginia, CSA . . *19* / 2. Editorial, "The Rebellion," *New York Times,* April 11, 1865 . . *21* / 3. Editorial "Lee Surrenders!" *New York Tribune,* April 12, 1865 . . *22* / 4. *Alexandria Gazette* of Virginia, April 12, 1865, reporting on the last public speech of Abraham Lincoln . . *23* / 5. Editorial, "Magnanimity in Triumph," *New York Tribune,* April 15, 1865 . . *24* / 6. Abolitionist Gerrit Smith, "Thoughts for the People," handbill, April 19, 1865 . . *25* / 7. Speech of President Andrew Johnson, April 21, 1865 . . *25* / 8. Editorial, "The Points to Be Secured before Reconstruction," *New York Times,* May 5, 1865 . . *26* / 9. Howell Cobb, former U.S. congressman, former governor of Georgia, former Confederate congressman and Confederate general, letter transmitted

3 *The Assassination* 48

4 *The Wild West* — 63

5 *Little Bighorn* — 74

6 *The Haymarket Affair* — 91

7 *Coxey's Army* 107

8 *The Race Question* 122

9 *The Philippine Question*   139

10 *The Tin Lizzie*   155

11 *The Triangle Shirtwaist Factory Fire* 175

12 *Margaret Sanger* 189

13 *World War I* 201

14 *Prohibition*   217

15 *Women's Suffrage*   235

16 *Scopes Trial*   255

17 *The New Deal*   271

18 *Pearl Harbor*   289

19 *Internment* 305

20 *Hiroshima* 324

21 *McCarthyism* 341

22 *The Guatemala Coup* 357

23 *The Sit-In Movement*   393

24 *The Cuban Missile Crisis* 409

25 *Vietnam*   430

26 *The Moon Landing*   448

27 *Watergate* 465

28 *The Exxon Valdez* 477

29 *Impeachment*   504

Web Sites

The following World Wide Web sites have been carefully researched and selected to support the text. At the appropriate location in each chapter, you will find the title of the Web site. The Web addresses (URLs) are listed below. We have made every effort to provide sites that will remain current, but Web sites sometimes change. We regret that any discrepancies are beyond our control.

Chapter 1 Civil War

1.1 The American Civil War Homepage
`http://sunsite.utk.edu/civil-war/warweb.html`
This Web page is an excellent, well-documented resource for the student of the Civil War. From here you can reach links about the secession crisis and before, images of wartime, documentary records, private/personal documents, various history sources, and many more Web sites pertaining to the Civil War.

1.2 Fort Pickens and Fort Sumter
`http://www.tulane.edu/~latner/Background/BackgroundForts.html`
This interesting Web site takes you through the history of these two forts during the Civil War, including the associated armies and ships.

1.3 The History Place: A Nation Divided
`http://www.historyplace.com/civilwar/index.html`
This Web site provides an excellent chronological overview of the Civil War. Click on "Abraham Lincoln" at the bottom of the page to read his autobiographies, speeches on slavery, and inaugural address as well as follow extensive links to battles and important generals in the war.

1.4 Civil War
`http://www.harlingen.isd.tenet.edu/coakhist/cwar.html`
This well-organized Web site informs the viewer about causes and effects of the Civil War, as well as the people and battles involved.

Chapter 2 One Nation, Indivisible

2.1 Robert E. Lee
`http://www.cfcsc.dnd.ca/links/bio/lee.html`
Visit this Web site and follow interesting links to General Robert E. Lee. Read the "Apotheosis of Robert E. Lee" and several biographies, and visit the Stratford Hall Plantation, birthplace of General Lee.

2.2 Civil War Resources on the Internet: From Abolitionism to Reconstruction
`http://www.libraries.rutgers.edu/rulib/socsci/hist/civwar-2.html`
This Web site contains many excellent links to the Civil War through Reconstruction. Sites include an abolition exhibit from the Library of Congress and political cartoons dealing with racial satire in the Civil War.

2.3 Civil Rights History Guide
`http://www.search-beat.com/civilrights.htm`
This Web site gives the viewer a comprehensive overview of the history of the civil rights movement. Follow links to learn more about slavery in colonial America, top civil rights Web sites, and key people and events.

Chapter 3 The Assassination

3.1 Abraham Lincoln: Sixteenth President
`http://www.whitehouse.gov/WH/glimpse/presidents/html/al16.html`
Read a short White House biography about the famous president, his inaugural addresses, or click on "Mary Todd Lincoln" for a biography of his wife.

3.2 The History Place Presents Abraham Lincoln
`http://www.historyplace.com/lincoln/`
This is an excellent, detailed timeline of President Lincoln's life, from his family to his years as president. View portraits of Lincoln, read letters to his wife, and see pictures of his box at Ford's Theatre.

3.3 Abraham Lincoln's Assassination

`http://members.aol.com/RVSNorton/Lincoln.html`

Visit this Web site for an informative and detailed description of Lincoln's assassination. Many aspects, such as an eyewitness account of Booth's capture, the 1865 Conspiracy Trial, and several photographs are presented.

Chapter 4 The Wild West

4.1 The Wild West

`http://www.calweb.com/~rbbusman/index.html`

Visit this interesting Web site for an informative trip back in time to early life in the American West. Click on "The Outlaws" and select John Wesley Hardin for his biography.

4.2 Links to Personalities of the West

`http://www.over-land.com/westpers4.html`

Visit this Web site to find out about all the famous characters of the nineteenth century American west. Click on "Legends of the West" to learn about the local lore.

4.3 The American West

`http://www.americanwest.com`

This Web site celebrates the pioneering spirit of the people who explored the American West. Click on the links to learn about gunslingers and outlaws, pioneer towns and forts, Native American tribes, and European emigration.

Chapter 5 Little Bighorn

5.1 Little Bighorn Associates

`http://lbha.netgate.net`

This Web site provides the reader with a comprehensive set of links to the Indian Wars on the Plains, the Native Americans, and General Custer. Click on "Treaties with the Indian Nations" for a detailed description of the Fort Laramie Treaties, military reports, and government documents.

5.2 The Battle of Little Bighorn

`http://www.mohicanpress.com/battles/ba04000.html`

Visit this interesting Web site for a thorough and well-presented replay of the events of the battle of Little Bighorn (click on "Custer's Last Stand"). Visit the Little Bighorn Photo Gallery and read about Daniel Kanipe, a sergeant in the Seventh Cavalry.

5.3 The Cavalry Man's Military History Site

`http://www.geocities.com/CollegePark/Classroom/1101/index.html`

This Web site contains many interesting links to General Custer and American military history. Tour the Gettysburg and Little Bighorn battlefields, view photos, learn about the life of George Custer and his 1867 court martial, and find out about the Little Bighorn coverup.

Chapter 6 The Haymarket Affair

6.1 Chicago: 1886 The Haymarket Riot

`http://cpl.lib.uic.edu/004chicago/timeline/haymarket.html`

Visit this Web site for history and many interesting photos of the Haymarket tragedy as well as links to other disturbances and disasters in Chicago, and a Chicago history timeline.

6.2 The Haymarket Martyrs

`http://www.kentlaw.edu/ilhs/haymkmon.htm`

This Web site from the Illinois Labor History Society provides a comprehensive summary of the Haymarket riot as well as photographs depicting the trial.

6.3 The Haymarket Tragedy

`http://www.kentlaw.edu/ilhs/haymarket.htm`

This Web site offers much information about the trial and pardon of the Haymarket prisoners, the eulogy for the martyrs, as well as photographs of the Haymarket plaque.

Chapter 7 Coxey's Army

7.1 Economic Depression

`http://iberia.vassar.edu/1896/depression.html`

Visit this interesting Web site for a history of the economic depression of the late 1800s and read Jacob Coxey's "Address on Behalf of the Industrial Army." Follow the links to read about Grover Cleveland and "Pitchfork" Ben Tillman and other important figures in nineteenth-century American radical tradition.

7.2 History Matters: Labor and Labor Movements

`http://chnm.gmu.edu/us/labor.taf`

This Web site provides the viewer with a broad range of links to many sites concerning the labor movement in nineteenth- and twentieth-century America.

7.3 Manuscripts in Labadie Collection

`http://www.lib.umich.edu/libhome/SpecColl.lib/LabadieManuscripts.html`

To gain a broader understanding of the labor struggles of the American people, read the brief summaries of influential people and organizations in the Labadie Collection, one of the oldest collections of radical history in the United States.

Chapter 8 The Race Question

8.1 Internet Modern History Sourcebook: Modern Social Movements

`http://www.fordham.edu/halsall/mod/modsbook56.html`

This Web site contains information about social movements such as feminism and minority movements. Look under "Black Power" for links to many of Booker T. Washington's speeches and links, essays by other influential black leaders, and the U.S. Civil Rights movement.

8.2 Booker T. Washington National Monument Homepage

`http://www.nps.gov/bowa/home.htm`

Learn about the life of Booker T. Washington, the plantation on which he worked during his early years, and the Tuskegee Institute by following links in this National Parks Service Web site. Click on "Where's 'Big House'?" to find out about the archaeological advances designed to uncover the location where Washington lived as a child.

8.3 The Advent of Modern America (1865 to 1920)

`http://www.berkshire.net/~quaboag/`
`modam.html`

This Web site is an excellent source for modern American history. Click on "Jim Crow Laws" for pictures of life during the period of segregation, and read in great detail about the case of *Plessy v. Ferguson*.

Chapter 9 The Philippine Question

9.1 Philippine Culture and History

`http://www.univie.ac.at/Voelkerkunde/`
`apsis/aufi/culhist.htm`

This Web site provides a detailed background to understanding the Filipino culture and history. Find out about the ethnic communities and folk tales, view photographs, and read about the 1896 rebellion against the Spanish as well as a contemporary interpretation of the Filipino-American struggle.

9.2 The History Guy: Philippine-American War

`http://www.historyguy.com/`
`PhilipineAmericanwar.html`

Visit this interesting Web site for an excellent overview of the American occupation of the Philippines. Read about the events leading up to the occupation and the consequences of the conflict.

9.3 William McKinley

`http://lcweb.loc.gov/rr/hispanic/1898/`
`mckinley.html`

This Web site provides a short biography of President McKinley with links to his involvement in the Philippines.

9.4 Today in History: George Dewey

`http://memory.loc.gov/ammem/today/`
`dec26.html`

This Web site details the life of George Dewey, offering links to all aspects of his life, including the Spanish-American War, and photographs of the American troops in Manila, as well as a unique viewing of the war as documented by Thomas Edison's film crew.

Chapter 10 The Tin Lizzie

10.1 Henry Ford Museum and Greenfield Village

`http://www.hfmgv.org`

This interesting Web site is full of photographs of Ford's inventions and a short description of "The Making of an Innovator." Click on "Exhibits" and "Featured Artifacts" to view the many facets of Henry Ford's life and "Online Exhibits" for stories of the inventor.

10.2 Henry Ford and the Model T

`http://www.wiley.com/products/subject/`
`business/forbes/ford.html`

This is the interesting story of Ford's dream, his work, and his success and devotion to the Model T.

10.3 Automotive History

`http://www.autoshop-online.com/auto101/`
`histtext.html`

This comprehensive Web site traces the history of the automobile, from the Greeks' three-wheeled vehicles, to the first electric-powered road vehicle in Scotland, the clash between horse-drawn carriages and automobiles, and the beginnings of the auto industry in the United States. Also featured is a commentary on the social impact of the automobile.

Chapter 11 The Triangle Shirtwaist Factory Fire

11.1 The Triangle Shirtwaist Factory Fire

`http://www.ilr.cornell.edu/`
`trianglefire/`

Visit this Web site for an excellent, comprehensive history of the New York city factory fire. Included are topics such as political cartoons, photographs, oral histories, and a detailed description of an investigation into the fire.

11.2 The Triangle Fire

`http://www.assumption.edu/HTML/Academic/`
`history/Hi113net/TriangleTofC/`

This Web site provides links to many of the events occurring during and after the fire. The firsthand accounts of many strike participants, survivors' stories, and physicians' testimonies are provided.

11.3 A Short History of American Labor

`http://www.unionweb.org/history.htm`

This Web site describes the struggle and story of American workers, the emergence of labor unions, and cases of federal intervention.

11.4 Women in the Workplace: Labor Unions

`http://www.thehistorynet.com/`
`WomensHistory/articles/19967_text.htm`

Visit this informative Web site for a history of women's condition in the workplace and the formation of trade unions and labor associations for women.

Chapter 12 Margaret Sanger

12.1 The Margaret Sanger Papers
http://www.nyu.edu/projects/sanger/

This Web site provides an excellent overview of Margaret Sanger's life and includes some of her letters and writings and many links to related subjects.

12.2 Margaret Sanger's "Deeds of Terrible Virtue"
http://www.neh.fed.us/html/magazine/98-09/sanger.html

Visit this Web site for the summary of a new historical documentary that recreates the world of Margaret Sanger.

12.3 Family Planning in America
http://www.plannedparenthood.org/ABOUT/NARRHISTORY/fpamnar.html

Visit this Web site for a narrative history of the family planning movement, from the time of Margaret Sanger's first birth control clinic and public opposition to the Comstock laws to birth control under the Reagan and Bush administrations.

12.4 Criminalizing Women
http://www.igc.org/solidarity/atc/feeley76.html

This Web site covers the history of the illegalization of abortion and the story of the birth control movement.

Chapter 13 World War I

13.1 Trenches on the Web:
http://www.worldwar1.com/tlss1914.htm

This Web site will provide you with a solid understanding of the events leading up to the assassination of Archduke Franz Ferdinand and the beginning of World War I. Learn about significant events such as the formation of deadly alliances, the Bosnian crisis, and war plans of the major countries.

13.2 Fateful Voyage of Lusitania
http://www.thehistorynet.com/MHQ/articles/1999/spring99_cover.htm

This informative Web site brings to life the devastating journey of the Lusitania. Click on "Full Text" and read the thoughts of German U-boat commander Walther Schweiger as he commanded the torpedoes to be fired.

13.3 The Great War Series
http://www.wtj.com/wars/greatwar/

Visit this Web site for a comprehensive overview of World War I, the Great War.

13.4 The World in the Era of Great Wars
http://www.berkshire.net/~quaboag/gtwar.html

This Web site is an excellent resource for all students of World War I history. Choose from dozens of interesting links to learn more about the causes, effects, and military course of the Great War.

Chapter 14 Prohibition

14.1 Temperance and Prohibition
http://www.history.ohio-state.edu/projects/prohibition/default.htm

This interesting Web site gives insight into many aspects of Prohibition, including the Women's Crusade of 1873–74, the Anti-Saloon League, cartoons from the Prohibition era, and arguments for and against the movement.

14.2 Prohibition: A Lesson in the Futility (and Danger) of Prohibiting
http://www.mcwilliams.com/books/aint/402.htm

This Web site contains a good overview of the events occurring in 1920 at the beginning of the Noble Experiment, and some of the effects of Prohibition.

14.3 Alcohol Prohibition Was a Failure
http://www.cato.org/pubs/pas/pa-157.html

Visit this Web site to read a comprehensive essay summarizing the effects of Prohibition and the reasons it failed.

Chapter 15 Women's Suffrage

15.1 History of the Suffrage Movement
http://www.pbs.org/onewoman/suffrage.html

This Web site from PBS Online is an excellent reference to the women's movement which culminated in the 1920 ratification of the Nineteenth Amendment.

15.2 Links to Sites Concerning Suffrage and Women's History
http://www.frontiernet.net/~lhurst/sbahouse/sufflink.htm

This Web site is an excellent resource to aid in the understanding of the role and history of women in early America. Links include a History of the Movement, Suffragist Biographies, and Distinguished Women of the Past and Present.

15.3 Selections from the NAWSA Collection, 1848–1921
http://lcweb2.loc.gov/ammem/rbnawsahtml/nawshome.html

Browse the NAWSA collection by subject or author to learn more about the National American Woman Suffrage Association, bibliographies of some of the pioneering women, and timelines of the events.

Chapter 16 Scopes Trial

16.1 Scopes Trial Homepage:

http://www.law.umkc.edu/faculty/
projects/ftrials/scopes/scopes.htm

This Web site provides detailed, well-organized documentation of the famous Scopes trial. Trial pictures and cartoons, biographies of the participants, excerpts from the trial transcript, and H. L. Mencken's account are some of the subjects covered.

16.2 The Scopes 'Monkey Trial'

http://www.dimensional.com/~randl/
scopes.htm

This interesting Web site is full of newspaper headlines about the trial and various articles and commentaries.

16.3 Inherit the Wind

http://xroads.virginia.edu/~UG97/
inherit/contents.html

Visit this Web site for an excellent, detailed background of the Scopes trial as well as the history and making of the movie *Inherit the Wind,* a historical drama which brought the trial back to the headlines.

Chapter 17 The New Deal

17.1 The Great Depression

http://members.xoom.com/smithwil/
grdepression.htm

This Web site is an excellent resource to aid in your understanding of the causes of the Great Depression and of the New Deal. Read about the Civilian Conservation Corps, browse through a "Then and Now" table of prices, discover the "Great Myths of the Great Depression," learn about the music and lyrics of the time, and read the memories and browse through scrap books of some Great Depression survivors.

17.2 New Deal Network

http://newdeal.feri.org

This comprehensive Web site includes a vast number of articles, images, and links to all aspects of the New Deal. Read American slave narratives, research the document library to find out about New Deal legislation, and read letters to Eleanor Roosevelt as well as her responses.

17.3 The FDR Years

http://www.washingtonpost.com/wp-srv/
local/longterm/tours/fdr/front.htm

Visit this *Washington Post* Web site for insight into the life, presidential campaigns, presidency, and New Deal policies of FDR, and learn about his impact on Washington D.C.

17.4 New Deal Cultural Programs

http://www.wwcd.org/policy/US/newdeal.
html

Visit this Web site to learn about FDR's policies regarding U.S. government intervention in cultural development, including the Treasury Section of Fine Arts, the Works Progress Administration, and the birth of "Federal One."

Chapter 18 Pearl Harbor

18.1 The History Place: World War II

http://www.historyplace.com/worldwar2/
timeline/pearl.htm

This Web site offers a complete outline of events taking place on the island of Oahu on December 7, 1947. Included are incredible photos of the bombings and explosions. Click on "WW II Timeline" for a detailed record of the events of World War II and many links.

18.2 Investigation of the Pearl Harbor Attack

http://metalab.unc.edu/pha/pha/
congress/part_0.html

Visit this Web site to read an official document of the U.S. Congress: the report of the Joint Committee on the investigation into Japan's devastating attack of Pearl Harbor.

18.3 The Avalon Project: Pearl Harbor Documents

http://www.yale.edu/lawweb/avalon/
wwii/pmenu.htm

This Web site contains three interesting historical documents concerning Pearl Harbor. Included are a U.S. note to Japan in November 1941, a message from the president to the emperor of Japan, and a note from Japan to the United States on the day of the bombings.

18.4 The New American: Pearl Harbor

http://www.thenewamerican.com/
departments/feature/070499.htm

Visit this site for an interesting present-day commentary on the Pearl Harbor attack and how it might have been avoided. Read about the U.S. government's successful attempt to crack the Japanese code, the "east wind, rain" message, war warnings, and the prelude to the attack.

Chapter 19 Internment

19.1 Internment and Evacuation of the San Francisco Japanese

http://www.sfmuseum.org/war/evactxt.
html

This Web site is an excellent resource to aid in the understanding of what happened to Japanese Americans during World War II. Links to ten weeks' worth of articles from the *San Francisco News* provide an interesting and accurate image of Japanese evacuation from this West Coast city. In addition, background articles are provided to give you a better political context.

19.2 Race and Racism in American Law

http://www.udayton.edu/~race/japanam.
htm

This Web site covers the legal issues surrounding internment and redress. Topics include statutes, cases, legislative history, and law reviews.

19.3 Japanese American Internment–Santa Clara Valley

    http://scuish.scu.edu/SCU/Programs/
    Diversity/exhibit1.html

Visit this Web site for an informative, well-designed exhibit on Japanese internment in Santa Clara, California. View original documents calling for evacuation, a map of the affected area, internment camps, and follow the links to view photos of many other internment camps in the West.

Chapter 20 Hiroshima

20.1 Atomic Bomb: Decision

    http://www.dannen.com/decision/

This Web site is an excellent, well-documented resource for students of World War II. It contains many documents which were Top Secret in 1945, such as the minutes of the Los Alamos Target Committee, arguments and recommendations of the scientific panel, and the official bombing order. Also included are Truman's diaries, Leo Szilard's petitions against use of the atomic bomb, and radiation monitoring at the trial bombing in New Mexico.

20.2 Outline of Atomic Bomb Damage in Hiroshima

    http://www.city.hiroshima.jp/C/City/
    ABombDamage/01.html

This powerful Web site brings home the image of war and destruction. Follow the series of events (by clicking "Next") to learn about Hiroshima before the bombing, and read of the instantaneous effects of the bomb: damage from the shock wave and blast, high temperature fires, radiation, and what it did to the human body.

20.3 Hiroshima: Was It Necessary?

    http://www.he.net/~douglong/index.html

This interesting Web site contains a plethora of information regarding Hiroshima and the atomic bomb. Read an article by the author debating the necessity of dropping the bomb, excerpts from the diaries and personal papers of President Truman and the secretary of War, and a "Who's Who" list of important figures in the decision to bomb. In addition, follow links to sites relating to Hiroshima and nuclear weapons.

Chapter 21 McCarthyism

21.1 The Cold War at Home

    http://expert.cc.purdue.edu/~phealy/
    mccarthy.html

Visit this Web site to learn about the rise and fall of McCarthyism and the political "witch hunts" of his

Committee in the 1950s. Read some opinions about McCarthyism and follow the links to sites regarding other events of the fifties.

21.2 Joseph McCarthy

    http://history.hanover.edu/20th/
    mccarthy.htm

Read several bibliographies about Joseph McCarthy and his movement. Topics include the impact of McCarthyism and an interpretation of the events which took place.

21.3 The Real McCarthy Record

    http://www.thenewamerican.com/tna/
    1996/vo12no18/vo12no18_mccarthy.htm

Visit this Web site to read an interesting, detailed account of the "real" stories behind Joseph McCarthy and his movement. Find out whether he spoke out against communism prior to his famous West Virginia speech, whether he was backed by the communists in his 1946 campaign, the purpose of the Tidings Committee, and his attack on General George Marshall.

Chapter 22 The Guatemala Coup

22.1 The United Fruit Company

    http://www.mayaparadise.com/ufc1e.htm

Visit this Web site for a history of this American-owned corporation and find out about the labor conditions and economic impact in Guatemala.

22.2 Documents Relating to American Foreign Policy

    http://www.mtholyoke.edu/acad/intrel/
    coldwar.htm

This Web site contains excellent references to students learning about the cold war and U.S. foreign policy during that time. Scroll down to "1954" for many interesting articles pertaining to Guatemala. Topics include "The Intelligence Oversight Board Report" and CNN and *New York Times* reports and articles as well as many documents relating to the cold war.

22.3 CIA Involved in Guatemala Coup—1954

    http://www.english.upenn.edu/
    ~afilreis/50s/guatemala.html

Visit this Web site for a brief overview of the role of the CIA in the Guatemala Coup. Click on "United Fruit Company" and then "U.S. Invasion of Guatemala" for an excerpt from Howard Zinn's *A People's History of the United States.*

22.4 U.S. Policy in Guatemala, 1966–96

    http://www.gwu.edu/~nsarchiv/NSAEBB/
    NSAEBB11/docs/index.html

Visit this National Security Archives Web site for formerly top-secret information and documents about the United States policy regarding Guatemala.

Chapter 23 The Sit-In Movement

23.1 Greensboro Sit-Ins

http://vh0333.infi.net/sitins/timeline
.htm

Visit this Web site for an informative timeline and many interesting photos about the National Civil Rights Timeline of the Sit-Ins for a closer look at the Greensboro events.

23.2 Student Nonviolent Coordinating Committee

http://www.worldbook.com/fun/aajourny/
html/bh087.html

This Web site includes background information about the SNCC and its leaders. Links within the "African American Journey" are provided to the Civil Rights Movement and its many organizations and leaders.

23.3 The Martin Luther King, Jr. Papers Project

http://www.stanford.edu/group/King/

This Web site provides excellent, extensive information about this famous civil rights leader. Read some of King's papers, documents, letters, and his Nobel Prize acceptance speech. Follow many links to related sites.

Chapter 24 The Cuban Missile Crisis

24.1 Fourteen Days in October: The Cuban Missile Crisis

http://hyperion.advanced.org/11046/

This well-organized Web site offers a comprehensive look at the events of the Cuban Missile Crisis. Visit the "Crisis Center" for an in-depth account and analysis of the crisis, the "Situation Room" for letters between Kennedy and Khrushchev, the "Reconnaissance Room" to view photos of the missiles that Kennedy first saw, and learn about "the players" through detailed biographies.

24.2 Archives of the *New York Times:* The Cuban Missile Crisis

http://www.nytimes.com/books/97/10/19/
home/missile.html

Visit this interesting Web site to read articles in the *New York Times,* that ran during and after the crisis. They analyze the events and offer opinions and interpretations.

24.3 NSA and the Cuban Missile Crisis

http://www.nsa.gov:8080/docs/cuba/

Read about the activities of the National Security Agency during the Cuban missile crisis. In addition, find out about the new roles of human and photographic intelligence and visit the "Document Archive" for declassified files from the crisis.

Chapter 25 Vietnam

25.1 The Vietnam War Internet Project

http://www.lbjlib.utexas.edu/shwv/
shwvhome.html

This Web site provides a detailed account of all aspects of the war in Vietnam, including documents and photos relating to the war, a resource index, military unit home pages, personal narratives and accounts, and a recommended reading list.

25.2 Vietnam War

http://www.geocities.com:80/Athens/
Forum/9061/USA/Vietnam/vietnam.html

This informative Web site provides links to excellent Vietnam War sites. Also included are an electronic newsletter created by and for Vietnam veterans, and an extensive photo gallery.

25.3 The History Net: Vietnam Article Index

http://www.thehistorynet.com/general/
articleindex/vietnam.htm

Visit this Web site for a comprehensive list of History Net articles concerning Vietnam. Read about the battles, personal narratives of survivors, and the controversy surrounding the U.S. policy.

25.4 Vietnam Yesterday and Today

http://servercc.oakton.edu/~wittman/

This Web site provides a broad overview of the war in Vietnam. Read about the chronology, characteristics, and statistics of the war, follow the links to other valuable Vietnam sites, and find out about excellent research materials and resources.

Chapter 26 The Moon Landing

26.1 Apollo to the Moon

http://www.nasm.edu/galleries/attm/
enter.html

Visit this Web site to learn about the events and competition surrounding the space race between the United States and the Soviet Union. Click on "Space Race" and read the well-documented resources provided by the National Air and Space Museum. Topics include "The Military Origins of the Space Race," "Secret Eyes in Space," and "A Permanent Presence in Space."

26.2 Red Star: The Soviet Moon Program

http://www.hbo.com/apollo/cmp/
redstar3_moon.html

This interesting Web site from HBO contains detailed information about the Soviet space program. Some features include Soviet space history, the vision of Soviet chief designer Sergei Korolev, and the Soviet Moon Story.

26.3 Project Apollo

http://www.ksc.nasa.gov/history/apollo/
apollo.html

Visit this NASA Web site to learn about the Apollo missions and relive the moment when a man first landed on the Moon. Find out about the spacecraft and read NASA History Series documents about the moon landing. Under Manned Missions, click on "Apollo 11" for a detailed, exciting, firsthand description from the astronauts about their revolutionary flight.

Chapter 27 Watergate

27.1 AllPolitics: Watergate

http://cnn.com/ALLPOLITICS/1997/gen/resources/watergate/

This Web site from CNN provides a comprehensive overview of the Watergate scandal. Read about *Time* magazine's coverage of the episode from 1972 to 1974, current analyses of the effects of Watergate, public cynicism as a result of Watergate, the hearings, and Nixon's resignation.

27.2 WashingtonPost.com: Watergate

http://www.washingtonpost.com/wp-srv/national/longterm/watergate/front.htm

This interesting site from the *Washington Post* details all the incidents and controversy surrounding the political scandal of Watergate. Read a chronology of events, learn about the key players, gain insight from the Nixon tapes, and analyze the mystery of Deep Throat.

27.3 Illusion and Delusion: The Watergate Decade

http://www.journale.com/watergate.html

This Web site takes you on a journey into the political turbulence of the 1970s. The detailed chronology of events is divided into several sections and contains many interesting photos.

Chapter 28 The *Exxon Valdez*

28.1 Trans Alaska Pipeline System

http://aurora.ak.blm.gov/arcticinfo/topics/pipe-1.htm

Visit this Web site to read about the building of the massive pipeline through Alaska. Read firsthand accounts of the workers and view photographs of the pipeline.

28.2 The Exxon Valdez Oil Spill Restoration Site

http://www.oilspill.state.ak.us

This Web site, by the *Exxon Valdez* Oil Spill Trustee Council, outlines the settlement and restoration plan after the spill, and details the path from injury to recovery of the affected people and wildlife.

28.3 Survivors of the *Exxon Valdez* Oil Spill

http://www.exxonvaldez.org/

Visit this Web site for a perspective of the Alaska fishermen and environmentalists on the tenth anniversary of the oil spill. Some topics include the environmental, psychological, and economic impact, ongoing litigation, and newspaper articles .

28.4 Response to the Exxon Valdez Spill

http://response.restoration.noaa.gov/intro/valdez.html

Visit this Web site from the National Oceanic and Atmospheric Administration to learn about the initial and long-term cleanup of the 1989 oil spill. Read about the Prince William Sound ecosystem and view photos of the spill.

Chapter 29 Impeachment

29.1 WashingtonPost.com Special Report: Clinton Accused

http://www.washingtonpost.com/wp-srv/politics/special/clinton/stories/shadow061399.htm

This Web site includes articles by *Washington Post* staff writer Bob Woodward, and links to "How the Research Was Conducted" and "Hillary Clinton's Anguish."

29.2 The Impeachment of William Jefferson Clinton

http://www.lib.umich.edu/libhome/Documents.center/impeach.html

This comprehensive Web site from the University of Michigan includes many government documents surrounding the presidential scandal. Included are the Clinton and Lewinsky testimony to the Grand Jury, the report of the Independent Counsel, and the *Jones v. Clinton* case.

29.3 The Clinton Crisis Front Page

http://msnbc.com/news/CLINTONUNDERFIRE_Front.asp

This Web site outlines the controversy surrounding President Clinton's acquittal. Read articles about the Senate trial, House impeachment, Paula Jones, and Linda Tripp.

Chapter 1

Civil War

Fort Sumter Is Fired Upon   *April 12, 1861*

Never before had the White House been captured by a candidate whose electoral majority had been won without the vote of even a single southern elector. The significance of Abraham Lincoln's victory was clear to southerners: The days when they could direct the course of the country were now a part of the past. South Carolina seceded from the United States on December 20, 1860. Mississippi, Alabama, Florida, Georgia, and Louisiana declared in January of 1861 that they, too, were no longer members of the American Union. Texas joined the new confederation created by these seceding states in February.

Following their secession from the Union, the states of the South assumed control of all federal property within their borders. This assumption was accomplished without resistance in most instances. Two federal outposts, however, refused to submit to the imposition of Confederate control: Fort Pickens in Pensacola, Florida, and Fort Sumter, a military installation situated on an island in Charleston Harbor, South Carolina. The continuing federal control of these outposts was an irritant to the South and a potentially volatile burden for the North.

☞ *First Impressions*

The Move toward Confrontation

As Lincoln formed his new Republican administration, there were important questions awaiting answer. Should his government abandon Forts Pickens and Sumter, or reinforce and attempt to hold them? This question was inseparable from a far more fundamental policy issue. Would the dissolution of the United States occur peaceably? Would it be allowed to occur at all? The answers to these questions did not come until the morning of April 12, 1861.

1.1 The American Civil War Homepage

Source 1   *Diary of Gideon Welles,* Secretary of the Navy

On the 6th of March, 1861, two days after the inauguration of President Lincoln, Secretary Holt, who continued to discharge the duties of Secretary of War, ... called at the Navy Department with the compliments of General Scott and requested my attendance at the War Department on matters of special importance. I went immediately with him to the office of the Secretary of War, where were

Generals Scott and Totten, and I think Secretary Cameron, and perhaps one or two others.

General Scott commenced with a statement of the perilous condition of the country and of the difficulties and embarrassments he had experienced for months past; related the measures and precautions he had taken for the public safety, the advice and admonitions he had given President Buchanan, which, however, had been disregarded, and, finally, his apprehensions, perhaps convictions, that hostilities were imminent and, he feared, inevitable. He had . . . taken the responsibility of ordering a small military force to Washington for the protection of the government and the public property and archives. . . . His statement was full, clear in its details, and of absorbing interest. . . . Among other matters, and that for which he had especially requested our attendance that morning, was certain intelligence of a distressing character from Major Anderson at Fort Sumter, stating that his supplies were almost exhausted, that he could get no provisions in Charleston, and that he with his small command would be totally destitute in about six weeks. Under these circumstances it became a question what action should be taken, and for that purpose, as well as to advise us of the condition of affairs, he had convened the gentlemen present.

The information was to most of us unexpected and astounding, and there was, on the part of such of us as had no previous intimation of the condition of things at Sumter, an earnest determination to take immediate and efficient measures to relieve and reinforce the garrison. But General Scott, without opposing this spontaneous resolution, related the difficulties which had already taken place, and stated the formidable obstacles which were to be encountered from the numerous and well-manned batteries that were erected in Charleston Harbor. Any successful attempt to reinforce or relieve the garrison by sea he supposed impracticable. An attempt had already been made and failed. The question was, however, one for naval authorities to decide, for the army could do nothing.

(Confidential)

Navy Department, April 5, 1861

Captain Samuel Mercer, commanding U.S. Steamer Powhatan . . .

The United States Steamers Powhatan, Pawnee, Pocahontas, and Harriet Lane will compose a naval force under your command, to be sent to the vicinity of Charleston, S.C., for the purpose of aiding in carrying out the objects of an expedition of which the War Department has charge.

The primary object of the expedition is to provision Fort Sumter. . . . Should the authorities at Charleston permit the fort to be supplied, no further particular service will be required of the force under your command. . . .

1.2 Fort Pickens and Fort Sumter

Should the authorities at Charleston, however, refuse to permit, or attempt to prevent the vessel or vessels having supplies on board from entering the harbor, or from peaceably proceeding to Fort Sumter, you will protect the transports or boats of the expedition in the object of their mission, disposing your force in such manner as to open the way for their ingress, and afford as far as practicable security to the men and boats, and repelling by force if necessary all obstructions toward provisioning the fort and reinforcing it; for in case of a resistance to the peaceable primary object of the expedition, a reinforcement of the garrison will also be attempted. . . .

I am, respectfully,
Your Obd't Serv't,
Gideon Welles, Secretary of the Navy

Source 2   *Alexandria Gazette and Virginia Advertiser*

FROM CHARLESTON

Charleston, April 9.—At last the ball has opened.

The state authorities last night received official notification that supplies would be furnished to Anderson at any hazard—peaceably if possible, by force if necessary.

Immense preparations immediately were commenced suitable to the emergency.

Orders were issued to the entire military force of the city, held in reserve, to proceed to their station without delay.

Four regiments of a thousand men each have been telegraphed for from the country. . . .

The community has been thrown into a fever of excitement by the discharge of seven guns from Citadel square, the signal for the assembling of all the reserves ten minutes afterward.

Hundreds of men left their beds, hurrying to and fro toward their respective destinations. In the absence of sufficient armories, [at] the corners of the streets, public squares, and other convenient points companies were formed, for all night the long roll of the drum, and the steady tramp of the military, and the gallop of the cavalry, resounding through the city, betokened the close proximity of the long anticipated hostilities. . . .

South Carolinians are anxious to meet the enemy at the point of the bayonet rather than . . . an exchange of iron compliments. The latter is a too deliberate style of fighting to suit the impetuous nature of the most desperate set of men ever brought together. . . .

No attempt is likely to be made upon the city. Officers acquainted with the caliber of Major Anderson's guns say the longest shot will fall short three-eighths of a mile.

FROM WASHINGTON

THE GAZETTE'S SPECIAL DISPATCH.

Washington, April 10.—I am authorized to say by a member of the Cabinet that the steamers for Charleston carried no arms and no men, but a supply of provisions for the garrison at Fort Sumter, and also that Gov. Pickens was notified that that was the object of the steamers' visit.

FROM CHARLESTON

Charleston, April 10, 1 P.M.—All is still quiet up to this hour. . . . It is believed that no order for attack on Fort Sumter has as yet been received from Montgomery. Nothing outside the bar.

The floating **battery** having been finished, mounted, and manned, was taken out of the dock last evening and anchored in a cove near Sullivan's Island, ready for service.

Our people are not excited, but there is a fixed determination to meet the issue.

An additional regiment of one thousand men is hourly expected from the interior.

Governor Pickens was in secret session with the State Convention to-day before their final adjournment, which took place at 1 o'clock.

About 1,000 troops were sent to the fortifications to-day, and 1,800 more will go down to-morrow. . . .

Large numbers of the members of the convention, after adjournment, volunteered as privates.

About 7,000 troops are now at the fortifications, the "beginning of the end" is coming to a final closing.

Washington, April 11.—The general excitement occasioned here yesterday by the calling out [of] the volunteer militia of the District to be mustered into the federal service has abated, and to-day four or five more companies marched to the War Department and took the army oath, namely; "to bear true allegiance to the United States and serve them honestly and faithfully against all their enemies and opposers, whomsoever, and observe and obey the orders of the President of the United States and the orders of the officers appointed over them, according to the rules and articles for the government of the United States."

Previous to taking the oath, the volunteers were informed that the obligation was for three months, unless they were sooner discharged.

Montgomery, April 11.—The War Department is overwhelmed with applications from Regiments, battalions, and companies to enter the service. Over 7000 men from the Border States offer their services besides two thousand Indian warriors, who have signified a desire to co-operate with the Confederate forces. Numbers of companies are daily arriving at Charleston, Savannah, and Pensacola.

Charleston, April 11, P.M.—A collision is hourly expected.

Northern dispatches state that attempts will be made to-day to reinforce Sumter in small boats protected by schooners lined with sand bags, the war vessels in the meantime to protect the landing party on Morris Island.

It is reported that Gen. Beauregard has demanded the immediate surrender of Fort Sumter.

EDITORIAL

What is Sumter . . . worth, in comparison with the preservation of the public peace, and the avoidance of civil war? Why hinge upon the question of a formal *recognition* of the Confederate States—when the Confederate States have a government, an army, a civil, political, and military organization? Why have the public been left under the impression for weeks past, that Sumter was to be relinquished, without disturbance? Has not the reported "military necessity" for its evacuation been acquiesced in by reasonable people everywhere, North and

South? We believe, not only in the "military necessity," but, under the circumstances, in the propriety of its evacuation. Patriots and statesmen have to look at things as they find them, and to deal with them accordingly. Will holding on to Sumter, or reinforcing the garrison, make *Secession* less a reality than it is—alter the condition of South Carolina—or, in any degree, injure the Confederate States—supposing injury to be intended? Will it strengthen the United States, or any position of the States yet in the Union? Will it strengthen the Union feeling in any of the Southern States which have not yet seceded? Will it not irritate and heighten angry feelings? Will it not, finally, and most of all, . . . tend to, and probably produce, a *civil war*?

Charleston, April 11, 8 o'clock P.M.—It has now been ascertained that a demand for the surrender of the fort was made to-day at 2 o'clock. . . . Thousands of people are assembled on the Battery this evening anticipating the commencement of the fight. . . .

The steamer Harriet Lane is reported off the bar, and signals are being displayed by the guard boats and answered by the batteries, but what is indicated cannot be more than guessed at.

Source 3   Diary of Mary Boykin Chesnut, wife of General Beauregard's aide-de-camp, James Chesnut

April 12— . . . I do not pretend to go to sleep. How can I? If Anderson does not accept terms at 4 o'clock, the orders are he shall be fired upon.

I count four by St. Michael's chimes, and I begin to hope. At half past four, the heavy booming of a cannon! I sprang out of bed and on my knees, prostrate, I prayed as I never prayed before.

There was a sound of stir all over the house, a pattering of feet in the corridor. All seemed hurrying one way. I put on my double-gown and a shawl and went to the house top. The shells were bursting. In the dark I heard a man say: "Waste of ammunition!" I knew my husband was rowing about in a boat somewhere in that dark bay, and that the shells were roofing it over, bursting toward the Fort. If Anderson was obstinate, Mr. Chesnut was to order the Forts on our side to open fire. Certainly fire had begun. The regular roar of the cannon, there it was! And who could tell what each **volley** accomplished in death and destruction.

The women were wild, there on the house top. Prayers from the women and imprecations from the men; and then a shell would light up the scene.

Source 4   *Alexandria Gazette and Virginia Advertiser*

SURRENDER OF FORT SUMTER

Charleston, April 13, 10½ A.M.—At intervals of fifteen minutes the firing was kept up all night on Sumter. Anderson ceased fire at six in the morning. All night he was engaged in repairing damages, and protecting the **barbette** guns on the top of Sumter. He commenced to return the fire this morning at seven o'clock.

An explosion has occurred at Sumter, as a dense volume of smoke was seen suddenly to rise. Anderson has ceased to fire for above an hour. His flag is still up. . . .

April 13—Forenoon—Fort Sumter is undoubtedly on fire. Major Anderson has thrown out a raft, and men are passing up buckets of water from it to extinguish the flames. The fort is scarcely discernible in the smoke. The men on the raft are now subjected to the fire from the Cummings Point batteries. With good glasses, balls can be seen skipping along the surface of the water and occasionally striking near the raft, creating great consternation among the men thereon.

The flames can now be seen issuing from all the portholes, and the destruction of all combustible matter in the fort appears to be inevitable. . . .

A reliable source states that up to 10 a.m. no one at Fort Moultrie had been killed. Eleven shots had penetrated the famous floating battery below her water line. The few shots fired by Anderson, early in the morning, knocked the bricks and chimneys of the officers quarters in Moultrie like a whirlwind.

It seems to be Anderson's only hope to hold out for aid from the fleet.

Two ships are making in towards Morris Island, apparently with a view to land troops to silence the destructive battery. . . .

April 13, 1 p.m.—Anderson's flag and mast are down. Supposed to have been shot away.

The federal flag has again been hoisted. Wm. Porcher Miles, under a white flag, has gone to Sumter.

Anderson has hauled down the federal flag, and hoisted a white one.

The batteries have all stopped firing, and two boats with Confederate flags are on their way to the fort.

Fort Sumter has surrendered. The Confederate flag has been hoisted.

Source 5 Jefferson Davis's message to the Confederate Congress

April 29, 1861

The declaration of war made against this Confederacy, by Abraham Lincoln, President of the United States, . . . renders it necessary . . . to devise the measures necessary for the defence of the country. . . .

The war of the Revolution was successfully waged, and resulted in the treaty of peace with Great Britain in 1783, by the terms of which the several States were each by name recognized to be independent. . . .

It was by the delegates chosen by the several States . . . that the Constitution of the United States was formed in 1787, and submitted to the several States for ratification.

Strange, indeed, must it appear to the impartial observer, that . . . an organization created by the States, to secure the blessings of liberty and independence against foreign aggression, has been gradually perverted into a machine for their control in their domestic affairs.

The creature has been exalted above its Creator—the principals have been made subordinate to the agent appointed by themselves.

The people of the Southern States, whose almost exclusive occupation was agriculture, early perceived a tendency in the Northern States to render a common government subservient to their own purposes by imposing burthens on commerce as protection to their manufacturing and shipping interests.

Long and angry controversies grew out of these attempts . . . to benefit one section of the country at the expense of the other. . . .

When the several States delegated certain powers to the United States Congress, a large portion of the laboring population were imported into the colonies by the mother country. In twelve out of the fifteen States, negro slavery existed, and the right of property existing in slaves was protected by law; this property was recognized in the Constitution, and provision was made against its loss by the escape of the slave. . . .

The climate of the Northern States soon proved unpropitious to the continuance of slave labor, while the reverse being the case at the South, made unrestricted free intercourse between the two sections unfriendly.

The Northern States consulted their own interests by selling their slaves to the South and prohibiting slavery between their limits. . . .

As soon, however, as the Northern States, that had prohibited slavery within their limits, had reached a number sufficient to give their representation a controlling vote in Congress, a persistent and organized system of hostile measures against the rights of the owners of slaves in the Southern States was inaugurated and gradually extended. A series of measures was devised and prosecuted for the purpose of rendering insecure the tenure of property in slaves.

Fanatical organizations . . . were assiduously engaged in exciting amongst the slaves a spirit of discontent and revolt. Means were furnished for their escape from their owners, and agents secretly employed to entice them to abscond.

The constitutional provision for their rendition to their owners was first evaded, then openly denounced. . . . Often owners of slaves were mobbed and even murdered in open day solely for applying to a magistrate for the arrest of a fugitive slave. . . .

Finally, a great party was organized for the purpose of obtaining the administration of the Government, with the avowed object of using its power for the total exclusion of the slave States from all participation in the benefits of the public domain. . . . This party, thus organized, succeeded in the month of November last in the election of its candidate for the Presidency of the United States. . . .

Early in April the attention of the whole country was attracted to extraordinary preparations for an extensive military and naval expedition in New York and other Northern ports. These preparations commenced in secrecy, for an expedition whose destination was concealed, and only became known when nearly completed, and on the 5th, 6th, and 7th of April, transports and vessels of war with troops, munitions and military supplies, sailed from Northern ports bound southward. . . .

According to the usual course of navigation, the vessels composing the expedition, and designed for the relief of Fort Sumter, might be looked for in Charleston harbor on the 9th of April. . . . [O]ur flag did not wave over the battered walls until after the appearance of the hostile fleet off Charleston. . . .

The people of Charleston for months had been irritated by the spectacle of a fortress held within their principal harbor as a standing menace against their peace and independence—built in part with their own money— . . . intended to be used . . . for their own protection against foreign attack. How it was held out with persistent tenacity as a means of offence against them by the very Government which they had established for their own protection, is well known. . . .

Scarcely had the President of the United States received intelligence of the failure of the scheme which he had devised for the reinforcement of Fort Sumter, when he issued a declaration of war against the Confederacy.

Source 6 President Abraham Lincoln's Special Session message

July 4, 1861

Fellow-Citizens of the Senate and House of Representatives:

1.3 The
History Place:
A Nation
Divided

Having been convened on an extraordinary occasion, your attention is not called to any ordinary subject of legislation.

At the beginning of the present Presidential term, four months ago, the functions of the Federal Government were found to be generally suspended within the several States of South Carolina, Georgia, Alabama, Mississippi, Louisiana, and Florida, excepting those of the Post Office Department.

Within these States all the forts, arsenals, dockyards, custom-houses, and the like . . . had been seized and were held in open hostility to this Government, excepting only Forts Pickens, Taylor, and Jefferson, on or near the Florida coast, and Fort Sumter, in Charleston Harbor, South Carolina. . . .

The forts remaining in the possession of the Federal Government in and near these States were either besieged or menaced by warlike preparations, and especially Fort Sumter was nearly surrounded by well-protected hostile batteries. . . .

On the 5th of March, the present incumbent's first full day in office, a letter of Major Anderson, commanding at Fort Sumter, . . . received at the War Department on the 4th of March, was by that Department placed in his hands. This letter expressed the professional opinion of the writer that reenforcements could not be thrown into the fort within the time for his relief rendered necessary by the limited supply of provisions. . . . The whole was immediately laid before Lieutenant-General Scott, who at once concurred with Major Anderson in opinion. . . . In a purely military point of view this reduced the duty of the Administration in the case to the mere matter of getting the garrison safely out of the fort.

It was believed, however, that to so abandon that position under the circumstances would be utterly ruinous; that the *necessity* under which it was done would not be fully understood; that by many it would be construed as a part of a *voluntary* policy; that at home it would discourage the friends of the Union, embolden its adversaries, and go far to insure to the latter a recognition abroad; that, in fact, it would be our national destruction consummated. This could not be allowed. . . . [I]t was resolved . . . to notify the governor of South Carolina that he might expect an attempt would be made to provision the fort, and that if the attempt should not be resisted there would be no effort to throw in men, arms, or ammunition without further notice, or in case of attack upon the fort. This notice was accordingly given, whereupon the fort was attacked and bombarded to its fall, without even awaiting the arrival of the provisioning expedition.

It was thus seen that the assault upon and reduction of Fort Sumter was in no sense a matter of self-defense on the part of the assailants. . . . They knew that this Government desired to keep the garrison in the fort, not to assail them, but merely to maintain visible possession, and thus to preserve the Union from actual and immediate dissolution, trusting, . . . to time, discussion, and the ballot box for final adjustment; and they assailed and reduced the fort for precisely the reverse object. . . .

It might seem at first thought to be of little difference whether the present movement at the South be called "secession" or "rebellion." The movers, however, well understand the difference. At the beginning they knew they could never raise their treason to any respectable magnitude by any name which implies *violation* of the law. . . . They invented an ingenious sophism, which, if conceded, was followed by perfectly logical steps through all the incidents to the complete destruction of the Union. The sophism itself is that any State may *consistently* with the National Constitution, and therefore, *lawfully* and *peacefully,* withdraw from the Union without the consent of the Union or of any other State. . . .

This sophism derives much . . . of its currency from the assumption that there is some omnipotent and sacred supremacy pertaining to a *State*—to each State of our Federal Union. Our States have neither more nor less power than that reserved to them in the Union by the Constitution, no one of them ever having been a State *out* of the Union. The original ones passed into the Union even before they cast off their British colonial dependence, and the new ones each came into the Union directly from a condition of dependence, excepting Texas. . . . Having never been States, either in substance or in name, *outside* of the Union, whence this magical omnipotence of "State rights," or asserting a claim of power to lawfully destroy the Union itself? Much is said about the "sovereignty" of the States. . . . What is a "sovereignty" in the political sense of the term? Would it be far wrong to define it "a political community without a political superior?" Tested by this, no one of our States, except Texas, ever was a sovereignty; and even Texas gave up the character on coming into the Union, by which act she acknowledged the Constitution of the United States . . . to be for her the supreme law of the land. The States have their status in the Union, and they have no other legal status. If they break from this, they can do so only against law and by revolution. The Union, and not themselves separately, procured their independence and their liberty. By conquest or purchase the Union gave each of them whatever of independence and liberty it has. The Union is older than any of the States, and, in fact, it created them as States. . . .

Our popular Government has often been called an experiment. Two points in it our people have already settled—the successful *establishing* and the successful *administering* of it. One still remains—its successful *maintenance* against a formidable internal attempt to overthrow it. It is now for them to demonstrate to the world that those who can fairly carry an election can also suppress a rebellion; that ballots are the rightful and peaceful successors of bullets, and that when ballots have fairly and constitutionally decided there can be no successful appeal back to bullets; that there can be no successful appeal except to ballots themselves at succeeding elections. Such will be a great lesson of peace, teaching men that what they cannot take by an election neither can they take it by a war. . . .

The Constitution provides, and all the States have accepted the provision, that "the United States shall guarantee to every State in this Union a republican form of government." But if a State may lawfully go out of the Union, having done so it may also discard the republican form of government; so that to prevent its going out is an indispensable *means* to the end of maintaining the guaranty mentioned. . . .

It was with the deepest regret that the Executive found the duty of employing the war power in defense of the Government forced upon him. He could but perform this duty or surrender the existence of the Government.

Second Thoughts

Why Did North and South Go to War?

1.4 Civil War

Great events in history seldom admit of easy explanation. So it is with the American Civil War. While all agree that the war started at Fort Sumter, few agree on why. Theories cite Northern aggression or Southern secession, slavery and racism, abolitionist agitation and Southern paranoia, capitalism vanquishing feudalism, the inevitable tension between incompatible cultures locked into an artificial union, bumbling political leadership, the assumption of power by a regional rather than a national party, and even an excess of democratic zeal. Some find the origin of the war in the tensions resulting from the expansion of the nation's borders. Samuel Eliot Morison viewed the struggle between North and South for control of the west as key, declaring that "with no Mexican War there would have been no Civil War, at least not in 1861." Though the Civil War remains one of the most momentous events in the history of the United States, neither those who waged it nor those who have since studied it have ever reached agreement on its causes.

Source 7   Henry Wilson, Radical Republican, speech to the United States Senate, May 1, 1862

How can any man looking over this broad land today and seeing flashing from every quarter of the heavens the crimes of human slavery against this country, labor to uphold, strengthen, and support human slavery in America? It is the cause and the whole cause of this rebellion. We talk about "Jeff" Davis, Slidell, Mason, and Toombs, and their treasonable confederates; but they are not the cause of this rebellion; they are simply the hands, the tools, the heart, the brain, the soul is slavery; the motive power is slavery. Slavery is the great rebel; Davis and his compeers are but its humble tools and instruments.

Slavery for thirty years has been hostile to and aggressive upon the free institutions of America. There is not a principle embodied in our free institutions, there is not an element of our government that elevates or blesses mankind, there is not anything in our government or our institutions worth preserving, that slavery for a generation has not warred against and upon.

It smote down thirty years ago the right of petition in these halls. It destroyed in large sections of the country the constitutional freedom of the press. It suppressed freedom of speech. It corrupted presses, churches, and political organizations. It plunged the nation into a war for the acquisition of slave-holding territory. It enacted a fugitive-slave law, inhuman, unchristian, disgraceful to the country and to the age. It repealed the prohibition of slavery over a half a million square miles in the central regions of the continent. It seized the ballot boxes in Kansas; it usurped the government of the Territory; it enacted inhuman and unchristian laws; it made a slave constitution and attempted to force it upon a free people; it bathed the virgin sods of that magnificent Territory with the blood of civil war. It mobbed, flogged, expelled, and sometimes murdered Christian men and women in the slave-holding States for no offence against law, humanity, or religion. It turned the hearts of large masses of men against their brethren, against the institutions of their country, against the glorious old flag, and the constitution of their fathers. It has now plunged this nation into this unholy rebellion, into this gigantic civil war that rends the country, and stains our waters and reddens our fields with fraternal blood.

Sir, I never see a loyal soldier upon a cot of sickness, sorrow, or death, without feeling that slavery has laid him there. I never gaze upon the wounds of a loyal soldier fallen in support of the flag of the republic without feeling that slavery inflicted those wounds upon him. I never see a loyal soldier wounded and maimed hobbling through your streets without feeling he was wounded and maimed by slavery. I never gaze upon the lowly grave of a loyal soldier dying for the cause of his country without feeling he was murdered by slavery. I never see a mourning wife or sorrowing children without realizing that slavery has made that mourning wife a widow and those children orphans.

Sir, all these sacrifices of property, of health, of life, all this sorrow, agony, and death, now upon us, are born of slavery. Slavery is the prolific mother of all those woes that blight our land and fill the heart of our people with sorrows.

Slavery pronounced long ago against the free elements of our popular institutions; it scoffed at the Declaration of Independence; it pronounced free society a failure; it jeered and sneered at the laboring masses as mudsills and white slaves. Scoffing at everything which tended to secure the rights and enlarge the privileges of mankind, it has pronounced against the existence of democratic institutions in America. Proud, domineering, defiant, it has pronounced against the supremacy of the government, the unity and life of the nation.

Sir, slavery is the enemy, the clearly pronounced enemy of the country. Slavery is the only enemy our country has on God's earth. There it stands. Hate is in its heart, scorn in its eye, defiance in its mein. It hates our cherished institutions, despises our people, defies our government. Slavery is the great rebel, the giant criminal, the murderer striving with dirty hands to throttle our government and destroy our country.

Source 8 Clement L. Vallandigham, Democratic congressman for Ohio, "Speech on the War and Its Conduct," January 14, 1863

Sir, I am one of that number who have opposed abolitionism, or the political development of the anti-slavery sentiment of the North and West, from the beginning. . . . Sir, it is but the development of the spirit of intermeddling, whose children are strife and murder. Cain troubled himself about the sacrifices of Abel and slew his brother. Most of the wars, contentions, litigations, and bloodshed, from the beginning of time have been its fruits. The spirit of non-intervention is the very spirit of peace and concord.

I do not believe that if slavery had never existed here we would have had no sectional controversies. This very civil war might have happened fifty, perhaps a hundred, years later. Other and stronger causes of discontent and of disunion, it may be, have existed between other states and sections, and are now being developed into maturity. The spirit of intervention assumed the form of abolitionism because slavery was odious in name and by association to the Northern mind, and because it was that which most obviously marks the different civilizations of the two sections.

The South herself, in her early and later efforts to rid herself of it, had exposed the weak and offensive parts of slavery to the world. Abolition intermeddling taught her at last to search for and defend the assumed social, economic, and political merits and values of the institution. But there never was an hour from the beginning when it did not seem to me as clear as the sun at broad noon that the agitation in any form, in the North and West, of the slavery question must sooner or later end in disunion and civil war.

Source 9   Edward Pollard, editor of the *Richmond Examiner*, *The Lost Cause: A New Southern History of the War of the Confederates,* 1866

No one can read aright the history of America, unless in the light of a North and a South; two political aliens existing in a Union imperfectly defined as a confederation of states. . . .

The slavery question is not to be taken as an independent controversy in American politics. It was not a moral dispute. It was the mere incident of a sectional animosity, the causes of which lay far beyond the domain of morals. Slavery furnished a convenient line of battle between the disputants; it was the most prominent ground of distinction between the two sections; it was, therefore, naturally seized upon as a subject of controversy, became the dominant theatre of hostilities, and was at last so conspicuous and violent, that occasion was mistaken for cause, and what was merely an incident came to be regarded as the main subject of controversy. . . .

The North naturally found or imagined in slavery the leading cause of the distinctive civilization of the South, its higher sentimentalism, and its superior refinements of scholarship and manners. It revenged itself on the cause, diverted its envy in an attack on slavery. . . . [T]he slavery question was not a moral one in the North, unless, perhaps, with a few thousand persons of disordered conscience. It was significant only of a contest for political power, and afforded nothing more than a convenient ground of dispute between two . . . opposite civilizations.

In the ante-revolutionary period, the differences between the populations of the Northern and Southern colonies had already been strongly developed. The early colonists did not bear with them from the mother-country to the shores of the New World any greater degree of congeniality than existed among them at home. They had come not only from different stocks of population, but from different feuds in religion and politics. There could be no congeniality between the Puritan exiles who established themselves upon the cold and rugged and cheerless soil of New England, and the Cavaliers who sought the brighter climate of the South. . . .

[T]he intolerance of the Puritans, the painful thrift of the Northern colonists, their external forms of piety, their jaundiced legislation, their convenient morals, their lack of sentimentalism . . . , and their unremitting hunt after selfish aggrandizement are traits of character which are yet visible in their descendents. On the other hand, the colonists of Virginia and the Carolinas were from the first distinguished by their polite manners, their fine sentiments, their attachment to a sort of feudal life, their landed gentry, their love of field-sports and dangerous adventure, and the prodigal and improvident aristocracy that dispensed its stores in constant rounds of hospitality and gaiety.

Slavery established in the South a peculiar and noble type of civilization. . . . The South had an element in its society—a landed gentry—which the North envied, and for which its substitute was a coarse ostentatious aristocracy that smelt of trade, and that, however it cleansed itself and aped the elegance of the South, and packed its houses with fine furniture, could never entirely subdue a sneaking sense of its inferiority. There is a singular bitter hate which is inseparable from a sense of inferiority.

Source 10   Alexander H. Stephens, former vice president of the Confederacy, *A Constitutional View of the Late War between the States,* 1868

It is a postulate, with many writers of this day, that the late war was the result of two opposing ideas, or principles, upon the subject of African Slavery. Between these, according to their theory, sprung the "irrepressible conflict," in principle, which ended in the terrible conflict of arms. Those who assume this postulate, and so theorize upon it, are but superficial observers.

That the War had its origin in *opposing principles* . . . may be assumed as an unquestionable fact. But the opposing principles which produced these results in physical action were of a very different character from those assumed in the postulate. They lay in the organic Structure of the Government of the States. The conflict in principle arose from different and opposing ideas as to the nature of what is known as the General Government. The contest was between those who held it to be strictly Federal in its character, and those who maintained that it was thoroughly National. It was a strife between the principles of Federalism, on the one hand, and Centralism, or Consolidation, on the other.

Source 11   Vice President Henry Wilson, a radical Republican, *The History of the Rise and Fall of Slavepower in America,* 1877

By means illegitimate and indefensible, reckless of principle and of consequences, a comparatively few men succeeded in dragooning whole States into the support of a policy the majority condemned, to following leaders the majority distrusted and most cordially disliked. . . . [A] class of men who despised the colored man because he was colored, and the poor whites because they were poor, inspire[d] the latter with a willingness, an enthusiasm even, to take up arms, subject themselves to all the hardships and hazards of war, for the express purpose of perpetuating and making more despotic a system which had already despoiled them of so much, and was designed to make still more abject their degradation.

Source 12 James Ford Rhodes, *Lectures on the American Civil War,* 1913

[O]f the American Civil War it may be safely asserted that there was but a single cause, slavery. . . . The question may be isolated by the incontrovertible statement that if the Negro had never been brought to America, our Civil War would never had occurred.

Source 13 Charles A. and Mary R. Beard, *The Rise of American Civilization,* 1933

The Civil War . . . , called in these pages the "Second American Revolution," was merely the culmination of the deep-running transformation that shifted the center of gravity in American society between the inauguration of Jackson and the election of Lincoln. . . .

[T]he so-called Civil War, or the War between the States, . . . was a social war, ending in the unquestioned establishment of a new power in the government, making vast changes in the arrangement of classes, in the accumulation and distribution of wealth, in the course of industrial development, and in the Constitution inherited from the Fathers. Merely by the accidents of climate, soil, and geography was it a sectional struggle. If the planting interest had been scattered evenly throughout the industrial region, had there been a horizontal rather than a perpendicular cleavage, the irrepressible conflict would have been resolved by other methods. . . .

In any event neither accident nor rhetoric should be allowed to obscure the intrinsic character of the struggle. If the operations by which the middle classes of England broke the power of the king and the aristocracy are to be known collectively as the Puritan Revolution, if the series of acts by which the bourgeois and peasants of France overthrew the king, nobility, and clergy is to be called the French Revolution, then accuracy compels us to characterize by the same term the social cataclysm in which the capitalists, laborers, and farmers of the North and West drove from power in the national government the planting aristocracy of the South. Viewed in the light of universal history, the fighting was a fleeting incident; the social revolution was the essential, portentous outcome.

Source 14 Allan Nevins, *The Emergence of Lincoln,* 1950

The main root of the conflict (and there were minor roots) was the problem of slavery with *its complementary problem of race-adjustment;* the main source of the tragedy was the refusal of either section to face these conjoined problems squarely and pay the heavy costs of a peaceful settlement. Had it not been for the difference in race, the slavery issue would have presented no great difficulties. But as the racial gulf existed, the South inarticulately but clearly perceived that elimination of this issue would still leave it the terrible problem of the Negro. Those historians who write that if slavery had simply been left alone it would soon have withered overlook this heavy impediment.

Source 15 David Donald, *Lincoln Reconsidered*, 1961

The Civil War, I believe, can best be understood neither as the result of accident nor as the product of conflicting sectional interests, but as the outgrowth of social processes which affected the entire United States during the first half of the nineteenth century. . . .

In the early nineteenth century all sections of the United States were being transformed with such rapidity that stability and security were everywhere vanishing values; nowhere could a father predict what kind of world his son would grow up in. . . .

In a nation so new that, as President James K. Polk observed, its history was in the future, in a land of such abundance, men felt under no obligation to respect the lessons of the past. . . . Every aspect of American life witnessed this desire to throw off precedent and to rebel from authority. Every institution which laid claim to prescriptive right was challenged and overthrown. The Church . . . was first disestablished . . . and then strange new sects . . . appeared to fragment the Christian community. The squirearchy, once a powerful conservative influence in the Middle States and the South, was undermined by the abolition of primogeniture and entails. . . . All centralizing economic institutions came under attack. The Second Bank of the United States, which exercised a healthy restraint upon financial chaos, was abolished during the Jackson period. . . .

Nowhere was the American rejection of authority more complete than in the political sphere. . . . By the 1850's the authority of all government in America was at a low point; government to the American was, at most, merely an institution with a negative role, a guardian of fair play.

Declining power of government was paralleled by increased popular participation in it. The extension of the franchise in America has rarely been the result of a concerted reform drive, . . . rather it has been part of the gradual erosion of all authority, of the feeling that restraints and differentials are necessarily anti-democratic, and of the practical fact that such restrictions are difficult to enforce. . . .

Possibly in time this disorganized society might have evolved a genuinely conservative solution for its problems, but time ran against it. At a stage when the United States was least capable of enduring shock, the nation was obliged to undergo a series of crises, largely triggered by the physical expansion of the country. . . .

These crises . . . were not in themselves calamitous experiences. Revisionist historians have correctly pointed out how little was actually at stake: slavery did not go into New Mexico or Arizona; Kansas, after having been opened to the peculiar institution for six years, had only two Negro slaves; the Dred Scott decision declared an already repealed law unconstitutional; John Brown's raid had no significant support in the North and certainly aroused no visible enthusiasm among Southern Negroes. When compared to crises which other nations have resolved without great discomfort, the true proportions of these exaggerated disturbances appear.

But American society in the 1850's was singularly ill-equipped to meet any shocks, however weak. It was a society so new and so disorganized that its nerves were rawly exposed. It was . . . a land which had . . . no resistance to strain. The very similarity of the social processes which affected all sections of the country—the expansion of the frontier, the rise of the city, the exploitation of great natural wealth—produced not cohesion but individualism. The structure of the American political system impeded the appearance of conservative statesmanship, and the rapidity of the crises in the 1850's prevented conservatism from crystallizing. The crises themselves were not world-shaking, nor did they inevitably produce war. They were, however, the chisel strokes which revealed the fundamental flaws in the block of marble, flaws which stemmed from an excess of democracy.

Source 16 Eugene Genovese, *The Political Economy of Slavery,* 1967

I do say that the struggle between North and South was irrepressible. From the moment that slavery passed from being one of several labor systems into being the basis of the Southern social order, material and ideological conflict with the North came into being and had to grow worse. If this much is granted, the question of inevitability becomes a question of whether or not the slaveholders would give up their world, which they identified properly with slavery itself, without armed resistance. The slaveholders' pride, sense of honor, and commitment to their way of life made a final struggle so probable that we may safely call it inevitable without implying a mechanistic determinism against which man cannot avail.

Source 17 Howard Zinn, *A People's History of the United States,* 1980

Behind the secession of the South from the Union . . . was a long series of policy clashes between South and North. The clash was not over slavery as a moral institution—most northerners did not care enough about slavery to make sacrifices for it, certainly not the sacrifice of war. It was not a clash of peoples (most northern whites were not economically favored, not politically powerful; most southern whites were poor farmers, not decisionmakers) but of elites. The northern elite wanted economic expansion—free land, free labor, a free market, a high protective tariff for manufacturers, a bank of the United States. The slave interests opposed all that; they saw Lincoln and the Republicans as making continuation of their pleasant and prosperous way of life impossible in the future.

So, when Lincoln was elected, seven states seceded from the Union. Lincoln initiated hostilities by trying to repossess the federal base at Fort Sumter, South Carolina, and four more states seceded. The Confederacy was formed; the Civil War was on.

Questioning the Past

1. Did Lincoln intentionally provoke the incident at Fort Sumter? Was South Carolina at fault for firing on the Fort? Which side was responsible for the firing on Fort Sumter? With the benefit of hindsight, should either Lincoln or South Carolina have handled the incident any differently?

2. Present the various theories offered to explain why North and South went to war. What theory, or theories, seem most valid?

3. What role did slavery play in producing the tensions that led to war?

4. Historian Samuel Eliot Morison wrote that "with no Mexican War there would have been no Civil War, at least not in 1861." What rationale could be offered in support of this thesis?

5. Suppose Lincoln had not resisted the effort of the southern states to secede, and the Confederacy had been allowed to establish itself as a sovereign nation. In what ways might the history of America since 1860 have been different? What would North America be like today?

Chapter 2

One Nation, Indivisible

Robert E. Lee Surrenders the Army of Northern Virginia, April 9, 1865

While at church services on the afternoon of the second day of April, 1865, President Jefferson Davis received an urgent message from General Robert E. Lee: Confederate forces could no longer defend Richmond against the swelling Union troops who were besieging it. The government must be evacuated without delay.

Later that evening observers described a tremendous series of explosions in the capital city of the Confederacy, "resembling an earthquake, and being heard for miles around." The Confederates had blown up their forts and they had destroyed their **iron-clads** and **rams** on the James River. The warship *Virginia* had been sent to the bottom of the river. The James River bridges had been demolished. The business and industrial districts of Richmond were set ablaze. Flames from eight hundred burning buildings could be seen at great distance. Officials of the Confederate government slipped away under cover of the night. By morning, Lee had pulled what was left of the Army of Northern Virginia out of its defensive trench works around Richmond and Petersburg and had begun a westward retreat.

After four exhausting years of war, and a nine-month siege of Richmond, Union troops at last entered and occupied the Confederate capital. The flag of the United States was again raised over the city after a long absence. President Lincoln accompanied the occupying troops and toured the burned-out remains of the city. The war was not yet over, but an end was within reach.

Word of the fall of Richmond took only hours to reach the capital of the Union a hundred miles to the north. "Cannons were fired, bells rung, flags hung out, processions formed, crowds collected, and speaking in all quarters," according to the local press. "The Court adjourned, the public schools were dismissed, the Engine companies turned out. All accounts represent the enthusiasm and excitement to have surpassed anything ever before seen in Washington." As a crowd gathered in front of his residence, Vice President Andrew Johnson took the opportunity to discuss the winning of the peace that would follow the winning of the war. "I am in favor of leniency, but, in my opinion, evil deeds should be punished," Johnson told the assembly which loudly shouted back its approval. "Treason is the highest crime known in the catalogue of crimes, and for him that is guilty of it—for him that is willing to lift his impious hand against the authority of the nation—I would say death is too easy a punishment."

❧ *First Impressions*

A Union Restored and Purified

Lee moved his army westward toward Lynchburg, hoping to evade the Union armies pursuing him and link up with another Confederate army in North Carolina commanded by General Joseph Johnston. But Union troops in superior numbers outmaneuvered Lee's Army of Northern Virginia and sealed off his path of retreat.

Source 1   Correspondence between General U.S. Grant, United States Army, and General Robert E. Lee, commanding the Army of Northern Virginia, CSA

2.1 Robert E. Lee

April 7, 1865

General R. E. Lee, Commanding C.S.A.

GENERAL: The result of the last week must convince you of the hopelessness of further resistance on the part of the army of Northern Virginia in this struggle. I feel that it is so, and regard it as my duty to shift from myself the responsibility of any further effusion of blood, by asking of you the surrender of that portion of the Confederate army, known as the Army of Northern Virginia.

> Very respectfully, your obedient servant,
> U.S. Grant, Lieut. General
> Commanding Armies United States

April 7, 1865

To Lieut. Gen. U.S. Grant, Commanding Armies of the United States:

GENERAL: I have received your note of this date. Though not entirely of the same opinion you express of the hopelessness of the further resistance on the part of the Army of Northern Virginia, I reciprocate your desire to avoid useless effusion of blood, and therefore, considering your proposition, ask the terms you will offer on condition of its surrender.

> R. E. Lee, General

April 8, 1865

Gen. R. E. Lee, Commanding C.S.A.:

GENERAL: Your note of last evening, in reply to mine of same date, asking conditions on which I will accept the surrender of the Army of Northern Virginia, is just received. In reply, I would say that peace being my first desire, there is but one condition I insist upon, viz:

That the men surrendered shall be disqualified for taking up arms again against the Government of the United States, until properly exchanged. I will meet you, or designate officers to meet any officers you may name for the same purpose, at any point agreeable to you, for the purpose of arranging definitely the terms upon which the surrender of the Army of Northern Virginia will be received.

Very respectfully, your obedient servant,
U.S. Grant, Lieutenant General

April 8, 1865

GENERAL: I received at a late hour your note of to-day, in answer to mine of yesterday. I did not intend to propose the surrender of the Army of Northern Virginia, but to ask the terms of your proposition. To be frank, I do not think the emergency has arisen to call for the surrender of this army, but as the restoration of peace should be the sole object of all, I desire to know whether your proposals would tend to that end. I cannot, therefore, meet you with a view to surrender the Army of Northern Virginia; but as far as your proposition may affect the Confederate States forces under my command, and tend to the restoration of peace, I should be pleased to meet you at 10 A.M., to-morrow, on the old stage road to Richmond, between the picket lines of the two armies.

Very respectfully, your ob't serv't,
R. E. Lee, General, C.S.A.

April 9, 1865

Gen. R. E. Lee, Commanding C.S.A.

GENERAL: Your note of yesterday is received. As I have no authority to treat on the subject of peace, the meeting proposed for 10 A.M. to-day could lead to no good. I will state, however, General, that I am equally anxious for peace with yourself, and the whole North entertains the same feeling. The terms upon which peace can be had are well understood. By the South laying down their arms they will hasten that desirable event, save thousands of human lives, and hundreds of millions of property not yet destroyed.

Sincerely hoping that all our difficulties may be settled without the loss of another life, I subscribe myself, very respectfully,

Your obedient servant,
U.S. Grant, Lieutenant General

April 9, 1865

GENERAL: I received your note of this morning at the picket line, whither I had come to meet you, to ascertain definitely what terms were embraced in your proposition of yesterday. With reference to the surrender of this army, I now request an interview in accordance with the offer contained in your letter of yesterday for that purpose.

Very respectfully, your obedient servant,
R. E. Lee, General, C.S.A.

April 9, 1865

General R. E. Lee, Commanding Confederate States Army

Your note of this date is but this moment, 11:55 A.M., received, in consequence of my having passed from the Richmond and Lynchburg to the Farmville and Lynchburg road. I am at this moment about four miles west of Walter's Church and will push forward to the front for the purpose of meeting you. Notice sent to me on this road where you wish the interview to take place, will meet me.

> Very respectfully, your obedient servant,
> U.S. Grant, Lieut. General

Appomattox, C.H.,
April 9, 1865

General R. E. Lee, Commanding C.S.A.:

In accordance with the substance of my letter to you of the 8th inst., I propose the surrender of the Army of Northern Virginia, on the following terms, to wit:

Rolls of all the officers and men to be made in duplicate, one copy to be given to an officer designated by me, the other to be retained by such officer or officers as you may designate.—The officers to give their individual paroles not to take up arms against the Government of the United States until properly exchanged, and each company or regimental commander to sign a like parole for the men of their commands. The arms, artillery, and public property to be packed and stacked, and turned over to the officers appointed by me to receive them. This will not embrace the side arms of the officers, not their private horses or baggage. This done, each officer and man will be allowed to return to their homes, not to be disturbed by the United States authority so long as they observe the laws in force where they may reside.

> Very respectfully,
> U.S. Grant, Lieut. General

April 9, 1865

Lieutenant Gen. U.S. Grant, Commanding, United States Armies:

GENERAL: I have received your letter of this date containing the terms of surrender for the Army of Northern Virginia, as proposed by you. As they are substantially the same as those expressed in your letter of the 8th inst., they are accepted. I will proceed to designate the proper officers to carry the stipulations into effect.

> Very respectfully, your obedient servant,
> R. E. Lee, General

Source 2   Editorial, "The Rebellion," *New York Times,* April 11, 1865

If one had looked yesterday to see our people go into extravagant demonstrations over the surrender of the rebel army—which is the surrender of the rebellion itself—he is by this time undeceived. Had we not been fully aware of the deep and solemn earnestness of the loyal heart, we should indeed wonder at what might almost be characterized as indifference. But still waters run deep. Four years of trial such as no nation on the earth has lived through: four year of unequaled financial pressure; of mental and physical tension, to the top of our bent, of armies till now unknown in history for numbers, for courage, for endurance, for achievement; four years of wrestling with a foe of our own blood and birth, a foe however grievously at fault still "worthy of our steel," four years in which no sun has set that did not pale its fire over newly bereaved hearthstones, and rekindle its morning rays amid the tears of widows and orphans; four such years have sobered and chastened our hearts to feelings more in accordance with our sufferings and our hopes than could be expressed in any wild bacchanalian revelry.

Source 3   Editorial "Lee Surrenders!" *New York Tribune*, April 12, 1865

Lee has surrendered! Three words only, but how much they mean! On Sunday night at 11 o'clock this news reached us, and before we had finished reading the dispatch cheer upon cheer rung through the night air, so quickly had the intelligence, not ten minutes off the wires, escaped to the street to be carried, like the beacon-flash from mountain-top to mountain-top that gathered the clans from a whole country-side, into thousands of households to be repeated in prayers of thanksgiving from thousands of family altars. In October, 1781, on a dark and stormy night, the little town of Boston was startled from its slumbers by the clear voice of a solitary watchman who cried: "Twal o'clock and Cornwalis be taken!" Three words—Cornwalis is taken! but how much they meant! The liberties of a whole people were achieved; the struggle of eight years was ended; the long, dark night of war was over; the bright dawn of Peace had broken; England was conquered! Now Lee has surrendered; our struggle is over; the new birth of the Nation is accomplished; the Revolution, begun a hundred years ago, is fulfilled; Republicanism, tried by the severest test to which it can ever be put, is triumphant; domestic treason is utterly suppressed and punished; freedom is extended to all the people; that "all men are created free and equal" is no longer an abstract principle, but the faith and foundation of a nation; the South is conquered, the Rebellion over, and peace immediate with a Union restored and purified! . . .

Shall we not bless God? We were more unbelieving than infidels if we did not. It is "His Kingdom come" inasmuch as it is the triumph of right over wrong. The great and holy cause of the Rights of Man, of Free Government, which the world has been fighting for these many centuries, is established as no man living ever dared hope to see. The People reign; there is presently to be "peace and good will to man." This is the meaning of the end of the Rebellion. This is what peace in the United States means to all the people of all the earth.

A New Social Order

In the weeks following the surrender of the Army of Northern Virginia, other Confederate forces across the South laid down their arms. The war was over. The peace was yet to be won.

The victory of the North on the battlefield had forced the South to stop fighting, but was that enough? Did the United States go to war against the South solely to suppress a rebellion? If so, then an end to armed resistance was a fitting enough peace. If the war was waged to preserve the Union, then forcing the Southern states back into a constitutional relationship with the rest of the country was an appropriate outcome of the conflict. But was a peace that yielded no more than a return to the way things were before the firing on Fort Sumter, or before the Southern states announced an intention to secede, enough?

Now that the North had the upper hand, should it check its strength in an act of mercy? Should it forgive and forget in hopes of achieving a lasting reconciliation between North and South? Bayonets may win battles over an enemy but they do not win over the enemy's heart and mind. Would leniency and compassion win the allegiance of the South to the Union?

Or did the sacrifice of more than half a million lives—lives tragically abbreviated through the horrors of war—call out for justice, revenge, and even retribution? Should a peace forcing change be imposed upon the South? Should the peace include an end to slavery, or more: a new social order in the South?

These were weighty questions to ponder. And their answer involved equally complex legal issues. If secession was, as Lincoln had always argued, unconstitutional, then the Southern states had never legally left the Union. With the end of the fighting, the Southern States and their citizens should be expected to resume their normal functions within the federal system. But if the South had indeed separated from the United States to form a new country, then the South had no claim to the protections of the Constitution. The victorious North could treat the Confederacy as a conquered country.

In 1865, these questions seemed open to no easy answer.

Source 4   *Alexandria Gazette* of Virginia, April 12, 1865, reporting on the last public speech of Abraham Lincoln

Numbers of persons assembled in front of the President's House in Washington, last night, and upon their call, the President came out, and addressed them. After an allusion to the causes of the rejoicing, &c, he went on to discuss the subject of the reconstruction of Louisiana, and . . . proceeded as follows:

"We all agree that the seceded States, so called, are out of their proper practical relation with the Union, and that the sole object of the Government, civil and military, in regard to those States, is to again get them into that proper practical relation. I believe that it is not only possible, but in fact easier, to do this without deciding or even considering whether these States have ever been out of the Union, than with it. . . . Finding themselves safely at home, it would be utterly immaterial whether they had ever been abroad. Let us all join in doing the acts necessary to restoring the proper practical relations between these States and the Union, and each forever after innocently indulge his own opinion whether in doing the acts he brought the States from without into the Union, or only gave them proper assistance, they never having been out of it.

The amount of constituency, so to speak, on which the new Louisiana government rests, would be more satisfactory to all, if it contained fifty, thirty, or even twenty thousand, instead of only about twelve thousand, as it really does. It is also unsatisfactory to some, that the elective franchise is not given to the colored man. I would myself prefer that it were now conferred on the very intelligent, and on those who serve our cause as soldiers. Still the question is not whether the Louisiana government, as it stands, is quite all that is desirable. The question is 'Will it be wiser to take it as it is, and help to improve it; or to reject and disperse it?' 'Can Louisiana be brought into proper practical relation with the Union sooner by sustaining, or by discarding her new State government?'

Some twelve thousand voters in the heretofore slave State of Louisiana have sworn allegiance to the Union; assumed to be the rightful political power of the State; held elections; organized a free government; adopted a free State constitution, giving the benefit of public schools equally to black and white, and empowering the Legislature to confer the elective franchise upon the colored man. Their legislature has already voted to ratify the constitutional amendment, recently passed by Congress, abolishing slavery throughout the nation. These twelve thousand persons are thus fully committed to the Union, and to perpetual freedom in the States—committed to the very things, and nearly all the things, the nation wants—and they ask the nation's recognition and its assistance to make good that committal.

Now, if we reject and spurn them, we do our utmost to disorganize and disperse them. We in effect say to the white man, 'You are worthless, or worse, we will neither help you nor be helped by you.' To the blacks, we say, 'This cup of liberty which these, your old masters, hold to your lips, we will dash from you, and leave you to the chances of gathering the spilled and scattered contents, in some vague and undefined when, where, and how.' If this course, discouraging and paralyzing both white and black, has any tendency to bring Louisiana into proper practical relations with the Union, I have, so far, been unable to perceive it.

If, on the contrary, we recognize and sustain the new government of Louisiana, the converse of all this is made true. We encourage the hearts and nerve the arms of the twelve thousand to adhere to their work, and argue for it, and proselytize for it, and fight for it, and feed it, and grow it, and ripen it to a complete success. The colored man, too, seeing all united for him is inspired with vigilance, and energy, and daring to the same end. Grant that he desires the elective franchise. Will he not attain it sooner by saving the already advanced steps toward it than by running backward over them? Concede that the new government of Louisiana is only to what it should be as the egg is to the fowl, we shall sooner have the fowl by hatching the egg than by smashing it. (Laughter.). . .

I repeat the question: 'Can Louisiana be brought into proper practical relation with the Union sooner by sustaining or by discarding her new State government?' What has been said of Louisiana will apply generally to the other States."

Source 5   Editorial, "Magnanimity in Triumph," *New York Tribune*, April 15, 1865

We hear men say—"Yes, forgive the great mass of those who have been misled into rebellion, but punish the leaders as they deserve." But who can accurately draw the line between leaders and followers in the premises? Some of the arch-plotters of Disunion have never taken up arms in its support, nor have they held any important post in its civil services. Where is your touchstone of leadership? We know none. . . .

But we cannot believe it wise or well to take the life of any man who shall have submitted to the National authority. The execution of even one such would be felt as a personal stigma by every one who had ever aided the Rebel cause. Each would say to himself, "I am as culpable as he; we differ only in that I am deemed of comparatively little consequence." A single Confederate led out to execution would be evermore enshrined in a million hearts as a conspicuous hero and martyr. We cannot realize that it would be wholesome or safe—we are sure it would not be magnanimous—to give the overpowered disloyalty of the South such a shrine. . . .

We plead against passions certain at this moment to be fierce and intolerant; but on our side are the Ages and the voice of History. We plead for a restoration of the Union, against a policy which would afford a momentary gratification at the cost of years of perilous hate and bitterness.

Source 6   Abolitionist Gerrit Smith, "Thoughts for the People," handbill, April 19, 1865

Let the first condition of Peace with them be that no people in the Rebel States shall ever either lose or gain civil or political rights by reason of their race or origin. God would have no right, social, ecclesiastical, nor any other, turn on such peculiarities. . . . A Peace, which denies the ballot to the black man, would be war:—and perhaps the worst of wars—a war of races.

2.2 Civil War Resources on the Internet: Abolitionism to Reconstruction

Let the second condition of Peace be that our black allies in the South— those saviors of our nation—shall share with their poor white neighbors in the subdivisions of the large landed estates of the South. And this, not merely to compensate them for what we owe them:—and not merely because they are destitute of property:—and not merely because they have ever been robbed of their earnings and denied the acquisition of property:—but, more than all these, because the title to the soil of the whole South is equitably in them, who have ever tilled it, and profusely shed upon it their sweat and tears and blood.

Let the only other condition be that the rebel masses shall not, for, say, a dozen years, be allowed access to the ballot-box, or be eligible to hold office; and that the like restrictions be for life on their political and military leaders. Without such restrictions there would be no safety for either the blacks or loyal whites of the South; and no adequate security against the nation's sinking into a condition worse in some respects than that from which she is now emerging.

Source 7   Speech of President Andrew Johnson, April 21, 1865

Some are satisfied with the idea that States . . . are to lose their character as States. But their life-breath has only been suspended, and it is a high constitutional obligation we have to secure each of these States in the possession and enjoyment of a republican form of Government. A State may be in the Government with a peculiar institution, and by the operation of a rebellion lose that feature. But it was a State when it went into a rebellion, and when it comes out without the institution it is still a State.

Source 8   Editorial, "The Points to Be Secured before Reconstruction,"
New York Times, May 5, 1865

The government has always demanded, and has now substantially obtained of the rebels, an unconditional submission. This does not mean simply an unconditional submission to the Federal Constitution and the laws of the land. It takes an antecedent submission to military rule. Until an amnesty is declared by President Johnson . . . all Southern rebels have no civil **status** whatever. So far as their *civil rights* and *franchises* are concerned, they are to-day practically as much outside of the pale of the Federal Constitution as the people of Russia. They are subject to military rule only.

This condition of things must be terminated as soon as possible. It is humiliating to the South, and, what is worse, it is altogether repugnant to our free institutions. The great question is how this state of things can be terminated, *justly* and *safely*. The submission has been without qualification; but the rehabilitation must have qualifications. What?

First—Some satisfaction must be rendered to justice for treason. The Constitution which makes treason a crime, and the statute of law, which attaches to it the penalty of death, must be vindicated. This will be effected by visiting capital punishment upon the guiltiest of the leaders who fall into the hands of the government. Commutation to a lighter penalty may be made in favor of those less criminal.

Second—Some safeguard must be established for the protection of the government against future sedition. The government is bound, in justice to itself, to see that the institution from which sprang the rebellion, is rooted out beyond all power of a new growth. It, therefore, is perfectly right, in exerting its influence, as far as possible, with the people of some of the redeemed States, to cause them to ratify the constitutional amendment forever interdicting slavery throughout the land. . . .

But there are, and long will be, bad men in every Southern State, who are filled with the most rancorous hate of the government, and whose whole study hereafter will be how to do it injury. All such men can be shut out of Congress by the very stringent oath of allegiance which is now required before allowing a seat in either body. . . .

When the government has thus supplemented its final annihilation of slavery, the cause of the rebellion, by practically disfranchising and shutting out of public office all who are rebellious in spirit, its work, as far as relates to its own protection, will be at an end. . . .

Third—Some security must be provided for the freedmen of the South. They have been unswervingly loyal to the government from the beginning of the rebellion, and that alone is enough to entitle them to its special protection. Moreover, the government, for its own purposes, made them what they are, and it therefore is bound to take care that emancipation shall be a blessing to them, and not a curse. The fulfillment of these duties is really the hardest difficulty, the very gordian knot of reconstruction. . . .

The Southern people may not any longer look upon the blacks as mere chattels; but yet they will regard them as an inferior and servile race. They will naturally be disposed to withhold from them the privileges which are indispensable to their civil and social elevation, and to keep them in a benighted and abject condition, best fit for passive service, and which will only be slavery under another name. . . .

How shall the government counteract it? Some say by giving all the Southern blacks the elective franchise, and thus enabling them to protect their rights. But the right of suffrage, without an intelligent mind behind it, would not afford this protection. Knowledge is power, politically as well as in every other way. A vote would no more make an ignorant freedman independent than it would a child five years old. The great point is not so much to secure suffrage for these poor people as education. Give the black multitudes of the South the advantages of good instruction, and there is no danger but that they and their children will in due time obtain all the political power they are qualified to exercise, and be able to protect themselves from wrong in every form. . . .

We have mentioned all the preliminaries which the government ought to assure before the reinstatement of the Southern people. The rebel leaders should be punished. So much for the general justice. Slavery should be utterly destroyed; and all who will not swear fidelity to the national government, should be disfranchised, and debarred from all eligibility to office. So much for security to the government. The freedmen should be secured from all further oppression, and to this end should be especially guaranteed public instruction. So much for justice to the race which has served us. These three ends provided for, the restoration of the South to its equality with every other part of the republic cannot be too quick or too complete. Every loyal man will hail the day when it is accomplished.

Source 9 Howell Cobb, former U.S. congressman, former governor of Georgia, former Confederate congressman and Confederate general, letter transmitted to President Johnson, June 14, 1865

I was a secessionist, and counselled the people of Georgia to secede. When the adoption of that policy resulted in War, I felt it my duty to share in the privations of the struggle, and accordingly at the commencement of the contest, I entered the army. . . . I was an earnest supporter of the cause throughout the struggle. Upon the surrender of General Johnston I regarded the contest at an end, and have since that time conformed my action to that conviction. . . .

The contest has ended in the subjugation of the South. The parties stand towards each other in the relative positions of conqueror and conquered; and the question for statesmen to decide, is, the policy and duty of the respective parties. With the latter the course is plainly marked out alike by the requirements of duty and necessity. . . . A return to the peaceful and quiet employments of life; obedience to the constitution and laws of the United States; and the faithful discharge of all the duties, and obligations, imposed upon them by the new state of things, constitute their plain and simple duty.

The policy to be adopted by the other party, is not so easily determined. . . . The hour of triumph, is not necessarily, an hour for calm reflection, or wise judgments. . . .

The whole country (of the Southern states) has been more or less devastated. Their physical condition in the loss of property, and the deprivation of the comforts of life . . . is as bad, as their worst enemy could desire. . . .

Looking to the future interests not only of the Southern people, but of the whole country, it is desirable that the bitter animosities . . . should be softened, as much as possible; and a devastated country restored . . . to comparative prosperity. To effect these results requires the exercise of virtues, which the history of the World shows, are not often, if ever found, in the hearts of the conquerors, magnanimity and generosity. The World is sadly in need of such an example. Let the United States furnish it. There never was a more fitting opportunity. It will never be followed by more satisfactory results. . . .

The prejudices and passions which have been aroused in this contest, crimsoned in the blood of loved ones, from every portion of the land, will yield only to the mellowing influences of time,—and the youngest participant in the struggle will scarcely live to see the last shadow pass away. It is for those in whose hands the power is entrusted, to deal with a brave and generous though conquered people, in such a spirit, as will most certainly and speedily ensure the desired result. The confidence of such a people can be won by kindness and generosity. I leave it for those who counsel a different policy, to foreshadow the effects of a contrary course. They may be able to see, how more blood, and more suffering will sooner restore kindlier feelings. I cannot. In the sufferings already endured, and the privations of the present, there appears to me ample atonement, to satisfy the demands of those, who would punish the South for the past. For the security of the future no such policy is required.

Giving to these general principles the form of practical recommendation, I would say that, all prosecutions and penalties should cease, against those who stand charged alone with the offense of being parties to, and supporters of the Southern cause. . . . The time for the exercise of this power of general amnesty with which the President is clothed, will arrive when he is satisfied, that the people of the South have abandoned the contest, and have in good faith returned to their allegiance to the United States. . . . In such a policy there would be exhibited a spirit of magnanimity, which would find its reward in the happiest results.

Source 10 Christopher G. Memminger, former Confederate secretary of the treasury, letter to President Johnson, September 4, 1865

I take it for granted that this whole Southern Country accepts emancipation from Slavery as the condition of the African race; but neither the North nor the South have yet defined what is included in that emancipation. The boundaries are widely apart which mark on the one side, political equality with the white races, and on the other, a simple recognition of personal liberty. With our own race, ages have intervened between the advance from one of these boundaries to the other. . . . The question now pending is, as to the station in this wide interval which shall be assigned to the African race. Does that race possess qualities, or does it exhibit any peculiar fitness which will dispense with the training which our own race has undergone, and authorize us at once to advance them to equal rights? It seems to me that this point has been decided already by the laws of the free States. None of them have yet permitted equality, and the greater part assert this unfitness of the African by denying him any participation in political power.

Source 11 President Andrew Johnson, "Danger in Negro Suffrage,"
October 3, 1865

It would not do to let the negro have universal suffrage now; it would breed a war of races. There was a time in the Southern States when the slaves of the large owners looked down upon non-slave owners because they did not own slaves; . . . this has produced hostility between the mass of the whites and the negroes. The outrages are mostly from non-slaveholding whites against the negro, and from the negro upon non-slaveholding whites. The negro will vote with the late master, whom he does not hate, rather than with the non-slaveholding white, whom he does hate. Universal suffrage will create another war, not against us, but a war of races.

Source 12 Governor B. G. Humphreys of Mississippi, message to the
Mississippi legislature, November 20, 1865

By the sudden emancipation of over three hundred thousand slaves, Mississippi has imposed upon her a problem of vast magnitude, upon the proper solution of which depends the hopes and future prosperity and welfare of ourselves and of our children.

Under the pressure of federal bayonets, urged on by the misdirected sympathies of the world on behalf of the enslaved African, the people of Mississippi have abolished the institution of slavery, and have solemnly declared in their State constitution that "the legislature should provide by law for the protection and security of person and property of the freedmen of the State, and guard them and the State against any evils that may arise from the sudden emancipation." We must now meet the question as it is, and not as we would like to have it. The rule must be justice. The negro is free, whether we like it or not; we must realize that fact now and forever. *To be free, however, does not make him a citizen, or entitle him to social or political equality with the white man.* But the constitution and justice do entitle him to protection and security in his person and property. . . .

To the guardian care of the Freedmen's Bureau has been entrusted the emancipated slaves. The civil law and the man outside of the Bureau have been deprived of all jurisdiction over them. . . . Idleness and vagrancy have been the result. Our rich and productive fields have been deserted for the filthy garrets and sickly cellars of our towns and cities. From producers they are converted into consumers, and, as winter approaches, their only salvation from starvation and want is federal rations, plunder and pillage. *Four years of cruel war conducted on principles of vandalism disgraceful to the civilization of the age, were scarcely more blighting and destructive on the homes of the white man, and impoverishing, degrading to the negro, than has resulted in the last six or eight months from the administration of this black incubus.* Many of the officers connected with that bureau are gentlemen of honor and integrity, *but they seem incapable of protecting the rights and property of the white man against the villanies of the vile and villanous with whom they are associated.*

How long this *hideous curse,* permitted of Heaven, is to be allowed to rule and ruin our happy people, I regret it is not in my power to give any assurance, further than can be gathered from the public and private declarations of President Johnson, that "the troops will all be withdrawn from Mississippi, when, in the opinion of the government, the peace and order and civil authority has been restored, and can be maintained without them." In this uncertainty as to what will satisfy the government of our loyalty and ability to maintain order and peace and civil government, our duty under the Constitution to guard the negro and the State from the evils arising from sudden emancipation must not be neglected. Our duty to the State, and to the freedmen, seems to me to be clear, and I respectfully recommend—1st. That negro testimony should be admitted in our courts, not only for the protection of person and property of freedmen, but for the protection of society against the crimes of both race. 2d. That the freedmen be encouraged at once to engage in some pursuit of industry for the support of his family and the education of his children, by laws assuring him of friendship and protection. Tax the freedmen for the support of the indigent and helpless freedmen, and *then with an iron will and the strong hand of power take hold of the idler and the vagrant and force him to some profitable employment.* 3rd. Pass a militia law that will enable the militia to protect our people against the insurrection, or any possible combination of vicious white men and negroes.

Source 13 President Andrew Johnson, "Functions of the States Suspended," December 4, 1865

The true theory is that all pretended acts of secession were from the beginning null and void. The States can not commit treason nor screen the individual citizens who may have committed treason any more than they can make valid treaties or engage in lawful commerce with any foreign power. The States attempting to secede placed themselves in a condition where their vitality was impaired, but not extinguished; their functions suspended, but not destroyed.

Source 14 Thaddeus Stevens, "The Conquered Provinces," *Congressional Globe*, December 18, 1865

The President assumes, what no one doubts, that the late rebel States have lost their constitutional relations to the Union, and are incapable of representation in Congress, except by permission of the Government. It matters but little, with this admission, whether you call them States out of the Union, and now conquered territories, or assert that because the Constitution forbids them to do what they did do, that they are therefore only dead as to all national and political action, and will remain so until the Government shall breathe into them the breath of life anew and permit them to occupy their former position. In other words, that they are not out of the Union, but are only dead carcasses lying within the Union. In either case, it is very plain that it requires the action of Congress to enable them to form a State government and send representatives to Congress. Nobody, I believe, pretends that with their old constitutions and frames of government they can be permitted to claim their old rights under the Constitution. They have torn their constitutional States into atoms, and built on their foundations fabrics of a totally different character. Dead men cannot raise themselves. Dead States cannot restore their existence "as it was." Whose especial duty is it to do it? In whom does the Constitution place the power? Not in the judicial branch of Government, for it only adjudicates and does not prescribe laws. Not in the Executive, for he only executes and cannot make laws. Not in the Commander-in-Chief of the armies, for he can only hold them under military rule until the sovereign legislative power of the conqueror shall give them law. Unless the law of nations is a dead letter, the late war between two belligerents severed their original compacts and broke all the ties that bound them together. The future condition of the conquered power depends on the will of the conqueror. They must come in as new states or remain as conquered provinces. Congress . . . is the only power that can act in the matter. . . .

It is obvious from all this that the first duty of Congress is to pass a law declaring the condition of these outside or defunct States, and providing proper civil governments for them. Since the conquest they have been governed by martial law. Military rule is necessarily despotic, and ought not to exist longer than is absolutely necessary. As there are no symptoms that the people of these provinces will be prepared to participate in constitutional government for some years, I know of no arrangement so proper for them as territorial governments. There they can learn the principles of freedom and eat the fruit of foul rebellion. . . .

But this is not all we ought to do before inveterate rebels are invited to participate in our legislation. We have turned, or are about to turn, loose four million slaves without a hut to shelter them or a cent in their pockets. The infernal laws of slavery have prevented them from acquiring an education, understanding the common laws of contract, or of managing the ordinary business of life. The Congress is bound to provide for them until they can take care of themselves. If we do not furnish them with homesteads, and hedge them around with protective laws; if we leave them to the legislation of their late masters, we had better have left them in bondage.

If we fail in this great duty now, when we have the power, we shall deserve and receive the execration of history and of all future ages.

Source 15 Thirteenth Amendment to the Constitution of the United States, ratified December 18, 1865

SECTION 1. Neither slavery nor involuntary servitude, except as a punishment for crime whereof the party shall have been duly convicted, shall exist within the United States, or any place subject to their jurisdiction.

SECTION 2. Congress shall have power to enforce this article by appropriate legislation.

Source 16 Congressman Ignatius Donnelly, on the floor of the United States House of Representatives, January 18, 1866

Through the clouds of a great war and the confusion of a vast mass of legislation we are at length reaching something tangible; we have passed the "Serbonian bog," and are approaching good dry land.

This is the logical conclusion of the war. The war was simply the expression of the determination of the nation to subordinate the almost unanimous will of the white people of the rebellious States to the unity and prosperity of the whole country. Having gone thus far we cannot pause. We must still subordinate their wishes to our welfare. . . .

Government having, by the acknowledgement of the President, ceased to exist, law being swept aside, and chaos having come again in those rebellious states, by what principle shall the law—making power of the nation—the Congress—govern itself? Shall it bend its energies to renew old injustice? Shall it receive to its fraternal embrace only that portion of the population which circumstance or accident or century-old oppression may have brought to the surface? Shall it—having broken up the armies and crushed the hopes of the rebels—pander to their bigotries and cringe to their prejudices? Shall it hesitate to do right out of deference to the sentiments of those who but a short time since were mowed down at the mouth of its cannon?

It is to my mind most clear that slavery having ceased to exist the slaves became citizens; being citizens they are a part of the people; and being a part of the people no organization deserves a moment's consideration at our hands which attempts to ignore them. If they were white people whom it was thus sought to disfranchise and outlaw not a man in the nation would dare to say nay to this proposition; every impulse of our hearts would rise up in indignant remonstrance against their oppressors. But it has pleased Almighty God, who takes counsel of no man, not even of the founders of the rebellion, to paint them of a different complexion, and that variation in the *pigmentum mucum* is to rise up as a perpetual barrier in our pathway toward equal justice and equal rights.

For one, with the help of God, I propose to do what I know to be right in the face of all prejudices and all obstructions; and so long as I have a seat in this body I shall never vote to reconstruct any rebellious State on any such basis of cruelty and injustice as that proposed by the Opposition here.

Take the case of South Carolina. She has 300,000 whites and 400,000 blacks; and we are asked to hand over the 400,000 blacks to the unrestrained custody and control of the 300,000 whites. We are to know no one but the whites; to communicate with no one but the whites; this floor is to recognize no one but white representatives of the whites. The whites are to make the laws, execute the laws, interpret the laws, and write the history of their own deeds; but below them, under them, there is to be a vast population—a majority of the whole people—seething and writhing in a condition of suffering, darkness, and wretchedness unparalleled in the world.

And this is to be an American State! This is to be a component part of the great, humane, Christian Republic of the world. This is to be the protection the mighty Republic is to deal out to its poor black friends who were faithful to it in its hour of trial; this is the punishment it is to inflict upon its perfidious enemies.

No, sir, no sophistry, no special pleading, can lead the American people to this result. Through us or over us it will reconstruct those States on a basis of impartial and eternal justice. Such a mongrel, patchwork, bastard reconstruction as some gentlemen propose, even if put into shape, would not hold together a twelvemonth. Four million human beings consigned to the uncontrolled brutality of 7,000,000 human beings! The very thought is monstrous. The instinct of justice which God implanted in every soul revolts at it. The voice of lamentation would swell up from that wretched land and fill the ears of mankind. Leaders and avengers would spring up on every hilltop of the north. The intellect, the morality, the soul of the age would fight in behalf of the oppressed, and the structure of so-called reconstruction would go down in blood.

Does any man think it is in the American people, who rose at the cry of the slave under the lash of his master, to abide in quiet the carnival of arson, rapine, and murder now raging over the south? Sir, a government which would perpetuate such a state of things would be a monstrous barbarism; the legislative body which would seek to weave such things into the warp and woof of the national life would deserve the vengeance of Almighty God.

The Issues Central to Reconstruction

The period following the Civil War witnessed one of the most contentious struggles ever waged between the executive and legislative branches of the federal government. At issue was not only how the country would be made whole again, but who would take the lead in bringing about the Reconstruction of the United States.

President Lincoln assumed that the responsibility for organizing governments for the rebellious states belonged to the executive branch. Since the president was of the view that the rebellion was the act of individuals within Southern states and that the States themselves had never left the Union, establishing state governments was merely a matter of finding loyalists in the rebellious areas and entrusting Southern governments to them. In December of 1863, Lincoln issued a Proclamation of Amnesty and Reconstruction. Under this offer, a full pardon would be granted to Southerners—with the exception of high Confederate military and governmental leaders—who swore both to "henceforth faithfully support, protect, and defend the Constitution of the United States and the Union of States thereunder" and to accept the emancipation of the slaves. Whenever the citizens of a state "not less than one-tenth in number of the votes cast at the presidential election" of 1860 signed this pledge of allegiance, such loyalists would be permitted to set up a state government and send representatives to the federal Congress. With regard to the former slaves, Lincoln expected the reconstructed Southern states to provide for their "permanent freedom" and education, but did not insist that the freedmen have the right to vote or be accorded equal treatment to that of whites.

During the Civil War and in the years that immediately followed it, the Congress of the United States was under the control of the Republican Party. Though Republicans were not of one mind on all issues regarding Reconstruction, they were in agreement that slavery must be ended and that those who had led the South out of the Union should not be placed in position to lead the South again. Some Republicans wished to see the federal government use the opportunity it now possessed to elevate black Americans to the level of opportunity and liberty already enjoyed by whites.

In response to the relatively lenient proposals of President Lincoln, the Republicans in Congress passed the Wade-Davis Bill. This legislation, if signed by the president, would have required loyalty oaths from at least fifty percent of Southern voters before the process of restoring states to the Union could begin. But Lincoln did not sign the Wade-Davis Bill, choosing to let the congressional plan die through a technique called the "pocket veto." For the time being, control of the Reconstruction process remained in the executive branch.

The assassination of Abraham Lincoln raised Vice President Andrew Johnson, a Southern Democrat and racist, to the White House. Johnson continued the mild and forgiving policies of his predecessor, though he excluded a larger number of Southerners—particularly those of the wealthier classes—from political life. Johnson presided over the recreation of governments in all the Southern states, but these governments only grudgingly conceded the end of slavery and quickly passed Black Codes to place the freedmen under conditions as brutal as slavery itself.

Congressional Republicans were not pleased. They tried to take action to protect the recently freed slaves from the new Southern governments. But in so doing they encountered increasing resistance from the president. Congress passed legislation to strengthen the authority of the Freedman's Bureau to protect the black population of the South, but Johnson vetoed it. Congress passed a Civil Rights Bill to counter the Southern Black Codes, but Johnson vetoed that as well. The actions of the president began to swell support for the more Radical Republicans who wished to ensure racial equality. On April 9, 1866, the Congress did what no previous Congress had ever been able to do: it mustered the two-thirds vote necessary in both houses of Congress to override a presidential veto and it wrote its Civil Rights Bill into law.

With its veto override, Congress began to take charge of Reconstruction. To further counter the Black Codes, the Republicans in Congress proposed passage of the Fourteenth Amendment, perhaps the most revolutionary alteration ever made to the American Constitution. President Johnson took to the campaign trail, touring the nation in his "swing around the circle," in a bid to rally opposition to Congressional Republicans and the proposed amendment. But his style and message backfired and the elections of November 1866 gave the Republicans a veto-proof Congress. Over the months and years that followed, Congressional Republicans dismantled presidential Reconstruction and took radical steps. They placed much of the South under military jurisdiction. They created governments in Southern states composed of loyal whites from the South, recent emigrants from the North, and African Americans. They secured ratification of the Fourteenth and Fifteenth Amendments. They passed legislation to protect Southern blacks. They even impeached the president, falling just one vote short in the Senate of removing Andrew Johnson from office.

These actions taken by the Republicans represented a radical departure from the past and resistance grew.

Source 17 Speech of Republican congressman Oliver Perry Morton, "On the Issues of 1868," January 6, 1868

There are two ideals paramount in the American mind antagonistic and irreconcilable, each struggling for the supremacy.

One is the justice and propriety of the war to put down the rebellion and preserve the integrity of the Union.

The other is the rightfulness of the rebellion and the wickedness and injustice of the government of the United States in putting it down by force of arms. The contest between these two ideas will, as in 1864, constitute the issue in 1868 and all other questions will be off-shoots from them and will arrange themselves upon one side or the other.

Whoever shall vote the so-called "Conservative" or Democratic ticket in 1868, whether he intend it or not, will thereby endorse the rebellion; and whoever shall vote the Republican ticket will utter his voice in favor of union, liberty, and justice. Whoever believes in the justice of the war and the preservation of the Republic will be in favor of reconstruction upon such terms as will give protection to all loyal men and guaranties against future rebellion; and whoever believes in the rightfulness of the rebellion will be in favor of the immediate restoration of the rebels, without condition or limitation, to civil and political rights, just as if there had been no war and nothing had happened.

Source 18 Democratic Party Platform of 1868

The Democratic Party in National Convention assembled, reposing its trust in the intelligence, patriotism, and discriminating justice of the people; standing upon the Constitution as the foundation and limitation of the powers of the government, and the guarantee of the liberties of the citizen; and recognizing the questions of slavery and secession as having been settled for all time to come by the war, or the voluntary action of the Southern States in Constitutional Conventions assembled, and never to be renewed or reagitated; does, with the return of peace, demand,

First. Immediate restoration of all the States to their rights in the Union, under the Constitution, and of civil government to the American people. . . .

Second. Amnesty for all past political offenses, and the regulation of the elective franchise in the States, by their citizens. . . .

In demanding these measures and reforms we arraign the Radical party for its disregard of right, and the unparalleled oppression and tyranny which have marked its career.

After the most solemn and unanimous pledge of both Houses of Congress to prosecute the war exclusively for the maintenance of the government and the preservation of the Union under the Constitution, it has repeatedly violated that most sacred pledge, under which alone was rallied that noble army which carried our flag to victory.

Instead of restoring the Union, it has, so far as in its power, dissolved it, and subjected ten States, in time of profound peace, to military despotism and negro supremacy.

It has nullified there the right of trial by jury; it has abolished the *habeas corpus,* that most sacred writ of liberty; it has overthrown the freedom of speech and of the press; it has substituted arbitrary seizures and arrests, and military trials and secret star-chamber inquisitions, for the constitutional tribunals; it has disregarded in time of peace the right of the people to be free from searches and seizures; it has entered the post and telegraph offices, and even the private rooms of individuals, and seized their private papers and letters without any specific charge or notice of affidavit, as required by the organic law; it has converted the American capitol into a Bastile; it has established a system of spies and official espionage to which no constitutional monarchy of Europe would now dare to resort; it has abolished the right of appeal, on important constitutional questions, to the Supreme Judicial tribunal, and threatens to curtail, or destroy, its original jurisdiction, which is irrevocably vested by the Constitution; while the Chief Justice has been subjected to the most atrocious calumnies, merely because he would not prostitute his high office to the support of false and partisan charges preferred against the President. Its corruption and extravagance have exceeded anything known in history, and by its frauds and monopolies it has nearly doubled the burden of the debt created by the war; it has stripped the President of his constitutional power of appointment, even of his own Cabinet. Under its repeated assaults the pillars of the government are rocking on their base, and should it succeed in November next and inaugurate its President, we will meet, as a subjected and conquered people, amid the ruins of liberty and the scattered fragments of the Constitution.

And we do declare and resolve, That ever since the people of the United States threw off all subjection to the British crown, the privilege and trust of suffrage have belonged to the several States, and have been granted, regulated, and controlled exclusively by the political power of each State respectively, and that any attempt by congress, on any pretext whatever, to deprive any State of that right, or interfere with its exercise, is a flagrant usurpation of power, which can find no warrant in the Constitution; and if sanctioned by the people will subvert our form of government, and can only end in a single centralized and consolidated government, in which the separate existence of the States will be entirely absorbed, and an unqualified despotism be established in place of a federal union of co-equal States; and that we regard the reconstruction acts so-called, of Congress, as such an usurpation, and unconstitutional, revolutionary, and void.

Source 19 Fourteenth Amendment to the Constitution of the United States, ratified July 28, 1868

SECTION 1. All persons born or naturalized in the United States, and subject to the jurisdiction thereof, are citizens of the United States and of the State wherein they reside. No State shall make or enforce any law which shall abridge the privileges or immunities of citizens of the United States; nor shall any state deprive any person of life, liberty, or property, without due process of law; nor deny to any person within its jurisdiction the equal protection of the laws.

SECTION 2. Representatives shall be apportioned among the several States according to their respective numbers, counting the whole number of persons in each State, excluding Indians not taxed. But when the right to vote at any election for the choice of electors for President and Vice President of the United States, representatives in Congress, the executive and judicial officers of a State, or the members of the legislature thereof, is denied to any of the male inhabitants of such State, being twenty-one years of age, and citizens of the United States, or in any way abridged, except for participating in rebellion, or other crime, the basis of representation therein shall be reduced in the proportion which the number of such male citizens shall bear to the whole number of male citizens twenty-one years of age in such State.

SECTION 3. No person shall be a senator or representative in Congress, or elector of President or Vice President, or hold any office, civil or military, under the United States, or under any State, who having previously taken an oath, as a member of Congress, or as an officer of the United States, or as a member of any State legislature, or as an executive or judicial officer of any State, to support the Constitution of the United States, shall have engaged in insurrection or rebellion against the same, or given aid or comfort to the enemies thereof. But Congress may by a vote of two thirds of each House, remove such disability.

SECTION 4. The validity of the public debt of the United States, authorized by law, including debts incurred for payment of pensions and bounties for services in suppressing insurrection or rebellion, shall not be questioned. But neither the United States nor any State shall assume or pay any debt or obligation incurred in aid of insurrection or rebellion against the United States, or any claim for the loss or emancipation of any slave; but all such debts, obligations, and claims shall be held illegal and void.

SECTION 5. The Congress shall have the power to enforce, by appropriate legislation, the provisions of this article.

Source 20 Fifteenth Amendment to the Constitution of the United States, ratified March 30, 1870

SECTION 1. The right of citizens of the United States to vote shall not be denied or abridged by the United States or by any State on account of race, color, or previous condition of servitude.

SECTION 2. The Congress shall have power to enforce this article by appropriate legislation.

Source 21 United States Civil Rights Act of 1875, March 1, 1875

Whereas, it is essential to just government we recognize the equality of all men before the law, and hold that it is the duty of government in its dealings with the people to mete out equal and exact justice to all, of whatever nativity, race, color, or persuasion, religious or political; and it being the appropriate object of legislation to enact great fundamental principles into law: Therefore,

2.3 Civil Rights History Guide

Be it enacted, ... That all persons within the jurisdiction of the United States shall be entitled to the full and equal enjoyment of the accommodations, advantages, facilities, and privileges of inns, public conveyances on land and water, theatres, and other places of public amusement; subject only to the conditions and limitations established by law, and applicable alike to citizens of every race and color, regardless of any previous condition of servitude. . . .

That any person who shall violate the foregoing section . . . shall, for every such offense, forfeit and pay the sum of five hundred dollars to the person aggrieved thereby . . . and shall also, for every such offense, be deemed guilty of a misdemeanor, and, upon conviction thereof, shall be fined not less than five hundred dollars nor more than one thousand dollars, or shall be imprisoned not less than thirty days nor more than one year.

📖 *Second Thoughts*

Reconstruction: Noble Venture or Misguided Effort?

Reconstruction had a short life. In the spring of 1867 and for the seven years that followed, Republicans interested in promoting fundamental changes in race relations were able to sway Congress and chart the course for the nation. These Republicans—Thaddeus Stevens, Ben Wade, Charles Sumner, Carl Schurz, and others—pushed passage of the Thirteenth, Fourteenth, and Fifteenth Amendments and Civil Rights legislation. But in the congressional elections of 1874, conservatives south and north, marshalled by the Democratic Party, won control of the House of Representatives and, in 1877, Republicans bargained away the Reconstruction effort in a successful bid to hang onto the White House.

After 1877, the federal government turned away from the plight of African Americans and southern governments came once more under the control of a conservative white aristocracy. The gains made by the post–Civil War generation in human rights slowly eroded. By the turn of the century, African Americans had been disenfranchised, segregated from their fellow citizens, and relegated to only those tasks in society that whites wished not to do. It was not until the midpoint of the twentieth century that a new attempt was made to realize the promises of the Civil War amendments.

***Source 22* Congressman Hilary A. Herbert of Alabama, *Why the Solid South? Or, Reconstruction and Its Results,* 1890**

The days during which the reconstruction governments ruled in the several Southern states were the darkest that ever shrouded any portion of our country. The slaughter and the sacrifices during our great civil war were terrible indeed, but those dark days were lighted by the shining valor of the patriot soldier; the storm clouds were gilded with glory. But there was . . . nothing but wretchedness and humiliation, and shame, and crime begetting crime. There was no single redeeming feature, except the heroic determination of the better classes in the several states to restore good government. . . .

The political earthquake that convulsed the Southern States for years, some of them from 1865 to 1876, of course left great fissures, some of which are not yet closed. . . . It was and is the misfortune of the Southern people to have to deal with the problems arising out of race prejudice. The negro had neither the will nor the power to resist the forces which arrayed him against his late master, and the solidification of his vote, by those who were to profit by it, meant, of course, a black man's party; for its majority sentiment determines the complexion of every political party. The domination of the black man's party, officered as it was, meant ruin. To avert ruin white men united; and then came a struggle, the issue of which was in all the States the same. It could not anywhere be doubtful. The race against which the negro had allowed himself to be arrayed has never yet met its master. It could not go down before the African.

No true friend of the colored man would, except in ignorance, precipitate such a conflict. . . .

When the reconstruction laws gave the negro the ballot the party that passed these laws claimed of the colored man his vote and secured it. The negroes went to the polls in solid masses for that party. We have seen the results. Wherever they got power their leaders robbed and plundered. Wherever the negro majorities were greatest the degradation of society was most complete and despoliation the most absolute.

Source 23 John W. Burgess, dean of the Faculty of Political Science, Columbia University, *Reconstruction and the Constitution, 1866–1876,* 1902

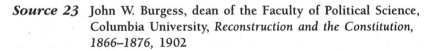

Slavery was a great wrong, and secession was an error and a terrible blunder, but Reconstruction was a punishment so far in excess of the crime that it extinguished every sense of culpability upon the part of those whom it was sought to convict and convert. More than a quarter of a century has now passed since the blunder-crime of Reconstruction played its baneful part in alienating the two sections of the country. Until four years ago little progress had been made in reconciling them. It is said that the recent war with Spain, in which men from the North and men from the South marched under the same banner to battle and victory, has buried the hatchet forever between them. But they had done this many times before, and yet it did not prevent the attempt to destroy the Union. It cannot be in this alone that the South feels increased security against the doctrines and the policies and interferences of the Republican party with regard to the negro question, the great question which has made and kept the South solidly Democratic. It is something far more significant and substantial than this. It is to some the pleasing, though to others startling, fact, that the Republican party, in its work of imposing the sovereignty of the United States upon eight millions of Asiatics, has changed its views in regard to the political relation of races and has at last virtually accepted the ideas of the South upon the subject. The white men of the South need now have no further fear that the Republican party, or Republican Administrations, will ever again give themselves over to the vain imagination of the political equality of man. It is this change of mind and heart on the part of the North in regard to this vital question of Southern "State" polity which has caused the now much-talked-of reconciliation.

Source 24 James Ford Rhodes, *The History of the United States, from the Compromise of 1850 to the Final Restoration of Home Rule at the South in 1877,* 1906

Truly the negro's fate has been hard. Torn from his native land he was made a slave to satisfy the white man's greed. At last, owing to a great moral movement, he gained the long-wished-for boon of freedom; and then when in intellect still a child, instead of being trained as a child, taught gradually the use of his liberty and given rights in the order of his development, he, without any demand of his own, was raised at once to the white man's political estate, partly for the partisan designs of those who freed him. His old masters, who understood him best and who, chastened by defeat and by adversity, were really his best friends, were alienated. He fell into the hands of rascals who through his vote fattened on the spoils of office. He had a brief period of mastery and indulgence during which his mental and moral education was deplorable and his worst passions were catered to. Finally by force, by craft and by law his old masters have deprived him of the ballot and, after a number of years of political power, he has been set back to the point, where he should have started directly after emancipation. He is trying to learn the lesson of life with the work made doubly hard by the Saturnalia he has passed through.

The Congressional policy of Reconstruction was short-sighted even from the partisan point of view in that it gave the South a grievance. In that balancing of rights and wrongs, which must be made in a just consideration of a great human transaction, the North at the end of the war could appeal to Europe and to history for the justification of its belief that there was on its side a large credit balance. Some of this it has lost by its repressive, uncivilized and unsuccessful policy of Reconstruction.

Source 25   Professor William A. Dunning of Columbia University, *Reconstruction: Political and Economic, 1865–1877*, 1907

To the ambitious northern whites, inexperienced southern whites, and unintelligent blacks who controlled the first reconstructed governments, the grand end of their induction into power was to put their states promptly abreast of those which led in the prosperity and progress at the North. Things must be done, they believed, on a larger, freer, nobler scale than under the debased regime of slavery. Accordingly, both by the new constitutions and by legislation, the expenses of the governments were largely increased: offices were multiplied in all departments; salaries were made more worthy of the now regenerated and progressive commonwealths; costly enterprises were undertaken for the promotion of the general welfare, especially where that welfare was primarily connected with the uplifting of the freedmen. The result of all this was promptly seen in an expansion of state debts and an increase of taxation that to the property-owning class were appalling and ruinous. . . .

In the maladministration that brought ruin to the finances, inefficiency and corruption played about equal parts. The responsible higher officials were in many cases entirely honest, though pathetically stupid, in their schemes to promote the interests of their states. But the governments numbered in their *personnel*, on the other hand, a host of offices to whom place was merely an opportunity for plunder. The progressive depletion of the public treasuries was accompanied by great private prosperity among radical politicians of high and low degree. First to profit by their opportunity were generally the northerners who led in radical politics; but the "scalawag" southerners and negroes were quick to catch the idea. Bribery became the indispensable adjunct of legislation, and fraud a common feature in the execution of the laws. The form and manner of this corruption, which has given so unsavory a connotation to the name "reconstruction," were no different from those which have appeared in many another time and place in democratic government. . . . The really novel and peculiar element in the maladministration in the South was the social and race issue which underlay it. . . .

The negro had no pride of race and no aspiration or ideals save to be like the whites. With civil rights and political power, not won, but almost forced upon him, he came gradually to understand and crave those more elusive privileges that constitute social equality. A more intimate association with the other race than that which business and politics involved was the end towards which the ambition of the blacks tended consciously or unconsciously to direct him. The manifestations of this ambition were infinite in their diversity. It played a part in the demand for mixed schools, in the legislative prohibition of discrimination between the races in hotels and theatres, and even in the hideous crime against white womanhood which now assumed new meaning in the annals of outrage. But every form and suggestion of social equality was resented and resisted by the whites with the energy of despair. The dread of it justified in their eyes modes of lawlessness which were wholly subversive of civilization. Charles Sumner devoted the last years of his life to a determined effort to prohibit by Federal law any discrimination against the blacks in hotels, churches, and cemeteries. His bill did not pass till 1875, after his death, but his idea was taken up and enacted into law by most of the southern radical legislatures. The laws proved unenforceable and of small consequence, but the discussion of them furnished rich fuel to the flames of race animosity, and nerved many a hesitating white, as well as many an ambitious black, to violent deeds for the interest of his people.

Source 26 Walter L. Fleming, professor of history, West Virginia University, *Documentary History of Reconstruction*, 1907

A year before Georgia was fully reconstructed the undoing of Reconstruction began with the re-franchisement (1869) of ex-Confederates in Tennessee and the consequent transfer of the state government to them. The border states began to go Democratic in 1870 and in that year North Carolina and Virginia returned to the control of the Conservative whites, while Georgia followed a year later. The Ku Klux Klan movement greatly aided in the recovery of these states, and also assisted the whites so that after 1871 although the reconstructionists held seven state governments, within those states they controlled only in the black counties, the majorities from the black districts overcoming the majorities from the white counties.

As the Reconstruction governments grew more corrupt the better class of whites deserted the Radical party, leaving only 3000 to 5000 whites, principally office holders, in each state to organize and control the blacks. Sympathy for the South grew in the North and the Democrats carried several states. But the Southern Radicals were now greatly aided by the Enforcement laws and by Federal control of elections. Disputed elections and dual governments were always decided in favor of the Radicals. Consequently by 1874 the whites were exasperated to the point of rebellion. In this year there was a revolution in Louisiana, and revolutionary elections in Alabama, Arkansas, and Texas gave control to the whites. These successes were made possible only by the use of extreme methods by the whites—intimidation, force, social and business ostracism, purchase of votes, drawing the color line, discharge from employment, forced resignations, the "shot gun plan," and "Rifle Clubs." Most of these were simply carpetbag methods adopted by the whites, but the whites were at a disadvantage in not having the support of the federal troops and marshals, and in not being able to use fraud in counting ballots. Conservative intimidation checked Radical intimidation and made it possible for a few thousand negroes in each state to vote with the whites. The disputed election of 1876 gave the opportunity to the Southern whites to make a "bargain" by which the troops were withdrawn from the South in return for the election of Hayes. South Carolina, Louisiana, and Florida then drove out the Radical officials. The South, now "solid," proceeded to eliminate the negro from politics by the use of election and registration laws, and other methods that the Radicals had used, and by new schemes, until finally the negro vote was either suppressed or brought mainly under Democratic control. Meanwhile individual amnesty acts and the Amnesty Act of 1872 restored the franchise to most of the whites. The use of the army in elections was forbidden by law in 1878 and 1880. No appropriations were made for deputy marshals at elections, and in 1884 the statutes were repealed. The United States Supreme Court aided in the undoing of Reconstruction Acts by interpreting the Fourteenth and Fifteenth Amendments as applying to violations by states, not by individuals. Consequently the Enforcement Acts were gotten out of the way. The Civil Rights Act was also declared to relate to matters not under the control of Congress. So within eight years after the initiation of the Congressional Plan of Reconstruction, all of the carpetbag and negro State governments, though strongly supported by the Washington administration, gave place to control by the whites; and within another eight-year period, the most important of the Enforcement laws were declared unconstitutional or were repealed, and the Federal control of state affairs ceased to a great extent.

Source 27 W. E. B. Du Bois, *Black Reconstruction,* 1935

The treatment of the period of Reconstruction reflects small credit upon American historians as scientists. We have too often a deliberate attempt so to change the facts of history that the story will make pleasant reading for Americans. . . . In order to paint the South as a martyr to inescapable fate, to make the North the magnanimous emancipator, and to ridicule the Negro as the impossible joke in the whole development, we have in fifty years, by libel, innuendo and silence, so completely misstated and obliterated the history of the Negro in America and his relation to its work and government that today it is almost unknown. This may be fine romance, but it is not science. It may be inspiring, but it is certainly not the truth. And beyond this it is dangerous. It is not only part foundation of our present lawlessness and loss of democratic ideals; it has, more than that, led the world to embrace and worship the color bar as social salvation. . . .

We shall never have a science of history until we have in our colleges men who regard the truth as more important than the defense of the white race, and who will not deliberately encourage students to gather thesis material in order to support a prejudice or buttress a lie.

Three-fourths of the testimony against the Negro in Reconstruction is on the unsupported evidence of men who hated and despised Negroes and regarded it as loyalty to blood, patriotism to country, and filial tribute to the fathers to lie, steal or kill in order to discredit these black folks. This may be a natural result when a people have been humbled and impoverished and degraded in their own life; but what is inconceivable is that another generation and another group should regard this testimony as scientific truth. . . . With a determination unparalleled in science, the mass of American writers have started out so to distort the facts of the greatest critical period of American history as to prove right wrong and wrong right. . . .

One fact and one alone explains the attitude of most recent writers toward Reconstruction; they cannot conceive Negroes as men; in their minds the word "Negro" connotes "inferiority" and "stupidity" lightened only by unreasoning gaiety and humor. Suppose the slaves of 1860 had been white folk. Stevens would have been a great statesman, Sumner a great democrat, and Schurz a keen prophet, in a mighty revolution of rising humanity. Ignorance and poverty would easily have been explained by history, and the demand for land and the franchise would have been justified as the birthright of natural freemen.

But Burgess was a slaveholder, Dunning a Copperhead and Rhodes an exploiter of wage labor. Not one of them apparently ever met an educated Negro of force and ability. Around such impressive thinkers gathered the young post-war students from the South. They had been born and reared in the bitterest period of Southern race hatred, fear and contempt. Their instinctive reactions were confirmed and encouraged in the best American universities. Their scholarship, when it regarded black men, became deaf, dumb, and blind. The clearest evidence of Negro ability, work, honesty, patience, learning and efficiency became distorted into cunning, brute toil, shrewd evasion, cowardice and imitation—a stupid effort to transcend nature's law.

For those seven mystic years between Johnson's "swing 'round the circle" and the panic of 1873, a majority of thinking Americans in the North believed in the equal manhood of black folk. They acted accordingly with clear-cut decisiveness and thorough logic, utterly incomprehensible to a day like ours which does not share this human faith; and to Southern whites this period can only be explained by deliberate vengeance and hate.

Source 28 Carl N. Degler, *Out of Our Past: The Forces That Shaped Modern America,* 1970

The first attempts to carve out a place for the black man in a white-dominated America were undertaken in the dozen years after 1865, which have come to be called the Reconstruction period. That era, despite the cataclysmic character of the War for the Union, is best understood as a continuation of the history of the previous thirty years. The conflicts of the Reconstruction period are deeply rooted in the previous generation of sectional struggle over the issue of Negro slavery. The war, it is true, removed slavery from the congressional debates as effectively as it destroyed the South, but it failed to reconcile the opposite moral values which lay behind the two sections' conceptions of what slavery was and what the Negro was.

Many of the Northern Republicans, for example—men like Ben Wade, Charles Sumner, Thaddeus Stevens, William Fessenden, and John Bingham—had been in Congress during the anti-slavery struggle of the 1850's. They were still there when the Reconstruction of the former Confederacy was begun. For such men, the experiences of the years of anti-slavery and nationalistic agitation made it unthinkable that the South should be restored to the Union untouched by the fires in which they themselves had been tempered. And what was true of the leaders was true of the thousands of ordinary men of the North whose lives were permanently altered by the moral fervor of the anti-slavery crusade and the emotionalism of the great War for the Union.

But the South, too, had a history by which its people had been molded. The Southerner's image of the Negro was shaped by the slave past, and its contours were shaken not at all by the rhetoric of the anti-slavery North or by the guns which finally destroyed the "peculiar institution." When the South came to legislate a status for the freedman, it would understandably draw upon the experience under slavery.

Under such circumstances, the cessation of hostilities between the sections brought not peace, but a political cold war, one which was more full of hate, bitterness, and misunderstanding than the hot war which preceded it. Since neither section had been able to transcend its historically derived conceptions about the nature of the Union, it was hardly to be expected that either would be able to rise above its history when dealing with the emotionally charged question of the freed Negro.

As the war overturned American thinking about slavery and the nature of the Union, so the Reconstruction re-educated the American people on the place the Negro should occupy in the United States. When the war ended, the position of the newly freed black man was ambiguous throughout the nation. In the North, though he was a citizen, society discriminated against him, and he was denied the ballot in all states except New York and five in New England. Moreover, as a measure of the North's attitude, within the previous five years the people of several northern states had overwhelmingly refused to extend the vote to Negroes. In the South, the Negro's ambiguous position was summed up in the fact that he was neither a slave nor a citizen.

But within half a decade, under the driving will of the Radical Republicans all this was reversed. The adoption of the Fourteenth and Fifteenth Amendments to the Constitution signified that the Negro was now to be a full citizen, equal in civil rights and voting privileges with white men. Insofar as modern Americans take pride from this inclusion of the Negro in the American dream of equality and opportunity, then it is to the Radicals that they are indebted. For it was solely because of the Radicals' control over the South that the requisite number of states were brought to ratify the two amendments. If not written into the Constitution then, when the conservative South was powerless to resist and the North was still imbued with its mission of reform, then the principle of Negro equality would probably never have been included in the national charter. This achievement of the Radicals is at least as much a part of the legacy of Reconstruction as the better-known corruption and the imposition of alien rule.

The accomplishment of the Radicals is essentially noteworthy because the obstacles were so formidable—not only in the South, but in the North as well. We have already seen that few states in the North in 1865 were prepared to grant Negroes the privilege of participating in the government. The North did, however, believe that the war had put a final end to Negro slavery. It was when that decision seemed to be challenged by the vanquished South that the equalitarian Radicals were presented with an opportunity to enlarge the area of the Negro's rights and privileges.

Source 29 Barbara Jeanne Fields, *Slavery and Freedom on the Middle Ground: Maryland during the Nineteenth Century,* 1985

Throughout the South the abolition of slavery worked a revolution in the social relations of the countryside. But nowhere did a new order arise immediately from the ashes of the old. Instead, a period of transition set in, so protracted in certain parts of the South as to engender a mistaken doubt in the minds of many scholars that a revolution occurred at all. The survival intact, at least temporarily, of a good many antebellum landholdings, and the rapid improvisation of means of coercing labor that to incautious observation might appear a simple continuation of slavery by other means, contributed to an illusory appearance of stasis. . . .

Regrettably, reflections of this kind sometimes tempt historians into odd and altogether inadmissible conclusions. If conditions after emancipation proved so unfavorable, the reasoning goes, were black people not, after all, better off as slaves? The only valid answer to such a question is that the question itself is improper. Slavery and freedom are incommensurable qualities, the differences between them an existential matter touching the dignity and worth of human life. People suffer, certainly, in freedom as well as in slavery. But that unquestionable truth does not license anyone to tote up the suffering of one—in dollars of gold, calories of food, or pounds of flesh—and weigh it against the suffering of the other, in order to determine in which state people are better off. Nor should historians deceive themselves that they can tiptoe around the impropriety of the question by distinguishing the "material" from the "moral" or "psychological" dimension of slavery and freedom. If human beings were vegetables, it would be proper to conclude that they are best off materially when most amply and efficiently provided with what they require for vegetation. But human beings are not vegetables, and their material and moral needs overlap to a degree that makes nonsense of any effort to measure the one in the absence of the other. What mechanistic and unimaginative scholars would probably call the moral or psychological dimension of freedom consists in no small part of exercising discretion in the manner of satisfying material needs. Was Frederick Douglass stating a moral or a material objection to slavery when he condemned the monotonous slave diet of ash cake and fat meat and justified the slaves' unauthorized forays into their owners' pantries and smokehouses?

Black people in Maryland's countryside during the decades following emancipation confronted, beyond doubt, a bleak situation. The ending of slavery placed in their hands at best only modest resources to meet it: land in marginal amounts; some access, though progressively restricted, to the produce of the water; the right to marriage and family relationships; and formal rights of citizenship. The importance of these resources, poor as they were, was that they were attributes of free men and women and, as such, preconditions for facing those challenges that do not arise in slavery but belong uniquely to the domain of freedom. If, possessing these few resources, black people could not construct a secure future for themselves, it must at least be said that they had no hope of doing so without them.

Source 30 Eric Foner, *Reconstruction: America's Unfinished Revolution, 1863–1877,* 1988

Over a century ago, prodded by the demands of four million men and women just emerging from slavery, Americans made their first attempt to live up to the noble professions of their political creed—something few societies have ever done. The effort produced a sweeping redefinition of the nation's public life and a violent reaction that ultimately destroyed much, but by no means all, of what had been accomplished. From the enforcement of the rights of citizens to the stubborn problems of economic and racial justice, the issues central to Reconstruction are as old as the American republic, and as contemporary as the inequalities that afflict our society. . . .

Perhaps the remarkable thing about Reconstruction was not that it failed, but that it was attempted at all and survived as long as it did.

Source 31 George M. Fredrickson et al., *America: Past and Present,* 1998

During the relatively brief period when they were in power in the South—varying from one to nine years depending on the state—the Republicans chalked up some notable achievements. They established (on paper at least) the South's first adequate systems of public education, democratized state and local government, and appropriated funds for an enormous expansion of public services and responsibilities. . . .

Furthermore, southern corruption was not exceptional, nor was it a special result of the extension of suffrage to uneducated African Americans, as critics of Radical Reconstruction have claimed. It was part of a national pattern during an era when private interests considered buying government favors to be a part of the cost of doing business, and many politicians expected to profit by obliging them.

Blacks bore only a limited responsibility for the dishonesty of the Radical governments. Although sixteen African Americans served in Congress—two in the Senate—between 1869 and 1880, only in South Carolina did blacks constitute a majority of even one house of the state legislature. Furthermore, no black governors were elected during Reconstruction. The biggest grafters were opportunistic whites. . . .

If blacks served or supported corrupt and wasteful regimes, it was because they had no alternative. Although the Democrats, or Conservatives as they called themselves in some states, made sporadic efforts to attract African American voters, it was clear that if they won control, they would attempt to strip blacks of their civil and political rights. But opponents of Radical Reconstruction were able to capitalize on racial prejudice and persuade many Americans that "good government" was synonymous with white supremacy.

Contrary to myth, the small number of African Americans elected to state or national office during Reconstruction demonstrated on the average more integrity and competence than their white counterparts. Most were fairly well educated, having been free Negroes or unusually privileged slaves before the war.

⚔ Questioning the Past

1. As Lee prepared to surrender to Grant at Appomattox Court House, at least one of Lee's generals suggested that the Army of Northern Virginia disperse in small bands into the mountains and wage a guerrilla war against the Northern invaders. With support from a sympathetic countryside, such a war, as the twentieth century has proven, might be waged for years and perhaps even waged with success. Southern leaders also urged the Confederate forces to fight on. And understandably so, many Northerners were already proposing the executions of Southern political and military leaders. Speculate about the short- and long-term political outcomes of endings at Appomattox less amiable than that chartered by Lee and Grant.

2. With the surrender of General Lee and other units of the Confederate forces, the North secured a victory in the war against the secessionists. What actions should the North have then taken to secure a meaningful peace?

3. The Civil War brought slavery in America to an end, but the generation who freed the slaves did not resolve any of the problems slavery had created: the freedmen were impoverished, landless, homeless, and illiterate. It would have been absurd to think they had an equal opportunity to succeed in American society, and the legacy of the gap between whites and blacks, established by slavery, still haunts the nation at the turn of the twenty-first century. What steps might the post–Civil War generation have taken to erase the effects of slavery and move America more rapidly toward an egalitarian society?

4. Was Reconstruction a noble and laudable venture or a misguided effort, a success or a failure?

5. Thaddeus Stevens proposed that the great plantations of the South be confiscated, divided, and parceled out to the former slaves. Present the arguments in support and in opposition to this proposal. Which case is the more persuasive? Defend your answer.

6. "All history teaches us that man would be safer in the claws of wild beasts than in the uncontrolled custody of his fellow men," Ignatius Donnelly argued during the debates over enfranchising the former slaves. "And can any man doubt that he who lives in a community and has no share in the making of the laws which govern him is in the uncontrolled custody of those who make the laws?" Explain and evaluate his point.

7. Account for the evolution of views among historians regarding Reconstruction.

Chapter 3

The Assassination

Lincoln Is Shot at Ford's Theatre   *April 14, 1865*

3.1 Abraham
Lincoln: Sixteenth
President

Ford's Theatre was packed for the final performance of *Our American Cousin,* and the mood of the audience was a relaxed and merry one. Not only were people out to enjoy a fine play, they were out to enjoy the first Friday night in four years when the omnipresence of war did not weigh heavily on their minds. General Lee had surrendered the Army of Northern Virginia to General Grant five days earlier, and the end of the terrible conflict was at last in sight. Even the president had come to Ford's for an evening at ease.

But while the audience was being seated at Ford's Theatre, a band of conspirators was gathering a few blocks away at the Surratt Boarding House. For months this band had plotted against the leadership of the United States. At first they plotted to kidnap the president and take him to Richmond as a hostage. An attempt to carry out such a venture had failed in March. Now, their plans took a more drastic turn: They would on this evening attempt to assassinate the three highest-ranking officials of the federal government. Lewis Payne would target the secretary of state, William Henry Seward. George Atzerodt would attempt to kill the vice president of the United States, Andrew Johnson. The organizer of the conspiracy, John Wilkes Booth, would proceed to Ford's Theater, where he expected to find the president with his guard down.

The play was well into its second act when a man in riding boots and spurs stepped through the front door of Ford's. He did not appear dressed for the theater, but he ascended the stairs to the balcony without meeting any challenge. He then walked down the aisle along the wall to a door that led to an anteroom, beyond which was the presidential box. The door was not guarded. Booth entered the anteroom and braced the door shut behind him with a board. Only one door now separated Booth from the president of the United States.

Through a small hole in the door he could see the back of the president's head. Quietly, Booth opened the door, pointed a small, 44-caliber single-shot derringer at Lincoln's head, and pulled the trigger.

Many in the audience thought the noise of the gunshot to be a part of the performance. But Major Rathbone, the guest of President and Mrs. Lincoln for the evening, leaped to his feet and rushed at the assassin. Booth stopped Rathbone's advance with the point of a dagger. The wounded Rathbone reeled backwards, and Booth jumped over the railing at the front of the box. As he did, one of his boots became entangled in the banner that draped the box, and his spur caught the edge of a portrait hanging on the box front. Consequently, he landed off balance on the stage 12 feet beneath the box and fractured his leg.

The injury slowed him only slightly, however; and after dramatically brandishing his dagger at the audience and shouting in Latin, "Thus be it ever to Tyrants!" Booth dashed out through the stage door into the alley behind Ford's Theatre, mounted his horse, and made good his escape.

✌ *First Impressions*
A Nation Will Weep for Him

Abraham Lincoln had spent a lifetime in public service. He had led his country through its most tragic era. And for that, Abraham Lincoln earned a place in our history books. John Wilkes Booth, by firing one shot taking less than a second, had caused his own name to be placed on the same page as that of Abraham Lincoln. Such is the irony of history.

3.2 The History Place Presents Abraham Lincoln

Source 1   **Statement of Secretary of War Edwin M. Stanton**

War Department,
Washington, D.C.,
April 15—1:30 A.M.

Last evening, at 10:30 p.m., at Ford's Theatre, the President, while sitting in his private box with Mrs. Lincoln, Miss Harris, and Major Rathbone, was shot by an assassin who suddenly entered the box. He approached behind the President. The assassin then leaped upon the stage, brandishing a dagger or knife, and made his escape by the rear of the theatre. The pistol ball entered the back of the President's head. The wound is mortal. The President has been insensible ever since it was inflicted, and is now dying.

About the same hour an assassin, either the same or another, entered Mr. Seward's house, and under pretense of having a prescription, was shown to the Secretary's sick chamber. The Secretary was in bed, a nurse and Miss Seward with him. The assassin immediately rushed to the bed, inflicting two or three stabs on the throat, and two in the face. It is hoped the wounds may not be mortal. My apprehension is that they will prove fatal. The nurse alarmed Mr. Frederick Seward, who was in an adjoining room, and hastened to the door of his father's room, where he met the assassin, who inflicted upon him one or more dangerous wounds. The recovery of Frederick Seward is doubtful.

It is not probable that the President will live through the night.

Source 2   **Washington *Evening Star,* April 15, 1865**

From the Associated Press:
President Lincoln and wife, together with other friends, last evening visited Ford's Theater for the purpose of witnessing the performance of the American Cousin. It was announced in the newspapers that General Grant would also be present, but that gentleman, instead, took the late train of cars for New Jersey. The theater was densely crowded, and everybody seemed delighted with the scene before them.

During the third act, and while there was a temporary pause for one of the actors to enter, a sharp report of a pistol was heard, which merely attracted attention, but suggesting nothing serious, until a man rushed to the front of the President's box, waving a long dagger in his right hand, and exclaiming "Sic Semper Tyrannis," and immediately leaped from the box, which was of the second tier, to the stage beneath, and ran across to the opposite side, thus making his escape, amid the bewilderment of the audience, from the rear of the theater, and mounting a horse, fled.

The screams of Mrs. Lincoln first disclosed the fact to the audience that the President had been shot, when all present rose to their feet, rushing toward the stage, exclaiming, "Hang him!" "Hang him!"

The excitement was of the wildest possible character; and, of course there was an abrupt termination of the theatrical performance. . . .

On hasty examination it was found that the President had been shot through the head, above and back of the temporal bone, and that some of the brain was oozing out. He was removed to the private residence of Mr. Peterson, opposite to the theater, and the Surgeon General of the army and other surgeons sent for to attend to his condition.

On examination of the private box blood was discovered on the back of the cushioned rocking chair in which the President had been sitting, also on the partition and on the floor.

A common single barrelled pocket pistol was found on the carpet.

A military guard was placed in front of the private residence to which the President had been conveyed.

An immense crowd was in front of it, all deeply anxious to learn the condition of the President. . . .

The shock to the community was terrible. . . .

When the excitement at the theater was at its wildest height, reports were circulated that Secretary Seward had also been assassinated.

On reaching this gentleman's residence a crowd and a military guard were found at the door, and on entering, it was ascertained that the reports were based upon truth.

Everybody was so much excited that scarcely an intelligible account could be gathered. . . .

The entire city last night presented a scene of wild excitement, accompanied by violent expressions of indignation, and the profoundest sorrow. Many persons shed tears.

3.3 Abraham Lincoln's Assassination

The military authorities have dispatched mounted troops in every direction, in order, if possible to arrest the assassins. . . .

Vice President Johnson is in the city, and his hotel quarters are guarded by troops.

Source 3   *National Intelligencer, April 15, 1865*

THE TRAGEDY OF LAST NIGHT

Our heart stands almost still as we take our pen to speak of the tragedy of last night. We have no words at command by which to express anything that we feel. Before this paper shall go to press, the fact may reach us that the President has been assassinated! We already know enough to be compelled to record the fact that he was shot in the Theatre, and that the ball entered his head. God Almighty grant that his life may be preserved! Still we have hope. . . .

And, horror upon horrors! It seems that the house of Mr. Seward was entered on a pretext by a murderer or murderers, who, it is represented to us on authority which we cannot doubt, beat and stabbed his son, the Hon. F. Seward, wounded others of his household, and who finally succeeded in stabbing the Secretary of State. The fact seems to be that his throat is cut. Up to this hour—2 A.M.—we have no assurance that the perpetrators of this terrible crime have been arrested. Nor are we advised as to the condition of the Secretary or of his son.

Rumors are so thick and contradictory, the excitement at this hour is so intense, that we rely entirely upon our reporters to advise the public of the details and result of this night of horrors.

Evidently conspirators are among us! To what extent does the conspiracy exist? This is a terrible question! When a spirit so horrible as this is abroad, what man is safe? We can only advise the utmost vigilance and the most prompt measures by the authorities. We can only pray God to shield us, His unworthy people, from further calamities like these.

If the President is dead, a noble and good man has fallen at his post, and the only one among us who had the power and the will to do as much as he could have done, and as humanely, and liberally, for the whole country. A nation will weep for him. The loss of the Secretary of State would be irreparable. But our heart is too full to say more.

Saturday Morning, 2½ O'Clock.—The President is still alive, but is growing weaker. The ball is lodged in his brain, three inches from where it entered the skull. He remains insensible, and his condition is utterly hopeless.

The Vice President has been to see him, but all company, except the Cabinet, his family, and a few friends, are rigidly excluded.

Large crowds still continue in the street, as near to the house as the line of guards allow.

Source 4   Secretary of War Edwin M. Stanton's communiques to Lieutenant General Grant

> War Department,
> Washington, D.C., 3 A.M.,
> April 15, 1865.

Lieutenant General Grant:
The President still breathes, but is quite insensible, as he has been ever since he was shot. He evidently did not see the person who shot him, but was looking on the stage, as he was approached behind.

Mr. Seward has rallied, and it is hoped he may live. Frederick Seward's condition is very critical. The attendant who was present was stabbed through the lungs, and is not expected to live. . . .

Investigation strongly indicates J. Wilkes Booth as the assassin of the President.

War Department,
Washington, D.C.
April 15,—4:10 A.M.

The President continues insensible, and is sinking. Secretary Seward remains without change. Frederick Seward's skull is fractured in two places, besides a severe cut upon the head. The attendant is still alive, but hopeless. . . .

It is now ascertained with reasonable certainty that two assassins were engaged in the horrible crime—Wilkes Booth being the one that shot the President; the other, a companion of his, whose name is not known, but whose description is so clear that he can hardly escape.

Source 5 Washington *Evening Star*, afternoon of April 15, 1865

EXTRA
THE DEATH OF THE PRESIDENT

At 22 minutes past seven o'clock the President breathed his last, closing his eyes as if falling to sleep, and his countenance assuming an expression of perfect serenity. There were no indications of pain, and it was not known that he was dead until the gradually decreasing respiration ceased altogether.

Rev. Dr. Gurley, (of the New York Avenue Presbyterian Church) immediately on its being ascertained that life was extinct, knelt at the bedside and offered an impressive prayer, which was responded to by all present.

Dr. Gurley then proceeded to the front parlor, where Mrs. Lincoln, Capt. Robert Lincoln, Mr. John Hay, the Private Secretary, and others were waiting, when he again offered prayer for the consolation of the family. . . .

Immediately after the President's death a Cabinet meeting was called by Secretary Stanton, and held in the room in which the corpse lay. Secretaries Stanton, Welles, and Usher, Postmaster General Dennison, and Attorney General Speed present. The results of the Conference are as yet unknown.

Shortly after nine o'clock this morning the remains were placed in a temporary coffin and removed to the White House, six young men of the Quartermaster's Department carrying the body to the house.

Source 6 *Richmond Whig*, April 17, 1865

The heaviest blow which has ever fallen upon the people of the South has descended. Abraham Lincoln, the President of the United States, has been assassinated. . . . The thoughtless and the vicious may affect to derive satisfaction from the sudden and tragic close of the President's career, but every reflecting person will deplore the awful event. Just as everything was happily conspiring to a restoration of tranquility, under the benignant and magnanimous policy of Mr. Lincoln, comes this terrible blow. God grant that it may not rekindle excitement or inflame passion again.

That a state of war, almost fratricidal, should give rise to bitter feelings and bloody deeds in the field was to be expected, but that the assassin's knife and bullet should follow the great and best loved of the nation in their daily walks, and reach them when surrounded by their friends, is an atrocity which will shock and appall every honorable man and woman.

Source 7   Washington *Evening Star,* April 18, 1865

EXTRA

THE ASSAILANT OF SECRETARY SEWARD ARRESTED!!

About three o'clock this morning a man clad in laboring clothes, covered with mud and bearing a pick-axe on his shoulder, was arrested entering a house occupied by members of the Surratt family on H street, between 9th and 10th. On removing the mud from his person he turned out to be of much more genteel appearance than his disguise indicated.

He has since his arrest been confronted with those at Secretary Seward's, who saw the Secretary's assailant on Friday night, and he was at once identified as the man.

It is reported that his name is Paine, but the full particulars have not yet transpired.

Surratt, it is now believed, was not a direct actor in the assassination, but seems to have been in some way implicated in the plot.

Upon the prisoner being brought to General Augur's headquarters this morning, Mr. Seward's colored servant, who was at the door at the time the assassin applied for admission, was sent for. The servant had no knowledge of the arrest of the prisoner, but upon entering the room in which the prisoner and a number of persons were, instantly exclaimed, "Why, here is the man that cut Mr. Seward."

Source 8   Washington *Evening Star,* April 21, 1865

THE REMAINS OF PRESIDENT LINCOLN

Yesterday the throng of persons visiting the remains of the late President, as they laid in state in the Capitol, continued until dark, at which time the doors were closed and the guard for the night . . . set. The number of visitors is estimated at about forty thousand, and but for the inclement weather the number would have been probably twice as many.

Source 9   Washington *Evening Star,* April 22, 1865

ARREST OF THE SURRATT FAMILY

Colonel Wells, Provost Marshall General of this Department, was pursuing investigation into the recent assassinations. He had decided to arrest Mrs. Surratt, who resides in this city at 541 H street, but subsequently decided to arrest the whole family, including her daughter Kate, two young ladies, whom she calls her nieces, and two colored servants. . . . Major Smith, Assistant Adjutant on General Augur's staff, proceeded to the house about 11 o'clock.

Major Smith proceeded up the steps alone, the house being a three story brick, with high stoop, and rapped. A woman raised a window, and asked, who is there? The reply was, "I'm an officer; let me in." The door was opened and the Major entered. Immediately after, the rest of the party entered one by one, until all were in. The purpose of the visit was announced and the inmates seemed somewhat surprised, the daughter especially being frightened, but the mother took it calmly as though she had been expecting it.

They were all assembled in the parlor, and not allowed to communicate with each other while the officers hunted up the bonnets, shawls, and shoes of the ladies, preparatory to conveying them to Colonel Ingraham's office. This took some little time, during which Miss Kate Surratt broke out into sobs, while her mother chided her for such an exhibition of her feelings.

Source 10 Washington *Evening Star*

PRESIDENT LINCOLN'S REMAINS IN NEW YORK

New York, April 24.—Business is generally suspended.

On the arrival of the funeral cortege Broadway was crowded to the utmost by people anxious to witness the funeral car and accompanying escort. The utmost quiet prevailed on the route, and the dense masses remained uncovered as the procession slowly wended its way to City Hall. The coffin was conveyed by eight soldiers to the Governor's room, and one thousand singers sang a mournful dirge as it was borne to its temporary resting place. . . . Immense crowds, numbering thousands, are in the streets, awaiting an opportunity to view for the last time the face of Abraham Lincoln.

New York, April 25.—The action of the Common Council against the colored citizens appearing in the procession to morrow is overruled by the Police Commissioner. The Secretary of War to-day telegraphed General Dix, expressing a desire that there should be no discrimination respecting color.

CEREMONIES AT ALBANY

Albany, April 26.—From the time the remains of the President were deposited in the Capitol until now, persons have been pressing thither. This morning the line of people extends at least a mile and a half. The place presents a solemn scene. There in the presence of death, hearts are bowed with grief, which often finds relief in tears.

OFFICIAL BULLETIN

War Department,
Washington, D.C.,
April 27, 1865.

J. Wilkes Booth and Harrold were chased from the swamp in St. Mary's county, Md., pursued yesterday morning to Garrett's farm, near Port Royal, on the Rappahannock, by Col. Baker's force.

The barn in which they took refuge was fired.

Booth in making his escape was shot through the head and killed, lingering about three hours, and Harrold taken alive.

Booth's body and Harrold are now here.

Edwin M. Stanton, Secretary of War

PRESIDENT LINCOLN'S REMAINS AT CLEVELAND

Cleveland, April 28.—All along the route from Buffalo to this city, which was reached this morning, the usual demonstrations of sorrow were witnessed.

The remains were escorted by a large military and civic procession to a beautiful constructed temple prepared to receive them, and soon thereafter the face of the honored dead was open to thousands of spectators, who in admirable order entered and retired from the enclosure.

EDITORIAL
"The End of the Assassin"

The manner of death of J. Wilkes Booth though at first a disappointment to the public has in some respects a peculiar fitness. For sympathy with his deed he received the fiercest execration; instead of a brilliant escape to a refuge of safety the officers of justice hunted the crippled fugitive like a starved beast from swamp to swamp, and at last, exhausted by hunger and pain, the wretch died the death of a cur. What may have been the anguish of his craven soul as the tolls closed around him no man may ever know. Whatever torture a frenzied people might have inflicted upon his carcass had he fallen into their hands alive has been exceeded by the misery of his flight. . . .

It is best that he should have passed beyond human passion as he did. The wretch whom a righteous trial might have invested with some degree of respectful detestation, is now only the despised malefactor, dying the death of a mad dog in an out house.

THE PRESIDENT'S REMAINS

Springfield, Ill., May 3.—The funeral train arrived at 8 o'clock this morning. All the way from Chicago, on the road, funeral arches were erected and mourning emblems displayed. An immense crowd assembled at the principal depot here. The remains were conveyed to the Capitol, where the apartments were decorated in the most elaborate manner. Deep solemnity prevailed, bells tolled, and minute guns were fired. Thousands of persons were here from adjoining States, contributing to swell the proportions of the vast multitude which assembled to honor the illustrious dead.

THE OBSEQUIES IN SPRINGFIELD—THE CLOSING EXERCISES

Springfield, May 4.—About noon the remains of President Lincoln were brought from the State-house and placed in the hearse. . . .

The procession consisting of the governors of seven States, members of Congress, State and municipal authorities, delegations from adjoining States, Free Masons, Odd Fellows, and citizens, including the colored procession, arrived at Oak Ridge Cemetery at 1 o'clock. . . .

There was a platform on which singers and an instrumental band were engaged in singing and playing appropriate music. On the right was the speakers' stand. The vault is at the foot of a knoll in a beautiful part of the ground which contains forest trees and all other varieties. It has a Doric gable, resting on pilasters; the main wall being rustic. The vault is fifteen feet high, and about the same in width, with semicircular wings projecting from its hillsides. The material is limestone. . . .

After a hymn by the choir, Rev. Mr. Hubbard read the last inaugural of President Lincoln. Next a dirge was sung by the choir, when Bishop Simpson delivered the funeral address, which was in the highest degree solemn and patriotic; portions were applauded. Then followed another dirge and another hymn, when the benediction was pronounced by Rev. Dr. Gurley. The procession then reformed and returned.

Our mournful duty of escorting the mortal remains of Abraham Lincoln hither is performed. We have seen them deposited in the tomb. Bereaved friends, with saddened faces and grief-stricken hearts have taken their adieu and turned their faces homeward, ever to remember the affecting and impressive scene they have witnessed.

The injunction so often repeated on the way, "Bear him gently to his rest," has been obeyed, and "the great heart of the nation throbs heavily at the portals of the tomb."

 ## *Second Thoughts*

Avenging a Martyr's Death

The assassination of Abraham Lincoln traumatized a nation that thought itself inured to violence following years of internecine bloodshed. Millions mourned Lincoln's passing. The timing of his death at the concluding moments of the Civil War and the coincidence of his being taken on Good Friday made him a martyr. He attained after death a popularity greater than he had ever enjoyed while alive. As Samuel Eliot Morison wrote in 1972, John Wilkes Booth "gave fresh life to the very forces of hate and vengeance which Lincoln himself was trying to kill."

Eight people were arrested in the days immediately following the assassination and brought before a military court. Four—Lewis Payne, George Atzerodt, David E. Herold, and Mary Surratt—were found guilty and met death on the gallows. Three others—including the physician who set Booth's broken leg—were sentenced to life imprisonment. Another of the conspirators was condemned to a prison term of six years. John Surratt, yet another of the conspirators, managed to flee the country but was brought back to stand trial in 1867. His trial ended in a hung jury.

Source 11   Walt Whitman, "O Captain, My Captain," 1865

O Captain! My Captain! our fearful trip is done,
The ship has weathered every rack, the prize we sought is won,
The port is near, the bells I hear, the people all exulting,
While follow eyes the steady keel, the vessel grim and daring,
    But O heart! heart! heart!
      O the bleeding drops of red,
        Where on the deck my Captain lies,
          Fallen cold and dead.

O Captain! My Captain! rise up and hear the bells;
Rise up—for you the flag is flung—For you the bugle trills,

> For you bouquets and ribboned wreaths—For you the shores
> a-crowding,
> For you they call, the swaying mass, their eager faces turning;
> Here Captain! dear father!
> This arm beneath your head!
> It is some dream that on the deck,
> You've fallen cold and dead.
>
> My Captain does not answer, his lips are pale and still,
> My father does not feel my arm, he has no pulse nor will,
> The ship is anchor'd safe and sound, its voyage closed and done,
> From fearful trip the victor ship comes in with object won;
> Exult O shores and ring, O bells!
> But I with mournful tread,
> Walk the deck my Captain lies,
> Fallen cold and dead.

Source 12   Presidential Proclamation, May 2, 1865

Whereas it appears from evidence in the Bureau of Military Justice that the atrocious murder of the late President, Abraham Lincoln, and the attempted assassination of the Hon. William H. Seward, Secretary of State, were incited, concerted, and procured by and between Jefferson Davis, late of Richmond, Va., and Jacob Thompson, Clement C. Clay, Beverley Tucker, George N. Sanders, William C. Cleary, and other Rebels and traitors against the Government of the United States harbored in Canada:

Now, therefore, to the end that justice may be done, I, Andrew Johnson, President of the United States, do offer and promise for the arrest of said persons, or either of them, within the limits of the United States, so that they can be brought to trial, the following rewards:

One hundred thousand dollars for the arrest of Jefferson Davis.

Twenty-five thousand dollars for the arrest of Clement Clay.

Twenty-five thousand dollars for the arrest of Jacob Thompson, late of Mississippi.

Twenty-five thousand dollars for the arrest of George N. Sanders.

Twenty-five thousand dollars for the arrest of Beverly Tucker.

Ten thousand dollars for the arrest of William C. Cleary, late clerk of Clement C. Clay.

The Provost-Marshal-General of the United States is directed to cause a description of said persons, with notice of the above rewards, to be published.

In testimony whereof I have hereunto set my hand and caused the seal of the United States to be affixed.

Source 13   Editorial, "The Trial of Jeff. Davis," *New York Times*, May 5, 1865

It is extremely desirable that the charges which have been solemnly made against Jefferson Davis, Jacob Thompson & Co., in the President's Proclamation, should be fully borne out on the trial.

If they are, and we have no doubt they will be, it will fix very accurately the place which the rebellion will occupy in history. The course which it has run has been simple and consistent from the commencement. It began with an attempt to found an empire upon wholesale robbery of servants' wages, and if its last act was really the murder of the President, Mr. Davis has the satisfaction of knowing that he has run through the whole gamut of crime in the short space of four years. There is a completeness and unity in the movement of which he has been the chief, which, whatever its moral complexion may be, must always entitle it to the highest place as an attempt to apply the rules of war to the commission of villainy.

Source 14 Horace Greeley, *The American Conflict: A History of the Great Rebellion,* 1867

That President Lincoln was the victim of a conspiracy of partisans of the Rebellion is established by undeniable proof; not so the charge that the chiefs and master-spirits of the Confederacy were implicated in the crime. Booth himself was, so far as had been shown, the projector and animating soul of the monstrous plot. . . . Booth was simply one of the many badly educated, loose-living young men infesting the purlieus of our great cities, who, regarding Slavery as the chief bulwark of their own claim to birthright in a superior caste, and the Federal Constitution as established expressly and mainly to sustain and buttress Slavery, could never comprehend that any political action adverse to whatever exactions and pretensions of the Slave Power could possibly be other than unjustly aggressive and treasonable. Few of this class were radically Disunionists; they sympathized with the Rebellion, not because it aimed at a division of the Republic, but because it was impelled by devotion to Slavery; and was thus hallowed, in their view, as a laudable effort, however irregular, to achieve and firmly secure the chief end of both the Constitution and the Union. There is no particle of evidence that Booth, or any of his fellow conspirators, had been in any-wise offended by, or that they cherished any feeling of aversion to, the President, save as the 'head center' of resistance to the Slaveholders' Rebellion. . . .

The quiet accession to the Presidency of Vice-President Johnson—the funeral honors to the good, beloved President, so suddenly snatched away at the moment when long years of trial and disaster had at length been crowned by a fullness of triumph and gladness rarely paralleled—the flight, pursuit, and capture of Booth, so severely wounded by his captors that he died a few hours afterward—the arraignment, trial, and conviction before a military court of Payne and several of their fellow-conspirators or accomplices—may here be hurriedly passed over, as non-essential to this history. Not so the burst of unmeasured, indignant wrath, the passionate grief, the fierce cry for vengeance, which the crime of the assassins very generally incited. Mr. Lincoln was widely known as radically, immovably averse to aught that savored of severity in dealing with the defeated insurgents. No 'railing accusations,' no incitements to severity or bitterness on the part of the loyal, had ever found utterance through his lips. Inflexibly resolved that the Rebellion should be put down, he was equally determined that its upholders, having submitted to the Nation's authority, should experience to the utmost the Nation's magnanimity. . . . And now, the butchery of this gentle, forbearing spirit, by the hand, hardly less blundering than bloody, of a pro-Rebel assassin, incited a fierce, agonized, frantic yell for retaliation . . . ; and the appearance of an official proclamation, signed by the new President . . . charging that the appalling crime of Booth and his associates had been "incited, concerted, and procured by and between Jefferson Davis . . . and other Rebels and traitors against the Government of the United States" was widely hailed as justifying the suspicions already current, and rendering the Confederates as a body morally guilty of the murder of Mr. Lincoln, and justly liable therefor to **condign** punishment.

Source 15 **Remarks of John H. Surratt, son of hanged conspirator Mary Surratt, Rockville, Maryland, December 6, 1870**

In the fall of 1864 I was introduced to John Wilkes Booth, who, I was given to understand, wished to know something about the main avenues leading from Washington to the Potomac. We met several times, . . . as he seemed to be very reticent with regard to his purposes, . . . but finally said he would make known his views to me provided I would promise secrecy. . . . He then said, "I will confide my plans to you; but before doing so I will make known to you the motives that actuate me. In the Northern prisons are many thousands of our men whom the United States Government refuses to exchange. You know as well as I the efforts that have been made to bring about that much desired exchange. Aside from the great suffering they are compelled to undergo, we are sadly in want of them as soldiers. We cannot spare one man, whereas the United States Government is willing to let their own soldiers remain in our prisons because she has no need of the men. I have a proposition to submit to you, which I think if we can carry out will bring about the desired exchange." There was a long and ominous silence which I at last was compelled to break by asking, "Well, Sir, what is your proposition?" He sat quiet for an instant, and then . . . in a whisper said, "it is to kidnap President Lincoln, and carry him off to Richmond!" "Kidnap President Lincoln!" I said. . . . I was amazed—thunderstruck—and in fact, I might also say, frightened at the unparalleled audacity of his scheme. After two day's reflection I told him I was willing to try it. I believed it practicable at that time, though I now regard it as a foolhardy undertaking. I hope you will not blame me for going thus far. I honestly thought an exchange of prisoners could be brought about could we have once obtained possession of Mr. Lincoln's person. And now reverse the case. Where is there a young man in the North with one spark of patriotism in his heart who would not have with enthusiastic ardor joined in any undertaking for the capture of Jefferson Davis and brought him to Washington? There is not one who would not have done so. And so I was led on by a sincere desire to assist the South in gaining her independence. I had no hesitation in taking part in anything honorable that might tend towards the accomplishment of that object. Such a thing as the assassination of Mr. Lincoln, I never heard spoken of by any member of the party. Never! . . .

　　It may be well to remark here that this scheme of abduction was concocted without the knowledge or assistance of the Confederate government in any shape or form. Booth and I often consulted together as to whether it would not be well to acquaint the authorities in Richmond with our plan, as we were sadly in want of money, our expenses being very heavy. In fact the question arose among us as to whether, after getting Mr. Lincoln, if we succeeded in our plan, the Confederate authorities would not surrender us to the United States again, because of doing this thing without their consent or knowledge. But we never acquainted them with the plan, and they never had anything in the wide world to do with it. In fact, we were jealous of our undertaking and wanted no outside help. I have not made this statement to defend the officers of the Confederate government. They are perfectly able to defend themselves. What I have done myself I am not ashamed to let the world know.

Source 16 Abraham Lincoln's former law partner, William H. Herndon, *The Life of Lincoln,* 1888

In the death of Lincoln the South, prostrate and bleeding, lost a friend; and his unholy taking-off at the very hour of the assured supremacy of the Union cause ran the iron into the heart of the North. His sun went down suddenly, and whelmed the country in a darkness which was felt by every heart; but far up the clouds sprang apart, and soon the golden light, flooding the heavens with radiance, illuminated every uncovered brow with the hope of a fair tomorrow. His name will ever be the watchword of liberty. His work is finished, and sealed forever with the veneration given to the blood of martyrs. Yesterday a man reviled and abused, a target for the shafts of malice and hatred: today an apostle. Yesterday a power: today a prestige, sacred, irresistible. The life and the tragic death of Mr. Lincoln mark an epoch in history from which dates the unqualified annunciation by the American people of the greatest truth in the bible of republicanism—the very keystone of that arch of human rights which is destined to overshadow and remodel every government upon the earth. The glorious brightness of that upper world, as it welcomed his faint and bleeding spirit, broke through upon the earth at his exit—it was drawn of a day growing brighter as the grand army of freedom follows in the march of time. . . .

This is the true lesson of Lincoln's life: real and enduring greatness, that will survive the corrosion and abrasion of time, of change, and of progress, must rest upon character. . . . Not eloquence, nor logic, nor grasp of thought; not statesmanship, nor power of command, nor courage; not any nor all of these have made him what he is, but these, in the degree in which he possessed them, conjoined to those qualities comprised in the term character, have given him his fame—have made him for all time to come the great American, the grand, central figure in American—perhaps in the world's—history.

Source 17 Lincoln's secretary John Nicolay and statesman John Hay, *Abraham Lincoln: A History,* 1890

The death of Lincoln awoke all over the world a quick and deep emotion of grief and admiration. If he had died in the days of doubt and gloom which preceded his reelection, he would have been sincerely mourned and praised by the friends of the Union, but its enemies would have curtly dismissed him as one of the necessary and misguided victims of sectional hate. They would have used his death to justify their malevolent forebodings, to point the moral of new lectures on the instability of democracies. But as he had fallen in the moment of a stupendous victory, the halo of a radiant success enveloped his memory and dazzled the eyes even of his most hostile critics.

Source 18 William A. Dunning, *Reconstruction: Political & Economic,* 1907

The first six weeks of Johnson's administration were dominated by the emotions which the assassination of his predecessor excited in all parts of the land. At Washington affairs fell largely under the direction of the secretary of war, whose total loss of self-control in the crisis contributed to intensify the panicky and vindictive feeling that prevailed. The idea that leading Confederates were concerned in Booth's plot . . . strengthened the hands of those who were demanding that the conquered people as a whole should receive harsh treatment. . . .

When, however, the excitement caused by the assassination of Lincoln subsided, and the suspicions that Davis and his associates had been concerned in the deed were seen by sane minds to be unfounded, conservative northern sentiment began to show alarm at the vindictive course to which the president seemed tending.

Source 19 W. E. B. Du Bois, *Black Reconstruction in America,* 1934

The tragic death of Lincoln has given currency to the theory that the Lincoln policy of Reconstruction would have been far better and more successful than the policy afterward pursued. If it is meant by this that Lincoln would have more carefully followed public opinion and worked to adjust differences, this is true. But Abraham Lincoln himself could not have settled the question of Emancipation, Negro citizenship and the vote, without tremendous difficulty.

Source 20 Kenneth M. Stampp, *The Era of Reconstruction,* 1965

To Lincoln, restoring the old relationship between the southern states and the Union was the essence of reconstruction. . . . For him, reconstruction was to be essentially a work of restoration, not of innovation; it was the old Union—the Union as it was—that he hoped to rebuild. . . .

Lincoln's plan of reconstruction, then, was designed to restore the southern states to the Union with maximum speed and with a minimum of federal intervention in their internal affairs. The great majority of white southerners would receive amnesty and full power to re-establish loyal state governments; Confederate leaders, with few exceptions, would receive special pardons when they applied for them. . . . The Negroes, if they remained, would be governed by the white men among whom they lived, subject only to certain minimum requirements of fair play. Such a program, in Lincoln's mind, was at once humane, politically practical, and constitutionally sound.

For a few years after Lincoln's death, a combination of northern humanitarians and radical Republicans overturned this conservative plan of reconstruction and came near to imposing upon the South a far-reaching social revolution, particularly in the relations of the two races. During the 1870's, however, conservative men regained control of the southern state governments, and the struggle to give political and legal equality to Negroes was virtually abandoned. . . .

This being the case, there would seem to be cause to revise somewhat the traditional images we have of the radical Republicans and of Lincoln. In some respects the radical leaders, rather than Lincoln, proved to be the sentimental idealists.

 ## Questioning the Past

1. What immediate and long-term effects did the assassination of Lincoln have on the development of America? Had Lincoln lived, would the restoration of the South to the Union and the reconstruction of the relations between the races have progressed any differently?

2. Though General Lee surrendered the Army of Northern Virginia on April 9, 1865, other Confederate armies continued to fight for several more weeks. The last land battle of the Civil War, a Confederate victory, was waged on May 12–13, 1865, along the Rio Grande at Palmetto. Confederate forces west of the Mississippi under General Kirby-Smith negotiated a surrender on May 26, 1865. Tens of thousands of northern and southern lives were lost before Lincoln's murder. Many lives, northern and southern, were lost following Lincoln's death. Why is the reaction of history more horrified by the wartime murder of a governmental leader than by the wartime deaths of 600,000 soldiers? Should a commander-in-chief be considered any less legitimate a target than the forces he commands?

3. A majority of the voters of the Union elected Lincoln to a second term in the White House. One man vetoed the decision of this majority. Since Lincoln's murder, other assassins have made attempts upon the lives of other presidents, three of which were successful. Can a democratic people have access to their public servants and protect them too? Can elected officials whose contact with their constituents must be filtered through a wall of security maintain an accurate feel for the public mood?

Chapter 4

The Wild West

Deputy Charles Webb Draws on John Wesley Hardin   *May 26, 1874*

The cattle kingdom rose and fell on the Great Plains in the years after the Civil War. With it came and passed the era of the western gunfighter. And of all the men who strapped on a gunbelt and drove cattle up the Chisholm Trail to the railheads in Kansas, none was deadlier than John Wesley Hardin.

The son of a Methodist minister, Wes Hardin seemed an unlikely candidate for the West's most notorious gunman. He was slight of build, standing five feet ten inches and weighing 160 pounds, and had what were described as "mild blue eyes." He was intelligent, articulate, and well-mannered. Yet before he was out of his teens, he was already a killer without a conscience.

John Wesley Hardin was in large measure a victim of time and place. The collapse of the Confederacy brought economic depression and military occupation to Texas. To survive, many Texans began to round up the wild longhorns that grazed by the millions on the grasslands of the southern part of the state. Cattle in Texas were worth about $5 a head; in the cities of the East they brought $40 apiece. The supply of Texas and the demand of the East met in Kansas at the places where the south-to-north cattle trails intersected the east-west rail lines. Great herds were soon moving north to the cow towns that sprang up beside the tracks. Still more herds were being moved out onto the Great Plains to take advantage of the open range lands. This Cattle Kingdom preceded the law onto the Plains: those living in cattle country had to be able to protect their lives and property through their own devices.

In 1868, at the age of 15, John Wesley Hardin killed his first man. A wrestling match with a former slave escalated into an incident in which Wes Hardin shot the freedman. Though Hardin shot the man in self-defense, his father feared that Wes would not be accorded a fair hearing by the federal troops then administering justice in Texas. He told young Hardin to go into hiding. A short time later, three soldiers came looking for Wes, but he killed all three, and local people helped him dispose of the bodies. Having killed four times before he turned 16, he found it easy after that.

As a fugitive, John Wesley Hardin found many friends and relatives in Texas willing to harbor him, as well as many enemies and adventurers wishing to challenge him for fame and fortune. He tried taking root and teaching school, but his past caught up with him. He became a cow-puncher and drover and was able to move freely through cattle country with a reputation that cleared most obstacles from his path. Where the reputation was not enough, his revolvers were. Forty-four men are said to have met death in front of his six-shooters. All of them, according to Hardin, needed to be killed, including the man in Dodge whom he shot through a hotel wall. The man's snoring was bothering the guests and had to be stopped. But the murder for which Hardin was finally imprisoned, ironically, was one that was probably justifiable.

ᴥ *First Impressions*

Gunfight at Comanche

4.1 The Wild West

Tales of gunmen with lightning-quick draws and deadly aims are founded more often in fiction than in fact. Though legends no doubt enhanced the career of Hardin as well, he was by all accounts both fast and accurate with a revolver, and was party to more documented gunfights than any other person of the Old West.

Source 1   *The Life of John Wesley Hardin, as Written by Himself,* 1894

It was April [1874] now, and I soon started my cattle for Wichita, Kansas, and put Joe Clements in charge. I was to receive the cattle in June at or near Wichita, but was not going with the cattle myself.

About this time my brother Joe and my cousin, Aleck Barrickman, went home to Comanche, and my wife and baby went with them to visit my parents there. It was understood that I should spend a week with them on my way up to Kansas.

Jim Taylor and I agreed to start another herd. . . . In about two weeks we had complied with the laws and had started another herd of about 1,000 head. We placed Dr. J. B. Brosius in charge with instructions to go by Hamilton, in Hamilton County, and they were to send me word at Comanche, where I would be with my parents.

About the 23rd of April, 1874, Jim Taylor and I left Gonzales, bound for Comanche and then for Wichita. . . . There was . . . a reward of $500 offered for Jim Taylor.

We got to Comanche on or about the 28th of April, having Rondo and two other race horses with us. It was not long before I made two races to be run on the Comanche tracks on the 26th of May, 1874. I was to run Rondo against a mare that had beaten him before. My brother had a horse named "Shiloh" which I also matched, and a cousin of mine, Bud Dixon, matched a horse of his called "Dock."

The 26th of May was my birthday. About the 5th, Jim Taylor and I went with my brother and the sheriff's party some twenty miles into Brown County to get some cattle that belonged to my brother. The cattle were in possession of the Gouldstones, and we got them and started back without any trouble. Night overtaking us, we stopped at Mrs. Waldrup's to pen our cattle. At the supper table Mrs. Waldrup told us how one Charles Webb, a deputy sheriff of Brown County, had come to her house and arrested Jim Buck Waldrup and had cursed and abused her. She had told him no gentleman would curse a woman.

Of course, we all agreed with her. This was the first time I had heard of Charles Webb. There were present that night at the supper table Bill Cunningham, Bud and Tom Dixon, Jim and Ham Anderson, Aleck Barrickman, Jim Taylor and Jim Milligan (deputy sheriffs), Joe Hardin, . . . and myself. We were all first cousins to each other except Jim Taylor. There is no doubt but that we all sympathized with Mrs. Waldrup, who had been so abused by Charles Webb. . . .

We drove the cattle home next morning to Comanche, and from that until the 26th but one more incident worthy of note occurred.

Henry Ware was a bully from Canada, and from some cause or other he disliked my brother Joe. He came to the herd one day and claimed a cow, and my brother told him he could not get it. Ware persisted and put his hand to his Winchester, when my brother ordered him out of the herd at the point of a **six-shooter**, an order the Hon. Henry Ware promptly obeyed, and he did not get his cow.

The 26th of May saw a big crowd at the races. . . . Rondo ran first and won easily. Shiloh came next and had a walk over. Next came Dock, which was a close race, but he won by six feet. So I and my friends won everything in sight. I won about $3000 in cash, fifty head of cattle, a wagon or two, and fifteen head of saddle horses. I set more than one man afoot and then loaned them the horses to ride home on.

I had heard that morning that Charles Webb, the deputy sheriff from Brown County, had come over to Comanche with fifteen men to kill me and capture Jim Taylor for the reward. I also heard that he had said that John Karnes, the sheriff of Comanche, was no man or sheriff because he allowed a set of murderers to stay around him, headed by the notorious John Wesley Hardin, and as he (Karnes) would not attend to his business, he would do it for him. . . .

He did not make any breaks at the race tracks, but when we all came back to town, he swore time and time again that he would kill me and capture Jim Taylor, and that this would be done before the sun went down. When I was told this, I laughed and said I hoped he would put it off till dark or altogether.

We were going from bar to bar, trying to spend some of the money we had won. I remember in one saloon I threw a handful of $20 gold pieces on the counter and called for the drinks. Some of my friends picked them up and thought I was drinking too freely, and told me if any scrap came up, I would not be able to protect myself. I assured them I was all right, but at last thought I had better go home to avoid any possible trouble. . . .

We invited the whole crowd up to Jack Wright's to take a last drink. Frank Wilson, a deputy sheriff under Karnes, came up and locked arms with me just as I was going to drink and said, "John, I want to see you."

I said all right.

This saloon was situated on the northwest corner of the square, the front facing the square to the east, with a door in front, and another door to the north near the west end of the saloon. Frank Wilson and I went out at the north door and then west for about ten steps, when I told him that was far enough and stopped on the back street west of the saloon. Frank said, "John, the people here have treated you well; now don't drink any more, but go home and avoid all trouble."

I told him Jeff (Hardin) had gone for the buggy, and I was going as soon as he came. He said, "You know it is a violation of the law to carry a pistol."

I knew now that he was trying to pump me, so I told him my pistol was behind the bar and threw open my coat to show him. But he did not know I had a good one under my vest. I looked to the south and saw a man, a stranger to me, with two six-shooters on coming towards us. I said to Frank, "Let's go back to the saloon. I want to pay my bill and then go home."

We went into the saloon and we were stopped by Jim Taylor, who said, "Wes, you have drank enough; let us go home; here is Jeff with the buggy."

I said, "Let us go in and get a cigar, then we will go home."

About this time Dave Karnes remarked, "Here comes that damned Brown County sheriff."

I turned around and faced the man whom I had seen coming up the street. He had on two six-shooters and was about fifteen steps from me, advancing. He stopped when he got to within five steps of me, then stopped and scrutinized me closely, with his hands behind him. I asked him, "Have you any papers for my arrest?"

He said, "I don't know you."

I said, "My name is John Wesley Hardin."

He said, "Now I know you, but have no papers for your arrest."

"Well," I said, "I have been informed that the sheriff of Brown County has said that Sheriff Karnes of this county was no sheriff or he would not allow me to stay around Comanche with my murdering pals."

He said, "I am not responsible for what the sheriff of Brown County says. I am only a deputy."

So Dave Karnes spoke up and said, "Men, there can be no difference between you about John Karnes," and said, "Mr. Webb, let me introduce you to Mr. Hardin."

I asked him what he had in his hand behind his back, and he showed me a cigar. I said, "Mr. Webb, we were just going to take a drink or a cigar; won't you join us?"

He replied, "Certainly." As I turned to go in the north door, I heard some one say, "Look out, Jack." It was Bud Dixon, and as I turned around, I saw Charles Webb drawing his pistol. He was in the act of presenting it when I jumped to one side, drew my pistol, and fired.

In the meantime, Webb had fired, hitting me in the left side, cutting the length of it, inflicting an ugly and painful wound. My aim was good and a bullet hole in the left cheek did the work. He fell against the wall, and as he fell he fired a second shot, which went into the air.

In the meantime, my friends, Jim Taylor and Bud Dixon, seeing that Webb had taken the drop on me and had shot me, pulled their pistols and fired on him as he was falling not knowing that I had killed him. Each shot hit him in the side and breast.

At my first attempt to shoot, Frank Wilson started to draw his pistol, but as soon as I had fired on Webb and before Wilson had time to draw, I covered him and told him to hold up his hands, which he did.

Several men were standing at the east end of the building next to the public square. When the shooting commenced, they started to rush over to the saloon, but soon retreated.

I afterwards learned the plan was for Charles Webb to assassinate me and then for the crowd to rush up and with Frank Wilson's help to rush in and overpower Jim Taylor, thus getting the reward. They expected my relatives and friends to stand still while they did their bloody work. They believed they could not arrest Taylor without killing me, hence they attacked me.

The crowd outside ran back, as I stated above, and cried out, "Hardin has killed Charley Webb; let us hang him."

The sheriff of the county, John Karnes, who was my friend, came in with a shotgun and asked, "Who did this work?"

I told him I had done it, and would surrender to him if he would protect me from the mob. I handed him my pistol to show my good faith.

About ten men ran around the east corner and commenced firing on us and Jim Taylor. Bud Dixon and Aleck Barrickman drew their pistols and started to fire, when they ran back behind the corner. They were reinforced and charged again, John Karnes met them at the door and demanded that they disperse. They overpowered and disarmed him of his gun and were trying to get my pistol away from him. I told my friends that there was no protection for us there, and told Jim Taylor to come with me and the other two to go back west. So Jim and I ran across the street to some horses that were hitched near by, and as I ran I pulled my knife out of my pocket and cut the hitching ropes.

I now saw that my wife and sister Mat were in the crowd crying and looking down towards my brother's law office. I saw my father and brother Joe coming toward the scene with shotguns.

I concluded the best thing to do to avoid bloodshed was to get out of town. Jim Taylor wanted to charge the mob, but I said, "For God's sake, don't do that; you may hit the wrong one." I caught his horse and kept him from shooting. We turned and went running out of town, the mob firing on us and the sheriff's party trying to protect us.

Dixon and Anderson, seeing we were safely out of town, got on their horses also, and we met again at my father's, where my father and brother joined us with the sheriff.

I was willing to surrender, but the sheriff said he could not protect me; that the mob was too strong.

Everyone Carried a Gun

After the killing of Deputy Webb, the State of Texas offered a reward of $4,000 to anyone who could take Hardin dead or alive. The Texas Rangers were ordered to track him as well. Hardin managed to stay ahead of the bounty hunters and Rangers for three years, but was captured in July 1877 when Texas Rangers assisted by local law officers took him by surprise aboard a train in Florida. Brought back to trial in Comanche, Hardin was convicted of second degree murder and sentenced to 25 years at hard labor in the Texas penitentiary. In March 1894, Governor James F. Hogg granted Hardin a full pardon and restored his rights of citizenship.

John Wesley Hardin spent his years in prison studying law. Upon being released and pardoned, Hardin passed the bar exam and began to practice law in Gonzales, Texas. One of his cases took him to El Paso in the spring of 1895, and there, awaiting the conclusion of the trial of his client, the notorious Jim "Killer" Miller, Hardin became a regular at such establishments as the Gem Saloon and Gambling Emporium, the Wigwam Saloon, Roy Barnum's Show Saloon, and the Acme Saloon.

4.2 Links to Personalities of the West

On the evening of August 19, 1895, John Wesley Hardin was at the Acme Saloon shaking dice with an acquaintance when Deputy Sheriff John Selman stepped through the swinging doors and shot Hardin in the back of the head. Hardin died instantly. Within eight months of his murder of Hardin, Selman was himself gunned down by ex-Sheriff George Scarborough. Scarborough, in turn, was killed by Will Carver. Will Carver was killed by Elijah Briant.

The West has been saddled with the reputation of a wild and lawless land. Certainly, not unlike the present day, guns were to be found in abundance and their use was not uncommon. But while everyone carried a gun in the West of the late nineteenth century, not everyone earned a living with one. The professional gunfighters—those for whom a gun was the primary tool of their trade—were found in such occupations as buffalo hunter, cattle rustler, law officer, robber, army scout, hired killer, or detective, and it was not unusual to find them passing with ease from one side of the law to the other. Manning Clements—a cousin of Wes Hardin and a man who once stated, "For three hundred dollars I'd cut anybody in two with a sawed-off shotgun"—was a rustler, murderer, and, at the time of his death in a barroom shoot-out, a candidate for sheriff of Runnels County, Texas. But beyond the professionals, the average westerner was prone to break the law on occasion.

4.3 The American West

📖 *Second Thoughts*

The Law of the Frontier

As Walter Prescott Webb pointed out, easterners made the laws for westerners and those laws often reflected eastern rather than western realities. For example, cattle and horse theft were relatively minor offenses in the East, but cattle were the primary property of the West, and horses were essential for survival. Consequently, the westerners took the law into their own hands to make the penalty fit the importance of the crime.

Source 2   *The Life of John Wesley Hardin, as Written by Himself, 1894*

The simple fact is that Charles Webb had really come over from his own county that day to kill me, thinking I was drinking and at a disadvantage. He wanted to kill me to keep his name, and he made his break on me like an assassin would. He fired his first shot at my vitals when I was unprepared, and who blames a man for shooting under such conditions? I was at a terrible disadvantage in my trial. I went before a court on a charge of murder without a witness. The cowardly mob had either killed them or run them out of the county. I went to trial in a town in which three years before my own brother and cousins had met an awful death at the hands of a mob. Who of my readers would like to be tried under these circumstances? On that jury that tried me sat six men whom I knew to be directly implicated in my brother's death. No, my readers, I have served twenty-five years for the killing of Webb, but know ye that there is a God in high heaven who knows that I did not shoot Charles Webb through malice, nor through anger, nor for money, but to save my own life.

True, it is almost as bad to kill as to be killed. It drove my father to an early grave; it almost distracted my mother; it killed my brother Joe and my cousins Tom and William; it left my brother's widow with two helpless babes; Mrs. Anderson lost her son Ham, and Mrs. Susan Barrickman lost her husband, to say nothing of the grief of countless others. I do say, however, that the man who does not exercise the first law of nature—that of self-preservation—is not worthy of living and breathing the breath of life.

Source 3   *El Paso Daily Herald,* August 20, 1895

Last night between 11 and 12 o'clock San Antonio street was thrown into an intense state of excitement by the sound of four pistol shots that occurred at the Acme saloon. Soon the crowd surged against the door, and there, right inside, lay the body of John Wesley Hardin, his blood flowing over the floor and his brains oozing out of a pistol shot wound that had passed through his head. Soon the fact became known that John Selman, constable of Precinct No. 1, had fired the fatal shots that had ended the career of so noted a character as Wes Hardin, by which name he is better known to all old Texans. For several weeks past trouble has been brewing and it has been often heard on the streets that John Wesley Hardin would be the cause of some killing before he left town. . . .

The wounds on Hardin's body were on the back of the head, coming out just over the left eye. Another shot in the right breast, just missing the nipple, and another through the right arm. The body was embalmed by Undertaker Powell and will be interred at Concordia at 4 P.M.

Source 4   Walter Prescott Webb, *The Great Plains,* 1931

The West was lawless for two reasons: first, because of the social conditions that obtained there during the period under consideration; secondly, because the law that was applied there was not made for the conditions that existed and was unsuitable for those conditions. It did not fit the needs of the country, and could not be obeyed. . . .

We know . . . that in the early period the restraints of law could not make themselves felt in the rarefied population. Each man had to make his own law because there was no other to make it. He had to defend himself and protect his rights by his force of personality, courage, and skill at arms. All men went armed and moved over vast areas among other armed men. The six-shooter was the final arbiter, a court of last resort, and an executioner. How could a man live in such a **milieu** and abide by the laws that obtained in the thickly settled portions of the country, where the police gave protection and the courts justice? Could the plainsman go unarmed in a country where danger was ever present? Could a man refuse to use those arms where his own life was at stake? . . .

In the absence of law and in the social conditions that obtained, men worked out an extra-legal code or custom by which they guided their actions. The code demanded what Roosevelt called a **square deal**; it demanded fair play. According to it one must not shoot his adversary in the back, and he must not shoot an unarmed man. In actual practice he must give notice of his intention, albeit the action followed the notice as a lightening stroke. Failure to abide by the code did not necessarily bring formal punishment for the act already committed; it meant that the violator might be cut off without benefit of notice in the next act. Thus was justice carried out in a crude but effective manner, and warning given that in general the code must prevail.

Under the social conditions the taking of human life did not entail the stigma that in more settled regions is associated with it. Men were all equal. Each was his own defender. His survival imposed upon him certain obligations which, if he were a man, he would accept. If he acted according to the code he not only attested his courage but implied that he was skilled in the art of living. Murder was too harsh a word to apply to his performance, a mere incident, as it were. But how could the Easterner, surrounded and protected by the conventions, understand such distinctions?

Theft was another form of lawlessness common on the Great Plains. But the code of the West had its way of interpreting and punishing theft. Of petty thievery there was practically none on the Plains. Property consisted of horses and cattle. There were horse thieves and cattle thieves.

There was no greater crime that to steal a man's horse, to set him afoot. It was like stealing the sailor's ship, or the wings of the bird. There were no extenuating circumstances and little time for explanation or prayer. The penalty was death. The cow thief was not nearly so bad in public estimation. A cow was mere property, but a horse was life itself to the plainsman. . . .

The land laws were persistently broken in the West because they were not made for the West and were wholly unsuited to any arid region. The homestead law gave a man 160 acres of land and presumed he should not acquire more. Since a man could not live on 160 acres of land in many parts of the region, he had to acquire more, or starve. Men circumvented this law in every possible way, and managed to build up estates sufficient to yield a living. Major Powell pointed out that the land unit in the arid region should be 2650 acres, instead of 160 as in the East. But the lawmakers could never see the force of the argument. . . .

One other example will be sufficient. Congress passed what was known as the Timber Act, which granted land free—a modified homestead law—on condition that the grantee grow forests on it. To the credit of Congress be it said that it did not require the prairie dogs to climb the trees or to live in the forests. The records do not reveal that Congress passed a law increasing the rainfall. . . .

Therefore the West was a lawless place. It was turbulent in the early days because there was no law. It was lawless in the later period because the laws were unsuited to the needs and conditions. Men could not abide by them and survive. . . . The blame for a great deal of Western lawlessness rests more with the lawmaker than with the lawbreaker.

Source 5   Cowboy E. C. "Teddy Blue" Abbott, *We Pointed Them North,* 1938

One time [in 1874] I remember I was in a saloon [in Lincoln, Nebraska], and I heard a fellow talking about the Yankees. He said, "I was coming down the road and I met a damn blue-bellied abolitionist, and I paunched him (shot him through the stomach). And he laid there in the brush and belched like a beef for three days, and then he died in fits. The bastard!"

He told that before a whole crowd of men. I don't know that he ever done it. But that was the way he talked to get a fight. Those early-day Texans was full of that stuff. Most of them that came up with the trail herds, being from Texas and Southerners to start with, was on the side of the South, and oh, but they were bitter. That was how a lot of them got killed, because they were full of the old dope about the war and they wouldn't let an abolitionist arrest them. The marshals in those cow towns on the trail were usually Northern men, and Southerners wouldn't go back to Texas and hear people say: "He's a hell of a fellow. He let a Yankee lock him up." Down home one Texas Ranger could arrest the whole lot of them, but up North you'd have to kill them first.

I couldn't even guess how many was killed that way on the trail. There was several killed at every one of those shipping points in Kansas, but you get different people telling the same story over and over again and the number is bound to be exaggerated. Besides, not all that were killed were cowboys; a lot of saloon men and tinhorn gamblers bit the dust. While I saw several shooting scrapes in saloons and sporting houses, I never saw a man shot dead, though some died afterwards.

But in the seventies they were a hard bunch, and I believe it was partly on account of what they came from. Down in Texas in the early days every man had to have his six-shooter always ready, and every house kept a shotgun loaded with buckshot, because they were always looking for a raid by Mexicans or Comanche Indians. What is more, I guess half the people in Texas in the seventies had moved out there on the frontier from the Southern states and from the rebel armies, and was a type that did not want any restraints.

But there is one thing I would like to get straight. I punched cows from '71 on, and I never saw a cowboy with two guns. I mean two six-shooters. Wild Bill carried two guns and so did some of those other city marshals, like Bat Masterson, but they were professional gunmen themselves, not cowpunchers. The others that carried two guns were Wes Hardin and Bill Longley and Clay Allison and them desperadoes. But a cowboy with two guns is all movie stuff, and so is this business of a gun on each hip. The kind of fellows that did carry two would carry one in the scabbard and a hide-out gun down under their arm.

Source 6   C. L. Sonnichsen, *I'll Die before I'll Run,* 1951

John Wesley Hardin . . . built up an enormous reputation as a gunman . . . ; his coolness and bravery under fire were almost legendary; and his sleight of hand with his pistols was something to tell stories about. "He is the man," said a humorous reporter, "who can make Catherine-wheels of a pair of six-shooters and drop a man with every barrel." Just why Billy the Kid has beaten John Wesley out for first honors (or dishonors) in the nation is hard to say, for Hardin had more on the ball in every way than the buck-toothed little rustler from New Mexico.

Source 7   Lewis Nordyke, *John Wesley Hardin: Texas Gunman,* 1957

This was the era in our national history when gunmanship—killing—was a profession. Some men were killers just as some were teachers. Economic, social, and political stresses and the growing pains of the westward movement must have been at least partially responsible. To say the least, nearly all the men in the biggest and most colorful crop of noted bad men in the West and the Middle Border—Billy the Kid, the James boys of Missouri and their close associates, Bill Longley, Ben Thompson, Sam Bass—were born within five to ten years of the birthday of John Wesley Hardin. . . .

Hardin probably killed more men in personal combat than any other man in the nation. He was easily the most sensational gunfighter of the gun-fighting Old West. . . .

To the end he remained an unfathomable mystery, the extreme of the period of the furious frontier and the tragic era of the Civil War and Reconstruction in the most recalcitrant of the defeated Southern states.

He was a rebel's rebel.

He despised man-made bans as he did injustice, falsehood, cowardice, and all half-gods.

Source 8   Ramon F. Adams, *The Book of the West*, 1963

The typical cowboy did very little shooting. From a practical standpoint, cartridges cost money and his pay was around a dollar a day. Certainly, he packed a gun and, like every other item of his equipment, it had a purpose: self-defense. . . .

The West was wild. Law officers were few and mainly confined to the towns. Renegades were everywhere; lurking . . . rustlers were often more dangerous than rattlesnakes. . . . And, where almost every man carried "five beans in the wheel," arguments could terminate in gunsmoke.

The cowboy has often been confused with the professional gunman. . . . These characters lived by virtue of their gun speed. They were not averse to "heisting" a stage or holding up a bank. They would hire out as "gun hands" during a range war. Their trigger fingers were "itchy" and they were "cat-eyed," for they never knew when some aspiring gunman or avenging foe might blast a hole in them for sheer glory or plain hatred. They were the "lobos" of the range country and inevitably, sooner or later, they were concrete proof of the Biblical proverb: "They that take the sword shall perish with the sword."

The average puncher could never approach the professional gunman's skill because that entailed hours of practice until the "draw" became a conditioned reflex, literally as fast as lightning.

Source 9   Bill O'Neal, *Encyclopedia of Western Gunfighters*, 1979

No western image is so deeply ingrained as the picture of two men approaching each other with hands poised over their gun butts, bound to determine who could draw and fire faster. Suddenly there is a blur of motion and two nearly simultaneous gunshots, and one man drops, hit by the first bullet. Common variations of this myth include one gunman shooting his adversary in the hand or, with even greater sportsmanship, letting his opponent draw first.

In real gunfights, however, the primary consideration was not speed but accuracy. Gunfighters frequently did not even carry their weapons in holsters. Pistols were shoved into hip pockets, waistbands, or coat pockets, and a rifle or shotgun was almost always preferred over a handgun. The primary concern in a shootout was not hitting the other man first or in the right spot but just *hitting* him. In gunfight after gunfight . . . men emptied their weapons at their adversaries without wounding them, or inflicting only minor wounds. The speed of the draw was insignificant. As anyone knows who has tried to hit a moving target with a pistol or has tried to "fan" a revolver, a snap shot rarely hits anything but the ground or the sky. If western gunfighters were reincarnated today, they would be astonished by the emphasis on the fast draw; in their day it was so unimportant that it was hardly worth mentioning.

Source 10 **Political scientist John Spanier,** *Games Nations Play,* **1993**

The usual explanation for the alleged immorality of states is that their concern for their security requires them to do "whatever must be done." In a domestic system with law and order, the resulting sense of security allows individuals and groups to act with at least some degree of morality, but in the international system the absence of law and order means that all states, like the cowboys in a lawless western town, must go armed, and must be prepared to shoot when their lives are endangered. According to the philosophy of Thomas Hobbes, the war of every man against every other man in a state of nature arose not from fear of death but from fear of *violent* death at the hands of another. In the resulting state of perpetual war nothing was unjust. The idea of right and wrong, justice and injustice simply had no place. The present state system is essentially a Hobbesian jungle; in a jungle, one must behave appropriately. The "nice guy" is devoured.

 Questioning the Past

1. A majority of the gunfights involving professional gunmen in the West occurred in five states: Texas, Oklahoma, Arizona, Kansas, and New Mexico, an area that included the cow towns and cattle trails. What made the Cattle Kingdom prone to violence?

2. Was John Wesley Hardin the product of the South and Reconstruction or of the West and the frontier? Present arguments for each view.

3. John Spanier compared the community of the Wild West to the current state of the international community. Does this comparison contribute to a better understanding of either the West of the late nineteenth century or of the world of today? Explain.

4. John Wesley Hardin stated that "the man who does not exercise the first law of nature—that of self-preservation—is not worthy of living." Is this a valid statement? Should citizens depend first upon themselves or upon society for protection?

5. Compare and contrast the gun violence of the Old West with the gun violence in America today. If towns such as Comanche had not permitted the possession of handguns inside city limits, could incidents such as the Webb-Hardin shoot-out have been prevented? Would a ban on civilian possession of handguns, assault rifles, and other weapons whose primary target is human be effective in reducing violence today?

Chapter 5

Little Bighorn

The Lakotas Defeat Custer *June 25, 1876*

Tatanka Yotanka, Sitting Bull, had no wish to surrender his freedom. Nor did he wish to trade his way of life and beliefs for those of the whites whose growing presence on the Great Plains threatened the very survival of his people. "It is not necessary for eagles to be crows," he said. "If the Great Spirit desired me to be a white man he would have made me so in the first place." When the soldiers came to demand that all the Lakotas, or Sioux of North and South Dakota, abandon their homelands on the northern plains and move onto a reservation where the government would care for them, Sitting Bull told them he would not go.

For generations, the Lakota people had lived and prospered on the northern plains. By the midpoint of the nineteenth century, however, this prosperous existence was under challenge. The discovery of gold in California and the opening of the Pacific coast to settlement lured caravans of wagons across the plains and through the hunting grounds of the Sioux and the native nations with whom the Sioux shared the great bison herds. At first the wagon trains were allowed to pass uncontested, since they seemed to pose no visible threat. But the wagons carried a deadly, invisible cargo: diseases imported from the Old World against which even the strongest of the plains warriors had no defense. One half of the Cheyenne nation died in the first summer of the gold rush, and the losses of other nations were equally staggering. As the native nations of the Great Plains began to sense a connection between the coming of the whites and the growing misery of their people, they began to resist the cross-plains migration.

Responding to the rising tensions, the United States government negotiated treaties to secure transit rights across Native American lands. In the Fort Laramie Treaty of 1851, Cheyenne, Crow, Arapaho, and Sioux consented to the establishment of roads and military outposts on their lands in exchange for American recognition of the inviolability of their established boundaries. Continued encroachments by whites, however, produced the Powder River War of 1866–1867, a war that the Sioux won, forcing the U.S. Army to abandon its forts on Lakota lands and negotiate the Fort Laramie Treaty of 1868.

The 1868 treaty brought the Powder River War to an end and established a reservation stretching over the western half of present-day South Dakota for those Sioux who wished to take up the white man's ways. For those Sioux who wished to continue their traditional life, all the land from the reservation westward to the Bighorn Mountains of Montana and Wyoming was declared an "unceded Indian territory" where "no white person or persons shall be permitted to settle upon or occupy

5.1 Little Bighorn Associates

any portion of the same." Some Sioux accepted the offer of the reservation. Others, led by Sitting Bull, had no desire to surrender their free way of life on the plains.

For a time, the Laramie Treaty of 1868 was honored by all its signatories, and peace prevailed on the Northwest plains. But in 1872, the U.S. government violated the treaty by agreeing to allow the Northern Pacific Railroad to lay track across Sioux land. Military escorts were sent to protect survey crews. Violence erupted as the Lakotas struggled to protect their lands and treaty rights. By the mid-1870s, bison hunters were systematically eradicating the Lakota's food supply while thousands of gold prospectors invaded the Black Hills of South Dakota and Wyoming, a sacred land within the unceded Sioux territory. Both the hunting and the prospecting violated treaty provisions. The U.S. Army, which by law was obligated to keep whites out of Sioux lands, protected the invaders from those invaded, appearing eager to provoke an incident that might ignite what General Sheridan claimed would be a "war of extermination" against the Sioux.

The Army gave the Sioux an ultimatum: all Sioux must move onto the reservation by January 1, 1876.

✎ *First Impressions*

"A Catastrophe in Our Indian Warfare"

Sitting Bull was a man whose courage and devotion to his people was legendary. His wisdom and his judgment had earned him the responsibilities of a chief of his Hunkpapa tribe of the Lakotas by the time he reached the age of 30. The deadline set by the United States came and passed, and Sitting Bull made no move to comply. His band, as well as many others who accepted his leadership, stayed with him in the non-reservation Sioux territories. In February, the United States declared "hostile" all Sioux who were not in residence at the Sioux reservation. An army was sent into the field to hunt these "hostiles" down.

Source 1   Sitting Bull, a chief of the Hunkpapa Sioux, 1875

Behold, my brothers, the spring has come; the earth has received the embraces of the sun and we shall soon see the results of that love!

Every seed is awakened and so has all animal life. It is through this mysterious power that we too have our being and we therefore yield to our neighbors, even our animal neighbors, the same right as ourselves, to inhabit this land.

Yet, hear me, people, we have now to deal with another race—small and feeble when our fathers met them but now great and overbearing. Strangely enough they have a mind to till the soil and the love of possession is a disease with them. These people have made many rules which the rich may break but the poor may not. They take tithes from the poor and weak to support the rich who rule. They claim this mother of ours, the earth, for their own and fence their neighbors away; they deface her with their buildings and their refuse. That nation is like a spring freshet that overruns its banks and destroys all who are in its path.

We cannot dwell side by side. Only seven years ago we made a treaty by which we were assured that the buffalo country should be left to us forever. Now they threaten to take that away from us. My brothers, shall we submit or shall we say to them: "First kill me before you take possession of my Fatherland?"

Source 2   **Letter from Lt. Richard E. Thompson to his family, June 1876**

> Camp in the Field.
> Forty miles from Fort Lincoln.

I am off, as you see from the heading of this, on the Big Horn expedition against the hostile Sioux. Already we have penetrated nearly to their stronghold, and in less than a week will be upon them, if they do not give us the slip. The command numbers 1,200 souls, including officers, troops, teamsters, herders, and all employed, so that we are strong enough for any force that is likely to offer us battle. I am fortunate in being on the staff of the commander (Gen. Terry). Gen. Custer is in command of his regiment, which forms part of the force, and you will probably soon hear of some engagement. As I am now writing at Gen. Custer's desk, it is reported that Indians are seen several miles off— probably their scouts, who are out to watch our movements. This goes back in a few moments by couriers, who are to take the mail through by night. Of course they carry their lives in their hands, and some of them may never reach. I shall send word, so as to keep you posted, at each opportunity. You will see plenty of newspaper accounts of our doings, and I know they will be the more interesting to you that I am concerned in all that is done out here.

Source 3   **"Uncle Sam's Crook: Will He Straighten the Sinuous Sioux of the Yellowstone?" *Chicago Times*, July 1, 1876**

In 1869 the United States concluded a treaty with the Indians ... known generally as the Sioux, whereby the eastern half of this enormous region was set apart for their occupation and use. The western line of the region thus ceded to the Indians was the 104th meridian, which runs through the western portion of the Black Hills, leaving about two-thirds of them in the region ceded to the Sioux. It was also agreed in this treaty that all the country lying between the 104th meridian and the Big Horn Mountains and between the North Platte and the Yellowstone should be unceded Indian territory; and that no white person should be permitted to occupy or settle upon the same, or even to pass through it without the consent of the Indians. It was further agreed that the line of federal posts ... running across the southwestern portion of the area should be abandoned. By this treaty the east half of this area of 240,000 square miles was given to the Indians for occupation—agencies, farms, schools, and the like— while the western half was made unceded Indian territory, on which no white man could settle, or over which a white man could not cross without the consent of the Indians. In the fullest possible sense, the entire area was turned over to the Indians, and guaranteed to them by a solemn treaty.

That treaty is in existence today, having never been repealed or modified in any particular.

From these statements, the public will be prepared to easily comprehend the causes of the present war and its extent. In brief, without any abrogation of the treaty with the Sioux, the Black Hills country was invaded by immigrants in search of gold. The Sioux resented this invasion, and commenced to attack immigrant trains. They in turn were attacked by United States troops. . . .

As to the moral quality of the Indian question, in reference to the present outbreak, there might be much said, were it an appropriate occasion. Whether a war is just or not should be settled either before or after its occurrence and not during its operation. Now that the war is in progress, it should be fought out, until the hostile Indians are thoroughly subdued. When that shall be done, then will it be in order to debate this truth; our people have just the same right to go into the Black Hills, while the present treaty stands unrepealed, that the people of Mexico would have to raid into, and take possession of, the city of Chicago; and that the Indians have the same right to defend their country against invasion that have Americans, or any other nation or community.

Source 4 **General William Tecumseh Sherman, newspaper interview, July 6, 1876**

Our purpose is to drive these Indians, who are of the wildest and most savage sort, down on the reservation. Montana is the most promising of our territories. It is settled by an intelligent people, among whom are many old soldiers, and it is the richest and most promising of our settlements. These Indians have been annoying the settlers; and we are to drive them down on the reservation. You can say that we will do it now or exterminate them.

Custer Makes an Audacious Decision

A three-pronged attack was launched into Lakota country in the spring of 1876. General George Crook set out from Fort Fetterman in Wyoming. Colonel John Gibbon marched from Fort Ellis in Montana. And General Alfred Terry, with a force that included George Custer and the Seventh Cavalry, moved out from Fort Lincoln in the Dakota Territory. The three columns were to converge and mount a concerted attack on the principal concentrations of Sioux in the region around the Bighorn River.

General Crook's force was delayed by engagements with Cheyenne and Sioux under the leadership of Crazy Horse, an Oglala Sioux war chief. The columns under General Terry and Colonel Gibbon met at the mouth of the Powder River. A reconnaissance party found the tracks left by a large group of Sioux leading up the Rosebud River Valley. General Custer and 12 companies of the Seventh Cavalry were sent out to follow this trail.

The trail led up the Rosebud and then into the valley of the Little Bighorn. Discovering this, Custer took his troops across the divide and onto the ridge overlooking the Little Bighorn River. From this vantage point he could see that the encampment was a large one. It was so large, in fact, that it extended some three miles along the river banks. Sitting Bull and his band were there. Crazy Horse and his band were there. And Northern Cheyenne had joined them. Most commanders would have backed away from a confrontation, preferring to await the arrival of the main force under Terry. But Custer was unlike most commanders. He had

5.2 The Battle of Little Bighorn

won a reputation at Gettysburg and in the Shenandoah Valley for his daring, and he had added to this reputation by his courage in campaigns against the warriors of the Great Plains. He divided his forces and prepared to hit the encampment from three sides.

Source 5   "Massacre of Our Troops," *New York Times*, July 6, 1876

5.3 The Cavalry Man's Military History Site

Salt Lake, July 5.—The special correspondent of the Helena [Montana] *Herald* writes from Stillwater, Montana, under date of July 2, as follows:

Muggins Taylor, a scout for Gen. Gibbon, arrived here last night direct from Little Horn River, and reports that Gen. Custer found the Indian camp of 2,000 lodges on the Little Horn, and immediately attacked it. He charged the thickest portion of the camp with five companies. Nothing is known of the operations of this detachment, except their course is traced by the dead. Major Reno commanded the other seven companies, and attacked the lower portion of the camp. The Indians poured a murderous fire from all directions. Gen. Custer, his two brothers, his nephew, and brother-in-law were all killed, and not one of his detachment escaped. . . .

The Indians surrounded Major Reno's command and held them one day in the hills cut off from water, until Gibbon's command came in sight, when they broke camp in the night and left. The Seventh fought like tigers, and were overcome by mere brute force. . . .

This report is given as Taylor told it, as he was over the field after the battle. The above is confirmed by other letters which say Custer has met a fearful disaster.

Source 6   "Massacre by the Indians," *Morning News,* Savannah, Georgia, July 7, 1876

Chicago, July 6.—A dispatch confirming the report of Gen. Custer's fight on the Little Big Horn river has just been received at Gen. Sheridan's headquarters. . . .

General Hancock, Secretary Chandler, and Postmaster Jewell were with the President today in consultation over the Indian situation. The War Department received this afternoon confirmatory reports of the newspaper accounts, which gave them the first intimation of the disaster. The following was received this evening from Sheridan's headquarters at Chicago, signed by Adjutant General Donan:

"Dispatches from General Terry dated at his camp at the mouth of the Big Horn, confirm the newspaper reports of a fight on the 25th of June on the Little Big Horn and of Custer's death. Terry has fallen back to his present camp. I have sent full dispatches to the Lieutenant General, who will probably communicate them. I have not yet received General Terry's report of the action or a list of casualties."

Source 7   Tribute to Custer, *State Journal*, Columbus, Ohio, July 7, 1876

He was a very severe disciplinarian, and it was only by the most supernatural daring in the face of the enemy that he was able to maintain a place in the esteem of his men. . . . Custer was a very striking figure, with his long yellow hair floating over his shoulders, his red neck-tie, his dashing hussar jacket, and a wide-brimmed, bandit-looking hat thrown backward on his head. . . . If Custer is gone, the Army has lost its most impetuous and daring cavalryman.

Source 8 "Custer's Last Battle," Washington *Evening Star,* July 7, 1876

Custer went into battle with companies C, L, I, F, and E, of the Seventh Cavalry, and the staff and non-commissioned staff of his regiment, and a number of scouts and only one Crow scout remained to tell the tale. All are dead.

Custer was surrounded on every side by Indians, and horses fell as they fought on skirmish line or in line of battle. Custer was among the last who fell, but when his cheering voice was no longer heard the Indians made easy work of the remainder. The bodies of all save the newspaper correspondents were stripped, and most of them were horribly mutilated. Custer was shot through the body and through the head. . . . The Crow scout survived by hiding in a ravine. He believes the Indians lost more than the whites. The village numbered 1,800 lodges, and it is thought there were four thousand warriors.

Gen. Custer was directed by Gen. Terry to find and feel of the Indians, but not to fight unless Terry arrived with infantry and with Gibbon's column.

Source 9 Editorial, "An Indian Victory," *New York Times,* July 7, 1876

Sitting Bull's band of Sioux left their reservation with hostile intent. They refused negotiations for peace. They defied the power and authority of the United States. They invited war. A force was sent against them. This force became divided, and Gen. Custer, with five companies, coming up to the main body of the Sioux, attacked them impetuously, without waiting for the support of the remainder of the column. The result was that the entire body of men . . . fell into a death trap; they were overwhelmed by superior numbers and were all slaughtered. The precise particulars of that horrible catastrophe will never be known. There were no survivors. The course of the detachment, after it began the attack, is traced only by the bodies of the slain. . . . No such catastrophe has happened in our Indian warfare since the Florida war [of the 1830s with the Seminoles].

It is useless to attempt to discover all the causes which have led to this disaster. The general management of the campaign may have been faulty. It is well known that military operations in the North-west have been crippled by the mistaken policy of retrenchment adopted by the present House of Representatives. Gen. Custer was a brave, dashing, but somewhat imprudent soldier, and his natural desire to save his superior officer the responsibility of an attack, may have hastened his fatal descent upon the enemy. Then, behind this, we cannot help seeing the needless irritation caused by the expedition into the Black Hills country last Summer. Sitting Bull's band were alienated and enraged at that time.

Source 10 Editorial, "The Little Big Horn Massacre," *Morning News,* Savannah, July 7, 1876

In our telegraphic column this morning will be found an account of a most shocking disaster that has befallen our troops in the Indian country. The news of the defeat and massacre of General Custer and his entire command by the Sioux Indians will cause a thrill of horror throughout the country. . . .

For this record of blood and massacre a fearful responsibility rests somewhere. There is good reason to believe that the present Indian war is the fruit of a reckless, corrupt and faithless Indian policy on the part of the government. Be that as it may, since the war has been provoked the government should at least employ prompt and effective means to put an end to the conflict. A few such experiences as that just reported, will convince the authorities at Washington that it is more than imprudent, that it is criminal to send out small bodies of troops to cope with the infuriated savages of the Northwestern frontier. The trouble in the Black Hills country has been brewing for the year past, and the government ought to have taken measures to conciliate the Indians or it should long since have exhibited a force on the frontier sufficient either to deter them from hostilities, or to speedily subdue them. But instead of concentrating its troops within striking distance of the hostile tribes, and keeping a watchful eye on their movements, the soldiers have been scattered through the peaceful and law-abiding communities of the Southern States, and the military authorities have been more occupied with preparations for a military Presidential campaign in the South, than with measures to protect the Indian frontier. And now that the Indians are on the war path, small detachments of troops are exposed to surprise and massacre by overwhelming numbers of wily and ferocious savages, while thousands of soldiers are idling away their days in inglorious ease in Southern garrisons.

A protracted Indian war may be a good thing for the post-traders, army contractors and ring speculators, but it will be a most costly and dangerous speculation for the tax payers and the frontier settlers. Such a war must be prevented if possible. The Seminole war [of 1835] . . . lasted seven years, cost the government over forty millions of dollars and thousands of valuable lives. The Seminoles had at no time more than one thousand warriors in the field, and yet they held the larger portion of the peninsula of Florida against five times their own number of troops, under able Generals. The Sioux are not less warlike and stubborn. They are vastly greater in numbers and if the government does not mean to repeat the experiences of the Seminole war, it will abandon its military surveillance of the South, withdraw its troops from unnecessary post duty in the Southern towns, relieve the redoubtable **Piegan** hero, General Sheridan, from the duty of looking after Louisiana "banditti" and Southern Ku-Klux, and turn him loose at once with ample force against the bloodthirsty warriors of the Black Hills country.

Source 11 From Gen. Philip Sheridan, commander against the Lakotas, July 7, 1876

Gen. W. T. Sherman, Washington, D.C.: . . .
I think it premature to think of asking for volunteer cavalry with the attendant expense. If the six companies of the Twenty-second Infantry are given to Terry, he will have about 2,000 men. Crook in a few days will have 1,500 men, and I sent him Merritt's eight companies of the Fifth Cavalry, 400 strong, which will make him over 2000 strong. We are all right. Give us a little time. I deeply deplore the loss of Custer and his officers and men. I fear it was an unnecessary sacrifice due to misapprehension and a super-abundance of courage, the latter extraordinarily

developed in Custer. I will keep in constant communication with you, and if I should see the slightest necessity for additional mounted men, . . . I will not hesitate to ask for them; and if Congress will give the $200,000 which I have asked for the past two years for the establishment of the posts at Tongue River and the mouth of the Big Horn, it will be in the interest of economy and will settle the Sioux question.

It should be remembered that the loss of Custer and the men with him must have been attended by at least a corresponding loss on the part of the Indians.

P. H. Sheridan, Lieutenant-General.

Source 12   "What Is Thought in Washington," *New York Times*, July 8, 1876

Washington, July 7.—It is agreed on all hands that there must now be an Indian war till the hostile Indians of the North-west have been chastised and subjugated. The cause and the responsibility of the Little Big Horn massacre are matters of small moment in deciding what shall be done. Western men freely predict that unless extraordinary efforts at defense are immediately made the miners in the Black Hills and the principal settlements in Montana will be harassed and many of them destroyed. The regular Army is not believed to be sufficiently strong to protect them, and a resort to volunteers is thought by many to be necessary. What shall be done cannot, however, be decided hastily in the absence of fuller information which official reports will contain. . . .

The facts as now understood dispose most people here to lay the blame for the slaughter upon Gen. Custer's imprudence and probable disobedience of orders. But criticism is kindly and charitable in tone, as it would not be had he not fallen with his command in the thickest of the battle. A forced march of seventy-eight miles in twenty-four hours, if made as reported, would unfit any army to fight till after rest and refreshment. The men would be for the most part unable to dismount or to stand up and fight or run if they were thrown out of the saddle; the horses could hardly be driven out of a walk, even by the excitement of a battle, while with fresh horses Custer could certainly have ridden through any Indian camp without losing all his men. . . .

The affair will be made use of as an argument by those who insist upon transferring the Indian Bureau to the War Department, and also by those who oppose such legislation. It will be made an excuse for increasing the Army, and held up as a reason for cutting it down, so diverse are the opinion and feelings aroused by the misfortune.

Source 13   Gen. Alfred H. Terry, official report to the headquarters of Gen. Sheridan, describing Gen. Custer's engagement, released July 8, 1876

> Headquarters Department of Dakota,
> Camp on Little Big Horn River.
> June 27, 1876.

It is my painful duty to report that, day before yesterday, the 25th inst., a great disaster overtook Gen. Custer and the troops under his command. At 12 o'clock on the 22d he started, with his whole regiment and a strong detachment of scouts and guards, from the mouth of the Rosebud. Proceeding up that river about twenty miles he struck a very heavy Indian trail, which had previously been discovered, and pursuing it, found a village of almost unexampled extent, and at once attacked it with that portion of his force which was immediately at hand. Major Reno with three companies, A, G, and M, of the regiment was sent into the valley of the stream at the point where the trail struck it. Gen. Custer, with five companies, C, E, F, I, and L, attempted to enter it about three miles lower down. Reno forded the river, charged down its left bank, dismounted and fought on foot, until finally completely overwhelmed by numbers he was compelled to mount, recross the river, and seek refuge on the high bluffs which overlooked its right bank. Just as he recrossed, Capt. Benteen, who with three companies, D, H, and K, was some two miles to the left of Reno when the action commenced, but who had been ordered by Gen. Custer to return, came to the river, and rightly concluding that it would be useless for his force to attempt to renew the fight in the valley, he joined Reno on the bluffs. Capt. McDougall with Company B was at first at some distance in the rear with a train of pack-mules. He also came to Reno soon. This united force was nearly surrounded by Indians, many of whom, armed with rifles, occupied positions which commanded the ground held by the cavalry, ground from which there was no escape. Rifle-pits were dug and the fight was maintained with heavy loss, from about 2:30 o'clock of the 25th till 6 o'clock of the 26th, when the Indians withdrew from the valley, taking with them their village.

Of the movements of Gen. Custer and the five companies under his immediate command scarcely anything is known from those who witnessed them, for no soldier or officer who accompanied him has yet been found alive. His trail from the point where Reno crossed the stream passes along and in the rear of the crest of the bluffs on the right bank for nearly or quite three miles, then it comes down to the bank of the river, but at once diverges from it as if he had unsuccessfully attempted to cross; then turns upon itself, almost completes a circle and closes. It is marked by the remains of his officers and men, the bodies of his horses, some of them dropped along the path, others heaped where halts appear to have been made. There is abundant evidence that a gallant resistance was offered by the troops, but they were beset on all sides by overpowering numbers. . . .

At the mouth of the Rosebud I informed Gen. Custer that I should take the supply steamer Far West up the Yellowstone to ferry Gen. Gibbon's column over the river; that I should personally accompany that column, and that I would in all probability reach the mouth of the Little Big Horn on the 26th inst. The steamer reached Gen. Gibbon's troops, near the mouth of the Big Horn, early in the morning of the 24th, and at 4 o'clock in the afternoon all his men and animals were across the Yellowstone. At 5 o'clock the column, consisting of five companies of the Seventh Infantry, four companies of the Second Cavalry, and a battery of Gatling guns, marched out to and across Tullock's Creek, starting soon after 5 o'clock in the morning of the 25th. The infantry made a march of twenty-two miles over the most difficult country which I have ever seen, in order that scouts might be sent into the Valley of the Little Big Horn. The cavalry, with the battery, was then pushed on thirteen or fourteen miles further, reaching camp at midnight. The scouts were sent out at 4:30 on the morning of the 26th. The scouts discovered the Indians, who were at first supposed to be Sioux, but when overtaken they proved to be Crows, who had been with Gen. Custer. They brought the first intelligence of the battle. Their story was not credited. It was supposed that some fighting, perhaps severe fighting, had taken place, but it was not believed that disaster could have overtaken so large a force as twelve companies of cavalry. The infantry, which had broken camp very early soon came up, and the whole column entered and moved up the Valley of the Little Big Horn. During the afternoon, efforts were made to send scouts through to what was supposed to be Gen. Custer's position, and to obtain information of the condition of affairs; but those who were sent out were driven back by parties of Indians, who, in increasing numbers, were seen hovering in Gen. Gibbon's front.

At 8:40 o'clock in the evening the infantry had marched between twenty-nine and thirty miles. The men were very weary, and daylight was fading. The column was therefore halted for the night, at a point about eleven miles in a straight line above the stream. This morning the movement was resumed, and after a march of nine miles, Major Reno's entrenched position was reached. The withdrawal of the Indians from around Reno's command and from the valley was undoubtedly caused by the appearance of Gen. Gibbon's troops.

Major Reno and Capt. Benteen, both of whom are officers of great experience, accustomed to see large masses of mounted men, estimated the number of Indians engaged as not less than 2,500. Other officers think that the number was greater than this. The village in the valley was about three miles in length, and about a mile in width. . . . It is believed that the loss of the Indians was large. I have yet received no official reports in regard to the battle but what is here stated is gathered from the officers who were on the ground then, and from those who have been over it since.

Source 14 Editorial, Washington *Evening Star,* July 10, 1876

Justice to the memory of a peerless soldier demands that Custer's fame should not be dimmed by a charge of disobedience of orders without the fullest evidence. That he was rash, and that in the case of the Little Big Horn disaster his judgment at once was at fault, must be admitted, but that he actually disobeyed orders would seem to be disproved by the orders of Gen. Terry, indicated in the following extract:

> "The Brigadier General commanding directs that as soon as your regiment can be made ready for the march you proceed up the Rosebud in pursuit of the Indians whose trail was discovered by Major Reno a few days since. It is, of course, impossible to give any definite instructions in regard to this movement, and, were it not impossible to do so, the department commander places too much confidence in your zeal, energy and ability to wish to impose upon you precise orders which might hamper your action when nearly in contact with the enemy. He will, however, indicate to you his own views of what your actions should be, and he desires that you conform to them unless you see sufficient reason for departing from them."

Quite possibly it may yet appear that Gen. Custer acted in direct opposition to the "views" indicated by Gen. Terry, but while this fact would relieve the latter of the responsibility for the disaster, it would not, under the permission given to Custer to act upon his own judgment, lay him open to the charge of positive disobedience of orders.

 Second Thoughts

Flagrant Blunders or Superior Strength?

Following the Battle of the Little Bighorn, warfare between the Lakotas and the United States continued. Many of the bands eventually were forced onto the reservation. Sitting Bull, however, led his band into exile in Canada in May 1877. In 1881 he returned to the United States and onto the reservation, following an offer of amnesty from the U.S. government. In 1890, Sitting Bull was killed in a melee that resulted when reservation police attempted to arrest him. Two weeks after his death the Seventh Cavalry opened fire with **Hotchkiss guns** on a peaceful band of Lakotas under Chief Big Foot, killing close to 300 men, women, and children. These shots fired at Wounded Knee were the last of the Plains Wars.

Source 15 John F. Finerty, *War-Path and Bivouac*, 1890

[Finerty covered the Bighorn expedition for the *Chicago Times* while accompanying the column led by General Crook.]

Custer . . . saw at a glance that he was overpowered, and did the only thing proper under the circumstances in leading his command to higher grounds where it could defend itself to some advantage. Even in that dread extremity his soldier spirit and noble bearing held the men under control, and the dead bodies of the troopers . . . found by General Gibbon's command lying in ranks as they fell, attested the cool generalship exhibited by the heroic leader in the midst of deadly peril.

It had always been General Custer's habit to divide his command when attacking Indian villages. His victory over **Black Kettle** on the Washita was obtained in that manner, but the experiment proved fatal to Major Eliot and a considerable squad of soldiers. It was the general opinion in Crook's command at the time that had an officer of more resolution been in Major Reno's place he would have attempted to join Custer at any cost. Reno was, no doubt, imposed upon by Indian strategy, and his retreat to the bluffs was, to say the least of it, premature. But in the light of after events it does not seem probable that he could have reached the fatal heights upon which Custer and his men perished. Had Custer taken his entire regiment into the fight he might still have sustained a repulse, but would have escaped annihilation. It is always a tactical error to divide a small command in face of the enemy. This was Custer's error.

Source 16 Stanley Vestal, *Sitting Bull: Champion of the Sioux*, 1932

[Vestal's account is based on interviews with surviving Sioux.]

It was a lazy day. In spite of the warnings, people did not expect enemies. Some of the young men were fishing, and the hills west of the river were dotted with women digging **tipsin**.

Just then Far Bear dashed to the council tipi. Brown Back had brought the news, he said. That morning early, two young Hunkpapa boys were out looking for stray horses. They crossed a soldier trail, and found a lost pack. Curious to see what they had found, they broke it open. It was full of hard bread. Hungry as boys will be, they sat down and began to eat. While they were eating, some soldiers came back on the trail, saw them, and began to shoot. The soldiers killed Deeds, but Hona's brother made his getaway!

Sitting Bull sprang up and, throwing aside the door flap of the council lodge, limped as fast as he could toward his own tipi, not far off. It was nearest to the soldiers. While he was hurrying, there was a yell of alarm. A man was pointing, yelling, and everyone turned to look where he pointed—south—up-river. There in the bottoms they saw a tower of dust coming, and in it, as it came, the blue shirts of soldiers, the heads of horses! While they stared, the column of soldiers widened into a line, smoke boomed from its front, and they heard the snarl of the carbines.

Sitting Bull hurried to his tipi to get his arms. He had a revolver, calibre .45, and an 1873 model carbine Winchester.... In the tent he found One Bull bent on the same errand.... Already the bullets were whining overhead, and one of the tent poles was splintered above them....

Sitting Bull was buckling on his cartridge belt. Already someone had caught up his war horse.... Sitting Bull leaped upon its bare back.

All around him was confusion. Old men were yelling advice, women and children rushing off afoot and on horseback to the north end of that three-mile camp, fleeing from the soldiers. They left their tents standing, grabbed their babies, called their older children, and hurried away, frightened girls shrinking under their shawls, matrons puffing for breath, hobbling old women, wrinkled and peering, with their sticks, making off as best they could, crying children, lost children, dogs getting in everybody's way and being kicked for their pains, nervous horses resisting the tug of the reins, and over all the sound of the shooting. First of all, Sitting Bull saw that his old mother was safely mounted and on her way....

The Hunkpapa stood their ground bravely, covering the retreat of their women and children down the flat. Veterans of the fight say, "It was sure hard luck for Major Reno that he struck the Hunkpapa camp first." ...

As fast as the Sioux were mounted, they rode out to meet the soldiers on the flat. Those who had guns fired occasionally, falling back slowly, trying to cover the retreat of the women streaming to the north. Every moment reinforcements came up, and the firing grew constantly heavier, until there were enough Indians to stop the soldiers in their tracks. While this was going on, the Sioux on the right flank swept down on the Ree scouts, recaptured the pony herd they had taken, and sent the Rees flying....

And now the soldiers stopped sure enough, got off their horses and began to shoot and fight on foot. The Sioux took courage. The women and children were safe. They charged the soldiers from the west side, as well as from the north, and the soldiers began to give way and drop back eastward into the timber. Pretty soon their line was behind a cutback among the trees. . . . The Sioux were all around them. . . .

Sitting Bull was puzzled by Reno's behavior. He had come against the huge camp with a handful, and then—instead of charging, the only way he could hope to fight his way through—he had dismounted his men and was fighting them afoot. Sitting Bull thought Reno was acting like a fool. But Sitting Bull was much too intelligent to underestimate his enemy. He wondered what was up. Therefore he remained with the warriors to the north of the troops, between the camp and the enemy. "Look out!" he yelled, "there must be some trick about this."

Meanwhile One Bull was over on the west side of the soldiers with other young men. As Sitting Bull's nephew, wearing his shield, he considered himself their leader. As the troops fell back . . . these young men charged the soldiers. . . .

By that time the soldiers in the timber had mounted their horses, dashed from the trees, and were galloping up the west bank of the river as hard as they could go, all strung out, looking for a place to cross. The moment Sitting Bull saw them running like that, without order, every man for himself, he knew that Reno's attack on the village had not been inspired by unusual bravery. He guessed the answer to his puzzle then: those soldiers had been *waiting* for somebody to come and help them. . . . Right away Sitting Bull surmised that there was another war party of enemies somewhere around. After that he did not urge the young men to charge the soldiers. . . .

Some of the warriors had crossed, and the last of the soldiers were scrambling up the steep bluffs. Last of all went four horse holders who had been left behind. One Bull and his comrades, hot with victory, started to plunge into the stream, ford it, and kill these. But Sitting Bull objected. "Let them go!" he yelled. "Let them go! Let them live to tell the truth about this battle." He wanted the white men to know that this fight had been begun by the soldiers, not the Sioux. They came shooting and fired the first shot. . . .

Sitting Bull rode north through the abandoned camps, one after the other. The tents stood empty and forlorn, their gaping doors open to the hungry, prowling dogs which sneaked in looking for meat, hardly able to believe that their good luck was real. . . . Sitting Bull hurried on up the flat to the north and west. He could see the women and children gathered there, boys and old men trying to keep them together. By this time they had learned that the soldiers had been routed upriver and were streaming back to their tents again.

But just then another war party of enemies was seen upon the bluffs across the river to the east, Custer's five companies trotting along the ridge, apparently looking for a place to cross. Sitting Bull's hunch was justified: there *was* a second war party!

Instantly, the women who had started back to the tents ran out on the prairies again. . . . Meanwhile, One Bull was dashing downriver on the east bank with the other young men to meet this new danger. They had just killed many soldiers, they were confident they could kill many more. . . .

The white soldiers were trotting along the hilltop in a cloud of dust, making toward the ford. Four Cheyenne rode out to face them, only four at first.

But these four—Bob-Tail-Horse was one—seemed to daunt them. At any rate, the soldiers stopped. Shooting began. The smoke rolled down the hill in a dense cloud. The Indians were all around, more and more of them. With the dust and the smoke there was not much to see.

One Bull was eager to go and join the fighting. He urged his uncle to go with him. But Sitting Bull replied:

"No, Stay here and help protect the women. Perhaps there is another war party of enemies coming. There are plenty of Indians yonder to take care of those." By "those," of course, he meant Custer's immediate command. . . . Having been greatly puzzled by Reno's strange behavior, he was even more puzzled by Custer's. Why, *why,* had he halted just when he should have charged? Unless he was waiting for someone. Once more, Sitting Bull's hunch was right. If Benteen had not been delayed, he might have struck the village from the west side.

Such skill in forecasting the enemy's movements, such canny sizing-up of a situation, were what made Sitting Bull peerless as a leader of the warlike Sioux. Brave men were plenty in their camps: but a man who combined intelligence and skill and courage as Sitting Bull did was hardly to be found. He knew, as Napoleon knew—and said—that "battles are won by the power of the mind."

Source 17 Milo Milton Quaife, editor of Custer's autobiography, *My Life on the Plains*, 1951

General George A. Custer was perhaps the most brilliant cavalry leader America has produced. His solid claim to military fame rests upon his achievements in the Civil War, yet paradoxically he is chiefly remembered by reason of his death in the minor action of the Little Big Horn in June, 1876.

Over it, as over much else in Custer's career and character, warm controversy still wages. Custer, in short, was an exceedingly complex character whose military brilliance and admirable qualities were marred by certain outstanding defects of character and temperament. In life he won devoted friends and admirers, and no less outspoken and bitter enemies. Nor did his tragic death suffice to still the tumult.

Source 18 Mari Dandoz, biographer of Crazy Horse, *The Battle of the Little Big Horn*, 1966

In the face of the great trail before him, the advice of his scouts, Indian and white, and the knowledge he should have had of the ancient summer conference [of the Sioux], Custer's division of his small force into three parts is inexplicable, unless one assumes that it was of overwhelming importance that neither Benteen nor Reno share in any victory. How the fight would have ended if the command had not been divided must remain pure speculation. That the Indians were powerful enough in numbers and in determination to defeat the entire force cannot be doubted; whether the worn horses of the troops were strong enough to carry any beyond the reach of the pursuing warriors is debatable. At best the carnage would have been appalling. The unit was, after all, planned for scouting, not for combat without reinforcements by infantry, more cavalry, and **Gatling guns**.

Source 19   **Attorney and Standing Rock Sioux Vine Deloria Jr.,** *Custer*
                   Died for Your Sins, 1969

All tribes, even those thousands of miles from Montana, feel a sense of accomplishment when thinking of Custer. Custer binds together implacable foes because he represented the Ugly American of the last century and he got what was coming to him.

Some years ago we put out a bumper sticker which read "Custer Died For Your Sins." It was originally meant as a dig at the National Council of Churches. But as it spread around the nation it took on additional meaning until everyone claimed to understand it and each interpretation was different.

Originally, the Custer bumper sticker referred to the Sioux Treaty of 1868 signed at Fort Laramie in which the United States pledged to give free and undisturbed use of the lands claimed by Red Cloud in return for peace. Under the covenants of the Old Testament, breaking a covenant called for a blood sacrifice for atonement. Custer was the blood sacrifice for the United States' breaking the Sioux Treaty. That, at least originally, was the meaning of the slogan.

Custer is said to have boasted that he could ride through the entire Sioux nation with his Seventh Cavalry and he was half right. He got halfway through. . . .

Since the battle it has been a favorite technique to boost the numbers on the Indian side and reduce the numbers on the white side so that Custer stands out as a man fighting against insurmountable odds. One question no pseudo-historian has attempted to answer, when changing the odds to make the little boy in blue more heroic, is how what they say were twenty thousand Indians could be fed when gathered into one camp. What a tremendous pony herd must have been gathered there, what a fantastic herd of buffalo must have been nearby to feed that amount of Indians, what an incredible source of drinking water must have been available for fifty thousand animals and some twenty thousand Indians!

Just figuring water needs to keep that many people and animals alive for a number of days must have been incredible. If you have estimated correctly, you will see that the Little Big Horn was the last great *naval* engagement of the Indian Wars.

Source 20   **Robert M. Utley,** *Cavalier in Buckskin: George Armstrong*
                   Custer and the Western Military Frontier, 1988

How could it have happened? What flagrant blunders produced so awful a debacle? How could a commander and a regiment widely perceived as the best on the frontier succumb so spectacularly to a mob of untrained, unlettered natives?

The simplest answer, usually overlooked, is that the army lost largely because the Indians won. To ascribe defeat entirely to military failings is to devalue Indian strength and leadership. The Sioux and the Cheyennes were strong, confident, united, well led, well armed, outraged by the government's war aims, and ready to fight if pressed. Rarely had the army encountered such a mighty combination in an Indian adversary. Perhaps no strategy or tactics could have prevailed against Sitting Bull's power.

But this explanation exonerates all the military chiefs and yields no scape-goat in blue. George Armstrong Custer is the favored candidate. Driven to win a great victory . . . he rushed up the Rosebud and plunged into battle before the cooperating units could get in place. He disobeyed Terry's orders by taking a direct rather than a circuitous route to his destination. He attacked . . . with an exhausted command and without adequate reconnaissance. Violating an elementary military maxim, he divided his force in the face of a superior enemy and then lost control of all but the element retained under his personal direction, and perhaps, in the end, even of that.

Analysis of this indictment must take account of the character of the evidence on which it rests. No sooner had Custer's body been buried on Custer Hill than all the principals—Terry, Gibbon, Brisbin, Reno, Benteen—began to recompose the history of recent events. Eager to explain the calamity and avert any culpability of their own, they conveniently forgot some things that had happened and remembered some things that had not happened. . . .

This self-serving evidence is not without historical value. But only by rigorously comparing it with evidence dating from before the fatal last hour on Battle Ridge can a true understanding of the dynamics of the disaster be reached. . . .

In such a comparison and analysis most of the charges against Custer collapse. Undoubtedly he hoped to win a great victory for himself and the Seventh Cavalry. But he did not rush up the Rosebud any faster than had been planned on the *Far West* [the steamboat which served as Terry's headquarters]. He did not disobey Terry's orders; they were entirely discretionary and, because of the uncertain location of the Indians, could not have been otherwise. . . . Custer's mission was to attack the Indians whenever and wherever he found them. Custer did not take an exhausted regiment into battle; the men were tired, as soldiers in the field usually are, but no more so than normal on campaign.

That Terry intended Custer to use his own judgment in finding and striking the Indians is made abundantly clear by the written orders. . . .

Custer was not concerned with how many Indians he would encounter, only with preventing their flight. Knowledge of their actual strength would not have changed his disposition. He had total confidence in the capability of the Seventh Cavalry to whip any number of Indians.

So did all the other generals, from Sheridan down. Most experience with Indian warfare showed that a charge into a village, however large, wrought panic and fleeing Indians. . . . Custer cannot be faulted for a mindset shared with his fellow commanders.

It was a mindset, indeed, shared with all his fellow citizens and thus in large part derived from them. That the generals had such contempt for the fighting prowess of their foes as to care little for their numbers was but one symptom of society's attitudes toward Indians. The cultural and racial arrogance of the American people found expression in their generals. Combined with the personal conceit of Custer, this was a deadly mixture.

Questioning the Past

1. What happened at the Little Bighorn on June 25, 1876, and why did it happen? Why did Custer charge Sitting Bull's encampment?

2. Was Custer to blame for the massacre? Argue the case for and against Custer's responsibility for the deaths of his troopers.

3. How did the newspapers of the time react editorially to the defeat of Custer and his troops? What motivations lay behind the positions taken by these papers?

4. Historian Samuel Eliot Morison wrote that "Custer became a hero to the boys who grew up in that era, and his bright and joyous figure, his long yellow locks, and trooper's swagger shine through the murk of controversy over who was to blame for the massacre on the Little Big Horn." Indeed, the memory of "Custer's Last Stand" has remained etched in the American memory for more than a century. An 1895 painting by Otto Becker showing a besieged Custer with a revolver in one hand and a sabre in the other, surrounded in his final moments by his loyal but overwhelmed troops, was made into a lithograph and hung on walls throughout the nation. Why did Custer come to symbolize American heroism? Why did the Battle of the Little Bighorn come to symbolize the Indian wars?

5. Between 1778 and 1871, the United States ratified close to 400 treaties with Native American nations. The earliest treaties respected the Native American nations as free and independent powers and did not attempt to assert U.S. control over them. Indeed, the first treaty was with the Delawares, and it granted that nation the right, if it so chose, to join the United States with full congressional representation. After 1812, however, there was a slow shift toward the view that native nations were "domestic dependent nations." The first treaty "reserving" land within the United States for a particular native nation was ratified in 1818. In a treaty with the Navajo in 1849, the U.S. asserted for the first time a right to "pass and execute in [Navajo] territory such laws as may be deemed conducive to the prosperity and happiness of said Indians." By what legitimate rationale could the United States treat with native nations in any way that did not recognize native independence, autonomy, and sovereignty? The Sioux still live on the Great Plains today in reservations. Should U.S. control of the Lakotas and their lands continue in perpetuity?

Chapter **6**

The Haymarket Affair

Tensions Explode in Chicago   *May 4, 1886*

Following the Civil War, America began in earnest the transformation from agrarian to industrial nation. From the time of the settlement at Jamestown to the eve of the rebellion, the farm had been the primary workplace of the American people and the principal source of their income. The factory so rapidly emerged as a place of employment following the war that in 1899 the value of American manufactured goods for the first time surpassed the value of America's crops. By the time of World War I, the United States had become the greatest manufacturing country in the world.

Rapid industrialization did not come without a social cost, however. For most of the great industrialists, the drive to maximize profits was more compelling than their concern for the public good. While the owners of the factories and the heads of the corporations earned millions in annual income, the workers they employed subsisted on wages that kept them in poverty. Workdays were long. Working conditions were often intolerable. With no laws to protect worker safety, thousands of people per year lost limbs—or their lives—on the job. When workers became too ill or too old, they could expect to be dismissed with no greater regard given for their future than would be displayed for the broken and worn-out parts of the machines over which they toiled.

What could working people do to change such conditions? A wide range of opinion existed. Radical reformers—socialists, communists, anarchists—offered grand schemes by which the workers themselves would take control of the factories where they worked and share in their management and profits. The Knights of Labor, America's largest labor organization, sought to bring the weight of working people to the task of broad reforms in the American economic, social, and political processes. The American Federation of Labor pursued still more modest goals: the immediate improvement of working conditions. All of these diverse groups came together, however, in a national campaign to establish an eight-hour workday in 1886.

The average worker in America during the 1880s put in a 10-hour workday and was on the job six days out of every seven. Ninety-hour workweeks were not uncommon. And bakers in New York City were accustomed to spending 120 hours of every week on the job.

6.1 Chicago:
1886 The
Haymarket Riot

May Day of 1886 witnessed spectacular demonstrations of worker support for the eight-hour workday throughout the country. Workers at 12,000 factories walked away from their jobs. There were parades, rallies, picnics, picket lines in industrial centers from coast to coast. In most places, these demonstrations passed without incident. In Chicago, however, where at least 80,000 workers took part in May Day events, developments followed a different course. Business and civic leaders in that city felt threatened by the advances being made by the labor movement and were anxious for an opportunity to silence its leaders.

First Impressions

"Revenge! Workingmen, to Arms!"

That chance came on May 3. Workers at the McCormick Works had been on strike for months prior to the May Day demonstrations. Their wages had been cut at a time when company profits were rising. A rally outside the factory gates on May 3 drew 6,000 striking McCormick workers to hear anarchist August Spies, who had been invited to speak by the local union. While Spies was speaking, the bell sounded at the McCormick Plant, signalling the end of the work day. When a few of the strikers began to taunt the strike-breakers leaving work, a detachment of some 200 policemen advanced on the rally participants, wielding clubs and then opening fire on the crowd with revolvers. Though two workers were killed at the McCormick Rally by police, newspaper reports initially put the number of dead at six. Spies, who joined the crowd in dodging the nightsticks and bullets while fleeing the scene, was incensed, as were many other working people in Chicago. Returning to his newspaper office, Spies wrote his notorious "Revenge Circular." Enraged labor leaders and radicals obtained a permit for a rally to be held at Haymarket Square on May 4.

Source 1   August Spies, anarchist and editor of *Arbeiter Zeitung* (Worker's Paper), "The Revenge Circular," May 3, 1886

6.2 The
Haymarket
Martyrs

Revenge! Workingmen, to arms! Your masters sent out their bloodhounds, the police. They killed six of your brothers at McCormick's this afternoon; they killed the poor wretches because they had the courage to disobey the supreme will of your bosses; they killed them because they dared to ask for the shortening of the hours of toil; they killed them to show you, free American citizens, that you must be satisfied and contented with whatever your bosses condescend to allow you or you will get killed. You have for years suffered unmeasurable inequities; you have worked yourselves to death; you have endured the pangs of want and hunger; your children you have sacrificed to the factory lords,—in short, you have been miserable and obedient slaves all these years. Why? To satisfy the insatiable greed, to fill the coffers of your lazy thieving masters. When you ask them now to lessen the burden they send their bloodhounds out to shoot you—kill you. If you are men, if you are the sons of your grandsires who shed their blood to free you, then you will rise in your might, Hercules, and destroy the hideous monster that seeks to destroy you! To arms! We call you to arms!

Your Brothers.

Source 2   Handbill circulated in Chicago on the afternoon of May 4, 1886

ATTENTION, WORKINGMEN! Great Mass-meeting to-night at 7:30 o'clock, at the Haymarket, Randolph Street, between Desplaines and Halsted. Good speakers will be present to denounce the latest atrocious acts of the police—the shooting of our fellow-workmen yesterday afternoon.

The Executive Committee.

Source 3   "NOW IT IS BLOOD!" Chicago *Inter Ocean*, May 5, 1886

The anarchists of Chicago inaugurated in earnest last night the reign of lawlessness which they have threatened and endeavored to incite for years. They threw a bomb into the midst of a line of 200 police officers, and it exploded with fearful effect, mowing down men like cattle. Almost before the missile of death had exploded the anarchists directed a murderous fire from revolvers upon the police. . . . The collision between the police and the anarchists was brought about by the leaders of the latter, August Spies, Sam Fielden, and A. R. Parsons, endeavoring to incite a large mass-meeting to riot and bloodshed.

Source 4   August Spies's description of the rally at Haymarket Square

A. Fischer, one of our compositors, asked me if I would not come to a general mass-meeting which would take place at the Haymarket in the evening and "make a speech" on the brutality of the police and the situation of the eight-hour striker. About 11 o'clock a member of the Carpenters' Union called on me and asked that the handbill he showed me be printed in the *Arbeiter Zeitung* as an announcement. It was the circular calling the Haymarket meeting, and at the bottom it contained the words—"Workingmen, bring your arms along!"

"This is ridiculous!" said I to the man, and had Fischer called. I told him that I would not speak at the meeting if his was the circular by which it had been called.

"None of the circulars are as yet distributed; we can have these words taken out," the man said. Fischer assented, and I told them that if they did that it would be all right. . . .

After supper my brother Henry called at our house. I asked him to come along to the meeting, which he did. . . . It was about 8:15 o'clock when we arrived. . . . Small and large groups of men were standing around, but there was no meeting. Not seeing anyone who might be supposed to be entrusted with the management of the meeting, I jumped upon a wagon, inquired for Mr. Parsons, and called the meeting to order. . . . I spoke about twenty minutes.

Then Parsons spoke. The audience was very quiet and attentive. Parsons confined himself to the eight-hour question, but spoke at great length. While he was speaking, I asked Mr. Fielden if he would not make a few remarks. He didn't care to speak, but would say a few words and then adjourn the meeting. . . . It was about ten o'clock when Fielden began to speak. A few minutes later a dark and threatening cloud moved up from the north. The people—or, at least, two thirds of them—fearing it would rain, left the meeting. "Stay," said Fielden, "just a minute longer; I will conclude presently." There were now not more than two hundred persons remaining. One minute later two hundred policemen formed into line at the intersection of Randolph Street and marched upon the little crowd in double quick step.

Raising his cane in an authoritative way, Captain Ward—directing his words to Fielden—said: "In the name of the people of the state of Illinois I command this meeting to disperse!"

"Captain, this is a peaceable meeting," retorted Mr. Fielden, while the captain turned around to his men and gave a command which I understood to be, "Charge upon them!" At this juncture I was drawn from the wagon by my brother and several others, and I had just reached the ground when a terrible detonation occurred. "What is that?" asked my brother. "A cannon, I believe," was my reply. In an instant the **fusillade** of the police began. Everybody was running. All this was as unexpected as if suddenly a cloud had burst. I lost my brother in the throng and was carried away toward the north. People fell, struck by the bullets, right and left. As I crossed the alley north of Crane's factory, a lot of officers ran into the alley, some of them exclaiming that they were hurt. They had evidently been shot by their own comrades, and sought protection in the alley. I was in a parallel line with them, and the bullets whistled around my head like a swarm of bees. I fell once or twice over others who had "dropped," but otherwise escaped unhurt into Zepf's saloon, at the corner of Lake Street. Here I heard for the first time that the loud report had been caused by an explosion, which was thought to have been the explosion of a bomb. I could learn no particulars, and about a half hour afterward took a car and rode home to see if my brother had been hurt. He had received a dangerous wound. Turning aside when I had answered, "It's a cannon, I believe," he beheld the muzzle of a revolver deliberately aimed at my back. Grasping the weapon, the bullet stuck him in a vital part.

The next morning the papers reported that the police had been searching for me all night and that they had orders to arrest me. Nobody had been at my house during the night; the report was a lie. I went to the office at my regular hour and began to work. About nine o'clock Detective Jim Bonfield made his appearance and told me the chief of police wanted to talk with me. I went along with him to the central station.

Source 5   Editorial, "The Chicago Murders," *New York Times,* May 6, 1886

No disturbance of the peace that has occurred in the United States since the war of the rebellion has excited public sentiment throughout the Union as it is excited by the Anarchists' murder of policemen in Chicago on Tuesday night. We say murder with the fullest consciousness of what that word means. It is silly to speak of the crime as riot. All the evidence goes to show that it was concerted, deliberately planned, and coolly executed murder. The deadly bomb was thrown with careful aim in the ranks of the policemen, as they approached, and before they had reached the leaders of the meeting or had given indication of any purpose other than to disperse the assembly which was threatening the public peace. The explosion of the bomb was a signal for the Anarchists to close around the police, momentarily thrown into confusion, and to open fire upon them from all directions and from behind boxes and wagons which served as breastworks. This could not have been done on the spur of the moment....

The laws of all the States are substantially the same regarding the crime of murder, and the definition of what constitutes a "principal," or one directly guilty of that crime.... As to the persons guilty of this crime, it was by no means only those who threw the bomb or fired the shots. The [New York] Penal Code, section 28, says: "A person concerned in the commission of a crime, whether he directly commits the act constituting the offense or aids and abets in its commission, and whether present or absent, and a person who directly or indirectly counsels, commands, induces, or procures another to commit a crime is a principal." This is the New York definition of a principle of law that prevails in every State of the Union.... It will not be difficult to get evidence sufficient to show that some of the men now under arrest in Chicago were engaged in "counseling, inducing, and procuring" the murder of the policemen. The dictates of justice, the safety of society, and above all the safety of the brave men on whom the safety of society rests, require that the cowardly savages who plotted and carried out this murder shall suffer the death they deserve....

[W]henever there is reason to suppose that the Anarchist element is to be met, it should be met with rifles and Gatling guns beyond the reach of their unhuman bombs. The Anarchists' methods are open and avowed. They themselves give ample warning to all decent people to keep away from them. If they meet in public with violent purposes and professions in spite of the preventive measures which should be taken against them, and it becomes necessary to put them down, let it be done, no matter at what cost of their lives, without needless risk of the lives of the guardians of the rights and the safety of the community. The life of any one of the faithful officers who fell in Chicago was worth more than those of all the savage gang at whose hands he fell.

Source 6   Testimony of Carter H. Harrison, mayor of Chicago, at the Haymarket Eight Trial, August 2, 1886

Question: Did you attend the Haymarket meeting on Desplaines Street on the 4th of May last?

Harrison: A part of it, not the whole. During May 4th, probably about noon, information came to me of the issuance of a circular of a very peculiar character, and a call for a meeting at the Haymarket that very night. I called the chief of police and directed him that if anything should be said at that meeting as was likely to call out a recurrence of such proceedings as at McCormick's factory the meeting should be immediately dispersed. I believed that it was better for myself to be there and to disperse it myself instead of leaving it to any policemen. I thought my order would be better obeyed. I went there then for the purpose, if I felt it necessary for the best interests of the city, to disperse that meeting.

Q: How long did you remain at the meeting?

A: It was about five minutes before eight o'clock when I arrived. . . . I left the meeting between 10 and 10:05 o'clock. I heard all except probably a minute or a minute and a half of Mr. Spies' speech, and all of Mr. Parsons' up to the time I left, with the exception of a break when I left him talking and went over to the [police] station. I was absent five or ten minutes. It was near the close of Parsons' speech. . . . I went to the station to speak to Captain Bonfield, and had determined to go home, but instead of going home I went back to hear a little more, and then left.

Q: Up to the time that you went to the station and had this interview with Mr. Bonfield, what was the tenor of the speeches?

A: With the exception of a portion in the earlier part of Mr. Spies' address, which, for probably a minute, was such that I feared it was leading up to a point where I should disperse the meeting, it was such that I remarked to Captain Bonfield that it was tame. The portion of Mr. Parsons' speech attracting most attention was the statistics as to the amount of returns given to labor from capital, and showing, if I remember rightly now, that capital got eighty-five per cent and labor fifteen per cent. . . .

Q: Was any action taken by you while you were at the meeting looking to the dispersal of the meeting?

A: No.

Q: Do you recollect any suggestion made by either of the speakers looking toward the immediate use of force or violence toward any person?

A: There was none. If there had been I should have dispersed them at once.

Q: How long was the interview that you had with Inspector Bonfield?

A: Probably five minutes.

Q: Will you please state what it was?

A: I went back to the station and said to Bonfield that I thought that the speeches were about over: that nothing had occurred yet or was likely to occur to require interference, and I thought he had better issue orders to his reserves at the other stations to go home. He replied that he thought about the same way, as he had men in the crowd who were reporting to him.

Q: Did you see any weapons in the hands of the audience?

A: No, sir; none at all.

The Anarchists: Felons or Scapegoats?

Why the police decided to disperse the crowd at Haymarket Square is still unclear. And despite the best efforts of detectives at the time and historians ever since, the identity and motivation of the Haymarket bomber is still a mystery.

But the conduct of the police and the conduct of the bomber were of secondary concern almost from the moment the smoke cleared from the blast. The primary concern was the roundup and trial of the very vocal advocates of anarchism.

On the morning after the Haymarket Riot, the city of Chicago was placed under martial law. Union halls, newspaper offices, and private homes were raided without search warrants as police sought evidence. Hundreds were arrested. Eight anarchists—August Spies, Michel Schwab, Oscar Neebe, Adolph Fischer, Louis Lingg, George Engel, Samuel Fielden, and Albert Parsons—were charged with the murder of the policemen.

6.3 The
Haymarket
Tragedy

The trial that followed raised questions about the quality of American justice, and was closely followed across the country and around the world. The defendants were clearly on trial for opinions they had publicly voiced. No one claimed that the eight, either in concert or individually, had thrown the bomb that killed the policemen. Indeed, five of the accused had not even attended the Haymarket Rally. The judge and jury, the public and the press, however, were openly biased against them. All were sentenced to be executed except Neebe, who was given 15 years at hard labor in an Illinois penitentiary.

The bomb tossed into the police ranks on May 4, 1886, had caused the deaths of seven policemen and left 66 more wounded. The retaliation of the police in firing point blank into the crowd killed four and wounded as many as 200. Four of the convicted anarchists would die on the gallows. But the impact of the bomb was greater than the immediate pain it inflicted. The Haymarket bomb served to further alienate the mass of Americans from the radical reformers. It all but crushed the anarchist movement in America. It associated the Knights of Labor with violence and set that organization on a path toward implosion. It left the American Federation of Labor to guide working people on a cautious course.

Source 7   Editorial, New Orleans *Times-Democrat*, August 21, 1886

All the chapters in that dramatic and horrible Haymarket tragedy have been written save one, all the acts finished save the last. It was a drama attended by **saturnalian** lights and scenes. Act I represented the conspirators gathered in the ill-lighted gloom of their secret halls . . . among heaps of deadly bombs. Act II showed a wild mob turned loose on the streets, with murder in their flaming eyes, and the terrible weapons of assassins in their hands. . . . Act III represents Justice standing as a Nemesis before a group of cowering criminals. . . . When the curtain rolls up again with a nation of spectators, to show the final tableau in Act IV, it will disclose a row of **gibbetted** felons, with haltered throats and fettered hands and feet, swinging slowly to and fro, in the air: then it will be rung down again, and the people will breathe freer, feeling that anarchism, nihilism, socialism, communism are forever dead in America!

Source 8   Judge Joseph E. Gary, in denying the motion of the convicted anarchists for a new trial, October 7, 1886

Whether these defendants, or any of them, did participate or expect the throwing of the bomb on the night of the 4th of May is not a question which I need to consider. The jury were not instructed to find them guilty if they believed that they participated in the throwing of the bomb, or encouraged or advised the throwing of that bomb, or had knowledge that it was to be thrown, or anything of that sort. The conviction has not gone upon the ground that they did have any actual participation in the act which caused the death of Degan, but upon the ground . . . that they had generally, by speech and print, advised a large class to commit murder, and had left the occasion, time and place to the individual will, whim and caprice of the individuals so advised; and that in consequence of that advice and in pursuance of it, and influenced by it, somebody not known did throw the bomb that caused Degan's death.

Source 9   Albert R. Parsons, from an eight-hour statement to the court prior to pronouncement of sentence, October 9, 1886

The oppressions of which we complain is such as . . . nearly all the people of the United States are crying out against. You need not think that we stand alone. Some are crying out in more desperate tones than others, but all in tones that it will not do for any government, much less . . . a pretended government of the people . . . [to] disregard.

Now, in this state of things a murder is committed by some one. Not by us, nor by any of us; but by someone as yet unknown. We are confessed by the chief agent in procuring our conviction to be innocent, and have had abundant proof of our innocence. . . . But the government which, in the opinion of those despairing millions, whose woes and whose miseries we voice here today, the government is responsible for their wrongs, but the government does not brook any forcible resistance by even so much as a single man. It regards this single man as a torch that would explode vast numbers of others. It therefore demands not only a victim, but victims. Victims they must have, whether they be innocent or whether they be guilty. . . . So, being unable to discover the guilty man, the machinery is set to work to convict seven innocent ones in his stead.

Source 10   Defense attorney William Perkins Black, Illinois Supreme Court, March 13, 1887

For aught which appears in this record, your honors upon your consciences will be compelled to say that the bomb may have been thrown by somebody in no way connected with these defendants, directly or indirectly. It may have been done by an enemy of theirs. It may have been done by some man acting upon his own mere malice and ill-will. It was thrown outside of the purpose of the Haymarket meeting. It was thrown in disregard of the arrangement and understanding for that meeting. It was thrown to the overthrow of the labor and the effort that these men were giving their lives to, namely, the establishment of the eight-hour day. It brought an end to their efforts. It was not of their devising. The record shows it.

The record fails to show who threw that bomb. And the question is, whether upon the barbaric **lex talionis**, that whenever a man was slain a man of the opposing faction must be slain, these seven men shall die because seven policemen, whom they did not like as a class, and who certainly did not love them, have died? You know the barbarians never stopped to fix individual responsibility for the crime. They simply said, "One of ours is dead, and we cannot rest till one of theirs die for him." It has been so here.

Source 11   Editorial, "The Executions," *New York Times*, November 12, 1887

The decent solemnity with which the victims of the Chicago massacre were avenged compared with the savage fury with which they were done to death completed the contrast, already so conspicuous, between anarchy and law. . . . The stolidity of the German criminals, though in their demeanor also there was something theatrical, was much less repulsive than the posing of PARSONS, and it marked them as much more dangerous and implacable conspirators than the vain, loose-tongued American. . . . They made it evident that if their lives had been spared they would have employed the time that remained to them in making war upon the human race. . . . An expression of sympathy for the fate of such criminals is itself a crime.

The martyrs of the law are thus at last avenged. For the first time immigrants from countries in which vast armies and great bodies of policemen are employed to suppress opinion have been admonished that Americans' wide tolerance of all opinions and of all modes of expressing them cease when mad opinions are translated into lawless acts. The lesson has not come before it was sorely needed. . . .

The police of Chicago were but a handful against the mob that murdered them; but they stood for all the millions of the American people, and every American felt it to be a duty to do his part toward bringing their murderers to justice, as every American would have felt it as a personal disgrace if their murderers had escaped justice. The vengeance taken upon them is not that of a single class or of a single community. It is that of the whole Nation. The odds of the mob against the police seemed great, but how puny would all the elements of crime and disorder and anarchy in Chicago or the country seem if they could be fairly set in array against the millions of honest and peaceable and law-abiding men and women who and whose like have made this country what it is, and who will keep it for order and for progress in trust for mankind in spite of all the human refuse that Europe has emptied or may yet empty on our shores? "Justice travels with a leaden foot but she strikes with an iron-hand." It is to be hoped that the disturbers of our peace may be so warned by the events of yesterday that her hand need not fall upon them yet more heavily, for if a still severer lesson is needed assuredly it will be given.

Second Thoughts

A Contest between Anarchists and Society

On November 10, 1887, it was reported that convicted anarchist Louis Lingg had bitten down on a dynamite cap in his prison cell—blowing away half his skull—in a successful suicide attempt. Illinois governor Oglesby, acting in response to petitions from the public, commuted the sentences of Schwab and Fielden to life imprisonment. On November 11, 1887, August Spies, Adolph Fischer, George Engel, and Albert Parsons were hanged. Protest rallies were held across the United States and in Europe. May Day was adopted in Paris at the Centennial of the French Revolution, July 14, 1889, as an international labor day in remembrance of the executed Chicago anarchists. On June 26, 1893, Illinois governor Altgeld signed papers granting pardons to Neebe, Schwab, and Fielden. On October 6, 1969, the monument to the felled policemen at Haymarket Square was blown up by an unknown bomber. The monument was rebuilt and replaced on May 4, 1970, and destroyed again by a bomb five months later. In February 1972, the police monument was removed from Haymarket Square to the security of Chicago Central Police Headquarters.

Source 12   Supreme Court justice Oliver Wendell Holmes, the majority
opinion for *Schenck v. United States,* 1919

The most stringent protection of free speech would not protect a man in falsely
shouting fire in a theatre, and causing a panic.... The question in every case
is whether the words used are used in such circumstances and are of such a
nature as to create a clear and present danger that they will bring about the
substantive evils that Congress has a right to prevent.

Source 13   James Ford Rhodes, *History of the United States,* 1919

The general strike on May 1 for an eight-hour day produced results in Chicago of national significance. Some while previous there had been a local
trouble at the McCormick Reaper Works which at this time was operated by
men who had not joined the strikers, "scabs," as they were called in derision.
The large number of idle men consequent upon the eight-hour strike was
the cause of the mischief that ensued. Many of them on the afternoon of
May 3 gathered at the McCormick works, listened to an incendiary speech
by an anarchist and attacked the so-called "scabs" as they emerged from the
works on their way home. Police came to their defence, charged the rioters
and, using their revolvers freely, overpowered the mob of whom a number
were hurt but no one killed, although one died later from injuries received
during the conflict. Reporting that six men had been killed the anarchists
called a meeting of working-men for the next evening "to denounce the latest
atrocious act of the police"; one of their circulars was headed "Revenge!
Working-men to Arms!!!"

   From this time forward the story has nothing to do with the eight-hour
movement or with diligent workingmen striking for a better day. We have now
to do with a contest between the anarchists on the one hand and society on
the other as represented for the moment by the Chicago police.... Under the
screen of high regard for the laborer the anarchists used his supposed grievances
to propagate their ideas and support their overt acts.... The misery in the
world, they argued, "arises out of the institution of private property": it must
therefore be abolished. Had they confined themselves to writing and to preaching
they would have been left unmolested, but they advocated "a destruction of the
existing order of society by rebellion and revolution" and proposed to bring this
about by the use of an explosive which had been adapted to peaceful pursuits.
"Dynamite!" declared one of their newspapers.... "One man with a dynamite
bomb is equal to a regiment of militia." It is hardly surprising that such preaching constantly repeated was soon translated into action....

   There can be no question that the punishment meted out to the anarchists
was legally just. "In law the anarchists were rightly punished," wrote Judge Gary,
"not for opinions but for horrible deeds." Judge, jury, and two Supreme Courts
after careful and impartial consideration were at one.

   The historical judgment confirms the legal. The anarchists attacked Society
and Society defended itself under due forms of law; the anarchists then took
every advantage of the quirks and **quiddities** of the law which they had derided.
All thoughtful citizens must have been interested to note that six out of the
eight who stood trial were Germans, as was also the thrower of the bomb. This

fellow had lived in this country not more than two years and could not speak English; he might however have emulated the courage of the American anarchist and, instead of fleeing from the country, surrendered himself to justice.

Source 14   Samuel Gompers, president, American Federation of Labor, *Seventy Years of Labor,* 1925

Inasmuch as the Haymarket bomb in Chicago destroyed the eight-hour movement, we trade unionists had no reason to sympathize with the cause of the anarchists as such. However, labor must do its best to maintain justice for the radicals or find itself denied the rights of free men.

Because there was no direct evidence showing that these men were guilty of throwing the bombs, there were numbers of men who believed that clemency should be exercised by commutation of sentence from death to imprisonment. About the seventh or eighth of November, 1887, I was sitting in my small back office of Union No. 144 when Ed King and James Lynch (of the Carpenters) came to me and asked me to go to Springfield to make a plea before Governor Oglesby for commutation of the sentence.

They presented to me the idea that because of my being well and favorably known and that I was regarded as a conservative man, my plea would help. Without further ado I closed my office door, and without any belongings other than those which I wore I went directly to the train and with them to Springfield.

The hearing was in the Governor's chamber. . . . Very earnest pleas were made.

There were in the group representatives of trade unionists, farmers, the Legislature, women's organizations, and nearly every social group.

I said in part:

> I have differed all my life with the principles and methods of the condemned, but know no reason why I should not ask the governor to interpose and save condemned men from the gallows. The execution would not be one of justice. . . . If these men are executed it would simply give impetus to this so-called revolutionary movement which no other thing on earth could give. These men would, apart from any consideration of mercy or humanity, be looked upon as martyrs. Thousands and thousands of labor men all over the world would consider that these men had been executed because they were standing up for free speech and free press.
>
> We ask you, sir, to interpose your great power to prevent so dire a calamity. If this great country could be great and magnanimous enough to grant amnesty to Jeff Davis, it ought to be great and magnanimous enough to grant clemency to these men.

I remember speaking coolly and calmly, and I pleaded as strongly as I could. . . . At the close of my statement Governor Oglesby arose to greet me, and thanked me and added that my appeal made the strongest impression upon his mind. However, all the appeals were of no avail for the governor declined to stay the execution. The men were executed on November 11, 1887.

Source 15 **Anarchist Alexander Berkmen, "Now and After," 1929**

[Berkman attempted to assassinate industrialist Henry Frick during the 1892 Homestead Steel Strike.]

I want to tell you about Anarchism. . . .

I want to tell you about it, because I believe that Anarchism is the finest and biggest thing man has ever thought of; the only thing that can give you liberty and well-being, and bring peace and joy to the world.

But before I tell you what Anarchism is, I want to tell you what it *is not*. . . .

It is *not* bombs.

It is *not* robbery and murder.

It is *not* war of each against all.

It is *not* a return to barbarism or to the wild state of man.

Anarchism is the very opposite of all that.

[I]t is capitalism and government which stand for disorder and violence. Anarchism means . . . order without government and peace without violence. . . .

Yes, Anarchists have thrown bombs and have sometimes resorted to violence. . . .

But . . . does it necessarily mean that Anarchism means violence? . . . When a citizen puts on a solder's uniform, he may have to throw bombs and use violence. Will you say, then, that citizenship stands for bombs and violence?

You will indignantly resent the imputation. It simply means, you will reply, that *under certain conditions* a man may have to resort to violence. The man may happen to be a Democrat, a Monarchist, a Socialist, Bolshevik, or Anarchist. . . .

What is this thing we call government? Is it anything else but organized violence? The law orders you to do this or not to do that, and if you fail to obey, it will compel you by force. . . . [T]he right to compel you is called authority. Fear of punishment has been made into duty and it is called obedience.

In this atmosphere of force and violence, of authority and obedience, of duty, fear and punishment we all grow up; we breathe it throughout our lives. We are so steeped in the spirit of violence that we never stop to ask whether violence is right or wrong. We only ask if it is legal, whether the law permits it.

You don't question the right of the government to kill, to confiscate and imprison. If a private person should be guilty of the things the government is doing all the time, you'd brand him a murderer, thief, scoundrel. . . .

We are all still barbarians who resort to force and violence to settle our doubts, differences, and troubles. Violence is the method of ignorance, the weapon of the weak. The strong of heart and brain need no violence, for they are irresistible in their consciousness of being right. The further we get away from primitive man and the hatchet age, the less recourse we shall have to force and violence. The more enlightened man will become, the less he will employ compulsion and coercion. The really civilized man will divest himself of all fear and authority. He will rise from the dust and stand erect: he will bow to no tsar either in heaven or on earth. He will become fully human when he will scorn to rule and refuse to be ruled. He will be truly free only when there shall be no more masters.

Anarchism is the ideal of such a condition; of a society without force and compulsion where all men shall be equals, and live in freedom, peace, and harmony.

The word Anarchy comes from the Greek, meaning without force, without violence or government, because government is the very fountainhead of violence, constraint, and coercion. . . .

[T]here can be no justice as long as we live under conditions which enable one person to take advantage of another's need, to turn it to his profit, and exploit his fellow man.

There can be no justice as long as one man is ruled by another; as long as one has the authority and power to compel another against his will.

There can be no justice between master and servant.

Nor equality.

Justice and equality can exist only among equals. Is the poor street-cleaner the social equal of Morgan? Is the washerwoman the equal of Lady Astor? . . . Let the washerwoman and Lady Astor enter any place, private or public. Will they receive equal welcome and treatment? . . . The washerwoman may have toiled hard all her life long, may have been a most industrious and useful member of the community. The Lady may have never done a stroke of work, never been of the least use to society. For all that it is the rich lady who will be welcomed, who will be preferred. . . .

It is money and the influence and authority which money commands, that alone count in the world.

Not justice, but possession. . . .

The industrial lords know that it is good for them to keep you unorganized and disorganized, or to break up your unions when they get strong and militant. By hook and crook they oppose your every advance as a class-conscious worker. . . . They will spare neither expense nor energy to stifle any thought or idea that may reduce their profits or threaten their mastery over you.

The movement for the eight-hour workday started in Chicago, on May 1, 1886, gradually spreading throughout the country. . . . The armed fist of the law immediately hastened to the aid of the employers. . . . The most vicious attack took place at the McCormick works, where the conditions of employment were so unbearable that the men were compelled to go on strike. . . . At this place the police and Pinkertons deliberately shot a volley into the assembled workers, killing four and wounding a score of others.

To protest against the outrage a meeting was called at Haymarket Square on the 4th of May, 1886. . . . Without . . . warning the police threw themselves upon the people, mercilessly clubbing and beating men and women. There was an explosion, as of a bomb. Seven policemen were killed and about sixty wounded.

It was never ascertained who threw the bomb. . . .

There had been so much brutality by the police and Pinkertons against the strikers that it was not surprising that some one should express his protest by such an act. Who was he? The industrial masters of Chicago were not interested in this detail. They were determined to crush rebellious labor, to down the eight-hour movement, and to stifle the voice of the spokesmen of the workers. They openly declared their determination to "teach the men a lesson." . . .

The Haymarket tragedy, as the case is known, is a striking illustration of the kind of "justice" labor may expect from the masters. It is a demonstration of its class character and of the means to which capital and government will resort to crush the workers.

Source 16   Matthew Josephson, *The Robber Barons: The Great American Capitalists, 1861–1901,* 1934

By 1885 the Noble Order of Knights of Labor held a certain terror for the rulers of great industries. A victorious strike against Jay Gould's Missouri Pacific Railroad in this year brought numerous recruits to the banners of the Order, which aroused immense hopes among the workers through having conquered the man who was reckoned both the strongest and the wiliest of capitalists. . . .

But . . . after 1886, even greater force and sovereign authority was marshalled on behalf of the alarmed industrial chieftains. Pinkerton detectives and industrial spies were used to weed out union men. The lockout, especially used by Carnegie, and the blacklist or "iron-clad oath" (not to participate in a union) were enforced by monopolists acting in concert. Finally, after the Haymarket riot in Chicago, where the explosion of a deadly bomb stirred public opinion to boiling pitch, all the forces of law and order, from local magistrates and militia to the President and the Supreme Court, united to crush the "conspiracy" of labor.

Source 17   Henry David, *The History of the Haymarket Affair,* 1936

The Haymarket bomb was responsible for the first major "red scare" in American history, and produced a campaign of "red-baiting" which has rarely been equalled. So expertly was this campaign waged that it molded the popular mind for years to come, and played its part in conditioning the mass response to the imaginary threat of the "social revolution" frequently displayed in the United States since 1886. It led to the immediate popular condemnation of Socialism, Communism, and Anarchism.

Source 18   Foster Rhea Dulles, *Labor in America,* 1960

Not only Chicago but the entire country was outraged by the bomb throwing. The anarchists were at once blamed and there was universal demand that they be hunted down and brought to trial. The police combed the city for suspects, and finally eight known anarchist leaders were arrested and charged with murder. In a frenzied atmosphere compounded equally of fear and the desire for revenge, they were thereupon found guilty—seven of them sentenced to death and the eighth to fifteen years imprisonment. There was no evidence whatsoever connecting them with the bombing. They were condemned out of hand for their revolutionary views and the incitements to violence which had supposedly caused the bombing. "Convict these men, make examples of them, hang them," urged the state's attorney, "and you save our institutions. . . ."

The capitalistic enemies of labor were seeking to hang upon the labor movement this "millstone of odium" by charging that the Knights of Labor and the unions generally were permeated by the spirit of anarchism and communism. An hysterical public appeared ready to believe it. The whole labor movement was blackened by the bomb tossed by some unknown hand into the police squad at Haymarket Square. It did not matter that its responsible leaders and the overwhelming mass of the workers were as opposed to both anarchism and communism as any other group in society. All labor was thrown on the defensive.

Source 19　Joseph G. Rayback, *A History of American Labor,* 1966

The Haymarket affair, which accented anarcho-syndicalist principles, drove the terror deeper into the nation's mentality and turned it into hysteria. A violent antilabor campaign followed. Fear-gripped state legislatures rushed laws curbing freedom of action of labor organizations onto the statute books. The courts began to convict union members of conspiracy, intimidation, rioting in whole-sale lots. Employers, taking advantage of the situation, instituted widespread antiunion campaigns, with Pinkertons, lockouts, black lists, and yellow-dog contracts.

Source 20　Paul Avrich, *The Haymarket Tragedy,* 1984

Haymarket, with its manifold effects, was a major event in American history. For the first time it brought anarchism to the attention of the general public, identifying it with terrorist violence and inspiring a horror of its teachings and practices. Equally important, it marked the climax of one of the most bitter industrial struggles in America's experience, interrupting the eight-hour move-ment and turning labor away from radical doctrines for years to come. Haymar-ket, on the other hand, forms part of the foundation on which the heritage of American labor rests. For, besides its connection with the eight-hour struggle, it gave to the labor movement its first revolutionary martyrs, whose sense of outrage against economic and social injustice, whose vision of a society in which the resources of production are available for the benefit of all, provided a source of inspiration for workers of every stripe. . . .

　　Although Haymarket was by no means the only instance where Ameri-can justice has failed, it was nonetheless a black mark on a legal system that professes truth and fairness as its highest principles. The defendants, all dying like men, all protesting their innocence, were put to death with a ferocity that shocked the enlightened world. As a barbarous act of power it was with-out parallel in American legal history. Naked force, it appeared to many, was to be the final answer of the authorities when the dispossessed insisted on pressing their claims.

 ## Questioning the Past

1. What were the causes and consequences of the Haymarket Affair?
2. Argue the case for and against the guilt of the eight anarchists who were put on trial in Chicago.
3. Samuel Fielden, who spoke at the Haymarket Rally and was convicted along with the seven other anarchists, commented in court prior to receiving his sentence:

"Now, policemen generally are not men of very intellectual calibre. They are not men who ought in any civilized community to be made the censors of speech or of the press." If there are to be limits on freedom of expression, who should be entrusted to be the "censors" and under what circumstances and procedures?

4. It has been argued that the Haymarket bomber was an anarchist. It has also been argued that the bomber was an agent provocateur. What possible motivation would an anarchist have for tossing the bomb? What would be the motivation for an agent provocateur?

5. Adolph Fischer, one of the convicted anarchists, wrote shortly before he was hanged: "I am sure that coming ages will look upon our trial, conviction, and execution as the people of the eighteenth century regard the barbarities of past generations—as the outcome of intolerance and prejudice against advanced ideas." How did the "coming ages" view this affair? What judgment may be made about it today?

Chapter 7

Coxey's Army

An Industrial Army Invades Washington   *May 1, 1894*

Times were hard, and Jacob Coxey was a man of compassion. One cold and rainy December night as he drove his buggy home to Massillon, Ohio, his mind raced over the problems of the unemployed as his rein hand guided his team around the potholes in the road. It was the convergence of these two concerns that inspired Coxey to a novel solution to both. Why not hire the unemployed to fix the potholes?

The idea seemed so simple and so beneficial. The federal government could come up with the money. It could offer this money in wages to any and all who were willing to work. It could loan money to local governments in exchange for long-term, noninterest-bearing bonds, and these localities could in turn hire the unemployed to build parks, playgrounds, roads, schools, hospitals. This infusion of funds to meet national and local needs would put more money into circulation in a time of tight money and economic depression. It would restore dignity to the unemployed and permit them again to provide food and shelter for their families. By setting a fair wage and establishing an eight-hour work day, the government could cause private employers to do the same or risk losing their employees to this new public works program. And, the potholes would be fixed.

To implement these ideas, Coxey drafted two measures he hoped Congress would consider: a "Good Roads Bill" and a "Noninterest-Bearing Bond Bill." But how could one modest, mild-mannered, yet sincere businessman in rural Ohio take his idea to the public and transform it into the will of the majority? He found the answer in collaboration with an unlikely partner, Carl "Old Greasy" Browne.

Browne and Coxey were an odd couple. Coxey was reserved, well-dressed, respectable. Browne was a big, burly, loud fellow, who wore an exaggerated western costume and was philosophically opposed to bathing. But the weaknesses of the one were erased by the strengths of the other, and together they came up with an idea to petition Congress on behalf of the powerless. Their petition would not, however, join countless other pleas from the poor in congressional wastebaskets. Their petition would wear boots. It would be a living petition of tens of thousands of unemployed Americans, marching on Washington, D.C., to deliver their plea in person. No one had ever attempted such a demonstration before.

The plan devised by Coxey and Browne sent a shudder of fear across the country. What would happen when 100,000 angry, unemployed workers surrounded the Capitol? General Washington had a force only a tenth that size at Yorktown. There had been half that number at

7.1 Economic
Depression

107

Fredericksburg. The nation's capital braced itself for the assault. The nation pondered the potential for revolution.

On March 25, 1894, the day the great march was to step off from Massillon, reporters were gathered for the event from around the world. Unfortunately for Coxey and Browne, there were more reporters than marchers. Rather than 100,000, the marchers numbered closer to 100. The power structure of America breathed a sigh of relief. The press was embarrassed at having swallowed Coxey and Browne's grandiose claims. Fortunately for the reporters, the 100 marchers turned out to include an entertaining assortment of harmless eccentrics: in addition to "Old Greasy," there was Oklahoma Sam, a cowboy with an impressive repertoire of roping and riding tricks; "Cyclone" Kirtland, an astrologer who foresaw Coxey's Army as "invisible in war, invincible in peace"; Douglas McCallum, author of the book *Dogs and Fleas, By One Of the Dogs;* "The Great Unknown," a mysterious man who organized and disciplined the troops; and a half-dozen other equally colorful characters. Rather than presenting to the people the progress of a revolutionary force, the march coverage became more the story of a comedy in boots. Every day, papers across the country carried the latest antics of the motley army.

✐ *First Impressions*

A Petition in Boots

Although the public laughed, they respected what Coxey was trying to do. His inarticulate plea for the poor struck a responsive chord, and as his army marched through the snow, endured time in jail, suffered hardships and public ridicule, but kept on coming, thousands lined his way to cheer. Coxey's Army, grown to 500 strong, reached the District of Columbia border by the end of April. On May 1, the marchers were ready to take their message to Capitol Hill.

Source 1   "Coxey Declares He Will Speak if He Goes to Jail for It," *Washington Post,* May 1, 1894

This morning brings the trial of the great test case of the Commonweal vs. the plutocrats. At least that is the way Gen. Coxey and Chief Marshall Browne profess to look at it in making arrangements for their procession to the Capitol to protest against the existing order of things and bring peace and prosperity to the people through taking the governor off the engine in the Bureau of Engraving and Printing. The great movement, so far as this army of the Commonweal is concerned, has grown to be very much of a farce, and the only inference to be drawn from the attitude of the leaders is that, failing to make a big demonstration of their parade, they are throwing themselves in direct opposition to the law, hoping to be arrested and to pose as martyrs to the cause of liberty.

Mr. Coxey spent the greater part of the day yesterday skirmishing through the city between the Capitol, the District Buildings, and the Health Office, first in search of a permit for a parade, and then in search of a pretext for mixing up with the police. His interview with the District Commissioners went very pleasantly till he intimated that he would speak from the steps of the Capitol, when he was informed that under no circumstances would that be permitted. He thereupon announced his intention of testing the law by having his procession and speaking in defiance of authorities.

Source 2   Speech of Carl Browne, chief marshal, Coxey's Army, to the marchers, May 1, 1894

This beautiful day ushers in a new dawn in history, and from now on it will be a continuous 1st of May until the bills we have come to present to Congress have become laws. The people of America in the future will look back upon the 1st day of May, 1894, as the most important date in history, marking, as it does, the birth of a new and fuller and freer liberty for the now down-trodden masses of the American common people.

This movement, mark you, will not cease with the American people, but will spread its beneficent influences until the whole world is touched and softened and sweetened by it.

I am not sure that interference with our plans would not be better for the movement. Such action would still further inspire the sympathies of the great masses of the people with our object and accentuate in their minds the impression so generally entertained, that the plutocrats will not brook any interference, no matter how peaceful it may be, with their determination to tighten their grasp on the country's throat.

I feel within me—my reincarnation tells me that no matter what happens and despite any and all circumstances the eventual success of our movement is assured. . . .

Whether or not we will be permitted to speak, I cannot say, but you must be careful to preserve the peace. . . . People said we wouldn't march up Pennsylvania Avenue when we reached here. Yet the police department yesterday informed Brother Coxey that we could march. We are here on time and will go to the grounds on time. All are certainly on deck. Yesterday it looked as though we wouldn't have many, but now we will go in with spirits as bright as the May day on which we march. Mr. Crisp refused yesterday to let us speak on the Capitol steps . . . [but] we will go to the Capitol grounds as individuals. They can't stop us from doing that. . . .

This demonstration will be more powerful than force, than guns, than bombs.

Source 3   "The March on the Capitol: A Spectacle Unlike Anything Ever Before Witnessed in Washington," *Washington Post*, May 2, 1894

The Army of the Commonweal looked about as hard and indifferent to all things spiritual or material as they had appeared since the start from Massillon. This may have been the contrast of the long line of ragged, dusty, sunburned and weather-beaten men shown against the background of handsome houses, and gayly dressed people that lined the sidewalks. But, however that may have been, the column looked strikingly woebegone and hopeless. This was not helped by the fluttering rags at the end of their peace sticks.

Their shoes were mostly on the verge of dissolution and yellow with the dust of the country roads; their coats, whatever might have been their original color, were weathered to an almost uniform blackish green. Their hats would have furnished a study for the modern realistic novelist, and at the side of nearly every one a rusty, dented, and battered canteen flapped with a dismal hollow clank.

The wagons that were sandwiched in at intervals between the **communes** were almost as battered and dusty as the men, and the horses even had a tired look as though they would be glad when it was all over. . . .

The line moved at a snail's pace, as though it was unanimously weary so that the procession which was only half a dozen squares in length, took a quarter of an hour to pass a given point. . . .

There was little or no excitement till the procession reached Pennsylvania Avenue. The spectators filled the sidewalks and a good-sized crowd, the usual advance guard of boys, negroes, and ne'er-do-wells, marched on Fourteenth Street and at the head of the band. But when the procession turned into the Avenue the crowd swelled to a size such as is seldom outside of a Presidential inauguration.

Apparently no preparations had been made to clear the way for the procession as is the habit with any large parade where the authorities are favorably interested. The procession was hardly big enough to clear the way for itself, and the four or five mounted officers were completely lost in the crowd that pushed out from the sidewalks, overflowed the car tracks, and surged back and forth around the horses of the leaders and through the decimated band. . . . The crowd of curiosity-seekers tried literally to climb into the carriage where Mr. and Mrs. Coxey were riding, and the correspondents who had followed the Commonweal on its march across country constituted a cordon of special police about the vehicle to keep off intruders. . . .

By this time the good-natured crowd had begun to cheer and hurrah, not so much from enthusiasm as from excitement and a general desire to make a noise. It filled the Avenue from curb to curb and choked and surged at the narrow turn by the Peace Monument like a glut in a log stream. The police almost gave up fighting their way, and fell back to breathe their sweating horses, while the crowd yelled and cheered Coxey and the Commonweal and everything else connected with the movement with which they were acquainted.

Coxey looked out over the heads of the crowd and bowed and smiled, and then looked up at the towering dome of the great white Capitol and the black lines of human beings swarming up the steps and terraces, filling the porches and windows, and massed up in pyramids around the Peace Monument, tree boxes, and lamp posts. And then the crowd would yell again and Coxey would bow and smile again. What he was thinking he did not say, but he evidently felt that he had made an impression.

Source 4   "EXTRA! EXCITING SCENE AT THE CAPITOL," Washington *Evening Star,* May 1, 1894

The Coxey army reached the Capitol grounds a few minutes before 1 o'clock. When the attempt was made to enter the grounds a small riot occurred, during which a number of heads were severely pounded by the police and some arrests were made. When the procession reached the Peace monument at the foot of the Capitol, instead of turning to go up the north side, as had been expected, it marched up South B street. Meanwhile thousands of curious people, seeking a view of the army, poured into the Capitol grounds from all directions, until the crowd was almost as large as at an inauguration. The lawns were trampled over, the shrubbery and flowers disregarded, but this overriding was entirely by the curious people on the outside. The army on reaching New Jersey avenue southeast, instead of marching directly into the Capitol grounds, marched up to 1st street southeast, the police and guard of the grounds following them. At that point a break was made by Browne and Coxey for the Capitol steps. They were followed by a bodyguard of their own men and an immense crowd of people who so swelled the confusion that people were trampling each other and the mass was so thick that the police could with difficulty move about on their horses. Browne rushed for the steps of the House and Coxey for the steps of the Senate, for the purpose of addressing the crowd.

The police charged the Coxeyites as they entered the grounds and immediately a fight began, in which there were not many participants, but which was very exciting and sent terror through the crowd, many of whom were women. Some of the Coxeyites seized the horses of the police by the bridle and struck at the officers with their fists or with anything at hand, and the policemen used their clubs freely on everyone who made any demonstration. Just as Browne, who had got [to] the head of the crowd momentarily out of reach of the police, rushed through the shrubbery on to the asphalt immediately in front of the main staircase of the House, a squad of four or five of the police who had ridden around came upon him, and seized him by the collar. He made a desperate fight and the mounted officers made a circle around him still holding him, while he struck right and left at them with his arms, which he had succeeded in keeping free, and his little body guard surrounded the officers and pelted and pounded at them with a desperation which was harmless only because they were without weapons. Browne was taken out of the grounds by two mounted police, one holding him on either side, and the other police continued with the few struggling Coxeyites who were determined not to yield and who on every occasion would slip around behind an officer and deal him a blow or try to pull him from his horse. The immense crowd gave the fight a much more serious aspect than the amount of fighting and number of people engaged in it warranted, and it was over in but a few minutes.

Meanwhile Coxey had reached the Senate steps and was there arrested by the police without resistance, but very vigorously protesting. . . .

The scene on the Capitol steps was one of the most remarkable ever witnessed in this or any other city. People were crowded up and down the steps until the whole line was black. Mr. Coxey, escorted by a squad of policemen on horse and on foot, was pushed through the crowd and on to the lower landing of the main east front steps. Here he was met by the captain of the Capitol police, Capt. Austin, . . . and a number of other officials of the police department. Mr. Coxey was cool and calm, but in a moment his voice became excited as he addressed the captain of the Capitol police.

"Is this the representative of Col. Bright?" he said.

"I am the captain of the Capitol police."

"Then," said Mr. Coxey, "I demand the right to deliver an address to the people. I make this demand in the name of the people of the American nation, and I demand the assistance and protection of the Capitol police while I do so."

A crowd of more than 10,000 people was standing around watching for the next developments. The conversation was held to a low tone of voice, and audible to a few people only.

"You can't make any address here," said the captain of the police.

"Then I wish to enter and read a protest," said Mr. Coxey, and he drew out of his pocket a typewritten paper of a couple of pages. He offered to read the paper, but was told that he must not do so, if it was lengthy or in any way resembled an address or harangue.

"Then I will submit this paper to you," said Mr. Coxey, and he handed it to the captain.

Then Mr. Coxey turned around and was forcibly rather than politely taken in charge by a detachment of police. A way was cleared for him by mounted officers through the crowd that packed the grounds to the very farthest limit. Again and again the officers raised their clubs, but they did not strike, and no one was hurt, with the exception of those who were thrown down and trampled by the mob.

Source 5   "Coxey Silenced by Police," *New York Times,* May 2, 1894

Washington, May 1.— . . . Through Washington's streets, which have seen many a brilliant and glorious pageant, trudged toward the Capitol today a disreputable crowd of tramps audaciously claiming to be the representatives of millions of respectable wage earners and bearing ridiculous banners and devices.

The parade was witnessed by thousands of people, but few of them, however, were weak-minded enough to feel anything but contempt for the marching travesty.

Most of the people, to be sure, looked at the scene with great interest, though with interest akin to that with which a specialist in insanity might regard a new form of the disease.

In spite of Coxey's bombastic declaration that he would defy the law and Federal authorities and speak his sophistry on the Capitol's steps, he did not do it.

Stalwart policemen seized him with the courtesy due to a violator of the law, and hustled him away without much resistance on the part of the Massillon horse dealer and leader of the tramps. It was an inglorious moment for Coxey. Coxey's tramps were remarkably meek. The sight of a large number of athletic policemen, who eyed the Coxeyite ranks with unfriendly eyes and carried big clubs, served to keep them from attempting to do anything which might cause them to be given a severe thrashing.

All told, about 600 men out of the originally-promised 300,000 marched up the Capitol hill and then marched down again.

Pioneers of the Unemployed

When Coxey and his Army turned the corner onto Pennsylvania Avenue on May Day in 1894, they not only heard the cheers of 40,000 spectators, they saw at the foot of Capitol Hill a solid wall of policemen armed with clubs and prepared to block their access to the Capitol grounds. They saw also 200 mounted officers and 1,500 regular army troops with fixed bayonets. It is no wonder that Coxey's Army made its abrupt turn just short of its intended destination. But Coxey had not come so far to be stopped so close. His dash through the shrubs, across the lawn and up the steps was a determined attempt to complete his mission. He never got the chance to read his speech. The best he could do was toss a copy to reporters as the police hauled him away.

As Coxey was being removed from the grounds, the spectators began to shout his name over and over again, "Coxey, Coxey, Coxey." The police lost their heads and began to club the spectators indiscriminately. At least 50 people were injured. While the police and spectators skirmished, Coxey's Army, true to Cyclone Kirtland's prophecy, remained "invisible in war," observing the whole bizarre scene from a block away.

Coxey, Browne, and another leader of the movement, Christopher Columbus Jones, were brought to court to face charges of carrying flags and banners supporting the "Good Roads Bill" onto the Capitol grounds where they also "did then and there step upon certain plants, shrubs, and turf then and there being and growing." Found guilty, the three were sentenced to 20 days in jail and a $5 fine each.

Coxey's march on Washington left no permanent imprint on the Capitol lawn. It did, however, inspire the emergence of other "Industrial Armies" around the country who imitated and associated themselves with Coxey's Commonweal army. These armies marched across the countryside, they commandeered trains, they captured headlines. All of these activities served to publicize the plight of the poor and unemployed during the depression. The measures they advocated in the depression of 1894, however, were not to be seriously considered for almost two more generations, when the country fell into the Great Depression of the 1930s.

Source 6 Jacob Coxey's (undelivered) speech on the Capitol steps, May 1, 1894

The Constitution of the United States guarantees to all citizens the right to peacefully assemble and petition for redress of grievances, and, furthermore, declares that the right of free speech shall not be abridged.

We stand here to-day to test these guarantees of our Constitution. We chose this place of assemblage because it is the property of the people, and if it be true that the right of the people to peacefully assemble upon their own premises and with their petitions has been abridged by the passage of laws in direct violation of the Constitution we are here to draw the eyes of the people to this shameful fact.

Here, rather than at any spot upon the continent, it is fitting that we should come to mourn our dead liberties, and by our protest arouse the imperiled nation to such action as shall rescue the Constitution and resurrect our liberty. Upon these steps where we now stand has been spread a carpet for the royal feet of a foreign princess, the cost of whose lavish entertainment was taken from the public treasury. . . .

Up these steps the lobbyists of trusts and corporations have passed unchallenged on their way to committee rooms to which we, the representatives of the toiling wealth producers have been denied. We stand here today in behalf of millions of toilers whose petitions have been buried in committee rooms, whose prayers have been unresponded to, and whose opportunities for honest, remunerative productive labor have been taken from them. We come here to remind Congress here assembled of the declarations of a United States Senator "that for a quarter of a century the rich have been growing richer, the poor, poorer. . . ."

We stand here to declare by our march of over 500 miles through difficulties and distress, a march unstained by even the slightest act which will bring the blush of shame to any, that we are law-abiding citizens, and as such our actions speak louder than words. We are here to petition for legislation which will furnish employment for every man able and willing to work, for legislation which will bring universal prosperity and emancipate our beloved country from financial bondage to the descendants of King George.

We have come to the only source which is competent to aid the people in their day of dire distress. We are here to tell our representatives, who hold their seats by the grace of our ballots, that the struggle for existence has become too fierce and relentless. We come and throw up our defenseless hands and say, "help or we and our loved ones must perish." We are engaged in a bitter and cruel war with the enemies of all mankind. A war with hunger, wretchedness, and despair, and we ask Congress to heed our petitions.

Source 7   O. O. Howard, major-general, United States Army, "The Menace of Coxeyism-I," *North American Review*, June 1894

Whatever be the cause or causes, a financial depression has come upon our country and still exists. . . . The latest phase of the struggle on the part of some of the people to recover their usual economic equilibrium is this "Coxey movement." It is unique in its inception, different from any other in the history of our country, and, indeed, quite unlike ordinary revolutionary experiments. The attempt to affect United States legislation by organizing the unemployed into peaceful hosts and marching them, without previous furnishing of supplies, by the precarious means of begging their way for hundreds of miles, to the Capital appears to ordinary minds the height of absurdity. Yet notwithstanding an almost unanimous press against their contemplated expedition, notwithstanding the discouragement by members of Congress with hardly a dissenting voice, and all legal checks put upon them by State and United States executive power, Coxey's first contingent is already in Washington, Kelly's from San Francisco at Des Moines, Ia., Frye's, organized in Los Angeles, Cal., is in Pennsylvania; the Rhode Island body, calling itself a delegation of unemployed workmen, has passed New York; and many other companies under different designations are organizing, or have already accomplished miles en route.

The idea of the organization of a "Commonweal Army" originated in the mind of one man, living in Massillon, Ohio, Jacob Sechler Coxey. Mr. Coxey had no special prominence before this time. His scheme, new enough and surprising, first brought his name before the public. He took the side of the unemployed and all unfortunates in his harangues; and he called himself one of them. . . .

It is difficult to judge of the motives of men. The desire for notoriety, doubtless, enters largely. Yet Coxey's ideas are not inconsistent with sincerity on his part, because the notion that those who occupy the seats of power can issue fiat money is, as I understand it, the doctrine of a large number of our citizens. With this political doctrine . . . , it is not illogical for him to call upon the government officials to relieve immediate want by public works and public money.

Source 8 **Thomas Byrnes, superintendent of the New York Police Department, "The Menace of Coxeyism-II," *North American Review,* June 1894**

The men who compose these so-called armies are, so far as I can learn, what are ordinarily called tramps. That is, they are men who do not earn and have not earned a living and supported themselves. They have banded together, a menace to the communities in which they were, and they propose to demand that Congress pass certain laws. Their avowed object is to assemble in front of the Capitol in Washington, and there, by their presence and numbers, to so intimidate the Congress of the United States as to force that body to pass certain laws dictated by them. Think of it for a moment: these idle useless dregs of humanity—too lazy to work, too miserably inefficient to earn a living—intend to "demand" that Congress shall pass laws at their dictation. "Demand," that is the word they use in their so-called proclamations. Two thousand, three thousand, five thousand tramps—whatever their number may be—"demand" when they speak to the government of the greatest country on earth! No wonder the people laugh.

Source 9 **Alvah H. Doty, chief of the Bureau of Contagious Diseases, New York Board of Health, "The Menace of Coxeyism-III," *North American Review,* June 1894**

The recent movement under the leadership of certain hare-brained men, which has resulted in the banding together in different parts of the country of a number of so-called workmen, has been variously ascribed to political and other motives. There is one aspect, however, which has received very little, if any, attention, although it may be productive of serious consequences. I refer to the probability of the different groups of Coxeyites acting as carriers and propagators of contagious disease. . . . [T]his un-American and unsanitary movement has been much encouraged by the citizens of the different places visited by these men. It would seem that the health official of every town or city throughout the country should be clothed with sufficient power to prevent the entrance into their respective places of any assemblage which, in their opinion, is dangerous to the public health.

Source 10 **Preamble of the constitution of Fry's Army, Spring 1894**

[Fry's was one of the several industrial armies inspired by Coxey's efforts.]

We have reached that point on our own road to ruin where three percent of the population own seventy-six percent of all the wealth. . . . The daily grind of pinching poverty, linked with the thought of a hopeless future, kills even the deep material instinct. The greatest crime perpetrated by a nation is to allow her people to be idle and sink into debauched servitude. The strange tragical questions confront us on every hand.

Why is it that those who produce food are hungry?

Why is it that those who make clothes are ragged?

Why is it that those who build palaces are homeless?

Why is it that those who do the nation's work are forced to choose between beggary, crime or suicide, in a nation that has fertile soil enough to produce plenty to feed and clothe the world; material enough to build palaces to house them all, and productive capacity, through labor-saving machinery, of forty thousand million man-power, and only sixty-five million souls to feed, clothe, and shelter.

Second Thoughts

A Clamor for Work for the Workless

7.2 History Matters: Labor and Labor Movements

Jacob Coxey continued his campaign on behalf of the unemployed for the remainder of his long life. In 1932, Coxey, by then the mayor of Massillon, was permitted to explain his ideas to Franklin Roosevelt, and when the latter ultimately included the Works Progress Administration and other public relief programs in his New Deal, Coxey pointed out, "I said the same things and they put me in jail for it." Coxey died in 1951 at the age of 97.

Source 11 Henry Vincent, official historian of Coxey's Army,
The Story of the Commonweal, 1894

The first announcement of the movement was received with derision and sneers all over the land. . . . The newspapers of the country treated it as a low comedy with every trace of seriousness eliminated. They demonstrated to their own satisfaction, at least, that nothing could possibly come of the proposed "On to Washington" march beyond an ill-assorted journey of a few miles by a motley company which would rival that of the **pot-valiant Falstaff**. The editorial paragraphs were jocose, satirical and frequently downright funny. It would seem that they made the mistake of failing to appreciate the value of earnestness in any given cause, as well as the benefit that might accrue to this one in particular by the wide notoriety which they gave it.

Discontent with the existing order of things was widespread. The army of the unemployed was an immense one, as the result of the shutting down of factories and the many business failures, and to many the message of Coxey came as the rain upon the thirsty ground. Men touched with the same spirit as Coxey, with compassion for the unemployed masses, . . . proceeded diligently to work enlisting recruits for the great crusade. Now, in direct disproof of the prediction of the sneerer and the scorner, not less than seventeen separate and distinct armies are plodding wearily yet resolutely toward the National Capitol.

Source 12 W. T. Stead, editor of the *American Review of Reviews,*
        "Coxeyism: A Character Sketch," 1894

It seemed almost impossible [in 1894] to contrive any device by which this
grim and worn-out topic could be served up in good salable newspaper articles. But Coxey did the trick. Coxey compelled all the newspapers of the
continent to devote from a column to six a day to reporting Coxeyism, that
is to say, with echoing the inarticulate clamor for work for the workless.
That was a great achievement. To have accomplished it shows that Coxey is
not without genius. No millionaire in all America could, without ruining
himself, have secured as much space for advertising his wares as Coxey commanded without the expenditure of a red cent by the unique device of his
petition in boots.

Source 13 Donald L. McMurry, *Coxey's Army: The Story of the Industrial
        Army Movement of 1894,* 1929

The armies could hardly have been moved about and fed as they were without
a great deal of popular sympathy in their favor, but this was not the only thing
that assisted them in their travels. . . . An Army was a source of embarrassment
to the locality in which it camped. It was expensive to feed it, but humanity
and local pride forbade that it should be allowed to starve. An Army was a
potential danger, especially if starved or thwarted into desperation. Workingmen saw possible competition in a labor market already sadly overstocked, and
property owners feared depredations. Thus, sympathy, where there was any, was
reinforced by interest in the army's departure, and the expedient course was to
feed it and speed it on its way, even if transportation had to be paid. Business
men, labor organizations, Populist farmers, and railroads, impelled by various
mixtures of philanthropy, fear, and discretion, played their parts in this game
of "passing the buck," and the armies made the most of it. Some of their leaders
were very clever men. . . .

There was found in the men of the industrial armies certain apparently
contradictory qualities . . . —a superficial lawlessness, combined with deep-
seated capacity for self-government and respect for certain fundamentals of law
and order. Most of them were frontiersmen or the descendants of frontiersmen.
They were self-reliant, and they knew what they wanted, and they adapted
available means to their ends without being much embarrassed by consideration
for the finer points of the law. When they wanted to go somewhere on a mission
that they thought was worth while, when trains were available and they thought
the railroads ought to carry them (the railroads represented plutocratic monopoly, anyway), they took the trains. . . . Even when this was done without the
consent of the owners, the trains might be considered borrowed rather than
stolen. They seldom took anything else, except, occasionally, food when they
were starving. They followed leaders who were able to obtain their respect . . . ,
and who offered to help their followers obtain the desired ends. They submitted
to a discipline which, in the best organized of the armies, at least, was a marvel
to those who observed it.

Source 14 Russel B. Nye, *A Baker's Dozen: Thirteen Unusual Americans,* 1956

[O]n May 18, 1951, Jacob Coxey died quietly at his Massillon home, surrounded by his pamphlets, a half-completed letter on his desk.

With Coxey died the great nineteenth-century American radical tradition of **Ignatius Donnelly**, of **James Weaver**, of **Pitchfork Ben Tillman** [see chapter 8, Source 5], **Sockless Jerry Simpson**, and the remainder of the hell-raising school of American politics. It had its share of crackpots and fanatics, but it was, for all that, a lively, native, bumptious American thing that meant a man could think what he wished, say what he pleased, and stand up to be counted. Coxey, like his generation of radicals, was a doggedly purposeful man, willing to be laughed at, but he was earnest, selfless, utterly devoted to his cause.

With his anachronistic stiff collar suggesting an illustration out of Dickens and his private bug buzzing in his brain, Jacob Coxey became a sort of comic figure in his own lifetime. It was easy to find him amusing. The phrase "Coxey's Army" generated smiles for two generations, and historians (when they mentioned him at all) tended to classify him among the crackpots and reformers. Yet there was in the man something that commanded respect, a sincerity and dignity that made the title of "General," once bestowed in amusement, appropriate and fitting. He died fighting the same battle, he firmly believed, that his idols Jefferson and Jackson had fought before him, for mankind's security, contentment, and plenty. "Nobody is going to be discontented or unhappy," he wrote in 1946, "when I win." He did not win, but General Coxey never surrendered.

Source 15 Richard Hofstadter, William Miller, Daniel Aaron, Winthrop Jordan, and Leon F. Litwack, *The United States,* 1976

As the depression [which began in 1893] deepened, the public mood grew ever more sullen. Thousands of unemployed roamed the country, sometimes in large gangs. Since the government offered no relief to the destitute, agitators proposed schemes of their own. In 1894, Jacob S. Coxey, of Massillon, Ohio, a rich man himself, convinced frightened property holders that a revolution had actually begun. Coxey proposed that Congress authorize a half-billion-dollar public works program. To dramatize his plan, he organized a march on Washington. "We will send a petition to Washington with boots on," he announced. Soon "armies" all over the country were heading for the national capital. Not all the marchers made it: 18-year-old Jack London, for example, who had joined the Reno Industrial Army, landed in the Niagara Falls jail, charged with being a common vagrant; 30 days later, even more confirmed in his radicalism, he emerged from the Erie County penitentiary and hopped a train back to California. Of the thousands who had initially formed the march, only Coxey's Army of about 300 men managed to reach Washington, D.C. Police speedily dispersed them. . . . Nevertheless, Coxey's march helped make unemployment a well-aired national issue.

Source 16 Carlos A. Schwantes, *Coxey's Army: An American Odyssey,* 1985

In the depression year of 1894 there arose suddenly out of the ranks of America's unemployed a grass-roots movement known popularly as Coxey's Army. For six or seven weeks it captured the attention of the nation. Other protesters had marched on local institutions of government . . . but never before on the nation's capital, unless Robert E. Lee's Army of Northern Virginia so qualified. Indeed, in the minds of many observers, the Coxey movement did reawaken unpleasant memories of Civil War strife, for not since the days of Lincoln had security about the White House and on Capitol Hill been so strict. . . .

In a way, the Coxey movement represented a double-barreled assault on the fundamental beliefs of Americans. Not only did it seek to educate them into accepting a certain amount of federal responsibility for the economic health of the nation; but the very existence of the crusade—and especially its prominence in the West—undermined the popular belief that the fertile agricultural lands of the frontier represented America's most practical form of social security and a wise alternative to governmental paternalism.

The numerous cases of train piracy in Montana, Oregon, and other parts of the West by armies of unemployed men helped to direct attention to the dwindling supply of free land in America. What did it mean when the nation's supposedly inexhaustible supply of fertile, easily obtainable farmland ran out? A Seattle newspaper succinctly expressed the popular belief when it editorialized in early 1894, "All social problems solve themselves in the presence of a bound-less expanse of vacant fertile land." Free land was for Americans their God-given inheritance, distinguishing them from the less richly endowed inhabitants of Old World nations. Thus they had a right to wonder whether the numerous episodes of train stealing by the unemployed signalled the end of the free-land era. Was the unnerving spectacle of lawlessness a portent of troubled times to come? Many observers thought so. . . .

Especially during periods of hard times, the West had long been seen as having a special quality, its free land mythologized into a kind of safety valve relieving the discontent that arose among dwellers in the nation's densely popu-lated industrial neighborhoods. Free land was thereby supposed to prevent the kind of massive social disruptions that Americans chauvinistically identified with European social and economic systems.

But historians writing in more recent times have challenged the mythology of the free-land safety valve; some have used statistics to show that more people moved from the country to the city during periods of economic distress than the other way around. The fact remains that a good many nineteenth-century Americans believed in the free-land safety valve and formulated their outlooks and actions accordingly. People, in other words, responded to perceptions of reality as if they were dealing with reality itself. And so long as even a handful of people escaped the industrial city for the free lands of the West, the dream seemed real enough. . . .

[U]ltimately the mythology of the free-land safety valve proved to be a poor tool to deal with massive unemployment in an urban industrial society. But it took the hard times of the 1890s and such disorders as the Coxey move-ment and the Pullman strike to hasten the process of exploding the myth. Only when people discarded the environmental approach to unemployment were they able to recognize that the state might deal directly with the problem without using free land as an intermediary. Eventually the idea voiced by the Coxey crusaders—that the federal government should provide them with public-works jobs—found its way onto the nation's political agenda and was finally accepted by the president and Congress during the hard times of the 1930s. . . . In short, the modern welfare state was a response by government to some of the social and economic problems that the free-land safety valve once supposedly addressed.

Although Coxey's proposal for noninterest-bearing bonds was never accepted by Congress, the public-works principle of his crusade was embodied in the New Deal's relief and recovery programs that put the nation's unemployed to work building roads, dams, and a host of other projects during the Great Depression of the 1930s. In the Employment Act of 1946, the federal government finally assumed legal responsibility for full employment.

Historian Henry Steele Commager described the 1890s as a watershed. On one side lay an America predominantly agricultural, self-contained, and self-reliant. On the other side lay modern America, urban and industrial. . . . The Coxey movement straddled that great divide. Its origin was a popular belief in the continued viability of grass-roots democracy, and from its many opponents it elicited condemnations firmly grounded in the self-reliant, agrarian tradition of the older America. To many supporters, on the other hand, Coxeyism also underscored the economic and political problems confronting modern America and offered a reasonable solution to one of the worst of these—unemployment. In common with the Populist revolt, Coxeyism was a democratic movement that called into question the underlying values of the new industrial society.

Source 17 John A. Garraty and Robert A. McCaughey, *The American Nation: A History of the United States,* 1987

During 1894 and 1895, while the nation floundered in the worst depression it had ever experienced, a series of events further undermined public confidence. In the spring of 1894 an "army" of unemployed led by Jacob S. Coxey, an eccentric Ohio businessman, marched on Washington to demand relief. . . . When Coxey's group of demonstrators . . . reached Washington, he and two other leaders were arrested for trespassing on the grounds of the Capitol. Their followers were dispersed by club-wielding policemen. This callous treatment convinced many Americans that the government had little interest in the suffering of the people, an opinion strengthened when Cleveland, in July 1894, used federal troops to crush the Pullman Strike.

Source 18 John L. Thomas, *The Great Republic: A History of the American People,* 1992

7.3 Manuscripts in the Labadie Collection

The American economy hit bottom in 1894. Five hundred banks closed their doors, 16,000 business firms collapsed, and unemployment reached nearly 20 percent. New issues on the New York Stock Exchange plummeted from $100 million to $37 million, and 2.5 million jobless workers tramped winter streets looking for work. Municipal governments and private charity organizations could not cope with the large numbers of destitute men who wandered aimlessly from city to city, finding factory gates closed and long lines at soup kitchens. Not since the dark days of the Civil War had the country seemed so threatened. . . .

The specter of masses of starving men marching on the nation's cities to plunder and pillage in an uprising of the dispossessed turned into farce in the spring of 1894 with the arrival in Washington of Coxey's Army. . . . The Cleveland administration's reaction to this living petition was a measure of its fear of mass upheaval: Coxey's followers were dispersed and their leader jailed on a technicality, while rumors of revolution swept through the city.

 ## Questioning the Past

1. On the evening before his army marched into Washington, Jacob Coxey met with Speaker of the House Crisp to obtain permission to speak on the Capitol steps on behalf of "millions of unemployed and starving people." The Speaker refused to give him a permit. "How are you the representatives of the people?" the Speaker asked Coxey. "By what authority do you undertake to represent the 65,000,000 people of this country? The people's representatives are the 356 Representatives elected to Congress and vested with authority under the provisions of our government." Coxey replied that Congress was not truly representative of the people. "Then," Speaker Crisp responded, "your remedy is at the ballot box. Under our system of government, the government itself is the people, subject to frequent changes when the people indicate at the ballot box that they want a change. You appear to be a self-constituted representative of the people." Coxey replied that there was an immediate need for relief and the ballot box would be too slow. Speaker Crisp next labeled Coxey's tactic an attempt to intimidate Congress and reiterated his decision to deny the permit. Was the Speaker's position valid? Did Coxey have a right to speak? Were Coxey's methods of trying to influence government policy legitimate or illegitimate?

2. Why did the America of 1894 reject Coxey's plans to help the unemployed? Present arguments for and against Coxey's proposals. Which arguments are the stronger?

3. What was the significance and the impact of Coxey's march on Washington?

4. Does an examination of the sources illustrate that time has altered opinion on Coxey and his mission? Explain.

5. It has been argued that implicit in the "inalienable rights" to "life, liberty, and the pursuit of happiness" is the right to a job. Should government be the employer of last resort? Should the American nation ensure a job for everyone willing and able to work? Present both sides of the issue.

Chapter **8**

The Race Question

Booker T. Washington Suggests a Compromise

September 18, 1895

Having decided that African Americans were no longer to be slaves, white America was slow to accept the idea that African Americans were to be as free they themselves were. In the years following the Civil War there was great variation from place to place in the degree of liberty and opportunity accorded the freed slaves and their descendants. By the 1890s, however, a uniform pattern of separation of the races was setting in. Some Americans, both blacks and whites, resisted this development. Many welcomed it. Still others tried to live with it.

The Civil War Amendments to the Constitution—Thirteenth, Fourteenth, and Fifteenth—had proclaimed the slaves free, guaranteed them the equal protection of the law, and promised that their color would not be deemed a proper reason to deny them the vote. It became quickly clear that these amendments were more a goal than a guarantee. Though some progress was made toward the implementation of these amendments during the period of Reconstruction, whatever momentum had been generated was lost when the last federal troops were withdrawn from the South in 1876 and the Democratic Party again picked up the reins of southern politics.

❧ *First Impressions*

Separate but Equal

8.1 Internet Modern History Sourcebook: Modern Social Movements

As the weight of racial segregation pressed ever more heavily upon African Americans, America's leaders, black and white, grappled with the question of what might be the proper relationship between the country's white majority and its largest racial minority, and what might be done to establish this relationship. In a speech to the Atlanta Exposition in 1895, Tuskegee Institute president Booker T. Washington suggested what came to be called the "Atlanta Compromise."

Source 1 Booker T. Washington, "The Atlanta Exposition Address," September 18, 1895

One-third of the population of the South is of the Negro race. No enterprise seeking the material, civil, or moral welfare of this section can disregard this element of our population and reach the highest success. . . .

Ignorant and inexperienced, it is not strange that in the first years of our new life we began at the top instead of at the bottom; that a seat in Congress or the state legislature was more sought than real estate or industrial skill; that the political convention or stump speaking had more attractions than starting a dairy farm or truck garden.

A ship lost at sea for many days suddenly sighted a friendly vessel. From the mast of the unfortunate vessel was seen a signal, "Water, water; we die of thirst!" The answer from the friendly vessel came back, "Cast down your bucket where you are." A second time the signal, "Water, water; send us water!" ran up from the distressed vessel, and was answered, "Cast down your bucket where you are." And a third and fourth signal for water was answered, "Cast down your bucket where you are." The captain of the distressed vessel, at last heeding the injunction, cast down his bucket, and it was full of fresh, sparkling water from the mouth of the Amazon River. To those of my race who depend on bettering their condition in a foreign land or who underestimate the importance of cultivating friendly relations with the Southern white man, who is their next-door neighbour, I would say: "Cast down your bucket where you are"—cast it down in making friends in every manly way of the people of all races by whom we are surrounded.

Cast it down in agriculture, mechanics, in commerce, in domestic service, and in the professions. . . . Our greatest danger is that in the leap from slavery to freedom we may overlook the fact that the masses of us are to live by the productions of our own hands, and fail to keep in mind that we shall prosper in proportion as we learn to dignify and glorify common labour and put brains and skill into the common occupations of life; shall prosper in proportion as we learn to draw the line between the superficial and the substantial, the ornamental gewgaws of life and the useful. No race can prosper till it learns that there is as much dignity in tilling a field as in writing a poem. It is at the bottom of life we must begin, and not at the top. Nor should we permit our grievances to overshadow our opportunities.

To those of the white race who look to the incoming of those of foreign birth and strange tongue and habits for the prosperity of the South, were I permitted I would repeat what I say to my own race, "Cast down your bucket where you are." Cast it down among the eight millions of Negroes whose habits you know, whose fidelity and love you have tested in days when to have proved treacherous meant the ruin of your firesides. Cast down your bucket among these people who have, without strikes and labor wars, tilled your fields, cleared your forests, builded your railroads and cities, and brought forth treasures from the bowels of the earth. . . . Casting down your bucket among my people, helping and encouraging them as you are doing on these grounds, and to education of head, hand, and heart, you will find that they will buy your surplus land, make blossom the waste places in your fields, and run your factories. While doing this, you can be sure in the future,

8.2 Booker T. Washington National Monument Homepage

as in the past, that you and your families will be surrounded by the most patient, faithful, law-abiding, and unresentful people that the world has seen. As we have proved our loyalty to you in the past, in nursing your children, watching by the sick-bed of your mothers and fathers, and often following them with tear-dimmed eyes to their graves, so in the future, in our humble way, we shall stand by you with a devotion that no foreigner can approach, ready to lay down our lives, if need be, in defense of yours, interlacing our industrial, commercial, civil, and religious life with yours in a way that shall make the interests of both races one. In all things that are purely social we can be as separate as the fingers, yet one as the hand in all things essential to mutual progress.

There is no defence or security for any of us except in the highest intelligence and development of all. If anywhere there are efforts tending to curtail the fullest development of the Negro, let these efforts be turned into stimulating, encouraging, and making him the most useful and intelligent citizen. Effort or means so invested will pay a thousand per cent interest. These efforts will be twice blessed—"blessing him that gives and him that takes."

There is no escape through law of man or God from the inevitable:

> The laws of changeless justice bind
> Oppressor with oppressed;
> And close as sin and suffering joined
> We march to fate abreast.

Nearly sixteen millions of hands will aid you in pulling the load upward, or they will pull against you the load downward. We shall constitute one-third and more of the ignorance and crime of the South, or one-third its intelligence and progress; we shall contribute one-third to the business and industrial prosperity of the South, or we shall prove a veritable body of death, stagnating, depressing, retarding every effort to advance the body politic. . . .

The wisest among my race understand that the agitation of questions of social equality is the extremest folly, and that progress in the enjoyment of all the privileges that will come to us must be the result of severe and constant struggle rather than of artificial forcing. No race that has anything to contribute to the markets of the world is long in any degree ostracized. It is important and right that all privileges of the law be ours, but it is vastly more important that we be prepared for the exercises of these privileges. The opportunity to earn a dollar in a factory just now is worth infinitely more than the opportunity to spend a dollar in an opera-house.

In conclusion, . . . I pledge that in your effort to work out the great and intricate problem which God has laid at the doors of the South, you shall have at all times the patient, sympathetic help of my race; only let this be constantly in mind, that, . . . from the product of field, of forest, of mine, of factory, letters, and art, much good will come, yet far above and beyond material benefits will be that higher good, that, let us pray God, will come, in a blotting out of sectional differences and racial animosities and suspicions, in a determination to administer absolute justice, in a willing obedience among all classes to the mandates of law. This, this, coupled with our material prosperity, will bring into our beloved South a new heaven and a new earth.

Separate Lives and Subservient Roles

At the time Washington offered his suggestion for establishing a relationship between the races, the situation of African Americans was bad and deteriorating. Across the nation, blacks were being forced into lives segregated from the majority of their countrymen. They were restrained by law and custom from attaining their full potential intellectually and economically. They were denied the educational opportunities presented to white Americans. Their choice in life was between accepting a role of subservience in society or being accorded no role at all. Lynching was commonplace—a socially tolerated means of dealing with blacks who did not show proper deference to their white neighbors.

During the decade of the 1890s, state governments systematically stripped African Americans of their right to vote and hold political office. Once black citizens had lost all vestiges of political power, government was unwilling to extend the protection of the law to this weak minority. Indeed, the Supreme Court gave the stamp of constitutional legitimacy to racial segregation when the case of a citizen named Plessy came before it. By the turn of the century, virtually every feature of life was regulated by the **Jim Crow** laws. There were separate schools, waiting rooms, washrooms, water fountains, park benches, even separate Bibles in southern courtrooms to prevent a holy book touched by one race from being touched by the other. Though both black and white citizens paid taxes, blacks were barred from entering federal government offices used by white people, beginning in the administration of Woodrow Wilson. A nation that sought to make the world safe for democracy had rendered democracy tenuous at home.

8.3 The Advent of Modern America (1805–1920)

Source 2 Supreme Court justice Henry B. Brown, majority opinion, *Plessy v. Ferguson,* 1896

The case turns upon the constitutionality of an act of the General Assembly of the State of Louisiana, passed in 1890, providing for separate railway carriages for the white and colored races. . . .

The information filed in the criminal District Court charged in substance that Plessy, being a passenger between two stations within the State of Louisiana, was assigned by officers of the company to the coach used for the race to which he belonged, but he insisted upon going into a coach used by the race to which he did not belong . . . , and was ordered by the conductor to vacate said coach and take a seat in another assigned to people of the colored race, and having refused to comply with such demand he was forcibly ejected with the aid of a police officer, and imprisoned in the parish jail to answer a charge of having violated the above act.

The constitutionality of this act is attacked upon the ground that it conflicts both with the Thirteenth Amendment of the Constitution, abolishing slavery, and the Fourteenth Amendment. . . .

That it does not conflict with the Thirteenth Amendment . . . is too clear for argument. A statute which implies merely a legal distinction between the white and colored races—a distinction which is founded in the color of the two races, and which must always exist so long as the white men are distinguished from the other race by color—has no tendency to destroy the legal equality of the two races, or re-establish a state of involuntary servitude. . . .

The object of the [Fourteenth] amendment was undoubtedly to enforce the absolute equality of the two races before the law, but in the nature of things it could not have been intended to abolish distinctions based upon color, or to enforce social, as distinguished from political, equality, or a commingling of the two races on terms unsatisfactory to either. Laws permitting, and even requiring, their separation in places where they are liable to be brought into contact do not necessarily imply the inferiority of either race to the other. . . .

So far, then, as a conflict with the Fourteenth Amendment is concerned, the case reduces itself to the question whether the statute of Louisiana is a reasonable regulation, and with respect to this there must necessarily be a large discretion on the part of the legislature. In determining the question of reasonableness it is at liberty to act with reference to the established usages, customs and traditions of the people, and with a view to the promotion of their comfort, and the preservation of the public peace and good order. Gauged by this standard, we cannot say that a law which authorizes or even requires the separation of the two races is unreasonable. . . .

We consider the underlying fallacy of the plaintiff's argument to consist in the assumption that the enforced separation of the two races stamps the colored race with a badge of inferiority. If this be so, it is not by reason of anything found in the act, but solely because the colored race chooses to put that construction upon it. . . . The argument also assumes that social prejudices may be overcome by legislation, and that equal rights cannot be secured to the negro except by an enforced commingling of the two races. We cannot accept this proposition. If the two races are to meet upon terms of social equality, it must be the result of natural affinities, a mutual appreciation of each other's merits and a voluntary consent of individuals. . . . Legislation is powerless to eradicate racial instincts or to abolish distinctions based upon physical differences, and the attempt to do so can only result in accentuating the difficulties of the present situation. If the civil and political rights of both races be equal one cannot be inferior to the other civilly or politically. If one race be inferior to the other socially, the Constitution of the United States cannot put them upon the same plane.

Source 3   Justice John M. Harlan, dissenting opinion, *Plessy v. Ferguson,* 1896

In respect of civil rights, common to all citizens, the Constitution of the United States does not, I think, permit any public authority to know the race of those entitled to be protected in the enjoyment of such rights. . . . If a white man and a black man choose to occupy the same public conveyance on a public highway, it is their right to do so, and no government, proceeding alone on the grounds of race, can prevent it without infringing the personal liberty of each. . . . The white race deems itself to be the dominant race in this country. And so it is, in prestige, in achievements, in education, in wealth and in power. So, I doubt not, it will continue to be for all time, if it remains true to its great heritage and holds fast to the principles of constitutional liberty. But in view of the

Constitution, in the eye of the law, there is in this country no superior, dominant, ruling class of citizens. There is no caste here. The Constitution is color-blind, and neither knows nor tolerates classes among citizens. In respect of civil rights, all citizens are equal before the law. The humblest is the peer of the most powerful. The law regards man as man, and takes no account of his surroundings or of his color when his civil rights as guaranteed by the supreme law of the land are involved. It is, therefore, to be regretted that this high tribunal, the final expositor of the fundamental law of the land, has reached the conclusion that it is competent for a State to regulate the enjoyment by citizens of their civil rights solely on the basis of race.

 ## *Second Thoughts*
Separate, but Inseparable

> The struggle to establish a relationship between the races consistent with America's libertarian and egalitarian ideals has continued over the course of the twentieth century. Though some members of both races have called from time to time for a total severance of the connections between white and black Americans, most have sought to find some basis for a working relationship. For nearly four centuries the two races have lived and worked together in the New World. Neither race has any greater right than the other to call itself American. Each has an indisputable claim to enjoy those rights that Jefferson termed inalienable.

Source 4   W. E. B. Du Bois, *The Souls of Black Folks,* 1903

Easily the most striking thing in the history of the American Negro since 1876 is the ascendancy of Mr. Booker T. Washington. It began at a time when war memories and ideals were rapidly passing; a day of astonishing commercial development was dawning; a sense of doubt and hesitation overtook the freedmen's sons—then it was that his leading began. Mr. Washington came, with a single definite programme, at the psychological moment when the nation was a little ashamed of having bestowed so much sentiment on Negroes, and was concentrating its energies on Dollars. His programme of industrial education, conciliation of the South, and submission and silence as to civil and political rights, was not wholly original; the Free Negroes from 1830 up to wartime had striven to build industrial schools . . . and others had sought a way of honorable alliance with the best of the Southerners. But Mr. Washington first indissolubly linked these two things. . . .

It startled the nation to hear a Negro advocating such a programme after many decades of bitter complaint; it startled and won the applause of the South, it interested and won the admiration of the North; and after a confused murmur of protest, it silenced if it did not convert the Negroes themselves.

To gain the sympathy and cooperation of the various elements comprising the white South was Mr. Washington's first task; and this . . . seemed, for a black man, well-nigh impossible. And yet . . . it was done in the words spoken at Atlanta: "In all things purely social we can be as separate as the five fingers, and yet one as the hand in all things essential to mutual progress." This "Atlanta Compromise" is by all odds the most notable thing in Mr. Washington's career. The South interpreted it in different ways: the radicals received it as a complete surrender of the demand for civil and political equality; the conservatives, as a generously conceived working basis for mutual understanding. So both approved it, and to-day its author is certainly the most distinguished Southerner since Jefferson Davis, and the one with the largest personal following. . . .

Mr. Washington represents in Negro thought the old attitude of adjustment and submission; but adjustment at such a peculiar time as to make his programme unique. This is an age of unusual economic development, and Mr. Washington's programme naturally takes an economic cast, becoming a gospel of Work and Money to such an extent as apparently almost completely to overshadow the higher aims of life. Moreover, this is an age when the more advanced races are coming in closer contact with the less developed races, and the race-feeling is therefore intensified; and Mr. Washington's programme practically accepts the alleged inferiority of the Negro races. Again, in our own land, the reaction from the sentiment of war time has given impetus to race-prejudice against Negroes, and Mr. Washington withdraws many of the high demands of Negroes as men and American citizens. In other periods of intensified prejudice all the Negro's tendency to self-assertion has been called forth; at this period a policy of submission is advocated. In the history of nearly all other races and peoples the doctrine preached at such crises has been that manly self-respect is worth more than lands and houses, and that a people who voluntarily surrender such respect, or cease striving for it, are not worth civilizing.

In answer to this, it has been claimed that the Negro can survive only through submission. Mr. Washington distinctly asks that black people give up, at least for the present, three things:

First, political power,
Second, insistence of civil rights,
Third, higher education of Negro youth—

and concentrate all their energies on industrial education, and accumulation of wealth, and the conciliation of the South. This policy has been . . . triumphant for perhaps ten years. As a result of this tender of the palm-branch, what has been the return? In these years there have occurred:

1. The disenfranchisement of the Negro.
2. The legal creation of a distinct status of civil inferiority for the Negro.
3. The steady withdrawal of aid from institutions for the higher training of the Negro.

These movements are not, to be sure, direct results of Mr. Washington's teachings; but his propaganda has, without a shadow of doubt, helped their speedier accomplishment. The question then comes: Is it possible, and probable, that nine millions of men can make effective progress in economic lines if they are deprived of political rights, made a servile caste, and allowed only the most meagre chance for developing their exceptional men? If history and reason give any distinct answer to these questions, it is an emphatic *No*. And Mr. Washington thus faces the triple paradox of his career:

1. He is striving nobly to make Negro artisans business men and property-owners; but it is utterly impossible, under modern competitive methods, for workingmen and property-owners to defend their rights and exist without the right of suffrage.
2. He insists on thrift and self-respect, but at the same time counsels a silent submission to civic inferiority such as is bound to sap the manhood of any race in the long run.
3. He advocates common-school and industrial training, and depreciates institutions of higher learning; but neither the Negro common-schools, nor Tuskegee itself, could remain open a day were it not for teachers trained in Negro colleges, or trained by their graduates.

This triple paradox in Mr. Washington's position is the object of criticism by two classes of colored Americans. One class is spiritually descended from **Toussaint the Saviour**, through **Gabriel**, **Vesey**, and **Turner**; and they represent the attitude of revolt and revenge; they hate the white South blindly and distrust the white race generally, and so far as they agree on definite action, think that the Negro's only hope lies in emigration beyond the borders of the United States. And yet, by the irony of fate, nothing has more effectually made this programme seem hopeless than the recent course of the United States toward weaker and darker peoples in the West Indies, Hawaii, and the Philippines—for where in the world may we go and be safe from lying and brute force?

The other class of Negroes who cannot agree with Mr. Washington has hitherto said little aloud. They deprecate the sight of scattered counsels, of internal disagreement; and especially they dislike making their just criticism of a useful and earnest man an excuse for a general discharge of venom from small-minded opponents. Nevertheless, the questions involved are so fundamental and serious that it is difficult to see how . . . this group . . . can much longer be silent. Such men feel in conscience bound to ask of this nation three things:

1. The right to vote.
2. Civic equality.
3. The education of youth according to ability.

They acknowledge Mr. Washington's invaluable services in counseling patience and courtesy in such demands; . . . they know that the low social level of the mass of the race is responsible for much discrimination against it, but they also know, and the nation knows, that relentless color prejudice is more often a cause than a result of the Negro's degradation. . . .

[Washington's] doctrine has tended to make the whites, North and South, shift the burden of the Negro problem to the Negro's shoulders and stand aside as critical and rather pessimistic spectators; when in fact the burden belongs to the nation, and the hands of none of us are clean if we bend not our energies to righting these great wrongs. . . .

So far as Mr. Washington preaches Thrift, Patience, and Industrial Training for the masses, we must hold up his hands and strive with him, rejoicing in his honors and glorying in the strength of this Joshua called of God and of man to lead the headless host. But so far as Mr. Washington apologizes for injustice, North or South, does not rightly value the privilege and duty of voting, belittles the emasculating effects of caste distinctions, and opposes the higher training and ambitions of our brighter minds—so far as he, the South, or the Nation, does this—we must unceasingly and firmly oppose them.

Source 5   Senator "Pitchfork" Ben Tillman of South Carolina, speech to the Senate, January 21, 1907

It was 1876, thirty years ago, and the people of South Carolina had been living under negro rule for eight years. There was a condition bordering on anarchy. Misrule, robbery, and murder were holding high carnival. The people's substance was being stolen, and there was no incentive to labor. Our legislature was composed of a majority of negroes, most of whom could neither read nor write. They were the easy dupes and tools of as dirty a band of vampires and robbers as ever preyed upon a prostrate people. . . . We felt the very foundations of our civilization crumbling beneath our feet, that we were sure to be engulfed by the black flood of barbarians who were surrounding us and had been put over us by the Army under the reconstruction acts. The sun of hope had disappeared behind a cloud of gloom and despair, and a condition had arisen such as has never been the lot of white men at any time in the history of the world to endure. Life ceased to be worth having on the terms under which we were living, and in desperation we determined to take the government away from the negroes.

We reorganized the Democratic party with one plank, and only one plank, namely, that "this is a white man's country and white men must govern it." Under that banner we went to battle. . . .

Look at our environment in the South, surrounded, and in a very large number of counties and in two States outnumbered, by the negroes—engulfed, as it were, in a black flood of semi-barbarians. Our farmers, living in segregated farmhouses, more or less scattered through the country, have negroes on every hand. For forty years these have been taught the damnable heresy of equality with the white man, made the puppet of scheming politicians, the instrument for the furtherance of political ambitions. Some of them have just enough education to be able to read, but not always to understand what they read. Their minds are those of children, while they have the passions and strength of men.

Source 6   William English Walling, *Independent*, Springfield, Illinois, September 3, 1908

[Walling, a white liberal, visited Springfield during a riot by whites that led to the lynchings of two African Americans, the mob murder of six, and the forced evacuation of more than 2,000 black residents from Lincoln's hometown. His call for a new "abolitionist" style crusade helped coalesce activists into founding the National Association for the Advancement of Colored People.]

On arriving in the town I found that the rioting had been continued thruout the night and was even feared for the coming evening, in spite of the presence of nearly the whole militia of the State. . . .

We at once discovered, to our amazement, that Springfield had no shame. She stood for the action of the mob. She hoped the rest of the negroes might flee. She threatened that the movement to drive them out would continue. I do not speak of the leading citizens, but of the masses of the people, of workingmen in the shops, the storekeepers in the stores, the drivers, the men on the street. . . . The *Illinois State Journal* of Springfield exprest the prevailing feeling even on its editorial page:

"While all good citizens deplore the consequences of this outburst of the mob spirit, many even of these consider the outburst was *inevitable,* at some time, from existing conditions, needing only an overt act . . . to bring it from latent existence into active operation. The implication is clear that conditions, not the populace, were to blame and that many good citizens could find no other remedy than that applied by the mob. It was not the fact of the whites' hatred toward the negroes, but of the negroes' own misconduct, general inferiority or unfitness for free institutions that were at fault."

On Sunday, August 16th [1908], the day after the second lynching, a leading white minister recommended the Southern disfranchisement scheme as a remedy for *negro* (!) lawlessness. . . . Besides suggestions in high places of the negro's brutality, criminality and unfitness for the ballot we heard in lower ranks all the opinions that pervade the South—that the negro does not need much education, that his present education has been a mistake, that whites cannot live in the same community with negroes except where the latter have been taught their inferiority, that lynching is the only way to teach them. . . .

Either the spirit of the abolitionists, of Lincoln and Lovejoy, must be revived and we must come to treat the negro on a plane of absolute political and social equality, or [Mississippi Senator James] Vardaman and Tillman will soon have transferred the race war to the North.

Already Vardaman boasts "that such sad experiences as Springfield is undergoing will doubtless cause the people of the North to look with more toleration upon the methods employed by the Southern people."

The day these methods become general in the North every hope of political democracy will be dead, other weaker races and classes will be persecuted in the North as in the South, public education will undergo an eclipse, and American civilization will await either a rapid degeneration or another profounder and more revolutionary civil war, which will obliterate not only the remains of slavery but all the other obstacles to a free democratic evolution that have grown up in its wake.

Yet who realizes the seriousness of the situation, and what large and powerful body of citizens is ready to come to their aid?

Source 7 Senator James K. Vardaman of Mississippi, speech to the Senate, February 6, 1914

God Almighty never intended that the negro should share with the white man in the government of this country; and you can not improve upon the plans of God Almighty or defeat His purposes, either, by legislative enactments. Do not forget that. It matters not what I may say or others may think; it matters not what constitutions may contain or statutes provide, wherever the negro is in sufficient numbers to imperil the white man's civilization or question the white man's supremacy the white man is going to find some way around the difficulty. And that is just as true in the North as it is in the South. You need not deceive yourselves about that. The feeling against the negro in Illinois when he gets in the white man's way is quite as strong, more bitter, less regardful of the negro's feelings and conditions than it is in Mississippi. . . .

Mr. President, I am not the negro's enemy. I know what is best for him. I think I can measure his productive capacity. I know the influences that move him. I am familiar with the currents of passion which sweep through his savage blood. I understand his hates, his jealousies, and his attachments. In a word, I think I know him as he really is. And knowing him, I believe I know what is best for him. You can not measure the negro by the standard you would measure accurately the white man. He is different from the white man physically, morally, and mentally. The pure-blooded negro is without gratitude. He does not harbor revenge. He is not immoral—he is unmoral. I have never known one who ever felt the guilt of sin, the goading of an outraged conscience, or the binding force of a moral obligation. The pure-blooded negro reaches mental maturity soon after he passes the period of puberty. The cranial sutures become ossified by the time he reaches 20 years of age, and it is not uncommon to find one who reads fluently at 15 years of age not to know a letter in the book at the age of 25 or 30. . . .

The white man and the negro of the South are not enemies. They may be made so if you continue to insist on trying to bring them into abnormal relationship. The relations that existed between them before and immediately succeeding the war was akin to that of father and son. . . . The negroes in Mississippi know that I am not their enemy. I would not permit them to vote, but I would protect them in the enjoyment of their life, liberty, and the pursuit of happiness and the product of their toil. And if the white people of the South are permitted to proceed along proper rational lines, knowing and recognizing the negro's inferiority, desiring, however, his betterment . . . , very much more progress will be made for the negro's uplifting . . . than will be made if it shall be directed by men who do not know any more about it personally than I do about the political economy of the planet Mars.

Source 8 W. E. B. Du Bois, "The Immediate Program of the American Negro," *The Crisis*, April 1915

The American Negro demands equality—political equality, industrial equality and social equality; and he is never going to rest satisfied with anything less. He demands this in no spirit of **braggadocio** and with no obsequious envy of others, but as an absolute measure of self-defense and the only one that will assure to the darker races their ultimate survival on earth. . . .

The practical steps to this are clear. *First* we must fight obstructions; by continual and increasing effort we must first make American courts either build up a body of decisions which will protect the plain legal rights of American citizens or else make them tear down the civil and political rights of all citizens in order to oppress a few. Either result will bring justice in the end. It is lots of fun and most ingenious just now for courts to twist law so as to say I may not live here or vote there, or marry the woman who wishes to marry me. But when to-morrow these decisions throttle all freedom and overthrow the foundation of democracy and decency, there is going to be some judicial house cleaning.

We must *secondly* seek in legislature and Congress remedial legislation; national aid to public school education, the removal of all legal discriminations based simply on race and color. . . .

Third the human contact of human beings must be increased; the policy which brings into sympathetic touch and understanding, men and women, rich and poor, capitalist and laborer, Asiatic and European, must bring into closer contact and mutual knowledge the white and black people of this land. It is the most frightful indictment of a country which dares to call itself civilized that it has allowed itself to drift into a state of ignorance where ten million people are coming to believe that all white people are liars and thieves, and the whites in turn to believe that the chief industry of Negroes is raping white women.

Fourth only the publication of the truth repeatedly and incisively and un-compromisingly can secure that change in public opinion which will correct these awful lies. . . .

In education . . . we must watch with grave suspicion the attempt of those who, under the guise of vocational training, would fasten ignorance and menial service on the Negro for another generation. Our children must not in large numbers, be forced into the servant class; for menial service is still, in the main, little more than an antiquated survival of impossible conditions. . . . It is our duty then, not drastically but persistently, to seek out colored children of ability and genius to open up to them broader, industrial opportunity and above all, to find that Talented Tenth and encourage it by the best and most exhaustive training in order to supply the Negro race and the world with leaders, thinkers and artists.

Source 9   Speech of Marcus Garvey, leader of the Universal Negro
             Improvement Association, September 21, 1921

Dr. Du Bois says . . . "that Negroes must settle down where they are, in white communities, and work out their destiny there." Do you know what that means? It means that Dr. Du Bois tells us to remain here until we get killed [applause], remain here until we are ready to be killed! Because, according to the attitude of those white men who represent the Ku Klux Klan, America now is and always will be "a white man's country," and any attempt to the contrary is going to bring about civil warfare, in which the weaker must go down, as against the power of the stronger. It is only a question of time. . . .

Now, what has been the attitude of the white man toward the Negro since his emancipation from slavery? The white man's attitude has been one of wicked, diabolical prejudice, one of refusal to associate with the Negro; an attitude of Jim Crowism; an attitude of segregation; an attitude of drawing the line of de-marcation, based strictly on color, in the life industrial. Now, even though they have not reached the apex of their intention industrially as far as the development of this country is concerned, if they have demonstrated the degree of prejudice they have in these years since they started their plan, how much more prejudiced against us will they not become in the next hundred years. . . .

The Universal Negro Improvement Association comes forward, therefore, with a program which seeks not to let the Negro cast down his bucket where he is, but to have the bucket suspended and at the same time have a desire to build up himself as an independent force, as an independent factor in the country that God Almighty gave him—in a country that nature gave him—in a country that Providence gave him when He said "Let there be light." You cannot get away from the fact that the black man's—the colored man's—native habitat is Africa.

Source 10   Chief Justice Earl Warren of the Supreme Court, unanimous opinion in *Brown v. Board of Education of Topeka, Kansas,* 1954

We come then to the question presented: Does segregation of children in public schools solely on the basis of race, even though the physical facilities and other "tangible" factors may be equal, deprive the children of the minority group of equal educational opportunities? We believe that it does. . . .

To separate them from others of similar age and qualifications solely because of their race generates a feeling of inferiority as to their status in the community that may affect their hearts and minds in a way unlikely ever to be undone. The effect of this separation on their educational opportunities was well stated by a finding in the Kansas case by a court which nevertheless felt compelled to rule against the Negro plaintiffs:

"Segregation of white and colored children in public schools has a detrimental effect upon the colored children. The impact is greater when it has the sanction of the law; for the policy of separating the races is usually interpreted as denoting the inferiority of the Negro group. A sense of inferiority affects the motivation of a child to learn. Segregation with the sanction of law, therefore, has a tendency to retard the development of Negro children and to deprive them of some of the benefits they would receive in a racially integrated school system."

Whatever may have been the extent of psychological knowledge at the time of *Plessy v. Ferguson,* this finding is amply supported by modern authority. Any language in *Plessy v. Ferguson* contrary to this finding is rejected.

We conclude that in the field of public education the doctrine of "separate but equal" has no place. Separate educational facilities are inherently unequal. Therefore, we hold that the plaintiffs and others similarly situated for whom the actions have been brought are, by means of the segregation complained of, deprived of the equal protection of the laws guaranteed by the Fourteenth Amendment.

Source 11   The Reverend Martin Luther King Jr., *Why We Can't Wait,* 1964

For a hundred years since emancipation, Negroes had searched for the elusive path to freedom. They knew that they had to fashion a body of tactics suitable for their unique and special conditions. The words of the Constitution had declared them free, but life had told them that they were a twice-burdened people—they lived in the lowest stratum of society, and within it they were additionally imprisoned by a caste of color.

For decades the long and winding trails led to dead ends. Booker T. Washington, in the dark days that followed Reconstruction, advised them: "Let down your buckets where you are." Be content, he said in effect, with doing well what the times permit you to do at all. However, this path, they soon felt, had too little freedom in its present and too little promise in its future.

Dr. W. E. B. Du Bois, in his earlier years at the turn of the century, urged the "talented tenth" to rise and pull behind it the mass of the race. His doctrine served somewhat to counteract the apparent resignation of Booker T. Washington's philosophy. Yet, in the very nature of Du Bois's outlook there was no role for the whole people. It was a tactic for an aristocratic elite who would themselves be benefited while leaving behind the "untalented" 90 per cent.

After the First World War, Marcus Garvey made an appeal to the race that had the virtue of rejecting concepts of inferiority. He called for a return to Africa and a resurgence of race pride. His movement attained mass dimensions, and released a powerful emotional response because it touched a truth which had long been dormant in the mind of the Negro. There was reason to be proud of their heritage as well as of their bitterly won achievements in America. Yet his plan was doomed because an exodus to Africa in the twentieth century by a people who had struck roots for three and a half centuries in the New World did not have the ring of progress.

With the death of the Garvey movement, the way opened for the development of the doctrine which held the center stage for almost thirty years. This was the doctrine, consistently championed and ably conducted by the National Association for the Advancement of Colored People, that placed its reliance on the Constitution and the federal law. Under this doctrine, it was felt that the federal courts were the vehicle that could be utilized to combat oppression, particularly in southern states, which were operating under the guise of legalistics to keep the Negro down.

Under brilliant and dedicated leadership, the N.A.A.C.P. moved relentlessly to win many victories in the courts. . . . Yet the failure of the nation, over a decade, to implement the majestic implications of these decisions caused the slow ebb of the Negro's faith in litigation as the dominant method to achieve his freedom. In his eyes, the doctrine of legal change had become the doctrine of slow token change. . . .

It is an axiom of social change that no revolution can take place without a methodology suited to the circumstances of the period. During the fifties many voices offered substitutes for the tactic of legal recourse. Some called for a massive blood bath to cleanse the nation's ills. . . . But the Negro in the South in 1955, assessing the power of the forces arrayed against him, could not perceive the slightest prospect of victory in this approach. . . .

Perhaps even more vital in the Negro's resistance to violence was the force of his deeply rooted spiritual beliefs. . . . Throughout the South, . . . the Negro Church had emerged with increasing impact in the civil-rights struggle. Negro ministers . . . were making their influence felt throughout the freedom movement.

The doctrine they preached was a nonviolent doctrine. It was not a doctrine that made them yearn for revenge but one that called upon them to champion change. It was not a doctrine that asked an eye for an eye but one that summoned men to seek to open the eyes of blind prejudice. The Negro turned his back on force not only because he knew he could not win his freedom through physical force but also because he believed that through physical force he could lose his soul. . . .

Nonviolent action, the Negro saw, was the way to supplement—not replace—the process of change through legal recourse. It was the way to divest himself of passivity without arraying himself in vindictive force. Acting in concert with fellow Negroes to assert himself as a citizen, he would embark on a militant program to demand the rights which were his: in the streets, on the buses, in the stores, the parks and other public facilities. . . .

We are a nation that worships the frontier tradition, and our heroes are those who champion justice through violent retaliation against injustice. It is not simple to adopt the credo that moral force has as much strength and virtue as the capacity to return a physical blow; or that to refrain from hitting back requires more will and bravery than the automatic reflexes of defense.

Yet there is something in the American ethos that responds to the strength of moral force.

Source 12   C. Vann Woodward, *The Strange Career of Jim Crow*, 1966

If the psychologists are correct in their hypothesis that aggression is always the result of frustration, then the South toward the end of the 'nineties was the perfect cultural seedbed for aggression against the minority race. Economic, political, and social frustrations had pyramided to a climax of social tensions. No real relief was in sight from the long cyclical depression of the 'nineties, an acute period of suffering that had only intensified the distress of the much longer agricultural depression. . . . There had to be a scapegoat. And all along the line signals were going up to indicate that the Negro was an approved object of aggression. These "permissions-to-hate" came from sources that had formerly denied such permission. They came from the federal courts in numerous opinions, from Northern liberals eager to conciliate the South, from Southern conservatives who had abandoned their race policy of moderation in their struggle against the Populists, from the Populists in their mood of disillusionment with their former Negro allies, and from a national temper suddenly expressed by imperialistic adventures and aggressions against colored peoples in distant lands.

The resistance of the Negro himself had long ceased to be an important deterrent to white aggression. But a new and popuar spokesman of the race, its acknowledged leader by the late 'nineties, came forward with a submissive philosophy for the Negro that to some whites must have appeared an invitation to further aggression. It is quite certain that Booker T. Washington did not intend his so-called "Atlanta Compromise" address of 1895 to constitute such an invitation. But in proposing the virtual retirement of the mass of Negroes from the political life of the South and in stressing the humble and menial role that the race was to play, he would seem unwittingly to have smoothed the path to proscription.

Source 13   John Hope Franklin, *From Slavery to Freedom*, 1974

While there was much to be said for the position that Washington took, his doctrine contained some weaknesses that are perhaps more obvious today than they were then. He accepted uncritically the dominant philosophy of American business when he insisted that everyone had his own future in his own hands. . . . The Negro Business League, which Washington organized in 1900 to foster business and industry, was based on the philosophy that if a person could make a better article and sell it cheaper, he could command the markets of the world; that if one produced something someone wanted, the purchaser would not ask who the seller is. Add to this a generous amount of tact, good manners, resolute will, and a tireless capacity for hard work, and success in business would be the reward. . . . [T]his philosophy was an adaptation of the theories of free competition and political individualism that had been taught by the school of classical political economy and was becoming more fictitious than ever by 1900. The spread of "vertical and horizontal combinations capitalized in hundreds of millions was discrediting the idea that a man of small capital could raise himself to affluence and power through hard work and thrift." Washington showed little understanding of these realities as he developed a program for the economic salvation of Negroes.

The particular type of industrial education that Washington emphasized, with much attention to the development of a class of artisans, was outmoded at the time he enunciated it. He did not seem to grasp fully the effect of the Industrial Revolution upon the tasks that had been performed by the hands of workers for centuries. To be sure, brickmasons, carpenters, blacksmiths, and the like would still be needed, but their tasks were being reduced to a minimum in the industrial age; many of the occupations that Washington was urging Negroes to enter were disappearing almost altogether. . . . In speaking of organized labor, Washington went so far as to say that Negroes did not like an "organization which seems to be founded on a sort of impersonal enmity to the man by whom he is employed." He therefore utterly failed to see the relation of the laboring class to the Industrial Revolution and counseled an approach to the labor problem that had the effect of perpetuating the master-slave tradition.

In counseling blacks to remain in rural areas, Washington failed to see not only that the advent of expensive farm machinery put the impoverished Negro farmer at a serious disadvantage but also that the industrial urban community was infinitely more attractive to blacks as well as to whites. There were, on the surface at least, innumerable economic opportunities in the city. . . . If Washington wished for his people educational and economic opportunities that would facilitate their assimilation and acceptance, the urban centers seemed to be, by far, the oases in the desert of despair. . . .

Despite the fact that there were blacks who vigorously opposed Washington's leadership and that there were some valid exceptions to his program for the salvation of his people, he was unquestionably the central figure—the dominant personality—in the history of Negro Americans down to his death in 1915. The vast majority of blacks acclaimed him as their leader, and few whites ventured into the matter of race relations without his counsel. During his lifetime lynchings decreased only slightly, the Negro was effectively disfranchised, and the black workers were systematically excluded from the major labor organizations; but Washington's influence, sometimes for better and sometimes for worse, was so great that there is considerable justification in calling the period the Age of Booker T. Washington.

Questioning the Past

1. Compare and contrast the goals and tactics of Washington, Du Bois, Garvey, and King. From the perspective of the present, what were the strengths and weaknesses of each approach to the race issue?

2. Explain the Supreme Court's reasoning in *Plessy v. Ferguson* and in *Brown v. Board of Education*. How could the Court have used the Fourteenth Amendment to justify two such opposing opinions?

3. Did the policies proposed by Booker T. Washington shield African Americans from the venom of racism or merely expose them to it to a greater degree? Develop arguments in support of both conclusions.

4. Why have political and social equality been so difficult to obtain in a nation that embraces egalitarianism as a fundamental tenet?

Chapter 9

The Philippine Question

Commodore Dewey Sinks the Spanish Squadron at Manila Bay   *May 1, 1898*

On April 25, 1898, the Congress of the United States declared that the American people were at war with Spain. The American purpose in going to war was to free the Cuban people from Spanish rule.

But the war to liberate Cuba was less than a week old when the attention of the American people was suddenly diverted to a place half a world away from Havana Harbor. Word came that U.S. Admiral George Dewey and his naval force had won a stunning victory over a Spanish fleet at Manila Bay in the Philippine Islands.

✎ *First Impressions*
The Taking of the Philippines

Dewey's victory was a historic moment for reasons that transcended the war with Spain. That war lasted a mere four months. The American military presence in the Philippines would last almost a century.

9.1 Philippine Culture and History

Source 1   Admiral George Dewey's cable to the Secretary of the Navy, 1898

[Manila, May 1.]

Secretary of the Navy, Washington:

The Squadron arrived at Manila at daybreak this morning. Immediately engaged enemy and destroyed the following Spanish vessels: *Reina Christina, Castilla, Don Juan de Austria, Isla de Luzon, Isla de Cuba, General Lezo, Marquis del Duaro, El Curreo, Velasco,* one transport, *Isla de Mandano,* water battery at Cavite. I shall destroy Cavite arsenal dispensatory. The squadron is uninjured. Few men are slightly injured. I request the Department will send immediately from San Francisco fast steamer with ammunition.

[Admiral George] Dewey.

Source 2   Naval Secretary's reply to Admiral Dewey

Washington, May 3, 1898.

Dewey:

I send hearty congratulations to yourself and your officers and men. The President highly appreciates your achievement. I await report from you, on receipt of which further action will be taken and any supplies that you wish will be forwarded.

[Secretary of the Navy James D.] Long.

Source 3   Dewey's cable to Secretary Long

[Cavite, May 4, 1898.]

9.2 Today in History: George Dewey

Secretary of the Navy, Washington:

I have taken possession of the naval station at Cavite, Philippine Islands, and destroyed its fortifications. Have destroyed fortifications bay entrance, patroling garrison. Have cut cable to main land. I control bay completely and can take city at any time, but I have not sufficient men to hold. The squadron excellent health and spirits. . . . Will ammunition be sent? I request answer without delay. I can supply squadron coal and provisions for a long time. Much excitement at Manila.

Dewey.

Source 4   Secretary Long's reply to Dewey

Washington, May 7, 1898.

Dewey:

The President, in the name of the American people, thanks you and your officers and men for your splendid achievement and overwhelming victory. In recognition he has appointed you acting rear-admiral, and will recommend a vote of thanks to you from Congress as a foundation for future promotion. The *Charleston* will leave at once with what ammunition she can carry. Pacific Mail Steamship Company's steamer *Pekin* will follow with ammunition and supplies. Will take troops unless you telegraph otherwise. How many will you require?

Long.

Source 5   President McKinley's message to Cabinet member Russel A. Alger

May 19, 1898

To the Secretary of War:

Sir:—The destruction of the Spanish fleet at Manila, followed by the taking of the naval station at Cavite . . . have rendered it necessary . . . to send an army of occupation to the Philippines for the twofold purpose of completing the reduction of the Spanish power in that quarter, and of giving order and security to the islands while in the possession of the United States.

The first effect of the military occupation of the enemy's territory is the severance of the former political relations of the inhabitants, and the establishment of a new political power. Under this changed condition of things, the inhabitants, so long as they perform their duties, are entitled to security in their persons and property, and in all their private rights and relations. . . . It will . . . be the duty of the commander of the expedition, immediately upon his arrival in the islands, to publish a proclamation, declaring that we have come not to make war upon the people of the Philippines, nor upon any party or faction among them, but to protect them in their homes, in their employments, and in their personal and religious rights. All persons who, either by active aid or by honest submission, cooperate with the United States in its efforts to this beneficent purpose, will receive the reward of its support and protection.

William McKinley.

Source 6   Remarks of President McKinley to visiting clergymen, November 21, 1899

The truth is I didn't want the Philippines, and when they came to us, as a gift from the gods, I did not know what to do with them. . . .

    I sought counsel from all sides—Democrats as well as Republicans—but got little help. I thought first we would take only Manila; then Luzon; then other islands, perhaps, also. I walked the floor of the White House night after night until midnight; and I am not ashamed to tell you, gentlemen, that I went down on my knees and prayed Almighty God for light and guidance more than one night. And one night late it came to me this way—I don't know how it was, but it came: (1) That we could not give them back to Spain—that would be cowardly and dishonorable; (2) that we could not turn them over to France or Germany—our commercial rivals in the Orient—that would be bad business and discreditable; (3) that we could not leave them to themselves—they were unfit for self-government—and they would soon have anarchy and misrule over there worse than Spain's was; and (4) that there was nothing left for us to do but to take them all, and to educate the Filipinos, and uplift and civilize and Christianize them, and by God's grace do the very best we could by them, as our fellow men for whom Christ also died. And then I went to bed, and to sleep, and slept soundly, and the next morning I sent for the chief engineer of the War Department (our map-maker), and I told him to put the Philippines on the map of the United States, and there they are, and there they will stay while I am President!

Civilization Must Advance

William McKinley's prayers for direction with regard to the Philippine question led him to conclude that the United States had an obligation to "civilize and Christianize" the 7 million Filipinos and to take control of their more than 7,100 islands. But, regrettably, McKinley must have misunderstood whatever divine instructions he may have received, because 80 percent of the people of the Philippines were already Christians, and

9.3 William McKinley

they had no desire to have the American notion of civilized behavior imposed on them.

The presidential decision to take possession of the Philippine Islands and retain them as an American colony ignited a rebellion of the Filipinos against the Americans, whom they had heretofore regarded as their friends and liberators. The American capture of Manila and the subsequent removal from Philippine soil of Spanish troops had been accomplished only because of the support of tens of thousands of Filipino patriots who fought alongside Dewey's forces under the impression that the fight was for Philippine independence. Now, they felt angry and betrayed.

The resulting insurrection lasted nearly four years. It cost more American lives than had the Spanish-American War that had spawned it. It also cost the lives of some 200,000 of those very Filipinos whose well-being McKinley had professed a desire to protect. A war that was begun to liberate the Cuban people from the brutality of Spanish rule had become a war to subjugate the people of the Philippines. And before the insurrection was crushed, American troops had taken up tactics as barbarous as those they had gone to Cuba to put down.

The Philippine question also led to a bitter debate within the United States about the position the American nation should assume in world affairs.

Source 7 Senator Albert J. Beveridge, "The March of the Flag" September 16, 1898

Fellow Citizens, it is a noble land that God has given us; a land that can feed and clothe the world; a land whose coast lines would enclose half the countries of Europe; a land set like a sentinel between the two imperial oceans of the globe, a greater England with a noble destiny. It is a mighty people that He has planted on this soil: a people sprung from the most masterful blood of history; a people perpetually revitalized by the virile, man-producing workingfolk of all the earth; a people imperial by virtue of their power, by right of their institutions, by authority of their heaven-directed purposes—the propagandists and not the misers of liberty. It is a glorious history our God has bestowed upon his chosen people; a history whose keynote was struck by Liberty Bell; a history heroic with faith in our mission and our future; a history of statesmen who flung the boundaries of the republic out into unexplored lands and savage wildernesses; a history of soldiers who carried the flag across the blazing deserts and through the ranks of hostile mountains, even to the gates of the sunset; a history of a multiplying people who overran a continent in half a century; a history of prophets who saw the consequences of evils inherited from the past and martyrs who died to save us from them; a history divinely logical, in the process of whose tremendous reasoning we find ourselves today.

Therefore, in this campaign, the question is larger than a party question. It is an American question. It is a world question. Shall the American people continue their relentless march toward the commercial supremacy of the world? Shall free institutions broaden their blessed reign as the children of liberty wax in strength, until the empire of our principles is established over the hearts of all mankind?. . .

The Opposition tells us that we ought not to govern a people without their consent. I answer, The rule of liberty that all just government derives its authority from the consent of the governed applies only to those who are capable of self-government. I answer, We govern the Indians without their consent, we govern our territories without their consent, we govern our children without their consent. I answer, How do you presume that our government would be without their consent? Would not the people of the Philippines prefer the just, humane, civilizing government of this republic to the savage, bloody rule of pillage and extortion from which we have rescued them?. . .

And, regardless of this formula of words made only for enlightened, self-governing peoples, do we owe no duty to the world? Shall we turn these people back to the reeking hands from which we have taken them? Shall we abandon them to their fate, with the wolves of conquest all about them—with Germany, Russia, France, even Japan, hungering for them? Shall we save them from those nations, to give them a self-rule of tragedy? It would be like giving a razor to a babe and telling it to shave itself. It would be like giving a typewriter to an Eskimo and telling him to publish one of the great dailies of the world. . . .

They ask us how we will govern these new possessions. I answer, Out of local conditions and the necessities of the case methods of government will grow. If England can govern foreign lands, so can America. If Germany can govern foreign lands, so can America. If they can supervise protectorates, so can America. Why is it more difficult to administer Hawaii than New Mexico and California? Both had a savage and an alien population; both were more remote from the seat of government when they came under our dominion than Hawaii is to-day. . . .

Will you remember that we do but what our fathers did—we but pitch the tents of liberty further westward, further southward—we only continue the march of the flag.

The march of the flag!

In 1789 the flag of the republic waved over 4,000,000 souls in thirteen states, and their savage territory which stretched to the Mississippi, to Canada, to the Floridas. The timid minds of the day said that no new territory was needed, and, for the hour, they were right. But . . . Jefferson, the first imperialist of the republic—Jefferson acquired that imperial territory which swept from the Mississippi to the mountains, from Texas to the British possessions, and the march of the flag began!

The infidels to the gospel of liberty raved, but the flag swept on!. . .

A screen of land from New Orleans to Florida shut us from the gulf, and over this and the Everglade Peninsula waved the saffron flag of Spain; Andrew Jackson seized both, the American people stood at his back, and, under Monroe, the Floridas came under the dominion of the republic, and the march of the flag went on!

The Cassandras prophesied every prophesy of despair we hear, to-day, but the march of the flag went on! Then Texas responded to the bugle calls of liberty, and the march of the flag went on! And, at last, we waged war with Mexico, and the flag swept over the Southwest, over peerless California, past the Gate of Gold, to Oregon on the north, and from ocean to ocean its folds of glory blazed.

And now, obeying the same voice that Jefferson heard and obeyed, that Jackson heard and obeyed, that Monroe heard and obeyed, that Seward heard and obeyed, that Ulysses S. Grant heard and obeyed, that Benjamin Harrison heard and obeyed, William McKinley plants the flag over the islands of the seas, outposts of commerce, citadels of national security, and the march of the flag goes on! . . .

Distance and oceans are no arguments. The fact that all the territory our fathers bought and seized is contiguous, is no argument. In 1819 Florida was further from New York than Puerto Rico is from Chicago to-day; Texas, further from Washington in 1845 than Hawaii is from Boston in 1898; California, more inaccessible in 1847 than the Philippines are now. Gibraltar is further from London than Havana is from Washington; Melbourne is further from Liverpool than Manila is from San Francisco. The ocean does not separate us from lands of our duty and desire—the oceans join us, a river never to be dredged, a canal never to be repaired.

Steam joins us; electricity joins us—the very elements are in league with our destiny. Cuba not contiguous! Puerto Rico not contiguous! Hawaii and the Philippines not contiguous! Our navy will make them contiguous. Dewey and Sampson and Schley have made them contiguous, and American speed, American guns, American heart and brains and nerve will keep them contiguous forever.

But the Opposition is right—there is a difference. We did not need the western Mississippi Valley when we acquired it, nor Florida, nor Texas, nor California, nor the royal provinces of the far Northwest. We had no emigrants to people this imperial wilderness, no money to develop it, even no highways to cover it. No trade awaited us in its savage vastnesses. Our productions were not greater than our trade. There was not one reason for the land-lust of our statesmen from Jefferson to Grant, other than the prophet and the Saxon within them.

But, to-day, we are raising more than we can consume. To-day, we are making more than we can use. . . . Therefore we must find new markets for our produce, new occupation for our capital, new work for our labor. And so, while we did not need the territory taken during the past century at the time it was acquired, we do need what we have taken in 1898, and we need it now.

Think of the thousands of Americans who will pour into Hawaii and Puerto Rico when the republic's laws cover those islands with justice and safety! Think of the tens of thousands of Americans who will invade mine and field and forest in the Philippines when a liberal government, protected and controlled by this republic, if not the government of the republic itself, shall establish order and equity there! Think of the hundreds of thousands of Americans who will build a soap-and-water, common-school civilization of energy and industry in Cuba, when a government of law replaces the double reign of anarchy and tyranny!— think of the prosperous millions that Empress of Islands will support when, obedient to the law of political gravitation, her people ask for the highest honor liberty can bestow, the sacred Order of the Stars and Stripes, the citizenship of the Great Republic!

Source 8   Diplomat John Barrett, "The Problem of the Philippines," September 1898

The great European powers and Japan are deeply interested in the future of the Philippines. They recognize that the nation holding them—if one of the first magnitude—will have a vantage ground of inestimable strategical and commercial value; and they will watch with a . . . jealous attitude the disposition of these islands, matchless in wealth and location. . . .

The Philippines are the southern key to the Far East; they hold a position in the South not much less important than that of Japan in the North; the South China Sea, the pathway of the numerous steamers and ships that come to the Far East by the Suez and Cape Town routes, is under the eye, as it were, of Manila; a fleet of warships could sail from Manila Bay, scour this Mediterranean of the East, and return to signal **Corregidor** island in four days.

If anyone doubts the strategical and commercial importance of the Philippines, he should obtain a map of the Far East and study carefully that splendid coast line of Eastern Asia that reaches from Singapore and Bangkok to Tientsin and Vladivostock, with its many ports and mighty rivers, its general greatness and its sheltered seas guarded by such island lands as Japan, Formosa, the Philippines, Borneo, Java, and Sumatra. It has no equal in the wide world. And along this coast and among all these islands none stands out more prominently than the Philippines, over which the American flag may yet float.

Source 9   British Admiral P. H. Colomb, "The United States Navy under the New Conditions of National Life," October 1898

So long as the Empire of the United States of America was contained in a ring fence of land and sea frontiers, she had, in all international disputes, the enormous advantage of unattackability. No one could get at her from the outside with any hope of success. . . . But with outlying territories, especially islands, a comparatively weak power has facilities for wounding her without being wounded in return which did not hitherto exist. . . . [S]uch parts of the Philippines as may in the end pass to the United States, cannot in any case be held by her if she goes to war with a country possessing a superior navy to her own.

Source 10   Speech of William Jennings Bryan to the Virginia Democratic Association, February 22, 1899

When the advocates of imperialism find it impossible to reconcile a colonial policy with the principles of our government or with the canons of morality; when they are unable to defend it upon the ground of religious duty or pecuniary profit, they fall back in helpless despair upon the assertion that it is destiny. "Suppose it does violate the Constitution," they say; "suppose it does break all the commandments; suppose it does entail upon the nation an incalculable expenditure of blood and money; it is destiny and we must submit."

The people have not voted for imperialism; no national convention has declared for it; no Congress has passed upon it. To whom, then, has the future been revealed? Whence this voice of authority? We can all prophesy, but our prophesies are merely guesses, colored by our hopes and our surroundings. Man's opinion of what is to be is half wish and half environment. Avarice paints destiny with a dollar mark before it, militarism equips it with a sword. . . .

The ancient doctrine of imperialism, banished from our land more than a century ago, has recrossed the Atlantic and challenged democracy to mortal combat upon American soil.

Whether the Spanish war shall be known in history as a war for liberty or as a war of conquest; whether the principles of self-government shall be strengthened or abandoned; whether this nation shall remain a homogeneous republic or become a heterogeneous empire—these questions must be answered by the American people—when they speak, and not until then, will destiny be revealed.

Destiny is not a matter of chance; it is a matter of choice; it is not a thing to be waited for, it is a thing to be achieved. No one can see the end from the beginning, but every one can make his course an honorable one from beginning to end, and by adhering to the right under all circumstances. Whether a man steals much or little may depend upon his opportunities, but whether he steals at all depends upon his own volition.

So with our nation. If we embark upon a career of conquest no one can tell how many islands we may be able to seize and how many races we may be able to subjugate; neither can any one estimate the cost, immediate and remote, to the nation's purse and to the nation's character, but whether we shall enter upon such a career is a question which the people have a right to decide for themselves. . . .

The main purpose of the founders of our government was to secure for themselves and for posterity the blessings of liberty. . . . On each returning Fourth of July our people have met to celebrate the signing of the Declaration of Independence; their hearts have renewed their vows to free institutions and their voices have praised the forefathers whose wisdom and courage and patriotism made it possible for each succeeding generation to repeat the words:

> "My country, 'tis of thee,
> Sweet land of Liberty,
> of thee I sing."

This sentiment was well-nigh universal until a year ago. It was to this sentiment that the Cuban insurgents appealed; it was this sentiment that impelled our people to enter into the war with Spain. Have the people so changed within a few short months that they are now willing to apologize for the War of the Revolution and force upon the Filipinos the same system of government against which the colonists protested with fire and sword?

The hour of temptation has come, but temptations do not destroy, they merely test the strength of individuals and nations; they are stumbling blocks or stepping stones; they lead to infamy or fame; according to the use made of them.

Benedict Arnold and Ethan Allen served together in the Continental army and both were offered British gold. Arnold yielded to the temptation and made his name a synonym for treason; Allen resisted and lives in the affections of his countrymen.

Our nation is tempted to depart from its "standard of morality" and adopt a policy of "criminal aggression." But, will it yield?

If I mistake not the sentiment of the American people they will spurn the bribe of imperialism.

Source 11   Speech of Theodore Roosevelt, "The Strenuous Life," 1899

It is a base untruth to say that happy is the nation that has no history. Thrice happy is the nation that has a glorious history. Far better it is to dare mighty things, to win glorious triumphs, even though checkered by failure, than to take rank with those poor spirits who neither enjoy much nor suffer much, because they live in the gray twilight that knows not victory nor defeat. . . .

We cannot avoid the responsibilities that confront us in . . . the Philippines. . . . The timid man, the lazy man, the man who distrusts his country, the over-civilized man, who has lost the great fighting, masterful virtues, the ignorant man, and the man of dull mind, whose soul is incapable of feeling the mighty lift that thrills "stern men with empires in their brains"—all these, of course, shrink from seeing the nation undertake its new duties; shrink from seeing us build a navy and army adequate to our needs; shrink from seeing us do our share of the world's work, by bringing order out of chaos in the great, fair tropical islands from which the valor of our soldiers and sailors has driven the Spanish flag. These are the men who fear the strenuous life, who fear the only national life worth leading.

Source 12 Journalist and former senator Carl Schurz, "Address at the Anti-Imperialist Conference in Chicago," October 17, 1899

President McKinley assumed of his own motion the sovereignty of the Philippine Islands by his famous "benevolent-assimilation" order of December 21, 1898, through which our military was directed forthwith to extend the military government of the United States over the whole archipelago, and by which the Filipinos were notified that if they refused to submit, they would be compelled by force of arms. Having bravely fought for their freedom and independence from one foreign rule, they did refuse to submit to another foreign rule, and then the slaughter of our allies began—the slaughter by American arms of a once friendly and confiding people. And this slaughter has been going on ever since.

This is a grim story. Two years ago the prediction of such a possibility would have been regarded as a hideous nightmare, as the offspring of a diseased imagination. But to-day it is a true tale—a plain recital of facts taken from the official records. These things have actually been done in these last two years by and under the administration of William McKinley. This is our Philippine war as it stands. Is it a wonder that the American people should be troubled in their consciences?. . .

I confidently trust that the American people will prove themselves too clear-headed not to appreciate the vital difference between the expansion of the Republic and its free institutions over contiguous territory and kindred populations, which we all gladly welcome if accomplished peaceably or honorably, and imperialism which reaches out for distant lands to be ruled as subject provinces; too intelligent not to perceive that our very first step on the road of imperialism has been a betrayal of the fundamental principles of democracy, followed by disaster and disgrace; too enlightened not to understand that a monarchy may do such things and still remain a monarchy, while a democracy cannot do them and still remain a democracy; too wise not to detect the false pride, or the dangerous ambitions, or the selfish schemes which so often hide themselves under that deceptive cry of mock patriotism: "Our country, right or wrong!" They will not fail to recognize that our dignity, our free institutions, and the peace and welfare of this and coming generations of Americans will be

secure only as we cling to the watchword of true patriotism: "Our country—
when right to be kept right; when wrong to be put right."

Source 13 Mark Twain, *New York Herald,* October 16, 1900

I left these shores . . . a red-hot imperialist. I wanted the American eagle to go
screaming into the Pacific. It seemed tiresome and tame for it to content itself
with the Rockies. Why not spread its wings over the Philippines, I asked myself?
And I thought it would be a real good thing to do.

I said to myself, Here are a people who have suffered for three centuries.
We can make them as free as ourselves, give them a government and a country
of their own, put a miniature of the American constitution afloat in the Pacific,
start a brand new republic to take its place among the free nations of the world.
It seemed to me a great task to which we had addressed ourselves.

But I have thought some more, since then, and I have read the Treaty of
Paris, and I have seen that we do not intend to free, but to subjugate the people
of the Philippines. We have gone there to conquer, not to redeem. . . .

It should, it seems to me, be our pleasure and duty to make those people
free, and let them deal with their own domestic questions in their own way.
And so I am an anti-imperialist. I am opposed to having the eagle put its talons
on any other land.

Source 14 Democratic Party Platform, 1900

We condemn and denounce the Philippine policy of the present administration.
It has involved the Republic in an unnecessary war, sacrificed the lives of many
of our noblest sons, and placed the United States, previously known and applauded throughout the world as the champion of freedom, in the false and
un-American position of crushing with military force the efforts of our former
allies to achieve liberty and self-government. The Filipinos cannot be citizens
without endangering our civilization; they cannot be subjects without imperiling
our form of government; and as we are not willing to surrender our civilization
or convert the Republic into an empire, we favor an immediate declaration of
the nation's purpose to give the Filipinos, first, a stable form of government;
second, independence; and third, protection from outside interference.

Source 15 Republican Party Platform, 1900

In accepting by the Treaty of Paris the just responsibility of our victories in the
Spanish war, the President and the Senate won the undoubted approval of the
American people. No other course was possible than to destroy Spain's sovereignty throughout the West Indies and in the Philippine Islands. That course
created our responsibility before the world, and with the unorganized population
whom our intervention had freed from Spain, to provide for the maintenance
of law and order, and for the establishment of good government and for the
performance of international obligations. Our authority could not be less than
our responsibility; and wherever sovereign rights were extended it became the
high duty of the Government to maintain its authority, to put down armed

insurrection and to confer the blessings of liberty and civilization upon all rescued peoples. The largest measure of self-government consistent with their welfare and our duties shall be secured them by law.

Source 16 Mark Twain, "To the Person Sitting in Darkness," 1901

On the first of May, Dewey destroyed the Spanish fleet. This left the Archipelago in the hands of its proper and rightful owners, the Filipino nation. Their army numbered 30,000 men, and they were competent to wipe out or starve out the little Spanish garrison; then the people could set up a government of their own devising. Our traditions required that Dewey should . . . go away. But the Master of the Game happened to think of another plan—the European plan. He acted upon it. This was, to send out an army—ostensibly to help the native patriots put the finishing touch upon their long and plucky struggle for independence, but really to take their land away from them and keep it. That is, in the interest of Progress and Civilization. The Plan developed, stage by stage, and quite satisfactorily. We entered into a military alliance with the trusting Filipinos, and they hemmed in Manila on the land side, and by their valuable help the place, with its garrison of 8,000 or 10,000 Spaniards, was captured—a thing which we could not have accomplished unaided at that time. . . . We knew they supposed that we also were fighting in their worthy cause—just as we had helped the Cubans fight for Cuban independence—and we allowed them to go on thinking so. . . .

We and the patriots having captured Manila, Spain's ownership of the Archipelago and her sovereignty over it were at an end—obliterated—annihilated—not a rag or shred of either remaining behind. It was then that we conceived the divinely humorous idea of buying both of these specters from Spain! . . . In buying those ghosts for twenty millions, we also contracted to take care of the friars and their accumulations. (I think we also agreed to propagate leprosy and smallpox, but as to this there is doubt. But it is not important; persons afflicted with the friars do not mind other diseases.)

With our Treaty ratified, Manila subdued, and our Ghosts secured, we had no further use for . . . the owners of the Archipelago. We forced a war, and we have been hunting America's guest and ally through the woods and swamps ever since.

Source 17 Editorial, *Argonaut* of San Francisco, May 26, 1902

There has been too much hypocrisy about this Philippine business. . . . Let us all be frank.

WE DO NOT WANT THE FILIPINOS.
WE WANT THE PHILIPPINES.

All of our troubles in this annexation matter have been caused by the presence in the Philippine Islands of the Filipinos. Were it not for them, the Treaty of Paris would have been an excellent thing; the purchase of the archipelago for twenty millions of dollars would have been cheap. The islands are enormously rich; they abound in dense forests of valuable hardwood timber;

they contain mines of the precious metals; their fertile lands will produce immense crops of sugar cane, rice, and tobacco. Touched by the wand of American enterprise, fertilized with American capital, these islands would speedily become richer. . . .

But unfortunately, they are infested by Filipinos. There are millions of them there, and it is to be feared that their extinction will be slow. Still, every man who believes in developing these islands must admit that it cannot be done successfully while the Filipinos are there. They are indolent. They raise only enough food to live on; they don't care to make money; and they occupy land which might be utilized to better advantage by Americans. Therefore the more of them killed, the better.

It seems harsh. But they must yield before the superior race. . . . How shortsighted, then, to check the army in its warfare upon these savages.

The Intervening Years

American control of the Philippines continued without challenge from the time the Insurrection was crushed until the morning of December 7, 1941. On that date, and almost simultaneous to their surprise attack on Pearl Harbor, the Japanese commenced an airborne bombing raid on American fortifications in the Philippines. The bombing raids were followed the next morning by a Japanese invasion force. By May of 1942, with the surrender of the American military outpost at Corregidor, the Philippines fell under the rule of the Japanese Empire.

With the defeat in 1945 of Imperial Japan, the Philippines again came under American rule. But this time, the American control was short-lived. On July 4, 1946, independence was at last granted to the Filipino people. The United States retained, however, military installations in the Philippine Islands.

Sadly, the almost half-century of American rule did not immediately produce the stable democracy that the advocates of imperialism had prophesied. In 1965, Ferdinand Marcos came to the presidency of the nation and began to amass powers that made his rule an absolute dictatorship within a decade. With American backing, Marcos remained the strongman of the Philippines until he was overthrown by a popular uprising in 1986.

 ## *Second Thoughts*

The Continuing Controversy

9.4 The History Guy: Philippine-American War

Popular dissatisfaction with the continuing American military presence in the Philippines also led to pressures for an American withdrawal. In November 1992, at the request of the Philippine government, the last American military base on Philippine soil was closed and the final detachment of United States Marines set sail for home, 94 years after Dewey's arrival in the islands.

Source 18 Charles S. Olcott, *William McKinley*, 1916

The right to hold and govern territory and peoples as a result of purchase or conquest is one of the inherent attributes of sovereignty. The makers of the Constitution intended to create a nation—not with limited sovereign powers as compared with their neighbors, but a strong, self-sustaining nation with all the powers that make for legitimate growth. It was inconceivable, therefore, that the United States, having obtained possession of certain territory outside its borders, had no authority to retain and govern it.

President McKinley, while holding this view, took his stand upon ground even higher. His conception of nationality was as broad as humanity. The same Christian spirit which was the law of his personal life was also the law of the Chief Executive of his people. He was no Levite to pass by on the other side when he saw a man stripped and beaten and left half dead by robbers. The Filipinos were in just that condition. They were wounded and bleeding and unable to stand alone as the result of three centuries of selfish exploitation. Only a small minority . . . were sufficiently educated to learn the art of self-government and these were without experience. If the Filipinos dreamed of independence, it was only to escape the bondage of Spain. If they failed at first to understand the altruism of President McKinley and the American nation, it was because in all their experience they had never heard of such a thing as a philanthropic ruler. It is quite conceivable that the man who fell among thieves might have mistaken the good Samaritan for another robber before he felt the touch of his helping hand. . . .

William McKinley was the first of our Presidents to respond to the call of a broad philanthropy toward other less fortunate peoples. Lincoln heard a similar call and responded with the emancipation of four million slaves. But that was within our own boundaries. McKinley saw that the time had come when the United States, no longer a weakling nation threatened with dissolution, but strong and able, should take to itself the apostolic injunction, "now we that are strong ought to bear the infirmities of the weak. . . ." He realized that those inalienable rights of life, liberty, and the pursuit of happiness which our forefathers so ardently desired for themselves were not intended by the Creator as the exclusive privilege of our own countrymen, but were a part of the endowment of the people of . . . the Philippines as well.

Source 19 Thomas A. Bailey, *A Diplomatic History of the American People*, 1946

It has been fashionable to condemn the annexation of the Philippines as a grievous diplomatic error. But it must be remembered that McKinley was finally forced to choose among several possible courses, all of which presented momentous problems. He chose—perhaps wisely—the one that he and his advisors, and possibly a majority of the American people, thought the least undesirable. . . .

Perhaps the most serious avoidable mistake made by the United States during this period was the failure to quiet the fears of the Filipinos. They had been encouraged to believe—whether with proper authority or not—that they would be given their independence, and they had assisted materially in the capture of Manila. But when it dawned on them that they were merely going to exchange Spanish for American overlords, they rose in revolt, February 4, 1899.

This unfortunate outbreak might have been avoided if Congress had unequivocally declared, in January, 1899, that it would give the Filipinos their independence as soon as order was restored.

Source 20   George F. Kennan, *American Diplomacy*, 1951

[O]n April 20 [1898] Congress resolved that "it is the duty of the United States to demand, and the Government of the United States does hereby demand, that the Government of Spain at once relinquish its authority and government in the island of Cuba and withdraw its land and naval forces from Cuba and Cuban waters." . . . There was nothing in the resolution to indicate that Congress had any interest in any territory other than Cuba or that the President was authorized to use the armed forces for any purpose not directly related to the Spanish withdrawal from Cuba. . . . Yet it was only eleven days later that Admiral Dewey, sailing into Manila Bay in the early hours of morning, attacked and destroyed the Spanish fleet there. And only a few days later President McKinley authorized preparations for the dispatch of an army of occupation. The mission of this ground force was to follow up Dewey's victory, to complete "the reduction of Spanish power in that quarter," and to give "order and security to the islands while in the possession of the United States." The force proceeded to the Philippines and went into action there. By August it stormed and took the city of Manila. The effect of this action was later to constitute the most important and probably decisive consideration in our final decision to take the islands away from Spain and put them under the United States flag entirely; for this military operation shattered Spanish rule in the islands, made it impossible for us to leave them to Spain, and left us . . . no agreeable alternative but to take them ourselves.

Now, why did this happen? If there was no justification for the action against the Philippines in the origin of the war with Spain, what were the motives that lay behind it? Why, in other words, did we do things in May, 1898, that made it almost impossible for us later not to annex a great archipelago in the South Seas in which, prior to this time our interest had been virtually nil? . . .

The fact of the matter is that down to the present day we do not know the full answer to this question. We know that Theodore Roosevelt, who was then the young Assistant Secretary of the Navy, had long felt that we ought to take the Philippines; that he wangled Dewey's appointment to the command of the Asiatic fleet; that both he and Dewey wanted war; and that he had some sort of a prior understanding with Dewey to the effect that Dewey would attack Manila, regardless of the circumstances or the origin or the purpose of the war. We know that President McKinley, in defending Dewey's action at a later date, showed a very poor understanding of what was really involved and professed to believe a number of strategic premises that simply were not true. McKinley indicated that he had no thought of taking the Philippines at the time of the Battle of Manila and that Dewey's action was designed only to destroy the Spanish fleet and eliminate it as a factor in the war. But, if this is true, we are still mystified as to why McKinley authorized the sending of any army of occupation to the islands within a few days of Dewey's victory. We are not sure that we really know what passed between the government in Washington and Dewey prior to the battle. And we can only say that it looks very much as though, in this case, the action of the United States government had been determined primarily on the basis of a very quiet intrigue by a few strategically placed persons in Washington, an intrigue which received absolution, forgiveness, and a sort of a public blessing by virtue of war hysteria—of the fact that Dewey's victory was thrilling and pleasing to the American public—but which, had its results been otherwise, might well have found its ending in the rigors of a severe and extremely unpleasant congressional investigation.

So much, then, for the decisions underlying our conduct of hostilities. What about the broader political decisions . . . —the decisions which led to the final annexation not only of the Philippines but of Puerto Rico and Guam and the Hawaiian Islands? These were very important decisions from our own standpoint. They represented a turning point, it seems to me, in the whole concept of the American political system. These territorial acquisitions of the year 1898 represented the first extensions of United States sovereignty to important territories beyond the continental limits of North America. . . . They represented the first instances of sizable populations being taken under our flag with no wide anticipation that they would ever be accepted into statehood. . . .

[A]t the bottom of it all lay . . . the fact that the American people of that day, or at least many of their more influential spokesmen, simply liked the smell of empire and felt an urge to range themselves among the colonial powers of the time, to see our flag flying on distant tropical isles, to feel the thrill of foreign adventure and authority, to bask in the sunshine of recognition as one of the great imperial powers of the world. But a country which traces its political philosophy to the concept of the social compact has no business taking responsibility for people who have no place in that concept. . . . Kings can have subjects; it is a question whether a republic can.

Source 21 Samuel Flagg Bemis, *The United States as a World Power,* 1955

The Philippine Islands under the sovereignty of the United States became a monument to American good works and good will, a model for colonial dominion and administration in the world. They also became a military and a diplomatic liability. They were a hostage to Japan for American foreign policy in the Far East. Time and again Theodore Roosevelt and other American diplomats had to make concessions to Japanese aggression on the continent of Asia in return for Japanese disavowal, either explicit or implicit, of aggressive intentions toward the Philippines. The principal concern of the United States in the Islands became that of liquidating decently and honorably an uncomfortable imperialism there, leaving them able to sustain their independence in a sea of sharks.

Source 22 Robert H. Ferrell, *American Diplomacy,* 1969

The most fateful territorial acquisition of the Spanish-American War was the taking of the Philippines, after Dewey had sunk the Spanish squadron. Annexation of the Philippines was of large importance to the future of American diplomacy. It projected the United States far into the Western Pacific, and so close to Japan and China—two future trouble spots of the world—that American interests, once established in the Philippines, were almost bound to become involved and probably hurt in Far Eastern rivalries quite as remote from the American national interest as had been the European rivalries against which President Washington once had counseled. . . . This move into the Far East has seemed in retrospect very unwise.

Source 23 Samuel Eliot Morison, *Oxford History of the American People*, 1971

Military government [over the Filipinos] was succeeded in 1901 by a civilian Philippine Commission appointed by the President, with William H. Taft as chairman and governor general of the islands. . . . Under American rule they made a remarkable advance in education, well being, and self-government. . . . The Filipinos . . . cooperated with Taft and his successors to establish a new civil code, a complete scheme of education, sanitation, good roads, a native constabulary; in 1907 a representative assembly—and baseball. Seldom has there been so successful an experiment in the now despised "colonialism" or "imperialism" as American rule in the Philippines. None of the critics' predictions that the Republic had embarked on a Roman road leading to disaster came true.

Nevertheless, acquisition of the Philippines affected America's future far more than any other settlement following the Spanish War. . . . [R]esponsibility for the Philippines made the United States a power in the Far East, involved her in Asiatic power politics, and made an eventual war with Japan probable. Annexing the Philippines was a major turning point in American history.

 Questioning the Past

1. William McKinley stated, "When we received the cable from Admiral Dewey telling of the taking of the Philippines, I looked up their location on the globe. I could not have told where those darned islands were within 2,000 miles!" Doubtless, most of the American people were as ill-informed about the Philippines as their president. That being the case, why were the American people disposed to venture their lives and expend their resources in an effort to possess these islands?

2. Present the arguments for and against imperialism. Which argument is the more convincing? Defend your view.

3. Carl Schurz said, regarding the American decision to rule the Filipinos as a "subject people," that the American people were "too enlightened not to understand that a monarchy may do such things and still remain a monarchy, while a democracy cannot do them and still remain a democracy." Yet the United States still controls territory whose inhabitants do not enjoy the rights and obligations of American citizenship. Does this betray America's democratic aspirations?

4. Present the arguments in support of the American decision to annex the Philippine Islands. Present the arguments against annexation. Which arguments are the stronger?

5. What were the short- and long-term effects of the American decision to annex the Philippines? Do the positive effects outweigh the negative?

Chapter **10**

The Tin Lizzie

Henry Ford Unveils the Model T   *October 1, 1908*

Was the automobile destined to be a mere fad that faded as its novelty wore off? Could it ever be more than a noisy plaything of the rich? These questions went without answer at the turn of the twentieth century; indeed, it was likely that no one had yet thought even to ask them.

One who had an inkling of what could be was Henry Ford. He envisioned the possibility of manufacturing cars priced within reach of "the great multitude," and he was prepared to take bold initiatives to realize this vision. Putting aside the conventional wisdom of responsible business and the prevailing practices of the automobile industry, he presented the public with a car that would come to dominate the market, a car whose construction process would inspire a restructuring of the factory system in general, a car that caused America to rebuild itself upon a mobile foundation. And at a time when other manufacturers sought security through presenting consumers with a variety of options, Ford offered only one car, and he offered it in only one color. "The customer can have it any color he wants," said Ford, "as long as he wants it black."

10.1 Henry Ford Museum and Greenfield Village

✸✸ *First Impressions*

"One of the Absolute Necessities of Our Later Day Civilization"

On October 1, 1908, Henry Ford unveiled the Model T to the American public. The model that rolled off his assembly line that day was followed by millions more just like it. By the time the last Model T rolled off the line in May 1927, it was clear that America had, with Henry Ford's invention, turned a new corner in history.

10.2 Henry Ford and the Model T

Source 1   Ford Motor Company president Henry Ford, letter to the editor, *The Automobile*, January 11, 1906

There are more people in this country who can buy an automobile than in any other country on the face of the globe, and in the history of the automobile industry in this country the demand has never yet been filled. Some statisticians figure it that the factories of this country were only able to fill 75 per cent of the demand in the past season. In spite of increased facilities and a marked improvement in the construction of automobiles, the prospect of filling the

155

demand this season is exceedingly slim, and for this reason most of the factories building cars claim prices should be maintained and to put out a low-priced car is unjustifiable and suicidal.

The assertion has often been made that it would only be a question of a few years before the automobile industry would go the way the bicycle went. I think this is in no way a fair comparison and that the automobile, while it may have been a luxury when first put out, is now one of the absolute necessities of our later day civilization. The bicycle was a recreation and a fad. The automobile, while it is a recreation, is in no way a fad.

The greatest need today is a light, low-priced car with an up-to-date engine capable of ample horsepower, and built of the very best material. One that will go anywhere a car of double the horsepower will; that is in every way an automobile and not a toy; and, most important of all, one that will not be a wrecker of tires and a spoiler of the owner's disposition. It must be powerful enough for American roads and capable of carrying its passengers anywhere that a horse-drawn vehicle will go without the driver being afraid of ruining his car.

It must be a handy car, not too cumbersome, and one where a chauffeur will not be absolutely necessary either as a driver or because of his mechanical skill; a car which the owner can leave in front of his office and which will be ready to start at any time and take him wherever he wishes to go.

Source 2 Ford advertisement, June 1908

[See advertisement next page.]

Source 3 "Gives $10,000,000 to 26,000 Employees," *New York Times*, January 6, 1914

Detroit, Mich., Jan. 5.—Henry Ford, head of the Ford Motor Company, announced today one of the most remarkable business moves of his entire remarkable career. In brief it is:

To give to the employees of the company $10,000,000 of the profits of the 1914 business, the payments to be made semi-monthly and added to the pay checks.

To run the factory continuously instead of only eighteen hours a day, giving employment to several thousand more men by employing three shifts of eight hours each, instead of only two nine-hour shifts, as at present.

To establish a minimum wage scale of $5 per day. Even the boy who sweeps up the floor will get that much.

Before any man in any department of the company who does not seem to be doing good work shall be discharged, an opportunity will be given to him to try to make good in every other department. No man shall be discharged except for proved unfaithfulness or irremediable inefficiency.

The Ford Company's financial statement of September 20, 1912 showed assets of $20,815,785.63, and surplus of $14,745,095.57. One year later it showed assets of $35,033,919.86 and surplus of $28,124,173.68. Dividends paid out during the year, it is understood, aggregated $10,000,000. The indicated

From the collections of Henry Ford Museum and Greenfield Village

profits for the year, therefore, were $37,597,312. The company's capital stock, authorized and outstanding, is $2,000,000. There is no bond issue.

About 10 per cent of the employees, boys and women, will not be affected by the profit sharing, but all will have the benefit of the $5 minimum wage. Those among them who are supporting families, however, will have a share similar to the men of more than 22 years of age.

In all, about 26,000 employees will be affected. Fifteen thousand now are at work in the Detroit factories. Four thousand more will be added by the institution of the eight-hour shift. The other seven thousand employees are scattered all over the world, in the Ford branches. They will share the same as the Detroit employees.

Personal statements were made by Henry Ford and James Cousens, Treasurer of the company, regarding the move.

"It is our belief," said Mr. Cousens, "that social justice begins at home. We want those who have helped us to produce this great institution and are helping to maintain it to share our prosperity. We want them to have present profits and future prospects. Thrift and good services and sobriety, all will be enforced and recognized.

"Believing as we do, that a division of our earnings between capital and labor is unequal, we have sought a plan of relief suitable for our business. We do not feel sure that it is the best, but we have felt impelled to make a start, and make it now. We do not agree with those employers who declare, as did a recent writer in a magazine in excusing himself for not practicing what he preached, that 'movement toward the bettering of society must be universal.' We think that one concern can make a start and create an example for other employers. That is our chief object."

"If we are obliged," said Mr. Ford, "to lay men off for want of sufficient work at any season we propose to so plan our year's work that the lay-off shall be in the harvest time, July, August, and September, not in the Winter. We hope in such case to induce our men to respond to the calls of the farmers for harvest hands, and not to lie idle and dissipate their savings. We shall make it our business to get in touch with the farmers and to induce our employees to answer calls for harvest help.

"No man will be discharged if we can help it, except for unfaithfulness or inefficiency. No foreman in the Ford Company has the power to discharge a man. He may send him out of his department if he does not make good. The man is then sent to our 'clearing house,' covering all the departments, and is tried repeatedly in other work, until we find the job he is suited for, provided he is honestly trying to render good service."

Source 4   Ford advertisement, January 1914

[See advertisement next page.]

Source 5   Henry Ford interview, *Detroit News,* November 4, 1916

Bear in mind: every time you reduce the price of the car without reducing the quality, you increase the possible number of purchasers. There are many men who will pay $360 for a car who would not pay $440. We had in round numbers 500,000 buyers of cars on the $440 basis, and I figure that on the $360 basis we can increase the sales to possibly 800,000 cars for the year—less profit on each car, but more cars, more employment of labor, and in the end we get all the total profit we ought to make.   *(Continued on page 160)*

From the collections of Henry Ford Museum and Greenfield Village

And let me say right here, that I do not believe that we should make such an awful profit on our cars. A reasonable profit is right, but not too much. So it has been my policy to force the price of the car down as fast as production would permit, and give the benefits to users and laborers, with resulting surprisingly enormous benefits to ourselves. . . .

Dodge Brothers say I ought to continue to ask $440 for a car. I don't believe in such awful profits. I don't believe it is right.

So, would I be serving the interests of our firm best by holding up the price because the manufacturer of another automobile wants us to, or by reducing the price in the interest of our own customers, our own employees, and our own business standing, and profit? I think I am right in my policy.

Source 6   Ford advertisement, May 1925

[See advertisement next page.]

Prophet of a New Age

When Henry Ford began manufacturing at his first plant, his company was able to turn out 16 cars a week. By the mid-1920s, Ford's assembly line was turning out 16 cars a minute. A story was told that a mechanic on the line responsible for installing Part #453 had lost his job because he had dropped his wrench and a dozen cars had passed in the time it took him to reach down and pick it up. So efficient had the Ford assembly lines become by the early 1920s that a pile of raw materials could be transformed into a completed Model T in less than two days. A story was told about a farmer who had the ill-fortune to lose the tin roof of his barn to stormy weather. For some reason, he sent the pieces of this roof to the Ford plant in Detroit and received an encouraging message by return mail: "Your car is one of the worst wrecks we have seen, but we will be able to fix it."

The efficiency and innovative techniques Ford employed in his production earned him a reputation as a mechanical genius. His success in marketing the Model T and winning dominance over the automobile market won him the reputation of being a business genius. His dramatic decision to establish the $5 work day made him a national celebrity whose opinions on any and all topics were carefully considered by the press and by the public. John B. Rae, one of the most prominent historians of the auto industry, observed that Henry Ford came to be viewed as "the prophet and oracle of a new industrial age" and an "industrial miracle worker." John Kenneth Galbraith, an economist and a critic of Ford, conceded that the father of the Model T was by the 1920s "the nation's most astonishing man."

The astonishment came from more than the Model T. Drawing upon his fortune and his celebrity status, Henry Ford chartered a ship, filled it with prominent pacifists, and sailed to Europe in 1915 in a futile effort to convince the warring factions to call a halt to World War I. This "peace ship" project was widely ridiculed as the brainchild of a naive idealist, though the "realist" politicians of the day who ordered foot soldiers to charge to a certain death across the killing zones between opposing trenches seemed not to suffer similar ridicule. In 1920, Ford's newspaper,

the Dearborn *Independent,* launched an ugly and misinformed campaign against Jews, a campaign that Ford had apparently ordered but later rebuked. Such forays away from the business of the automobile industry showed that Ford's ability to master one field was not a genius that would necessarily transfer to another. Still, within his primary field of operation, Ford achieved phenomenal results.

 ## *Second Thoughts*

Transforming the Way People Lived

Henry Ford and his Model T had a tremendous impact in shaping twentieth-century America. The census for the year 1900 cited no statistics on the automobile because the industry was considered "too indefinite" for

10.3 Automotive History

serious consideration. The census conducted at the midpoint of the century found 40,339,000 registered automobiles. The most recent census, that of 1990, cited a figure of 143,026,000 automobiles registered in the United States. Life in the United States—and increasingly in the world as a whole—has come to be organized around the universal availability and use of this individualized means of transportation.

Source 7   Henry Ford, *My Philosophy of Industry,* 1928

To know what is growing and in what direction it is growing comprises the highest providential wisdom—it is the ability to read the signs of the times, not of the times that are, but of the times that are to be.

People who try to understand only the immediate times are somewhat behind the times. Those who know the times at all began to understand them before they existed. Signs of the times, then, are the signs of things to come. The signs of the times that now are were given long ago. By the time they emerge into actuality they are no longer signs, they are the times themselves. It is one thing to see a thing, another thing to see through a thing. There is very little of life on the surface. We see today as the product of distant yesterdays; yet hidden in today is a root of distant tomorrows, and it is the man who knows the coming tomorrows who really sees most of life. To read the signs of the times one must do a kind of original work—read what few are reading, or, I might say, read what isn't printed yet, reach original conclusions, deal with fundamental values which lie beneath and behind all other values. One leads the way for himself instead of following others, one looks to principles, to a deep foundation upon which rest the changes that afterward occur. The signs of the times demand our learning a new language, observing fundamental things, doing original thinking, getting at naked facts, and being sure they *are* facts, not simply theories. Life is a river which constantly changes its course, and the way of understanding is to follow this river—not the dried up and deserted river bed.

Source 8   Charles Merz, *And Then Came Ford,* 1929

Henry Ford, inventor of his own motor car, protagonist of the art of mass production, and prophet of a new age of standardization, had been a significant figure on the American scene for at least a decade, but neither the press nor the nation had discovered him. . . .

Ford had been breaking ground in industry for at least five years before 1913. He had been building up a fortune by defying the accepted theory that the only way to find a market for a product as expensive as a motor car was to vary his production constantly, and he had filled a young nation with hundreds of thousands of new vehicles of cheap and rapid transportation. He was the same man in midsummer 1913 and in midsummer a year later. But between these dates the picture changed entirely. In 1913 he was a man known only to the motor trade and his fellow townsmen in Detroit: a successful manufacturer whose name inevitably appeared in print from time to time, but a man unheard of by the nation. One year later reporters were dogging his footsteps with demands for interviews, photographers were hopping out at him from behind fence posts and motor trucks to snap his picture, personal impressions of him, written by eyewitnesses, were selling magazines from one end of the country to the other, and editors were telegraphing him for his opinion on the next election, the price of copper, and the war in Europe.

Something happened between midsummer 1913 and midsummer 1914 that made Ford a first-page feature.

The factor that brought Ford suddenly and dramatically to the centre of the stage was neither his car nor his mass production nor his millions, but his five-dollar wage. On the evening of January 5, 1914, newspapers all over the country carried the announcement. . . . It was a good story for a news-hungry press, and a good story especially for one reason. It turned upside down the conventional relationship of employer and employee and staged the spectacle of a corporation head apparently cutting his own profits in two for the purpose of putting unskilled men in his plant on a par with skilled men in other factories, at a time when unskilled men were ready to work for him at less than half his price.

Out of a clear sky and on a lavish scale a successful business man had chosen suddenly to experiment with the divine law of supply and demand by paying double the market value for his labour.

Year by year the galloping figures of Ford's income and production brought fresh proof to the average man that here, in fact, was a magician capable of working wonders. . . . In February, 1926, . . . the Ford Company built the motor car that brought its total contribution to the mobile power of the world to three hundred million horsepower. Out on the broad macadam highways that lined a busy modern nation with gas tanks, roadside cafeterias and rooms for boarders, it had turned loose, to date, the potential power of ninety-eight Niagara Falls.

It was a gigantic enterprise that had evolved from Ford's experimental theory of a motor car "built for the multitude" in 1908. The net worth of this company stood at some six hundred million dollars in the first month of 1926. In eighty-eight plants scattered over the face of the earth . . . Ford cars were manufactured and assembled. More than a hundred and fifty thousand men and women laboured in the vast labyrinth of the Ford industries. Two million cars came off the assembly lines each year. . . . Every principle of production with which the manufacture of the first Model T had been embarked upon in 1908 had arrived by 1926 at a spectacular conclusion. . . .

So fine had the process of manufacturing a motor car been drawn that by 1926 it was a matter of thirty-three hours from the time iron ore left the bottom of a Great Lakes freighter until a new Ford honked for clearance on the open road.

Source 9   Novelist and social critic Upton Sinclair, *The Flivver King,* 1937

The public had got the idea that the Ford Motor Company was going to pay each of its men not less than five dollars a day; the men got the same idea, and there was some dismay when it was discovered that this was not the program. The former wages were to remain unchanged; but every two weeks the men were to receive a bonus—provided they had "qualified." There was a catch in that word, and it was a complicated catch, which some of the men never did solve.

There were three groups. Married men had to be "living with and taking care of their families." Single men over twenty-two had to be "living wholesomely," and "of proud thrifty habits." Young men under twenty-two, and all women, had to be "the sole support of some next of kin." To ascertain these facts concerning fourteen thousand employees of a manufacturing company was no small task of research; to perform it, Henry Ford set up a Social Department of the Ford Motor Company, with a staff of fifty moral and properly certified young gentlemen to assist him. Two years later he persuaded an Episcopal clergyman, the dean of St. Paul's Cathedral in Detroit, to resign that honorable job and take charge of the morals of the Ford workers.

Henry and his new staff agreed upon the elementary principles. They were going to break up the evil habit of the foreign workers taking boarders into their homes, which made the home a money-making device and undoubtedly gave opportunity for promiscuity. They were going to compel unmarried men to visit a clergyman or a justice of the peace before they set up housekeeping. They were going to break up the habit of boys running away from home and failing to support their elderly relatives. They were going to stop at least the worst drinking, and see that homes were kept clean, and that children and sick people were taken care of. These were worthy aims, and the prize to the worker who would assist the Social Department was a check every fortnight amounting to somewhere between twenty-five and fifty dollars. . . .

But human nature is notoriously perverse, and many of the men grumbled bitterly about having their private lives investigated, and they changed the name of the new department from "Social" to "Snooping." Instead of complying loyally with the terms of the agreement, they set to work to circumvent it by diabolical schemes. The foreigners turned their boarders into brothers or brothers-in-law; the young men hid their girl friends for a while, or put them forth as orphan sisters; some evil ones even went so far as to hire an aged relative pro tem, in order to do their qualifying. Some of these tricks were caught up with, and the tricksters were fired, and there was not a little spying and tale-bearing and suspicion.

Source 10   Keith Sward, *The Legend of Henry Ford,* 1948

Organizers of the I.W.W. approached Ford's workers. The leaders of this colorful, loose-knit body had been filtering into Detroit for a number of years, propagating the gospel of "one big union" and transplanting a tradition of revolt that was native to the wheat fields and to the mines and lumber-camps of the Northwest.

The insurgence of the I.W.W. took root among a certain number of the employees of the Ford Motor Company. In the summer of 1913, "wobbly" organizers began to concentrate their fire on Highland Park. Their papers, *Solidarity* and *The Emancipator,* started to focus on working conditions at the Ford Motor Company. They pilloried "Henry Ford, the Speed-up King," naming him as the proprietor of a "sweat shop" which paid wages of twenty-five cents an hour, frequently discharging his men to rehire them at twenty cents. The "one big union" showered Ford's workmen with handbills. I.W.W. orators carried the slogans of the organization and the eight-hour day to the very doorstep of the Ford Motor Company.

The Ford management tried to ward off this challenge first from the outside. After a few preliminary appearances in Highland Park, certain I.W.W. speakers were carted off to jail as soon as they mounted the soapbox at the plant gates. Then the Company arrived at a more drastic formula. Before the wobbly penetration, Ford's workers had enjoyed the right to saunter out of doors at lunch time. But once the I.W.W. had put in its appearance, the outdoor lunch privileges were summarily withdrawn.

Thus far, Ford and Couzens were only dabbling with symptoms. The men were still quitting at the appalling rate of 40 to 60 per cent a month. Nor had the I.W.W. really been driven to cover. The dogged missionaries reappeared. The handbills continued to circulate, and the grapevine had it that the wobblies were planning to strike Ford in the summer of 1914.

Then James Couzens, Ford's business manger, came to the rescue. Confronted by a spontaneous labor insurrection from within and by the threat of union organization from without, Couzens late in 1913 conceived the Five-Dollar Day. He announced it to the world on January 5, 1914, and he did so with consummate showmanship. He presented the plan in terms of a large and disinterested humanitarianism. . . .

While holding forth as the champions of labor, Ford and Couzens had not thrown caution to the winds. Nor had either man overlooked for a moment the considerations of self-interest or of cold business expediency.

Source 11 Frederick Lewis Allen, editor, *Harper's Magazine*, *The Big Change: America Transforms Itself, 1900–1950*, 1952

As his sales of the Model T increased, Ford deliberately dropped the price—and they increased still further. In 1913 he put in his first assembly line, and by the beginning of 1914 he was producing his first entire car on the assembly-line principle. Each workman performed a single operation; each element of the car went on a power-driven moving conveyor platform past a series of these workmen, each of whom added or fixed in place some part of it; and these various assembly lines converged upon a main conveyor platform on which the chassis moved to completion.

In principle this method of manufacture was far from new. It depended upon Eli Whitney's great discovery of the principle of interchangeable parts. It owed much to the refinement of that principle by such men as Henry Leland (founder and head of Cadillac), who had shown what close machining could do to make these interchangeable parts fit with absolute precision. Moreover, many a manufacturer had used the assembly-line principle to some extent. Cyrus McCormack, for instance, had done so in his reaper works as far back as the eighteen-fifties; and in particular the packers had used an overhead conveyor to carry slaughtered animals past a series of workers. Ford was indebted, too, to Frederick Winslow Taylor for his studies in "scientific management," the careful planning of manufacturing processes so as to save steps and motions. And Ransom Olds had already put a single type of automobile into quantity production—until his financial backers forced him back into the luxury market.

Nevertheless the Ford assembly line, with its subassemblies, was unique as a remorselessly complete application of all these ideas.

When his manufacturing system was complete, in January, 1914, Ford made an announcement which echoed round the world.

At that time the going wage in the automobile industry averaged about $2.40 per nine-hour day. Ford announced he would pay his men a minimum of $5 per eight-hour day. . . .

The public reaction to the announcement was terrific. Most businessmen were indignant: Ford was ruining the labor market, he was putting crazy ideas into workmen's heads, he would embarrass companies which couldn't possibly distribute such largess, he was a crude self-advertiser. There was much scoffing of the sort that a Muncie, Indiana, newspaper indulged in many years later: "Henry Ford thinks that wages ought to be higher and goods cheaper. We agree with him, and let us add that it ought to be cooler in the summer and warmer in the winter." People with tenderer minds hailed Ford for his generosity and said that he was showing what a noble conscience could achieve in the hitherto unregenerate precincts of industry. Meanwhile the Ford plant was mobbed by applicants for jobs.

What Ford had actually done—in his manufacturing techniques, his deliberate price cutting, and his deliberate wage raising—was to demonstrate with unprecedented directness one of the great principles of modern industrialism: the dynamic logic of mass production. This is the principle that the more goods you produce, the less it costs to produce them; and that the more people are well off, the more they can buy, thus making this lavish and economical production possible.

Every successful manufacturer had followed this principle up to a point. But few had been able to follow it far; or, if able to, had been able to resist the human temptation to cease expanding their output unduly and then cash in by charging what the traffic would bear. . . . Henry Ford—a cranky and self-willed man, in many respects an ignorant and opinionated man, and a merciless competitor—followed the dynamic logic of mass production all the way, and the results were uncanny.

In 1909–10 his price per car had been $950. It went down to $780, to $690, to $600, to $550, to $490, to $440, to $360; then, after an increase due to the shortages and inflation of World War I, went down again until by 1924 the price of a Ford was only $290. Meanwhile production had expanded by slow-degrees from 18,664 cars all the way to 1,250,000 in 1920–21. . . .

In the meantime, however, Ford's experiment had had what Paul Hoffman [an advertising consultant in the 1950s] has called "multiplier value." For he had advertised a principle which, though more often honored in the breach than in the observance, has a place of some sort in the thinking of every industrial manager today. The continuing discovery and demonstration of this principle has been one of the most powerful forces in the making of twentieth-century America. For it has had its corollaries: that a nation of men and women secure against exploitation and acute poverty is a nation of delighted buyers of goods, to everybody's profit; that it pays better to produce the same sort of food, clothing, and equipment for people of all income levels, than to produce luxury goods for a few, and that therefore one can make money by lowering the barriers. Thus is Marxism confounded—not by dogma, but by the logic of advanced industrialism itself; or, to put it an another way, by capitalism turned to democratic ends.

Source 12   Merrill Denison, *The Power to Go*, 1956

Henry Ford and his principal product, the Model T, may prove to be the greatest revolutionaries of all time: the creative forces that instituted changes more truly significant and more extensive than any attributed to rival revolutionary couples, Brutus and Cassius, Robespierre and Danton, Marx and Lenin.

It was Ford who showed the way to a world economy of abundance based on the energy resources of the internal combustion engine. Had it not been Ford, it must, of course, have been someone else. The American environment made the coming of the mass-produced automobile inevitable. But it was not someone else. It was a man named Henry Ford—Dearborn farm boy, apprentice machinist, watch repairer, gasoline-engine experimenter, electric powerhouse superintendent, racing car driver, company promoter, unsuccessful and successful automobile manufacturer, and, finally, creator of the Model T—Henry Ford, and the host of creative men he attracted to him.

Puddle jumper, road house, tin lizzie, flivver: terms of disdain or endearment, they became a part of the American vocabulary during the Golden Age of Motordom; the Elysian decade and a half when to own and drive an automobile was to be part Mercury and part Columbus. A daring experiment in the beginning, and successively a joke, a nuisance, an institution, and a tradition, the Ford Model T and its progeny put America on wheels, led to the building of a million miles and more of roads, revolutionized our industrial progress, and brought about changes in our social, economic, and political life still beyond any final reckoning.

Scorned by the owners of bigger, more expensive cars, regarded by the trade as an impudent experiment, kidded by vaudeville jokesters and comic artists, the unpretentious open touring cars and runabouts, with all their rattles and their strangely temperamental ways, proved to be exactly the car for which thousands had been waiting. It cost less. It took you there, and it brought you back. America, priding itself on its ability to know a good thing when it saw it, bought Model T's and kept on buying them until a total of 15,000,000 had rolled off the production lines. . . .

[T]he epic of the Model T remains . . . the story of an idea, tentatively conceived, stubbornly nurtured, and brilliantly executed by a remarkable man. What Henry Ford accomplished was the domestication of power by placing within the reach of millions of people a simple, standardized, mobile power plant and transportation tool whose sole purpose was utilitarian.

Source 13   Historians Allan Nevins and Frank Ernest Hill, *Ford Expansion and Challenge*, 1957

All told, when the last Model T passed from wareroom to customer, the number manufactured came to 15,458,781. . . .

As the Model T vanished from the assembly line and joined the historic vehicles of the past, men could see that its most vital quality had been . . .

integrity. Its pioneering usefulness had depended on its utility, its dependability, its versatility, and its tenacious endurance, all traits which reflected the honesty of its construction. Charles Merz called it "the first log cabin of the Motor Age," an apt image, for it sheltered almost precisely half of the automobile owners of the United States in their swarming conquest of roads and lanes. It had the homely strength, economy, all-round usefulness of the log cabin, and like it, fitted the demands of a hard-working, practical people venturing into a new domain. A farmer of the Pacific Northwest told a story eloquent of its characteristics. In 1915 he bought a second-hand roadster two years old. In the next thirteen years, using it as a farm truck, he took the Model T to the repair shop only twice. The engine never required overhauling, and the car was never laid up. During these years, the owner, apart from the cost of demountable rims and a set of fenders, spent $40 on upkeep. "I do not know how many hundreds of thousands of miles it has run," he wrote, "as the speedometer was worn out when I bought it and I never put another one on, but it was in constant use." That car had integrity. Perhaps nothing in it was beautiful—but nothing in it was false.

It would be easy to fill pages with impressive statistics about the Model T. No other model has ever been produced in such numbers, and it is safe to say on this score alone its record will never be matched. . . . The Model T, teaching the industry (indeed, numerous industries) the immense possibilities of mass production of goods, greatly stimulated the growth of the national economy. Before it was discontinued, automobile manufacturing was firmly established as the leading industry of the United States, and a pillar of world prosperity.

More striking than such statistics, however, are the innumerable evidences of the sturdy serviceability of the Model T to tens of millions of families, its extraordinary durability, and its impact upon social change. . . . It is proof of the durability of the Model T that in March, 1927, nearly nineteen years after the first one had been made, 11,325,521 of its kind were registered in the United States. As late as 1949 more than 200,000 were still registered, a figure exceeding the registration of all American cars in the year the Model T was born. . . .

The social impact of the Model T is not easily measured, and awaits the systematic assay of experts in the various social studies. That it helped to change the national psychology and national manners and mores as well as the national economy, cannot be questioned. No other single machine, in all probability, did so much to induce people of provincial mind to begin thinking in regional and national terms; none did more to create the sense of a freer and more spacious life. As a single item in the long roster of effects, a historian of the country store notes that the Model T gave people a new liberty about what they would buy and where. Statisticians even reduced this liberty to figures: the farm buyer would travel on the average six to eight miles for hardware, fourteen for furniture, and twenty for women's fashions. Countless city wage earners gained from the humble, honest flivver the same command over distance: their ideas changed as suburban living became feasible, and country escapes easy. Rural villages began to wither and county seats to expand. The pressure toward uniformity, in one sense, increased; but in another sense people found a far greater variety in life.

In the two decades of the Model T, a new nation had been born—and partly at its behest.

Source 14   John B. Rae, *The American Automobile: A Brief History*, 1965

The American automobile industry has grown into the largest manufacturing operation in the world, its annual performance is the most important single indicator of the condition of the American economy, and American life is organized predominantly on the basis of the universal availability of motor transportation. All this would have been an impressive accomplishment over a period of centuries: as it was, it took place in two generations.

Source 15   John Jerome, *The Death of the Automobile: The Fatal Effect of the Golden Era, 1955–1970*, 1972

Once the air-pollution problem is solved (if it can be), we can go on to the next crisis resulting from the overproduction, overpromotion, oversale, and overuse of the private automobile. . . .

But maybe we will solve all those new problems, too. Assume for a moment that we can. Assume an industry that is totally socially responsible. Assume that the solutions are found: no more crises in environmental pollution, land rape, traffic death tolls, exhaustion of natural responses. The way completely cleared for unlimited expansion of the private automobile as the sole workable transportation system not just for the nation but for the whole planet. World-wide, up to the limit of the populace to pay for this private unlimited mobility. Whole continents to conquer—with pavement, traffic lights, stop signs, parking lots, commercial strips. Snow tires for the Himalayas! Antifreeze for Antarctica! Dune buggies for the Sahara! The very thought is enough to make our salesmen's hearts start pounding.

Unfortunately, there seems little likelihood that we'll have a chance to fill out the invoices. In the unlikely event that the directly automobile-related crises evaporate to allow unlimited growth, we'll run out of fossil fuels to combust. . . .

The rate we are burning fossil fuels has already overtaken the balance of nature, and we are generating carbon dioxide faster than we are oxygen. . . . One car, driving from Santa Monica to Pasadena, burns up more oxygen than the total population of Los Angeles County breathes in the same forty-five-minute period that the motor trip takes. . . .

Making fun of the prophets of doom is almost as entertaining as the delicious terror of contemplating the doom itself. In the meantime, no serious citizen can question the advisability of doing what we can to forestall the apocalypse. . . . Funny—all smog was at first was a stink. But it tipped the balance. It made us see, finally, that the automobile is the enemy.

Source 16   Andrew Rolle, *Los Angeles: From Pueblo to City of the Future*, 1981

Preoccupation with the automobile was central to Los Angeles's growth. Form did, indeed, follow function as Los Angeles sprawled. . . . Long ago demographers foresaw that Los Angeles would become a speeded-up prototype of that urbanization which today threatens to engulf the major cities of the world. This urban sprawl, with its satellite residential suburbs, has accompanied a massive shift from an agricultural to an industrial society. . . .

An up-dated epithet about Los Angeles no longer describes it jokingly as a group of suburbs in search of a city but now as a city connected by concrete and smog. Los Angeles depends on the automobile as does no other metropolis. As it struggles to accommodate three million autos, smog has become one of its most serious problems. . . .

Had Los Angeles maintained its original rapid transit system, the problem of pollution would surely have taken a different turn. But . . . [n]ow the city is sometimes referred to as "four thousand acres of parking lots." Lewis Mumford once estimated that two-thirds of its central area is occupied by facilities devoted to automobiles: garages, service stations, and streets.

Source 17 John B. Rae, *The American Automobile Industry,* 1984

The Model T, "Tin Lizzie," was put on the market in 1908, the answer to Ford's quest for the car for the mass market and the most famous automobile ever built. It was sturdily constructed to withstand hard use, mounted high to negotiate the rutted country roads of the day, and easy to operate and maintain. Owners could do much of their own repair work. It had a simple four cylinder 20 h.p. engine and a planetary transmission giving two speeds forward and one in reverse. Shifting gears, reversing, and braking were all done by foot pedals operating through bands on the transmission drums, so that a confused driver could always stop the car by pushing any two pedals. Like all motor vehicles of that era, the engine was started with a crank handle—the electric starter did not come until 1912 and was never standard equipment on the Model T. This technique demanded care. The crank handle on any car could kick back unexpectedly and broken arms and jaws were not uncommon. . . .

"Tin Lizzie" was an immediate and spectacular success. . . . The success of the Model T was so great that Henry Ford decided to abandon all other Ford models and concentrate his company's resources exclusively on the production of Model T's. This was a critical decision and a bold one. The rapidly mounting demand for the car appeared to justify the risk, but the market for motor vehicles was still new and untested: a change in public taste would have been disastrous. However, Ford made the right choice; Model T sales continued to rise geometrically. . . .

After much experimentation the moving assembly line came to fruition in 1913. . . . The key elements of this system were first, moving the work to the worker instead of vice versa; and second, having each worker perform a single operation, requiring as little skill as could be devised. In short, the concept was basically simple, but the execution was not. It required elaborate planning, complex and expensive tooling, and exact synchronization of the movement of materials through the plant and along main and subsidiary assembly lines. These first Ford assembly lines were in fact crude by later standards. . . .

It was still a revolution in methods of production and was immediately recognized as such. The adoption of the moving assembly line was the second of the fundamental decisions that put Ford at the top of the automotive world, the first being the decision to make only Model T's. . . . [B]y 1920 three-fifths of all the motor vehicles in the United States and half of those in the world were Model T Fords.

This feat attracted worldwide attention to the Ford Motor Company, greatly magnified when on 5 January 1914 the company announced a basic wage rate of five dollars a day, roughly twice the prevailing rate in Detroit at the time. Eager job seekers descended on the Ford plant and a few days after the announcement the crowds had to be dispersed with firehoses. As with virtually everything else Henry Ford did, the motivations for the five-dollar day have been exhaustively examined without any satisfactory conclusion being reached. Ford had a way of rationalizing his actions after the event, or having them rationalized for him, and it is seldom possible to pinpoint what really motivated him at the time. The five-dollar day has been attributed to a wish to share the company's enormous profits with its work force, to raise wages so as to create a market for Ford cars, to forestall possible I.W.W. activity, to reduce labor turnover, or simply to give order to the company's wage structure. One feature of the five-dollar day that has been overlooked is that half of it was regarded by the company as wages, which put the Ford Motor Company at the top of the current prevailing wage level in Detroit. The other half was considered to be a distribution of profits, a privilege rather than a right, so that in Henry Ford's eyes conditions could properly be imposed requiring a worker to be "worthy" of his share in the company's profits.

In this respect the five-dollar day was an example of the "welfare capitalism" that was coming into favor at that time. . . . The five-dollar wage was hedged with qualifications in practice, . . . but it was all magnificent publicity for the Ford Motor Company, and Henry Ford had an acute sense for publicity.

Source 18   Robert Lacey, *Ford: The Men and the Machines,* 1986

The Model T turned out to be exactly what was needed by a restless population trying to fill up a continent. . . . They swarmed everywhere, transforming the way people lived and thought and had fun—family outings, picnics, lovers' trysts. The freedom which the car offered loosened existing ties and created new ones. Together with radio, it was the people's car which transformed America from a continent of separate settlements into one vast neighbourhood. . . .

The Model T converted a plaything of the European rich into the birthright of the American masses, and it started off that strangest of love affairs, the enduring emotional relationship between the American and his car.

Source 19   Michael Renner, "Rethinking Transportation," *State of the World,* 1989

Since the days of Henry Ford, societies have enacted a steady stream of laws to protect drivers from each other and themselves, as well as to protect the general public from the unintended effects of massive automobile use. Legislators have struggled over the competing goals of unlimited mobility and the individual's right to be free of the noise, pollution, and physical dangers that the automobile often brings.

Prior to the seventies, the auto's utility and assured role in society were hardly questioned. Even worries about escalating gas prices and future fuel availability subsided in the eighties almost as quickly as they had emerged. . . .

The most alarming effect of mass motorization may not be the depletion of fossil fuels but the large-scale damage to human health and the natural environment. Researchers at the University of California estimate that the use of gasoline and diesel fuel in the United States alone may cause up to 30,000 deaths every year. And the American Lung Association estimates that air pollution from motor vehicles, power plants, and industrial fuel combustion costs the United States $40 billion annually in health care and lost productivity.

Cars, trucks, and buses play a prominent role in generating virtually all the major air pollutants, especially in cities. In OECD member countries, they contribute 75 percent of carbon monoxide emissions, 48 percent of nitrogen oxides, 40 percent of hydrocarbons, 13 percent of particulates, and 3 percent of sulphur oxides. Worldwide, the production and use of automobile fuels accounts for an estimated 17 percent of all carbon dioxide (CO_2) released from fossil fuels. Transportation is also the primary source of lead pollution. The adverse health effects of all these pollutants are fairly well established, though the threshold of effects remains uncertain.

Perhaps more significant are the synergistic effects. The best known and most pervasive of these is photochemical smog—the brown haze that causes health disorders, restricts visibility, erodes buildings and monuments, reduces crop yields, and is at least partly responsible for the massive forest damage afflicting central Europe. Ozone, the most important component of smog, is the product of complex reactions between nitrogen oxides and hydrocarbons in the presence of sunlight.

In 1986, between 40 and 75 million Americans were living in areas that failed to attain National Ambient Air Quality Standards for ozone, carbon monoxide, and particulates. If these standards were in force elsewhere, they would routinely be exceeded in many cities: Athens, Budapest, Cairo, Mexico City, New Delhi, and São Paulo are among those with the world's most polluted air.

Nitrogen and sulphur oxides, together with unburnt hydrocarbons, are the principal components of the phenomenon commonly known as acid rain. Acid precipitation is destroying freshwater aquatic life and forests throughout central Europe and North America and degrading marine life in Atlantic coastal waters.

The most serious long-term consequence of automotive emissions, however, is the atmospheric buildup of CO_2 and other "greenhouse gases"—nitrous oxide, methane, and ozone. There is now virtual consensus among scientists that if the concentration of CO_2 in the atmosphere doubles from preindustrial levels, a substantial increase in average global temperature will occur. Indeed, such a rise is already underway. The impending climate change could shift global precipitation patterns, disrupt crop-growing regions, raise sea levels, and threaten coastal cities worldwide with inundation.

Source 20 **Deborah Gordon, analyst for the Union of Concerned Scientists, *Steering a New Course*, 1991**

The breakdown of the transportation system will not occur tomorrow, or even next year. Without corrective action, however, a serious disintegration of service is likely by the end of the decade. One of the most ominous warnings is the alarming increase in congestion. The US General Accounting Office has calculated that if present trends continue, road congestion in the United States will *triple* in only fifteen years. . . .

Already two-thirds of the rush hour travellers on urban interstate highways experience delays. Americans spend one billion hours a year stuck in traffic, wasting two billion gallons of gasoline and costing the economy anywhere from $10 billion to $30 billion—enough to fund the entire federal environmental program. By the time congestion triples, it will cost the nation up to $50 billion a year, more than the federal government now spends on low-income housing, veterans benefits, and the war on drugs combined.

Traffic has gotten worse because there are simply too many passenger cars and trucks driven too many miles, with too few people in them, for our roads to handle. An estimated one-half of all trips Americans take, and at least three-quarters of all commutes, are made by a single person alone in a car. To accommodate this habit, we now own enough cars to put every American in one—and no one would have to sit in the back seat. We drove those vehicles nearly two trillion miles last year, and the number is growing at the rate of 3 per cent a year. . . .

Americans cherish their freedom, and to most of us this means the freedom to choose. But for passenger transportation in the 1990s, there is no true choice: most of us are limited to the gasoline-powered automobile. While the car once provided cheap, nearly unlimited mobility, today it is the cause of pollution, congestion, and a nationwide addiction to ever greater oil imports. Moreover, our hundreds of millions of passenger vehicles, each emitting its weight in carbon annually, are threatening climate stability by adding dangerous levels of carbon dioxide to the atmosphere.

The time is overdue for addressing these issues. As the problems caused by our inefficient use of transportation resources mount, we will pay a high price in reduced productivity, damage to the environment, and diminished human health and welfare. Transportation policy must steer a new course; we cannot afford to wait.

Source 21 Odil Tunali, "A Billion Cars: The Road Ahead," *World Watch*, January/February 1996

At the mid-point of the twentieth century, when there were 2.6 billion people on Earth, there were 50 million cars. Now, as we near the end of the century, the human population has more than doubled, but the car population has increased tenfold—to 500 million. Today, everyone seems to want a car. And within another 25 years there may be 1 billion cars on the world's roads.

It is not already car-dominated Los Angeles, Paris, or Rome where this is happening, but in the booming cities of the developing world. In China, for example, there are just 1.8 million passenger cars today—one for every 670 people. In ten years, there may be twice as many, and by 2010, that number is projected to rise to 20 million. Such a scenario seems likely to be repeated in most parts of the developing world.

The potential effects of this automotive explosion—on the quality of human life and the sustainability of all life—are staggering. But perceptions of what those effects will mean vary widely, depending on who is doing the perceiving. The world's automotive industries view the projected growth in car demand as a stupendous business opportunity, and a great economic windfall for those countries whose factories can meet the growing demand.

This view is shared by the governments of fast-developing countries like China, India, and Brazil, whose own industries are beginning to flourish. Since the American automotive boom of the 1950s and 60s, which coincided with a rapid rise in U.S. economic output and affluence, the standard prescription for development has held that any country aspiring to economic growth must rely on the auto industry as a central industrial pillar.

Increasingly affluent consumers in the developing countries, who represent the potential auto market of the near future, also share this excitement. The vast majority of that market will be in Asia and Latin America, and in formerly Communist countries of Eastern Europe, which are now bent on catching up with their affluent neighbors to the west. To these consumers, cars are not just transportation; they symbolize the highest rewards of the consumer culture: a proof of wealth, power, and personal freedom.

Yet consumers, industrialists, and economic planners are all neglecting the prodigious strains that automotive expansion is placing on both human and environmental health. Motor vehicle transport accounts for half of the world's total oil consumption, generates nearly one-fifth of all greenhouse gas emissions, and has pervasive impacts on land use and air quality. Tailpipe exhaust is now the single largest source of air pollution—surpassing wood fires, coal-burning power plants, and chemical manufacturing—in nearly half the cities of the world. And cities everywhere are choking on the sheer numbers of motor vehicles and the roads that attempt to accommodate them. The result is a declining quality of life in car-dominated cities worldwide.

 ## Questioning the Past

1. What was the significance of the Model T and the manner in which it was produced?

2. List the possible motives behind the decision of the Ford Motor Company to institute the $5 work day. Which motive, or motives, seem most plausible? Was Ford motivated by a sense of altruism or was the move merely a good business decision?

3. "The automobile has remade America in its own image," wrote Christopher Finch in *Highways to Heaven: The AUTO Biography of America*, "and that formidable work will not easily be undone." In what ways has the automobile shaped the America of the twentieth century? What are the attractions and the detractions of a lifestyle that revolves around the automobile? Should America try to find alternatives to an automobile-based transportation system?

4. "Reading the signs of the times is a method of information open to every one," Henry Ford wrote. "Those who know the times at all began to understand them before they existed. Signs of the times, then, are the signs of the times to come." What are the signs of the times with regard to the automobile, and what use could an entrepreneur such as Henry Ford make of such information?

5. If over a ten-year period, 2½ million people died in war or from disease, it would be considered a terrible tragedy, and world opinion would galvanize to stop the killing. Yet the death rate from traffic accidents is around 250,000 per year globally, and millions more suffer devastating injury. Do such deaths seem more acceptable than those wrought by war or disease?

Chapter 11

The Triangle Shirtwaist Factory Fire

A Tragedy Moves a Nation *March 25, 1911*

After the turn of the twentieth century much of the factory work in New York City, particularly in the garment industry, was located in "skyscrapers," buildings that rose 10 stories or more above street level. By the second decade of the century, in excess of half a million people in Manhattan worked in factories located at least eight stories high. In testimony before a New York State Assembly investigating committee on December 28, 1910, the New York City fire chief, Edward Croker, was asked the maximum reach of his department's firefighting potential. "Not over eighty-five feet," or about seven stories, was his reply. "I think if you want to go into the so-called workshops which are along Fifth Avenue and west of Broadway and east of Sixth Avenue, twelve-, fourteen- or fifteen-story buildings they call workshops," Croker stated, "you will find it very interesting to see the number of people in one of these buildings with absolutely not one fire protection, without any means of escape in case of fire."

11.1 The Triangle Shirtwaist Factory Fire

First Impressions
"My God, Will the Fire Department Never Come?"

March 25, 1911, blossomed into the kind of Saturday afternoon in early spring that gives rise to thoughts of a picnic in the park. But picnics were not part of the weekend routine for the 600 people who worked at the Triangle Shirtwaist Factory. Saturday and Sunday found them, not unlike any other day of the week, busy at their sewing machines on the eighth, ninth, and tenth floors of the Asch Building. Mostly ranging in age from 13 to 23, these employees—over 80 percent of whom were young women who had recently emigrated from Germany, Italy, Hungary, or Russia—had been lured to their jobs by a wage of $6 to $10 for a 60- to 72-hour workweek. They were just completing the day's work and preparing to

175

receive their pay envelopes when the first puffs of smoke were seen on the eighth floor.

Source 1 **"154 Killed in Skyscraper Factory Fire,"** *New York World,* **March 26, 1911**

At 4:35 o'clock yesterday afternoon fire springing from a source that may never be positively identified was discovered in the rear of the eighth floor of the ten-story building at the Northwest corner of Washington place and Greene street, the first of three floors occupied as a factory of the Triangle Waist Company. . . . At 2 o'clock this morning Chief Croker estimated the total number dead as one hundred and fifty-four. . . .

It was the most appalling horror since the Slocum disaster and the Iroquois Theatre fire in Chicago. Every available ambulance in Manhattan was called to cart the dead to the Morgue—bodies charred to unrecognizable blackness or reddened to a sickly hue—as was to be seen by shoulders or limbs protruding through flame eaten clothing. Men and women, boys and girls were of the dead that littered the street; that is actually the condition—the streets were littered.

The fire began in the eighth story. The flames licked and shot their way up through the other two stories. All three floors were occupied by the Triangle Waist Company. The estimate of the number of the employees at work is made by Chief Croker at about 1,000. The proprietors of the company say 700 men and girls were in their place.

Whatever the number, they had no chance of escape. Before smoke or flame gave signs from the windows the loss of life was fully under way. The first signs that persons in the street knew that these three top stories had turned into red furnaces in which human creatures were being caught and incinerated was when screaming men and women and boys and girls crowded out on the many window ledges and threw themselves into the streets far below.

They jumped with their clothing ablaze. The hair of some of the girls streamed up of flame as they leaped. Thud after thud sounded on the pavements. It is the ghastly fact that on both the Greene and the Washington place sides of the building there grew mounds of the dead and dying.

And the worst horror of all was that in this heap of the dead now and then there stirred a limb or sounded a moan.

Within the three flaming floors it was as frightful. There flames enveloped many so that they died instantly. When Fire Chief Croker could make his way into these three floors he found sights that utterly staggered him—that sent him, a man used to viewing horrors, back and down into the street with quivering lips.

The floors were black with smoke. And then he saw as the smoke drifted away bodies burned to bare bones. There were skeletons bending over sewing machines. . . .

The curious, uncanny feature about this deadly fire is that it was not spectacular from flame and smoke. The city had no sign of the disaster that was happening. The smoke of the fire scarcely blackened the sky. No big, definite clouds rose to blot out the sunshine and the springtime brightness of the blue above.

Concentrated, the fire burned within. The flames caught all the flimsy lace stuff and linens that go into the making of spring and summer shirtwaists and fed eagerly upon the rolls of silk.

The cutting room was laden with the stuff on long tables. The employees were rolling over such material at the rows and rows of machines. Sinisterly the spring day gave aid to the fire. Many of the window panes facing south and east were drawn down. Draughts had full play.

The experts say that the three floors must each have become a whirlpool of fire. Whichever way the entrapped creatures fled they met a curving sweep of flame. Many swooned and died. Others fought their way to the windows or the elevator or fell fighting for a chance at the fire-escape—the single fire-escape leading into the blind court that was to be reached from the upper floors by climbing over a window sill!

On all of the three floors, at a narrow window, a crowd met death trying to get out to that one slender fire-escape ladder.

Source 2 James Cooper, "World Reporter Passing When Fire Started Saw Girls Jump to Death," *New York World,* March 26, 1911

As the first whiffs of smoke came from the windows of the factory building . . . yesterday afternoon, I was passing that corner. Here follows a description of what occurred as witnessed by myself and hundreds of spectators during the first five minutes and later by thousands of men and women:

11.2 The Triangle Fire

For fully a minute the spectators seemed in doubt as to whether the smoke meant a fire in the building or was merely simply some unusual smoke that might come from a machine used for manufacturing purposes. Then a little tongue of flame appeared just over the top of an eight-story window on the west side of the Washington place side of the building.

"That's a sure enough fire! I'm going to send in an alarm!" said one man on the edge of a little group of men watching the fire. He set out on a run for Broadway, and as he did so there was a little ripple of fire ran around the tops of other windows on the eighth floor.

Within another minute the entire eighth floor of the building was spouting little jets of flame from the windows, as if the floor was surrounded by a row of incandescent lights. From the street there was not the slightest indication that the fire was of a serious nature. As a policeman arrived at the corner opposite the building a man remarked to him:

"It's mighty hard work burning one of these fire-proof buildings, but I guess it's lucky it's Saturday afternoon. It looks as if every one was out of the place."

The increasing light of the flames attracted a large crowd within three minutes. No sign of life in the building had been observed by the spectators on the street front when suddenly something that looked like a bale of dark dress goods was hurled from an eighth story window.

"Somebody's in there all right," exclaimed a spectator. "He's trying to save the best cloth."

Another seeming bundle of cloth came hurtling through the same window, but this time a breeze tossed open the cloth and from the crowd of 500 persons there came a cry of horror.

The breeze had disclosed the form of a girl shooting down to instant death on the stone pavement beneath. Before the crowd could realize the full meaning of the horror another girl sprang upon another window ledge. It seemed she had broken open the window with her fists. Her hair, streaming down her back, was all ablaze and her clothing was on fire.

She stood poised for a moment with her arms extended and then down she came.

A united murmur of dread went up from the watching multitude, rising to a loud note of despair as three other girls at the same moment threw themselves from various windows and other girls could be seen clinging to the window frames, struggling for breath and trying to decide between death within the factory room and the death on the stone pavement and sidewalk below.

What seemed like a full minute passed before the next girl jumped. As she took the fatal leap a wave of flame followed her from the window, giving the spectators some idea of conditions in the building.

A policeman came running from the Mercer street station just in time to witness this girl's death. "My God," he cried, "will the Fire Department never come?" He ran away to telephone and just then two more girls came down together, seemimgly with their arms about each other.

As with one accord the throng of spectators, now numbering in the thousands, turned away their heads. "It seems a crime to see such a thing and be unable to do anything to help," they said.

A shout of terror from a score or more girls who lined the upper windows of the high buildings on the opposite side of the street apprised those of us on the sidewalk of a new terror. They could see what we could not, a rush of girls on the ninth and tenth floors of the building toward the windows on the Washington place front.

Until that moment there had appeared no signs of fire on the two upper floors, but puffs of smoke came from the windows and then a girl burst right through a window on the topmost floor and sprang out to death. Fire followed her, but disappeared for a time while the little lights began playing by the score about the upper window casings.

I heard many men volunteer to carry the burned, crushed bodies of the girls from the sidewalk and street where they fell, but a thin line of police had been formed to cut off the building pending the arrival of the firemen, and quantities of falling glass and bits of cornice made the place beneath the burning factory so dangerous that the police waved back the volunteers with the word:

"We would all go if it would do any good, but a wall may fall and you must all stand back."

The gladdest sound that had ever come to the ears of the spectators was the clanging of the bell announcing the first of the fire apparatus was coming from Broadway.

Then a man who was standing close beside me and who was crying said dully: "What's the use? It's only a chemical wagon and a hook and ladder. They haven't sent in enough alarms."

The chemical so valuable at small fires was absolutely of no use, and the hook and ladder men raised a ladder as far as the fifth story but could do no better. Scarcely had the ladder been raised when the firemen received their first idea of the work in store.

Another bundle of burning dresses enclosing a girl came twisting and turning through the air from a ninth story window. The poor girl struck upon the upper rounds of the useless ladder. For an instant we all thought she had caught there, and three firemen were on the ladder in a moment. But the girl was unable to sustain her hold, and after what seemed a real struggle on her part to cling to the ladder, she came hurtling down the remaining five stories to the street.

As she lay upon the sidewalk her hair was burning and a fireman ran to her and beat out the flames with his bare hands. He knelt over the girl for a minute and then returned to the wagon.

"It's no use touching her now," he said to a group of us, "she's battered to pieces."

Suddenly the streets began to fill with weeping girls, some supporting others who had fainted. Men and boys with hands and faces slashed by glass appeared inside the police lines asking for a doctor, and for the first time we in the crowd of spectators learned that a large majority of the 600 employees of the factory had succeeded in reaching the street in safety. But all had left friends in the burning rooms, and all were so dazed that they could scarcely speak. The climax of the terrors on the street front came just as the first water tower came dashing into the street, at sight of which the crowd welled with delight. While the tower was scarcely one block distant three girls leaped at practically the same moment from the tenth story windows.

I could see the throng that from three streets witnessed this fall. From the moment of the first deep moan that told of the girls' fall every one turned face about, and it is doubtful if any one witnessed the end. . . .

Before the first water tower could be put into action the crowd was treated to a sight of coolness and heroism that for a moment gave some relief to the tension.

Adjoining the factory building on the west is the New York University Law School building. It is also ten stories in height, but slightly overtops the burned structure. Several men appeared upon the roof of the University building and lowered ropes to the window farthermost west in the tenth story of the factory.

From the street we had been unable to see whether or not any girls were left alive on the top floor, but the minute the first rope was lowered it was grasped by a girl, who was pulled to safety on the roof of the University building.

So much smoke was coming from the upper windows that it was impossible to judge how many were saved in this way, but what appeared to be ten or twelve bundles, representing saved human beings, were pulled to the roof.

Source 3 "Law Students Save Twenty," *New York World,* March 26, 1911

Twenty members of the practice class of the Law School of the New York University, which lies just to the east of the fire-swept structure, were attending a lecture by Prof. Frank A. Sommer when the scream of a girl drew them to the windows of the room. Through the smoke and flame that poured from the factory they saw a long line of operatives making their way. . . to the roof of a lower building immediately adjoining that of the University.

Prof. Sommer immediately marshalled his students, led them to the roof of the university building, where two wooden ladders were found, and lowered them to the roof where the girls were gathering, many with dresses afire. As quickly as was possible twenty of these girls were helped to the roof of the university, from which they were led to the elevators and carried to the street.

"But we could serve only a part of those who had fled to this roof," Prof. Sommer said. "As many others, I am sure, would not wait for us, in their pain and terror. I saw girl after girl leap down the airshaft in the rear of this building on which they had sought refuge.

"It was thirty-five feet from this roof to the top of the university. Comparatively far away as we were, the flames actually menaced the wooden ladders that we used . . . I am sure they could not have been saved in any other way, for as they came to us many of them were in flames, some of them had their hair afire."

Source 4   Statement of Professor H. G. Parsons, witness from the ninth floor of the university building

The sight that I caught from the windows of our building was more ghastly than I shall ever be able to put into words. When that first scream came I did not need to be told or to look to see what had happened. I knew.

But when I did go to the windows it was to be confronted by things more terrible than I could ever have imagined. I saw a fire escape literally gorged with girls from the ninth to the first floors. The ladder that led from the lowest landing place to the street was not working. I cannot even guess how many girls were caught in that trap.

As I took my horrified view of them a great tongue of flame reached out and swept the fire escape from top to bottom. Then the girls who had been there dropped out of my sight like flies over the mouth of a furnace. They were swept away in a breath. Not one escaped. The second glance that I compelled myself to take confirmed that.

Source 5   Statement of Morris Katz, survivor of the fire

I was working with my sister Gussie on the eighth floor. If the fire had started five minutes later we would all have been out of the building. The girls were beginning to get on their hats and coats when some one shouted, "fire." I looked up and saw a tiny little fire starting close by the Greene street stairway down which all the employees go.

Before you could scarcely think the fire was running all around the room. There was a lot of light muslin in the room and heaps of packing paper. I ran first toward the Washington place entrance, but there was a crowd there, and the girls cried that they could not get the door open. Some of us ran back to the Greene street entrance, but the fire was all over there, so I took my sister by the hand and ran for the fire escapes.

Lots of us got down that way, but at the bottom we found ourselves all shut in. I cut my hand breaking a basement window, and we crawled through to the basement. It was pitch dark, but some of us groped our way through to the Washington place side, where there is a freight elevator running to the sidewalk. I climbed up the wire rope of this and managed to make myself heard by some men on the sidewalk.

They found some way of lowering the elevator, and we all came out through that hole.

A Narrow Instruction

Less than 30 minutes from the time it was first noticed, the fire at the Asch Building was under control. But in that short, frantic half-hour, 46 people had taken the leap from the upper stories of the factory. None survived the jump. Some hit the sidewalk so hard that their bodies cracked the pavement. They fell through the nets held by the firemen. They lay in heaps on the sidewalk for two hours while the fireman drenched the smoldering structure with hoses.

When they were able to enter the building, the firemen found still bolted the door to the stairs on the eighth floor. They also found the bodies of nineteen more women who had jumped down the elevator shafts. Eighty-two other bodies were strewn around in the debris. The building, as advertised, was indeed fireproof and showed no structural damage.

At dawn on the morning after the blaze, the families of the victims lined up at the gates of a makeshift morgue on the Charity Dock at the foot of East 26th Street. They then began the ordeal of walking along the rows of coffins in hopes of identifying which of the bodies were those of their loved ones. Most of the victims had been burned beyond recognition. Seven victims were never identified.

A memorial parade of five hours' duration drew 100,000 marchers and 500,000 spectators on April 5, 1911. It rained throughout the event. The *New York World* reported that the "skies wept" along with the mourners.

On April 11, the owners of the Triangle Shirtwaist Company, Isaac Harris and Max Blanck, who called themselves "the Shirtwaist Kings," were indicted for manslaughter. The trial opened on December 5, amid a near-riot by parents of the victims, who screamed "Murderers! Murderers!" as Harris and Blanck were escorted into the courtroom. The trial revealed that the Shirtwaist Kings had been warned of the hazardous conditions in their facility. There had been a number of nonfatal fires in the factory over the years, it was disclosed. Yet Harris and Blanck had ignored the advice of the city and held no fire drills. They admitted to a policy of locking the exits from the factory as a method of preventing "tardiness" and "theft." Under cross-examination Harris disclosed that his known losses from theft in 1910 amounted to less than $12.

After 16 days of testimony from survivors, firemen, and city inspectors, the case was presented to the jury. Surprisingly, the jury found the defendants not guilty. Interviews given by jurors following the trial indicated that the panel believed that Harris and Blanck were indeed guilty; their decision reflected a narrow instruction to the jury from the judge. The jurors were instructed that they could not find the Triangle Shirtwaist proprietors guilty because of any general policy of bolting the exit doors, but rather only if they found "the defendants had knowledge that the door was locked" at the moment the fire began. This point had defied proof.

Source 6   Statement of Dr. George M. Price, chairman of special
task force, the Fire Prevention Investigating Committee,
March 27, 1911

What was expected has happened. Those who knew of the flimsy fire protection
in the loft buildings of New York long ago predicted just such a disaster as
occurred in Washington Square. If, however, this building were the only one of
those unprotected against fire the situation would not be so terrible, but the
fact is that there is hardly a large loft building in New York which is better
protected against fire, or where there is special care taken to safeguard the limbs
and lives of operatives.

The Joint Board of Sanitary Control employed eight Inspectors . . . and the
data gathered by these Inspectors throws much light upon the inadequacy of
the fire-prevention facilities in most of the 1,243 shops inspected by the board.

In 14 shops no fire escapes at all have been found. In 65 shops the fire
escapes were provided with straight ladders, which are, as is well known, very
dangerous, and which hardly anyone who is not an experienced ladder climber
can make use of.

In 101 shops no drop ladders at all were found, or those found were placed
out of reach.

In 491 shops, or 40 per cent of all shops inspected, there were no other
exits in case of fire except one fire escape.

In 28 shops the doors leading to halls and stairways were found locked
during the day.

In 60 shops the halls were less than three feet wide.

In 1,173 shops, or 97.5 percent of all shops, the doors leading to halls
were opened in instead of out as the law requires.

In a word, the investigation has shown that even with the low standards
for fire protection as demanded at present by the labor laws, there are hundreds
and thousands of violations in one industry alone.

When we consider the existing regulations about fire protection, we must
admit that they are far inadequate and, indeed, a delusion and a sham.

There is no reason why the so-called fireproof buildings . . . where such
large numbers are working and women are massed, there is no reason why these
should not be compelled to provide fire escapes. Nor is there any reason why
the shops which are required to have fire escapes should have but one, no matter
how many persons work therein. According to the present law, if a building is
provided with one fire escape it answers the purpose of the law, whether ten
persons or ten hundreds work thereat.

Source 7   Editorial, "Murdered by Incompetent Government,"
New York World, March 27, 1911

After the disastrous factory fire in Newark last November Chief Croker said:

"There are buildings in New York where the danger is every bit as great
as in the building destroyed at Newark, and a fire in the daytime would be
accompanied by loss of life. We can see that the law is complied with, but that
is as far as we can go. What we should have is an ordinance requiring fire-escapes

on every building used for manufacturing purposes. Take for instance some of the large loft buildings below Twenty-third street. The employees go up to their work in the elevators and many of them do not even know where the stairways are. I have appeared before many committees trying to have the ordinance amended so that fire-escapes would be required on these buildings. The absence of fire-escapes on the buildings where persons work subjects them to a risk which they should not be compelled to take."

The *World* and other newspapers seconded Chief Croker's demand but nothing was done to prevent in New York a calamity greater than that in Newark. Saturday it came; and more than 150 persons died horrible deaths in the worst disaster since the burning of the *General Slocum*, victims of official negligence and incompetency in the face of the clearest warning.

Because the building where the fire occurred was of the approved "loft" type, "partly fireproof but not death-proof," as Chief Croker well describes it, there was but one narrow, flimsy fire-escape. It led not to the street and safety but to a courtyard below the street level from which at that hour there was no exit. This building is one which the Fire Department had "recommended" should be equipped with escapes, but the department has no authority to order fire-escapes put on.

A ten-story loft building, no matter how nearly fireproof it may be, is commonly filled with inflammable material. It should be equipped with automatic sprinklers on every floor. This building was not. It should have broad and ample stairways with wide treads and low risers, inclosed in a fireproof well. This building had two stairways, each no wider than those in a private house; and on the fatal ninth floor, a door opening inward prevented quick access to one of them. The doors of public school buildings open outward. That is the law. Loft buildings should be subject to the same rule.

The elevators in a loft building are expected to carry all its inmates up and down. They are ample for the purpose except in emergency. There are doubtless many of the girls who, as Chief Croker says, did not know where the stairs were. . . . Fire-drills are held in schools which are but four stories high. In this loft building of ten stories, in which at times 2,000 girls were gathered, none was ever held. Loft buildings by the dozen are being built today in New York which are legal death-traps. An enormous army of working men and women must starve, or in the law phrase "assume the risk" of working in them.

By what the Washington Place building had not and was not, we know what a loft building should have and should be. If already constructed, it should be equipped at once with ample fire-escapes to the street—not steep and flimsy, but substantial, wide, easy to use. It should have automatic sprinklers, doors opening outward, compulsory fire-drills, placards of instruction, arrows on the walls pointing to stairways and windows, free access to the roof at all times. And no new building of this type should ever again be erected in New York without a well in which nothing that can burn is permitted.

Against such reasonable safeguards we may expect architects to protest lest their designs be "disfigured," and owners and tenants to raise objections of expense. But if such arguments outweigh the mute appeal of those rows of charred bodies in the Morgue, of the yawning holes in the sidewalk through which young girls crashed to the vaults below, of the shafts in which dying wretches flung themselves on top of the halted elevators—then what is to-day New York's sorrow will live and last as its shame.

📖 *Second Thoughts*
A Sense of Stricken Guilt

11.3 A Short
History of
American Labor

Harris and Blanck actually turned a nice profit from the Triangle Fire. They collected from their insurance company $64,925 above the value of the property they lost in the blaze. On September 26, 1913, Blanck was convicted of locking the exit door of his new factory with a chain. He was fined $20. He was convicted on December 1, 1913, of forcing a 19-year-old woman to work on Sunday, in violation of city ordinance. His fine was again $20. On March 11, 1914, Harris and Blanck settled the claims of the relatives of Washington Place victims by compensating them $75 for the lives of their loved ones. Meanwhile, the State of New York and the governments of other jurisdictions were moved by the Triangle Fire to enact new codes to ensure the health and safety of workers.

Source 8 **Abram I. Elkus, chief counsel, Factory Investigating Commission of New York State, October 14, 1911**

A man may be killed by a tenement house as truly as by a club or gun. A man may be killed by a factory and the unsanitary conditions in it as surely as he may be killed by a fire.

It is not less true that the slaughter of men and women workers by the slow process of unsanitary and unhealthful conditions is not immoral and anti-social, but the state is beginning to declare that it is legally indefensible and therefore must, through carefully considered legislation, be made virtually impossible. . . .

The so-called unavoidable or unpreventable accidents which, it is said, were once believed to be the result of the inscrutable decrees of Divine Providence are now seen to be the result in many cases of unscrupulous greed or human improvidence.

Source 9 **Editorial, "Triangle Fire Anniversary,"** *New York Times,* **March 25, 1961**

This is a day for remembrance, appreciation and a resolve to do better—the fiftieth anniversary of the Triangle factory fire on Washington Place that, because of inadequate fire prevention and protection, took no less than 146 garment workers' lives.

The public outcry that followed this tragedy gave strength to those valiant leaders who first investigated the conditions that made the catastrophe possible and then brought about the "golden age" of social legislation in New York that set the pace for other states—Alfred E. Smith, Robert F. Wagner, Frances Perkins, Dr. George M. Price and Rose Schneiderman. Without their indefatigable efforts many more lives would surely have been lost during the past half century. . . .

This is a good day also to take account of what still needs to be done. Within the past three years three fires in the downtown loft district of Manhattan have added thirty-three to the toll of unnecessary deaths. In spite of all the legal protections of the past half century none of the three buildings had automatic sprinklers. All of them revealed some of the same sort of "housekeeping" and structural fire hazards that killed so many people fifty years ago. And the 21,000 searching factory inspections, first ordered by Fire Commissioner Cavanagh in 1958, have found 30,000 violations of existing laws since last November and have resulted in no less than 1,130 orders to install sprinklers.

Source 10 Remarks of Frances Perkins, secretary of labor from 1933 to 1945, March 25, 1961

It was a fine, bright spring afternoon. We heard the fire engines and rushed into the Square to see what was going on. We saw the smoke pouring out of the building. We got there just as they started to jump. I shall never forget the frozen horror which came over us as we stood with our hands on our throats watching that horrible sight, knowing that there was no help. They came down in twos and threes, jumping together in a kind of desperate hope. . . .

Out of that terrible episode came a self-determination of stricken conscience in which the people of this state saw for the first time the individual worth and value of each of those 146 people who fell or were burned in that great fire. And we saw, too, the great human value of every individual who was injured in an accident by a machine.

There was a stricken conscience of public guilt and we all felt that we had been wrong, that something was wrong with that building which we had accepted or the tragedy never would have happened. Moved by this sense of stricken guilt, we banded together to find a way by law to prevent this kind of disaster.

And so it was that the Factory Commission that sprang out of the ashes of the tragedy made an investigation that took four years to complete, four years of searching, of public hearings, of legislative formulations, of pressuring through the legislature the greatest battery of bills to prevent disasters and hardships affecting working people, of passing laws the likes of which has never been seen in any four sessions of any state legislature. . . .

The stirring up of the public conscience and the act of the people in penitence brought about not only these laws which make New York State to this day the best state in relation to factory laws; it was also that stirring of conscience which brought about in 1932 the introduction of a new element into the life of the whole United States. We had in the election of Franklin Roosevelt the beginning of what has come to be called a New Deal for the United States. But it was based upon the experiences that we had had in New York State and upon the sacrifices of those who, we faithfully remember with affection and respect, died in that terrible fire on March 25, 1911. They did not die in vain and we will never forget them.

Source 11   Leon Stein, *The Triangle Fire,* 1962

Harris and Blanck had made their fortunes manufacturing shirtwaists for ladies. They were the largest firm in the business, and the garment they made was aimed at mass sales. It was of medium quality and sold for $16.50 to $18 a dozen—wholesale.

More than any other item of feminine apparel, the shirtwaist symbolized the American female's new-found freedoms. It was a cool and efficient bodice garment, generally worn with a tailored skirt. Early in the new century it became standard attire for thousands of young ladies taking positions with industry and commercial enterprises. The popular artist, Charles Dana Gibson, immortalized the shirtwaisted female. He pictured her as a bright-eyed, fast-moving young lady, her long tresses knotted in a bun atop her proud head, ready to challenge the male in sport, drawing room, and, if properly equipped with paper cuff covers, even in the office.

The shirtwaist was topped at the neck by a recognizable variant of an open or buttoned mannish collar. In sharp contrast to the masculine stringency thus achieved, it descended in a broad expanse across the bosom, then by means of tucks, darts, or pleats tapered dramatically to a fitted waistline. The secret of its perennial popularity was in its lines and the fabric of which it was generally made. Crisp, clean, translucent—and more combustible than paper—the sheer cotton fabrics produced opposite but pleasing effects. The bouffant quality of the fabric enhanced the figure it enfolded. At the same time its sheerness piquantly revealed the dainty shape beneath.

At the start of the new century the garment industry began a move out of the slum workshops and railroad flats in which entire families labored over bundles of cut garments farmed out to them by jobbers. By 1903, . . . in New York, 70 percent of coat production was done in factories in contrast to the old farming-out system. . . .

The advantages of locating in one of the new towering loft buildings were described by Arthur E. McFarlane as including "cheaper insurance because loft buildings were fireproof. . . ." But the more important advantage arose from the New York factory law requirement that each worker be provided with 250 cubic feet of air. In the new buildings, the ceilings were higher than in the old with the result that more workers could be crowded into a given area. In terms of square feet per worker, the new factories provided less, not more space for each employee.

Because of this, firms like Triangle could, in effect, draw together under one roof the scores of homework units and sweatshops they would have had to utilize under the old farming-out system. Instead, these now became self-organized teams of workers.

Triangle would hire a good machine operator and allocate to him half a dozen machines out of the 240 on the ninth floor. In turn, this operator, in reality a contractor for the firm, would hire the young girls, immigrants and women from his hometown across the sea, as learners. He would teach them how to make the separate parts of the garment which he, as master craftsman, would join together. . . . Only he knew the value of the work done by his team because only he bargained with the company for the rate on each style.

"The girls never knew," says Joseph Flecher [a cashier at Triangle and a fire survivor]. "For them there was no fixed rate. They got whatever the contractor wanted to pay as a start. In two or three weeks they knew how to sew very well. Never mind. For a long time they still got the same low pay. Triangle and the inside contractor got the difference."

The company dealt only with its contractors. It felt no responsibility for the girls. Its payroll listed only the contractors. It never knew the exact total of its workers.

On Saturdays, it was the inside contractor who paid the girls. In each case he took into account the skill and speed, the family relationships or the defenselessness of the individual worker. She, in turn, showed her appreciation by being docile and uncomplaining.

Source 12 Joseph G. Rayback, *A History of American Labor,* 1966

An issue of great importance in the nineteenth century—that of safety and health in factories, tenements, and mines—might have been forgotten in the early twentieth century if it had not been for the Triangle Shirt Waist Factory fire in New York City in 1911. The tragedy . . . renewed the older movement. Under the pressure of the Progressives, led in this case by state federations of labor, northern and western states refurbished their old laws, defining safety regulations in factories more specifically and providing more severe punishment for violations. Some states also enacted more exacting tenement- and mine-safety laws.

11.4 Women in the Workplace: Labor Unions

Source 13 Allen Weinstein and R. Jackson Wilson, *Freedom and Crisis,* 1974

Who was to blame for the tragedy? This question haunted New Yorkers in the weeks that followed the Triangle disaster. . . . The city's fire department bore a share of the responsibility, despite the bravery of those who fought the blaze. The department had failed to enforce even those few mild safety laws that were on the books. Moreover, its equipment was inadequate for fighting fires in the city's new loft buildings. The tallest fire ladders reached only the sixth floor, although half the city's factory workers worked in lofts above this floor. Some of the department's safety nets were so weak that they broke under the force of falling bodies.

The City Buildings Department too had to accept a measure of the blame. The Asch Building, like most of New York City's garment shops, lacked adequate safety features. Several months earlier, a factory inspector had warned the owners of the Asch Building of such violations as insufficient exits and locked stairway doors. But the department made no effort to ensure that these conditions were corrected. There were 47 inspectors in Manhattan to check over 50,000 buildings. Of these buildings 13,600 had been listed as dangerous by the fire department the previous month. Inspectors managed to visit 2,000 buildings in March, but the Asch Building was not among them.

Nor were the fire insurance companies innocent of blame. Insurance brokers in New York suffered heavy losses from the numerous fires that occurred in the city's loft buildings. Yet the insurance industry failed to insist on safety standards that might have reduced fire hazards. Rather, they preferred to pay off after a fire and then raise a company's premiums. Higher policy rates also meant higher commissions for insurance brokers. During the 1890s a group of insurance companies attempted to offer cheaper rates to manufacturers who installed sprinkler systems in their factories. These companies were soon driven out of business by the city's powerful insurance industry. It was simply easier and more profitable to leave the "fireproof" firetraps alone and settle afterward.

On April 11, a week after the public funeral for the Triangle victims, Isaac Harris and Max Blanck were indicted by a grand jury and charged with manslaughter. . . . If Harris and Blanck had been convicted, the Triangle fire might have been forgotten more easily. The public might have been satisfied that justice had been done. As it turned out, the acquittal of Harris and Blanck sparked a new effort to improve the conditions under which New York City's laborers worked.

 ## Questioning the Past

1. Search the sources presented and list the various causes they cite for the tragedy at the Asch Building on March 25, 1911. Which of these seem plausible and which do not? What might have prevented the loss of life that occurred?

2. The manner in which the work force of the Triangle Shirtwaist Company was organized is known as the **padrone** system. How did this system function and what were the advantages and disadvantages of it to the workers, contractors, and factory owners?

3. Argue the case for and against the assumption by federal, state, and local government of a responsibility to inspect and regulate privately owned businesses and factories in an effort to guarantee a safe and healthy working environment.

Chapter 12

Margaret Sanger

The First Birth Control Clinic Is Opened

October 16, 1916

"No woman can call herself free who does not control her own body," Margaret Sanger wrote. "No woman can call herself free until she can choose conscientiously whether she will or will not be a mother." Acting on this premise, Sanger took what seemed a bold step in 1916. She rented a storefront in Brooklyn and opened the first birth control clinic in America. Her intent in establishing the clinic was to disseminate information on contraception and provide literature on sex education. Each person wishing a consultation was to be charged a fee of ten cents.

The clinic was an immediate success. Young women waited in line for the opportunity to talk with Sanger or her sister, Ethel Byrne, both nurses. The only problem with the clinic was that distributing information of this kind was against the law. It was illegal under the laws of the state of New York, and it violated the Comstock Law, passed by the federal government in 1873.

The Comstock Law provided for a penalty of $5,000 in fines and up to five years of imprisonment for "every obscene, lewd, or lascivious book, pamphlet, picture, paper, writing, print, or other publication of an indecent character, and every article or thing designed, adapted, or intended for the prevention of conception or procuring of abortion." The laws of New York paralleled that of the federal government: no person could give another information about contraception.

On October 25, 1916, officers of the New York City vice squad raided Margaret Sanger's birth control clinic. They seized literature and confiscated files detailing the case histories of the clinic's clients. They also arrested Margaret Sanger and members of her staff.

Anthony Comstock, who inspired and gave his name to the law prohibiting the dissemination of books and other literature on birth control, set the standards of decency in America during the Victorian Age. "If you open the door to anything," he warned in a 1915 interview in *Harper's Weekly,* "the filth will all pour in and the degradation of youth will follow." Any public mention of sex could arouse "impure" thoughts, corrupt youth, and bring civilization crashing down in horrific collapse.

189

✑ *First Impressions*
Matters of Life—and Death

In his efforts to shore up civilized society, Comstock had the backing of the law and prevailing attitudes. Sexual intercourse was to occur only within marriage, and it was to occur for the purpose of procreation, nothing more, nothing less. It was against such attitudes that Margaret Sanger had to pursue her goal of educating the public on the importance of birth control.

Source 1   Anthony Comstock, president of the Society for the Suppression of Vice, *Traps for the Young*, 1883

Satan is permitted to place his traps where they will do him the most good and the children the most harm. . . . This moral vulture steals upon our youth in the home, school, and college, silently striking its terrible talons into their vitals, and forcibly bearing them away on hideous wings to shame and death. Like a cancer, it fastens itself upon the imagination, and sends down into the future life thousands of roots, poisoning the nature, enervating the system, destroying self-respect, fettering the will-power, defiling the mind, corrupting the thoughts, leading to secret practices of most foul and revolting character, until the victim tires of life, and existence is scarcely endurable. It sears the conscience, hardens the heart, and damns the soul. It leads to lust and lust breeds unhallowed living, and sinks man, made in the image of God, below the level of the beasts. There is no force at work in the community more insidious, more constant in its demands, or more powerful and far-reaching than lust. *It is the constant companion of all other crimes.* It is honeycombing society. Like a frightful monster, it stands peering over the sleeping child, to catch its first thoughts on awakening. This is especially true when the eye of youth has been defiled with the scenes of lasciviousness in the weekly crime newspapers, or by their offspring, obscene books and pictures. . . . Think of the homes that are wrecked by unbridled passion. . . . From the first impure thought til the close of the loathsome life of the victim, there is a succession of sickening, offensive, and disgusting scenes before the mind, until life, to such a one, must be made up of disease, wounds, and putrefied sores. Suicide dances before his vision in his moments of despondency as the only means by which to hide his shame. . . .

I repeat, *lust is the boon companion of all other crimes.* There is no evil so extensive, none doing more to destroy the institutions of free America. It sets aside the laws of God and morality; marriage bonds are broken, most sacred ties severed, State laws ignored, and dens of infamy plant themselves in almost every community, and then reaching out like immense cuttlefish, draw in, from all sides, our youth to destruction. . . .

The thing I mention now [free love] crushes self-respect, moral purity, and holy living. Sure ruin and death are the end to the victims caught by this doctrine. . . . It is a bid to the lowest and most debased forms of living, and is dangerous to youth and adults alike. . . . It should be spelled l-u-s-t, to be rightly understood. . . .

As advocated by a few indecent creatures calling themselves reformers— men and women foul of speech, shameless in their lives, and corrupting in their influences—we must go to a sewer that has been closed, where the accumulations of filth have for years collected, to find a striking resemblance to its true character. I know of nothing more offensive to decency or more revolting to good morals. . . . With them, marriage is bondage; love is lust; celibacy is suicide; while fidelity to marriage vows is a relic of barbarism. All restraints which keep boys and girls, young men and young maidens pure and chaste, which prevent our homes from being turned into voluntary brothels, are not to be tolerated by them.

Nothing short of turning the whole human family loose to run wild like the beasts of the forest, will satisfy the demands of the leaders and publishers of this literature.

Source 2 **Handbill distributed in English, Yiddish, and Italian in the Brownsville section of Brooklyn, autumn 1916**

MOTHERS!
    Can you afford to have a large family?
    Do you want any more children?
    If not, why do you have them?
    DO NOT KILL, DO NOT TAKE LIFE, BUT PREVENT
    Safe, Harmless, Information can be obtained of trained Nurses at
      46 AMBOY STREET
    Near Pitkin Ave.—Brooklyn
    Tell your Friends and Neighbors. All Mothers Welcome. A registration
      fee of 10 cents entitles any mother to this information.

Source 3 Margaret Sanger, *An Autobiography,* 1938

The morning of October 16, 1916—crisp but sunny and bright after days of rain—Ethel, Fania, and I opened the doors of the first birth control clinic in America, the first anywhere in the world except the Netherlands. I . . . believe this was an event of social significance.

Would the women come? Did they come? Nothing, not even the ghost of Anthony Comstock, could have kept them away. We had arrived early, but before we could get the place dusted and ourselves ready for the official reception, Fania called, "Do come outside and look." Halfway to the corner they were standing in line, at least one hundred and fifty, some shawled, some hatless, their red hands clasping the cold, chapped, smaller ones of their children. . . .

Newly married couples with little but love, faith, and hope to save them from charity, told of the tiny flats they had chosen, and of their determination to make a go of it if only the children were not born too soon. A gaunt skeleton suddenly stood up one morning and made an impassioned speech. "They offer us charity when we have more babies than we can feed, and when we get sick with more babies for trying not to have them they just give us more charity talks!"

Women who were themselves already past childbearing age came just to urge us to preserve others from the sorrows of ruined health, overworked

12.1 The Margaret Sanger Papers

husbands, and broods of defective and wayward children growing up on the streets, filling dispensaries and hospitals, filing through the juvenile courts.

We made records of every applicant and, though the details might vary, the stories were basically identical. All were confused, groping among the ignorant sex-teachings of the poor, fumbling without guidance after truth, misled and bewildered in a tangled jungle of popular superstitions and old wives' remedies. Unconsciously they dramatized the terrible need of intelligent and scientific instruction in these matters of life—and death. . . .

Day after day the waiting room was crowded with members of every race and creed; Jews and Christians, Protestants and Roman Catholics alike made their confessions to us, whatever they may have professed at home or in church. I asked one bright little Catholic what excuse she might make to the priest when he learned she had been to the clinic. She answered indignantly, "It's none of his business. My husband has a weak heart and works only four days a week. He gets twelve dollars, and we can barely live on it now. We have enough children."

Her friend, sitting by, nodded approval. "When I was married," she broke in, "the priest told us to have lots of children and we listened to him. I had fifteen. Six are living. I'm thirty-seven years old now. Look at me! I might be fifty!"

That evening I made a mental calculation of fifteen baptismal fees, nine baby funerals, masses and candles for the repose of nine baby souls, the physical agony of the mother and the emotional torment of both parents, and I asked myself, "Is this the price of Christianity?" . . .

Although the line outside was enough to arouse police attention, nine days went by without interference. . . . The next day Ethel and Fania were both absent from the clinic. The waiting room was filled almost to suffocation when the door opened and the woman [Margaret Whitehurst] . . . came in.

"Are you Mrs. Sanger?"

"Yes."

"I'm a police officer. You're under arrest."

The doors were locked and this Mrs. Margaret Whitehurst and other plain-clothes members of the vice squad—used to raid gambling dens and houses of assignation—began to demand names and addresses of the women, seeing them with babies, broken, old, worried, harrowed, yet treating them as though they were inmates of a brothel. Always fearful in the presence of the police, some began to cry aloud and the children on their laps screamed too. For a few moments it was like a panic, until I was able to assure them that only I was under arrest. . . . After half an hour I finally persuaded the policemen to let these frightened women go.

All of our four hundred and fifty case histories were confiscated, and the table and demonstration supplies were carried off through the patient line outside. The more timid had left, but many had stayed. This was a region where a crowd could be collected by no more urgent gesture than a tilt of the head skyward. Newspaper men with their cameras had joined the throng and the street was packed. Masses of people spilled out over the sidewalk on the pavement, milling excitedly.

The patrol wagon came rattling up to our door. I had a certain respect for uniformed policemen—you knew what they were about—but none whatsoever for the vice squad. I was white hot with indignation over their unspeakable attitude towards the clinic mothers and stated I preferred to walk the mile to the court rather than sit with them. Their feelings were quite hurt. "Why, we didn't do anything to you, Mrs. Sanger," they protested. Nevertheless I marched ahead, they following behind. . . .

I stayed overnight at the Raymond Street jail, and I shall never forget it. The mattresses were spotted and smelly, the blankets stiff with dirt and grime. The stench nauseated me. It was not a comforting thought to go without bed-clothing when it was so cold, but, having in mind the diseased occupants who might have preceded me, I could not bring myself to creep under the covers. Instead I lay down on top and wrapped my coat around me. The only clean object was my towel, and this I draped over my face and head. For endless hours I struggled with roaches and horrible-looking bugs that came crawling out of the walls and across the floor. When a rat jumped up on the bed I cried out involuntarily and sent it scuttling out.

Choosing to Be Jailed

Margaret Sanger's night in the Raymond Street Jail was not her first time behind bars, and it would not be her last. On the afternoon of October 22, she was released on bail. Undaunted by the experience, she immediately reopened the clinic. It was not long before Mrs. Sanger found herself in a patrol wagon on her way back to the Raymond Street Jail. This time, she was charged with "maintaining a public nuisance."

12.2 Margaret Sanger's "Deeds of Terrible Virtue"

On January 22, 1917, for the crime of disseminating information on birth control, Ethel Byrne was sentenced to 30 days in the workhouse on Blackwell's Island. She protested this verdict by announcing her intention to die for her cause and then launched a well-publicized hunger strike. Thousands of women died each year in New York from the complications of unwanted pregnancies and illegal abortions, she argued, what was one life compared to so many others? Mrs. Byrne refused both food and liquids, and in the 103rd hour of her strike, she suffered the distinction of becoming the first woman in American history to be force-fed by the government. A rubber tube was forced down her throat and liquid nourishment poured directly into her stomach. A year passed following her release before her health was restored.

A three-judge panel began hearing testimony in the case of Margaret Sanger on the morning of January 29, 1917. On the evening of that day, several thousand people gathered at Carnegie Hall in a show of support for her cause. When the court reconvened several days later, the panel offered Mrs. Sanger a choice between serving time in the Blackwell's Island workhouse, or "extreme clemency," provided she would promise not to break the law again. She chose the workhouse.

Source 4   "Mrs. Sanger Defies Courts Before 3,000," *New York Times,* January 30, 1917

Three thousand persons in mass meeting at Carnegie Hall last night started a concerted movement for the repeal of the law forbidding the dissemination of birth control knowledge.

Mrs. Margaret Sanger . . . made a speech in which she threw all caution aside and removed all doubt as to her purpose when she declared, while the crowd cheered her wildly, that she had devoted her life to the cause of voluntary motherhood, and would continue the fight for birth control, courts or no courts, workhouse or no workhouse. Mrs. Sanger is a sister of Ethel Byrne, who is on a hunger strike in the Blackwell's Island workhouse, serving a 30 days sentence. Most of the crowd were women—women of all classes, old, young, poor, and rich. The two upper galleries were filled, because the admission charge there was only 25 cents. The admission on the lower floor, which was two-thirds full, was 75 cents. The boxes, which were allotted by subscription, were filled with richly dressed persons, many of them socially prominent. The money from the admissions, with deductions for the hall, went for a fund to pay lawyers to fight the anti-birth control measure in the courts and at Albany. The leaders of the "cause" said that if it had not rained and kept away the poor people the hall would have been filled.

There was no age limit to the admission. Many girls were in the audience who might have been high school students—few of them had escorts. The spirit of the crowd was bubbling. Every mention of the name of Mrs. Sanger and of Mrs. Byrne brought prolonged cheers.

The promoters of the meeting had expected trouble with the police over the distribution of the first number of *The Birth Control Review,* published by the New York State Birth Control League. But no one interfered while the ushers sold the magazine at 15 cents a copy.

Dr. Mary Hunt, a well-known physician, made an attack on "Fifth Avenue doctors," who, she said, practiced birth control in their own families and in the families of their rich patients, but stood in the way of poor women obtaining that knowledge.

Miss Helen Todd, who presided, introduced Mrs. Sanger as a woman who, with Mrs. Byrne, "was making a bridge over which womankind could pass to freedom."

It was noted that Mrs. Sanger departed from the prepared copy of her speech in that she was not so severe on the judiciary as she had intended to be. . . . "I come to you tonight," she said, "from a crowded courtroom, a vortex of persecution. I come not from the stake at Salem, where women were burned for blasphemy, but from the shadow of Blackwell's Island, where women are tortured for 'obscenity.'

"Birth control is the one means by which the working man shall find emancipation. I was one of eleven children. My mother died when I was 17 because she had had too many children and had worked herself to death. I became a nurse to help support my family, and I soon discovered that . . . the average person was as ignorant of sex matters as our most primitive ancestors. There has been progress in every department of our lives except in the most important—creation. So I came to the conclusion that the greatest good I could do was to help poor women to have fewer children to be brought up in want and poverty. . . .

"Colonel Roosevelt goes all around the country telling people to have large families and he is neither arrested nor molested. But can he tell me why I got sixty-three letters in one week from poor mothers in Oyster Bay asking me for birth control information? No woman can call herself free until she can choose the time she will become a mother.

"My purpose in life is to arouse sentiment for the repeal of the law. It is we women who have paid for the folly of this law, and it is up to us to repeal it."

Second Thoughts
Her Vision Realized beyond Her Dreams

Margaret Sanger devoted a lifetime to educating the public about the importance of birth control. Through her challenges to the prevailing laws and attitudes, she tested the patience of judges and lawmakers, and she tested the constitutionality of their rules. In the end, she won over the public and won over the law.

Source 5   Heywood Broun and Margaret Leech, *Anthony Comstock: Roundsman of the Lord,* 1927

The advocates of birth control had always evoked Comstock's wrath. In his old age he saw these people growing more numerous, more brazen. To a woman reporter for the *Tribune,* in May, 1915, he reluctantly spoke on this delicate subject. "Are we to have homes or brothels?" he cried, and "Can't everybody, whether rich or poor, learn to control themselves?" Margaret Sanger's pamphlet, *Family Limitation,* had aroused his horror. "In my opinion, this book is contrary not only to the law of the State, but to the law of God," said Justice McInerney at the trial of William Sanger in September, 1915. "If some of these women who go around advocating Woman Suffrage would go around and advocate women having children, they would be rendering society a greater service." So, only a few days before the Old Man's death, the voice of his period judicially spoke, and perhaps he died content in the knowledge that there were many left to carry on his work. William Sanger had been arrested in January, 1915, for distributing his wife's pamphlet. The evidence was secured by an agent of the Society for the Suppression of Vice, and this must have been one of the last trials in which Anthony Comstock gave testimony. Sanger, despite his protests in the courtroom that he was himself the father of "three lovely children," was convicted, and chose to go to jail for thirty days rather than pay a fine of $150.

Source 6   Margaret Sanger, *My Fight for Birth Control,* 1931

[M]y three children and my later nursing work combined to give me many and various problems to think about. Constantly I saw the ill effects of childbearing on women of the poor. Mothers whose physical condition was inadequate to combat disease were made pregnant, through ignorance and love, and died. Children were left motherless, fathers were left hopeless and desperate, often feeling like criminals, blaming themselves for the wife's death—all because these mothers were denied by law knowledge to prevent conception.

My own motherhood was joyous, loving, happy. I wanted to share these joys with other women. I longed to see Motherhood come into its own—the flower of Womanhood. I had thought and thought, and pondered over it all. Since the birth of my first child I had realized the importance of spacing babies, but only a few months before had I fully grasped the significant fact that a powerful law denied and prevented mothers from obtaining knowledge to properly space their families. This was so outrageous, so cruel, so useless a law that

I could not respect it. I could not believe that it would have the force of the government behind it were it challenged. I believed at the time that when the government knew the facts it would not and could not put that law into operation. I longed to prove its bad effects, to show up its destructive force on women's and children's lives. I was convinced in my heart that the *spirit* of the law would be interpreted and not the *letter* of the law. Little did I anticipate the future battle royal: Women's, mother's, children's lives against a worn-out parchment!

Source 7   Pope Paul VI, "Humanae Vitae," 1968

The problem of birth, like every other problem regarding human life, is to be considered . . . in the light of an integral vision of man and his vocation, not only his natural and earthly, but also his supernatural and eternal vocation. And since, in the attempt to justify artificial methods of birth control, many have appealed to the demands both of conjugal love and "responsible parenthood," it is good to state very precisely the true concept of these two realities of married life. . . .

Conjugal love reveals its true nature and nobility when it is considered in its supreme origin, God, who is love, "the Father, from whom every family in heaven and on earth is named."

Marriage is not, then, the effect of chance or the product of evolution of unconscious natural forces; it is the wise institution of the Creator to realize in mankind His design of love. By means of the reciprocal personal gift of self, proper and exclusive to them, husband and wife tend towards the communion of their beings in view of mutual personal perfection, to collaborate with God in the generation and education of new lives. . . .

Responsible parenthood . . . above all implies a more profound relationship to the objective moral order established by God, of which a right conscience is the faithful interpreter. The responsible exercise of parenthood implies, therefore, that husband and wife recognize fully their own duties towards God, towards themselves, towards the family and towards society, in a correct hierarchy of values.

In the task of transmitting life, therefore, they are not free to proceed completely at will, as if they could determine in a wholly autonomous way the honest path to follow; but they must conform their activity to the creative intention of God. . . .

These acts, by which husband and wife are united in chaste intimacy, and by means of which human life is transmitted, are as the [Second Vatican] Council recalled, "noble and worthy". . . . [A]s experience bears witness, not every conjugal act is followed by a new life. God has wisely disposed natural laws and rhythms of fecundity which, of themselves, cause a separation in the succession of births. Nonetheless the Church, calling men back to the observance of the norms of the natural law, as interpreted by their constant doctrine, teaches that each and every marriage act must remain open to the transmission of life. . . .

Upright men can even better convince themselves of the solid grounds on which the teaching of the Church in this field is based, if they care to reflect upon the consequences of methods of artificial birth control. Let them consider, first of all, how wide and easy a road would thus be opened up towards conjugal infidelity and the general lowering of morality. Not much experience is needed in order to know human weakness, and to understand that men—especially the young, who are so vulnerable on this point—have need of encouragement to be faithful to the moral law, so that they must not be offered some easy means of eluding its observance. It is also to be feared that the man, growing used to the employment of anti-conceptive practices, may finally lose respect for the woman and, no longer caring for her physical and psychological equilibrium, may come to the point of considering her as a mere instrument of selfish enjoyment, and no longer as his respected and beloved companion.

Source 8 Emily Taft Douglas, *Margaret Sanger: Pioneer of the Future,* 1970

When she started her crusade, in 1914, federal, state and local laws were against her. She was jailed eight times. The medical profession denounced her, the churches excoriated her, the press condemned her and even liberal reformers shunned her. She entered the fight alone, a frail woman without much education, with no social or financial backing, and nothing but conviction. Yet step by step, she made her points and eventually won her battles.

At first even her friends opposed her tactics. Those who approved her goal said that she must change the laws as reformers did in other fields. But at that period, legislative relief at any government level was as remote as the chance for Negroes in the Deep South to gain their civil rights by state action. Indeed, for all the later efforts of many people, including herself, most of the laws still remain on the books exactly as they were when she began her fight.

Her winning strategy was to secure new interpretations of existing laws. After challenging the restraints, she appealed the judgments of the lower courts and was upheld by the broader views of the upper courts. Thus she won *de facto* repeal of restrictions long before the civil rights leaders followed the same course.

And what had these legal changes accomplished? . . . Birth control instruction, which she had introduced at the Brownsville clinic, had spread across the nation to countless clinics, hospitals, and health services. That was not all, for she had carried her message around the globe on mammoth lecture tours. . . .

In the twenties, she conceived and set up the first World Population Conference at Geneva. After World War II, when she was seventy-three, she organized the International Planned Parenthood Federation, and as its President for six years, she built its strength. . . .

But the test of her work, as Margaret Sanger always insisted, was not measured in abstractions, but in the reduction of human tragedies. Today birth control not only saves the lives of countless mothers, but enhances the health and happiness of many times that number. Where it is used, it ends the nightmare of constant pregnancy and of bearing more children than the parents can support. It introduces the spacing of babies for optimum welfare and gives mothers the basic right of determining their maternity.

Perhaps above all, her influence was in teaching people to accept sex as it is, a part of life that needs a rational response. When she was young, the very word was outlawed in polite society. Nice girls grew up in ignorance of their own anatomy, while, on the other hand, boys were encouraged to face the facts with guffaws, in brothels and accommodated by a white slave traffic. . . . Today public schools teach the physiological facts for which she was once censored.

Source 9   David M. Kennedy, *Birth Control in America*, 1970

12.3 Family
Planning in
America

She began by defying old conventions and ended the lionized champion of new ones. By the time of her death at age 82, said *Time,* "her vision had been realized beyond her dreams." History records few examples of such successful advocacy of important social change. . . .

Mrs. Sanger's career in behalf of birth control embraced a period in American history during which contraception was first advocated in an organized way, initially rejected, at least officially, and finally accepted both privately and publicly. The congruence of that cycle with Mrs. Sanger's active life was no accident: indeed, she did much to shape its development. . . . There are historical moments perfectly fitted to the temperaments and personalities of certain individuals. The time from 1912 to the Second World War was such a moment for Margaret Sanger. For innovation and rejection, she was ideally suited. . . .

American society quite possibly needed to go through a phase of rejection and revulsion before it could accept something so new as the widespread practice of artificial contraception. Mrs. Sanger thrived on rejection. She loved combat. She needed enemies. She found joy in revulsion and shock. In temperament and personality, she was the ideal figure to lead and sustain the birth control movement in that early phase. The 1940's brought a new phase, in which birth control began to enjoy substantial social and official acceptance. Not surprisingly, Mrs. Sanger then slipped quietly from the position of leadership she had enjoyed for twenty-five years. So effectively had she educated society that it seemed no longer to need her.

Source 10   Ellen Chesler, *Woman of Valor,* 1992

12.4
Criminalizing
Women

For nearly half a century, Sanger dedicated herself to the deceptively simple proposition that access to a safe and reliable means of preventing pregnancy is a necessary condition of women's liberation and, in turn, of human progress. Her most exquisite triumphs were her last. She was past seventy when the world finally began to heed her concern for unchecked population growth, past eighty when the team of doctors and scientists she had long encouraged first marketed the oral, anovulant birth control pill. She lived to see the realization of her repeated efforts as a litigant and a lobbyist through the landmark 1965 ruling of the Supreme Court in *Griswold v. Connecticut,* which guaranteed constitutional protection to the private use of contraceptives. She died just as Lyndon Johnson incorporated family planning into America's public health and social welfare programs and committed at least a fraction of the nation's foreign policy resources to it, fulfilling her singular vision of how best to achieve peace and prosperity at home and abroad.

Since her death the rebirth of a vigorous feminist movement has given new resonance to her original claim that women have a fundamental right to control their own bodies. Her direct legacy endures in the far-reaching international family planning movement that descends from her pioneering organizational efforts. She has become an occasional scapegoat of extremists opposed to abortion. . . . But by and large, she shares the ignoble fate of so many iconoclasts like her who have lived to see the routine acceptance of ideas once considered disturbing. She has been forgotten.

Every woman in the world today who takes her sexual and reproductive anatomy for granted should venerate Margaret Sanger.

Sanger envisioned a united front of women who would claim the legalization of contraception . . . as a fundamental right. . . . Birth control, she argued, would enhance the opportunities of women beyond the promises of economic reformers, on the one hand, and of suffragists on the other. It would be a tool for redistributing power fundamentally, in the bedroom, the home, and the larger community. Women would achieve personal freedom by experiencing their sexuality free of consequences, just as men have always done, but in taking control of the forces of reproduction they would also lower birthrates, alter the balance of supply and demand for labor, and therein accomplish the revolutionary goals of workers without the social upheaval of class warfare. Bonds of gender would transcend divisions of ethnicity, race, or class. Not the dictates of Karl Marx, but the refusal of women to bear children indiscriminately, would alter the course of history.

Source 11   Timothy Wirth, counselor, U.S. State Department, daily press briefing, January 11, 1994

This year we have a very ambitious agenda in the global affairs area. A top priority for everybody are our commitments on population. As all of you know, I believe, the world population is currently 5.5 billion. If we do nothing, the world's population will double again sometime in the next 35 to 40 years, and will move on to 13 to 15 billion people before it is estimated that it will level off.

To imagine a world in which the population doubles in this fashion is unfathomable and clearly does not allow us any way that we're going to be able to maintain the quality of life or respect for the individuals that are fundamental to what we believe in the United States, nor would it allow us to maintain an environment with any integrity whatsoever or to conserve what many would call God's creation.

As a consequence, the United States has moved very dramatically into the population area. . . . [T]he United States is this year providing close to $500 million . . . in world population programs. Our goal . . . is to provide family planning services, comprehensive family planning packages, to every woman in the world who wants them by the year 2000.

 Questioning the Past

1. Debate the validity of Margaret Sanger's assertion that "No woman can call herself free who does not control her own body."
2. Present the arguments for and against birth control.
3. When Margaret Sanger appeared in court in January 1917, the following exchange occurred:

   "The Court: You have been in court during this time that your counsel made the statement that pending the prosecution of appeal neither you nor those affiliated with you in this so-called movement will violate the law; that is the promise your counsel makes for you. Now, the Court is considering extreme clemency in your case.

Possibly you know what extreme clemency means. Now, do you personally make that promise?

The Defendant: Pending the appeal.

The Court: If Mrs. Sanger will state publicly and openly that she will be a law-abiding citizen without any qualifications whatsoever, this Court is prepared to exercise the highest degree of leniency.

The Defendant: I'd like to have it understood by the gentlemen of the Court that the offer of leniency is very kind and I appreciate it very much. It is with me not a question of personal imprisonment or personal disadvantage. I am today and always have been more concerned with changing the law regardless of what I have to undergo to have it done.

The Court: . . . Since you are of that mind, am I to infer that you intend to go on in this matter, violating the law, irrespective of the consequences?

The Defendant: I haven't said that. I said I am perfectly willing not to violate Section 1142 [Prohibition on distribution of birth control materials]—pending the appeal.

Judge Hermann: The appeal has nothing to do with it. Either you do or you don't. . . .

The Court: . . . It is the law for you, it is the law for me, it is the law for all of us until it is changed; and you know what means and avenues are open to you to have it changed, and they are lawful ways. You may prosecute those methods and no one can find fault with you. If you succeed in changing the law, well and good. If you fail, then you have to bow in submission to the majority. . . . All we are concerned about is this statute, and as long as it remains the law will this woman promise here and now unqualifiedly to respect it and obey it? Now, it is yes or no. What is your answer, Mrs. Sanger? Is it yes or no?

The Defendant: I can't respect the law as it stands today.

The Court: . . . Refusal to obey the law becomes an open defiance of the rule of the majority. . . . The judgment of the Court is that you be confined to the Workhouse for the period of thirty days."

Explain and defend the Court's position in this exchange. Explain and defend Margaret Sanger's position. Which side is the more persuasive?

4. H. G. Wells, a friend of Sanger's, wrote: "Alexander the Great changed a few boundaries and killed a few men. Both he and Napoleon were forced into fame by circumstances outside of themselves and by currents of the time, but Margaret Sanger made currents and circumstances. When the history of our civilization is written, it will be a biological history and Margaret Sanger will be its heroine." Explain his point.

5. What similarities and differences are there between Margaret Sanger's movement for birth control and the current controversy regarding abortion?

6. How does it happen that the government arrested Margaret Sanger in 1916 for doing what the State Department now proclaims is a "top priority" of American foreign policy?

Chapter 13

World War I

Wilson Takes America to War   *April 2, 1917*

Just as the pulling of a single thread can cause an entire fabric to unravel, the assassination of one man in 1914 led to an unraveling of world order. The nations of Europe were so interwoven in a tangle of alliances that the murder of the heir to the throne of the Austro-Hungarian Empire by a Serbian nationalist pulled apart the fabric of peace.

Imperial and economic rivalries had created considerable underlying tension within Europe. But the war followed the assassination of Archduke Franz Ferdinand on June 28, 1914, by a process that seemed almost separate and apart from the real intentions of the nations involved.

Following the assassination, Austria mobilized its troops in a show of righteous indignation against Serbia, which it considered to be the primary instigator of Austria's domestic tensions. Russia, viewing itself as the champion of Slavic peoples, mobilized its troops to support Serbia, a Slavic state. Germany, because of its commitment under the Triple Alliance, mobilized to support Austria. France, under obligation to stand with Russia under terms of the Triple Entente, mobilized in response to the potential German and Austrian threat to Russia. Britain, the third member of the Triple Entente, mobilized in support of France. And without even a conference to discuss the rapidly deteriorating situation, the rival parties found themselves in a war that probably none of them wanted.

13.1 Trenches on the Web

ᘓᘖ *First Impressions*
From Neutrality to Belligerency

The question for Americans in 1914 was, would this unraveling of the peace continue to spread outward from Europe until it destroyed the peace of the whole world?

Source 1   Woodrow Wilson's open letter to the American people, August 19, 1914

My Fellow Countrymen:

I suppose that every thoughtful man in America has asked himself, during these last troubled weeks, what influence the European war may exert upon the United States, and I take the liberty of addressing a few words to you in order to point out that it is entirely within our own choice what its effects upon us

201

will be and to urge very earnestly upon you the sort of speech and conduct which will best safeguard the Nation against distress and disaster. . . .

The people of the United States are drawn from many nations, and chiefly from the nations now at war. It is natural and inevitable that there should be the utmost variety of sympathy and desire among them with regard to the issues and circumstances of the conflict. Some will wish one nation, others another, to succeed in the momentous struggle. It will be easy to excite passion and difficult to allay it. Those responsible for exciting it will assume a heavy responsibility, responsibility for no less a thing than that the people of the United States . . . may be divided in camps of hostile opinion, hot against each other. . . .

Such divisions among us would be fatal to our peace of mind and might seriously stand in the way of the performance of our duty as the one great nation at peace, the one people holding itself ready to play a part of impartial mediation and speak the counsels of peace and accommodation, not as a partisan, but as a friend.

I venture, therefore, my fellow countrymen, to speak a solemn word of warning to you against that deepest, most subtle, most essential breach of neutrality which may spring out of partisanship, out of passionately taking sides. The United States must be neutral in fact as well as in name during these days that are to try men's souls. We must be impartial in thought as well as in action, must put a curb upon our sentiments as well as upon every transaction that might be construed as a preference of one party to the struggle before another.

Source 2   Secretary of State William Jennings Bryan, message to Great Britain, February 10, 1915

The department has been advised . . . that the British Government . . . on January thirty-first explicitly authorized the use of neutral flags on British merchant vessels presumably for the purpose of avoiding recognition by German naval forces. The department's attention has also been directed to reports in the press that the captain of the *Lusitania*, acting upon orders or information received from the British authorities, raised the American flag as his vessel approached the British coasts, in order to escape anticipated attacks by German submarines. . . .

The formal declaration of such a policy of general misuse of a neutral's flag jeopardizes the vessels of the neutral visiting those waters in a peculiar degree by raising the presumption that they are of belligerent nationality regardless of the flag which they may carry.

In view of the announced purpose of the German Admiralty to engage in active naval operations in certain delimited sea areas adjacent to the coasts of Great Britain and Ireland, the Government of the United States would view with anxious solicitude any general use of the flag of the United States by British vessels traversing those waters.

Source 3   Secretary of State Bryan's message to Germany, February 10, 1915

The Government of the United States, having had its attention directed to the proclamation of the German Admiralty issued on the fourth of February, that the waters surrounding Great Britain and Ireland, including the whole of the English Channel, are to be considered as comprised within the seat of war; that all enemy merchant vessels found in those waters after the eighteenth instant will be destroyed . . . and that neutral vessels expose themselves to danger within this zone of war because, in view of the misuse of neutral flags . . . , it may not be possible always to exempt neutral ships from attacks intended to strike enemy ships, feels it to be its duty to call the attention of the Imperial Government of Germany . . . to the very serious possibilities of the course of action apparently contemplated under that proclamation. . . .

If the commanders of German vessels of war should act upon the presumption that the flag of the United States was not being used in good faith and should destroy on the high seas an American vessel or the lives of American citizens, it would be difficult for the Government of the United States to view the act in any other light than as an indefensible violation of neutral rights.

Source 4   Notice in the *New York Times,* May 1, 1915

NOTICE!

TRAVELERS intending to embark on the Atlantic voyage [of the *Lusitania*] are reminded that a state of war exists between Germany and her allies and Great Britain and her allies; that the zone of war includes the waters adjacent to the British Isles; that in accordance with formal notice given by the Imperial German Government, vessels flying the flag of Great Britain, or of any of her allies, are liable to destruction in those waters and that travelers sailing in the war zone on ships of Great Britain or her allies do so at their own risk.

> IMPERIAL GERMAN EMBASSY
> Washington, D. C. April 22, 1915.

Source 5   Editorial, *New York Times,* May 8, 1915

[On May 7, 1915, a German submarine torpedoed the *Lusitania* off the coast of Ireland. The ship sank with the loss of 1,198 lives, including 128 Americans. Newspaper editorials on the following day amounted to a nearly nationwide outcry.]

From our Department of State there must go to the Imperial Government at Berlin a demand that the Germans shall no longer make war like savages drunk with blood, that they shall cease to seek the attainment of their goals by the assassination of non-combatants and neutrals. In the history of wars there is no single deed comparable in its inhumanity and its horror to the destruction, without warning, by German torpedoes of the great steamship *Lusitania.*

13.2 Fateful Voyage of *Lusitania*

Source 6   Editorial, *New York Herald,* May 8, 1915

If ever wholesale murder was premeditated this slaughter on the high seas was. By official proclamation of an intention to disregard all rules of blockade and international law, Germany declared that her submarines would sink every ship that sought to enter or leave the ports of the United Kingdom and of France.

By official advertisement all passengers were warned not to take passage on British ships from the United States for England. By letter and telegram passengers were warned not to go by the *Lusitania*. The ship had been marked for slaughter. The warnings were disregarded, but she was doomed from the moment she passed out of the three-mile limit. . . .

Henceforth is international anarchy to be the controlling factor in marine warfare? Henceforth is piracy on the high seas to be recognized and go unprotested and unpunished? Henceforth is the wanton murder of neutrals and noncombatant passengers to be treated as regrettable incidents and let go at that?

It is for the neutral countries, and above all for the United States, to answer these questions. It is a time of gravity in American history unmatched since the civil war.

This cold-blooded, premeditated outrage on colossal scale will cause . . . a blinding white light of indignation throughout the neutral portions of the world.

Source 7   Editorial, *Richmond Times-Dispatch,* May 8, 1915

Germany surely must have gone mad. The torpedoing and sinking of the *Lusitania* . . . evince a reckless disregard of the opinions of the world in general and of this country in particular—a determination to win by any method and at any cost—only compatible with the assumption that blood lust has toppled reason from the throne.

Through centuries of incessant struggle, in the ascent of the race from savagery, civilization has wrung from war certain guarantees of the sanctity of human life. These guarantees are expressed in the code that enlightened nations recognize.

Source 8   Editorial, *San Francisco Chronicle,* May 8, 1915

With the torpedoing of the *Lusitania* Germany scores her largest individual triumph in the war on British commerce. . . . Up till a few days ago British officials were boasting of the fact that the submarine blockade had not proved an effective bar to commerce. . . .

The question as to whether there were American citizens on board the Lusitania does not call for discussion. Our people have had ample warning, and should know that when they step aboard a British ship they are consigning themselves to the protection of a nation which at present can offer very little security for those at sea.

Source 9   German foreign secretary Alfred Zimmerman's message to the German Embassy in Mexico City, January 17, 1917

On the first of February we intend to begin submarine warfare unrestricted. In spite of this, it is our intention to endeavor to keep neutral the United States of America.

If this attempt is not successful, we propose an alliance on the following basis with Mexico: That we shall make war together and together make peace. We shall give general financial support, and it is understood that Mexico is to reconquer the lost territory in New Mexico, Texas and Arizona. The details are left to you for settlement.

You are instructed to inform the President of Mexico of the above in the greatest confidence as soon as it is certain there will be an outbreak of war with the United States.

Source 10   Walter Lippmann, "The Defense of the Atlantic World," *New Republic,* February 17, 1917

All along the Germans have seen two great truths: first, that British command of the sea has become absolute, and has abolished the neutral rights which interfere with it; second, that America's policy has been to protest feebly and without effect against Britain while Germany has been held by threat of war from using the submarine fully to relieve the pressure. The Germans have pointed out quite accurately that the result of this policy has been to close the road to Germany and hold open the road to Britain and France. The German highway we have allowed the Allies to bar, the Allied highway we were ready to keep open at the risk of war. We have not merely been committed theoretically to selling munitions and supplies to anyone who can come and fetch them. We have in fact permitted the Allies to cut off Germany, we have been in fact prepared for war to deliver munitions and foodstuffs to the Allies.

Source 11   Editorial, "Draw the Sword of Liberty," *Washington Post,* April 1, 1917

Three courses are open to the United States in dealing with Germany:

It can abandon its rights and refuse to fight.

It can declare that a state of war exists and then carry on a half-hearted, partial, qualified, and therefore ineffectual war.

It can declare war and immediately utilize all its energies and resources for the prompt and complete defeat of the enemy.

The first course is suggested by the coward pacifists who demand peace at any price, including national honor.

The second course may be mistakenly advocated by men who are willing to defend the national honor, but shrink from the thought of prosecuting a vigorous aggressive war.

The third course is that which hard facts and past experience show to be advisable and necessary. . . .

The quarrel with Germany will never be settled right until Germany is whipped. A makeshift arrangement with an undefeated Germany would mean another war. Germany will cease to be a menace to the independence of the United States only when she is hammered to her knees and convinced by the only argument that appeals to her intellect—brute force. . . .

Germany made a frightful mistake when she thought she could crush France. She blundered when she thought England would refuse to fight. She now mistakes the temper of the people of Russia.

Let us show her that she made the greatest blunder when she dared to order the American flag off the ocean; when she sent out her pirates and murdered Americans.

Americans in Congress! Do not trifle with these savages. Do not underestimate their devilish skill and power. Do not take halfway measures against them. Declare war on them, and then drive the knife home to the hilt! Raise an army, not a pitiful corporal's guard for six months, but a million men for the duration of the war, and another million in reserve. Build airplanes, not by the dozens, but by the thousand. Give us a merchant marine. Rush the battle cruisers and battleships and submarines to completion. Increase the personnel of the navy to at least 125,000. Pass the espionage bill. Give the President $1,000,000,000 for war expenses.

Americans in Congress! The spirits of your fathers look down upon you and wait for you to let loose the thunderbolts of Liberty. Ancestral voices warn you that your time has come to guard this nation against the savage that assails it. You have a thousand times the strength and power that your forefathers had when they established this Union. Use this strength! Exert this power! Call into being the forces that will smite down and annihilate the barbarians who presume to tear the American flag from the skies!

Source 12   Editorial, "Traitorous Pacifists," *Washington Post,* April 1, 1917

Large advertisements are appearing in the metropolitan newspapers, skillfully written for the purpose of stirring up class hatred and suspicion and thus dissuading Americans from enlisting in the war that is coming. . . .

At this time, when the United States is on the verge of war, the Washington Post believes that the advertisements in question are an abuse of the right of free speech. It does not presume to judge other newspapers which print these advertisements, but for itself, it will not print them. . . .

An effort to prevent the voluntary enlistment of American citizens for the defense of their country is treasonable in time of war. It is sedition at any time. "The hope of impunity is a strong incitement to sedition," said Hamilton. The pacifists will not long enjoy impunity. If they are wise they will cease their agitation before they are legally classified as public enemies and punished accordingly.

Naive Expectations

13.3 The Great War Series

The United States had innocently imagined it possible to trade with both sides in the European conflict. Ships flying the American flag, it was thought, would be permitted to sail past British warships to deliver supplies to German ports, and to sail past German warships to make deliveries at British ports. Such expectations were fatally naive.

The British declared the waters around German ports to be a war zone. The Germans made the same declaration about the waters surrounding Britain. The British Navy was the mightiest in the world and could turn back ships that attempted to deliver supplies to its enemies. The Germans could not compete with the British Navy and had to wage a kind of guerrilla warfare from beneath the surface of the seas.

It was the code of "civilized warfare" that warning must be given before a merchant ship came under attack. Moreover, a warship had an obligation to rescue the passengers and crew from vessels it chose to sink. The British warships, in control of the surface of the seas and of the ports of Western Europe, could turn a merchant ship away from German ports, confiscate its cargo, and release the vessel without taking the lives of crew or passengers. Submarines could not.

A German U-boat on the surface was slow and ill-equipped for battle. It was at risk even from the deck guns of merchant ships. Its quarters were cramped and without space for cargo or rescued seamen. It had little choice but to attack from underwater and without warning, and it had little choice but to leave the passengers and crews of the vessels it destroyed to fend for themselves.

Moreover, the British were known to sail under the flags of neutrals. They used passenger ships to transport military supplies, placing the Germans in the position of losing face if they attacked such vessels and losing the war if they did not. The luxury liner *Lusitania* carried, in addition to the 128 Americans who met their deaths below her decks, 1,248 cases of three-inch shells, 4,927 cases of cartridges, and 2,000 boxes of small-arms ammunition. Secretary of State William Jennings Bryan, who left the Wilson administration in protest of the president's uneven response to British and German acts of belligerency, said, "Germany has a right to prevent contraband from going to the Allies, and a ship carrying contraband should not rely upon passengers to protect her from an attack—it would be like putting women and children in front of an army."

The Germans tried to respond to American complaints and, for a time, restrained their submarine warfare. But on January 31, 1917, the German government announced its intention to resume unrestricted use of the submarine. On February 3, the United States broke diplomatic relations with Germany in protest, and on April 2, 1917, Woodrow Wilson delivered a war message to Congress. A declaration of war passed Congress on April 6.

Source 13 President Woodrow Wilson's war message to Congress, April 2, 1917

I have called the Congress into extraordinary session because there are serious, very serious, choices of policy to be made, and made immediately, which it was neither right nor constitutionally permissible that I should assume the responsibility for making.

On the third of February last I officially laid before you the extraordinary announcement of the imperial German government that on and after the first day of February it was its purpose to put aside all restraints of law or of humanity and use its submarines to sink every vessel that sought to approach either the ports of Great Britain and Ireland or the western coasts of Europe. . . .

The new policy has swept every restriction aside. Vessels of every kind, whatever their flag, their character, their cargo, their destination, their errand, have been ruthlessly sent to the bottom without warning, and without thought of help or mercy for those on board. . . .

Property can be paid for; the lives of peaceful and innocent people cannot be. The present German submarine warfare against commerce is a war against mankind.

It is a war against all nations. American ships have been sunk, American lives taken, in ways which it has stirred us very deeply to learn of, but the ships and people of other neutral nations have been sunk and overwhelmed in the waters in the same way.

There has been no discrimination. The challenge is to all mankind. . . .

There is one choice we cannot make, we are incapable of making: We will not choose the path of submission and suffer the most sacred rights of our nation and our people to be ignored or violated. The wrongs against which we now array ourselves are no common wrongs; they cut to the very roots of human life.

With a profound sense of the solemn and even tragical character of the steps I am taking and of the grave responsibilities which it involves, but in unhesitating obedience to what I deem my constitutional duty, I advise that the Congress declare the recent course of the imperial German government to be in fact nothing less than war against the government and people of the United States. . . .

Neutrality is no longer feasible or desirable where the peace of the world is involved and the freedom of its peoples, and the menace to that peace and freedom lies in the existence of autocratic governments backed by organized force which is controlled wholly by their will, not by the will of their people. We have seen the last of neutrality in such circumstances. . . .

The world must be made safe for democracy. Its peace must be planted upon the tested foundations of political liberty. We have no selfish ends to serve.

We desire no conquest, no dominion. We seek no indemnities for ourselves, no material compensation for the sacrifices we shall freely make. We are but one of the champions of the rights of mankind. We shall be satisfied when those rights have been made as secure as the faith and the freedom of nations can make them. . . .

It is a distressing and oppressive duty, gentlemen of the Congress, which I have performed in thus addressing you. There are, it may be, many months of fiery trial and sacrifice ahead of us. It is a fearful thing to lead this great peaceful people into war, into the most terrible and disastrous of all wars, civilization itself seeming to be in the balance.

But the right is more precious than the peace, and we shall fight for the things which we have always carried nearest our hearts—for democracy, for the right of those who submit to authority to have a voice in their own governments, for the rights and liberties of small nations, for a universal dominion of right by such a concert of free peoples as shall bring peace and safety to all nations and shall make the world itself at last free. To such a task we can dedicate our lives and our fortunes, everything that we are and everything that we have, with the pride of those who know that the day has come when America is privileged to spend her blood and her might for the principles that gave her birth and happiness and the peace which she has treasured. God helping her, she can do no other.

Second Thoughts

To Make the World Safe for Democracy

13.4 The World in the Era of Great Wars

Whether the United States entered World War I to defend Western civilization, democracy, or selfish commercial interests has been debated by statesmen and historians throughout the eight and a half decades since Congress approved sending U.S. troops to Europe.

Source 14 Editorial, "Liberty Draws the Sword," *Washington Post*,
April 4, 1917

Americans are now witness of the unprecedented spectacle of democracy strip-
ping for a death-grapple with autocracy. Never before have democracy and autocracy met face to face in a knockout fight for domination of the world. The issue
heretofore has not been clearly defined, or the combatants have been unevenly
matched, or the field of battle has been too restricted. Usually autocracy was
too cunning to come into the open and fight a democracy that had been aroused.
It was only when democracy was unfledged or unprepared or in a stupor that
autocracy asserted all its brutality and mercilessness. When the sons of liberty
were awake and armed, autocracy avoided a finish fight by false pretenses of
peace and by making concessions.

The German autocracy deemed the time auspicious for asserting domination
of the world. Democracy seemed to be asleep. It was unprepared. Its borders were
unguarded, its weapons rusty, its spirit apparently debased by prosperity and cowardice. Autocracy, on the other hand, was armed to the teeth, and all its complicated
enginery of war organized for concerted action. The German people were molded
into a war machine, as obedient to their masters as clay is to the potter. As the
clay does not ask the potter why or wherefore, so the German people dared not
question their war lords. The hour was ripe for action, and the system of despotic
mandate and slavish obedience was in perfect working order. . . .

Now comes the great republic, the natural enemy and destroyer of autocracy. With insane rage autocracy has challenged the sovereignty of this nation.
It has struck squarely at the life of democracy, and boasts that it will overcome
the United States.

The spokesman of the world's free people has sounded the call to arms.
America is called upon to defend herself and destroy her assailant. There is not
room enough on earth or ocean for both autocracy and democracy. One or the
other must perish.

Source 15 Speech of labor leader and Socialist Party spokesman,
Eugene Debs, Canton, Ohio, June 16, 1918

[For this speech Debs was convicted of violating the Espionage Act and
sentenced to ten years in federal prison.]

[I]t is extremely dangerous to exercise the constitutional right of free speech in
a country fighting to make democracy safe in the world.

I realize that, in speaking to you this afternoon, there are certain limitations placed upon the right of free speech. . . . I may not be able to say all
I think; but I am not going to say anything that I do not think. I would
rather a thousand times be a free soul in jail than to be a sycophant and a
coward in the streets. . . .

Are we opposed to Prussian militarism? (Shouts from the crowd of "Yes,
Yes!) . . . I hate, I loathe, I despise Junkers and junkerdom. I have no earthly
use for the Junkers of Germany, and not one particle more for the Junkers in
the United States.

They tell us that we live in a great republic; that our institutions are democratic; that we are a free and self-governing people. This is too much even for a joke. . . .

To whom do the Wall Street Junkers in our country marry their daughters? After they have wrung their countless millions from your sweat, your agony and your life's blood, in a time of war and in a time of peace, they invest these untold millions in the purchase of titles of broken-down aristocrats, such as princes, dukes, counts and other parasites and no-accounts. Would they be satisfied to wed their daughters to honest workingmen? To real democrats? Oh, no! They scour the markets of Europe for vampires who are titled and nothing else. . . .

These are the gentry who are today wrapped up in the American flag, who shout from the housetops that they are the only patriots, and who have their magnifying glasses in hand, scanning the country for evidence of disloyalty, eager to apply the brand of treason to the men who dare to even whisper their opposition to junker rule in the United States. No wonder Sam Johnson declared that "patriotism is the last refuge of the scoundrel." He must have had this Wall Street gentry in mind, or at least their prototypes, for in every age it has been the tyrant, the oppressor and the exploiter who has wrapped himself in the cloak of patriotism, or religion, or both to deceive and overawe the people. . . .

Wars throughout history have been waged for conquest and plunder. In the Middle Ages when the feudal lords who inhabited the castles whose towers may still be seen along the Rhine Valley concluded to enlarge their domains, to increase their power, their prestige, their wealth they declared war upon one another. But they themselves did not go to war any more than the modern feudal lords, the barons of Wall Street go to war. The feudal barons of the Middle Ages, the economic predecessors of the capitalists of our day, declared all wars. And their miserable serfs fought all the battles. The poor, ignorant serfs had been taught to revere their masters; to believe that when their masters declared war upon one another, it was their patriotic duty to fall upon one another and to cut one another's throats for the profit and glory of the lords and barons who held them in contempt. And that is war in a nutshell. The master class has always declared the wars; the subject class has always fought the battles, while the subject class has had nothing to gain and all to lose—especially their lives.

Source 16 Harry Elmer Barnes, *The Genesis of the World War*, 1929

It must be remembered . . . that the resumption of German submarine warfare . . . was the excuse and not the real reason for our entering the war. President Wilson . . . had decided that we would come in at least a year before the submarine warfare was resumed by Germany.

The gist of the whole matter . . . appears to be that Mr. Wilson failed himself to observe the neutrality he enjoined upon his country at the outbreak of the war. By permitting England but not Germany to violate international law promiscuously he inevitably invited those reprisals which occurred. He then found in the action which he thus stimulated those ostensible causes for the war which he idealized after April, 1917. . . .

There is no doubt that he was a pacifist at heart, but he viewed the conflict as one in which England was upholding the cause of civilization. This led to his determination to enter the conflict if the entry of the United States should become essential to a British victory and if it was possible to put the country in as a unit. His policy, then, was one of combining a hope for an Entente victory with the preparation of the country for war in the event that England could not win without our assistance. . . .

Mr. Wilson was never in fact really neutral . . . [H]e had one set of concepts and procedures for Great Britain and the Entente and quite another for the Central Powers. . . . The German submarine warfare was a legitimate retaliation against the British violations of international law with respect to such matters as contraband, continuous voyage and blockade, against which Mr. Wilson refused to protest with adequate persistence and firmness. . . .

Mr. Wilson, while in favor of peace as against war in the abstract, decided to enter the War on the side of the Entente as soon as he was convinced that England could not win decisively without American aid. This decision on his part was arrived at before the close of the year 1915.

Source 17   James Duane Squires, *British Propaganda at Home and in the United States,* 1935

The American people launched themselves into the war with an emotional hysteria that can only be understood by realizing the power of propaganda in generating common action. . . . There will, of course, never be any agreement on the percentage of influence which British propaganda had in bringing about the decision of April 6, 1917. It was not the cause for American entrance into the World War. But that it was a cause, and a powerful one, it seems impossible for the historian today to deny.

Source 18   Charles Seymour, *American Diplomacy during the War,* 1936

It has sometimes been asserted that the entrance of the United States into the World War was the result of the influence of certain "interests," which for one reason or another desired American participation on the side of the Allies; that Wilson himself was caught in this influence, thoroughly impregnated as he was supposed to be with pro-Allied sentiment; that the declaration of the unrestricted submarine campaign was merely a pretext for belligerency which on one score or another would have been declared in any case.

There is no scrap of evidence supporting this thesis, and all that is available directly controverts it. At the beginning of the war Wilson declared and believed that it could not reach us, that if we kept clean neutral hands we were fulfilling our duty and preserving our security. He was speedily disabused. . . . The German submarine attacks shocked him, and for the first time he perceived that it might not be possible to carry through two purposes that might conflict—the preservation of the honor of the country and the preservation of its peace. The problems of neutrality were intolerable; they could be ended only if the war ended. . . .

As to the influence of "interests," whether pro-Ally or financial, if such influence existed, it did not touch Wilson. . . . Of his own conscience he made it [the decision to enter the war] because in no other way could he see how to protect American lives and property. It was the German submarine warfare and nothing else that forced him to lead America into war.

Source 19 Newton D. Baker, Wilson's secretary of war, *Why We Went to War,* 1936

I have spent practically all the leisure of the last year examining this subject, attempting to read all that has been published by our State Department and by the foreign offices of other governments and much of the discussion of these subjects by scholars and publicists. Out of it all I have come with the clear conviction that the entry of the United States into the World War was not in the least affected by munition makers or bankers, that the business interests of the country were a constant but, it seems to me, a proper object of solicitude of the Government, but that nothing done in furtherance of these business interests affected the ultimate decision. I am convinced also that our entrance into the war was caused directly and solely by the German use of the submarine and that to the last President Wilson worked to keep America out of the war.

Source 20 Charles A. Beard, *The Devil Theory of War,* 1936

In the summer of 1914 the American people were busy as ever making and trying to sell goods at an advantage. But things were not going at top-notch speed. Business had slowed down in the preceding winter. . . . There was a great deal of unemployment in the cities. Manufactures were not moving swiftly enough to suit the makers. The prices of farm produce did not satisfy farmers.

In other words, Americans could do a lot more business than they were doing. . . .

Then the big war broke with a bang. The American people got excited about it and evolved all kinds of passions, sentiments and theories pertaining thereunto. But in general they were peaceful and wanted to go on making and selling goods, at an advantage.

Very soon the Allies, for whom the seas were open, began to buy steel, manufactures and farm produce rather heavily. Industrialists and farmers were pleased to sell. Workers were pleased to have jobs. Merchants and bankers were pleased to facilitate the transactions of purchase and payment. . . .

It just so happened, perhaps unfortunately, that the best of the new customers were the Allied governments engaged in an unpacific enterprise. But they were good customers. They were in a hurry. They needed goods, in fact, very badly, and were not inclined to haggle too much over prices, commissions and fees.

At first they could pay for their purchases. They had gold to send over. They could muster American, Canadian and other foreign securities, and sell them to raise cash. . . . But there was a limit to the gold, securities and imports available to pay for American goods and keep Americans busy at peacetime pursuits.

Apparently a pinch was felt very early in the rush, for the French government soon sounded out the National City Bank on the possibility of a loan or credit. That would help. It would make American money available to pay American business men and farmers, engaged in peacetime pursuits. Bigger sales, bigger profits, bigger wages, bigger prices and bigger prosperity. It looked good to everybody—

manufacturers, farmers, bankers, wage-earners and politicians who wanted to stay in office. Perhaps some tears were shed, but they were not as big as millstones and did not get in the way of making and selling at an advantage.

But few realized how fateful in outcome their peaceful pursuit was to be. Few realized that war is not made by a *deus ex machina,* but comes out of ideas, interests and activities cherished and followed in the preceding months and years of peace. The notion that peace might make war did not enter busy heads.

The big question in 1915 was: How can the Allies "pay" for more and more goods, and enable Americans to follow peaceful pursuits happily?

New York bankers found the answer. They communicated it to Robert Lansing, Secretary of State, to William G. McAdoo, Secretary of the Treasury, to Colonel House, confidential advisor to the President of the United States. The question reached Woodrow Wilson. The answer reached him. Finding the solution agreeable, he approved it. The bankers' solution worked—for a time. Americans bought bonds to pay themselves for goods sold to the Allies. It was wonderful, the way it worked. . . . Americans could keep on with their peaceful pursuits, with bigger and bigger prospects—for a time, for a time.

But in time the Allies were in another jam. They were in danger of losing the War. . . . As Ambassador Page informed President Wilson in March, 1917, defeat for the Allies meant an economic smash for the United States. The following month, President Wilson called on Congress to declare war on the German Empire. . . .

War is not the work of a demon. It is our very own work, for which we prepare, wittingly or not, in ways of peace. But most of us sit blindfolded at the preparation.

Source 21 Thomas A. Bailey, *Diplomatic History of the United States,* 1946

There can be no doubt that both sets of belligerents had flagrantly violated American rights—or what the State Department declared were American rights. Throughout the entire period of neutrality the Allies did so more consistently than Germany. Why, then, did America not fight them? Why did she not declare war against both groups of belligerents, just as it had been proposed that she fight both Great Britain and France in 1812?

The basic reason appears to have been that Allied practices hurt only American property rights. The United States could lodge protests, and perhaps collect damages when the war was over. The German submarine took American lives. And there seemed to be no proper recompense for lives. So the United States fought Germany. As the Boston *Globe* remarked: one was "a gang of thieves"; the other was "a gang of murderers. On the whole, we prefer the thieves, but only as the lesser of two evils."

Source 22 Edward H. Buehrig, *Woodrow Wilson and the Balance of Power,* 1955

The central theme of American foreign relations in the nineteenth century was the mutual accommodation progressively achieved between ourselves and Great Britain. The main theme in the present century is quite different,

offering a melancholy contrast. At the turn of the century Germany and the
United States had already emerged as great powers, and Japan was in the
process of attaining that status. Presently Russia took on new form and vigor,
and Italy was to entertain high political ambition. Later still, India began to
emerge, as did China. Coincident with this revolutionary change in the old
order, the United States has come to blows twice with Germany and once
each with Japan and Italy. Moreover, we have fought China and must consider
the danger of war with the Soviet Union. At the halfway mark, the new
century has witnessed serious conflict between ourselves and all our rising
contemporaries save India. . . .

How shall we characterize these broad movements of history, and what is
the connection between them and our involvement in World War I?

We can see today, what was much less clearly visible at the time, that the
first World War signalized the decline of Europe from its pre-eminence in world
politics. . . . Sooner or later such a decline was bound to occur. In the actual
event, Europe did not succumb to superior alien forces but to her own internecine strife. German ambition, beyond the capacity of Continental Europe to cope
with, engaged the energies of Great Britain. In fact, Anglo-German rivalry became
a major point of tension. . . .

The United States and Germany became embroiled because of their differ-
ing attitudes toward British control of the seas. Germany felt that she must
challenge that control in the interest of her own freedom of action. . . . But
unlike Germany, the United States was not rebellious against Britain's predomi-
nant position. The argument that this showed subservience to Great Britain, so
long as American prosperity was not endangered, does not cover the whole
ground. It sprang mainly from the fact that the United States saw no threat to
its vital interests in Britain's position and, moreover, shrank from the prospect
of Germany supplanting British power. This essential difference between American and German attitudes toward Great Britain underlay the progressive es-
trangement and eventual rupture of German-American relations.

Source 23   H. Stuart Hughes, *Contemporary Europe: A History,* 1961

At its start the First World War was neither an ideological struggle nor in a real
sense a world conflict. It was an old fashioned European quarrel—the last and
greatest of a succession of such quarrels dating back nearly three centuries to
the Thirty Years War. Essentially it was fought for national, imperial aims. In
the origins of the conflict, ideological goals figured scarcely at all. At the start,
at least, the men in the trenches had little sense of fighting to preserve a specific
form of government or even a more vaguely realized "way of life." They thought
almost solely in national terms. The French and British, for example, felt very
simply that they were defending their countries rather than fighting to preserve
or extend an abstract principle like democracy. . . .

This lack of ideology was only natural. The warring coalitions were separated by no clear difference of political principle. The two great democracies, it
is true, were fighting alongside each other. But they were also in alliance with
Tsarist Russia, the most reactionary of the powers. Hence, at the start of the
war, the Entente had no real ideological cohesion. Its adversaries were more

closely linked by ideological ties: both Germany and Austria-Hungary were qualified autocracies or semi-parliamentary states.

In the ideological spectrum, the Entente occupied the two extremes, and the Central Powers lay somewhere in between. . . . Indeed certain Germans even argued that it was they rather than their adversaries who were fighting for democracy. The German Social Democrats, for example, soothed their Marxist consciences with the claim that by defending their country against Russia they were keeping "Asiatic" despotism out of Central Europe. . . .

In the crucial year 1917, all this changed. With the entrance of the United States, the conflict in truth became a world war. And with the first Russian Revolution, only a month before, the Entente attained an enviable ideological unity. Now that Italy and America had been added to the coalition—and Russia had cast off its exhausted despotism—five great democracies were ranged in one camp. For a few brief months, this illusion persisted.

Source 24 Barbara W. Tuchman, *The Zimmermann Telegram,* 1966

Had the telegram [see Source 9] never been intercepted or never been published, inevitably the Germans would have done something else that would have brought us in eventually. But the time was already late and, had we delayed much longer, the Allies might have been forced to negotiate. To that extent the Zimmermann telegram altered the course of history. But then, as Winston Churchill has remarked, the course of history is always being altered by something or other—if not by a horseshoe nail, then by an intercepted telegram. In itself the Zimmermann telegram was only a pebble on the long road of history. But a pebble can kill a Goliath, and this one killed the American illusion that we could go about our business happily separate from other nations. In world affairs it was a German Minister's minor plot. In the lives of the American people it was the end of innocence.

Source 25 Robert Ferrell, *American Diplomacy,* 1969

Perhaps one should conclude that the reasoning which took Wilson and the American people away from the feelings of August 1914 to the remarkable singleness of purpose on April 6, 1917, was a view of balance of power, but not the traditional view. The decision in 1917 was emotional, grounded in the belief, indeed conviction, that right, in the person of the Allies, was battling wrong, personified by the Central Powers. There was abroad, so Wilson and his fellow Americans believed, a highly organized, savage campaign against decency and morality, and in the early spring of 1917 evil was weighing heavily in the balance against good.

Questioning the Past

1. List and evaluate the merits of the various explanations offered for the entry of the United States into World War I. Which cause or causes seem most compelling? Was it inevitable that America would be drawn into the war?

2. Was the security of the United States in danger prior to the president's message of 1917? Can a nation justify going to war if its security is not threatened? What kinds of reasons, if any, justify war?

3. Explain the controversy of submarine warfare from both the Entente view and the Central Powers view. Did the Germans have any realistic alternatives to unrestricted submarine warfare? Is it likely that an alternative to the use of submarine warfare would have prevented American entry into the war?

4. In its editorial of April 4, 1917, "Liberty Draws the Sword," the *Washington Post* commented critically that "the German people were molded into a war machine, as obedient to their masters as clay is to the potter." The German people, the *Post* stated, "dared not question their warlords." Compare and contrast these sentiments with those expressed in the *Post*'s editorial of April 1, 1917, "Traitorous Pacifists."

5. Are citizens of a free country obligated to accept their government's decision to go to war? During World War I, Congress passed a Conscription Act that forced Americans to fight even if they did not wish to do so. Are citizens obligated to kill if ordered to do so by their government? Congress also passed in 1917 an Espionage Act and in 1918 a Sedition Act that set a penalty of up to $10,000 in fines and 20 years in prison for any citizen who encouraged disloyalty, interfered with the draft, or uttered "disloyal or abusive language" about the American government, the American Constitution, the American flag, or the uniform of American servicemen. Can Congress in wartime violate the First Amendment to the Constitution? Argue both sides of these questions.

Chapter **14**

Prohibition

The Eighteenth Amendment Takes Effect

January 16, 1920

It was the eve of America's Noble Experiment. The coming dawn, it was thought, would find America free at last from the grip of demon rum. Observances marked the occasion across the country. In Norfolk, 10,000 people had gathered at the tabernacle of America's greatest evangelist, Billy Sunday, for a mock funeral. The deceased was a 20-foot effigy of John Barleycorn, borne along the streets of the city in a solemn procession, escorted by 20 pallbearers, mourned only by a person masquerading as Satan. As the procession entered the tabernacle, Sunday called out to the corpse, "Good-bye, John! You were God's worst enemy. You were hell's best friend. I hate you with a perfect hatred. I love to hate you. The reign of tears is over. The slums will soon be a memory. We will turn our prisons into factories and our jails into storehouses and corncribs. Men will walk upright now, women will smile and the children will laugh. Hell will be forever for rent."

Colonial America saw little wrong in alcoholic drink. Workers were often paid in rum, and spiritous liquors were considered a necessary dietary supplement for those engaged in manual labor. Life insurance policies for those who consumed alcohol were normally lower than for those who abstained from drink, since liquor was thought to have medicinal value. Almost every ritual, event, or ceremony called for alcohol, and every evening meal was punctuated by a series by toasts. Clearly, the attitudes of the present differ from those of the past. The reason for this variation is the Temperance Movement that shifted American thinking in the intervening years. A movement of great magnitude, such as that which altered the national opinion on alcohol, invariably begins as the idea of a single person.

ᴥ *First Impressions*
"Hell Will Be Forever for Rent"

In the case of temperance, the idea was that of Dr. Benjamin Rush, a signer of the Declaration of Independence and the physician of the Continental Army during the American Revolution. In 1784, Rush wrote *An Inquiry into the Effects of Ardent Spirits,* which argued that liquor was harmful rather than healthful. To Rush's basic medical complaint was added in the 1820s the religious argument that fueled the reforming zeal

14.1 Temperance
and Prohibition

217

of the temperance societies. Support came next from a political movement and a women's crusade, until finally, early-twentieth-century America saw little good in alcoholic drink.

Source 1 Benjamin Rush, *An Inquiry into the Effects of Ardent Spirits upon the Human Body and Mind,* 1784

The effects of ardent spirits divide themselves into such as are of a prompt, and such as are of a chronic nature. The former discover themselves in drunkenness; the latter in a numerous train of diseases and vices of the body and mind.

I. I shall begin by briefly describing their prompt, or immediate effects, in a fit of drunkenness.

This odious disease (for by that name it should be called) appears with more or less of the following symptoms, and most commonly in the order in which I shall enumerate them.

1. Unusual garrulity.
2. Unusual silence.
3. **Captiousness**, and a disposition to quarrel.
4. Uncommon good humour, and an insipid simpering, or laugh.
5. Profane swearing, and cursing.
6. A disclosure of their own, or other people's secrets.
7. A rude disposition to tell those persons in company whom they know, their faults.
8. Certain immodest actions. I am sorry to say, this sign of the first stage of drunkenness, sometimes appears in women, who, when sober, are uniformly remarkable for chaste and decent manners.
9. A clipping of words.
10. Fighting; a black eye, or swelled nose, often mark this grade of drunkenness.
11. Certain extravagant acts which indicate a temporary fit of madness. These are singing, hallooing, roaring, imitating the noises of brute animals, jumping, tearing off clothes, dancing naked, breaking glasses and china, and dashing other articles of household furniture upon the ground, or floor. After a while the paroxysm of drunkenness is completely formed. The face now becomes flushed, the eyes project, and are somewhat watery, winking is less frequent than is natural; the upper lip is protruded,—the head inclines a little to one shoulder;—the jaw falls;—belchings, and hickup take place;—the limbs totter;—the whole body staggers;—The unfortunate subject of this history next falls on his seat,—he looks around him with a vacant countenance, and mutters inarticulate sounds to himself;—he attempts to rise and walk. In this attempt, he falls upon his side, from which he gradually turns upon his back. He now closes his eyes, and falls into a profound sleep, frequently attended by snoring, and profuse sweats, and sometimes with such a relaxation of the muscles which confine the bladder and the lower bowels, as to produce a symptom which delicacy forbids me to mention. In this condition, he often lies from ten, twelve, and twenty-four hours, to two, three, or four, and five days, an object of pity and disgust to his family and friends. . . .

II. Let us next attend to the chronic effects of ardent spirits upon the body and mind. In the body, they dispose to every form of acute disease; they moreover *excite* fevers in persons predisposed to them, from other causes. This has been remarked in all the yellow fevers which have visited the cities of the United

States. Hard drinkers seldom escape, and rarely recover from them. The following diseases are the usual consequences of the habitual use of ardent spirits, viz.

1. A decay of appetite, sickness at stomach, and a puking of bile or a discharge of a frothy and viscid phlegm by hawking, in the morning.

2. Obstructions of the liver . . .

3. Jaundice and dropsy of the belly and limbs, and finally of every cavity of the body . . .

4. Hoarseness, and a husky cough . . .

5. Diabetes . . .

6. Redness, and eruptions on various parts of the body . . .

7. A fetid breath, composed of every thing, that is offensive in putrid animal matter.

8. Frequent and disgusting belchings. Dr. Haller relates the case of a notorious drunkard having been suddenly destroyed in consequence of the vapour discharged from his stomach by belching, accidentally taking fire by coming in contact with the flame of a candle.

9. Epilepsy.

10. Gout, in all its various forms of swelled limbs, colic, palsy, and apoplexy. Lastly, 11. Madness.

Source 2 The Reverend Lyman Beecher, "Six Sermons on Intemperance," 1826

Could all the forms of evil produced in the land by intemperance come upon us in one horrid array, it would appall the nation, and put an end to the traffic in ardent spirit. If, in every dwelling built by blood, the stone from the wall should utter all the cries which the bloody traffic extorts, and the beam out of the timber should echo them back, who would build such a house, and who would dwell in it? What if in every part of the dwelling, from the cellar upward, through all the halls and chambers, babblings, and contentions, and voices, and groans, and shrieks, and wailings, were heard day and night! What if the cold blood oozed out, and stood in drops upon the walls, and, by preternatural art, all the ghastly skulls and bones of the victims destroyed by intemperance should stand upon the walls, in horrid sculpture, within and without the building! Who would rear such a building? What if at eventide and at midnight the airy forms of men destroyed by intemperance were dimly seen haunting the distilleries and stores where they received their bane, or following the track of the ship engaged in the commerce—walking upon the waves, flitting athwart the deck, sitting upon the rigging, and sending up, from the hold within and the waves without, groans, and loud laments, and wailings? Who would attend such stores? Who would labor in such distilleries? Who would navigate such ships?

Oh! were the sky over our heads one great whispering-gallery, bringing down about us all the lamentation and woe which intemperance creates, and the firm earth one sonorous medium of sound, bringing up around us from beneath the wailings of the damned, whom the commerce in ardent spirit had sent thither—these tremendous realities, assailing our senses, would invigorate our conscience, and give decision to the purpose of reformation. But these evils are as real as if the stone did cry out of the wall, and the beam answered it; as real as if, day and night, wailings were heard in every part of the dwelling, and blood and skeletons were seen upon every wall; as real as if the ghostly forms of departed victims flitted about stores and distilleries, and with unearthly voices screamed in our ears their loud lament. They are as real as if the sky over our heads collected and brought down about us all the notes of sorrow in the land, and the firm earth should open a passage for the wailings of despair to come up from beneath.

Source 3   Platform of the Prohibition Party, 1872

We, in National Convention assembled, as citizens of this free Republic, sharing the duties and responsibilities of its Government, in discharge of a solemn duty we owe to our country and our race, unite in the following declaration of principles:. . . .

That the trade in intoxicating beverages is a dishonor to Christian civilization, inimical to the best interests of society; a political wrong of unequal enormity, subversive of the ordinary objects of government, not capable of being regulated or restrained by any system of license whatever, but imperatively demanding for its suppression effective legal Prohibition by both State and National legislature. . . .

That there can be no greater peril to the nation than the existing party competition for the liquor vote; that any party not openly opposed to the traffic, experience shows, will engage in this competition, will court the favor of the criminal classes, will barter away the public morals, the purity of the ballot, and every object of good government, for party success. . . .

That while adopting national political measures for the Prohibition of the liquor traffic, we will continue the use of all moral means in our power to persuade men away from the injurious practice of using intoxicating beverages. . . .

That we invite all persons, whether total abstainers or not, who recognize the terrible injuries inflicted by the liquor traffic, to unite with us for its overthrow, and to secure thereby peace, order and the protection of persons and property. . . .

That competency, honesty and sobriety are indispensable qualifications for holding public office.

Source 4   Frances E. Willard, president of the Women's Christian Temperance Union, 1874

We paused in front of Sheffner's saloon, on Market Street. The ladies ranged themselves along the curbstone, for they had been forbidden in anywise to incommode the passers-by, being dealt with much more strictly than a drunken man or a heap of dry-goods boxes would be. At a signal from our gray-haired leader, a sweet-voiced woman began to sing. "Jesus the water of life will give," all our voices soon blending in the song. I think it was the most novel spectacle that I recall. There stood women of undoubted religious devotion and the highest character, most of them crowned with the glory of gray hairs. Along the stony pavement of that stoniest of cities rumbled the heavy wagons, many of them carriers of beer; between us and the saloon in front of which we were drawn up in line, passed the motley throng, almost every man lifting his hat, and even the little newsboys doing the same. It was American manhood's tribute to Christianity and to womanhood, and it was significant and full of pathos. The leader had already asked the saloonkeeper if we might enter, and he had declined, else the prayer meeting would have occurred inside his door. A sorrowful old lady, whose only son had gone to ruin through that very death-trap, knelt on the cold moist pavement and offered a broken-hearted prayer, while all our heads were bowed.

At a signal we moved on, and the next saloonkeeper permitted us to enter. I had no more idea of the inward appearance of a saloon than if there were no such place on earth. I knew nothing of its high, heavily corniced bar, its barrels with the ends all pointed toward the looker-on, each barrel being furnished with a faucet; its shelves glittering with decanters and cut glass, its floors thickly strewn with sawdust, and here and there a table with chairs—nor of its abundant fumes, sickening to healthy nostrils. The tall, stately lady who led us, placed her Bible on the bar and read a psalm. . . . Then we sang, "Rock of Ages" as I thought I had never heard it sung before, with a tender confidence to the height of which one does not rise in the easy-going, regulation prayer meeting, and then one of the older women whispered to me softly that the leader wished to know if I would pray. It was strange, perhaps, but I felt not the least reluctance as I knelt on the sawdust floor, with a group of earnest hearts around me, and behind them, filling every corner and extending out into the street, a crowd of unwashed, unkempt, hard-looking drinking men. I was conscious that perhaps never in my life . . . had I prayed truly as I did then. This was my Crusade baptism. The next day I went to the West, and within a week had been made president of the Chicago W.C.T.U.

Source 5   The Reverend James Long Jr., and J. Owen Long, "Rally Voters," 1907

Little drops of whiskey,
Little mugs of beer,
Bring the keenest sorrow,
To the children dear,

Little drinks of brandy,
Little sips of gin,
Swell the mighty torrents
Of disease and sin.

Rally voters
Heed no party sway
Show you're free men,
Voting as you pray.

E'en the glass of cider,
And the ruby wine,
Mar the strength and beauty
Of the form divine.

Little slips of paper
For the ballot cast
If for prohibition
Peace will bring at last.

Rally, then, ye voters,
Heed no party, party sway
Show the world you're free men
Voting as you pray.

Source 6   "The Effect of Alcohol on Sex Life," poster of the Anti-Saloon League, 1913

I. ALCOHOL INFLAMES THE PASSIONS, thus making the resisting of temptation to sex-sin unusually strong.

II. ALCOHOL DECREASES THE POWER OF CONTROL, thus making the resisting of temptation especially difficult.

III. ALCOHOL DECREASES THE RESISTANCE OF THE BODY TO DISEASE, thus causing the person who is under the influence of alcohol more likely to catch disease.

IV. ALCOHOL DECREASES THE POWER OF THE BODY TO RECOVER FROM DISEASE, thus making the result of disease more serious.

The influence of alcohol upon sex-life could hardly be worse.

AVOID ALL ALCOHOLIC DRINK ABSOLUTELY.

The control of sex impulses will then be easy and disease, dishonor, disgrace and degradation will be avoided.

Source 7   Evangelist Billy Sunday, "The Booze Sermon," 1915

I tell you it strikes in the night. It fights under cover of darkness and assassinates the characters that it cannot damn, and it lies about you. It attacks defenseless womanhood and childhood. The saloon is a coward. It is a thief; it is not an ordinary court offender that steals your money, but it robs you of manhood and leaves you in rags and takes away your friends, and robs your family. It impoverishes your children and it brings insanity and suicide. It will take the shirt off your back. It will steal the coffin from a dead child and yank the last crust of bread out of the hand of a starving child; it will take the last bucket of coal out of your cellar, and the last cent out of your pocket, and it will send you home bleary-eyed and staggering to your wife and children. It will steal the milk from the breast of the mother and leave her nothing with which to feed her infant. It will take the virtue from your daughter. It is the dirtiest, most low-down, damnable business that ever crawled out of the pit of Hell. It is a sneak, a thief and a coward.

It has no faith in God; has no religion. It would close every church in the land. It would hang its beer signs on the abandoned altars. It would close every public school. It respects the thief and it esteems the blasphemer; it fills the prisons and the penitentiaries. It despises Heaven, hates love, scorns virtue. It tempts the passions. Its music is the song of a siren. Its sermons are a collection of lewd, vile stories. It wraps a mantle about the hopes of this world and that to come. Its tables are full of the vilest literature. It is the moral clearinghouse for rot, and damnation, and poverty, and insanity, and it wrecks homes and blights lives today.

The saloon is a liar. It promises good cheer and sends sorrow. It promises health and causes disease. It promises happiness and sends misery. Yes, it sends the husband home with a lie on his lips to his wife; and the boy home with a lie on his lips to his mother; and it causes the employee to lie to his employer. It degrades. It is God's worst enemy and the devil's best friend. It spares neither youth nor old age. It is waiting with a dirty blanket for the baby to crawl into the world. It lies in wait for the unborn.

It cocks the highwayman's pistol. It puts the rope in the hands of the mob. It is the anarchist of the world and its dirty red flag is dyed with the blood of women and children. It sent the bullet through the body of Lincoln; it nerved the arm that sent the bullets through Garfield and William McKinley. Yes, it is a murderer. Every plot that was ever hatched against the government and law, was born and bred, and crawled out of the grog-shop to damn this country.

I tell you that the curse of God Almighty is on the saloon.

Source 8   Amendment XVIII, Constitution of the United States, ratified on January 16, 1919

Section 1. After one year from the ratification of this article the manufacture, sale, or transportation of intoxicating liquors within, the importation thereof into, or the exportation thereof from the United States and all territory subject to the jurisdiction thereof for beverage purposes is hereby prohibited.

Section 2. The Congress and the several States shall have concurrent power to enforce this article by appropriate legislation.

Section 3. This article shall be inoperative unless it shall have been ratified as an amendment to the Constitution by the legislatures of the several States, as provided in the Constitution, within seven years from the date of the submission hereof to the States by the Congress.

A Symbol of Dreaded Modernity

The movement that began with Benjamin Rush and grew steadily through the nineteenth century arrived at a time favorable to its message in the second decade of the twentieth century. America was at war. There was a general commitment to self-sacrifice on the part of those Americans who stayed safe and secure at home while their sons and brothers were at risk in the trenches of western Europe. And could any patriotic American sit serenely at a bar hoisting a bottle of Pabst or Busch or some other Germanic brew and stare at himself in the saloon mirror without guilt? An amendment to the Constitution prohibiting intoxicating drink swept through Congress and the legislatures of the states as a wartime expedient.

The imperialism of the early twentieth century instilled in white Americans a sense of obligation that they must remain morally and physically strong if they were to attempt to rule over and direct the lives of people of color at home and around the globe. Alcohol potentially weakened the white race. It also gave pleasure to people of other races. Will Rogers joked that Mississippi would stay dry as long as white voters could stagger to the polls.

A crusading zeal also marked the times. The Populist Movement of the 1890s, and the Socialist and Progressive movements of the new century had popularized the idea of reform. The Protestant Church was struggling to maintain its religious and moral leadership of the country in a time of rising Catholic and Jewish influence in America's urban centers. The lingering conservatism of Victorian morality and the realization of rural, agrarian America that it was losing power to the cities also led to a targeting of alcohol as a symbol of a dreaded modernity. Would not a ban of alcohol eliminate vice, misery, and immorality in the cities?

The constitutional amendment banning alcoholic drink was implemented by the Volstead Act. Anyone who manufactured or transported or sold a beverage containing more than one-half of one percent alcohol would be subject to a fine of $1,000 and six months in prison. For the second offense, the penalty was $2,000 and five years behind bars.

14.2 Prohibition: A Lesson in the Futility (and Danger) of Prohibiting

Source 9   Editorial, "Prospect and Retrospect," *Washington Post*, January 17, 1920

Prohibition is here. Before the United States stretch the Sahara sands, with no oasis in sight. Another step, we are told, has been taken toward the ideal existence for which the human heart yearns. . . .

Prohibition is a fact. As we ponder it our imagination travels back through the crowded events of a century and a half, and we see George Washington and Alexander Hamilton sitting before the open fireplace at Mount Vernon toasting their stockinged shins before a log fire and discussing matters of vital interest to the young republic whose destinies they are endeavoring to shape. As they sit in earnest converse on matters of state they sip with apparent relish goblets of rum from the West Indies—rum containing 60 per cent alcohol!

As we contemplate this picture of utter depravity we are driven to ask: Is it any wonder that Washington's will was weakened when he resorted thus to strong drink? Is it any wonder that Hamilton's mentality was dwarfed by alcohol? The pity of it!

Giving the imagination rein, we can see Grant in the field, in the dark days when the sovereignty of the nation was tottering in the balance, drinking raw whisky from a tin cup. We cannot but shudder and speculate what a tower of strength Grant would have been to his country had he been a total abstainer. . . .

We see upon the ways of American shipyards leviathan dreadnoughts and efficient destroyers, defenders of liberty and civilization, destined soon to take the water under a baptism of ginger ale or grape juice, in consonance with the policy of the bone dry navy. And the mind turns to the old frigate Niagara, now calmly resting in her final anchorage on Lake Erie. We wonder if the sailors of 1812 would have been braver and if Perry would have shown more personal courage had they been deprived of their regular ration of grog; and whether the old Niagara herself would not have proved a stauncher ship and added a more brilliant page to American history had she not been christened with the sparkling wine from the sun-kissed vineyards of France.

The world moves, and civilization progresses with it. Hence we must go forward harboring in our breasts the feeling that America is turning from her disgraceful past. Above the sands of the desert of prohibition the sun shines in the heavens and the night brings their cool relief. To beguile the journey an occasional mirage will flash upon the blue screen of the sky, picturing a long mahogany counter with a shiny brass rail in front, and behind it white-jacketed servitors cracking ice, working faucets and squirting siphons amid the incessant jangling of cash registers, their activities reflected in a massive mirror before which repose long rows of bottles and glasses and—

Then the mirage fades, and the eye beholds only the boundless waste of the hot sands.

Lead on, Crusaders; we follow! There's no other place to go.

Source 10 Sir A. C. Geddes, British ambassador to the United States, *Dispatch from His Majesty's Ambassador to Washington*, June 14, 1923

My Lord,

I have the honour to transmit to your Lordship herewith a memorandum on the subject of the effects of prohibition in the United States. Your Lordship is already familiar with the difficulty of obtaining reliable statistics on this controversial subject, and with the inevitable divergence between the figures furnished respectively by the supporters and opponents of prohibition. The enclosed memorandum is based on statistics supplied by the opposing factions as well as by the Federal Prohibition authorities.

I have, &c.
A.C. Geddes.

Memorandum.

Scope of the Present Legislation.

Since the Eighteenth Amendment to the Constitution of the United States came into force on the 29th January, 1920 (one year from the date of its ratification), it has been unlawful to manufacture, sell or transport intoxicating liquor. The "Volstead Act," passed by Congress in October 1919, defined intoxicating liquor as liquor which contained more than one-half of 1 per cent of alcohol. This Act provided for the licensing of sacramental wine in small quantities, and of whisky and wine, under stringent restrictions, for medicinal purposes. In forty-five of the forty-eight States local law has been passed in support of the Federal Act. In the remaining three States the federal prohibition agents are not assisted by the State police in making raids, &c., for the purposes of securing enforcement. These three States have recently been joined by the State of New York, the most populous State of the Union, where the local enforcement law has just been repealed, and the co-operation of the State police thus withdrawn.

Present Consumption of Intoxicating Liquor.

On this point the following figures have been compiled by the three bureaux, in which the most detailed statistics as to the effects of prohibition are available:—

	Anti-Saloon League	Association Against the Prohibition Amendment	Federal Prohibition Unit of the Treasury
Amount of intoxicating liquor now consumed on a 100 percent basis of that consumed formerly . . .	Percent 20	Percent at least 66	Percent 20

Prohibition of intoxicating liquor has on the whole been effective in the rural districts and in the smaller towns throughout the country. It is less effective on the eastern seaboard and in the vicinity of the Great Lakes, where powerful organizations of liquor-smugglers succeed in effecting a regular traffic in imported intoxicants.

Large quantities of home-made liquor are also brewed, but it has proved to be poisonous in many cases, and the practice is reported to be on the decrease. According to opinions given by the Association against the Prohibition Amendment, the fact that the consumption of intoxicating liquor is illegal has in itself been sufficient to lead many Americans who formerly drank little or nothing to conform to a fashionable habit at social gatherings of carrying small pocket-flasks of home-brewed or imported spirits.

Arrest for Drunkenness.

The following figures have been submitted by the bureaux named as a general estimate:—

	Anti-Saloon League	Association Against the Prohibition Amendment	Federal Prohibition Unit of the Treasury
Number of deaths, on a 100 percent basis of deaths formerly occurring	percent 20	percent 250	percent 20

The Anti-Saloon League quote the following statistics in respect of nine cities in support of their general estimate given above:—

Arrests for Drunkenness	in 1917	in 1921
Boston	72,000	31,000
Cincinnati	14,000	500
St. Louis	4,900	990
Washington, D.C.	10,800	5,800
New York City	13,800	6,200
San Francisco	15,100	6,500
Los Angeles	17,500	6,800
Portland, Oregon	6,700	2,900
Detroit	17,400	7,200

Deaths from Alcoholism.
The figures are as follows:

	Anti-Saloon League	Association Against the Prohibition Amendment	Federal Prohibition Unit of the Treasury
Number of deaths, on a 100 percent basis of deaths formerly occurring	percent 20	percent 250	percent 20

According to estimates supplied by the Department of State, the number of deaths from these causes rose slightly after 1920, although they had been decreasing steadily between 1917 and 1920. The State Department's figures are as follows:—

1917	1918	1919	1920	1921
3,922	2,216	1,367	900	1,611

Further statistics on this point compiled by the health authorities of nineteen cities, all having populations over 300,000, show that the deaths from alcoholism in 1922 were slightly more than in 1920 or 1921, but were 57 per cent fewer than the deaths which occurred from this cause in 1916 or 1917.

Effect on Crime.

Estimates of comparative criminal statistics for the period before and after prohibition are as follows:—

	Anti-Saloon League	Association Against the Prohibition Amendment	Federal Prohibition Unit of the Treasury
Amount of all crime on a 100 percent basis of crime formerly occurring	percent 40	percent 125	percent 100

A report published by the Department of Commerce shows that, between the 1st July, 1917, and the 1st July, 1922, the number of persons detained in State prisons increased from 72.4 to 74.5 per 100,000 of the population. During the same period the ratio of Federal prisoners per 100,000 of the population increased from 3 to 5.1.

Economic Effects.

Since the adoption of prohibition a marked increase, which is computed at 40 per cent, has taken place in the amount of deposits at savings banks. The supporters of prohibition in the United States claim that the average wage-earner now has considerably more money to spend on the education of his children, on the furnishing of his home, on dress, sports and amusements. They also affirm that prohibition has caused increased production in the factories, and that many employees who in former days absented themselves regularly on the Monday and even on the Tuesday of each week now work a full six-day week. So many other factors have contributed to restore economic conditions in the United States since the war that it is almost impossible to form any estimate of the extent to which prohibition has contributed to this recovery, or otherwise.

Source 11 Attorney Clarence Darrow, debating a supporter of Prohibition, 1924

I object to a man being drunk if he gets in the way of anybody else. I don't mind his being drunk alone. But if I want to take a drink and do not get drunk where I interfere with anybody else, should society then tell me that I can't drink? Or, if Brother Holmes . . . hasn't got any more sense than to get drunk, is that any reason why I, who do not get drunk, shall not have anything to drink? Now—is it? . . . Now, I don't believe in encouraging prohibitionists. There isn't anything that they would stop at. They would pass a law to make you go to church—as they have done. They did that in New England, and they picked out the church. They would send you to jail if you didn't do it. And then they passed a law against your sleeping in church—and that took all the pleasure out of religion.

I say nobody in their right senses would trust their individual liberty to the people who believe in that sort of legislation. . . .

Now, suppose we admit for the sake of argument, that sixty per cent of the people of this country would vote dry. If sixty percent of the people do not believe in something that the other forty per cent believe in, should they send the forty per cent to jail for what they do?

Now, there is your question. What proportion of a population should believe that certain acts are criminal before passing a criminal statute? If forty per cent of the people of this country believe that a thing is innocent, do you think that the sixty per cent who do not believe it would send that forty per cent to jail if they were a tolerant people?

I assume that sixty per cent of the people of this county believe in either the Protestant or Catholic religion, or think they do, and believe that it is very necessary to man's welfare on earth and absolutely necessary to his welfare in the hereafter. Are they justified in passing a criminal statute and sending heretics to jail? They have done it, and they may do it again, because intolerance is just as strong in the world today as it ever was. And when we permit it to have its way, nobody knows who will be the victims. . . .

If the doctrine should prevail that when sixty per cent of the people of a country believe that certain conduct should be a criminal offense and for that conduct they must send the forty per cent to jail, then liberty is dead and freedom is gone. They will first destroy the forty per cent, and then turn and destroy each other.

In this world of ours we cannot live with our neighbors without a broad tolerance. We must tolerate their religion, their social life, their appetites of eating and drinking, and we should be very slow, indeed, when we make criminal conduct of what is believed by vast numbers of men and women to be honest and fair and right.

This prohibition law has filled our jails with people who are not criminals, who have no conception or feeling that they are doing wrong. It has turned our federal courts into police courts, where important business is put aside for cases of drunkenness and disorderly conduct. It has made spies and detectives, snooping around doors and windows. It has made informers of thousands of us. It has made grafters and **boodlers** of men who otherwise would be honest. It is hateful, it is distasteful, it is an abomination, and we ought to get rid of it, and we will if we have the courage and the sense.

Source 12 Henry Ford, *My Philosophy of Industry*, 1929

In common decency the liquor generation should be allowed to die in silence. Its agonies should not be the constant topic of American journals.

Prohibition was intended to save the country and generations yet to come. There are a million boys growing up who have never seen a saloon, and who will never know the handicap of liquor, either in themselves or their relatives; and this excellent condition will go on spreading itself over the country when the wet press and the paid propaganda of booze are forgotten. There should be no mistake about it. The abolition of the commercialized liquor trade in this country is as final as the abolition of slavery. These are the two great reforms to which moral America committed itself from the beginning of its history.

Anything that interferes with our ability to think clearly, lead healthy, normal lives, and do our work well will ultimately be discarded, either as an economic handicap or from a desire for better personal health.

Source 13 "U.S. Prohibition Ends Today through Presidential Edict; Nation's Rum Flows at 3 P.M.," *Washington Post*, December 5, 1933

President Roosevelt and Acting Secretary of State William Phillips this afternoon—probably between 2 and 3 p.m.—will proclaim to the nation the repeal of the eighteenth amendment and the end of national prohibition.

Even before these proclamations are issued—in fact as soon as Pennsylvania, Ohio and Utah ratify the repeal amendment—trucks laden with authentic and legal whiskies, wines, gin and cordials will roll forth from warehouses in 24 States to supply the liquor with which Americans tonight will slake their theoretical 13-year-old thirst.

Source 14 Editorial, "Today's Meaning," *Washington Post*, December 5, 1933

The eighteenth amendment was applied in the mistaken notion that a great moral and social reform may be achieved by the mere enactment of a sumptuary law. We know now how absurd it was to think so. We know that with all its power, all its wealth, all its dignity and all its resources, the United States government is not able effectively to lay down a dictum and enforce it in the face of hostile or apathetic public sentiment.

We have at least learned from the eighteenth amendment and all its by-products—among others, racketeering and a general spirit of lawlessness bred in an otherwise law-abiding people—that the Federal Government is not able effectively to exercise local police powers; that measures requiring active and diligent use of such powers must proceed from local sentiment. They cannot be pressed down from above. National Prohibition came much too near to wrecking the fundamental respect for law essential to civilized government for us ever to make the same kind of mistake again.

Source 15 Amendment XXI, Constitution of the United States, ratified on December 5, 1933

Section 1. The eighteenth article of amendment to the Constitution of the United States is hereby repealed.

Section 2. The transportation or importation into any State, Territory, or possession of the United States for delivery or use therein of intoxicating liquors, in violation of the laws thereof, is hereby prohibited.

Section 3. This article shall be inoperative unless it shall have been ratified as an amendment to the Constitution by conventions in the several States, as provided in the Constitution, within seven years from the date of the submission hereof to the States by the Congress.

 Second Thoughts

Rural vs. Urban Morality

By the time the Eighteenth Amendment took effect, there were already 27 states enforcing some form of prohibition within their jurisdictions. With the repeal of the Eighteenth Amendment, all but seven states rescinded their own statutes. The last state to go "wet" was Mississippi in 1966. The repeal of state laws, however, often left to local communities the option of prohibiting or permitting alcoholic drink. Consequently, there are still localities in America where liquor sale, consumption, and transportation are illegal. In the larger sense, while the temperance movement did not eradicate ardent spirits, it did transform the public perception of liquor. It also left the country with a web of peculiar regulations and agencies not found in most other countries.

14.3 Alcohol
Prohibition
Was a Failure

Source 16 Charles A. and Mary R. Beard, *The Rise of American Civilization*, 1934

[T]hat hot desire to force ideas and moral standards on one's fellowmen [:] It was under this head that the critics of prohibition usually classed the associated effort which abolished, nominally at least, the manufacture and sale of intoxicating liquor as a beverage. Their assignment, however, is not altogether exact. It is true that since the middle of the nineteenth century there had been a well-organized temperance movement in America, inspired by moral fervor, and that it was given decided impetus by the Women's Christian Temperance Union founded in 1874 with Frances Willard as a dominant leader. It is also true that the Prohibition Party, which nominated its first candidate for the presidency in 1872 and continued its agitation with unabated zeal, was largely supported by religious ardor. But while these movements flourished, the liquor business likewise flourished.

It was not until the Anti-Saloon League, founded at Oberlin, Ohio, commenced its nation-wide campaign in 1895 that war on the traffic took on a formidable aspect. Now the Anti-Saloon League which bent its energies to abolishing the saloon in villages, towns, counties, and states in a piecemeal fashion no doubt made an appeal to the moral elements of the population . . . but it had also practical ends in view. It did not ask its members to take the total abstinence pledge: rather did it summon them to battle against the saloon, the workingman's club. In the South, the League was strongly supported by business men who saw in the abolition of the "dram shop" an increase in the sobriety and regularity of their colored personnel. In other parts of the country, especially in the West, employers of labor in quest of efficiency gave money and support to the new crusade, for drunken workmen were a danger as well as an economic loss to machine industry. . . .

Probably many supporters of the Anti-Saloon League were amazed when they discovered that the total abolition of the saloon implied the extreme doctrine of unconditional prohibition. Even as things turned out, the middle and upper classes with money to spare could always get good liquor of any kind, in any quantity, for a price. Therefore, from one point of view it is possible to say that, while prohibition was a failure, the abolition of the old-fashioned saloon was fairly successful. At all events, ascribing prohibition to nationalized Puritanism betrayed a forgetfulness of leading features characterizing colonial life, for the old Puritan loved fine liquor, mild and strong, and none of the original Puritan states was dry when the Eighteenth Amendment took effect. It was safe to venture a guess that the desire of business men for efficiency and safety in labor was as potent in bringing about the new regime as the wanton lust of moralists determined to impose their own standards upon the nation.

Source 17   Richard Hofstadter, *The Age of Reform,* 1955

[T]he crusade to protect fundamentalist religion from modern science . . . had its culmination in the Scopes trial; the defense of the eighteenth amendment at all costs; and the rallying of the Ku Klux Klan against the Catholics, the Negroes, and the Jews. . . . When the crusading **debauch** was over, the country's chief inheritance from the Yankee-Protestant drive for morality and from the tensions of the war period was Prohibition. To the historian who likes to trace the development of the great economic issues and to follow the main trend of class politics, the story of Prohibition will seem like a historical detour, a meaningless nuisance, an extraneous imposition upon the main course of history. The truth is that Prohibition appeared to the men of the twenties as a major issue because it *was* a major issue, and one of the most symptomatic for those who would follow the trend of rural-urban conflicts and the ethnic tensions in American politics. It is also one of the leading clues to the reaction against the Progressive temper. For Prohibition, in the twenties, was the skeleton at the feast, a grim reminder of the moral frenzy that so many wished to forget, a ludicrous caricature of the reforming impulse, of the Yankee-Protestant notion that it is both possible and desirable to moralize private life through public action.

To hold the Progressives responsible for Prohibition would be to do them an injustice. Men of an urbane cast of mind, whether conservatives or Progressives in their politics, had been generally antagonistic, or at the very least suspicious, of the pre-war drive toward Prohibition; and on the other side there were many advocates of Prohibition who had nothing to do with other reforms. We cannot, however, ignore the diagnostic significance of prohibitionism. For Prohibition was a pseudo-reform, a pinched, parochial substitute for reform which had a widespread appeal to a certain type of crusading mind. It was linked not merely to an aversion to drunkenness and to the evils that accompanied it, but to the immigrant drinking masses, to the pleasures and amenities of city life, and to the well-to-do classes and cultivated men. It was carried about America by the rural-evangelical virus: the country Protestant frequently brought it with him to the city when the contraction of agriculture sent him there to seek his livelihood. . . . Prohibition was a means by which the reforming energies of the country were transmuted into mere peevishness.

Source 18   Andrew Sinclair, *Era of Excess: A Social History of the Prohibition Movement,* 1962

The questions which occupied the American people in the first three decades of this century were not the questions which occupied their Presidents. While the White House was concerned with trusts and taxation and tariffs and foreign policy, the people worried over prohibition and Romanism and fundamentalism and immigration and the growing power of the cities of the United States. These worries lay under the surface of all political conflicts. For the old America of the village and farms distrusted the new America of the urban masses. Prohibition was the final victory of the defenders of he American past. On the rock of the Eighteenth Amendment, village America made its last stand. . . .

The Eighteenth Amendment was repealed by the Twenty-first. The old order of the country gave way to the new order of the cities. Rural morality was replaced by urban morality, rural voices by urban voices, rural votes by urban votes. A novel culture of skyscrapers and suburbs grew up to oust the civilization of the general store and Main Street.

Source 19   Paul Goodman and Frank Gatell, *America in the Twenties: The Beginnings of Contemporary America,* 1972

For fourteen years, the United States remained legally dry. In fact, however, the production and consumption of alcohol did not stop; it simply went underground. And in the end Prohibition turned into a nightmare. From the outset, millions refused to comply, including President Warren G. Harding, though he campaigned as a staunch dry. The Yale University Club laid in a 14 year supply of liquor, and those with less foresight and cash bought illegal booze from bootleggers. Two thousand badly paid prohibition agents had the impossible task of preventing drinking in a nation of 100 million people.

Production moved from the factory into the home. Eventually it became the special province of the underworld. Prohibition did not create organized crime—criminal syndicates already flourished in the big cities—but now gangsters, imitating Big Business, perceived the advantages of limiting competition, consolidating resources, and enlarging their take. Prohibition shifted an estimated $2 billion annually from the liquor manufacturers to the bootleggers and gave organized crime enormous sums of money for intimidating other businessmen. Big-time crime, like big business, was the achievement of powerful men such as Al Capone, the kingpin of the Chicago underworld. Unlike John D. Rockefeller, who bought out his competitors or drove them into bankruptcy, Capone cut them down with the Thompson submachinegun, or dropped them, weighted with chains, in Lake Michigan. At their height, the Chicago gang wars of the 1920s produced 400 murders in one year. . . .

Prohibition did not stop all Americans from drinking, but it did dry up large parts of America, those inclined to be dry anyway. . . . But if small-town and rural America was drier than ever, urban America was as wet as ever. New York City for instance had 32,000 speakeasies in the 1920s, evidencing the widespread erosion of respect for law among the law-abiding, especially among Americans of immigrant stock. As for millions of native-born Protestants who accepted modernity, Prohibition was a reminder that an older, rural America still held power. . . . Above all, Prohibition, like fundamentalism, represented a desperate effort to resist changes that were turning America into a pluralistic and secular society, in which no single culture ruled.

Source 20   Robert Dallek, *The Great Republic*, 1992

In 1920 most prominent citizens dutifully endorsed the Eighteenth Amendment. But in the course of the decade, although Prohibition brought a decline in alcoholism and especially in deaths from cirrhosis of the liver, successful Americans increasingly turned against it. Millions of citizens came to consider Prohibition an insufferable violation of their rights. Prohibition, they said, artificially created a new class of criminals—those who drank and those who supplied the liquor—and then increased taxes to pay for the enforcement of the law. Those who favored repeal assumed that the use of alcohol did not matter very much: drinking should be a question of individual choice.

 Questioning the Past

1. Argue the case for the prohibition of intoxicating drinks. Argue the case against such a prohibition. Which case is the more compelling? Present arguments for and against the prohibition of other drugs that impair the mind and negatively affect the body: cocaine, marijuana, heroin, tobacco. Do the lessons learned from the failure to prohibit alcohol apply in any way to the efforts to control other drugs?

2. Andrew Sinclair wrote that the "success of the Prohibitionists is . . . easier to understand than their defeat would have been." Why was America susceptible to the idea of prohibition? What arguments of the Prohibitionists appealed to the ideals and values of America?

3. Representative George Tinkham of Massachusetts commented during Prohibition, "The more advanced a country is, the higher its alcoholic content." While this may or may not be the case, there does seem to be among affluent nations a high incidence of abuse of alcohol and other escapist drugs. Why is this?

4. Richard Hofstadter wrote that the victory of Prohibition brought the "transformation of the drinker from a victim of evil to a lawbreaker." Debate this point.

5. The per capita consumption rate for alcohol in the United States is around 52 gallons each year. Alcoholism is the third largest cause of American deaths. Around 25,000 Americans lose their lives in alcohol-related auto accidents annually. If Prohibition was not an effective solution to the alcohol problem, what is?

Chapter **15**

Women's Suffrage

The Nineteenth Amendment Is Ratified

August 26, 1920

The movement to permit women to rise to their full potential as human beings, unfettered by social, political, and religious constraints, began in a small town in New York State in the middle of the nineteenth century. There, at the village of Seneca Falls in the summer of 1848, some 300 women and men met to draft a Declaration of Sentiments that addressed many of the ways in which American society suppressed women. The reaction to the Seneca Falls Convention from around the country was mostly one of ridicule. And to many observers of the time, the most ridiculous of the proposals set forth by the convention participants was the suggestion that women should be allowed to vote. It would take the convention delegates and those who later came to share their views some 70 years to change the public mind on this point.

Since the Constitution of the United States left the question of voting to state governments, the movement for women's suffrage had concentrated its efforts on winning the franchise on a state-by-state basis. The suffragists succeeded in winning voting rights for women in Wyoming Territory in 1869. When Wyoming was admitted to statehood in 1890, its constitution enfranchised women. Colorado, Utah, and Idaho granted women the right to vote during the last decade of the nineteenth century. By the time Woodrow Wilson had settled into the White House, Oregon, Arizona, Kansas, Nevada, and Montana were also permitting women to vote, as were a number of localities around the country. Illinois allowed voting rights for women in presidential elections. These were important victories, but they were but small recompense for the tremendous expenditures of talent and energy poured into the state-by-state efforts, most of which had ended in frustration and failure.

15.1 History of the Suffrage Movement

❧ *First Impressions*

"I Have No Son to Fight for Democracy Abroad, and So I Send My Daughter to Fight for Democracy at Home"

As the momentum of the movement seemed to be dissipating, the suffrage campaign got its second breath. This reinvigoration began with a demonstration in Washington on the eve of Woodrow Wilson's inauguration

235

in 1913, and it signaled a shift from a state-by-state strategy to an effort to amend the federal Constitution.

Source 1   "Suffrage Crusaders in Thrilling Pageant Take City by Storm," Washington *Evening Star*, March 3, 1913

15.2 Links to Sites Concerning Suffrage and Women's History

The modern crusade of "votes for women" this afternoon took Washington by storm. Marching determinedly along Pennsylvania Avenue with bands playing martial and religious music, five thousand earnest women passed between solidly packed masses of humanity to emphasize their demand for suffrage through a constitutional amendment, while there were being enacted on the south steps of the Treasury Building allegorical dances and tableaux interpreting the dreams and ambitions of militant womanhood.

Washington for a time was suffrage-mad. The huge crowds gathered in the city for the inauguration tomorrow gazed upon the procession and tableaux from sidewalks, windows, grandstands and every point of vantage. "Votes for women" signs were waved. Automobile horns were tooted. Women and men cheered and clapped their hands.

Showing the history and objects of the suffrage movement through beautifully decorated floats, through costumed paraders on foot and horseback and through mottoes on varied-colored banners, the procession pageant impressed the thousands of spectators by its beauty and size. Like modern Amazons marching on to battle, the suffragists looked neither to the right or left.

Reaching a climax in a great mass meeting in Memorial Continental Hall this afternoon, the great suffrage demonstration will pass into history as the greatest bid for public support ever made by any body of people.

Source 2   "Woman's Beauty, Grace, and Art Bewilder the Capital; Miles of Fluttering Femininity Present Entrancing Suffrage Appeal," *Washington Post*, March 4, 1913

Five thousand women, marching in the woman suffrage pageant yesterday, practically fought their way foot by foot up Pennsylvania Avenue, through a surging mass of humanity that completely defied the Washington police, swamped the marchers, and broke their procession into little companies. The women, trudging stoutly along under great difficulties, were able to complete their march only when troops of cavalry from Fort Myer were rushed into Washington to take charge of Pennsylvania Avenue. No inauguration has ever produced such scenes, which in many instances amounted to little less than riots.

Later, in Continental Hall, the women turned what was to have been a suffrage demonstration into an indignation meeting in which the Washington police were roundly criticized for their inactivity. . . . Miss Helen Keller, the noted deaf and blind girl, was so exhausted and unnerved by the experience in attempting to reach a grandstand where she was to have been a guest of honor that she was unable to speak later at Continental Hall.

The scenes which attended the entry of "General" Rosalie Jones and her "hikers" on Thursday, when the bedraggled women had to fight their way up Pennsylvania Avenue, swamped by a crowd with which a few policemen struggled in vain, were repeated yesterday, but on a vastly larger scale. The marchers had to fight their way from the start, and took more than one hour in making the first ten blocks. Many of the women were in tears under the gibes of the crowd that lined the route.

Although stout wire ropes had been stretched up and down the length of Pennsylvania Avenue from the Peace Monument to the Mall behind the White House, the enormous crowds that gathered early to obtain points of vantage overstepped them or crawled beneath. Apparently no effort was made to drive back the trespassers in the early hours, with the result that when the parade started it faced at almost every hundred yards a solid wall of humanity.

As a spectacle the pageant was entrancing. Beautiful women, posing in classic robes, passed in a bewildering array, presenting an irresistible appeal to the artistic, and completely captivating the hundreds of thousands of spectators who struggled for a view along the entire route.

But there were hostile elements in the crowd through which the women marched. Miss Milholland, herald of the procession, distinguished herself by aiding in riding down a crowd that blocked the way and threatened to disrupt the parade. Another woman member of the "petticoat cavalry" struck a man a stinging blow across the face with her riding crop in reply to a scurrilous remark as she was passing. The mounted police rode hither and yon, but seemed powerless to stem the tide of humanity.

A disorderly group gathered in front of the reviewing stand, in which sat Mrs. Taft and Miss Helen Taft and a half dozen invited guests from the White House. They kept up a running fire of caustic comment. Apparently no effort was made to remove them and, evidently disgusted, the White House party left before the procession had passed in its halting and interrupted journey toward Continental Hall, where the mass meeting was held. . . .

The tableaux on the steps of the Treasury Building, framed in the great columns and broad stairway of the government's treasury house, were begun when the parade started from its rendezvous at the base of the Capitol. Beautiful in coloring and grouping, the dramatic symbolization of women's aspirations for political freedom was completed long before the head of the parade was in sight. In their thin dresses and bare arms, the performers waited, shivering, for more than an hour until finally they were forced to seek refuge within the big building.

Around the Treasury Department the crowds were massed so tightly that the repeated charges by the police were seemingly ineffective. It was as though the bluecoats charged a stone wall. . . .

When the cavalry suddenly appeared, there was a wild outburst of applause in the reviewing stand. The men in brown virtually brushed aside the mounted and foot police and took charge. In two lines the troop charged the crowds. Evidently realizing they would be ridden down, the people fought their way back. When they hesitated, the cavalrymen, under the orders of their officers, did not hesitate. Their horses were driven into the throngs and whirled and wheeled until hooting men and women were forced to retreat. A space was quickly cleared.

The parade itself, in spite of the delays, was a great success. Passing through the two walls of antagonistic humanity, the marchers for the most part kept their temper. They suffered insult and closed their ears to jibs and jeers. Few faltered, although several of the older women were force to drop out from time to time.

Source 3   "Score the Police for Inefficiency," Washington *Evening Star,*
March 4, 1913

Demanding a congressional investigation to fix the blame for the overflowing
of huge crowds into Pennsylvania Avenue during their great procession and the
disgusting scenes attending the affair, the leaders and marchers of the suffrage
pageant of yesterday afternoon gathered in Memorial Continental Hall, following
the "votes for women" demonstration, and for more than an hour criticized the
policing of the city during the parade.

While the women were denouncing the "idiotic incompetency of the police
arrangements," as they described them, members of the House of Representatives
were equally free at the Capitol with their scathing criticisms of Maj. Sylvester
and his force. In the House a congressional investigation was demanded to learn
why Maj. Sylvester, superintendent of police, had disregarded a joint resolution
of Congress providing for adequate police protection. . . .

From every side yesterday and today came the most bitter denunciations
of the police "protection" afforded the suffragists. The statement said to have
been made by Maj. Sylvester last night that "the pageant was given the same
protection that will be given the inaugural parade," was greeted by jeers. A
member of the Senate, on hearing of this remark, declared that if this is the
case Washington would have a new superintendent before sundown today.

Miss Alice Paul, chairman of the procession committee, with other leaders,
today called attention to the fact that they had spent their entire time Saturday and
Sunday pleading for better protection. During the reception of "Gen." Rosalie Jones,
they said, they realized that the police were not trying to give protection, and they
asked Secretary of War Stimson and several governors for assistance. . . .

It was evident early in the afternoon that the police were making no real
effort to clear the streets for the pageant, and from every side came the query,
"Why don't the police do something, or, why doesn't Maj. Sylvester call for
troops from Fort Myer?"

It was not until the women managing the pageant got busy with the Secretary of War that details of the 15th Cavalry, from the Army post across the
river, were rushed to the city. When the troopers made their appearance at 15th
Street and the Avenue they found the police shooing the crowds in a futile sort
of way; waving their big batons and grinning fatuously as the crowds jostled
and pushed them out of the way. The troopers, forming two ranks, charged on
the surging crowd at the south side of the Treasury, and in less than three
minutes had the people back of the ropes, and held them there. . . .

More than 200 persons were hurt more or less seriously during the pageant,
and even the ambulances had to fight their way through the massed humanity
to get to the victims. At Emergency and Casualty Hospitals the extra forces of
physicians and nurses had their hands full all afternoon and until late at night,
and at both institutions the corridors were filled with extra cots upon which to
place the sick and injured women, men and children brought in.

And, according to the reports at police headquarters and the precinct stations, not a single arrest was made by the Washington police during the several
hours of unchecked rioting.

As a result of the lack of police protection, the monster pageant which, speaking impartially, otherwise would have been one of the most imposingly beautiful

spectacles ever presented in Washington, was broken up into fragments, halted a hundred times before it had traveled ten blocks, and scores of the women and girls participating in the demonstration were made the victims of ribald insults that, had the crowds been held behind the ropes, would have been impossible. . . .

"Policemen in uniform stood and jeered, along with ruffians and hoodlums, at the marchers in the suffrage parade," said Representative Hobson of Alabama, in the House early this morning. He charged that the police department had utterly ignored the resolution passed by Congress two days ago directing that Pennsylvania Avenue be kept free of traffic and open for the women's parade.

"I marched in the section set apart for senators and representatives," continued Hobson. "There were some twenty of us headed by Judge Rucker of Missouri. When we reached 7th Street the crowd had closed in upon us so closely that we were compelled to give up marching four abreast to march two abreast, and finally we walked single file, and even then we almost had to force our way through the crowds. And police, many of them, did nothing to put the crowd back, but occupied themselves in jeering at us." . . .

Mr. Hobson said that after Congress had ordered that Pennsylvania Avenue be cleared for the parade Maj. Sylvester had no right to let his personal feelings in regard to woman suffrage interfere with the performance of his duties. "Women were insulted, kicked and struck by ruffians," said Mr. Hobson, "and many of the policemen on the spot made no effort to stop these outrages."

Source 4   "Row in the House," *Washington Post*, March 4, 1913

When Representative Hobson last night rebuked Maj. Richard Sylvester from the floor of the House for not giving the women and young girls in yesterday's parade police protection, Minority Leader Mann retorted:

"They ought to have been at home."

"Does the gentleman from Illinois mean to say," asked Mr. Hobson, "that these young girls were not entitled to police protection? A woman has just telephoned me that her daughter on one of the floats was insulted by a ruffian, who jumped on the float where she was riding, grabbed her by the knee, and attempted to pull her off the float."

Representative Cooper, of Wisconsin, white with rage, hastened across the floor, shaking his fist in the direction of Mr. Mann, shouting: "Don't let the fact that you received a testimonial tonight make a damned blackguard of you."

Representative Kent, of California, whose daughter also was in the parade and was insulted, angrily retorted to Mr. Mann, who turned to the attack with a request for Mr. Kent to take himself off to a place where the climate is warmer than it is just now in Washington.

Source 5   Editorial, "The Women's Parade," Washington *Evening Star*, March 4, 1913

Regardless of yesterday's display of unchecked rowdyism, the parade of the women in this city was of a nature to command the highest praise. Had it been given scope between the lines allotted to it by Congress, it would have been one of the most impressive spectacles ever witnessed in Washington. It was the result of careful planning, thoughtful research, and self-sacrificing labors on the part of a great number of women from all parts of the country. It stood for a definite movement in American affairs and it was beautiful in itself and highly significant in its character. Had it been given a fair chance it would have made a high mark for Washington pageants of all kinds. The cause of woman suffrage is not injured by the comparative failure of this parade due to circumstances wholly beyond the control of its projectors and participants. On the contrary the pageant treatment accorded to the women who marched is certain to awaken sympathy not only here but elsewhere and it is to be believed that today as a result of yesterday's shameful performance here the cause of woman suffrage is stronger than ever.

A Schism in the Suffrage Movement

The march on Washington was sponsored by the nation's most prominent suffrage organization, the National American Woman Suffrage Association. But it was planned and staged by the Congressional Committee of that association.

15.3 Selections from the NAWSA Collection, 1848–1921

The National American Woman Suffrage Association was the product of a merger of two national organizations, both founded in the aftermath of the Civil War. One, the National Woman Suffrage Association, had been formed by woman who saw in the ratification of the Fifteenth Amendment an opportunity to win the same federal support for women's suffrage that the amendment had bestowed upon black men. Congress, however, proved unreceptive to the idea of a constitutional amendment enfranchising women, and the NWSA shifted its efforts to amending state constitutions to build grassroots support for the federal amendment. The American Woman Suffrage Association had from the start the objective of winning the vote for women by action at the state level. In 1890, the two organizations merged. Over decades of both separate and combined efforts, the members of the NAWSA mounted some 56 state campaigns for woman suffrage and logged countless hours of lobbying in the halls of state legislatures. These efforts secured voting rights for women in 13 states.

The Congressional Committee of the NAWSA was established to maintain a visible presence in Washington, in anticipation of the day when there would finally be a sufficiently strong state base of woman suffrage to move Congress to initiate amendment of the federal Constitution. In 1912, Alice Paul was appointed to chair the Congressional Committee. Paul had spent several years in England, where she had worked in the more aggressive British suffrage campaign. She brought a more militant attitude to the American movement and attracted a new generation of women who shared her attitudes and commitment to activism. It was Paul who provided leadership for the demonstration of March 3, 1913.

In the months that followed the demonstration, a gap appeared and began to widen between the attitudes of the leadership of the NAWSA and the leadership of its Congressional Committee. By 1916, this gap had widened to the point of a complete split. The result was the formation by Alice Paul and others of the National Woman's Party, a relatively small organization with a relatively large presence.

The National American Woman Suffrage Association had stressed nonpartisanship in its organizing campaigns. The National Woman's Party took the controversial stand of holding the party in power responsible for the enactment of a federal amendment. This meant that the NWP worked to defeat Woodrow Wilson and the candidates of his Democratic Party, regardless of the views any individual Democratic candidate might hold on the question of voting rights for women. This tactic, threatening as it was to Democrats sympathetic to the goals of the suffrage movement, embarrassed the leadership of the NAWSA.

This tactic, however, was overshadowed by an even more sensational one. On January 10, 1917, a dozen members of the National Woman's Party appeared in front of the White House carrying picket signs. Their messages read: "MR. PRESIDENT, WHAT WILL YOU DO FOR WOMAN SUFFRAGE?" and "HOW LONG MUST WOMEN WAIT FOR LIBERTY?" For the next year and a half, the National Woman's Party maintained a picket line outside the White House. The authorities tolerated the pickets until June 1917, when the police began to make arrests on the questionable charge of "obstructing the traffic." As women were hauled off to jail, others took their places in line.

Two hundred women went to jail, including Alice Paul. They refused to pay fines and were sentenced to anywhere from 3 days to as much as 7 months in a prison workhouse. Many began hunger strikes in jail and were force-fed by prison authorities. When pardoned by Wilson on November 28, 1917, the women resumed their activist stance, even burning the president's message on suffrage.

Whether because of such militancy or in spite of it, Congress began to move on the suffrage issue.

Source 6   Lucy Burns, address to the Convention of the National American Woman Suffrage Association, December 1913

The National American Woman Suffrage Association is assembled in Washington to ask the Democratic Party to enfranchise the women of America.

Rarely in the history of the country has a party been more powerful than the Democratic Party is today. It controls the Executive Office, the Senate, and more than two-thirds of the members of the House of Representatives. It is in a position to give us effective and immediate help.

We ask the Democrats to take action now. Those who hold power are responsible to the country for the use of it. They are responsible, not only for what they do, but for what they do not do. Inaction establishes just as clear a record as does a policy of open hostility.

We have in our hands today not only the weapon of a just case; we have the support of ten enfranchised States—States comprising one-fifth of the United States, one-seventh of the House of Representatives and one-sixth of the electoral vote. More than three million, six hundred thousand women have a vote in Presidential elections. It is unthinkable that a national government which represents women, and which appeals periodically to the Suffrages of women, should ignore the issue of their right to political freedom.

Source 7   Editorial, *The Suffragist,* weekly publication of the
Congressional Union, January 24, 1914

The policy of the Congressional Union is to ask for a Woman Suffrage Amendment from the Party in power in Congress and to hold them responsible for their answer to its request.

This policy is entirely non-partisan, in that it handles all Parties with perfect impartiality. If the Republicans were in power, we would regard them in their capacity as head of the Government as responsible for the enfranchisement of women. If the Progressives or Socialists should become the majority Party . . . we would claim from them the right to govern ourselves, and would hold them responsible for a refusal of this just demand. . . .

Let us by all means deal directly with the people who can give us what we want. The Democrats have it in their power to enfranchise women. . . . Assuming that the Democrats yield nothing in the present session, we can, when Congress closes, concentrate our forces on those points where the Party is weakest, and thus become a force worth bargaining with. . . . To defeat even a few Democratic Senators . . . would make a serious breach in the Party organization. . . . If, on the other hand, we set out to attack every anti-Suffragist in Congress we should have hundreds to defeat, and every man would be safe in whose constituency we did not organize. . . .

What should we do in our enfranchised States, if we confined ourselves to the plan of supporting individual Suffragists and attacking individual anti-Suffragists, irrespective of their Party affiliations? All the candidates for office in the enfranchised States are Suffragists. Is it suggested that we be inactive in the only places where we possess political power? Our problem at the present moment is to use the strength of women's votes in national elections so as to force attention to the justice of our claim from the present Administration.

Source 8   President Woodrow Wilson's address to a delegation of
suffragists, January 15, 1915

I want to say that nobody can look on the fight you are making without great admiration, and I certainly am one of those who admire the tenacity and the skill and the address with which you try to promote the matter that you are interested in.

But I, ladies, am tied to a conviction which I have had all my life that changes of this sort ought to be brought about State by State. If it were not a matter of female Suffrage, if it were a matter of any other thing connected with Suffrage, I would hold the same opinion. It is a long standing and deeply matured conviction on my part and therefore I would be without excuse to my own constitutional principles if I lend my support to this very important movement for an amendment to the Constitution of the United States.

Frankly I do not think that this is the wise or the permanent way to build.

Source 9   Editorial, *The Suffragist,* September 30, 1916

The effort of the Woman's Party will be directed toward the defeat of Mr. Wilson and the national Democratic ticket in the twelve equal suffrage states. . . . The

Woman's Party has been accused of "being out to punish Mr. Wilson." They are very indifferent indeed about Mr. Wilson. In thirty-six states they are not attempting to harm a political hair of Mr. Wilson's head. They would view with composure the re-election of Mr. Wilson—but *not* in the equal suffrage states and *not* by the help of women's votes. One thing we have to teach Mr. Wilson and his party—and all on-looking parties—that the group which opposes national suffrage for women will lose women's support in twelve great commonwealths controlling nearly a hundred electoral votes.

Source 10 Senator Joseph W. Bailey's testimony to the House Committee on Woman Suffrage, January 7, 1918

I am opposed to women voting anywhere except in their own societies; I would let them vote there but nowhere else in this country. . . . No free government should deny suffrage to any class entitled to it and no free government should extend suffrage to any class not entitled to it. For the ultimate success or failure of any free government will depend upon the average intelligence and patriotism of the electorate. I hope to show that as a matter of political justice and political safety women should not be allowed to vote. . . . The two most important personal duties of citizenship are military service and sheriff's service, neither of which is a woman capable of performing. . . . If an outlaw is to be arrested are you going to order a woman to get a gun and come with you? If you did she would sit down and cry, and she ought to keep on crying until her husband hunts you up and makes you apologize for insulting his wife. . . . A woman who is able to perform a sheriff's duty is not fit to be a mother because no woman who bears arms ought to bear children. . . . We agree, I think, that the women of this country will never go into our armies as soldiers or be required to serve on the sheriff's posse comitatus. That being true I hardly think they have the right to make the laws under which you and I must perform those services. . . .

The third personal duty of citizenship is jury service, and while women are physically capable of performing that service there are reasons, natural, moral and domestic, which render them wholly unfit for it. . . . We go to the courthouse for stern, unyielding justice. Will women help our courts to better administer justice? They will not. Nobody is qualified to decide any case until they have heard all the testimony on both sides but the average woman would make up her mind before the plaintiff had concluded his testimony. . . . Who will care for the children in the mother's absence? . . . They tell me they will require the unmarried women to act as jurors. There will be enough of them, for marrying will become a lost habit in our country if we apply ourselves much longer to this business of making women like men. . . .

Will women vote intelligently? Can they do it? What time will a woman have to prepare herself for these new duties of citizenship? Will she take it from her home and husband or from her church and children or from her charities and social pleasures? She must take it from one or all of them and will she make herself or the world better by doing so? . . .

We must have two sexes and if the women insist on becoming men I suppose the men must refine themselves into women. . . . I dread the effect of this woman's movement upon civilization because I know what happened to the

Roman Republic when women had attained their full rights. They married without going to church and divorced without going to court. . . .

A single standard of conduct for men and women is an iridescent dream. We cannot pay women a higher tribute than to insist that their behavior shall be more circumspect than ours.

Source 11 "Great Washington Crowd Cheers Demonstration at White House by National Woman's Party," *New York American*, September 17, 1918

With a great crowd cheering them for the first time instead of jeering them, and throwing to them rolled bills and change, the suffrage demonstrants of the National Woman's Party burned on the plinth of the Lafayette Statue, opposite the White House, this afternoon the words President Wilson uttered to another group of suffragists earlier in the day.

Holding a scrap of paper containing the President's statement to a blaze from a bronze flambeau and letting it burn to the last ash at her finger tips, Miss Lucy Branham, of Baltimore, protested inaction, concluding:

"We therefore take these empty words and consign them to the flames."

The message the President had given earlier in the day to a delegation from the National Woman Suffrage Association was:

"I am, as I think you know, heartily in sympathy with you. I have endeavored to assist you in every way in my power, and I shall continue to do so. I will do all I can to urge the passage of this amendment by an early vote."

Miss Branham, speaking of the message as she burned it, said:

"President Wilson still refuses any real support to the movement for political freedom of women. This afternoon he again expresses interest in their freedom, but does not take the necessary steps to see that freedom becomes an established fact. His expressions of interest, therefore, are merely empty words.

"Today the chairman of the Rules Committee of the Senate, spokesman of the administration, stated that suffrage was not on the program for this session and that the Senate was hoping to recess in a few days for the autumn election campaign."

Source 12 Debate in the United States Senate on the woman suffrage amendment, September 27–30, 1918

Mr. Jones of New Mexico: Mr. President, I move that the Senate proceed to the consideration of the unfinished business.

The motion was agreed to; and the Senate, as in Committee of the Whole, resumed the consideration of the joint resolution (H.J. Res. 200) proposing an amendment to the Constitution of the United States extending the right of suffrage to women. . . .

Mr. Pittman [of Nevada]: . . . I want to say now, as an opening statement, that for weeks—yes, for months—the Woman's Party, an organization which openly supported every Republican candidate during the last campaign for the Senate and House of Representatives, have constantly charged the Woman Suffrage

Committee of the Senate with attempting to obstruct a vote on this measure. They have gone further than that. They have, in their campaigns throughout the suffrage States, used the argument not only that the committee, a majority of whom are Democrats, were obstructing this vote, but that the President of the United States himself was responsible for the obstruction of it. To a country not familiar with the circumstances, that argument was exceedingly appalling. I confess now that it was having its effect as a campaign argument. . . .

Mr. Wolcott: Is the woman's party the party that has been conducting the picketing here in Washington?

Mr. Pittman: That is the party. There is a National American Woman's Suffrage Association which was headed by Dr. Shaw and is now led by Mrs. Catt. That association has never mixed in politics. It has the confidence, I know, of both sides of this Chamber. Every lady in it enjoys that confidence. It is composed of Democrats and Republicans. I do not know what the politics of any of them are, but I know that they have conducted their campaign in a ladylike, modest, and intelligent way, in wide contradiction to the method adopted by the adjunct of the Republican Party. . . .

Mr. Poindexter [of Washington]: I should like the Senator, so long as he is discussing the action of the pickets, to explain to the Senate whether or not it is the action of the pickets and the militant branch of the woman's party that caused the president to change his attitude on the subject. Was he coerced into supporting this measure—after he had for years opposed it—because he was picketed? . . .

Mr. Pittman: I should like the Senator to answer that question so that I can get on with my speech.

Mr. Poindexter: I will answer the question. I can only speak for myself. So far as the effect upon me is concerned, it would tend to antagonize me. I am not in favor of militancy in politics, nor of attempting to coerce an independent body into the support of any measure. I do not think that, generally speaking, such methods tend toward a favorable result; but I am asking the Senator whether or not it had that effect upon the President. My recollection is that the President did change his attitude, and I am very glad he changed it, he deserves credit for changing it, and for the position he now occupies; but so long as the Senator is going into an analysis of the political history of this proceeding, I should like him to complete it, and explain to us, in view of the partisan issue which he has injected into this question, just the motives that have brought about the change of attitude on the part of the leader of the Democratic Party.

Mr. Pittman: I will do that with a great deal of pleasure, of course, because nothing is pleasanter than to defend a man who needs no defense. . . . The President has taken the . . . ground that war has made it absolutely necessary to pass this amendment. . . .

Mr. Reed [of Missouri]: I am sorry that that issue has been raised. The fact, as everybody knows, is that the adoption of this amendment has nothing to do with the winning of the war. The truth of the matter . . . is that this is a political question, and men are voting for it here because they think that it will help their political fortunes.... [T]his body has been supposed to be the highest deliberative body in the world. That has been its boast for many years.

Here matters are thrashed out. In this crucible the dross is frequently burned away and the pure gold extracted. While we may talk long, while we may talk sometimes without much purpose, in the end the debates here clarify questions and bring about better results than would otherwise obtain.

But now we find a petticoat brigade awaits outside, and Senate leaders, like little boys, like pages, trek back and forth for others. If you accept that office, Senators, then put on cap and bells and paint your cheeks like clowns, as did the court fools of the middle centuries, and do your truckling in proper garb. . . .

Mr. Lewis [of Illinois]: . . . I have heard my distinguished friend, for whom I have an entertaining affection, characterize these women . . . as though they were enemies of the Government filling the lobbies of the Senate, as though these leaders were criminals of the country hiding in the purlieus of the Capitol. Indeed, as though they were vicious agents seeking to poison the avenues of legislation. I fear the Senator has conceived them in the image of some inhuman monster that was seeking to disgrace the Republic. . . .

Will it be urged by my eminent friend that there is an offense on the part of women who call out their public representatives, their public servants, to ascertain from them where they stand in respect to their personal rights?

Shall it be said they become criminals because they have assumed to say to their public servants the thing which they feel is their right and solicit of them the support of the thing which they feel is their justice?

Has it come that a distinguished Senator can on the floor indict these women for coming about and seeking to protect their rights, when every railroad lobbyist in America in the past could with freedom haunt this Capitol when a bill is before the body looking to the guardianship of the Republic, who would intercept the course of government for uses of their own private fortunes, when there was not a word to condemn them or their emissaries, however guilty has been their object and criminal has been their design? . . .

Mr. Reed: Mr. President—

Mr. Lewis: I must decline to yield to the Senator. I will yield later. . . .

Mr. President, there is but one question; let us meet it. . . . Eminent Senators have indulged at great length upon the constitutional distinctions of government. There is great foundation for those distinctions; there is great precedent to sustain them; but they are of the past. Sir, as I view this measure to-day and the issue involved in the question is not, *can* you give the women the suffrage, but *will* you? The minds of men may haunt the dusty tomes of the past to find some devious method or ponderous reason as their excuse and justification for the denial, *but to the popular mind of humanity there will still remain the plain fact that he could do it and did not.* If the answer be that we did not because there is a constitutional distinction between local State government and its privileges and the Federal Government and its powers, I reply to the eminent Senators that such obstruction has all been repealed. . . .

Mr. President, for myself I think there comes a time in all governments when the emergencies of justice repeal the influence of precedent.

Mr. Reed: Mr. President, I endeavored to halt the Senator from Illinois [Mr. Lewis] in his mad career in order to correct a fundamental error into which he had fallen, but he was so infatuated with the sublimity of his own thought and was so engulfed in the ocean of his words that he could not pause to allow a correction. I simply desired to have him understand . . . that nothing I said had reflected upon the character of any lady advocating the cause of woman suffrage and that any attempt to put that sort of construction upon my words would be unworthy of even a verbal juggler. . . .

I apologize for trying to corner the Senator. I ought to have known better, after the advertisement that appears in the morning paper of the big liberty-loan rally. I read: "Senator J. Hamilton Lewis, just back from France, speaker of the evening. Senator Lewis is just back from an extensive trip over the entire American battle front. He saw the boys at Chateau-Thierry. He talked with French and American staff officers. . . . He dodged 75's in a motor car."

Senators, I can not in a colloquy, by any verbal barrage or otherwise, corner any man who can dodge .75 shells in a motor car. (Laughter.) That is a degree of physical alacrity which is only equalled by the mental gymnastics you have just witnessed. . . .

I oppose this joint resolution because it is violative not of the Constitution, for . . . you may change the Constitution, but because it is violative of the spirit of our institutions. I oppose it because it seems to me the unjustest thing on earth to undertake to fix the qualifications of voters in my State, and for those qualifications to be fixed by men and women who never set foot upon our soil and who know nothing of the institutions of our State. . . .

Mr. President, this is a matter that belongs to the States; it has heretofore remained with the States. Under this system of government that has grown up we have prospered. If it were proposed tomorrow to amend . . . the Constitution so that the women of Wyoming could not vote, I should vote against doing so, because that is the business of Wyoming, and every other suffrage State. I would not vote to interfere with their right to let women vote; but I insist that they should not interfere with the right of other States to settle their own affairs. . . .

Mr. Benet [of South Carolina]: If the people in our State are not satisfied with our laws we can amend our constitution very readily. If the advocates of a measure are in a minority and are not satisfied with the result, then they have the redress of leaving our State. But if this constitutional amendment is adopted it will be the absolute, binding law on South Carolina for all time, no matter that the majority of her citizens now do not want it. . . .

The fact that the Fourteenth and Fifteenth Amendments were adopted has nothing to do with this question. South Carolina was then in the hands of a people foreign to her ideals, foreign to her hopes, foreign to her desires, and although we are set down in the Constitution as having ratified them, the people of South Carolina have never ratified those amendments in their hearts, and they believe that these amendments were forced on them by people who did not understand their situation. . . . .

Mr. Vardaman [of Mississippi]: . . . If I had my way about it, I should not permit a negro man or negro woman or a yellow man or yellow woman to vote in any State in this Republic. I should make of this absolutely a white man's Government. . . . It is my purpose to continue the fight for the repeal of the Fifteenth Amendment, and finally the complete elimination of the negroes, both male and female, from the politics of America. And I expect the white women of America to help me in that great undertaking. . . .

Mr. Shafroth [of Colorado]: The distinction is attempted to be made that this is a matter for State determination. If the principle is true that the just powers of government are derived from the consent of the governed, it applies to all governments. It applies to the State government. If the State does not permit that principle of law to prevail in the State, then it is not a democratic State; it is a State that violates the very fundamental principle of the Government. If a Nation which is a distinct Government itself, which elects its President, Vice President, and its Senators and Representatives, denies that principle of government, wherein can you say that it is a true democracy? . . .

Is it possible that when we elect a President of the United States we should deprive one-half of the people the right of participating in that election? The man says that the men represent the women. You might say, let the son represent the father, or let the father represent the sons. Of course there is some sympathy between them, and consequently you would not get extremely bad legislation; but if the principle is true that the just powers of government are derived from the consent of the governed you have no right without that person's consent to let somebody else represent him or her. . . .

Mr. Jones [of Washington]: When Wyoming, in 1869, gave its women the right to vote, it decreed the ultimate enfranchisement of all women in this Republic and throughout the whole civilized world. This nation can no more continue with the women of one State enjoying the highest boon of citizenship while the women of another State are denied that right than the Nation could remain half slave and half free.

Source 13   President Woodrow Wilson's address to the United States Senate, September 30, 1918

Mr. Vice President and gentlemen of the Senate, the unusual circumstances of a world war in which we stand and are judged in the view not only of our own people and of our own consciences but also in view of all nations and peoples will, I hope, justify in your thought, as it does in mine, the message I have come to give you. I regard the concurrence of the Senate in the constitutional amendment proposing the extension of the suffrage to women as vitally essential to the successful prosecution of the great war of humanity in which we are engaged. . . .

This is a people's war and the people's thinking constitutes its atmosphere and morale, not the predilections of the drawing room or the political considerations of the caucus. If we be indeed democrats and wish to lead the world to democracy, we can ask other peoples to accept in proof of our sincerity and our ability . . . nothing less persuasive and convincing than our actions. Our professions will not suffice. . . .

Through many, many channels I have been made aware what the plain, struggling, workaday folk are thinking. . . . They are looking to the great, powerful, famous Democracy of the West to lead them to the new day for which

they have so long waited; and they think, in their logical simplicity, that democracy means that women shall play their part in affairs alongside men and
upon an equal footing with them. . . . They have seen their own governments
accept this interpretation of democracy—seen old governments like Great Britain, which did not profess to be democratic, promise readily . . . this justice to
women. . . .

Are we alone to refuse to learn the lesson? Are we alone to ask and take
the utmost that women can give,—service and sacrifice of every kind—and still
say that we do not see what title that gives them to stand by our sides in the
guidance of the affairs of their nation and ours? We have made partners of the
women in this war; shall we admit them only to a partnership of sacrifice and
suffering and toil and not to a partnership of privilege and of right? This war
could not have been fought . . . if it had not been for the services of the women.
. . . We shall not only be distrusted but shall deserve to be distrusted if we do
not enfranchise them. . . .

I tell you plainly that this measure which I urge upon you is vital to the
winning of the war. . . . And not to the winning of the war only. . . . I for one
believe that our . . . comprehension of matters that touch society to the quick,
will depend upon the direct and authoritative participation of women in our
councils. We shall need their moral sense to preserve what is right and fine and
worthy in our system of life as well as to discover just what it is that ought to
be purified and reformed. Without their counsellings we shall be only half wise.

Source 14 **Amendment XIX, Constitution of the United States,**
August 26, 1920

The right of citizens of the United States to vote shall not be denied or abridged
by the United States or by any State on account of sex.

Congress shall have the power to enforce this article by appropriate legislation.

 Second Thoughts

"No Politician Could Be Unmindful"

There were all sorts of predictions of what the nation would become once
women were enfranchised. Some promised a new age of peace and morality and benevolence. Others warned of the imminent collapse of the
American family and a consequent social chaos. Both predictions were
predicated upon the premise that women would cast their ballots as a
bloc. This did not happen, and neither prediction was realized. Though
women constitute a majority of the American population and could con-
ceivably muster a majority of the popular vote behind women candidates
and "women's issues," they have most often been just as concerned with
the broad array of political questions and as varied in their answers as
their male counterparts.

Source 15 Inez Haynes Irwin, *The Story of the Woman's Party*, 1921

That procession [of March 3, 1913], which was really a thing of great beauty, brought Suffrage into prominence in a way the Suffragists had not for an instant anticipated. About eight thousand women took part. The procession started from the Capitol, marched up Pennsylvania Avenue past the White House and ended in a mass-meeting at the Mall of the Daughters of the American Revolution. Although a permit had been issued for the procession, and though this carried with it the right to the street, the police failed to protect the marchers as had been rumored they would. The end of the Avenue was almost impassable to the parade. A huge crowd, drawn from all over the country, had appeared in Washington for the Inauguration festivities. They chose to act in the most rowdy manner possible and many of the police chose to seem oblivious of what they were doing. Disgraceful episodes occurred. . . . Secretary of War Stimson had finally to send for troops from Fort Myer. There was an investigation of the action of the police by a Committee of the Senate. The official report is a thick book containing testimony that will shock any fine-minded American citizen. Ultimately, the Chief of Police for the District of Columbia was removed.

The investigation, however, kept the Suffrage procession in the minds of the public for many weeks. It almost overshadowed the Inauguration itself. . . .

The first great demonstration of the Congressional Committee [of the National American Woman Suffrage Association]—the procession of March 3—had been designed to attract the eyes of the country to the Suffragists. It succeeded beyond their wildest hopes.

Source 16 Ida Husted Harper, *The History of Woman Suffrage*, 1922

An outstanding feature of the present century has been the entrance of women into the industrial field, following the work which under modern conditions was taken from the homes to the factories. Thus without their volition they became the competitors of men in practically every field of labor. Unorganized and without the protection of a vote they were underpaid and a menace to working men. In self-defense, therefore, the labor unions were compelled to demand the ballot for women. They were followed by other organizations of men until hundreds were on record as favoring woman suffrage. Men trying to bring about civic or political reforms in the old parties or through new ones and feeling their weakness turned to women with their great organizations but soon realized their inefficiency without political power. The old objections were losing their force. The lessening size of families and the removal of the old time household tasks from the home left women with a great deal of leisure which they were utilizing in countless ways that took them out into the world, so that there was no longer any weight in the charge that suffrage would cause women to forsake their domestic duties for public life. Women of means began coming into the movement for the suffrage and relieving the financial stringency which had constantly limited the activities of the organized work. The opening of large national headquarters in New York, the great news center of the country, in 1909, marked a distinct advance in the movement which was immediately apparent throughout the country. Following the example of England, parades and processions and various picturesque features were introduced in New York and other large cities, which gave the syndicates and motion pictures material and interested the public. Woman suffrage became a topic of general discussion and women flocked into the suffrage organizations.

Source 17 Charles A. and Mary R. Beard, *The Rise of American Civilization,* 1933

Amid the turbulence connected with this reconstruction in political machinery [the Progressive Movement of the first two decades of the twentieth century], woman suffrage was once more brought out of the parlor and the academy, reviving an agitation which, after giving great umbrage to the males of the fuming forties, had died down during the Civil War. For this renewal of an old campaign a rallying command was given in the late sixties when Congress was attempting to nationalize suffrage by enfranchising the freedmen of the South and champions of the colored man were declaring that no person's civil liberties were safe without the ballot. With a relevancy that could hardly be denied, the feminists now asked why the doctrine did not apply to women, only to receive a curt answer from the politicians that sent them flying to the platform to make an appeal to the reasoning of the public at large.

For the purpose of giving a concrete point to their agitation they drafted a brief amendment to the federal Constitution, in express terms conferring the suffrage on women, and they secured its introduction in the House of Representatives in 1869. With that as a symbol of their high resolve, under the leadership of Elizabeth Cady Stanton and Susan B. Anthony, later supported by Anna Howard and Carrie Chapman Catt, they launched a campaign destined to last for half a century before attaining its goal.

The invincible minority of women who engineered this movement concentrated their forces on two redoubts of political power with varying emphasis. From time to time they were able to raise a debate on their federal amendment in Congress and occasionally they commanded for it a "respectful consideration," though seldom even that much honor. Discovering however that the drive on Washington brought scant results, the suffragists devoted more labor to winning the ballot in individual states each of which under the federal Constitution had the right to decide who should vote within its borders. Thus they hoped through state enfranchisement to get a leverage strong enough to move things at the national capital.

In that sphere also gains were exceedingly slow for the traditions of all the ages were against the measure. . . . For three decades the feminists beat their bare fists against granite, winning here and there the right to vote in some local elections, but awakening little more than amusement among those who sat on high political thrones.

Then the unexpected happened. Engulfed in the rising tides of populism which swept through the West in the early nineties, Colorado, Utah, and Idaho gave the ballot to women, leading the dauntless minority to announce the beginning of an immediate landslide. While their prophecy was somewhat premature, within but a few years their cause was lifted to the headlines by the militant suffragists of England striking hard blows, if not firing the customary shots heard round the world.

At last the avalanche really began to move. The progressive surge added Washington to the suffrage states in 1910 and before five years had gone, California, Oregon, Kansas, Arizona, Nevada, and Montana had completely enfranchised their women; while Illinois had given them a right to vote for President of the United States. Having now in their hands the fate of many presidential electors, Senators, and Representatives, the petitioners could no longer be scorned by the gentlemen who managed national affairs, for a minority of feminine votes, shifted from one side to the other, might elect or defeat a candidate.

Grasping that fact with clear understanding, a group of rebellious young advocates, who had not grown up in the state campaign atmosphere, led by Alice Paul and Lucy Burns, began to organize women voters in an effort to wring an endorsement of equal suffrage from the major political parties and carry the national amendment through Congress without further delay. Henceforth no politician with his ear to the ground in Washington or his eye on federal patronage for his home town could be unmindful of women already enfranchised, however indifferent he had been in the past.

Source 18   Eleanor Flexner, *Century of Struggle: The Woman's Rights Movement in the United States*, 1975

It is impossible not to conclude from the impact reflected in the Press from day to day that the issue of suffrage for women did gain enormous publicity from the picketing, the arrests, the jail sentences, and the hunger strikes. But while some support was gained by the women's gallantry, other support, in Congress and outside of it, was alienated. It is true that the pickets apparently posed the Administration with a problem whose eventual solution lay only in granting women the vote. But to say that the Woman's Party was the sole cause of the breakthrough which finally occurred is to ignore history. Other forces were at work; among the most obvious were the role of women in a country now totally at war and the mounting crescendo of suffrage work under the leadership of the National Suffrage Association.

Source 19   Nancy Woloch, *Women and the American Experience*, 1984

By the time Carrie Chapman Catt entered office [as president of the National American Woman Suffrage Association] in 1915, the NAWSA was shifting its tactics from "education" to more methodical modes of pressure, such as button-holing legislators. . . . Carrie Chapman Catt . . . had a master plan for victory. After converting President Wilson . . . and winning the pivotal New York battle, the NAWSA would overcome congressional lethargy, win a proposed suffrage amendment and wage state fights to get it ratified. Catt was able to carry her plan into effect even faster than she anticipated. But she also had to cope with two new developments that had not been part of the plan. One was the apostasy of dissident radicals within the NAWSA, which culminated in the formation of a rival suffrage organization, the National Woman's party, in 1916. The other was U.S. entry into World War I in 1917. . . .

The Woman's party was a considerable embarrassment to the NAWSA which felt that it would only alienate sympathetic Democrats. The NAWSA also believed that the suffrage movement should be above party politics. But the Woman's party's dramatic mode of agitation also drew attention to the cause. . . . Despite NAWSA objections to these new rivals, the militants probably had a positive impact. . . .

While the Woman's party pressured Congress and attracted attention, Carrie Chapman Catt increased the tempo of her master plan. The crucial New York state referendum . . . [was] won in 1917. . . . By now, tactics were more important than argument. In 1917, Catt announced that she did not know whether the vote was a right, a duty, or a privilege, but that "whatever it is, women want it." To ensure they got it, the NAWSA had to capitalize on all the good works that American women were now contributing to the war effort. . . .

The National Woman's party . . . refused to support U.S. entry into the war. The NAWSA, however, unable to oppose the popular tide of patriotism, dropped the cause of peace. Instead, it attempted to profit from war. Indeed, during the war NAWSA membership doubled, reaching its peak of 2 million by 1919. . . .

The war effort was extremely popular among activist middle-class women, especially clubwomen, who plunged into volunteer war work—selling bonds, saving food, and organizing benefits for the troops. . . . Now Carrie Chapman Catt was asking for passage of the woman suffrage amendment as a "war measure." The fight for democracy began at home, Catt argued. . . . The war also presented an additional "expediency" argument: it was unwise to deprive women of the vote just when their war work was needed. Taking the latter position, President Wilson, a convert to woman suffrage since 1916, urged the Senate in 1917 and 1918 to pass a woman suffrage amendment, contending that such a measure was "vital to the winning of the war." Despite the National Woman's party's rebellion and despite, or because of, the interruption of war, Catt's master plan was paying off.

Influenced by the Wilson administration, by the NAWSA (which was at last showing strength in numbers), and by favorable wartime public opinion, the House of Representatives finally passed a suffrage amendment on January 10, 1919. The recalcitrant Senate approved it in June 1919. Fourteen months after the Senate suffrage vote . . . the woman's vote was finally legal nationwide.

Source 20 Linda G. Ford, *Iron-Jawed Angels: The Suffrage Militancy of the National Woman's Party, 1912–1920,* 1991

The NWP [National Woman's Party] did move the great "center" of the suffrage movement toward greater activity by its own radical actions. The *Suffragist* said they were "a new squad that carried militancy ahead," making a new middle ground for the foot draggers of the "other" group [National American Woman Suffrage Association]. . . . The militants' stubborn protests, their non-violent resistance to the administration's authoritarian measures, reviled though they may have been, created a situation in which something had to be done. Alice Paul concluded that the militant demonstrations had been very effective in moving Wilson in particular. Each act of militancy was followed by government action— militancy worked. The NWP claimed the victory, but in analyzing the struggle, even they admitted that they had won it together with NAWSA. (NAWSA never reciprocated this credit.)

Questioning the Past

1. "They might as well have been a lot of wooden, painted policemen so far as their control over the crowds," said Senator Poindexter of the protection offered the suffragists in the March 3, 1913 demonstration. Based on the information presented from the press accounts, did the police attempt to sabotage the event? If so, what action, if any, should have been taken against them and on what grounds?

2. Present the arguments for and against an amendment to the federal Constitution extending voting rights to women.

3. Historian Gerda Lerner, speaking of the conditions at the turn of the twentieth century, noted: "When measured against the plight of children laboring long hours in factories and fields, the abysmal working conditions of female factory hands, the sweatshops, and the problems of immigrants in the slums, the subject of woman suffrage seemed less urgent, less dramatic, and less appealing." Given the myriad of urgent problems plaguing America in the early twentieth century, was the talent and energy devoted to the suffrage movement misplaced? How important is the right to vote? It is unusual when a majority of the eligible voters even bother to turn out for state and local elections, and barely half of the electorate participates in presidential elections. Why is this so?

4. "The men who sat and looked back through the ages of the past and read the story of mankind's struggles and woes and then sat down to plan a citadel of liberty so mighty that it could never be overthrown—the men who sat about that council chamber were the master spirits of the world. To them we might now offer almost our very prayers if it were not impiety to pray to any but Almighty God," Senator Reed argued on the Senate floor on September 27, 1918. "There was Jefferson, in whose brain was pictured the evils and the wrongs of all the past; Madison and Washington and Hamilton and all the immortals who here wisely planned and laid the foundations of the great temple of our liberty. When they thus planned and builded, sirs, they knew the dangers of concentrated power; they knew that authority feeds upon itself and, like a monster, grows from its own flesh until it will destroy the liberties of all. So they declared that there should be no powerful central government; that each State should keep complete and absolute sovereignty. . . . They left to the several States the absolute right to frame their own governments, only stipulating that they should be of republican form; they left to the States the right to say who should vote and how the affairs of the people should be conducted; they left to the States every right save the few rights that were delegated and which were essential to the stability of the Central Government." Discuss the strengths and weaknesses of Senator Reed's position.

16

The Scopes Trial

And on the Seventh Day, the Defense Rested

July 20, 1925

Dayton, Tennessee, a tiny town of 2,000 in the rural South, seemed an improbable place for a courtroom confrontation called by some "the trial of the century." Yet, here, in the Rhea County Courthouse on July 10, 1925, were gathered hundreds of spectators and reporters for a trial that would capture headlines around the world. Eight attorneys, including the Attorney General of Tennessee, sat at the prosecutor's table. Six attorneys sat at the defense table. The opposing teams of attorneys were led by two of the greatest orators America had ever produced. For the prosecution, there was one of the nation's political giants, William Jennings Bryan, the Great Commoner, who had mesmerized the Democratic Convention of 1896 with his eloquence, thrice been his party's nominee for president, served as secretary of state in the Wilson Cabinet, and now held sway as a leader of the Fundamentalist movement. Heading the defense team was Clarence Darrow, the nation's premier judicial advocate for the poor, the unpopular, the political heretic. And sitting next to Darrow at the defendant's table, almost lost in the clamor and controversy swirling around him, was the subject of the proceeding, a quiet high school biology teacher named John T. Scopes.

Scopes was charged with violating Tennessee's Butler Act. This law, enacted in March 1925, declared that "it shall be unlawful for any teacher in any of the Universities, Normals and all other public schools of the State . . . to teach any theory that denies the story of the Divine Creation of man as taught in the Bible, and to teach instead that man has descended from a lower order of animals." Scopes had violated this law by sharing with his students the theories on evolution developed by Charles Darwin in the nineteenth century and accepted by most scholars of the twentieth.

There was no doubt that Scopes had presented Darwin's ideas to his class. He admitted it. His students acknowledged it. The question was, as the defense saw it, did the state have a right to proscribe certain ideas from the classroom? And, could the state prescribe that a particular religious viewpoint be taught to students in public schools?

After the prosecution had rested its case, Darrow had hoped to call to the stand scholars and scientists from around the country to show that all Scopes had done was to present the truth to his students. But these experts were not allowed to testify. The question was not about the validity of Darwinian science, but, as the court saw it, whether or not John T. Scopes had violated the law of Tennessee by teaching the theory of

255

16.1 Scopes
Trial Homepage

evolution. The forum he had hoped for had been denied him, but Darrow responded with an unprecedented courtroom maneuver.

ᴗᴥᴕ *First Impressions*
Darrow Interrogates Bryan

Frustrated by the decision of the court that his planned defense for Scopes was inadmissible, Darrow responded on the seventh day of the trial with a most extraordinary tactic: he called to the stand, as the sole witness for the defense, the prosecuting attorney, William Jennings Bryan.

Source 1   *Tennessee v. John T. Scopes,* trial transcript, July 20, 1925

Mr. Darrow. You have given considerable study to the Bible, haven't you, Mr. Bryan?

Mr. Bryan. Yes, Sir, I have tried to. . . . I have studied the Bible for about fifty years, or some time more than that, but, of course, I have studied it more as I have become older than when I was but a boy.

Q. Do you claim that everything in the Bible should be literally interpreted?

A. I believe everything in the Bible should be accepted as it is given there; some of the Bible is given illustratively. For instance: "Ye are the salt of the earth." I would not insist that a man was actually salt, or that he had flesh of salt, but it is used in the sense of salt as saving God's people.

Q. But when you read that Jonah swallowed the whale—or that the whale swallowed Jonah—excuse me, please—how do you literally interpret that?

A. When I read that a big fish swallowed Jonah—it does not say whale.

Q. Doesn't it? Are you sure?

A. That is my recollection of it. A big fish, and I believe it, and I believe in a God who can make a whale and can make a man, and make both do what He pleases. . . .

Q. Now, you say, the big fish swallowed Jonah, and he there remained how long—three days—and then he spewed him upon the land. You believe that the big fish was made to swallow Jonah?

A. I am not prepared to say that; the Bible merely says it was done.

Q. You don't know whether it was the ordinary run of fish, or made for that purpose?

A. You may guess; you evolutionists guess.

Q. But when we do guess, we have a sense to guess right.

A. But do not do it often.

Q. You are not prepared to say whether that fish was made specially to swallow a man or not?

A. The Bible doesn't say, so I am not prepared to say.

Q. But do you believe He made them—that He made such a fish and that it was big enough to swallow Jonah?

A. Yes, sir. Let me add: One miracle is just as easy to believe as another. . . .

Q. Just as hard?

A. It is hard to believe for you, but easy for me. A miracle is a thing performed beyond what man can perform. When you get beyond what man can do, you get within the realm of miracles; and it is just as easy to believe the miracle of Jonah as any other miracle in the Bible.

Q. Perfectly easy to believe that Jonah swallowed the whale?

A. If the Bible said so; the Bible doesn't make as extreme statements as evolutionists do. . . .

Q. The Bible says Joshua commanded the sun to stand still for the purpose of lengthening the day, doesn't it, and you believe it?

A. I do.

Q. Do you believe at that time the entire sun went around the earth?

A. No, I believe the earth goes around the sun. . . .

Q. Have you an opinion as to whether—whoever wrote the book, I believe it is . . . the Book of Joshua, thought the sun went around the earth or not?

A. I believe that he was inspired.

Q. Can you answer my question?

A. When you let me finish the statement.

Q. It is a simple question, but finish it.

A. You cannot measure the length of my answer by the length of your question. (Laughter.)

Q. No, except that the answer will be longer. (Laughter.)

A. I believe that the Bible is inspired, an inspired author, whether one who wrote as he was directed to write understood the things he was writing about, I don't know. . . .

Q. Do you think whoever inspired it believed that the sun went around the earth?

A. I believe it was inspired by the Almighty, and He may have used language that could be understood at that time. . . .

Q. That means it is subject to construction?

A. That is your construction. I am answering your question. . . .

Q. Is it your opinion that passage was subject to construction?

A. Well, I think anybody can put his own construction upon it, but I do not mean necessarily that it is a correct construction. I have answered the question. . . .

Q. Can you answer my question directly? If the day was lengthened by stopping either the earth or the sun, it must have been the earth?

A. Well, I should say so. . . .

Q. Now, Mr. Bryan, have you ever pondered what would have happened to the earth if it had stood still?

A. No.

Q. You have not?

A. No, the God I believe in could have taken care of that, Mr. Darrow.

Q. I see. Have you ever pondered what would naturally happen to the earth if it stood still suddenly?

A. No. . . .

Q. You believe the story of the flood to be a literal interpretation?

A. Yes, sir.

Q. When was that flood? . . . .

A. I never made a calculation.

Q. A calculation from what?

A. I could not say. . . .

Q. What do you think?

A. I do not think about things I don't think about.

Q. Do you think about things you do think about?

A. Well, sometimes. (Laughter.)

Q. How long ago was the flood, Mr. Bryan?

A. Let me see Usher's calculation about it? [Bryan then looked at the margin notes printed in the Bible entered by him as trial evidence.] It is given here, as 2348 years B.C.

Q. Well, 2348 B.C. You believe that all the living things that were not contained in the ark were destroyed?

A. I think the fish may have lived. . . .

Q. Don't you know that the ancient civilizations of China are 6,000 or 7,000 years old . . . ?

A. No; but they would not run back beyond the creation, according to the Bible, 6000 years. . . .

Q. Have you any idea how old the earth is?

A. No.

Q. The book you have introduced in evidence tells you, doesn't it? [The Bible introduced in evidence carried a margin note based upon calculations of Bishop James Usher in the seventeenth century which set creation at 4004 B.C., at 9 o'clock in the morning.]

A. I don't think it does, Mr. Darrow. . . .

Q. It says B.C. 4004?

A. That is Bishop Usher's calculation.

Q. That is printed in the Bible you introduced?

A. Yes, sir.

Q. And numerous other Bibles?

A. Yes, sir. . . .

Q. Would you say that the earth was only 4,000 years old?

A. Oh, no; I think it is much older than that.

Q. How old?

A. I couldn't say. . . .

Gen. Stewart. I want to impose another objection. What is the purpose of this examination?

Mr. Bryan. The purpose is to cast ridicule on everybody who believes in the Bible, and I am perfectly willing that the world know these gentlemen have no other purpose than ridiculing every Christian who believes in the Bible.

Mr. Darrow. We have the purpose of preventing bigots and ignoramuses from controlling the education of the United States, and you know it, and that is all. . . .

Gen. Stewart. This is resulting in a harangue and nothing else. . . .

The Court. Are you about through, Mr. Darrow?

Mr. Darrow. I want to ask a few more questions about the creation. . . . Mr. Bryan, do you believe that the first woman was Eve?

Mr. Bryan. Yes.

Q. Do you believe she was made literally out of Adam's rib?

A. I do.

Q. Did you ever discover where Cain got his wife?

A. No, sir; I leave the agnostics to hunt for her.

Q. You have never found out?

A. I have never tried to find. . . .

Q. The Bible says he got one, doesn't it? Were there other people on the earth at that time?

A. I cannot say.

Q. You cannot say. Did that ever enter your consideration?

A. Never bothered me.

Q. There are no others recorded, but Cain got a wife.

A. That is what the Bible says.

Q. Where she came from you do not know? All right. Does the statement, "The morning and the evening were the first day," and "The morning and the evening were the second day," mean anything to you?

A. I do not think it necessarily means a twenty-four hour day.

Q. You do not? . . . What do you consider it to be?

A. I have not attempted to explain it. . . . The fourth verse of the second chapter says: "These are the generations of the heavens and of the earth, when they were created in the day that the Lord God made the earth and the heavens," the word "day" there . . . is used to describe a period. . . .

Q. Then when the Bible said, for instance, "and God called the firmament heaven. And the evening and the morning were the second day," that does not necessarily mean twenty-four hours? . . .

A. No. But I think it would be just as easy for the kind of God we believe in to make the earth in six days as in six years or in 6,000,000 years or in 6,000,000,000 years. . . .

Q. Do you think those were literal days?

A. My impression is they were periods, but I would not attempt to argue against anybody who wanted to believe in literal days. . . .

Q. Do you think the sun was made on the fourth day?

A. Yes. . . .

Q. They had evening and morning for four periods without the sun, do you think?

A. I believe in creation as there told, and if I am not able to explain it I will accept it. . . .

Monkey Business in Court

16.2 The Scopes "Monkey Trial"

By the time Bryan took the stand, the Rhea County Courthouse and its environs had in the eyes of the world assumed an almost carnival-like appearance. Banners with messages such as "Sweethearts, Come to Jesus!" and "Where Will You Spend Eternity?" were draped across the streets. Lemonade, hotdog, and sandwich vendors competed with street-corner preachers for the attention of passersby. Tents belonging to numerous religious revival groups surrounded Dayton's city limits.

The atmosphere inside the courtroom had taken on much of the same flavor. Darrow had objected to the prayers that preceded each day's testimony. He had demanded that either the banner over the jury box that proclaimed, "Read Your Bible" be removed or that it be supplemented by another banner advising, "Read Your Evolution." He had objected to the judge's references to Bryan by the title "colonel" and was granted his own commission as an "honorary colonel" in the Tennessee militia. All of the attorneys played to the crowd, and laughter punctuated with a smattering of "amens" frequently followed the pronouncements of attorneys and witnesses. So great was the crowd and so menacing the stress it placed on the courthouse structure that the trial was moved out onto the courthouse lawn for Darrow's examination of Bryan.

When the court reconvened the morning after Bryan's appearance on the witness stand, Judge Raulston refused to let Bryan resume his testimony. Instead, the case was given to the jury and a verdict of guilty was quickly returned.

Source 2 *New York Times,* July 22, 1925

BRYAN, MADE WITNESS IN OPEN AIR COURT, SHAKES HIS FIST AT DARROW AMID CHEERS
Big Crowd Watches Trial under Trees

Dayton, Tenn., July 20.—So-called Fundamentalists of Tennessee sat under the trees of the Rhea County Court House lawn listening to William J. Bryan defend his faith in the "literal inerrancy" of the Bible, and laughed.

Clarence Darrow, agnostic and skeptic, had called the leader of the Fundamentalists to the stand in an effort to establish by the testimony of Mr. Bryan himself that the Bible need not be interpreted literally, so that the defense might argue before the jury that Mr. Scopes did not teach a theory which contradicts the Bible.

The greatest crowd of the trial had come in anticipation of hearing Messrs. Bryan and Darrow speak, and it got more than it expected. It saw Darrow and Bryan in actual conflict—Mr. Darrow's rationalism in combat with Mr. Bryan's faith—and forgot for the moment that Bryan's faith was its own. The crowd saw only the battle, appreciated only the blows one dealt to the other and laughed with and at both.

To the crowd spread under the trees watching the amazing spectacle on the platform the fight seemed a fair one. There was no pity for the helplessness of the believer come so suddenly and so unexpectedly upon a moment when he could not reconcile statements of the Bible with generally accepted facts. There was no pity for his admissions of ignorance of things boys and girls learn in high school, his floundering confessions that he knew practically nothing of geology, biology, philology, little of comparative religion, and little even of ancient history.

These Tennesseans were enjoying a fight. That a great man, a Biblical scholar, an authority on religion, was being dispelled seemed to make no difference. They grinned with amusement and expectation, until the next blow by one side or the other came, and then guffawed again. And finally, when Mr. Bryan, pressed harder and harder by Mr. Darrow, confessed he did not believe the Bible should be taken literally, the crowd howled.

Source 3 Washington *Evening Star,* July 21, 1925

SCOPES CONVICTED

Courtroom, Dayton, Tenn., July 21, 1925.—A verdict was returned in the Scopes case at 11:20 a.m.

Scopes was summoned before the bar. Judge Raulston told him of his conviction by the jury and read a copy of the statute to him.

The judge then fixed the fine at $100.

"Have you anything to say, Mr. Scopes?" asked the judge.

"Your honor, I have been convicted of violating an unjust statute," replied Scopes. "Any action other than I have pursued would be in violation of my idea of academic freedom."

The judge repeated the fine of $100. . . .

"Anyone have anything they want to say?" asked Judge Raulston.

There was no response.

The final address . . . was made by Judge Raulston, who declared that "it sometimes takes courage to stand for a sentiment that stands in contravention to public opinion. . . . A man who is big enough to stand up for a principle is big indeed."

The judge paid tribute to small towns, saying many great men have come from villages.

"Two things in this world are indestructible," he said. "One, the truth and the other the word of God, given to man that man may use it."

"This little talk comes from my heart. . . . If I have made mistakes the higher courts will find it so."

Source 4   *The Times* of London, July 22, 1925

MR. SCOPES FOUND "GUILTY"

Dayton was the scene of the most amazing drama yesterday afternoon, enacted beneath the maple trees in Court House Square, whither the Judge adjourned the Court after lunch as he feared the collapse of the Court House floor owing to the great crowd of spectators. There, with the midsummer sun shining in a cloudless sky, the Evangelist, Mr. Bryan, the principal prosecutor, was called by the defence to enter the witness box and submit to a prolonged examination in regard to his beliefs by the agnostic, Mr. Clarence Darrow, leading counsel for the defence. It was a masterly stroke on the part of the defence. . . .

This morning more temperate counsels prevailed. It was agreed to expunge from the Court reports the whole of Mr. Bryan's testimony. The counsel on both sides abandoned the right to address the jury. . . . The Judge then proceeded to deliver his charge. The jury, after an absence of seven minutes, returned a verdict of Guilty, and Mr. Scopes was fined 106 dollars (£20). The defence entered notice of appeal and the trial was over.

Meanwhile all the United States, except the jury trying Mr. Scopes, can read in this morning's newspapers the evidence of eight competent scientists in regard to the validity of the theories of evolution. Despite its tragic-comic interludes, the trial has had the effect of arousing widespread interest in books on evolution, thus accomplishing the main purpose of the defence.

Source 5   Editorial, *Washington Post*, July 22, 1925

The Scopes trial ends as was expected, by the verdict of guilty. There was never any question of Scopes' guilt. The law was plain. . . .

Judge Raulston, evidently an honest man, allowed too much latitude to the lawyers of both sides. The questions propounded to William J. Bryan and his answers constituted an argument which had no place in the court. What Mr. Bryan believes or does not believe is irrelevant and immaterial. The court set itself right by expunging Mr. Bryan's testimony.

The Scopes case will be appealed to the State supreme court, where a decision as to the constitutionality of the "anti-evolution" law is expected. . . .

All the excited talk at Dayton goes into the wastebasket, where it belongs.

Source 6 Editorial, *New York Times*, July 22, 1925

ENDED AT LAST

On both sides the herd of the half-baked has raged violently about a non-existent issue. There was a legal question, which may be erected into a constitutional question. Yet we don't see the Federal courts, the Supreme Court, making themselves arbiters in a "war" between "religion" and "science." It is to be hoped that the higher courts in Tennessee will settle the constitutional validity of the anti-evolution law. If the Daytonian sense of humor is keen, Dayton has enjoyed itself and loses nothing in particular except its daily theatre, in and out of doors.

The sometime god of its idolatry has fared so ill as to inspire pity. It was a Black Monday for him when he exposed himself to the processes of involution and evolution. He was entangled, and made to turn himself inside out; and there was little or nothing inside. It has long been known to many that he was only a voice calling from a poorly furnished brain-room. But how almost absolutely unfurnished it was the public didn't know till he was forced to make an inventory. We are far from wishing to add to a humiliation some part of which must fall on his country. It may be doubted, however, if he is capable of feeling it or that his devotees will not applaud and glory in his shame. It is natural that to a man so prodigiously ignorant, evolution should be a dragon to be slain.

Source 7 The Reverend Thomas H. Nelson, *Moody Bible Institute Monthly*, September 1925

While in attendance at the Scopes trial in Dayton, Tenn., I came to the conclusion that the trial was misnamed.

It was God, our Father, Jesus Christ, our Saviour, Christianity and the true church, that was on trial there, while the whole world looked on.

With these mighty issues in the balance, it might well be, as the newspapers said, the greatest and most interesting subject ever discussed in this country, looked at from the angle of its having inspired more cablegrams, telegrams, telephones, and radiograms than were ever sent about any other subject.

I concluded further, that Jews and Unitarians had joined forces to push this antichristian conflict. It was very fitting that Clarence Darrow, a criminal lawyer and an avowed agnostic, should lead in the defense of this evolution case, for the teaching of creative evolution is both criminal and atheistic.

While ignorant reporters were belittling this case, and belying and abusing William Jennings Bryan as the real nemesis of creative evolution, I consider it to be the mightiest issue that has ever been joined since the trial of Jesus Christ before Pontius Pilate.

Second Thoughts
Causes and Consequences

The Tennessee Supreme Court began its hearings on the appeal of the Scopes conviction on June 1, 1926. On January 17, 1926, it issued its ruling. The Butler Act, the Court determined with but one dissenting vote, was indeed constitutional. The judgment of $100 levied against John T. Scopes, however, was set aside on a technicality.

At the time of the Scopes trial, 15 states were considering laws to stop the teaching of evolution in public schools. The Scopes trial—although it ended in a conviction of Scopes and an affirmation of the constitutionality of the law under which he was convicted—checked this movement. And though the law remained on the statute books of Tennessee for several decades, no teacher was again prosecuted under its provisions.

The census of 1920 found that for the first time in American history, a majority of the American people lived in urban areas, but the division between urban and rural folks was about equal. This caused great tension. William Jennings Bryan spoke for the rural population by defending fundamentalism. Cynic H. L. Mencken reported on the trial to an Eastern and urban audience. When Bryan died in a Dayton hotel room five days after the trial, Mencken's response was typical of his style of journalism.

Source 8   H. L. Mencken, *American Mercury,* October 1925

Has it been duly marked by historians that William Jennings Bryan's last secular act on this globe of sin was to catch flies? A curious detail, and not without its sardonic overtones. He was the most sedulous fly-catcher in American history, and in many ways the most successful. His quarry, of course, was not *Musca domestica* but *Homo neandertalensis*. For forty years he tracked it with coo and bellow, up and down the rustic backways of the Republic. Wherever the **flambeaux of Chautauqua** smoked and guttered, and the bilge of idealism ran in the veins, and Baptist pastors dammed the brooks with the sanctified, and men gathered who were weary and heavy laden, and their wives who were . . . as fecund as the shad (*Alosa sapidissima*), there the indefatigable Jennings set up his traps and spread his bait. He knew every country town in the South and West, and he could crowd the most remote of them to suffocation by simply winding his horn. The city proletariat, transiently flustered by him in 1896, quickly penetrated his **buncombe** and would have no more of him. . . . But out where the grass grows high, and the horned cattle dream away the lazy afternoons, and men still fear the powers and principalities of the air—out there between the corn-rows he held his old puissance to the end. . . .

It was hard to believe, watching him at Dayton, that he had traveled, that he had been received in civilized societies, that he had been a high officer of state. He seemed only a poor clod like those around him, deluded by a childish theology, full of an almost pathological hatred of all learning, all human dignity, all beauty, all fine and noble things. He was a peasant come home to the barnyard. Imagine a gentleman, and you have imagined everything that he was not. What animated him from end to end of his grotesque career was simply ambition—the ambition of a common man to get his hand upon the collar of his superiors, or, failing that, to get his thumb into their eyes. He was born with a roaring voice, and it had the trick of inflaming half-wits. His whole career was devoted to raising those half-wits against their betters, that he himself might shine.

His last battle will be grossly misunderstood if it is thought of as a mere exercise in fanaticism—that is, if Bryan the Fundamentalist Pope is mistaken for one of the bucolic Fundamentalists. There was much more in it than that. ... What moved him, at bottom, was simply hatred of the city men who had laughed at him so long, and brought him at last to so **tatterdemalion** an estate. He lusted for revenge upon them. He yearned to lead the anthropoid rabble against them, to punish them for their execution upon him by attacking the very vitals of their civilization. He went far beyond the bounds of any merely religious frenzy, however inordinate. When he began denouncing the notion that man is a mammal even some of the **hinds** at Dayton were agape. And when, brought upon Clarence Darrow's cruel hook, he writhed and tossed in a very fury of malignancy, bawling against the veriest elements of sense and decency like a man frantic—when he came close to that tragic climax of his striving there were snickers among the hinds as well as hosannas.

Upon that hook, in truth, Bryan committed suicide, as a legend as well as in the body. He staggered from the rustic courtroom ready to die, and he staggered from it ready to be forgotten. ...

Thus he fought his last fight. All sense departed from him. ... He descended into demagogy so dreadful that his very associates at the trial table blushed. His one yearning was to keep the yokels heated up—to lead his forlorn mob of imbeciles against the foe. That foe, alas, refused to be alarmed. It insisted upon seeing the whole battle as a comedy. Even Darrow, who knew better, occasionally yielded to the prevailing spirit. One day he lured poor Bryan into the folly I have mentioned: his astounding argument against the notion that man is a mammal. I am glad I heard it, for otherwise I'd never believe it. There stood the man who had been thrice a candidate for the Presidency of the Republic—there he stood in the glare of the world, uttering stuff that a boy of eight would laugh at.

Source 9   Clarence Darrow, *The Story of My Life,* 1932

An organization of men and women calling themselves fundamentalist had been very actively seeking to control the schools and universities of America. The members of this body claimed to believe that the various books that are bound together and are called "the Bible" are inspired in their every statement; that the whole of these books was virtually written by the Almighty and is in every part literally true. These books contain what is purported to be a story of the creation of the universe and man and what are regarded as the early activities on the earth.

The fundamentalists denied that these Bible stories are legends, opinions, poems, myths and guesses, and pronounced them history. It has not been long since all Christians held the same attitude toward the Bible. The books of the Old and New Testaments were written ages before the world had any knowledge of our science. To those old authors the world was flat, the sun was drawn across the horizon to light the day, and the moon to light the night. To lengthen the day it was only necessary to have the sun stand still. Man and every other animal were made mature and full-grown. Men believed that the stars were stuck into the firmament and that Jacob had a vision of angels going up and down on a ladder, which was the up-to-date mode of that day for that sort of a trip.

Finally men conceived the idea of taking a look at heaven, whereupon they started building a tower and got so near that it attracted the attention of the Lord who is said to have circumvented their bright idea by confounding the tongues of the workmen so that if one of them asked for mortar he would perhaps be given a pail of beer, and any one asking for more bricks might be handed water instead. This would make it impossible to proceed with the building. So they abandoned the project and it was called the Tower of Babel, and to this day the fundamentalists explain the many languages in the world as due to the confusing and befuddling of the tongues of those workmen. . . .

When Mr. Bryan took the stand, . . . I proceeded with questions that brought out points illustrating the fundamentalists' ideas of the Bible and religion. . . . Bryan twisted and dodged and floundered, to the disgust of the thinking element, and even his own people. That night an amount of copy was sent out that the reporters claimed was unprecedented in court trials. My questions and Bryan's answers were printed in full, and the story seems to have reached the whole world.

When the court adjourned it became evident that the audience had been thinking, and perhaps felt that they had heard something worth while. Much to my surprise, the great gathering began to surge toward me. They seemed to have changed sides in a single afternoon. A friendly crowd followed me toward my home. Mr. Bryan left the grounds practically alone. The people seemed to feel that he had failed and deserted his cause and his followers when he admitted that the first six days might have been periods of millions of ages long. Mr. Bryan had made himself ridiculous and had contradicted his own faith. I was truly sorry for Mr. Bryan.

Source 10 W. J. Cash, *The Mind of the South,* 1941

At the heart of it stood a great plexus of fears and hates, which, moving beneath the surface of the reigning optimism and faith in Progress, operated enormously to engage the attention and energies of the common whites . . . : the fears and hates which were to issue in such phenomena as the Ku Klux Klan and the anti-evolution campaign which heated up in the trial of John T. Scopes at Dayton, Tennessee.

In part these fears and hates were continuous with the vast neurosis which afflicted the whole of the United States, and even more the Western World in general, in the decade. Like Yankee soldiers and the soldiers of Europe, Southern soldiers had served for long months on the carrion fields of France—had stamped upon their shaken nerves for as long as they should live the macabre memory of interminable passage through a world of maggoted flesh, lice, mud, bedlam, and the waiting expectancy of sudden death. That, and the grim knowledge of how easy it had been to kill, and how easy it would be to kill again. . . .

With startled, horrified, and yet strangely eager gaze, they had seen the men of all the evening lands, themselves included, flinging away the established standards of their daily living and returning upon a savagery that was more savage than any savage had ever dreamed, because it used all the accumulated knowledge of civilization for its ferocious purpose. . . .

The world, in a word, clearly stood poised above disaster. Nobody might be sure that . . . civilization might not completely collapse into the chaos of recrudescent and blood-drinking barbarism. And so they were afraid, these Southerners, like all Americans and like all Western men. Afraid cloudily and, as always, without analysis, even subconsciously and blindly, but none the less really for all that. Afraid of all that stood without them, and perhaps even afraid of themselves. And because of their fears, desperately determined to hold fast, even in spite of themselves, to their old certainties—somehow to island themselves impregnably against the threatening flood. . . .

An authentic folk movement, beyond a doubt: such was the Klan. And such also, in only comparatively less measure, was the anti-evolution movement. For it cannot be dismissed as the aberration of a relatively small, highly organized pressure group made up of ignorant, silly, and fanatical people, as some writers have attempted to do. Having observed it at close range, I have no doubt at all that it had the active support and sympathy of the overwhelming majority of the Southern people. . . .

What stood at Dayton and demanded the conviction of Scopes under Tennessee law forbidding the teaching of evolution in the state-supported schools—what sat down before the legislatures of all the Southern states and demanded similar or more stringent laws—was far more than any band of hillbillies. And what actuated it and what it demanded were more than what appears on the surface. The Darwinian doctrine was indeed no more than the focal point of an attack for a program, explicit or implicit, that went far beyond evolution laws: a program proceeding not only from fundamentalist religious fears but from the whole body of the fears we have seen, and having as its objective the stamping out of all the new heresies and questioning in the schools and elsewhere—the restoration of that absolute conformity to the ancient pattern under the pain and penalties of the most rigid intolerance. . . .

The anti-evolution organizations were everywhere closely associated with those others which quite explicitly were engaged in attempting to wipe out all the new knowledge in the schools, to clear all modern books out of the libraries. "Yankee infidelity" and "European depravity" and "alien ideas" were their standard rallying cries. They warned constantly and definitely that evolution was certain to breed Communism. Just as clearly and constantly, they warned that it was breaking down Southern morals—destroying the ideal of Southern Womanhood. One of the most stressed notions which went around was that evolution made a Negro as good as a white man—that is, threatened White Supremacy. And always, as what I already say indicates, they came back to the idea of saving the South. . . .

In the very hour when they seemed to have it in their power to do what they had plainly set out to do, the people themselves showed a curious hesitancy and revulsion—a strange unreadiness to go through with it. The same disgust for the Klan's crimes and the same proud shrinking from the thought that the South was being treated as a comic land because of the anti-evolution laws and attacks on intelligence . . . probably had something to do with that.

After the Scopes trial, for all the indubitable majority opposition to Darwin, only two states went on to pass anti-evolution laws, . . . Mississippi and Arkansas.

Source 11   Richard Hofstadter, *The American Political Tradition*, 1948

16.3   *Inherit the Wind*

The Scopes trial, which published to the world Bryan's childish conception of religion, also reduced to the absurd his inchoate notions of democracy. His defense of the anti-evolution laws showed that years of political experience had not taught him anything about the limitations of public opinion. The voice of the people was still the voice of God. The ability of the common man to settle every question extended, he thought, to matters of science as well as politics and applied equally well to the conduct of schools as it did to the regulation of railroads or the recall of judges or the gold standard. In prosecuting Scopes the people were merely asserting their right "to have what they want in government, including the kind of education they want." Academic freedom? That right "cannot be stretched as far as Professor Scopes is trying to stretch it. A man cannot demand a salary for saying what his employers do not want."

So spoke the aging Bryan, the knight errant of the oppressed. He closed his career in much the same role as he had begun it in 1896: a provincial politician following a provincial populace in provincial prejudices.

Source 12   William E. Leuchtenburg, *The Perils of Prosperity*, 1958

The Scopes trial is usually seen simply as a struggle for academic freedom against Tennessee **Hottentots**. Certainly this was the most important substantive issue in the case, and there is little to be said for the bizarre attempt to force teachers to give their students a wholly inaccurate account of the evolution of man. Yet the case was not simply a morality play between the good forces of intellectual freedom and the evil spirits of obscurantism. In the Scopes trial, the provincialism of the city was arrayed against the provincialism of the country, the shallowness of Mencken against the shallowness of Bryan, the arrogance of the scientists against the arrogance of the fundamentalists.

Source 13   Ray Ginger, *Six Days or Forever*, 1958

Man has progressed by exercising a humble confidence in the might of his own mind, not by throwing up his hands and shrugging his shoulders. A quality of the scientific attitude was emphasized by Thorstein Veblen in 1897: "The modern scientist is unwilling to depart from the test of causal relation or quantitative sequence. When he asks the question, Why? he insists on the answer in terms of cause and effect. . . ." The scientist, said Veblen, recognizes only the colorless impersonal sequence of material cause and effect, and refuses to go behind that sequence in search of any purpose in the process. Apart from human purposes, no Purpose exists.

Working from this attitude, science has steadily expanded our knowledge of man and nature. The increments have come ever more rapidly: since every new idea, every new tool, is a combination of existing ideas or existing tools, it is inevitable that the larger the existing stock, the greater the number of possible new combinations. And the scientific knowledge has been accepted by more and more people, because it led to practical results, to a greater control of things and men which could be used to effect human purposes, and because the scientific habit of mind is itself cumulative.

Historically, religion has fought these encroachments. Nearly every major scientific idea was opposed by some creed. . . . The long-run result has been a withering away of religion, an expansion of the area within which material causes were thought to rule and a concomitant shrinking of the area within which God's rule was regarded as operative.

Only marginal Christian sects now agree with St. Augustine and Luther that the diseases of Christians show an infection by demons. Only the fundamentalists now regard the story of Creation as a historical account, but in the 17th century it was accepted by Anglican and Puritan alike. . . .

Of course science has its defects. It cannot prove that anything is impossible. It deals only with probabilities. To believers in the Virgin Birth, it can merely say that no case of a virgin birth has ever been authenticated (of course the biological possibility of nonmiraculous virgin birth is well established), while the cause of hundreds of millions of conceptions can be proved. Science knows nothing of Absolute Truth. While it carries us closer and closer to the truth about countless relations, it will never reach the complete truth about any of them. For those who need the amniotic warmth of certainty, dogma is the proper womb.

Source 14 Sheldon Norman Grebstein, *Monkey Trial*, 1960

However flamboyant and newsworthy its personalities, the case could not have attracted the enormous attention it did without some real and important issues at its heart. Even the carnival atmosphere of little Dayton, Tennessee, the frequent grandstand plays of the trial's participants, the threatened collapse of the courtroom floor, the presence of cheering and applauding spectators, the scores of reporters and photographers, the microphones (it was the first American trial to be nationally broadcast)—even all this could not obscure the fact that here powerful forces were in conflict. This was far more than the slight matter of a high school teacher who might have violated a state law and might be fined five hundred dollars. It was to become a case of Fundamentalism versus Modernism, theological truth versus scientific truth, literal versus liberal interpretation of the Bible, Genesis versus Darwin; and it was to have grave implications for democracy as well. Did the majority in Dayton or elsewhere have the right to dictate what should or should not be taught in public schools? Did the police powers of the state allow it to control the minds of its citizens? Were church and state really separate in America? Did America's tradition as a Christian nation also commit her to an acceptance of the Bible as part of the articles of government? Such were the issues of the trial, and they are still with us. For individual and academic freedom, the will and welfare of the majority, and the role of religion in the lives of men and of the communities to which they belong will be pertinent questions as long as our present mode of government survives.

Source 15 Winthrop S. Hudson, *Religion in America*, 1973

Fundamentalism can best be understood as a phase of the rural-urban conflict, drawing its strength from the tendency of many who were swept into an urban environment to cling to the securities of their childhood. . . . [I]n many ways Fundamentalism was as much a product of a cultural as a religious concern. It is significant that it arose among rural-oriented people in the cities before it penetrated the small towns and villages of the countryside. Furthermore, the mores which were emphasized as indispensable to the Christian life had, in the words of H. Richard Neibuhr, "at least as little relation to the New Testament and as much connection with social custom" as did those aspects of behavior which were condemned, while the cosmological and biological notions which were stressed as integral to the gospel were equally culturally conditioned. Fundamentalist sentiment also was not unrelated to the sweeping tide of hyperpatriotism which was so conspicuous a feature of the early 1920's. "One hundred per cent Americanism" tended to be regarded as the normal corollary of "old time religion," and "Back to the Christ, the Bible, and the Constitution" was a typical slogan. While Fundamentalism had no direct connection with the resurgent Ku Klux Klan of the 1920's, the more extreme wing of the Fundamentalist movement was in some respects a parallel phenomenon. . . .

By 1925, when a national comedy was acted out in the "monkey trial" at Dayton, Tennessee, with William Jennings Bryan and Clarence Darrow in the starring roles, the obscurantism, violent language, and "smear" tactics of the most vociferous Fundamentalists had so alienated public opinion generally that there was little prospect that the Fundamentalists would gain control of any major Protestant denomination.

 ## Questioning the Past

1. What forces in American society led to the confrontation at Dayton?

2. Bryan stated upon arrival at Dayton that "the trial uncovers an attack on revealed religion. A successful attack would destroy the Bible and with it revealed religion. If evolution wins, Christianity goes." Darrow responded with the statement: "Scopes isn't on trial; civilization is on trial. The prosecution is opening the doors for a reign of bigotry equal to anything in the Middle Ages. No man's belief will be safe." Argue both of these views. Which assertion, if either, was valid?

3. Bryan never entertained the thought of converting Darrow to fundamentalism; likewise, Darrow knew he could not convince Bryan to forsake his religious beliefs. Each was hoping to win over the audience. Read through the transcript and identify the places where each may have "scored points" in the debate. What was each trying to prove? Who was the more effective?

4. When the decision of the majority conflicts with the academic freedom of teachers and students, which principle should prevail? Why?

5. Throughout history, ideas contrary to the prevailing notions of religious, political, or moral thought have suffered suppression. Why?

Chapter **17**

The New Deal

Franklin Roosevelt Unveils a New Direction for the Nation   *March 4, 1933*

"I have no fears for the future of our country," Herbert Hoover told the American people in his inaugural address of March 4, 1929. "It is bright with hope." His optimism was shared by the millions who had confidently voted him into office. It was a time of unprecedented prosperity in America, and hardly anyone could imagine a future that was not even more prosperous. Economic growth seemed inevitable, and little more was required from the president than to be a good caretaker of the presidential mansion. Yet four years later the same electorate that had given Herbert Hoover an overwhelming vote of confidence in 1928 voted just as overwhelmingly to evict him from the White House. "Democracy," Hoover concluded, "is not a polite employer." The reason for Hoover's forced retirement was an economic disaster the likes of which the country had never before experienced.

The Great Depression settled over America late in 1929 like an oppressive fog that did not lift for more than a decade. As it settled, most Americans lost all sight of hope. The Depression caused millions of Americans to lose their jobs and left one-fifth of the population by 1932 with no source of income whatsoever. There was no unemployment insurance. Businesses failed. Ten thousand banks permanently closed their doors during the Depression's first five years. There was no deposit insurance. People lost their life's savings. Stocks on the New York Exchange lost more than 75 percent of their value in four years. Farm income dropped by 60 percent. Urban income was cut in half. There were no minimum wage laws. Many Americans could not keep up payments on their mortgages and lost their homes. Many subsisted on scraps of food. Some starved. There was no social security system, no food stamps, no aid to families with dependent children, no welfare. The leaders of the country had grown to maturity in an age when the doctrine of Social Darwinism held sway: the strong would prosper and the weak would fall by the wayside in a natural process of survival of the fittest. Government would damage this natural order if it intervened to give artificial support to those not strong enough to survive through their own devices.

17.1 The Great Depression

271

🐾 *First Impressions*

"This Nation Asks for Action, and Action Now"

Many leaders and politicians, including President Hoover, believed it normal for the economy to pass through periods of boom and bust and thought of government interference in this business cycle as potentially dangerous to the long-term economic health of the nation. By 1932, however, a sizable segment of the public had begun to question the practicality of this view. And a majority was willing to look beyond Hoover and his ideas for a new direction. The Democratic Party's nominee for the presidency, Franklin D. Roosevelt, offered the promise of change.

Source 1   President Herbert Hoover, "The Importance of the Preservation of Self-help and of the Responsibility of Individual Generosity as Opposed to Deteriorating Effects of Government Appropriations," February 3, 1931

This is not an issue as to whether people shall go hungry or cold in the United States. It is solely a question of the best method by which hunger and cold shall be prevented. It is a question as to whether the American people on the one hand will maintain the spirit of charity and mutual self-help through voluntary giving and the responsibility of local government as distinguished on the other hand from appropriations out of the Federal Treasury for such purposes. My own conviction is strongly that if we break down this sense of responsibility, of individual generosity to individual, and mutual self-help in the country in times of national difficulty, and if we start appropriations of this character, we have not only impaired something infinitely valuable in the life of the American people but have struck at the roots of self-government. Once this has happened it is not the cost of a few score millions but we are faced with the abyss of reliance in future upon Government charity in some form or other. The money involved is indeed the least of the costs to American ideals and American institutions. . . .

The basis of successful relief in national distress is to mobilize and organize the infinite number of agencies of self-help in the community. That has been the American way of relieving distress among our own people and the country is successfully meeting its problem in the American way today.

Source 2   Franklin D. Roosevelt, address on accepting the Democratic nomination for the presidency, July 2, 1932

17.2 New Deal Network

Chairman Walsh, my friends of the Democratic National Convention of 1932:. . . The appearance before a National Convention of its nominee for President, to be formally notified of his selection, is unprecedented and unusual, but these are unprecedented and unusual times. . . .

Let it also be symbolic that in so doing I broke traditions. Let it be from now on the task of our Party to break foolish traditions. We will break foolish traditions and leave it to the Republican leadership, far more skilled in that art, to break promises.

Let us now and here highly resolve to resume the country's march along the path of real progress, of real justice, of real equality for all of our citizens, great and small. . . .

There are two ways of viewing the Government's duty in matters affecting economic and social life. The first sees to it that a favored few are helped and hopes that some of their prosperity will leak through, sift through, to labor, to the farmer, to the small business man. That theory belongs to the party of Toryism, and I had hoped that most of the Tories left this country in 1776. . . .

My program . . . is based upon this simple moral principle: the welfare and the soundness of the Nation depend first upon what the great mass of the people wish and need; and second, whether or not they are getting it.

What do the people of America want more than anything else? To my mind, they want two things: work, with all the moral and spiritual values that go with it; and with work, a reasonable measure of security—security for themselves and for their wives and children. Work and security—these are more than words. They are more than facts. They are the spiritual values, the true goal toward which our efforts of reconstruction should lead. These are the values that this program is intended to gain; these are the values we have failed to achieve by the leadership we now have.

Our Republican leaders tell us economic laws—sacred, inviolable, unchangeable—cause panics which no one could prevent. But while they prate of economic laws, men and women are starving. We must lay hold of the fact that economic laws are not made by nature. They are made by human beings.

Yes, when—not if—when we get the chance, the Federal Government will assume bold leadership in distress relief. For years Washington has alternated between putting its head in the sand and saying there is no large number of destitute people in our midst who need food and clothing, and then saying the States should take care of them, if there are. . . .

I say that while primary responsibility for relief rests with localities now, as ever, yet the Federal Government has always had and still has a continuing responsibility for the broader public welfare. It will soon fulfill that responsibility. . . .

One word more: Out of every crisis, every tribulation, every disaster, mankind rises with some share of greater knowledge, of higher decency, of purer purpose. Today we shall have come through a period of loose thinking, descending morals, an era of selfishness, among individual men and among Nations. Blame not Governments alone for this. Blame ourselves in equal share. Let us be frank in acknowledgment of the truth that many amongst us have made obeisance to Mammon, that the profits of speculation, the easy road without toil, have lured us from the barricades. To return to higher standards we must abandon the false prophets and seek new leaders of our own choosing.

Never before in modern history have the essential differences between the two major parties stood out in such striking contrast as they do today. Republican leaders not only have failed in material things, they have failed in national vision, because in disaster they have held out no hope, they have pointed out no path for the people below to climb back to places of security and safety in our American life.

Throughout the Nation, men and women, forgotten in the political philosophy of the Government of the last years, look to us here for guidance and for more equitable opportunity to share in the distribution of national wealth.

On the farms, in the large metropolitan areas, in the smaller cities and villages, millions of our citizens cherish the hope that their old standards of living and of thought have not gone forever. Those millions cannot and shall not hope in vain.

I pledge you, I pledge myself, to a new deal for the American people. . . .

Source 3 Franklin D. Roosevelt, inaugural address, March 4, 1933

I am certain that my fellow Americans expect that on my induction into the Presidency I will address them with a candor and a decision which the present situation of our Nation impels. This is preeminently the time to speak the truth, the whole truth, frankly and boldly. Nor need we shrink from honestly facing conditions in our country today. This great Nation will endure as it has endured, will revive and will prosper. So, first of all, let me assert my firm belief that the only thing we have to fear is fear itself—nameless, unreasoning, unjustified terror which paralyzes needed efforts to convert retreat into advance. In every dark hour of our national life a leadership of frankness and vigor has met with that understanding and support of the people themselves which is essential to victory. I am convinced that you will again give that support to leadership in these critical times.

In such a spirit on my part and on yours we face our common difficulties. They concern, thank God, only material things. Values have shrunken to fantastic levels; taxes have risen; our ability to pay has fallen; government of all kinds is faced by serious curtailment of income; the means of exchange are frozen in the currents of trade; the withered leaves of industrial enterprise lie on every side; farmers find no markets for their produce; the savings of many years in thousands of families is gone.

More important, a host of unemployed citizens face the grim problem of existence, and an equally great number toil with little return. Only a foolish optimist can deny the dark realities of the moment.

Yet our distress comes from no failure of substance. We are stricken by no plague of locusts. Compared with the perils which our forefathers conquered because they believed and were not afraid, we have still much to be thankful for. Nature still offers her bounty and human efforts have multiplied it. Plenty is at our doorstep, but a generous use of it languishes in the very sight of the supply. Primarily this is because rulers of the exchange of mankind's goods have failed through their own stubbornness and their own incompetence, have admitted their failure, and have abdicated. Practices of the unscrupulous money changers stand indicted in the court of public opinion, rejected by the hearts and minds of men.

True they have tried, but their efforts have been cast in the pattern of an outworn tradition. Faced by failure of credit they have proposed only the lending of more money. Stripped of the lure of profit by which to induce our people to follow their false leadership, they have resorted to exhortations, pleading tearfully for restored confidence. They know only the rules of a generation of self-seekers. They have no vision, and when there is no vision the people perish.

The money changers have now fled from their high seats in the temple of our civilization. We may now restore that temple to the ancient truths. The measure of the restoration lies in the extent to which we apply social values more noble than mere monetary profit. . . .

Restoration calls, however, not for changes in ethics alone. This Nation asks for action, and action now.

Our greatest primary task is to put people to work. This is no unsolvable problem if we face it wisely and courageously. It can be accomplished in part by direct recruiting by the Government itself, treating the task as we would treat the emergency of a war, but at the same time, through this employment, accomplishing greatly needed projects to stimulate and reorganize the use of our natural resources. . . .

If I read the temper of our people correctly, we now realize as we have never realized before our interdependence on each other; that we cannot merely take but we must give as well; that if we are to go forward, we must move as a trained and loyal army willing to sacrifice for the good of a common discipline, because without such discipline no progress is made, no leadership becomes effective. We are, I know, ready and willing to submit our lives and property to such a discipline, because it makes possible a leadership which aims at a larger good. This I propose to offer, pledging that the larger purposes will bind upon us all as a sacred obligation with a unity of duty hitherto evoked only in time of armed strife.

With this pledge taken, I assume unhesitatingly the leadership of this great army of our people dedicated to a disciplined attack upon our common problems.

Action in this image and to this end is feasible under the form of government which we have inherited from our ancestors. Our Constitution is so simple and practical that it is possible always to meet extraordinary needs by changes in emphasis and arrangement without loss of essential form. . . .

It is to be hoped that the normal balance of Executive and legislative authority may be wholly adequate to meet the unprecedented task before us. But it may be that an unprecedented demand and need for undelayed action may call for temporary departure from the normal balance of public procedure.

I am prepared under my constitutional duty to recommend the measures that a stricken Nation in the midst of a stricken world may require. These measures, or such other measures as the Congress may build out of its experience and wisdom, I shall seek, within my constitutional authority, to bring to speedy adoption.

But in the event that the Congress shall fail to take one of these two courses, and in the event that the national emergency is still critical. I shall not evade the clear course of duty that will then confront me. I shall ask the Congress for the one remaining instrument to meet the crisis—broad Executive power to wage a war against the emergency, as great as the power that would be given to me if we were invaded by a foreign foe.

For the trust reposed in me I will return the courage and the devotion that befit the time. I can do no less.

We face the arduous days that lie before us in the warm courage of national unity; with the clear consciousness of seeking old and precious moral values; with the clean satisfaction that comes from the stern performance of duty by old and young alike. We aim at the assurance of a rounded and permanent national life.

We do not distrust the future of essential democracy. The people of the United States have not failed. In their need they have registered a mandate that they want direct, vigorous action. They have asked for discipline and direction under leadership. They have made me the present instrument of their wishes. In the spirit of the gift I take it.

Source 4   **Humorist Will Rogers, "Support the President!" March 1933**

America hasn't been as happy in three years as they are today. No money, no banks, no work, no nothing, but they know they got a man in the White House who is wise to Congress, wise to our big bankers and wise to our so-called big men. The whole country is with him. Even if what he does is wrong, they are with him. Just so he does something. If he burned down the Capitol, we would cheer him and say, Well, at least he got a fire started, anyhow.

We have had years of "Don't rock the boat!" Sink it, Mr. President. We just as well be swimming, as like the way we are.

The New Deal: Too Much or Not Enough?

17.3 The FDR Years

Franklin Roosevelt wasted no time taking action. He called Congress into special session on March 9, 1933. In the one hundred days of that special session, and in the five years that followed it, Roosevelt pushed through a remarkable package of legislative items collectively called the New Deal. Action supplanted ideology as Roosevelt seemed willing to try any measure that promised a reasonable prospect for success. He reached back into the past to borrow ideas from the Farmer's Alliances, Jacob Coxey, the Populist, Socialist, and Progressive movements. He listened to business and he listened to labor, and he accepted advice from the assortment of intellectuals and experts he had drawn into his administration.

Even before Congress arrived for the special session, Roosevelt had taken a bold step. His first act following his inauguration was to order a nationwide "bank holiday." The nation's banks were closed on March 5, 1933, to give time to restore confidence and cool the panic that was causing runs on the country's financial institutions. Before the special session was over, Congress had created the Federal Deposit Insurance Corporation to insure depositors against losses in the event of bank failure. A Home Owners Loan Corporation was also established to refinance mortgages and save people from losing their homes.

The New Deal extended federal subsidies to American farmers, financial assistance to businesses large and small, and federal recognition and respect to organized labor. It brought the stock market under federal regulation, tightened banking standards, established rules and regulations for "fair business practices," and set guidelines for corporate competition. Its relief programs placed the unemployed on the federal payroll and put them to the task of building public parks, playgrounds, erosion control dams, roads. The Works Progress Administration, most ambitious of the relief efforts, even attempted to place people in jobs for which they possessed talent and training: writers, musicians, actors, scholars were put to work on publicly funded arts and research projects. Electricity was brought to rural areas and, in a great socialist experiment, the Tennessee Valley Authority was formed to bring power and economic development into a seven-state section of the South that had never fully recovered from the devastation of the Civil War.

Permanent stabilizers were built into the economic system to assure that money would continue to circulate through the populace even in economically trying times. A minimum wage law was enacted to ensure that those who worked would at least earn enough to subsist. Child labor was eliminated both to see that children spent their days in the classroom rather than the factory and to assure that adults would no longer have to compete with poorly compensated minors for available jobs. Unemployment compensation was established to keep money coming to those out of work and, through them, to those still at work providing goods and services. Workmen's Compensation would help those injured in the workplace to survive until fit enough to return to their jobs, and Social Security would provide a pension for those permanently retired from the workplace.

The New Deal touched everyone in some way, and though it did not bring America out of the Depression, it at least made life less harsh and restored hope. Evidence that Franklin Roosevelt and his New Deal were popular with the people is offered by the fact that his tenure in the White House is the longest in the history of the country. In four consecutive elections Roosevelt was given the endorsement of the electorate. Critics, however, complained either that his New Deal went too far or that it did not go far enough.

17.4 New Deal
Cultural Programs

Source 5   Republican Party Platform of 1936

America is in peril. The welfare of American men and women and the future of our youth are at stake. We dedicate ourselves to the preservation of their political liberty, their individual opportunity and their character as free citizens, which today for the first time are threatened by Government itself.

For three long years the New Deal Administration has dishonored American traditions and flagrantly betrayed the pledges upon which the Democratic Party sought and received public support.

The powers of Congress have been usurped by the President.

The integrity and authority of the Supreme Court have been flouted.

The rights and liberties of American citizens have been violated.

Regulated monopoly has replaced free enterprise.

The New Deal Administration constantly seeks to usurp the rights reserved to the States and to the people.

It has insisted on the passage of laws contrary to the Constitution. . . .

It has created a vast multitude of new offices, filled them with its favorites, set up a centralized bureaucracy, and sent out swarms of inspectors to harass our people.

It has bred fear and hesitation in commerce and industry, thus discouraging new enterprises, preventing employment and prolonging the depression. . . .

It has coerced and intimidated voters by withholding relief to those opposed to its tyrannical policies.

It has destroyed the morale of our people and made them dependent upon government.

Appeals to passion and class prejudice have replaced reason and tolerance.

To a free people, these actions are insufferable. . . .

We pledge ourselves:

1. To maintain the American system of Constitutional and local self-government. . . .
2. To preserve the American system of free enterprise, private competition, . . . and to seek its constant betterment in the interests of all.

Source 6   American Communist Party Platform of 1936

The American people today face the greatest crisis since the Civil War. Extreme reaction threatens the country, driving toward Facism and a new world war. . . .

The collapse of the Hoover-Republican prosperity destroyed our boasted American standards of living. The New Deal failed to protect and restore our living standards. American capitalism is unable to provide the American people with the simple necessities of life.

Over 12,000,000 able-bodied and willing workers are without jobs. For a majority of these there is no hope of jobs.

The income of the working people has been cut in half. Half our farmers have lost their land. They are converted into a pauperized peasantry.

Millions of young people face a future without hope, with no prospect of ever being able to establish a home or rear a family.

The Negro people suffer doubly. Most exploited of working people, they are also victims of jim-crowism and lynching. They are denied the right to live as human beings. . . .

The peace, freedom, and security of the people are at stake. . . .

At the head of the camp of reaction stands the Republican Party—the party of Wall Street, the party of the banks and monopolies. . . .

Roosevelt is bitterly attacked by the camp of reaction. But he does not fight back these attacks. Roosevelt compromises. He grants small concessions to the working people, while making big concessions to . . . Wall Street, to the reactionaries. . . .

The Communist Party and its candidates stand on the following platform. . . .

Open the closed factories—we need all that our industries can produce. If the private employers will not or cannot do so, then the government must open and operate the factories, mills, and mines for the benefit of the people.

Industry and the productive powers of our nation must be used to give every working man and woman a real, American standard of living, with a minimum annual wage guaranteed by law. . . .

We demand a 30-hour week without reduction in earnings . . . in private industry and on public works. . . .

We demand higher wages and vacations with pay. We demand the abolition of the wage differential between the North and the South.

It is the obligation of the American government to establish an adequate system of social insurance for the unemployed, the aged, the disabled and the sick. . . .

We stand for adequate relief standards for all unemployed. . . .

We demand that social and labor legislation shall be financed and the budget balanced by taxation of the rich. We are opposed to sales taxes in any form . . . and call for their immediate repeal. The main source of government finance must be a system of sharply graduated taxation of incomes of over $5,000 a year, upon corporate profits and surpluses, as well as taxation upon the present tax-exempt securities and large gifts and inheritances. The people of small income, small property, and home owners must be protected against foreclosures and seizures and from burdensome taxes and high interest rates. . . .

We favor nationalization of the entire banking system. . . .

Our land is the richest in the world. It has the largest and most skilled working class. Everything is present to provide a rich and cultured life for the whole population. Yet millions starve. The whole nation suffers, because capitalism is breaking down, because profits are the first law and are put above human needs—and the capitalist rulers are turning to Fascism and war.

Second Thoughts

"And When There Is No Vision the People Perish"

Historians and critics have not known what to think of the New Deal. Some have called it state capitalism. Others have seen it as creeping socialism. Some have cursed it for establishing a welfare state. Some have criticized it for not tending enough to the public welfare. Whatever its strengths and shortcomings, both major parties have accepted its basic premises since the time of Franklin Roosevelt.

Source 7 Franklin D. Roosevelt, *The Public Papers and Addresses of Franklin D. Roosevelt,* 1938

On the occasion of the all-night session of the Democratic National Convention in Chicago, in 1932, I was at the Executive Mansion in Albany with my family and a few friends. While I had not yet been nominated, my name was still in the lead among the various candidates. Because I intended, if nominated, to make an immediate speech of acceptance at the Convention itself in order to get the campaign under way, we discussed what I should say in such a speech. From that discussion and our desire to epitomize the immediate needs of the Nation came the phrase "New Deal," which was used in that acceptance speech and which has very aptly become the popular expression to describe the major objectives of the Administration.

The word "Deal" implied that the Government itself was going to use affirmative action to bring about its avowed objectives rather than stand by and hope that general economic laws alone would attain them. The word "New" implied that a new order of things designed to benefit the great mass of our farmers, workers and business men would replace the old order of special privilege in a Nation which was completely and thoroughly disgusted with the existing dispensation.

The New Deal was fundamentally intended as a modern expression of ideals set forth one hundred and fifty years ago in the Preamble of the Constitution of the United States—"a more perfect union, justice, domestic tranquility, the common defense, the general welfare and the blessings of liberty to ourselves and our posterity."

But we were not to be content with merely hoping for these ideals. We were to use the instrumentalities and powers of government actively to fight for them.

Source 8   Charles A. and Mary R. Beard, *America in Midpassage*, 1939

The word "never" is to be used sparingly in history. It could be said with due respect for the record, however, that never before had Congress in the course of two years enacted legislation running so widely and so deeply into the American economy. Perhaps it would be no exaggeration to declare that all the federal legislation from the establishment of the Constitution down to the inauguration of Franklin D. Roosevelt in the spring of 1933 had not flouted so materially the presuppositions of "free enterprise" and the doctrine of laissez faire.

How did this happen, and what was its meaning? Was it, as heated imaginations suggested, a revolution or the beginning of a revolution? Or did it merely bring to a closer focus theories and practices long in process of development, without marking a sharp break in the course of events? . . .

On the verdict to be reached, history threw some light. Behind each statute of the New Deal legislation lay a long series of agitations, numerous changes in the thought and economy of American society, and pertinent enactments. Except for certain sections of the National Industrial Recovery Act, not a single measure passed by Congress in 1933 and 1934 was without some more or less relevant precedent. . . .

In this legislation was there anything revolutionary? If by revolution is meant the overthrow of one class by another, a sudden and wholesale transfer of property, then all the New Deal laws combined effected no revolution. Nor were they intended to do so. The Agricultural Adjustment Act deprived no farmer, planter, or wheat-raising corporation of land. The Recovery Act stripped no industrial concern of its tangibles. The two laws were designed to set agriculture and industry in motion without changing property holdings or property relations. . . .

If a change in things was thus effected, it was the change of tying private interests more closely into a single network and making the fate of each increasingly dependent upon the fate of all. From the process a revolution might develop, but that would be another historical illustration of events outrunning purposes. . . . When history was conceived not as handsprings into liberation but as the movement of ideas and interests in time, with occasional broad jumps occurring, then the events of 1933 and 1934 seemed merely to mark the dissolution of once firm assurances and a modification of many theories and practices.

Whatever the near or distant outcome might be, the New Deal legislation did indicate fundamental doubts respecting many ideas, long current, as good always and everywhere in American society. It marked a general surrender of the doctrine that poverty and unemployment come only from the improvidence of the poor and that the persons affected must take the consequences of their futile and evil lives. It repudiated the Darwinian law of the jungle by seeking to eliminate through concerted action—mutual aid—innumerable practices of competition once deemed right and just. . . . For more than forty years, statesmen and demagogues alike had sought by antitrust acts to intensify the ruthless struggles of competition, on the assumption that such conflicts in economy were wholesome and that the downward pressure of competition on labor was of no concern to the State or Society.

Source 9   John T. Flynn, *The Roosevelt Myth*, 1948

[M]any good people in America still cherish the illusion that Roosevelt performed some amazing feat of regeneration for this country. They believe he took our economic system when it was in utter disrepair and restored it again to vitality; that he took over our political system when it was at its lowest estate and restored it again to its full strength. He put himself on the side of the underprivileged masses. He transferred power from the great corporate barons to the simple working people of America. He curbed the adventurers of Wall Street, and gave security to the humble men and women of the country. And above all he led us through a great war for democracy and freedom and saved the civilization of Europe.

But not one of these claims can be sustained. He did not restore our economic system to vitality. He changed it. The system he blundered us into is more like the managed and bureaucratized, state-supported system of Germany before World War I than our own traditional order. Before his regime we lived in a system which depended for its expansion upon private investment in private enterprise. Today we live in a system which depends for its expansion and vitality upon the government. This is a pre-war European importation—imported at the moment when it had fallen into complete disintegration in Europe. In America today every fourth person depends for his livelihood upon employment either directly by the government or indirectly in some industry supported by government funds. In this substituted system the government confiscates by taxes or borrowings the savings of all the citizens and invests them in non-wealth-producing enterprises in order to create work. Behold the picture of American economy today: taxes which confiscate the savings of every citizen, a public debt of 250 billion dollars as against a pre-Roosevelt debt of 19 billion, a government budget of 40 billion instead of four before Roosevelt, inflation doubling the prices, and reducing the lower-bracket employed workers to a state of pauperism as bad as that of the unemployed in the depression, more people on various kinds of government relief than when we had 11 million unemployed, Americans trapped in the economic disasters and the political quarrels of every nation on earth and a system of permanent militarism closely resembling that we beheld with horror in Europe for decades, bureaucrats swarming over every field of life and the President calling for more power, more price-fixing, more regulation and more billions. Does this look like the traditional American scene? Or does it not look like the system built by Bismarck in Germany in the last century and imitated by all the lesser Bismarcks in Europe?

No, Roosevelt did not restore our economic system. He did not construct a new one. He substituted an old one which lives upon permanent crisis and an armament economy.

Source 10   Eric F. Goldman, *Rendezvous with Destiny*, 1952

The very tone of the New Deal was far more aggressively equalitarian than that of either Populism or progressivism. The Populists had never been able to win the workingman; all during the decades from 1865 to 1936, most of the Negroes had been voting Republican while most of the newer immigrants were voting Democratic. The New Deal, for the first time, brought all the low-status groups into one camp and produced an economic and social cleavage in voting unprecedented in the history of the country. Under the circumstances, New Deal liberalism naturally represented leveling to an unusual degree.

Source 11   David M. Potter, *People of Plenty*, 1954

Although hated in conservative circles as an expropriator and a fomenter of class antagonisms, Roosevelt in fact attempted to create a real balance between various class interests, such as those of labor and those of management; and this balance was predicated on an idea which was the very antithesis of the class struggle—the idea that no one need lose anything: debts were not scaled down, mortgages were not cancelled, imminent bankruptcies which would have paved the way for nationalization were not permitted to occur. Even "the unscrupulous money-changers," as Roosevelt called them, were not driven from the temples of finance. They were simply required to suspend operations for a brief time. Landlords collected farm benefits; industrialists under the NRA secured indulgence for monopolistic practices that had been under fire from more conservative administrations for forty years. . . . At the nadir of the Depression when capitalism was fearfully vulnerable and almost unresisting to attack and when many doctrinaires would have said that the overthrow of capitalism was the prerequisite to reform, Roosevelt unhesitatingly assumed that the country could afford to pay capitalism's ransom and to buy reform, too. One of his most irritating and most successful qualities was his habit of assuming that benefits could be granted without costs being felt.

Source 12   Former secretary of state Dean Acheson, *A Democrat Looks at His Party*, 1955

Government, as Mr. Hoover saw it, had a limited function, which became a wholly inadequate one as the disaster grew. The government in Washington should plan, advise, exhort, and encourage business and local government. But it should not act, direct, or order. It would be wrong for it to throw its own credit and resources into the gap left by the collapse of private, state, and municipal credit. The federal government had no responsibility and no authority to reactivate finance and industry or to deal with relief. To the millions who were suffering physical privation and the loss of their farms, homes, businesses, jobs, bank accounts, and investments this attitude seemed callous and defeatist.

　　The New Deal was under no such self-imposed limitation. After the new President had said in his inaugural address that the only thing we had to fear was fear itself, he proceeded to act on every front with imagination, vigor, and courage. He conceived of the federal government as the whole people organized to do what had to be done, and he galvanized its will to action. . . .

All the problems were attacked at once. Government credit was put behind the saving of homes and farms and the reopening of banks. Work programs were financed to provide relief and new purchasing power for business. Municipal, state, and federal public works stimulated the building and heavy industries. Agricultural production and prices were taken in hand by the Agricultural Adjustment Administration and industrial production by the National Recovery Administration. A road into future development was opened by the public power program to expand the fundamental requisite of an industrial civilization—energy. Housing projects, new labor legislation, the social security enactments, the school and youth programs carried the promise that recovery would also progress throughout the population.

It is not my purpose to write a history or eulogy of the New Deal's recovery legislation, but to recall its . . . basic attitude toward the function and responsibility of government. And I wish to recall something else—its essential conservatism. Its purpose and effect was to bring to new life and strength, to even wider acceptance and participation, the system of private ownership of property.

The New Deal did not turn to a system of collective farming, nor did it result in a vast increase in farmlands owned by mortgagors, the insurance companies and banks. It saved individual farming and increased it. There was no nationalization of banks and industries.

Source 13 Arthur M. Schlesinger Jr., *The Politics of Upheaval*, 1960

The assumption that there were two absolutely distinct economic orders, capitalism and socialism, expressed . . . a conviction that reality inhered in theoretical essences of which any working economy, with its compromises and confusions, could only be an imperfect copy. If in the realm of essences capitalism and socialism were wholly separate phenomena based on wholly separate principles, then they must be rigorously kept apart on earth. Thus abstractions became more "real" than empirical reality: both doctrinaire capitalists and doctrinaire socialists fell victim to . . . the "fallacy of misplaced concreteness." Both ideological conservatism and ideological radicalism dwelt in the realm of either-or. Both preferring essence to existence.

The distinction of the New Deal lay precisely in its refusal to approach social problems in terms of ideology. Its strength lay in its preference of existence to essence. The great central source of its energy was the instinctive contempt of practical, energetic, and compassionate people for dogmatic absolutes. Refusing to be intimidated by abstractions or to be overawed by ideology, the New Dealers responded by doing things. . . . The whole point of the New Deal lay in its faith in "the exercise of Democracy," its belief in gradualism, its rejection of catastrophism, its denial of either-or, its indifference to ideology, its conviction that a managed and modified capitalist order achieved by piecemeal experiment could best combine personal freedom and economic growth. . . .

Roosevelt hoped to steer between the extremes of chaos and tyranny by moving always, in his phrase, "slightly to the left of center." "Unrestrained individualism" had proved a failure; yet "any paternalistic system which tries to provide security for everyone from above only calls for an impossible task and a regimentation utterly uncongenial to the spirit of our people." He deeply agreed with Macaulay's injunction to reform if you would preserve. . . .

As Roosevelt saw it, he was safeguarding the constitutional system by carrying through reforms long-overdue. "The principle object of every Government all over the world," he once said, "seems to have been to impose the ideas of the last generation upon the present one. That's all wrong." As early as 1930 he had considered it time for America "to become fairly radical for at least one generation. History shows that where this occurs occasionally, nations are saved from revolution." In 1938 he remarked, "In five years I think we have caught up twenty years. If liberal government continues over another ten years we ought to be contemporary somewhere in the late nineteen forties."

Source 14 Senator Barry Goldwater, *Conscience of a Conservative,* 1961

The New Deal, Dean Acheson wrote approvingly in a book called *A Democrat Looks At His Party,* "conceived of the federal government as the whole people organized to do what had to be done." A year later Mr. Larson wrote *A Republican Looks At His Party,* and made much the same claim in his book for Modern Republicans. The "underlying philosophy" of the New Republicanism, said Mr. Larson, is that "if a job has to be done to meet the needs of the people, and no one else can do it, then it is the proper function of the federal government."

Here we have, by prominent spokesmen of both political parties, an unqualified repudiation of the principle of limited government. There is no reference by either of them to the Constitution, or any attempt to define the legitimate functions of government. The government can do whatever *needs* to be done; note, too, the implicit but necessary assumption that it is the government itself that determines *what* needs to be done. We must not, I think, underestimate the importance of these statements. They reflect the view of a majority of the leaders of one of our parties, and of a strong minority among the leaders of the other, and they propound the first principle of totalitarianism: that the State is competent to do all things and is limited in what it actually does only by the will of those who control the State.

It is clear that this view is in direct conflict with the Constitution which is an instrument, above all, for *limiting* the functions of government, and which is as binding today as when it was written.

Source 15 V. O. Key Jr., *Politics, Parties, and Pressure Groups,* 1964

The characteristics of the presidential election of 1932 correspond closely to those of the model of a landslide, marking a general withdrawal of popular confidence in the party in power. The Great Depression brought injury not only to farmers and industrial workers but to employers, financiers, merchants, and all classes of people. The Republican Administration floundered as disaster piled upon disaster, and Mr. Hoover became the symbol of the many ills that beset many people. The polling of 1932 unmistakably expressed discontent against Mr. Hoover and his party. . . .

The shift away from the Republican party between 1928 and 1932 occurred almost everywhere. . . . Although sample surveys were not then in operation, other evidence suggests that declines in Republican strength occurred in all income and occupational groups. The election was not a revolt of the downtrodden; rather an antipathy toward the Administration and a yearning for something different permeated all social strata. . . .

In the realignments in the voting of 1936 the coalition built by the New Deal jelled. The 1932 voting had been characterized by accessions to Democratic strength among all classes of people. The unfolding of the Rooseveltian legislative program cemented additional support to the Democratic party and simultaneously drove back to the Republican party many who had voted for change in 1932.

No survey data are available for 1932 and statements about the movement of voters between 1932 and 1936 must necessarily be guarded. Yet, on the basis of extensive analysis of the election returns, educated guesses are possible. The policies of the New Deal brought in 1936 substantial new support from their beneficiaries. Metropolitan, industrial workers turned in heavy Democratic majorities. The unemployed, and those who feared that they might become unemployed, voted Democratic in higher degree. Organized labor moved solidly into the Democratic ranks. . . .

Defections from the Democratic ranks were most notable in the business groups and in some rural areas. The Republican campaign against the New Deal voiced the resentment of business groups at new government regulations, expressed anxieties about the new role granted to organized labor, and assaulted welfare policies, such as the Social Security Act and unemployment relief. . . . The departure of the business elements from the Democratic party manifested itself graphically in party finance. Contributions by manufacturers and bankers to the Democratic war chest in 1936 aggregated less than half the sum from those sources in 1932. . . .

The return of a party to power under circumstances like those of the 1936 campaign gives such an election a special significance. Drastic innovations in public policy aroused bitter denunciation by the outs; the ins had to stand on their record. The electorate had before it the question whether to ratify these innovations, few of which had been clearly foreshadowed in the 1932 campaign. The result could only be interpreted as a popular ratification of the broad features of the new public policy.

Source 16 Carl N. Degler, *Out of Our Past: The Forces that Shaped Modern America,* 1970

Twice since the founding of the Republic, cataclysmic events have sliced through the fabric of American life, snapping many of the threads which ordinarily bind the past to the future. The War for the Union was one such event, the Great Depression of the 1930's was the other. And, as the Civil War was precipitated from the political and moral tensions of the preceding era, so the Great Depression was a culmination of the social and economic forces of industrialization and urbanization which had been transforming America since 1865. A depression of such pervasiveness as that of the thirties could happen only to a people already tightly interlaced by the multitudinous cords of a machine civilization and embedded in the matrix of an urban society.

In our history no other economic collapse brought so many Americans to near starvation, endured so long, or came so close to overturning the basic institutions of American life. It is understandable, therefore, that from that experience should issue a new conception of the good society. . . .

Perhaps the most striking alteration in American thought which the Depression fostered concerned the role of the government in the economy. Buffeted and bewildered by the economic debacle, the American people in the course of the 1930's abandoned, once and for all, the doctrine of laissez faire. This beau ideal of the nineteenth century economists had become, ever since the days of Jackson, an increasingly cherished **shibboleth** of Americans. But now it was almost casually discarded. . . .

Almost every one of the best-known measures of the federal government during the depression era made inroads into the hitherto private preserves of business and the individual. Furthermore, most of these measures survived the period, taking their places as fundamental elements in the structure of American life. For modern Americans living under a federal government of transcendent influence and control in the economy, this is the historic meaning of the Great Depression.

Much of what is taken for granted today as the legitimate function of government and the social responsibility of business began only with the legislation of those turbulent years. . . .

The conclusion seems inescapable that, traditional as the words may have been in which the New Deal expressed itself, in actuality it was truly a revolution in ideas, institutions and practices, when one compares it with the political and social world that preceded it. In its long history, America has passed through two revolutions since the first one in 1776, but only the last two, the Civil War and the Depression, were of such force as to change the direction of the relatively smooth flow of its progress. The Civil War rendered a final and irrevocable decision in the long debate over the nature of the Union and the position of the Negro in American society. From that revolutionary experience, America emerged a strong national state and dedicated by the words of its most hallowed document to the inclusion of the black man in a democratic culture. The searing ordeal of the Great Depression purged the American people of their belief in the limited powers of the federal government and convinced them of the necessity of the guarantor state. And as the Civil War constituted a watershed in American thought, so the Depression and its New Deal marked the crossing of a divide from which, it would seem, there could be no turning back.

Source 17 Ira Katznelson and Mark Kesselman, *The Politics of Power,* 1975

Particularly since Franklin D. Roosevelt, the balance of power among the three branches of government has tilted toward the president. The rapid growth in size and power of the presidency can be illustrated by one statistic. When Herbert Hoover served as president from 1928 to 1932, he was aided by a personal secretary and two assistants. Less than a half century later, the Executive Office of the President (EOP) exceeds five thousand staff members, including six hundred members of the White House staff. Every president for nearly half a century has probably been more powerful than even the most powerful presidents of the nineteenth century.

Source 18   Howard Zinn, *A People's History of the United States,* 1980

When the New Deal was over, capitalism remained intact. The rich still controlled the nation's wealth, as well as its laws, courts, police, newspapers, churches, colleges. Enough help had been given to enough people to make Roosevelt a hero to millions, but the same system that had brought depression and crisis—the system of waste, of inequality, of concern for profit over human need—remained.

Source 19   John A. Garraty and Robert A. McCaughey, *The American Nation,* 1987

On balance, the New Deal had an immense constructive impact. By 1939 the country was committed to the idea that the federal government should accept responsibility for the national welfare and act to meet specific problems in every necessary way. What was most significant was not the proliferation of new agencies or the expansion of federal power. These were continuations of trends already a century old when the New Deal began. The importance of the "Roosevelt revolution" was that it removed the issue from politics. "Never again," the Republican presidential candidate was to say in 1952, "shall we *allow* a depression in the United States." . . .

After the New Deal the federal government accepted its obligation to try to provide all the people with a decent standard of living and to pay some attention to achieving the Jeffersonian goal of happiness for all. If the New Deal failed to end the depression, it effected changes that have—so far, at least—prevented later economic declines from becoming catastrophes.

Source 20   Michael Parenti, *Democracy for the Few,* 1980

The first two terms of President Franklin D. Roosevelt's administration have been called the New Deal, an era commonly believed to have brought great transformations on behalf of "the forgotten man." Actually, the New Deal's central dedication was to business recovery rather than social reform. In attempting to spur production, the government funneled large sums from the public treasury into the hands of the moneyed few. In nine years the Reconstruction Finance Corporation alone lent $15 billion to big business. . . .

Faced with massive unrest, the federal government created a relief program that eased some of the hunger and starvation and—more importantly from the perspective of business—limited the instances of violent protest and radicalism. . . .

The disparity between the New Deal's popular image and its actual accomplishments remains one of the unappreciated aspects of the Roosevelt era. To cite specifics: the Civilian Conservation Corps provided jobs at subsistence wages for 250,000 out of 15 million unemployed persons. At its peak, the Works

Progress Administration (WPA) reached about one in four unemployed, often with work of unstable duration and wages below the already inadequate ones of private industry. Of the 12 million workers in interstate commerce who were earning less than forty cents an hour, only about a half million were reached by the minimum wage law. The Social Security Act of 1935 made retirement benefits payable only in 1942 and thereafter, covering but half the population and providing no medical insurance and no protection against illness before retirement. . . .

All this is not to deny that, in response to enormous popular pressure, the Roosevelt administration produced democratic gains. . . . Yet the New Deal era hardly adds up to a triumph for the people. They were ready to go a lot further than Roosevelt did, and probably would have accepted a nationalized banking system, a less begrudging and more massive job program, and a national health-care system. . . .

By 1940, the last year of peace, the number of ill-clothed, ill-fed, and ill-housed Americans showed no substantial decrease. Unemployment continued as a major problem. And the level of consumption and national income was lower than in 1929. . . . Only by entering the war and *remaining thereafter on a permanent war economy* was the United States able to maintain a shaky "prosperity" and significantly lower the Depression era unemployment.

 ## Questioning the Past

1. "Above all, one needs to recognize how markedly the New Deal altered the character of the State in America," historian William E. Leuchtenburg observed. "If you had walked into an American town in 1932, you would have had a hard time detecting any sign of a federal presence, save perhaps for the post office. . . . Washington rarely affected people's lives directly. There was no national old-age pension system, no federal unemployment compensation, no aid to dependent children, no federal housing, no regulation of the stock market, no withholding tax, no federal school lunch, no farm subsidy, no national minimum wage, no welfare state." There is no doubt that the New Deal changed the relationship of the federal government to the American people. Did it change this relationship for the better or for the worse? Argue both sides of this question.

2. Carl Degler asserted that the New Deal was "truly a revolution in ideas, institutions and practices." Was the New Deal a revolution? If so, what was revolutionary about it?

3. Did the New Deal save capitalism or discard it?

4. A democracy rests upon the dispersion of power in the hands of all the people; a dictatorship rests upon a concentration of power in the hands of one person. Argue that the powers Roosevelt was prepared to assume as proclaimed in his inaugural address were compatible with the values of a democratic society. Present the argument that Roosevelt's inaugural address contained ideas incompatible with democracy. Which is the stronger argument?

5. Franklin Roosevelt said, "While it isn't written in the Constitution, nevertheless it is the inherent duty of the Federal Government to keep its citizens from starvation." Debate this point.

Chapter **18**

Pearl Harbor

The Japanese Attack Hawaii   *December 7, 1941*

Dawn came peacefully to the islands of the Hawaiian chain on the Sunday morning of December 7, 1941. As the first rays of the sun warmed the beaches of this Pacific paradise, few could have imagined that within moments a catastrophic event would shatter not only the calm serenity of these American isles but the sense of security and peace that the American people had always drawn from their aloofness from the affairs of the world.

During the hours before dawn a powerful fleet had moved within striking distance of the American army and navy bases located on the island of Oahu. This fleet, consisting of submarines, destroyers, cruisers, battleships, and six aircraft carriers, had sailed for two weeks across the Pacific and arrived off the Hawaiian chain undetected by American military forces. By 7:40 A.M. the first wave of planes launched from the carriers was in sight of the American Pacific Fleet resting at anchor in Pearl Harbor. Minutes later the sound of droning engines was heard over Honolulu, and the sky was dotted by hundreds of Japanese planes—dive bombers, torpedo planes, horizontal bombers, fighter planes. At 7:55 the bombs began to fall. Three minutes later a radio message went out from Hawaii that shocked the American people and shifted the course of American foreign policy from that moment through the present: "AIR RAID ON PEARL HARBOR. THIS IS NO DRILL."

18.1 The History Place: World War II

✎ *First Impressions*

War Was Unavoidable

Japan justified its attacks on European presences in the East as a defense of "Asia for Asians." The United States immediately retaliated to defend its fleet, its citizens, and its interests. The two sides employed similar rhetoric to justify the Asian phase of World War II.

Source 1   Wire service report of Richard Haller, *Washington Post,* December 8, 1941

Honolulu, Dec. 7—Japanese war planes brought sudden death and undisclosed destruction to the beautiful Hawaiian Islands in their sudden raid this morning.

A flotilla of planes bearing the rising sun of Japan on their wingtips appeared out of the south while most of the city was sleeping. The planes dove immediately to the attack on Pearl Harbor and Hickman Field, the giant airbase lying near by.

There was a deafening roar of explosions.

Our antiaircraft units opened fire.

Three battleships were struck as they lay at anchor in the naval base.

One was reportedly set afire. Another we hear has been sunk along with another warship. . . .

I saw 15 planes of one attacking group subjected to heavy antiaircraft fire from batteries ringing Honolulu.

Several were shot down. . . .

I wasn't able to confirm reports that Japanese paratroops had landed. The report spread through Honolulu like wild fire.

From the rooftop of the Honolulu Advertiser building I saw a thick pall of smoke rising from the Pearl Harbor and Hickman Field areas. Three separate fires were raging there.

A staggering series of explosions came shortly after 10 o'clock when the attack was already two hours old. . . .

A few minutes later the Japanese planes, flying at an immense altitude, returned over Honolulu.

Our own fighter planes were in the sky in hot pursuit. A bomb fell in our direction. We took refuge as it screamed to earth only a short distance from the Honolulu Advertiser Building. . . .

Waikiki, the world famous resort beach, was also subjected to sudden attack as the raiders tried to silence the big guns of Fort de Russy, guarding the entrance to Honolulu Harbor.

The raiders again appeared over Diamond Head, flying from the south. There appeared to be 50 to 75 planes in the raiding group. . . .

The raiders fantailed over the residential districts and dropped what appeared to be incendiary bombs over Pacific Heights and Dowsett Highlands. Some fires were ignited.

Gov. Poindexter lost no time in proclaiming a state of emergency throughout the territory.

Source 2   Editorial, *New York Times*, December 8, 1941

18.2 Investigation of the Pearl Harbor Attack

There is only one possible answer to Japan's attack. That answer is an immediate declaration of war by the United States against Japan. . . .

We do not need at this stage to consider the reasons for the timing of this almost incredible assault upon the outposts of our defense by a nation whose emissaries in Washington were still expressing friendship for our people. Whether Japan has yielded at last to pressure from Hitler, who has obviously wished for many months to deflect American power from the Atlantic to the Pacific, or whether this is primarily and essentially an independent Japanese adventure, launched by a military clique in Tokyo whose powers of self-deception now rise to a state of sublime insanity, we cannot know until events have given more perspective. It is possible that the second hypothesis is the more credible one—since Hitler . . . can scarcely desire at this time the open and formal entrance of the United States into a war which will certainly and automatically find us openly and formally at war with Germany as well before that war is finished. These are conjectures of great interest and importance. But they do not count in the face of explosive facts. The only thing that matters now is that a deliberate attempt has been made by an enemy Power to destroy the defenses of America.

To that attempt we will reply. We will reply with our full force, without panic and without losing sight of our objectives. We will make war upon Japan and we will put an end to these interminable and unbearable threats of Japanese aggression. But in making war upon Japan, we will not overestimate the ability of Japan to do us harm; we will not mistake the lesser danger for the greater danger, and we will not forget that Hitler, and not Tokyo, is the greatest threat to our security. The real battle of our times will not be fought in the Far Fast. It will be fought on the English Channel. . . .

The Japanese attacks yesterday at Hawaii, at Guam, on the Philippines, on American ships within a few days' steaming distance of our own Pacific Coast, have blown away with the force of a hurricane the whole structure of myth upon which opposition to the President's policies has been based: the myth that we were "not in danger": the myth that it was "fantastic" even to imagine a direct attack on the defenses of the United States: the myth that the President has been "trying to drag us into war," instead of trying—as must now be so abundantly clear, even to the last skeptic—to find dependable allies for us in an hour of great need and to strengthen those allies for the test of strength that lay ahead.

Source 3   Editorial, *The Times* of London, December 8, 1941

Japan has struck. Faithful to what is now the well-established rule in Axis warfare and to the precedents followed by Hitler when he marched on Russia last June, she has attacked the United States without warning. While Mr. Kurusu and Admiral Nomura were actually in the State Department continuing their talks with Mr. Cordell Hull, large forces of Japanese areoplanes, apparently from naval aircraft carriers, bombed Pearl Harbour, the big American base in the Hawaiian Islands, and Manila, the capital of the Philippines. . . . The Japanese attacked without warning, but a declaration that a state of war exists between Japan and the United States and Great Britain "in the Western Pacific" has since been issued. . . . An American declaration of War must await the decision of Congress, but there can be no doubt of the decision when Congress assembles today. Both Houses of Parliament meet this afternoon, and Mr. Churchill's pledge that in case of war with Japan Britain will be at America's side within the hour is certain to be honoured.

Source 4   Editorial, *Washington Post*, December 8, 1941

The Japanese attack on Hawaii began precisely as many Navy and Army officers predicted it would. That is, Japanese planes took off from carriers at sea to lay their "eggs" on Oahu's strategic defenses. How successful they are is unclear. . . . It is disturbing, nevertheless, that enemy planes were apparently able to slip, under cover of darkness, through the protective cordon of ships and planes which the Navy had thrown about the islands. Ever since the war began in

Europe both services in Hawaii have been on emergency duty. For the Navy this has meant, among other things, incessant ship and plane patrol hundreds of miles at sea. The reason for such patrol has been, of course, to spot and radio the location of the enemy long before he could get within attacking distance of the islands. In theory, anyway, it is then the Army's job to send out its faster bombers, among them flying fortresses, to destroy the enemy. In the present instance, however, Japanese carriers and their protective craft seem to have escaped immediate detection. . . .

War broke out in the Pacific on the very day that Secretary Knox announced, in his annual report, that our Navy is now the equal of any fleet in the world. It is a matter of profound satisfaction to the American people that, as we meet this attack on Hawaii and the Philippines, our line of defense has been greatly strengthened.

Source 5   Statement of the Emperor of Japan, December 8, 1941

IMPERIAL WAR RESCRIPT

18.3 The
Avalon Project:
Pearl Harbor
Documents

We, by grace of Heaven, Emperor of Japan, seated on the Throne of a line unbroken for ages eternal, enjoin upon ye, Our loyal and brave subjects:

We hereby declare war on the United States of America and the British Empire. . . .

To insure the stability of East Asia and to contribute to world peace is the far-sighted policy which was formulated by Our Great Illustrious Imperial Grandsire and Our Great Imperial Sire succeeding Him, and which We lay constantly to heart.

To cultivate friendship among nations and to enjoy prosperity in common with all nations has always been the guiding principle of Our Empire's foreign policy. It has been truly unavoidable and far from Our wishes that Our Empire has now been brought to cross swords with America and Britain.

More than four years have passed since China, failing to comprehend the true intentions of Our Empire, and recklessly courting trouble, disturbed the peace of East Asia and compelled Our Empire to take up arms. Although there has been re-established the National Government of China, with which Japan has effected neighborly intercourse and cooperation, the regime which has survived at Chungking relying on American and British protection, still continues its fratricidal opposition.

Eager for the realization of their inordinate ambition to dominate the Orient, both America and Britain, giving support to the Chungking regime, have aggravated the disturbances in East Asia.

Moreover, these two powers, inducing other countries to follow suit, increased military preparations on all sides of Our Empire to challenge us. They have obstructed by every means Our peaceful commerce, and finally resorted to a direct severance of economic relations, menacing greatly the existence of Our Empire.

Patiently have We waited and long have We endured in the hope that Our Government might retrieve the situation in peace, but Our adversaries, showing not the least spirit of conciliation, have unduly delayed a settlement; and in the meantime, they have intensified the economic and political pressure to compel thereby Our Empire to submission.

This trend of affairs would, if left unchecked, not only nullify Our Empire's efforts of many years for the stabilization of East Asia, but also endanger the very existence of Our nation. The situation being such as it is, Our Empire for its existence and self-defense has no other recourse but to appeal to arms and to crush every obstacle in its path.

The hallowed spirits of Our Imperial Ancestors guarding Us from above, We rely upon the loyalty and courage of Our subjects in Our confident expectation that the task bequeathed by Our Forefathers will be carried forward, and that the sources of evil will be speedily eradicated and an enduring peace immutably established in East Asia, preserving thereby the glory of Our Empire.

Source 6   **President Franklin D. Roosevelt's war message to Congress, December 8, 1941**

Yesterday, December 7, 1941—a date which will live in infamy—the United States was attacked by naval and air forces of the Empire of Japan.

The United States was at peace with that nation and, at the solicitation of Japan, was still in conversation with its Government and its Emperor looking toward the maintenance of peace in the Pacific. Indeed, one hour after Japanese air squadrons had commenced bombing in the American Island of Oahu, the Japanese Ambassador to the United States and his colleagues delivered to our Secretary of State a formal reply to a recent American message. And while this reply stated that it seemed useless to continue the diplomatic negotiations, it contained no threat or hint of war or of armed attack.

It will be recorded that the distance of Hawaii from Japan makes it obvious that the attack was deliberately planned many days or even weeks ago. During the intervening time the Japanese Government has deliberately sought to deceive the United States by false statements and expressions of hope for continued peace.

The attack yesterday on the Hawaiian Islands has caused severe damage to American naval and military forces. I regret to tell you that many American lives have been lost. In addition American ships have been reported torpedoed on the high seas between San Francisco and Honolulu.

Yesterday the Japanese Government also launched an attack against Malaya.

Last night Japanese forces attacked Hong Kong.

Last night Japanese forces attacked Guam.

Last night Japanese forces attacked the Philippine Islands.

Last night the Japanese attacked Wake Island.

And this morning the Japanese attacked Midway Island.

Japan has, therefore, undertaken a surprise offensive extending throughout the Pacific area. The facts of yesterday and today speak for themselves. The people of the United States have already formed their opinions and well understand the implications to the very life and safety of our Nation.

As Commander in Chief of the Army and Navy I have directed that all measures be taken for our defense.

But always will our whole Nation remember the character of the onslaught against us.

No matter how long it may take us to overcome this premeditated invasion, the American people in their righteous might will win through to absolute victory.

I believe that I interpret the will of Congress and of the people when I assert that we will not only defend ourselves to the utmost but will make it very certain that this form of treachery shall never again endanger us.

Hostilities exist. There is no blinking at the fact that our people, our territory, and our interests are in grave danger.

With confidence in our armed forces—with the unbounding determination of our people—we will gain the inevitable triumph—so help us God.

I ask that the Congress declare that since the unprovoked and dastardly attack by Japan on Sunday, December 7, 1941, a state of war has existed between the United States and the Japanese Empire.

Source 7   Editorial, *Nichi Nichi,* Tokyo, Japan, December 8, 1941

What an arrogant attitude our enemies have assumed! How long have they procrastinated on the negotiations? How they tried to strangle us by economic blockade? We have no time to spread the whole list of their crimes. Both heaven and mankind will not tolerate the insatiable greed of possession of which they have become captive.

With a flash of the sabre, Japanese airforces, Army and Navy, are already scoring outstanding successes, and American and British bases in the Pacific are now being crushed one by one. This is a war of emancipation of East Asia, a war of reconstruction of East Asia. Look, the ominous clouds that have been hanging low over the Pacific are now being cleared every minute, and a bright horizon is now peeping beyond.

We have persevered but we have now come to the end of our patience and have at last risen. We have to purge both British and American influence from the Pacific, the South Seas and East Asia, root and branch.

Source 8   "Surprise Attacks Launched," *Mainichi,* Osaka, Japan, December 9, 1941

The Navy department of the Imperial General Headquarters on Monday, December 8, at 11:10 a.m. issued a communique regarding the progress of hostilities in the western Pacific.

1 The Imperial Navy on December 8 [December 7 Honolulu time] at dawn succeeded in staging a surprise attack on the American Fleet and air force in Hawaii.

2 The Imperial Navy on December 8 at dawn sunk the British gunboat Peterel berthed in Shanghai. The American gunboat Wake also in Shanghai surrendered to the Imperial Navy at the same time.

3 The Imperial Navy by raiding Singapore on December 8 at dawn accomplished great results.

4 The Imperial Navy on December 8 at dawn bombed enemy military establishments at Davao (in the Philippines), Guam, and Wake Island in the Pacific.

Source 9   Editorial, *Asahi,* Tokyo, Japan, December 9, 1941

Japan has entered a state of war with the United States and the British Empire. The move followed the failure of the effort to reach an accord with the United States on the problems of the Pacific.

From the first, we contended that the cancer of the Pacific was America's policy of applying fantastic principles to the situation in East Asia. The Americans spoke as though their appointed task was to police the world. The policy followed by it in dealing with Finland shows that the American conception of justice varies according to the circumstances in which America finds itself. The situation which has compelled this country to declare war on America and Britain is to be blamed on these countries. Both America and Britain deliberately closed their eyes to the actualities of the situation in East Asia and sent aid to the Chungking regime in its struggle with this country.

Source 10   Editorial, *Chugai Shogyo,* Japan, December 9, 1941

The state of war between Japan, and the United States and Great Britain is not accidental, and there are remote and immediate causes for it. It was unavoidable. There is a degree to prudence and limit to patience. How Japan has been prudent and patient in the recent negotiations with the United States is clearly told. But what has the United States done to us in return? It has merely mentioned imaginary and selfish principles and tried to force them upon Japan. There was not a speck of sincerity in its attitude. On the other hand, it strengthened the anti-Japanese encircling line, to wait the surrender of Japan. Such an attitude of insult and violence cannot be permitted. . . .

It is the peace of the Orient that Japan and its people have always desired and demanded, to contribute to the establishment of permanent world peace. . . .

But it was the United States and Great Britain that have tried to prevent us from attaining this great end. What they did in connection with the present China affair closely proves it. When we realize that the blood of our brothers was sacrificed because of those enemies behind the scene, our blood boils. War is now declared against these nations, and the people must be determined to service the nation at their sacrifice.

It has become clear that the two hostile nations have been long stimulating the disturbance in East Asia. Their final object was to obtain absolute control of the Orient. Thus they do not welcome our plan of establishing the East Asia Co-prosperity Sphere. That is to say, Japan has been obliged to rise for the nation's very existence and the honor of the state. Our ancestors' teaching has clearly taught us what to do when our nation is insulted. The glorious history of three thousand years should never be spoiled by any blot.

Source 11   Editorial, "Supremacy of the Seas in Our Hands," *Mainichi,* Osaka, Japan, December 12, 1941

The Imperial Navy, which destroyed the main force of the U.S. Pacific Fleet at Hawaii and its air force at the outbreak of the war, has again startled the world by annihilating the nuclei of the British Far Eastern Fleet in the sea off the coast of the Malay Peninsula on the third day. . . .

As a result of the destruction of the main strength of the American and British fleets, the supremacy of the Pacific and the Indian Oceans has been gripped by the Imperial Navy. . . . The American warships at Hawaii and the British men-of-war in the Malay region have proved extremely frail. . . .

The British and American Navies themselves should never have been weak. As is generally known, the U.S. Navy has indeed been the golden signboard of American defense. "A Navy Second to None" has been the goal of the United States for many years. And it looked as if that country had arrived at the goal. President Roosevelt, in particular, has been the foremost protagonist of this big navy, nay the No. 1 navy in the world.

However, once the Japanese Navy rose in arms, this golden signboard was smashed to pieces. The U.S. Navy used to boast about its trans-oceanic operations and took pride in her superior 5-5-3 naval ratio. Such things have already become dreams of the past. The Washington system which imposed the 5-5-3 ratio on our country has been crushed. . . .

The naval battle will go on. But in the Pacific and in the Indian Oceans, we can no longer meet a navy which will dare stage a frontal attack against the Grand Fleet of the Imperial Navy.

The Imperial Navy, which has been rated third in respect of tonnage, has demonstrated that it can beat the British and American Navies which held first and second places respectively. It stands to reason that we have now won the supremacy of the seas. Since her victory over the Spanish Armada, Britain has reigned as the Mistress of the Seas for three centuries. But the day has come for the supremacy to shift into the hands of Nippon.

Why Was the Attack a Surprise?

The Japanese attack on Pearl Harbor cost the lives of 2,403 American sailors, soldiers, and civilians. More than 1,000 Americans were wounded. Eight American battleships were put out of action. Many additional naval vessels were damaged and 149 American planes were destroyed. The attacking Japanese forces lost only 29 aircraft. It was a stunning blow.

Japanese leaders reasoned that such a blow—hopefully, a knockout punch—was needed to clear the way for what they envisioned would be a "Greater East Asia Co-prosperity Sphere." Japan had long resented European and American control of lands and peoples in East Asia. Japanese leaders denounced the exploitation of Asian resources and markets that accompanied the European and American occupation of Asian territories. They condemned the Western view that Europeans and Americans of European descent were racially superior to the people of Asia. To fully realize the Japanese vision of "Asia for Asians" required the ouster of the French from Indochina, the Dutch from the East Indies, the British from China and South Asia, the Americans from the Philippines.

Though wrapped in noble rhetoric, the Japanese ambitions for East Asia were based neither more nor less on altruism than those of the Europeans they sought to oust. The Japanese were intent on replacing the European empires in Asia with an Asian empire of their own, and had made significant progress toward this end in China prior to 1941. Japan saw itself as the political, military, and industrial center of the new Asia it hoped to build.

Japanese strategists believed that the future of their nation required access to the resources of Asia. Oil, in particular, was essential to Japanese industrial growth and military security. Consequently, a decision had been made to drive the European powers from East Asia and take control of the oil fields of the Dutch East Indies. Such an action, however, carried with it a high probability of producing a military confrontation with the United States. To preempt such a confrontation, the Japanese had decided to stage a surprise attack against the strongholds of American military might in the Pacific.

It was reasonable to expect that months, even years, might pass before the American strength could be rebuilt to a point where retaliation would be possible. In the meantime, the Japanese expected to so entrench themselves in their conquests that a challenge to their position in East Asia would be too costly to attempt. Also, over time, the Japanese hoped, the American anger would subside enough to let reason dictate America's course. The United States would hopefully come to see on the European front a threat so menacing that a war in the Pacific would appear a dangerous diversion.

But the leaders of Japan underestimated the intensity of emotion they unleashed when their bombs hit Pearl Harbor. Americans were united in the belief that the attack could neither be forgiven nor forgotten. War was declared immediately and without consideration of the practical question of how crippled the Pacific Fleet might or might not be.

While there was no question about American commitment to finish the war that was started on the morning of December 7, there were questions about how such an attack could have taken the United States completely by surprise. The government of the United States knew that Japan was preparing to launch a military offensive. A warning had been sent to all American commands in the Pacific a week before the bombs fell on Pearl Harbor, urging vigilance in anticipation of an attack. The War Department had cracked the Japanese code more than a year before the bombing of Pearl Harbor and even produced for the president a daily summary of the most secret of Japanese messages. These circumstances led many to wonder how the American military could have "lost" the Japanese Fleet for the two crucial weeks prior to the attack on Oahu.

Nevertheless, the United States had responded to Japanese military moves against China in ways that all but guaranteed a Japanese response. The United States joined Britain in encouraging and supplying the Chinese resistance to the Japanese operations in China. The United States raised moral objections to Japanese military tactics and applied increasingly severe economic pressure to alter the course of Japanese policy in China. Sales of iron and scrap metal to Japan were halted. Japanese assets in the United States were frozen. American oil exports to Japan were cut off despite the fact that Japan depended upon America to supply 80 percent of its petroleum needs. And when Japan began to contemplate seizing the oil fields of the Dutch East Indies, the United States warned that such a move could lead to war. The policies of the Roosevelt administration, critics argue, gave the Japanese a choice between submitting to economic strangulation or fighting back.

On the other hand, Roosevelt was criticized with equal ferocity by people who believed he had allowed America to abdicate its necessary role in the early containment of Axis and Japanese expansion.

Second Thoughts

A Necessary War or a Presidential Plot?

The surprise attack on Pearl Harbor destroyed resistance to the United States' role as a combatant in World War II. Within just a few years, however, American doves and hawks resumed their opposing dialogue. Some critics accused President Roosevelt of plotting the attack to force America into war, while others argued that he should have led the nation into battle long before December 1941.

Source 12   Thomas A. Bailey, *A Diplomatic History of the American People,* 1946

The historian may now record that the ghastly gamble of the Japanese was a blunder of the first magnitude. The damage at Pearl Harbor was heavy but not irreparable. If the Japanese had continued their Hitlerian tactics of piece-meal penetration, if they had moved step by step into Thailand, Malaya, and the Dutch East Indies, the problem of declaring war would have been put squarely before an America which had a large and very vocal isolationist bloc. It is probable that a vote for war might not have been mustered; or if mustered, not until after many months had passed, and then only after em-bittered debate, injured feelings, partisanship as usual, strikes as usual, grow-ing disunity, and a protracted postponement of the all-out war effort. The torpedoes that sank the American battleships in Pearl Harbor also sank "America Firstism." . . .

On December 8, 1941, the day after Pearl Harbor, the Senate approved the [declaration of war] resolution 82 to 0; the House, 388 to 1. On December 11, four days after Pearl Harbor, Germany and Italy announced that they regarded themselves as in a state of war with the United States. Again, American opinion was spared the confusion of a debate over fighting the European Axis, for the decision was taken out of the hands of Congress, which formally acted that same day. This time the vote in the Senate was 88 to 0 for war with Germany; in the House, 393 to 0. On the resolution to recognize a state of war with Italy the count was 90 to 0 in the Senate; 399 to 0 in the House. This unprecedented unanimity was in part a recognition of the fact that war had already come; in part, an answer to Pearl Harbor. . . .

Most Americans knew what they were fighting against rather than what they were fighting for: America had been attacked and her aggressors had to be punished and shackled. A year after Pearl Harbor nearly four out of ten persons could confess that they had no clear idea of why they were waging war. . . . There was even a strong reluctance to recognize that by the time of Pearl Harbor the global war had become America's war; as late as 1945 eight out of ten persons believed that in December, 1941, Roosevelt should have been trying to keep the country out of the conflict. One can only surmise what the disunity would have been if the perpetrators of Pearl Harbor had not electrified the nation.

Source 13 Secretary of War Henry L. Stimson and McGeorge Bundy, *On Active Service,* 1948

[T]he major responsibility for the catastrophe rested on the two officers commanding on the spot—Admiral Kimmel and General Short. It is true that the War and Navy Departments were not fully efficient in evaluating the information available to them, and of course it was also true that no one in Washington had correctly assessed Japanese intentions and capabilities. . . . The men in Washington did not foresee this attack, and they did not take the additional actions suggested by a retrospective view. But the fact remained: the officers commanding at Hawaii had been alerted like other outpost commanders; unlike other outpost commanders they proved on December 7 to be far from alert. It did not excuse them that Washington did not anticipate that they would be attacked. . . .

Much of the discussion of Pearl Harbor was confused and embittered by a preposterous effort to demonstrate that President Roosevelt and his advisors had for some unfathomable but nefarious reason "planned it that way." There was also a marked disposition to believe that men friendly to the President were hiding something of crucial importance. . . .

[T]he central importance of the Pearl Harbor attack lay not in the tactical victory carried off by the Japanese but in the simple fact that the months of hesitation and relative inaction were ended at one stroke. "When the news first came that Japan had attacked us, my first feeling was of relief that the indecision was over and that a crisis had come in a way which would unite all our people. This continued to be my dominant feeling in spite of the news of catastrophes which quickly developed. For I feel that this country united has practically nothing to fear, while the apathy and divisions stirred up by unpatriotic men have been hitherto very discouraging." [Stimson's Diary, December 7, 1941.]

In the attack on Pearl Harbor a curtain of fire was lowered over the problems and anxieties of the preceding months. . . . [N]o longer would the loud and bitter voices of a small minority be raised in horror at every forward step to block aggression. . . .

On December 7, 1941, for the first time in more than twenty years, the United States of America was placed in a position to take unified action for the peace and security of herself and the world. The Japanese attack at Pearl Harbor restored to America the freedom of action she had lost by many cunning bonds of her citizens' own contriving. The self-imprisoned giant was set free.

Source 14 Roosevelt critic John T. Flynn, *The Roosevelt Myth,* 1948

The President . . . declared he was for those who wanted to stay out of the war while he secretly decided to go into the war, and his public avowals were the precise opposite of his secret intentions. He did not tell the truth to the American people and from the beginning to the end pursued a course of deliberate deception of them about his plans. . . .

The President could not, without Congress, launch an attack. He knew that if he asked Congress for a declaration of war he would not get it. The week before Pearl Harbor, the polls showed 75 per cent of the people against going into the war. And he had been carrying on an undeclared war for many months. The events leading to Pearl Harbor have been extensively investigated, though there is yet much to be obtained. This much has been established completely and that is that the President and his war cabinet knew an attack was coming, though they did not know it was coming at Pearl Harbor. Whether or not they should have known is a point we cannot enter into here. The President had told the Japanese that if they made any further move in the Pacific the United States would have to act. The move was expected against the Kra Peninsula or perhaps Singapore itself, the Dutch East Indies or the Philippines. On November 27, just ten days before the attack, the President told Secretary Stimson, who wrote it in his diary, that our course was to maneuver the Japanese into attacking us. This would put us into the war and solve his problem. The attack did put us in the war. It did solve Roosevelt's problem. It was a costly solution. But it got him out of a difficult hole and into the one he maneuvered to get into—the war.

Source 15 Harry Elmer Barnes, *Perpetual War for Perpetual Peace*, 1953

The net result of revisionist scholarship applied to Pearl Harbor boils down essentially to this: In order to promote Roosevelt's political ambitions and his mendacious foreign policy some three thousand American boys were quite needlessly butchered. Of course, they were only a drop in the bucket compared to those who were ultimately slain in the war that resulted, which was as needless, in terms of vital American interests, as the surprise attack on Pearl Harbor.

Source 16 Robert A. Divine, *The Reluctant Belligerent*, 1965

From the first signs of aggression in the 1930's to the attack on Pearl Harbor, the United States refused to act until there was no other choice. The American people believed in the 1930's that they could escape the contagion of war. When the fall of France destroyed this illusion, they embraced the comforting notion that through material aid they could defeat Hitler without entering the conflict. When Japan threatened all Asia, Americans naively believed that economic pressure would compel her to retreat. Even when Japan responded with the attack of Pearl Harbor, the United States ignored the Axis alliance and waited for Hitler to force America into the European war.

American foreign policy was sterile and bankrupt in a period of grave international crisis. Although it was the single most powerful nation on the globe, the United States abdicated its responsibilities and became a creature of history rather than its molder. By surrendering the initiative to Germany and Japan, the nation imperiled its security and very nearly permitted the Axis powers to win the war. In the last analysis the United States was saved only by the Japanese miscalculation in attacking Pearl Harbor. Japan's tactical victory quickly led to strategic defeat as the United States finally accepted the challenge of aggression.

Source 17 Robert H. Ferrell, *American Diplomacy*, 1969

[T]he controversy over Pearl Harbor was an acrimonious affair. John T. Flynn, the well-known journalist, blew the lid off the Pearl Harbor controversy in 1945

. . . when he published his pamphlet *The Final Secret of Pearl Harbor*. He showed that the American government in the months before entry into the war had cracked the highest Japanese secret code, the so-called purple cipher, and had been reading Japan's innermost diplomatic and military secrets long before the attack of December 7, 1941. Pressure for a congressional investigation became overwhelming, and Congress authorized a special joint committee which sat from November 15, 1945, to May 31, 1946. Its record of hearings encompassed approximately 10,000,000 words, and this mountain of evidence was published in October in 39 volumes. But the joint committee came to no agreement as to the meaning of its evidence and publicly registered its uncertainty in a report containing dissenting majority and minority views.

Argument continued, with the key question being why the Pearl Harbor disaster occurred if the government was so well-informed on Japanese intentions. Some individuals chose to believe that there had been an intelligence lapse before the fleet disaster—that plenty of warnings had come from the decoded intercepts but they were not properly evaluated. . . . Another interpretation of the Pearl Harbor disaster, however, was that the intercepts and other important pieces of information were ignored . . . because President Roosevelt had "planned it that way." He had determined to expose the fleet so as to force the reluctant American nation into the Second World War. . . .

What can one make out of this sort of accusation? Have the revisionists ever succeeded in proving their case about Pearl Harbor? In actual fact they have not, for an enormous amount of scholarship, revisionist and antirevisionist, has been expended on the subject of Pearl Harbor, and no one has emerged with clear proof, even a trace of proof, that the American president in 1941 purposely exposed the Pacific fleet to achieve his goals in foreign policy. . . .

Admittedly a circumstantial case can be constructed in support of revisionist history. It is true that the authorities in Washington prior to December 7, 1941, badly bungled some warning messages to the various Pacific commands, messages based on information derived from the Japanese intercepts. These messages employed customary military circumlocution in an effort to seem mindful of all occasions and eventualities; the Pearl Harbor commanders interpreted the messages as a warning against sabotage—and among other precautions they bunched their planes on the runways where they made convenient targets for Japanese attack. . . .

The back-door theorists have borrowed support from the treatment of the army and navy commanders at the unfortunate Hawaii base, Admiral Kimmel and Lieutenant General Walter C. Short. They were hastily—and, the present writer believes, most unfairly—cashiered after the Japanese attack; their treatment by the Washington administration was so ungenerous as to suggest that they were needed as scapegoats to remove suspicion from higher authorities. . . .

But no one has really proved any untoward acts at Pearl Harbor. . . . Nearly all the records of the United States government have been opened . . . , and no proof of a presidential plot has yet appeared.

It ought to be possible, therefore, to settle the argument for revisionism by an argument drawn from what might be termed common sense. What man, one might ask, having risen to the presidency and enjoyed two successful terms in office, would jeopardize his life's reputation, not to speak of the fate of his country, to engage in a plot so crude that it sounds as if it came out of the sixteenth century, the era of Niccolo Machiavelli? Common sense refuses to believe in the possibility of such a course. Moreover, in so large and unwieldy an establishment as the government of the United States it is enormously difficult to set a conspiracy on foot without someone revealing it.

Source 18 Robert Dallek, *Franklin D. Roosevelt and American Foreign Policy, 1932–1945*, 1979

[C]ritics of Roosevelt's leadership argued that the President had provoked the Japanese attack as a "backdoor" to the European war. They even suggested that FDR expected the Pearl Harbor assault but allowed American forces to be surprised in order to assure unity at home. This argument . . . is without merit. . . . The country's political and military leaders simply discounted or underestimated the likelihood of a Japanese attack on Hawaii. Yet the authors of the assertion that FDR allowed American forces to be surprised did not enunciate it simply to discredit FDR. Voiced by a group of writers who believed the United States would have done better to stay out of the war, the refusal to see the Pearl Harbor attack as a surprise was essential to a vindication of old isolationist beliefs. Having consistently argued that American security was not at stake in the war, . . . diehard isolationists tried to answer a devastating refutation of this theme by placing the blame for Pearl Harbor on FDR. . . .

The isolationist tenet that described involvement in the war as certain to damage the nation's democratic institutions was a more realistic concern. By setting precedents for arbitrary use of Executive power, Roosevelt and subsequent Presidents gave meaning to isolationist warnings that the defense of democracy abroad would compromise it at home. It is an irony of history that in his determination to save democracy from Nazism, Roosevelt contributed to the rise of some undemocratic practices in the United States. But it is an even greater irony that the isolationist failure to appreciate the threat posed by Nazi might helped force Roosevelt into the machinations which later Presidents used to rationalize abuses of power on more questionable grounds.

Source 19 Journalist Haynes Johnson, *Washington Post*, December 7, 1991

It began at 7:55 a.m., Hawaiian time, 5,000 miles and five time zones away from Washington, in a place unknown to most Americans, and intruded on a capital where generals still rode horses, gentlemen didn't read each other's mail, even if they were intelligence agents, the Army trained with World War I ammunition and rifles, and blacks were called Negroes or colored people who existed in a totally segregated society.

As the clock inched toward 1 o'clock that Sunday afternoon, Washington and the nation stood in a state of suspended animation. Each tick of the second hand inexorably moved them closer to a historic fault line. Everything that went before represented the old America, an America that would never be the same. Everything that came after stood for a new America emerging reluctantly, painfully out of self-imposed and smug isolation to center stage on the world scene.

Source 20   Ninety-Ninth National Convention of the Veterans of Foreign Wars, "Resolution 441: Restore Pre-Attack Ranks to Admiral Husband E. Kimmel and General Walter C. Short," adopted unanimously, August 31, 1998

Whereas, Admiral Husband E. Kimmel and General Walter C. Short were the Commanders of Record for the Navy and Army Forces at Pearl Harbor, Hawaii, on December 7, 1941, when the Japanese Imperial Navy launched its attack; and

18.4 The New American: Pearl Harbor

Whereas, following the attack, President Franklin D. Roosevelt appointed Supreme Court Justice Owen J. Roberts to a commission to investigate such incident to determine if there had been any dereliction to duty; and

Whereas, the Roberts Commission conducted a rushed investigation in only five weeks. It charged Admiral Kimmel and General Short with dereliction of their duty. The findings were made public to the world; and

Whereas, the dereliction of duty charge destroyed the honor and reputations of both Admiral Kimmel and General Short, and due to the urgency neither man was given the opportunity to defend himself against the accusation of dereliction of duty; and

Whereas, other investigations showed that there was no basis for the dereliction of duty charges, and a Congressional investigation in 1946 made specific findings that neither Admiral Kimmel nor General Short had been "derelict of duty" at the time of the bombing of Pearl Harbor; and

Whereas, it has been documented that the United States military had broken the Japanese codes in 1941. With the use of a cryptic machine known as "Magic," the military was able to decipher the Japanese diplomatic code known as "Purple" and the military code known as JN-25. The final part of the diplomatic message that told of the attack on Pearl Harbor was received on December 6, 1941. With this vital information in hand, no warning was dispatched to Admiral Kimmel and General Short to provide sufficient time to defend Pearl Harbor in the proper manner; and

Whereas, it was not until after the tenth investigation of the attack on Pearl Harbor was completed in December 1995 that the United States Government acknowledged in the report of Under Secretary of Defense Edwin S. Dorn that Admiral Kimmel and General Short were not solely responsible for the disaster, but that responsibility must be broadly shared; and

Whereas, at this time the American public has been deceived for the past fifty-six years regarding the unfounded charge of dereliction of duty against two fine military officers whose reputations and honor have been tarnished; now, therefore

Be it Resolved, by the Veterans of Foreign Wars of the United States, that we urge the President of the United States to restore the honor and reputations of Admiral Husband E. Kimmel and General Walter C. Short.

Source 21   Remarks of Senator William Roth of Delaware prior to a 52 to 47 vote of the United States Senate to restore the reputations of Admiral Husband Kimmel and General Walter Short, May 24, 1999

Admiral Husband Kimmel and General Walter Short were the two senior commanders of U.S. forces deployed in the Pacific at the time of the disastrous surprise December 7, 1941, attack on Pearl Harbor. In the immediate aftermath of the attack, they were unfairly and publicly charged with dereliction of duty and blamed as singularly responsible for the success of that attack.

Less than 6 weeks after the Pearl Harbor attack, in a hastily prepared report to the President, the Roberts Commission—perhaps the most flawed and unfortunately most influential investigation of the disaster—leveled the dereliction of duty charge against Kimmel and Short—a charge that was immediately and highly publicized.

Admiral William Harrison Standley, who served as a member of this Commission, later disavowed its report, stating that these two officers were "martyred" and "if they had been brought to trial, they would have been cleared of the charge." . . .

The 1995 Department of Defense report put it best, stating that "responsibility for the Pearl Harbor disaster should not fall solely on the shoulders of Admiral Kimmel and General Short; it should be broadly shared." . . .

This resolution . . . is about justice, equity, and honor. Its purpose is to redress an historic wrong, to ensure that Admiral Kimmel and General Short are treated with the dignity and honor they deserve, and to ensure that justice and fairness fully permeate the memory and lessons learned from the catastrophe at Pearl Harbor.

As we approach Memorial Day and prepare to honor those who served to protect our great nation, it is a most appropriate time to redress this injustice. After 58 years, this correction is long overdue. I urge my colleagues to support this joint resolution.

Questioning the Past

1. From the Japanese viewpoint, present the arguments both for and against the strategy of simultaneous assaults on American and European positions in Asia and the Pacific. Was this strategy a gamble that offered reasonable prospects for success or an action that was, in the words of historian Robert H. Ferrell, "foolhardy and irresponsible in the extreme"? What alternatives to the surprise offensive, both military and diplomatic, might the Japanese have tried?

2. Thomas Bailey expresses the doubt that without the attack on Pearl Harbor, the American people would not have come to believe that "the global war had become America's war." In the absence of a direct attack on American soil, was this conflict being waged in the Eastern Hemisphere truly "America's war"? Why or why not?

3. Though the blame for the attack on Pearl Harbor rests with the Japanese, who is to blame for the success of the attack?

4. Why would the attack on Pearl Harbor produce such a dramatic reversal of American public opinion regarding entry into the Pacific and European conflicts?

Chapter 19

Internment

President Roosevelt Signs Executive Order No. 9066 *February 19, 1942*

The successful attack on the American fleet at Pearl Harbor shocked the American people. This shock was compounded in the days that followed by what appeared to be an unstoppable Japanese advance outward across the Pacific. Guam fell to the Japanese within a week. The British suffered their own "Pearl Harbor" as the Japanese Imperial Navy took out the great battleships H.M.S. *Prince of Wales* and H.M.S. *Repulse* off the Malay Peninsula. Thailand surrendered to Japan. Hong Kong was captured. Manila, the major city of the Philippines, was overrun, and the American and Filipino defenders of the Philippine Islands were forced to retreat to defensive positions on the Bataan Peninsula and on the island fortress of Corregidor. The Gilbert Islands were taken and Wake Island succumbed to Japan's might. Singapore came under attack, as did the oil fields of the Dutch East Indies. All this occurred before the war was even three weeks old.

With the Japanese Imperial forces on the move, Allied forces in retreat across a wide front, and the American fleet damaged and smoldering, what was there to stop a Japanese assault on the Pacific Coast of North America? The thought caused the American people deep anxiety, particularly those on the West Coast.

⌘ *First Impressions*

"A Gangster's Parody of Every Principle of International Honor"

The American fleet at Pearl Harbor had been so formidable, and yet the Japanese victory came at so little loss to the attackers. Could subversion and sabotage explain the ease with which the Japanese planes had moved upon their targets? Had they been guided by the tens of thousands of ethnic Japanese who resided in Hawaii? Many Americans could make sense of the devastation of the "Day of Infamy" in no other way. And from this premise, it was not far to the alarming supposition that the tens of thousands of ethnic Japanese in California, Oregon, Washington, and Alaska were also at work undermining America's West Coast defenses in preparation for the next Japanese assault. The hysteria sparked by Pearl Harbor thus inflamed long-simmering racial animosities and led Franklin Roosevelt to a historical moment the nation would later regret.

Source 1   Editorial, "Death Sentence of a Mad Dog," *Los Angeles Times,* December 8, 1941

Japan has asked for it. Now she is going to get it.

Ten years of honest effort on our part to preserve peace in the Pacific—10 years of insolent trickery and treaty-breaching on hers—came to their simultaneous and grimly appointed ends when the first of friendship-professing Tokyo's bombs fell without warning, literally from the blue, on our ocean outposts at dawn yesterday.

It was the act of a mad dog, a gangster's parody of every principle of international honor—and the self-signed death sentence of a murderous savage among enlightened governments. For its example and inspiration, one need hark back no farther than to the like deeds of Japan's fellow-assassins—Germany when she fell upon peaceful and unsuspecting Denmark, Norway, Holland and Belgium; Italy when she stabbed in the back mortally wounded France in the hope of looting the corpse. . . .

The one respect in which Tokyo's "coup" differs from those of Hitler is that she has attacked no weak and defenseless nation. Instead, she has invited her own destruction by the swiftest and most ruthless means by which it can be compassed. . . .

This is a time for every American to show his colors. It is a time for coolness and courage. It is a time to sink without trace not only the enemy abroad but the enemies within. . . .

Let us not underestimate the strength of our enemy nor ignore the probability that this one piece of trickery is her only one. It is inconceivable that the evident long preparations which Japan has been making for this attack upon us have been confined to the blows already struck. There is every reason to suppose that she has made plans to cripple our counteroffensive in every way possible; against them we must be acutely on our guard at every vulnerable point. It is not alarmism to point out that the Pacific Coast, from the Aleutians to the Canal, is a zone of danger in which alert, keen-eyed civilians can be of yeoman service in co-operating with the military and civil authorities against spies, saboteurs and fifth-columnists. We have thousands of Japanese here and in other Coast cities. Some, perhaps many, are loyal **Nesei**, or good Americans, born and educated as such. What the rest may be we do not know, nor can we take a chance in the light of yesterday's demonstration that treachery and double-dealing are major Japanese weapons. But let there be no precipitation, no riots, no mob law. Panic and confusion, even Jap tactics themselves, serve the enemy. Anything suspicious should be instantly reported to the nearest person in authority. . . .

War is a grim and terrible business. Our losses may be heavy; certainly our sacrifices will be great. But the conflict is not of our seeking. We have gone as far as, in self-respect and honor, we could go to avoid it. We have our quarrel just. With that knowledge we go to war a united nation, with cool heads, stout hearts and an unshakable determination that we shall not cease to fight till right and justice triumph, against whatever odds.

Source 2   "Japanese Aliens Roundup Starts," *Los Angeles Times,* December 8, 1941

A great man hunt was under way last night in Southern California as the Federal Bureau of Investigation agents sought 300 alien Japanese suspected of subversive activities.

19.1 Internment and Evacuation of San Francisco Japanese

As soon as war is declared against Japan, judged a certainty today when Congress meets, 3000 additional Japanese aliens are to be rounded up and placed in protective custody by government agents, the *Times* learned.

During the afternoon and night, close to 200 suspicious Japanese were rounded up by police, deputy sheriffs and special officers working under the direction of F.B.I. agents.

In West Los Angeles 18 were grabbed, 18 were taken into custody at Newton police station, 7 in Hollywood, 4 at Wilshire, between 30 and 40 went through the University station, 4 at Pasadena, 4 at Santa Monica, 3 at Hawthorne, 5 at Ingleside, 30 at Hollenbeck station, and on through the list of Los Angeles police stations and outlying cities.

Raids throughout Los Angeles, San Pedro, El Centro, Pomona, Brea and Newport were carried out last night by police and deputy sheriffs led by F.B.I. agents.

These culminate months of intensive investigation by F.B.I. agents . . . during which time an index file of suspicious Japanese has been collected. . . . Several truck loads of Japanese were seen passing through Brea toward Pomona, Brea police reported, and orders to stop all cars bearing Japanese and to confiscate maps and binoculars or radios were given.

At the time this order was issued, deputy sheriffs and California highway patrolmen were searching a knoll in Carbon Canyon, five miles east of Brea, for six Japanese reportedly seen on the hilltop with binoculars and maps.

Source 3   Lincoln's Birthday radio address of Los Angeles mayor Bowron, February 12, 1942

If Lincoln were alive today, what would he do . . . to defend the nation against the Japanese horde—the people born on American soil who have secret loyalty to the Japanese Empire?

There isn't a shadow of a doubt but that Lincoln, the mild-mannered man whose memory we regard with almost saint-like reverence, would make short work of rounding up the Japanese and putting them where they could do no harm. . . .

The removal of all those of Japanese parentage must be effected before it is too late.

Those little men who prate of civil liberties against the interest of the nation and the safety of the people will be forgotten in the pages of history, while an executive in Washington who will save the nation against invasion and destruction will be entitled to a secure place beside Lincoln.

Source 4   "Rapid Evacuation of Japanese Urged," *Los Angeles Times,*
February 13, 1942

Washington, Feb. 13.—Assured by government authorities here that the Army,
the Navy and agents of the Department of Justice are speedily rounding up all
dangerous enemy aliens along the Pacific Coast, Senators and Representatives
from California, Oregon, and Washington today asked President Roosevelt to
order immediate evacuation from strategic areas of "all persons of Japanese
lineage." . . .

In the recommendation approved and sent to Mr. Roosevelt today, the
President was requested to order "the immediate evacuation of all persons of
Japanese lineage and all others, aliens and citizens alike, whose presence shall
be deemed dangerous or inimical to the defense of the United States from all
strategic areas." . . .

The President was asked to define the strategic areas to be affected by the
evacuation program and to include in his orders military installations, war industries, water and power systems, oil fields and refineries and transportation
facilities.

It was suggested that he make provision for gradual extension of the strategic
areas until Alaska, Washington, Oregon and California should be cleared of citizens
and aliens whose presence might result in sabotage or disloyal acts. . . .

The committee chosen to present the Pacific Coast sabotage issue to the
President consists of Senators Holman of Oregon and Walgren of Washington,
and Representatives Englebright, Lea, Welch and Costello of California, and An-
gell of Washington. . . .

"We are aware of the gravity of asking the President of the United States
to order the evacuation from any area of thousands of men and women who
enjoy the rights of American citizenship," said a committee member, "but we
feel the situation justifies our position and will warrant any action he may take."

Source 5   Recommendation of Lt. General John L. DeWitt, commanding
general, Western Defense Command, to Secretary of War
Henry L. Stimson, February 14, 1942

In the war in which we are now engaged racial affinities are not severed by
migration. The Japanese race is an enemy race and while many second and third
generation Japanese born on United States soil, possessed of United States citizenship, have become "Americanized," the racial strains are undiluted. To conclude otherwise is to expect that children born of white parents on Japanese
soil sever all racial affinity and become loyal Japanese subjects, ready to fight
and, if necessary, to die for Japan in a war against the nation of their parents.
That Japan is allied with Germany and Italy in this struggle is no ground for
assuming that any Japanese, barred from assimilation by convention as he is,
though born and raised in the United States, will not turn against this nation
when the final test of loyalty comes. It, therefore, follows that along the vital
Pacific Coast over 112,000 potential enemies, of Japanese extraction, are at large
today. There are indications that these were organized and ready for concerted

action at a favorable opportunity. The very fact that no sabotage has taken place to date is a disturbing and confirming indication that such action will be taken.

Source 6   "Scores of Farmers Seek Land Evacuated by Jap Aliens," *Los Angeles Times*, February 19, 1942

Scores of American farmers reported to the office of the county agricultural commissioner yesterday seeking information on the ways and means of taking over lands left idle by evacuation of Japanese aliens from prohibited military areas.

Most of the applicants, according to Deputy Commissioner Howard Wilcomb, are either farming now or have had farming experience.

Applications will be taken at 808 N. Spring St. within a day or so, Wilcomb said, when W. S. Rosecrans, agricultural co-ordinator for the Los Angeles County Defense Council, moves his office to that location.

Source 7   Radio address of Los Angeles mayor Bowron, February 19, 1942

Would Americans born in Japan, to say nothing of American citizens residing there, have free access to the harbor of Yokohama and other ports on the Nipponese Island?

Mark you this, if there is a repetition of Pearl Harbor on the Pacific Coast, the responsibility is going to be fixed on somebody's shoulders . . . by the verdict of an enraged American people. . . .

Public opinion has crystallized. The people of California, the American citizens of California, say the Japanese, both alien and American-born, must go.

Source 8   Franklin D. Roosevelt, Executive Order No. 9066, February 19, 1942

WHEREAS the successful prosecution of the war requires every possible protection against espionage and against sabotage to national-defense material, national-defense premises, and national-defense utilities . . . ;

NOW, THEREFORE, by virtue of the authority vested in me as President of the United States, and Commander in Chief of the Army and Navy, I hereby authorize and direct the Secretary of War, and the Military Commanders whom he may from time to time designate, whenever he or any designated Commander deems such action necessary or desirable, to prescribe military areas in such places and of such extent as he or the appropriate Military Commander may determine, from which any or all persons may be excluded, and with respect to which, the right of any person to enter, remain in, or leave shall be subject to whatever restrictions the Secretary of War or the appropriate Military Commander may impose in his discretion. The Secretary of War is hereby authorized to provide for residents of any such area who are excluded therefrom, such transportation, food, shelter, and other accommodations as may be necessary, in the judgment of the Secretary of War or the said Military Commander, and until other arrangements are made, to accomplish the purpose of this order. . . .

I hereby further authorize and direct the Secretary of War and said Military Commander to take such other steps as he or the appropriate Military Commander may deem advisable to enforce compliance with the restrictions applicable to each Military area herein above authorized to be designated, including the use of Federal troops and other Federal Agencies, with authority to accept assistance of state and local agencies.

I hereby further authorize and direct all Executive Departments, independent establishments and other federal Agencies, to assist the Secretary of War or the said Military Commanders in carrying out this Executive Order, including the furnishing of medical aid, hospitalization, food, clothing, transportation, use of land, shelter, and other supplies, equipment, utilities, facilities, and services. . . .

Franklin D. Roosevelt
The White House

A Symptom of Pervasive Racism

19.2 Race and Racism in American Law

Acting upon the Executive Order issued by the president, federal troops first excluded all people of Japanese ancestry from militarily sensitive areas. Then notices were posted requiring all ethnic Japanese, whether citizens of the United States or not, to register themselves with federal authorities. This done, and a registry of all who were even of one-eighth Japanese ancestry compiled, Japanese Americans and resident Japanese aliens were ordered to report with such belongings as they could carry to designated assembly points. From these assembly points they were transported to one of 13 concentration camps, where they remained behind barbed wire and under military guard for more than two years. As individuals, none of the 120,000 people so detained was either accused or convicted of any crime. As a group, they were condemned without trial to imprisonment.

Americans have always thought of themselves as generous in sharing their citizenship and its benefits with newcomers. And generous they were to a point. The Naturalization Act of 1790—the first such legislation in the nation's history—offered immigrants the opportunity to become "naturalized" citizens with all rights and privileges save one: The one right reserved was the constitutionally mandated restriction that only a "natural born" citizen could become president. Generous as it was, however, the Naturalization Act was particular about which aliens would be admitted to citizenship. It specified that an alien wishing to become naturalized must be "a free white person."

The period after the Civil War witnessed a broadening of the basis for citizenship. With the end of slavery, citizenship rights were extended to "persons of African descent." But this extension was interpreted to mean that aliens of Asian ancestry could not be citizens, an interpretation confirmed by the United States Supreme Court. The Fourteenth Amendment to the Constitution, ratified in 1868, bestowed United States and state citizenship upon those born within the country, regardless of the citizenship status of their parents. Thus, ironically, immigrants from Asia would never be allowed American citizenship, but their children would be citizens from birth.

The denial of citizenship to Asian immigrants was a symptom of a pervasive racism that withheld the opportunities of America from those who immigrated to America from across the Pacific. As Asian immigrants began to arrive in numbers on the West Coast beginning in the 1850s, they experienced restrictions on their freedom, their employment possibilities, and their access to justice under American law. Efforts were made to exclude and segregate them. Children of Chinese, Japanese, and other Asian ancestries were not allowed to attend the same schools as the children whose ancestors had immigrated from Europe. The racial segregation of ethnic Japanese children in California schools produced an international incident that threatened to erupt into war between the United States and Japan in the first decade of the twentieth century. Negotiations in 1907 and 1908 eased the tensions somewhat through a "Gentlemen's Agreement": Theodore Roosevelt convinced the city of San Francisco to rescind its order that all children of Japanese descent be congregated at a single school, and the government of Japan agreed to restrict further immigration of its nationals to the United States. But tensions were never eliminated, and discrimination against Japanese Americans and other peoples of Asian descent continued, particularly in the Pacific Coast states where the vast majority of Asian Americans resided.

In 1913, California enacted legislation prohibiting "aliens ineligible to citizenship" from owning farmland in the state. Politically powerless, socially segregated, economically suppressed, and the victims of malicious racial stereotyping, the Japanese Americans were easy prey for the hysteria of wartime.

Source 9   Teru Watanabe, Japanese American evacuee from Los Angeles, describing the events of spring 1942

On May 16, 1942, my mother, two sisters, niece, nephew, and I left . . . by train. Father joined us later. Brother left earlier by bus. We took whatever we could carry. So much we left behind, but the most valuable thing I lost was my freedom.

Source 10   Report of Leonard Abrams, American serviceman assigned to the Santa Anita Race Track, an assembly point for Japanese American evacuees, spring 1942

We were put on full alert one day, issued full belts of live ammunition, and went to the Santa Anita Race Track. There we formed part of a cordon of troops leading into the grounds; buses kept arriving and many people walked along . . . many weeping or simply dazed, or bewildered by our formidable ranks.

19.3 Japanese American Internment: Santa Clara Valley

Source 11   Account of William Kochiyama, Japanese American evacuee, spring 1942

At the entrance . . . stood two lines of troops with rifles and fixed bayonets pointed at the evacuees as they walked between the soldiers to the prison compound. Overwhelmed with bitterness and blind with rage, I screamed every obscenity I knew at the armed guards, daring them to shoot me.

Source 12   Shizuko S. Tokushige, Japanese American evacuee,
           spring 1942

At Parker, Arizona, we were transferred to buses. With baggage and car-ryalls hanging from my arms, I was contemplating what I could leave behind, since my husband was not allowed to come to my aid. A soldier said, "Let me help you, put your arm out." He proceeded to pile everything on my arm. And to my horror, he placed my two-month-old baby on top of the stack. He then pushed me with the butt of the gun and told me to get off the train, knowing when I stepped off the train my baby would fall to the ground. I refused. But he kept prodding and ordering me to move. I will always be thankful [that] a lieutenant checking the cars came upon us. He took the baby down, gave her to me, and then ordered the soldier to carry all our belongings to the bus and see that I was seated and then report back to him.

Source 13   George Kasai, Japanese American evacuee, spring 1942

When we finally reached our destination, four of us men were ordered by the military personnel carrying guns to follow them. We were directed to unload the pile of evacuees' belongings from the boxcars to the semi-trailer truck to be transported to the concentration camp. During the interim, after filling one trailer-truck and waiting for the next to arrive, we were hot and sweaty and sitting, trying to conserve our energy, when one of the military guards, standing with his gun, suggested that one of us should get a drink of water at a nearby water faucet and try and make a run for it so he could get some target practice.

Source 14   Gladys Bell, member of the administrative staff at Camp
           Topaz in central Utah, summer 1942

[T]he evacuees . . . had only one room, unless there were around 10 in the family. Their rooms had a pot-bellied stove, a single electric light hanging from the ceiling, an Army cot for each person and a blanket for the bed. Each barrack had six rooms with only three flues. This meant that a hole had to be cut through the wall of one room for the stovepipe to join the chimney of the next room. The hole was large so that the wall would not burn. As a result, everything said and some things whispered were easily heard by people living in the next room.

Source 15   Assistant Secretary of State Breckinridge Long, memorandum
           to Cordell Hull, December 17, 1943

I have appeared before two committees of the Senate where the subject has been discussed and I may say where an avid interest in the future of the Japanese in the United States has been manifested. Legislation will be needed if any large-scale operation is desired—and a large-scale operation to get them out of the United States seems to be the hope of the members of those committees.

The problem has been complicated by our laws relating to citizenship and by the constitutional provision regarding the native-born character of the citizenship of those born here. The Attorney General is reported to have said recently to one of the Committees that he had a formula under one of our statutes by which native-born Japanese or one naturalized could be divested of his American citizenship—thus making him eligible for deportation. However, there has been no official ruling by the Attorney General on this point.

I think the far larger part of official sentiment is to do something so we can get rid of these people when the war is over—obviously we cannot while the war continues.

But sentiment is liable to wane if the authorization measures are not adopted before the war ends.

We have 110,000 of them in confinement here now—and that is a lot of Japs to contend with in postwar days, particularly as the West Coast localities where they once lived do not desire their return.

Source 16 Supreme Court justice Hugo Black, writing the majority opinion in *Korematsu v. United States of America,* October 1944

[The Court's 6–3 decision upheld the constitutionality of Executive Order 9066 and the conviction of Fred T. Korematsu.]

The petitioner, an American of Japanese descent, was convicted in a Federal district court for remaining in San Leandro, California, a "Military Area," contrary to Civilian Exclusion Order No. 34 of the Commanding General of the Western Command, U.S. Army, which directed that after May 9, 1942, all persons of Japanese ancestry should be excluded from that area. No question was raised as to the petitioner's loyalty to the United States. . . .

It should be noted, to begin with, that all legal restrictions which curtail the civil rights of a single racial group are immediately suspect. That is not to say that all such restrictions are unconstitutional. It is to say that courts must subject them to the most rigid scrutiny. Pressing public necessity may sometimes justify the existence of such restrictions; racial antagonism never can. . . .

Exclusion Order No. 34, which petitioner knowingly and admittedly violated, was one of a number of military orders and proclamations, all of which were substantially based upon Executive Order 9066. . . .

We uphold the exclusion order as of the time it was made and when the petitioner violated it. In doing so, we are not unmindful of the hardships imposed by it upon a large group of American citizens. But hardships are a part of war, and war is an aggregation of hardships. All citizens alike, both in and out of uniform, feel the impact of war in greater or lesser measure. Citizenship has its responsibilities as well as its privileges, and in time of war the burden is always heavier. Compulsory exclusion of large groups of citizens from their homes, except under circumstances of direst emergency and peril, is inconsistent with our basic governmental form. But when under conditions of modern warfare our shores are threatened by hostile forces, the power to protect must be commensurate with the threatened danger. . . .

It is said that we are dealing here with the case of imprisonment of a citizen in a concentration camp solely because of his ancestry, without evidence or inquiry concerning his loyalty and good disposition towards the United States.

Our task would be simple, our duty clear, were this a case involving the imprisonment of a loyal citizen in a concentration camp because of racial prejudice. To cast this case into outlines of racial prejudice, without reference to the real military dangers which were presented, merely confuses the issue. Korematsu was not excluded from the military area because of hostility to him or his race. He was excluded because we are at war with the Japanese Empire, because the properly constituted military authorities feared an invasion of our West Coast and felt constrained to take proper security measures, because they decided that the military urgency of the situation demanded that all citizens of Japanese ancestry be segregated from the West Coast temporarily, and finally, because Congress, reposing its confidence in this time of war in our military leaders—as it inevitably must—determined that they should have the power to do this.

Source 17 Supreme Court justice Owen Roberts, dissenting opinion, *Korematsu v. United States of America*

I dissent, because I think the indisputable facts exhibit a clear violation of Constitutional rights. . . . [I]t is a case of convicting a citizen as a punishment for not submitting to imprisonment in a concentration camp, based on his ancestry, and solely because of his ancestry, without evidence or inquiry concerning his loyalty and good disposition towards the United States.

Source 18 Hatsuye Egami, "Wartime Diary," 1944

In a camp, it can be said that food, above all things, is the center and the pleasure of life. It's natural to want to eat something good. I cannot help thinking about the old men standing with plates in their hands. Residents in America for forty or fifty years, they pursued gigantic dreams and crossed an expansive ocean to America to live. The soil they tilled was a mother to them, and their life was regulated by the sun. They were people who had worked with all they had, until on their foreheads wave-like furrows were harrowed. Everytime I see these oldsters with resigned, peaceful expressions meekly eating what is offered them, I feel my eyes become warm.

 ## *Second Thoughts*
A Sorry Episode in American History

Japanese Americans remained in the internment camps until December 1944. Internment caused them psychological and physical suffering. It cost them their homes, their businesses, and their farms as well as their freedom. It disrupted careers and damaged reputations. Nevertheless, despite the suffering they endured at the hands of their own government, 17,000 Japanese Americans, recruited largely from the internment camps, were enlisted into the United States Army. These "Nisei" troops, ultimately organized as the 442nd Regimental Combat Team, were among the most decorated American soldiers of World War II.

Source 19 T. Harry Williams, Richard Current, and Frank Freidel,
  A History of the United States, 1961

On the Pacific Coast, hatred of Americans of Japanese background became extreme. Wild stories circulated about sabotage at Pearl Harbor—later proven 100 per cent untrue. As sandbags were piled around Pacific Coast telephone offices, and **barrage** balloons were raised over shipyards, fear of Japanese-American espionage and sabotage became intense. Under public pressure, Roosevelt authorized the army to remove all people of Japanese ancestry. Some 117,000 people, two-thirds of them United States citizens . . . suffered the financial loss of at least 40 per cent of their possessions and for several years were barred from lucrative employment. Yet Japanese-Americans in Hawaii were left unmolested without incident throughout the war.

Source 20 James MacGregor Burns, *Roosevelt: The Soldier of Freedom,* 1970

During these weeks of stinging defeat the President ratified an action that was widely accepted at the time but came to be viewed in later years as one of the sorriest episodes in American history. This was the uprooting of tens of thousands of Japanese-Americans from their homes on the West Coast and their incarceration in concentration camps hundreds of miles away. . . .

It was the old story of a determined and vocal minority group of regional politicians and spokesmen with a definite plan united against an array of federal officials who were divided, irresolute, and not committed against racism. Hindsight would prove that there was little military necessity for mass evacuation. Hindsight would also put responsibility not only on the obvious factors of racism and frustration, but also on a great negative factor—the opposition never showed up. The liberal dailies and weeklies were largely silent. Only a strong civil-libertarian President could have faced down all these forces, and Roosevelt was not a strong civil libertarian.

Source 21 Sociologist Harry H. L. Kitano, *Race Relations,* 1974

The necessary conditions for placing groups behind barbed wire (or for more severe actions, such as extermination and genocide) are shaped by prior events, especially by prejudice, discrimination, and segregation. Prejudice, usually maintained by stereotyping, leads to the avoidance of a group; discrimination and segregation, maintained by laws, customs, and norms fosters disadvantage and isolation. For a group so cut off, stereotypes become the operating reality since there is no way of effectively correcting the biased information. If certain "incidents" crystallize the already negative sentiments, more permanent solutions (concentration camps, exile, isolation, and extermination) may be instituted.

For example, prior to 1954, the **Issei** could not become U.S. citizens; therefore certain basic civil rights had never been a part of their expectations: they were the targets of stereotyping and legal harassment. Issei could neither vote nor freely own land; nuisance laws prevented them from employing white girls and the prices of their California state fishing licenses were set deliberately high. Antimiscegenation laws discouraged the Issei from believing that they were equal to the white man. Stereotyped as less than human, and placed at a comparative disadvantage by laws and customs, they were limited in their opportunities for any kind of equal status contact.

The Nisei had been segregated into Little Tokyos and Osakas, usually in the older and less desirable areas of the cities. These Japanese communities were able to maintain effective social control over their members, and there were none of the usual signs of social disorganization such as high rates of crime and delinquency.

However, segregated ethnic groups lack any equal-access contact and are subject to ethnic stereotypes on the part of the dominant group. The problem is not solely with dominant group perceptions; other minorities may see the stereotypes as the reality, and even members of the target group may turn on each other—those with the "desired" qualities (e.g., who are more acculturated) may reject their peers. As a consequence, target minorities often find themselves stereotyped, isolated, avoided, and fighting among themselves. The Japanese in the United States at the time of Pearl Harbor were victims of all of the boundary-maintenance mechanisms; the Filipinos, Chinese, and Koreans had turned against them; most of the majority group thought in terms of the stereotype of the "sly, sneaky, tricky, Jap"; and politicians and journalists played upon popular anti-Japanese sentiments. The group itself was divided by generation (**Issei, Nisei, Kibei**) and by American and Japanese loyalties. Therefore, they were ripe for the events that followed the attack on Pearl Harbor. . . .

Immediately after December 7, 1941, the FBI rounded up selected enemy aliens, including 2,192 Japanese. Even this roundup, which was logical enough at the time, had its ludicrous moments. The arrested were those who had contributed money to Japan, who had achieved some degree of prominence, or who belonged to certain organizations. My father was taken away initially on the charge of possessing illegal contraband—which turned out to be several flashlights and a knife.

Source 22 President Gerald R. Ford, "Remarks upon Signing a Proclamation concerning Japanese-American Internment during World War II," February 19, 1976

February 19 is the anniversary of a very, very sad day in American history. It was on that date in 1942 that Executive Order 9066 was issued resulting in the uprooting of many, many loyal Americans. . . .

We now know what we should have known then—not only was that evacuation wrong but Japanese-Americans were and are loyal Americans. On the battlefield and at home the names of Japanese-Americans have been and continue to be written in America's history for the sacrifices and the contributions they have made to the well-being and to the security of this, our common Nation.

Executive Order 9066 ceased to be effective at the end of World War II. Because there was no formal statement of its termination, there remains some concern among Japanese-Americans that there yet may be some life in that obsolete document. This proclamation [4417] that I am signing here today should remove all doubt on that matter.

I call upon the American people to affirm with me the unhyphenated American promise that we have learned from the tragedy of that long ago experience—forever to treasure liberty and justice for each American and resolve that this kind of error shall never be made again.

Source 23 Michi Nishiura Weglyn, *Years of Infamy: The Untold Story of America's Concentration Camps,* 1976

Had the President, having perceived the racist character of the American public, deliberately acquiesced to the clearly punitive action knowing it would be rousingly effective for the flagging home-front morale?

Or could factors other than political expediency, perhaps a more critical wartime exigency, have entered into and inspired the sudden decision calling for mass action—made as it was at a time when the allied cause in the Pacific was plummeting, one reversal following another in seemingly endless succession?

A bit of personal conjecture: Shocked and mortified by the unexpected skill and tenacity of the foe (as the Administration might have been), with America's very survival in jeopardy, what could better insure the more considerate treatment of American captives, the unknown thousands then being trapped daily in the islands and territories falling to the enemy like dominoes, than a substantial *hostage reserve*? And would not a readily available *reprisal reserve* prove crucial should America's war fortune continue to crumble: should the scare propaganda of "imminent invasion" become an actual, living nightmare of rampaging hordes of yellow "barbarians" overrunning and making "free fire zones" of American villages and hamlets—looting, raping, murdering, slaughtering. . . . Within two months after the crippling blow dealt by the Japanese at Pearl Harbor, a fast-deteriorating situation in the soon untenable Philippine campaign moved [Secretary of War] Stimson to call for threats of reprisals on Japanese nationals in America "to insure proper treatment" of U.S. citizens trapped in enemy territory. On February 5, the very day when mass evacuation-internment plans began to be drawn up and formalized within the War Department, Stimson wrote [Secretary of State] Hull:

> General MacArthur has reported in a radiogram that American and British civilians in areas of the Philippines occupied by the Japanese are being subjected to extremely harsh treatment. The unnecessary harsh and rigid measures imposed, in sharp contrast to the moderate treatment of metropolitan Filipinos, are unquestionably designed to discredit the white race.
> I request that you strongly protest this unjustified treatment of civilians, and suggest that you present a threat of reprisals against the many Japanese nationals now enjoying negligible restrictions in the United States, to insure proper treatment of our nationals in the Philippines.

If a reprisal reserve urgency had indeed precipitated the sudden decision for internment, the emphasis, as the tide of the war reversed itself, switched to a buildup of a "barter reserve": one sizable enough to allow for the earliest possible repatriation of American detainees.

Source 24 Commission on Wartime Relocation and Internment of Civilians, an investigative panel appointed by the U.S. Congress, *Personal Justice Denied,* Part 1, 1983

The policy of exclusion, removal and detention was executed against 120,000 people without individual review, and exclusion was continued virtually without regard for their demonstrated loyalty to the United States. Congress was fully aware of and supported the policy of removal and detention; it sanctioned the exclusion by enacting a statute which made criminal the violation of orders issued pursuant to Executive Order 9066. The United States Supreme Court held the exclusion constitutionally permissible in the context of war. . . .

All this was done despite the fact that not a single documented act of espionage, sabotage or fifth column activity was committed by an American citizen of Japanese ancestry or by a resident Japanese alien on the West Coast.

No mass exclusion or detention, in any part of the country, was ordered against American citizens of German or Italian descent. Official actions against enemy aliens of other nationalities were much more individualized and selective than those imposed on the ethnic Japanese. . . .

After the tide of war turned with the American victory at Midway in June 1942, the possibility of serious Japanese attack was no longer credible; detention and exclusion became increasingly difficult to defend. Nevertheless, other than an ineffective leave program run by the War Relocation Authority, the government had no plans to remedy the situation and no means of distinguishing the loyal from the disloyal. Total control of these civilians in the presumed interest of state security was rapidly becoming the accepted norm.

Determining the basis on which detention would be ended required the government to focus on the justification for controlling the ethnic Japanese. If the government took the position that race determined loyalty or that it was impossible to distinguish the loyal from the disloyal because "Japanese" patterns of thought and behavior were too alien to white Americans, there would be little incentive to end detention. If the government maintained the position that distinguishing the loyal from the disloyal was possible and that exclusion and detention were required only by the necessity of acting quickly under the threat of Japanese attack in early 1942, then a program to release those considered loyal should have been instituted in the spring of 1942 when people were confined in the assembly centers.

Neither position prevailed. General DeWitt and the Western Defense Command took the first position and opposed any review that would determine loyalty or threaten continued exclusion from the West Coast. Secretary Stimson and Assistant Secretary McCloy took the second view, but did not act on it until the end of 1942 and then only in a limited manner. . . .

The loyalty review should have led to the conclusion that no justification existed for excluding loyal Americans from the West Coast. Secretary Stimson, Assistant Secretary McCloy and General Marshall reached this position in the spring of 1943. Nevertheless, the exclusion was not ended until December 1944. No plausible reason connected to any wartime security has been offered for this eighteen to twenty month delay in allowing the ethnic Japanese to return to their homes, jobs and businesses on the West Coast, despite the fact that the delay meant, as a practical matter, that confinement in the relocation camps continued for the great majority of evacuees for another year and a half.

Between May 1943 and May 1944, War Department officials did not make public their opinion that exclusion of loyal ethnic Japanese . . . no longer had any military justification. If the President was unaware of this view, the plausible explanation is that Secretary Stimson and Assistant Secretary McCloy were unwilling, or believed themselves unable, to face down political opposition on the West Coast. . . .

In May 1944 Secretary Stimson put before President Roosevelt and the Cabinet his position that the exclusion no longer had a military justification. But the President was unwilling to act to end the exclusion until the first Cabinet meeting following the Presidential election of November 1944. The inescapable conclusion from this factual pattern is that the delay was motivated by political considerations. . . .

The promulgation of Executive Order 9066 was not justified by military necessity, and the decisions which followed from it—detention, ending detention, ending exclusion—were not driven by analysis of military conditions. The broad historical causes which shaped these decisions were race prejudice, war hysteria and a failure of political leadership. Widespread ignorance of Japanese Americans contributed to a policy conceived in haste and executed in an atmosphere of fear and anger at Japan. A grave injustice was done to American citizens and resident aliens of Japanese ancestry who, without individual review or any probative evidence against them, were excluded, removed and detained by the United States during World War II.

Source 25 Editorial, "Final Payment for Japanese Internees," *New York Times,* April 26, 1988

Congress is about to pass a bill offering token payments and apologies to Japanese-Americans interned during World War II. But President Reagan is said to be uncertain about signing it. Not to do so would interrupt justice for all. This legislation responds to the needs of the victims, and to the nation's need to make amends.

The internment was a panicked response to the Japanese attack on Pearl Harbor in December 1941. President Franklin Roosevelt accepted the idea that Japanese-Americans might constitute a serious risk on the West Coast, where many of them lived.

Ultimately about 120,000—most of them U.S. citizens—were rounded up and sent to relocation camps where many lived under guard for the duration of the war. About half of those interned are still alive. Some recall having to abandon homes, possessions and businesses on a few hours' notice. After the war, some were able to recover their property. In 1948, Congress approved paying $37 million to settle 26,000 claims. But to date, nothing formal has been done to address the sense of grievance that has understandably weighed on so many internees through the years. The legislation about to emerge from Congress does just that. It offers a $20,000 payment to each actual victim of internment, along with a formal apology on behalf of the nation.

Opposition centers on cost: $1.3 billion in the Senate version, to be paid out over five years. Some opponents say that an apology alone ought to be sufficient, that adding cash somehow demeans it. But the apology ought to involve more than words on paper. Given the damage inflicted, $20,000 amounts to minimal compensation for pain and suffering. In any case, recipients of the offer may accept or reject it as they choose.

This long-overdue law constitutes an act of decency that would honor the President who signs it.

Source 26   Congress of the United States, Public Law 100-383, Sec. 2(a), August 10, 1988

The Congress recognizes that, as described by the Commission on Wartime Relocation and Internment of Civilians, a grave injustice was done to both citizens and permanent resident aliens of Japanese ancestry by the evacuation, relocation, and internment of civilians during World War II. As the Commission documents, these actions were carried out without adequate security reasons and without any acts of espionage and sabotage documented by the Commission, and were motivated largely by racial prejudice, wartime hysteria, and a failure of political leadership. The excluded individuals of Japanese ancestry suffered enormous damages, both material and intangible, and there were incalculable losses in education and job training, all of which resulted in significant human suffering for which appropriate compensation has not been made. For these fundamental violations of the basic civil liberties and constitutional rights of these individuals of Japanese ancestry, the Congress apologizes on behalf of the Nation.

Source 27   John Hersey, "Behind Barbed Wire," *New York Times Magazine*, September 11, 1988

The United States had declared war on Germany and Italy, as well as Japan, but no German or Italian enemy aliens, to say nothing of German-Americans or Italian-Americans, were subjected to these blanket Exclusion Orders. Only "Japanese aliens and non-aliens," as the official euphemism put it.

Each person who responded to the summons had to register the names of all family members and was told to show up at a certain time and place, a few days later, with all of them, bringing along only such baggage as they could carry by hand—for a trip to a destination unknown. Names had become numbers.

"Henry went to the control station to register the family," wrote a Japanese-American woman years later. "He came home with twenty tags, all numbered 10710, tags to be attached to each piece of baggage, and one to hang from our coat lapels. From then on, we were known as Family No. 10710." "I lost my identity," another woman would assert, describing the replacement of her name by a number. "I lost my privacy and dignity."

There followed a period of devastating uncertainty and anxiety. "We were given eight days to liquidate our possessions," one of the evacuees testified at an investigation by the Department of Justice many years later. The time allowed varied from place to place. "We had about two weeks," another recalled, "to do something. Either lease the property or sell everything." Another: "While in Modesto, the final notice came with a four day notice." Under the circumstances, the evacuees had to dispose of their businesses, their homes, and their personal possessions at panic prices to hostile buyers.

"It is difficult," one man would later testify, "to describe the feeling of despair and humiliation experienced by all of us as we watched the Caucasians coming to look over our possessions and offering such nominal amounts, knowing we had no recourse but to accept whatever they were offering because we did not know what the future held for us." One woman sold a 37-room hotel for $300. A man who owned a pickup truck, and had just bought a set of tires and a new battery for $125, asked only that amount of a prospective buyer. "The man 'bought' our pickup for $25." One homeowner, in despair, wanted to burn his house down. "I went to the storage shed to get the gasoline tank and pour the gasoline on my house, but my wife . . . said don't do it, maybe somebody can use this house; we are civilized people, not savages."

By far the greatest number of Nisei—the term for first-generation Japanese-Americans that came to be used as the generic word for all ethnic Japanese living in America—were in agriculture, growing fruit, vegetables, nursery plants and specialty plants. They had worked wonders in the soil. They owned about one-fiftieth of the arable land in the three Pacific Coast states, and what they had made of their farms is suggested by the fact that the average value per acre of all farms in the three states in 1940 was roughly $38, while an acre on a Nisei farm was worth, on average, $280.

But now the farmers had to clear out in a matter of days. The Mother's Day crop of flowers, the richest harvest of the year, was about to be gathered; it had to be abandoned. An owner of one of the largest nurseries in southern California, unable to dispose of his stock, gave it all to the Veterans Hospital adjoining his land. A strawberry grower asked for a deferral of his evacuation summons for a few days, so he could harvest his crop. Denied the permission, he bitterly plowed the berries under. The next day, the Federal Bureau of Investigation charged him with an act of sabotage and put him in jail. . . .

On the day of departure, evacuees found themselves herded into groups of 500, mostly at railroad and bus stations. They wore their numbered tags and carried hand-baggage containing possessions that they had packed in fear and perplexity, not knowing where they were going. They embarked on buses and trains. . . .

Each group was unloaded, after its trip, at one of 16 assembly centers, most of which were located at fairgrounds and racetracks. There, seeing barbed wire and searchlights, and under the guard of guns, these "aliens and non-aliens" were forced to realize that all among them—even those who had sons or brothers in the United States Army—were considered to be dangerous people. . . .

Toward the end of May 1942, evacuees began to be transferred from these temporary assembly centers to 13 permanent concentration camps—generally called by the more decorous name of "relocation centers"—where they would be held prisoner until several months before the end of the war. By Nov. 1, some 106,770 internees had been put behind barbed wire in six western states and Arkansas.

Thus began the bitterest national shame of the Second World War for the sweet land of liberty: the mass incarceration, on racial grounds alone, on false evidence of military necessity, and in contempt of their supposedly inalienable rights, of an entire class of American citizens.

Source 28   Roger Daniels, *Prisoners without Trial: Japanese Americans in World War II*, 1993

Once characterized as "our worst mistake," this was neither a mistake nor an error in judgment nor an inadvertence. The wartime abuse of Japanese Americans, it is now clear, was merely a link in a chain of racism that stretched back to the earliest contacts between Asians and whites on American soil. . . .

The reasons for the establishment of these concentration camps are clear. A deteriorating military situation created the opportunity for American racists to get their views accepted by the national leadership. The Constitution was treated as a scrap of paper not only by [Assistant Secretary of War John J.] McCloy, [Secretary of War Henry L.] Stimson, and Roosevelt, but also by the entire Congress, which approved and implemented everything done to the Japanese Americans, and by the Supreme Court of the United States, which in December 1944, nearly three years after the fact, in effect sanctioned the incarceration of the Japanese Americans.

The Court has always held that the "war power" and the right of national defense could stretch the limits of federal authority, and Roosevelt and the lawyers in the War Department who drafted Executive Order 9066 appealed to that power. But was there a "military necessity" for EO 9066? . . . [T]he general staff officer charged with assessing the West Coast situation did not think so, and the army's G-2 [intelligence] reported to General Marshall, on the very day Roosevelt signed the order, that its analysts believed that "mass evacuation [was] unnecessary." The decision made was not military but political: the general staff was not asked for its opinion, and its official recommendations were ignored. When the cases testing the constitutionality of the actions taken against the Japanese Americans came before the Supreme Court in 1943 and 1944, the War and Justice Departments not only suppressed this evidence but also . . . deliberately presented false reports of subversion to the Court.

Perhaps the best way to appreciate the difference between real and fictitious military necessity is to contrast the way in which the federal government treated the Japanese on the West Coast and the Japanese in Hawaii. On the West Coast, despite the continuing panic . . . , there had been only desultory and largely harmless shellings by two Japanese submarines. Hawaii had been severely bombed and seemed vulnerable to further attack. In California, Japanese of all generations constituted some 2 percent of the population, whereas in Hawaii every third person was of Japanese ethnicity. Yet in Hawaii there was only minimal incarceration of Japanese: out of a population of some 150,000, fewer than 1,500 persons were confined. And when, throughout the first few months of the war, politicians—most persistently, Secretary of the Navy Knox—called for mass incarceration in Hawaii, the nation's highest military commanders successfully resisted the pressure, not because of any concern for the civil rights of the Hawaiian Japanese, but because Japanese labor was crucial to both the civilian and the military economies in Hawaii.

Questioning the Past

1. Present the arguments for the internment of Japanese aliens and Americans of Japanese descent during World War II. Present the arguments against such internment. Which position is the more persuasive in the context of 1942? Which is the more persuasive today?

2. Does a reading of Executive Order No. 9066 betray its intent? Why would the wording be so circumlocutionary?

3. General DeWitt concluded his recommendation to Secretary Stimson, dated February 14, 1942, with the assertion regarding the threat of Japanese American sabotage that "The very fact that no sabotage has taken place to date is a disturbing and confirming indication that such action will be taken." Explain and evaluate the general's reasoning.

4. Why were Japanese Americans interned during World War II?

5. In 1988, Congress passed and President Reagan signed into law an apology for internment accompanied by an offer of $20,000 to each victim of internment in compensation for the suffering and deprivation inflicted by EO 9066. Is this an equitable conclusion to the internment issue?

6. What constitutional guarantees, if any, were violated by internment?

7. T. Harry Williams *et al.* wrote that internment "represented a serious erosion of civilian rights, since the Supreme Court in 1944 validated the evacuation, and in other decisions upheld military control over civilians. In time of war or national emergency, United States citizens could expect no court protection of their civil rights from military or executive authority." Discuss this point. Should constitutional guarantees apply equally in wartime and peacetime?

Chapter **20**

Hiroshima

The United States Drops an Atomic Bomb on Japan *August 6, 1945*

20.1 Atomic
Bomb: Decision

A single American aircraft flew six miles above the Japanese city of Hiroshima early on the morning of August 6, 1945. The people of the city gave the plane little notice, since they had grown accustomed to the appearance of a weather plane around 8 o'clock every morning. But this morning, the aircraft above them was no weather plane. It was a B-29, nicknamed the *Enola Gay,* and at 8:15, the American bombardier aboard this plane released the first atomic bomb ever dropped on a human population. The bomb detonated 2,000 feet above the central city with an explosive force equal to 14,000 tons of TNT. It was the beginning of a new age in history.

First Impressions
Weapons of Terrifying Destructiveness

Within a few days, reporters from outside Hiroshima were able to describe how thoroughly the city had been demolished; only three buildings remained. But the full extent of the devastation wrought by the atomic bomb on its human victims would not be clear for several years.

Source 1   Account of a Hiroshima resident, Aikono, August 6, 1945

I looked skyward as I heard the droning of an airplane and saw a black spot floating. At this instant, the spot shed blue and red lights like lightning. No sooner had I become dizzy, than a scorching heat struck my body.

Source 2   Account of a Hiroshima visitor, Seiichi Miyata, August 6, 1945

When the enemy **superforts** appeared over the city, I was at a hotel some kilometers from the central section. First I heard the faint roaring of a plane flying at a high altitude, so my friend and I realized that a B-29 was approaching. I went to one of the windows facing south, and my friend to the opposite side, and looked up at the sky. The roaring in the meantime stopped and suddenly a dazzling flash as bright as the flash of light used when taking photographs covered the whole area. Then in no time, I felt a hot pressure, which was immediately followed by a deafening detonation. My friend and I rushed into the room and flung ourselves flat on the floor. My friend got burnt in the corner of one of his eyes. Fortunately I was safe. . . .

Later, walking around the streets, I saw that most of the wooden buildings had been demolished, the glass windows of concrete buildings broken, and furniture thrown here and there. At a certain national school, children, who had been doing physical exercises in the open without much clothes on them, suffered severe burns. The skin was torn off, and they were in agony, though the scorched parts were not bleeding much. Some of them were suffering from water blisters. Most of the city residents who had the misfortune of being near the area where the bombs were dropped suffered from burns much more than from other wounds.

Source 3 Account of a young woman aboard a Hiroshima trolley, August 6, 1945

At that moment my eyes were suddenly blinded by a flash of piercing light and the neighborhood was enveloped in dense smoke of a yellow color like poison gas. Instantly everything became pitch dark, and you couldn't see an inch ahead. Then a heavy and tremendously loud roar. The inside of my mouth was gritty as though I had eaten sand and my throat hurt. I looked toward the east, and I saw an enormous black pillar of cloud billowing upward. "It's all over now," I thought.

20.2 Outline of Atomic Bomb Damage in Hiroshima

The End of World War II

Lightened by the release of its 10,000-pound payload, the *Enola Gay* surged upward and the pilot had to take the plane into a steep dive to return to the original altitude. Simultaneously, the B-29 banked sharply to the right, and the tail gunner was able to watch the atomic bomb fall toward Hiroshima. It fell for 43 seconds before detonating. As it did, a bright light filled the plane and the tail gunner, still looking at the point of detonation, observed that it was a "bubbling mass of purple-gray smoke, and you could see it had a red core to it and everything was burning inside." What he did not know was that the temperature at the center of Hiroshima at that moment had reached 300,000 degrees centigrade.

In an instant, somewhere between 75,000 and 175,000 men, women, and children ceased to exist. An exact total can never be known, since many people were simply vaporized in the blast, leaving no bodies to count or bury. Seventy-five percent of the structures in the city—about 90,000 buildings—were destroyed, and few of the structures that did survive were habitable. Fires burned out of control all over the city.

The atomic bomb was the closing curtain on a war that was forced upon the United States by the Japanese air attack on Pearl Harbor in December of 1941. The bomb itself was the product of one of the most impressive and secretive scientific research programs of all history. Concerned that the Germans were engaged in a program to develop weaponry by tapping the power of nuclear fission, President Roosevelt assembled a team of American and British scientists in 1941 to begin work on an American bomb.

Germany surrendered on May 8, 1945, without having solved the mystery of atomic weaponry, but the United States tested an atomic bomb in the New Mexican desert on July 16, 1945. President Truman later described the successful American atomic research project as the "greatest achievement of organized science in history."

By the time the American arsenal was strengthened by the addition of the atomic bomb, the end of World War II was already in sight. Mussolini and the Italian Fascists were defeated. Hitler was dead and Germany was occupied by American and Soviet forces. The only enemy still on the field of battle was Japan. The nearly four years of bitter warfare in the Pacific had, however, pushed back the frontiers of the Japanese Empire and left the Japanese forces in a defensive stance on their main islands.

With the European phase of the war successfully concluded, the Allies by the summer of 1945 were preparing to turn their full might against Japan. The Soviet Union, which had taken no part in the Pacific theatre of the war, had pledged to declare war on Japan 90 days after the close of conflict on the European front, which was August 8.

The leaders of the Allied Powers—The United States, Britain, France, China, and the Soviet Union—held a summit conference at Potsdam in July of 1945 and issued an ultimatum to Japan demanding immediate surrender. The ultimatum concluded with the threat that a failure to surrender unconditionally would result in the "prompt and utter destruction" of Japan.

Source 4   Statement of President Harry Truman, August 6, 1945

Sixteen hours ago an American airplane dropped one bomb on Hiroshima, an important Japanese army base. That bomb had more than 20,000 tons of T.N.T. It had more than two thousand times the blast power of the British "Grand Slam," which is the largest bomb ever yet used in the history of warfare.

The Japanese began the war from the air at Pearl Harbor. They have been repaid many fold. And the end is not yet. With this bomb we have now added a new and revolutionary increase in destruction to supplement the growing power of our armed forces. In their present form these bombs are now in production and even more powerful forms are in development.

It is an atomic bomb. It is a harnessing of the basic power of the universe. The force from which the sun draws its power has been loosed against those who brought war to the Far East. . . .

We are now prepared to obliterate more rapidly and completely every productive enterprise the Japanese have above ground in any city. We shall destroy their docks, their factories, and their communications. Let there be no mistake; we shall completely destroy Japan's power to make war.

It was to spare the Japanese people from utter destruction that the ultimatum of July 26 was issued at Potsdam. Their leaders promptly rejected that ultimatum. If they do not now accept our terms they can expect a rain of ruin from the air, the like of which has never been seen on this earth.

Source 5   Editorial, *The Times* of London, August 8, 1945

DARKNESS OVER HIROSHIMA

An impenetrable cloud of dust and smoke, standing over the ruin of the great Japanese arsenal at Hiroshima, still veils the undoubtedly stupendous destruction wrought by the first impact in war of the atomic bomb. A mist no less impenetrable is likely for a long time to conceal the full significance in human affairs of the release of the vast and mysterious power hitherto locked within the infinitesimal units of which the material structure of the universe is built up. All that can be said with certainty is that the world stands in the presence of a revolution in earthly affairs. . . .

Speculation can only peer a little way into the future that the new power opens for the world. The issue of the Japanese war, already certain, must be greatly hastened, whether the rulers of Tokyo acknowledge by surrender the demonstration that the allies hold them in the hollow of their hand, or insist on immolating their country before the irresistible power of the new weapon. . . . If they choose the second alternative, it seems likely that the Allies may be able to accomplish . . . the destruction of Japanese resistance in the home islands by air power alone, leaving to the army the role of occupation only. Beyond the Japanese war the consequences for strategy and grand tactics are vast but incalculable. Presumably all fortification, as it has been hitherto understood, becomes immediately obsolete: for nothing can resist the new force. Schemes for world security founded upon the maintenance of bases at the strategic points of the globe will call for exhaustive reconsideration.

All strategic calculation, however, becomes insignificant before the evident challenge to the people of the world to rise to the fateful occasion in such degree as to make strategy itself speedily irrelevant. Beyond all doubt, unless atomic power is turned to serve the aims of peace, it can speedily make an end of civilized life on earth.

Source 6   Text of President Truman's press conference, 3:00 P.M., August 8, 1945

I have only a simple announcement to make. I can't hold a regular press conference today; but this announcement is so important I thought I would call you in.

Russia has declared war on Japan! That is *all!* [Much applause and laughter, as the reporters raced out.]

Source 7   President Truman's "Radio Report to the American People on the Potsdam Conference," August 9, 1945

[A second atomic bomb was dropped on Nagasaki, Japan, killing some 80,000 people, on this date.]

Having found the atomic bomb we have used it. We have used it against those who attacked us without warning at Pearl Harbor, against those who have starved and beaten and executed American prisoners of war, against those who have abandoned all pretense of obeying international laws of warfare. We have used it in order to shorten the agony of war, in order to save the lives of thousands and thousands of young Americans.

We shall continue to use it . . . until we completely destroy Japan's power to make war. Only a Japanese surrender will stop us.

Source 8 Editorial, *Nippon Times*, Tokyo, August 10, 1945

A Moral Outrage Against Humanity

In the air attack on Hiroshima Monday morning, the enemy used a new type of bomb of unprecedented power. Not only has the greater part of the city been wiped out, but an extraordinary proportion of the inhabitants have been either killed or wounded. The use of a weapon of such terrifying destructiveness not only commands attention as a matter of a new technique in the conduct of war. More fundamentally and vitally it opens up a most grave and profound moral problem in which the very future of humanity is put at stake. . . .

This was no mere excess committed in the heat of battle. It was an act of premeditated wholesale murder, the deliberate snuffing out of the lives of tens of thousands of innocent civilians who had no chance of protecting themselves in the slightest degree. How deliberate and callous the enemy is in his unprincipled action is proved by the infamous threat of President Truman to use this diabolical weapon on an increasing scale. . . .

How can a human being with any claim to a sense of moral responsibility deliberately let loose an instrument of destruction which can at one stroke annihilate an appalling segment of mankind? This is not war; this is not even murder. . . . This is a crime against God and humanity which strikes at the very basis of human existence. . . .

The crime of the Americans stands out in ghastly repulsiveness all the more for the ironic contradiction it affords to their lying pretensions. For in all their noisy statements, they have always claimed to be the champions of fairness and humanitarianism. . . .

This hypocritical character of the Americans had already been amply demonstrated in the previous bombings of Japanese cities. Strewing explosives and fire bombs indiscriminately over an extensive area, hitting large cities and small towns without distinction, wiping out vast districts which could not be mistaken as being anything but strictly residential in character, burning or blasting to death countless thousands of helpless women and children, and machine-gunning fleeing refugees, the American raiders had already shown how completely they violate in their actual deeds the principles of humanity which they mouth in conspicuous pretense.

But now beside the latest technique of total destruction which the Americans have adopted, their earlier crimes pale into relative insignificance. What more barbarous atrocity can there be than to wipe out at one stroke the population of a whole city without distinction—men, women, and children; the aged, the weak, the infirm; those in positions of authority, and those with no power at all. . . .

For this American outrage against the fundamental moral sense of mankind, Japan must proclaim to the world its protest against the United States, which has made itself the arch-enemy of humanity.

Source 9 Imperial Japanese government's protest, through the Swiss government, August 10, 1945

The U.S. air force on August 6 dropped a new type of bomb on the urban area of Hiroshima city, thereby killing or injuring a large number of citizens and destroying the major part of the city in an instant. Being an ordinary city not possessing any particular military defense facilities or equipment, Hiroshima as a whole cannot be taken as a military object.

In his statement regarding this attack, United States President Truman said that the attack was aimed at destroying shipyards, factories, and traffic organs. . . . [T]he bomb in question explodes in the air and exerts its destructive effect on a very extensive area. It is clear, therefore, that it is technically utterly impossible to limit the effect of the attack by this bomb to a specific target. The United States authorities must know very well the efficiency of this bomb.

Upon inspecting conditions in the area stricken by the bomb, it was found that the damage was widespread and that everyone in the area, combatants and non-combatants, irrespective of age and sex, were killed or injured by the bomb blast and its radiant heat. From the size of the stricken area and the number of casualties, the bomb can be called the most atrocious and barbarous weapon ever produced.

That belligerents do not have unrestricted rights in selecting the means of killing the enemy and that they should not use arms, projectiles, or other materials which may give unnecessary pain to the enemy are the fundamental principles of Wartime International Law. . . .

Since the outbreak of the current World War, the U.S. Government has declared time and again that the use of poisonous gas and other inhuman war methods are unlawful for civilized societies and that the United States will not resort to these methods unless her opponent uses them first. But the new type of bomb far surpasses in effect poisonous gas and other arms, the use of which has hitherto been prohibited on account of their barbarous character.

In utter disregard of International Law and the fundamental principles of humanity, the United States has been carrying out extensive wanton attacks upon cities in the Nippon Empire, thereby killing or injuring numerous old men, women, and children and destroying or burning down shrines, temples, schools, hospitals, and houses of the people in general. Now she has begun using this new type of bomb, which is incomparable to any hitherto existing arms and projectiles in its indiscriminate and atrocious character.

The Imperial Nippon Government does hereby accuse the U.S. Government in its own name as well as in the name of entire mankind and its civilization.

Source 10   Editorial, Swedish newspaper *Svenska Morqenbladet,*
August 11, 1945

For the purpose of showing the power of the atomic bomb, the war leaders in the United States could have selected some other objective than a big city. If the United States felt the necessity of testing the atomic bomb against a city, she should have given the citizens sufficient time to evacuate from the city. The present attempt of the United States is astonishingly an inhuman undertaking.

Source 11 Japanese journalist's report, *Yomiuri Hochi,* August 12, 1945

Upon entering the suburbs of Hiroshima city, I found that all the windows of houses had been blown out and the tiles were covered with dust. The trunks of burnt trees were scorched black.

Only three buildings, including the Police Station remain in the city.

Source 12 Emperor of Japan's announcement to his subjects, August 14, 1945

IMPERIAL RESCRIPT

To Our good and loyal subjects:

After pondering deeply the general trends of the world and the actual conditions obtaining in Our Empire today, We have decided to effect a settlement of the present situation by resorting to an extraordinary measure.

We have ordered Our Government to communicate to the Governments of the United States, Great Britain, China and the Soviet Union that Our Empire accepts the provisions of their Joint Declaration.

To strive for the common prosperity and happiness of all nations as well as the security and well-being of Our subjects is the solemn obligation which has been handed down by Our Imperial Ancestors, and which We lay close to heart. Indeed, We declared war on America and Britain out of Our desire to ensure Japan's self-preservation and the stabilization of East Asia, it being far from Our thought either to infringe upon the sovereignty of other nations or to embark upon territorial aggrandizement. But now the war has lasted for nearly four years. Despite the best that has been done by everyone—the gallant fighting of military and naval forces, the diligence and assiduity of Our servants of the State and the devoted service of Our one hundred million people, the war situation has developed not necessarily to Japan's advantage, while the general trends of the world have all turned against her interest. Moreover, the enemy has begun to employ a new and most cruel bomb, the power of which to do damage is indeed incalculable, taking the toll of many innocent lives. Should We continue to fight it would not only result in an ultimate collapse and obliteration of the Japanese nation, but also it would lead to the total extinction of human civilization. Such being the case, how are We to save the millions of Our subjects; or to atone Ourselves before the hallowed spirits of our Imperial Ancestors? This is the reason why We have ordered the acceptance of the provisions of the Joint Declaration of the Powers.

Source 13 Dwight Macdonald, editorial, *Politics,* August 1945

[O]n the morning of August 6, 1945, an American plane dropped a single bomb on the Japanese city of Hiroshima. Exploding with the force of 20,000 tons of TNT, the bomb destroyed in a twinkling two-thirds of the city, including, presumably, most of the 343,000 human beings who lived there. No warning whatsoever was given. This atrocious action places "us," the defenders of civilization, on a moral level with "them," the beasts of **Maidanek.** And "we," the American people, are just as much and as little responsible for this horror as "they," the German people. . . .

Can one imagine that the atomic bomb could ever be used "in a good cause"? Do not such means instantly, of themselves, corrupt any cause?

Crossing a Boundary

"If you judge from the articles and editorials which have been written in the past twenty years, and all the prayers that have been prayed, and all the mourning and preaching that has been going on, you would judge that we crossed some kind of moral boundary with the use of these weapons," Air Force General Curtis Le May complained in 1965. "The assumption seems to be that it is much more wicked to kill people with a nuclear bomb, than to kill people by busting their heads with rocks." It is true that death is an end oblivious to the means used to reach it, but a boundary was crossed with the achievement of nuclear fission and its successful adaptation to destructive purposes: human beings discovered the key to a technology capable of destroying all living things on the planet, and of completing this destruction in a matter of minutes.

20.3 Hiroshima: Was It Necessary?

Nuclear weapons do differ from rocks and other conventional devices as tools of warfare. For one thing, the destructive force of nuclear weaponry dwarfs that of conventional warfare. The largest conventional bombs of the age that ended on the morning of August 6, 1945, were called "Blockbusters." Each Blockbuster contained one ton of trinitrotoluene, or TNT, a powerful explosive. The uranium-fueled atomic bomb that destroyed Hiroshima had the explosive impact of 13,000 Blockbusters. The plutonium-fueled bomb that fell on Nagasaki three days later was the equivalent of 20,000 tons of TNT.

Within seven years of the detonation of the fission bomb over Hiroshima, the United States had reached the next level in its nuclear research with the successful test of a thermonuclear weapon, a bomb so powerful that it employed a fission bomb just to serve as its trigger. In 1961, the Soviet Union exploded a thermonuclear weapon that had the equivalent explosive force of 58 million tons of TNT. Today, a single Trident class submarine with its cargo of missile-borne nuclear weapons carries the potential to inflict greater destruction than all of the bombs detonated in World Wars I and II.

More significantly, nuclear war is never over. Treaties may be signed, arms may be put away, but the impact of the radiation continues indefinitely, as does the death toll. More than 140,000 people died from the effects of the Hiroshima and Nagasaki bombs between the time the war ended and 1950. People continue to die from the bombing of Hiroshima five decades later.

 Second Thoughts

A Military Necessity or a Political Expedient?

Exactly why the United States dropped atomic bombs on two Japanese cities—and whether the motives justified the actions—has been debated during the intervening half-century by politicians, scientists, historians, and others. Few people in 1945 could have imagined how extensive the impact of the new technology would be. Likewise, few, including the scientists who develop them, can comprehend the explosive force in today's nuclear arsenals.

Source 14 Report of U.S. War Department's Strategic Bombing Survey, 1945

[C]ertainly prior to 31 December 1945, and in all probability prior to 1 November 1945, Japan would have surrendered even if the atomic bombs had not been dropped, even if Russia had not entered the war, and even if no invasion had been planned or contemplated.

Source 15 James F. Byrnes, secretary of state in 1945, *Speaking Frankly,* 1947

In these two raids there were many casualties but not nearly so many as there would have been had our air forces continued to drop incendiary bombs on Japan's cities. Certainly, by bringing the war to an end, the atomic bomb saved the lives of thousands of American boys.

No one who played a part in the development of the bomb or in our decision to use it felt happy about it. It was natural and right that men should worry about performing duty that would cost so many human lives. . . . But the truth is, war remains what General Sherman said it was.

Source 16 Secretary of War Henry L. Stimson, *On Active Service in Peace and War,* 1947

Two great nations were approaching contact in a fight to a finish which would begin on November 1, 1945. Our enemy, Japan, commanded forces of somewhat over 5,000,000 armed men. Men of these armies had already inflicted upon us, in our break-through of the outer perimeter of their defenses, over 500,000 battle casualties. Enemy armies still unbeaten had the strength to cost us a million more. As long as the Japanese Government refused to surrender, we should be forced to take and hold the ground, and smash the Japanese ground armies, by close-in fighting of the same desperate and costly kind that we had faced in the Pacific islands for nearly four years.

In light of the formidable problem which thus confronted us, I felt that every possible step should be taken to compel a surrender . . . before we had commenced an invasion. . . . The bomb seemed to me to furnish a unique instrument for that purpose.

My chief purpose was to end the war in victory with the least possible cost in the lives of the armies which I had helped to raise. . . . I believe that no man, in our position and subject to our responsibilities, holding in his hands a weapon of such possibilities for accomplishing this purpose and saving those lives, could have failed to use it and afterwards looked his countrymen in the face. . . .

The decision to use the atomic bomb was a decision that brought death to over a hundred thousand Japanese. No explanation can change that fact and

I do not wish to gloss it over. But this deliberate, premeditated destruction was our least abhorrent choice. The destruction of Hiroshima and Nagasaki put an end to the Japanese war. It stopped the fire raids, and the strangling blockade; it ended the ghastly specter of a clash of great land armies.

Source 17 Henry Stimson and McGeorge Bundy, *On Active Service*, 1948

Stimson believed, both at the time and later, that the dominant fact of 1945 was war, and that therefore, necessarily, the dominant objective was victory. If victory could be speeded by using the bomb, it should be used; if victory must be delayed in order to use the bomb, it should not be used. So far as he knew, this general view was fully shared by the President and all his associates.

Source 18 British scientist P. M. S. Blackett, *Fear, War, and the Bomb*, 1948

One can imagine the hurry with which the two bombs—the only two existing—were whisked across the Pacific to be dropped on Hiroshima and Nagasaki just in time, but only just, to insure that the Japanese Government surrendered to American forces alone. . . .

The hurried dropping of the bombs on Hiroshima and Nagasaki was a brilliant success, in that all the political objectives were fully achieved. American control of Japan is complete, and there is no struggle for authority there with Russia. . . . So we may conclude that the dropping of the atomic bombs was not so much the last military act of the second World War, as the first major operation of the cold diplomatic war with Russia.

Source 19 Hanson W. Baldwin, *Great Mistakes of the War*, 1950

To accept the Stimson thesis that the atomic bomb should have been used as it was used, it is necessary to first to accept the contention that the atomic bomb achieved or hastened victory. . . .

The atomic bomb was dropped in August. Long before that month started our forces were securely based in Okinawa, the Marianas and Iwo Jima; Germany had been defeated; our fleet had been cruising off the Japanese coast with impunity bombarding the shoreline; our submarines were operating in the sea of Japan; even interisland ferries had been attacked and sunk. Bombing, which started slowly in June, 1944, from China bases and from the Marianas in November, 1944, had been increased materially in 1945, and by August, 1945, more than 16,000 tons of bombs had ravaged Japanese cities. Food was short; mines and submarines and surface vessels and planes clamped an iron blockade around the main islands; raw materials were scarce. Blockades, bombing, and unsuccessful attempts at dispersion had reduced Japanese production capacity from 20 to 60 percent. The enemy, in a military sense, was in a hopeless strategic position by the time the Potsdam demand for unconditional surrender was made on July 26.

Such, then, was the situation when we wiped out Hiroshima and Nagasaki.

Need we have done it? No one can, of course, be positive, but the answer is almost certainly negative....

Not only was the Potsdam ultimatum merely a restatement of the politically impossible—unconditional surrender—but it could hardly be construed as a direct warning of the atomic bomb and was not taken as such by anyone who did not know the bomb had been created. A technical demonstration of the bomb's power may well have been unfeasible, but certainly a far more definite warning could have been given; and it is hard to believe that a target objective in Japan with but sparse population could not have been found. The truth is we did not try: we gave no specific warning. There were almost two months before our scheduled invasion in which American ingenuity could have found ways to bring home to the Japanese the impossibility of their position and the horrors of the weapon being held over them; yet we rushed to use the bomb as soon as unconditional surrender was rejected....

But, in fact, our only warning to a Japan already militarily defeated, and in a hopeless situation, was the Potsdam demand for unconditional surrender issued on July 26, when we knew Japanese surrender attempts had started. Yet when the Japanese surrender was negotiated about two weeks later, after the bomb was dropped, our unconditional surrender demand was made conditional and we argued, as Stimson had originally proposed we should do, for continuation of the Emperor upon his imperial throne.

We were, therefore, twice guilty. We dropped the bomb at a time when Japan already was negotiating for an end to the war but before those negotiations could come to fruition. We demanded unconditional surrender, then dropped the bomb and accepted conditional surrender, a sequence which indicates pretty clearly that Japan would have surrendered even if the bomb had not been dropped, had the Potsdam Declaration included our promise ... to permit the Emperor to remain on his imperial throne....

It is quite possible that the atomic bomb shortened the war by a day, a week, or a month or two—not more.

But at what a price!

Source 20   Interview of James F. Byrnes, *U.S. News & World Report,* August 15, 1960

Q Governor Byrnes, in light of what we now know, was it wrong to use the atomic bomb against Hiroshima and Nagasaki?

A I do not think so. Of course, Monday morning quarterbacking is a very pleasant pastime, but it is not a fruitful one....

Q Do any of the alternatives proposed in 1945 look any better today than they did then?

A Again, my answer is that I do not think so. For instance, I recall, among the alternatives suggested at that time to the Interim Committee of which I was a member, the suggestion that the bomb be dropped on an isolated island with representatives of Japan and other nations invited to witness the test. This was rejected.

Then there was the question of giving the Japanese fair warning about the time and place of the explosion but we rejected it because we feared the American prisoners of war would be brought into the designated area. We were told by experts, too, that, whatever the success of the test bomb, they could not guarantee that another bomb would explode when dropped.

Q It might be a "dud"?

A Yes. If we gave the Japanese advance notice of the time and place we would drop the bomb, and then the bomb failed to explode, our optimism would have played into the hands of Japanese militarists who were urging a continuation of the war, and who would say that our failure was proof that we were merely bluffing about possessing this bomb. . . .

Q Did we want to drop the bomb as soon as possible in order to finish the war before Russia got in?

A Of course, we were anxious to get the war over as soon as possible.

Q Was there a feeling of urgency to end the war in the Pacific before the Russians became too deeply involved?

A There certainly was on my part, and I'm sure that, whatever views President Truman may have had of it earlier in the year, that in the days immediately preceding the dropping of the bomb his views were the same as mine—we wanted to get through with the Japanese phase of the war before the Russians came in. On July 26, Jim Forrestal [then Secretary of the Navy, later Secretary of Defense] wrote in his "Diaries," page 78: "Talked with Byrnes now at Potsdam. Byrnes said he was most anxious to get the Japanese affair over with before the Russians got in."

Source 21 Interview of Dr. Leo Szillard, scientist and atomic bomb codeveloper, *U.S. News & World Report,* August 15, 1960

Q Dr. Szillard, what was your attitude in 1945 toward the question of dropping the bomb?

A I opposed it with all my power, but I'm afraid not as effectively as I should have wished.

Q Did any other scientists feel the same way you did?

A Very many other scientists felt this way. . . .

Q Do you feel that President Truman and those immediately below him gave full and conscientious study to all the alternatives to use of the atomic bomb?

A I do not think they did. They thought only in terms of our having to end the war with military means. . . .

I don't think Japan would have surrendered unconditionally without the use of force. But there was no need to demand the unconditional surrender of Japan. If we had offered Japan the kind of peace treaty which we actually gave her, we could have had a negotiated peace. . . .

Q Would a demonstration have been feasible?

A It is easy to see, at least in retrospect, how an effective demonstration could have been staged. . . . But again, I don't believe that staging a demonstration was the real issue, and in a sense it is just as immoral to force a sudden ending of a war by threatening violence as by using violence. My point is that violence would not have been necessary if we had been willing to negotiate. After all, Japan was suing for peace. . . .

Q Have your views on this subject changed at all since 1945?

A No, except that I can say much more clearly today what I was thinking at that time. . . . Today I would put the whole emphasis on the mistake of insisting on unconditional surrender. Today I would say that the confusion arose from considering the fake alternatives of either having to invade Japan or of having to use the bomb against her cities.

Q Would most other nations, including Russia, have done the same thing we did, confronted with the same opportunity to use the bomb?

A Look, answering this question would be pure speculation. I can say this, however: By and large, governments are guided by considerations of expediency rather than by moral considerations. . . .

Prior to the war I had the illusion that up to a point the American Government was different. This illusion was gone after Hiroshima.

Perhaps you remember that in 1939 President Roosevelt warned the belligerents against using bombs against the inhabited cities, and this I thought was fitting. . . .

Then, during the war, without any explanation, we began to use incendiary bombs against the cities of Japan. This was disturbing to me and it was disturbing to many of my friends.

Q Was that the end of the illusion?

A Yes, this was the end of the illusion. But, you see, there was still a difference between using incendiary bombs and using the new force of nature for purposes of destruction. There was still a further step taken here.

Source 22 Gar Alperovitz, *Atomic Diplomacy,* 1965

[T]o state in a precise way the question "Why was the atomic bomb used?" is to ask why senior officials did *not* seriously question its use. . . .

The first point to note is that the decision to use the bomb did not derive from overriding military considerations.

Despite Truman's subsequent statement that the weapon "saved millions of lives," Eisenhower's judgment that it was "completely unnecessary" as a measure to save lives was almost certainly correct. This is not a matter of hindsight; before the atomic bomb was dropped each of the Joint Chiefs of Staff advised that it was highly likely that Japan could be forced to surrender unconditionally, without the use of the bomb and without an invasion. . . .

In essence, the second of the two overriding considerations seems to have been that a combat demonstration was needed to convince the Russians to accept the American plan for a stable peace. And the crucial point of this effort was the need to force agreement on the main questions in dispute: the American proposals for Central and Eastern Europe. . . .

At present no final conclusion can be reached on this question. But the problem can be defined with some precision: Why did the American government refuse to attempt to exploit Japanese efforts to surrender? Or, alternatively, why did they refuse to test whether a Russian declaration of war would force capitulation? Were Hiroshima and Nagasaki bombed primarily to impress the world with the need to accept America's plan for a stable and lasting peace—that is, primarily, America's plan for Europe? The evidence strongly suggests that the view which the President's personal representative offered to one of the atomic scientists in May 1945 was an accurate statement of policy:

"Mr. Byrnes did not argue that it was necessary to use the bomb against the cities of Japan in order to win the war. . . . Mr. Byrnes's view [was] that our possessing and demonstrating the bomb would make Russia more manageable in Europe."

Source 23 Economist Herbert Feis, *The Atomic Bomb and the End of World War II, 1966*

[T]here was no good reason to refrain from the use of the atomic bomb, like any other weapon, against Japan. . . .

It may be contended with the grim support by history that no exceptional justification for the use of the atomic bomb need be sought or given. For the prevalent rule of nations except when "knighthood was in flower" has allowed the use of any and all weapons in war except any banned by explicit agreement; and this was the prevailing view at the time, qualified only by revulsion against use of weapons and methods deemed needlessly inhumane such as the poisoning of wells and torture. Did not, it should be borne in mind, every one of the contending nations strive its utmost to invent and produce more deadly weapons, faster planes of greater bomb capacity, new types of mines, rockets and buzz-bombs? And was not each and every improved sort of killing weapon brought into action without ado or reproach? For this reason alone, almost all professional military men, and those in uniform in 1945, would then have denied that any special justification for the use of the bomb was needed. . . .

These considerations seem to me conclusive defenses of our right, legal and historical, for the use of the atomic bomb against Japan. Those who made the decision took them for granted. They thus felt free to make it without scruples on these scores.

Their reckoning . . . was governed by one reason deemed paramount: that by using the bomb the agony of war might be ended most quickly and lives be saved. It was believed with deep apprehension that many thousands, probably tens of thousands, of lives of Allied combatants would have to be spent in the continuation of our air and sea bombardment and blockade, victims mainly of Japanese suicide planes. In spite of its confidence in ultimate success, our assailant naval force felt vulnerable, because of grim and agonizing experience. . . .

It was reliably known that the Japanese were assembling thousands of planes, of all kinds and conditions, to fling against the invasion fleet and the troop-carrying ships. Thus, should it prove necessary to carry out the plans for invasion, . . . American casualties alone might mount to hundreds of thousands. Our allies . . . would suffer corresponding losses.

But the people who would have suffered most, had the war gone on much longer and their country been invaded, were the Japanese. One American incendiary air raid on the Tokyo area in March 1945 did more damage and killed and injured more Japanese than the bomb on Hiroshima. Even greater groups of American bombing planes would have hovered over Japan, consuming the land, its people and its food, with blast and fire, leaving them no place to hide, no chance to rest, no hope of reprieve. . . .

In summary it can be concluded that the decision to drop the bombs upon Hiroshima and Nagasaki ought not to be censured. The reasons were—under the circumstances of the time—weighty and valid enough.

Source 24   William Appleman Williams, *The Tragedy of American Diplomacy,* 1972

This sense of urgency about using the bomb makes it possible to advance beyond the question of whether the United States dropped the bomb to end the war against Japan, or whether it did so in order to check the Russians. The evidence provided by the government archives and private American leaders converges on one explanation: The United States dropped the bomb to end the war against Japan and thereby stop the Russians in Asia, and give them sober pause in eastern Europe.

Source 25   Howard Zinn, *Postwar America: 1945–1971,* 1973

The motivation behind dropping the bomb on Hiroshima, despite the death and suffering of the Japanese . . . was political. That political motive was to keep the Russians out of the Pacific war so that the United States would play the primary role in the peace settlement in Asia. The circumstantial evidence for this conclusion . . . is that the strictly military need to end the war did not require such instant use of the bomb. Admiral William Leahy, Truman's chief of staff; General Henry Arnold, commanding general of the air force; General Carl Spaatz, commander of the Strategic Air Force; as well as General Douglas MacArthur, commander of the Pacific theater; and General Eisenhower, did not think use of the bomb was necessary. . . .

Hiroshima was not an unfortunate error in an otherwise glorious war. It revealed, in concentrated form, characteristics that the United States had in common with the other belligerents—whatever their political nomenclature. The first of these is the commission and easy justification of indiscriminate violence when it serves political aims. The second is the translation of the system's basic power motives into whatever catchall ideology can mobilize the population—"socialism" for socialist states, "democracy" for capitalist states, "the master race" for the Fascist states. The common denominator for all has been the survival of the system in power—whether socialist, Fascist, or capitalist. What dominated the motives for war among all the belligerents were political ends—power, privilege, expansion—rather than human ends—life, liberty, the pursuit of individual and social happiness.

Source 26 Gregory D. Black and Clayton R. Koppes, *Foreign Service Journal,* August 1974

In wartime, it is not unusual for nations to develop a dehumanized image of their enemies. Such an image can lead to conduct otherwise unthinkable. The World War II U.S. Office of War Information, among other things, analyzed the images of America's enemies as projected by Hollywood onto the nation's movie screens. In August of 1974, Gregory D. Black and Clayton R. Koppes published in the *Foreign Service Journal* the following conclusions based upon OWI studies:

> Hollywood had a distinct view of each of the enemies. Germans were gentlemen with whom it was possible to deal as equals. As soldiers they were efficient, disciplined, and patriotic: the. . . [Office of War Information studies were] unable to find a scene in which the Germans were morally corrupt or delighted in cruelty. Japanese soldiers were pictured as less military than their German counterparts, and were almost universally cruel and ruthless. Japanese were short, thin, and wore spectacles. They were tough but devoid of scruples. In almost every film showing American-Japanese battles, the enemy broke the rules of civilized warfare.

Source 27 Robert Dallek, *The Great Republic,* 1992

A new, inexperienced president, Harry S Truman, sat in the White House. An array of military and civilian advisors counseled the president to use the new weapon against Japan, explaining that it might eliminate the need for an invasion of the Japanese home islands. . . . Although the terrifying dimensions of atomic and nuclear weaponry became crystal clear only after World War II, at the time the weapon impressed many American military and government leaders as essentially a more efficient way of using air power to terrorize the enemy. It was also assumed that FDR would have used the weapon and that, so much tax money had been spent in developing the bomb, Congress and the public would expect the expenditures to be justified by dropping it. Finally, some American military and political leaders felt using the bomb would serve postwar peace by intimidating the Soviets.

 Questioning the Past

1. Four general viewpoints have emerged about the atomic bombing of Hiroshima. The first view was that taken by the president and his advisers, who asserted that the bomb was a legitimate weapon, that its use saved lives and shortened the war, and that it was a tool of righteous revenge. This is called the "orthodox" viewpoint. The second position is the "realist" view. This position argues that Truman did not need to use the bomb to end the war. The "revisionist" position asserts that though the bomb was dropped on Japan, its real target was the Soviet Union. The "moralist" view takes the position that the use of atomic weapons is a crime against humanity. By vaporizing tens of thousands of civilians without

warning, the moralists argue, the United States made itself morally indistinguishable from Nazi Germany. Present and evaluate the arguments that support each of these viewpoints.

2. Why did the United States drop atomic bombs on Hiroshima and Nagasaki?

3. What alternatives to the atomic bomb might the United States have tried in 1945?

4. Was the atomic bombing of Hiroshima justifiable? Was it justifiable to drop the second bomb on Nagasaki? Present a defense of your position on these questions.

5. It has been widely believed that the manner in which the atomic age was introduced to the world prompted an arms race among the great powers. Offer rationale for this belief.

Chapter **21**

McCarthyism

Senator McCarthy Accuses the State Department of Being "Infested" with Communists *February 9, 1950*

The United States emerged from World War II as the greatest power in the world. Indeed, it was the only surviving power. Its allies, competitors, and rivals on the international scene had been devastated by the war. America alone of the great powers came out of the war stronger than when it went in. Its factories were unscathed and, though its population accounted for only six percent of the world's total, the value of the goods and services its people produced was about equal to that of the rest of the human race combined. The American people quickly began to feel the material rewards of their economic supremacy, and their exclusive possession of the atomic bomb gave them a sense of military security.

Yet underlying the prosperous appearance of the American people was an uneasiness. The Soviet Union, the communist state that had been their ally against Nazi Germany, had become their enemy. The spread of Soviet influence across eastern Europe caused them deep concern. A cold war with the Soviets tested their resolve and their nerves. When they learned that the Soviets, too, had unleashed the power of the atom, and that this achievement had benefited from the betrayal of their own atomic secrets, they were shocked and angered. In 1949, the Chinese mainland came under communist rule, and the following year saw American troops fighting a hot war with communism on the Korean peninsula. It seemed to many as though all that they had achieved was now in danger.

It was disturbing enough to feel threatened by an ideology that seemed to be inching closer and closer to the outer walls of America's defenses. But what if this ideology were secretly at work inside the walls already? Suppose it were quietly boring from within America's institutions to leave them inwardly weak while appearing outwardly strong. Suppose trusted civil servants were preparing to unlatch the gates from the inside and open the way to a communist takeover. Suppose it were the clandestine complicity of these same civil servants that had enabled communism to spread so rapidly abroad. Suppose college professors, entertainers, journalists, even generals, were engaged in a conspiracy to ease Americans out of their freedom and their prosperity and into the hands of a totalitarian state. Such speculations, posed forcefully by Senator Joseph McCarthy, excited America to the point of hysteria in the decade following World War II.

21.1 The Cold War at Home

ᑲᓍᑫ *First Impressions*

The Enemy Within

A fear of communism had been a part of the American psyche for most of the twentieth century, sometimes latent, sometimes active, but ever present. It was to this phobia that Senator McCarthy appealed in his attempt to reveal a communist conspiracy within the nation.

Source 1   Senator Joseph McCarthy, "Wheeling Speech," February 9, 1950

21.2 Joseph McCarthy

Ladies and gentlemen, tonight as we celebrate the one-hundred and forty-first birthday of one of the greatest men in American history, I would like to be able to talk about what a glorious day today is in the history of the world. As we celebrate the birth of this man who with his whole heart and soul hated war, I would like to be able to speak of peace in our time, of war being outlawed, and of world-wide disarmament. These would be truly appropriate things to be able to mention as we celebrate the birthday of Abraham Lincoln.

Five years after a world war has been won, men's hearts should anticipate a long peace, and men's minds should be free from the heavy weight that comes with war. But this is not a period of peace. This is a time of the "cold war." This is a time when all the world is split into two vast, increasingly hostile armed camps—a time of a great armaments race.

Today we can almost physically hear the mutterings and rumblings of an invigorated god of war. You can see it, feel it, and hear it all the way from the hills of Indochina, from the shores of Formosa, right over into the very heart of Europe itself.

The one encouraging thing is that the "mad moment" has not yet arrived for the firing of the gun or the exploding of the bomb which will set civilization about the final task of destroying itself. There is still a hope for peace if we finally decide that no longer can we safely blind our eyes and close our ears to those facts which are shaping up more and more clearly. And that is that we are now engaged in a show-down fight—not the usual war between nations for land areas or other material gains, but a war between two diametrically opposed ideologies.

The great difference between our Western Christian world and the atheistic Communist world is not political, ladies and gentlemen, it is moral. There are other differences, of course, but those could be reconciled. For instance, the Marxian idea of confiscating the land and factories and running the entire economy as a single enterprise is momentous. Likewise, Lenin's invention of the one-party police state as a way to make Marx's idea work is hardly less momentous.

Stalin's resolute putting across of these two ideas, of course, did much to divide the world. With only these differences, however, the East and West could most certainly still live in peace.

The real difference, however, lies in the religion of immoralism—invented by Marx, preached feverishly by Lenin, and carried to unimaginable extremes by Stalin. This religion of immoralism, if the Red half of the world wins—and well it may—this religion of immoralism will more deeply wound and damage mankind than any conceivable economic or political system.

Karl Marx dismissed God as a hoax, and Lenin and Stalin have added in clear-cut, unmistakable language their resolve that no nation, no people, who believe in God, can exist side by side with their communistic state. . . .

While Lincoln was a relatively young man in his late thirties, Karl Marx boasted that the Communist specter was haunting Europe. Since that time, hundreds of millions of people and vast areas of the world have fallen under Communist domination. Today, less than 100 years after Lincoln's death, Stalin brags that this Communist specter is not only haunting the world, but is about to completely subjugate it.

Today we are engaged in a final, all-out battle between communistic atheism and Christianity. . . .

Six years ago, at the time of the first conference to map out the peace— Dumbarton Oaks—there were within the Soviet orbit 180,000,000 people. Lined up on the antittotalitarian side there were in the world at that point roughly 1,625,000,000 people. Today, only 6 years later, there are 800,000,000 people under the absolute domination of Soviet Russia—an increase of over 400 percent. On our side, the figure has shrunk to around 500,000,000. In other words, in less than 6 years the odds have changed from 9 to 1 in our favor to 8 to 5 against us. This indicates the swiftness of the tempo of Communist victories and American defeats in the cold war. As one of our outstanding historical figures once said, "When a great democracy is destroyed, it will not be because of enemies from without, but rather because of enemies from within."

The truth of this statement is becoming terrifyingly clear as we see this country each day losing on every front.

At war's end we were physically the strongest nation on earth and, at least potentially, the most powerful intellectually and morally. . . .

The reason why we find ourselves in a position of impotency is not because our only powerful potential enemy has sent men to invade our shores, but rather because of the traitorous actions of those who have been treated so well by this Nation. It has not been the less fortunate members of minority groups who have been selling this Nation out, but rather those who have had all the benefits that the wealthiest nation on earth has had to offer—the finest homes, the finest college education, and the finest jobs in Government we can give.

This is glaringly true in the State Department. . . . In my opinion the State Department, which is one of the most important government departments, is thoroughly infested with Communists.

I have in my hand 57 cases of individuals who would appear to be either card-carrying members or certainly loyal to the Communist Party, but who nevertheless are still helping to shape our foreign policy.

One thing to remember in discussing Communists in our Government is that we are not dealing with spies who get 30 pieces of silver to steal the blueprints of a new weapon. We are dealing with a far more sinister type of activity because it permits the enemy to guide and shape our policy.

Source 2   Senator Joseph McCarthy, "Statement on Drew Pearson,"
delivered to the Senate, December 15, 1950

Mr. President, the other night I told one of my fellow Senators that today I intended to discuss the background of one of the cleverest men who has ever prostituted one of the noblest professions—a man who, in my opinion, has been doing an infinite amount of damage to America and all of the institutions of our form of Government. When I told the Senator this, he said: "McCarthy, don't do it." He said it would be like having stood in the mouth of the **Cloaca Maxima** and having tried to stop the flow. He said: "You will be merely inundated by the slime and smear and he will still go on every day and every week polluting otherwise fine newspapers and poisoning the airwaves."

I realize that the task of exposing this man, or perhaps I should say this person, will be an unpleasant, disagreeable task, which will leave me more than a bit bloodied up also, but as I told the Senator the other night—when I was a boy on the farm my mother used to raise chickens. From those chickens the groceries for a large family were supplied, as well as mother's Christmas money. The greatest enemy the chickens had were skunks. In order to protect mother's chickens my three brothers and I had to dig out and destroy those skunks. It was a dirty, foul, unpleasant, smelly job. We learned early in life that the jobs that most badly need doing and are so often left undone are often the most difficult and unpleasant jobs.

I do not agree with the Senator who advised me the other night—I do not agree that this is an impossible task. I think that while it cannot be done overnight, this man can be exposed to the American people for what he is, at which time he will no longer be dangerous. . . .

It is impossible for me to understand how so many reputable newspapermen can buy the writings of this twisted, perverted mentality which so cleverly sugar-coats and disguises his fiendishly clever, long-range attempts to discredit and destroy in the minds of the American people all of the institutions which make up the heart of this Republic. . . .

The heads of any of our intelligence agencies will testify that one of the principal aims of the Communist Party is to gain control of our lines of communication; that is, newspapers, radio, television, motion pictures, and so forth. It, of course, would be a miracle if they had not recognized in Pearson the ideal man for them—an unprincipled, greedy degenerate liar—but with a tremendous audience both in newspapers and on the airwaves—a man who has been able to sugar-coat his wares so well that he has been able to fool vast numbers of people with his fake piety and his false loyalty.

Pearson has long had working for him—part of the time officially on his payroll, and part of the time in a slightly different status—one David Karr. The relationship is such that it is difficult to know who is the master and who is the servant.

[W]hile under questioning . . . before the House Committee on Un-American Activities, Karr admitted under oath that he knew the American League for Peace and Democracy, whose publicity he was handling, was a Communist-controlled organization. . . .

I have discussed this man Pearson with practically every former member of the Communist Party whom I have met during my recent and present investigation of Communists in Government. Almost to a man, they were agreed on a number of things—No. 1: That Pearson's all-important job, which he did for the Party without fail, under the directions of David Karr, was to lead the character assassination of any man who was a threat to international Communism. No. 2: That he did that job so well that he was the most valuable of all radio commentators and writers from the standpoint of the Communist Party. No. 3: In order to maintain his value, it was necessary that he occasionally throw pebbles at Communism, and Communists generally, so as to have a false reputation of being an anti-Communist.

It appears that Pearson never actually signed up as a member of the Communist Party and never paid dues. However, that has not in any way affected his value to the Party; nor has it affected his willingness to follow the orders of David Karr, who, of course, is a most active member of the party, and who carries instructions and orders to Pearson.

I ask those who are skeptical as to whether Pearson actually has been doing a job for the Communist Party to stop and review Pearson's record over the past ten years. You will find that he has always gone all-out to attack anyone who is attempting to expose individual and dangerous Communists. . . .

I say to the 150,000,000 normal people of America, the chips are down. They are truly down. The time has come for action. It is up to the American people, through their actions, to notify the sponsors of the voices of Communism that have been polluting the airwaves and the newspapers, that they, the American people, are through paying for the soapboxes for those who preach the Communist Party line. . . . If the American people take action and refuse to continue paying for the Pearson cabal, the Communist Party in the United States will have suffered a death blow.

Source 3   Kenneth Colegrove, "Senator McCarthy," *Congressional Record*, June 24, 1952

Without question, the charge of harboring Communists which Senator McCarthy brought against the State Department in his Wheeling address in February 1950 was a hard blow. But his sledge-hammer blows were a natural reaction to the hostility of a corrupt administration toward any adequate investigation of communism in the executive branch of Government. . . . President Truman had denounced honest efforts to search out subversives in the Federal Government. He had branded the probe of the Committee on Un-American Activities of the House of Representatives into Communist spying in the Federal Government as a "red herring." He accused congressional investigation of subversives in Government as an effort to promote public hysteria. . . .

The brutal charges of Senator McCarthy were thus a natural reaction to the pugnacious refusal of the Truman administration to assist congressional investigation of the loyalty of federal employees. The need for investigation was obvious to honest and alert citizens. The Western democracies were engaged in a cold war with the most dangerous dictatorship in modern history. By means of new techniques of infiltration and subversion, the Moscow-directed Communist Party was engaged in undermining constitutional government in every democratic country in the world. Even the Republican Party, both in and out of Congress, had proven to be lethargic and leaderless when confronted with the problem of subversive influences in the Federal Government. . . .

It was under these distressing circumstances that the smashing charges of the Wisconsin Senator awakened public opinion, prodded the Republican Members of Congress into action, and compelled Congress to inaugurate investigations that ultimately proved fruitful in exposing Communist operations to control American foreign policy.

All of this was not accomplished without an emotional convulsion. It cannot be denied that Senator McCarthy had deeply offended the innermost convictions of millions of American citizens. To some voters it appeared that he had trampled upon the American tradition that the accused is deemed innocent until convicted. To others it seemed that his broad charges, without complete supporting evidence, were unfair to the victims of the accusation and violated an American principle of fair play. To many soft liberals, who felt that freedom of speech required the absence of any restrictions upon the propaganda of Communists even when advocating the overthrow of the American Constitution by force, Senator McCarthy appeared as a violent enemy of constitutional liberty. . . .

Those who would preserve American liberty by permitting Communists to undermine American liberty were wittingly or unwittingly offering the conquest of their country to a foreign power. . . . It would be erroneous to brand President Truman and the Democrats who protected Communism in the Federal Government as traitors to their country. On the other hand, history will not award them the distinction of stalwart guardians of national security.

A frequent charge made against Senator McCarthy by President Truman, the State Department, and Democratic Congressmen was the allegation that he was engaged in the spread of public hysteria. The facts do not justify this accusation, for an examination of the record shows that most of the hysteria was found, not in the ranks of the pro-Americans and anti-Communists, but rather among the enemies of Senator McCarthy. Defenders of the State Department invented the word "McCarthyism" for propaganda effect. Into this symbol, the soft liberals poured all their opprobrium, venom, and contempt.

There may be severe hardships inflicted upon citizens who may be named as proper objects of investigation by Members of Congress, particularly in case the accused persons are innocent of the accusation. On the other hand, if the actions of the accused have given justifiable grounds for suspicion of subversive activities, there is no good reason why, in the name of the people, such persons should not be brought under legislative investigation. The freedoms of the Bill of Rights are indeed very precious liberties. But good citizens will conduct themselves in a manner to deserve the protection of these freedoms.

Source 4   Republican Party Platform of 1952

By the Administration's appeasement of Communism at home and abroad it has permitted Communists and their fellow travelers to serve in many key agencies and to infiltrate our American life. When such infiltrations became notorious through the revelations of Republicans in Congress, the Executive Department stubbornly refused to deal with it openly and vigorously. It raised the false cry of "red herring" and took other measures to block and discredit investigations. It denied files and information to Congress. It set up boards of its own to keep information secret and to deal lightly with security risks and persons of doubtful loyalty. It only undertook prosecution of the most notorious Communists after public opinion forced action. . . .

There are no Communists in the Republican Party. We have always recognized Communism to be a world conspiracy against freedom and religion. We never compromised with Communism and we have fought to expose it and to eliminate it in government and American life.

A Republican President will appoint only persons of unquestioned loyalty.

Source 5 Democratic National Committee, *Campaign Handbook: How to Win in 1952,* 1952

Democratic Congresses during Democratic Administrations have set up strong bars against Communist subversion. We have made it unlawful for a Communist to hold a government job. The Atomic Energy Act took control of atomic energy from the military, placed it in civilian hands, and set up rigid standards to prevent the leak of atomic secrets. All of the atomic leaks which have recently been exposed took place during military control—none under civilian control.

And the Loyalty Program for Federal Employees, set up by President Truman, utilized the FBI to screen each and every person on the payroll of the Federal government. Of its effectiveness, *Life* magazine said on October 1, 1951:

"If Houdini were a suspected Communist he couldn't get near a sensitive government payroll today."

Trial by Mere Accusation

When Senator McCarthy announced the existence of a Communist conspiracy inside the State Department, he claimed to hold in his hand a list containing the names of 57 Communists in America's foreign service. Over the next few days the number of Communists at the State Department was variously proclaimed to be 265, 57, or 207. But since no one but the Senator ever saw the list he held, the number of names it contained remains a mystery. Such inconsistencies, however, were a minor concern in the general excitement which followed the charge. Soon, McCarthy was pointing his accusing finger at journalists, academicians, entertainers, civil servants of all departments. It was not only Communists who were the targets of his accusations, it was reformers and liberals of all types. Before the reign of terror had run its course, millions of Americans had joined in the finger pointing. Anyone with ideas that differed from a narrow norm was the target of suspicion and, all too often, persecution.

Few dared challenge McCarthy or those who joined him in his "witch hunt." To do so was to risk becoming his prey. Politicians who did not join the crusade were branded "soft on Communists," a mark politically damaging. Private citizens who spoke out against the hysteria were accused of being either Communists themselves or "fellow travelers." Thousands of careers were ruined and lives damaged. No conspiracy was uncovered.

21.3 The Real McCarthy Record

As the months wore on, McCarthy went after bigger and bigger game. When the Army did not give him the kind of cooperation he demanded, he announced plans to expose Communist infiltration within the military. In 1954, the American people watched on their television screens as McCarthy took on the United States Army in hearings before his own Permanent Subcommittee on Investigations. What they saw left them disillusioned. McCarthy and his aides were arrogant and abusive. Support for the crusade began to collapse. By August, McCarthy had so fallen that the Senate at last was willing to accuse him of misconduct, though for his violation of Senate rules rather than his contempt for American values of decency and fairness.

Source 6   Senator McCarthy's questioning of General Ralph W. Zwicker, Army-McCarthy hearings, February 18, 1954

[Major Irving Peress, a dentist, was registered as a member of the American Labor Party, a legal but left-of-center political party in New York. When he declined to answer questions about his political beliefs, the Army ordered him discharged. When McCarthy learned that Peress would not identify his political views, Peress was called before McCarthy's subcommittee, where the Major invoked the protection of the Fifth Amendment. McCarthy called on the Army to court-martial Peress. Before that could happen, General Zwicker signed Peress's discharge papers, leading to the following confrontation.]

The Chairman: General, let's try and be truthful. I am going to keep you here as long as you keep hedging and hemming.

General Zwicker: I am not hedging.

The Chairman: Or hawing.

General Zwicker: I am not hawing, and I don't like to have anyone impugn my honesty, which you just about did.

The Chairman: Either your honesty or your intelligence; I can't help impugning one or the other, when you tell us that a major in your command who was known to you to have been before a Senate committee, and of whom you read the press releases very carefully—to now have you sit here and tell us that you did not know whether he refused to answer questions about Communist activities. I had seen all the press releases and they all dealt with that. So when you do that, General, if you will pardon me, I cannot help but question either your honesty or your intelligence, one or the other. I want to be frank with you on that.

Now, is it your testimony now that at the time you read the stories about Major Peress, that you did not know that he had refused to answer questions before this committee about his Communist activities?

General Zwicker: I am sure I had that impression. . . .

The Chairman: Did you also read the stories about my letter to Secretary of the Army Stevens in which I requested or, rather, suggested that this man be court-martialed, and that anyone who protected him or covered up for him be court-martialed?

General Zwicker: Yes, sir. . . .

The Chairman: Who ordered his discharge?

General Zwicker: The Department of the Army. . . .

The Chairman: Did you take any steps to have him retained until the Secretary of the Army could decide whether he should be court-martialed?

General Zwicker: No, sir. . . .

The Chairman: Could you have taken such steps?

General Zwicker: No, sir. . . .

The Chairman: Let me ask you this question. If this man, . . . prior to getting an honorable discharge, were guilty of some crime . . . could you then have taken steps to prevent his discharge . . . ?

General Zwicker: I would have definitely taken steps to prevent discharge. . . .

The Chairman: Let us say he went out and stole $50, the night before.

General Zwicker: He wouldn't have been discharged.

The Chairman: Do you think stealing $50 is more serious than being a traitor to the country as part of the Communist conspiracy?

General Zwicker: That, sir, was not my decision. . . .

The Chairman: You did learn, did you not, from newspaper reports, that this man was part of the Communist conspiracy or at least that there was strong evidence that he was? Didn't you think that was more serious than the theft of $50?

General Zwicker: He has never been tried for that, sir, and there was evidence, Mr. Chairman,

The Chairman: Don't give me that doubletalk. The $50 case, that he had stolen the night before, he has not been tried for that. . . .

General Zwicker: On all of the evidence or anything that had been presented to me as Commanding General of Camp Kilmer, I had no authority to retain him. . . .

The Chairman: Let's assume that John Jones is a major in the United States Army. Let's assume that there is sworn testimony to the effect that he is part of the Communist conspiracy. . . . Let's assume that Major John Jones is under oath before a committee and says, "I cannot tell you the truth about these charges because, if I did, I fear that might tend to incriminate me." Then let's say that General Smith was responsible for this man receiving an honorable discharge, knowing these facts. Do you think that General Smith should be removed from the military, or do you think he should be kept in it?

General Zwicker: He should be by all means kept if he were acting under competent orders to separate that man.

The Chairman: Let us say he is the man who signed the orders. Let us say General Smith is the man who originated the order. . . .

General Zwicker: That is not a question for me to decide, Senator.

The Chairman: You are ordered to answer it, General. You are an employee of the people.

General Zwicker: Yes, sir.

The Chairman: You have a rather important job. I want to know how you feel about getting rid of Communists.

General Zwicker:—I am all for it.

The Chairman: All right. You will answer that question, unless you take the Fifth Amendment. I do not care how long we stay here, you are going to answer it.

General Zwicker: Do you mean how I feel toward Communists?

The Chairman: I mean exactly what I asked you, General; nothing else. And anyone with the brains of a 5-year-old can understand that question. . . .

General Zwicker: I do not think he should be removed from the military.

The Chairman: Then, General, you should be removed from any command. Any man who has been given the honor of being promoted to general and who says "I will protect another general who protected Communists," is not fit to wear that uniform, General.

Source 7   "The Big Truth," *The Progressive,* April 1954

If the Kremlin could succeed in planting one of its own agents in the Senate of the United States, it could hardly hope for greater results in creating doubt, disunity, and fear in America than it has gained from McCarthy's operations.

If this judgement seems harsh and extreme, we can only reply that the hard facts . . . make it clear that—

- McCarthy has struck violently at the very principles of freedom and fair play which distinguish democratic self-government from Communist regimentation.
- McCarthy has sown seeds of suspicion and disunity among the nations of the free world at the very moment they most need unity against the threat of Communist aggression.
- McCarthy has flagrantly demoralized the civil and military establishments of our government at a time of unparalleled world crisis.

By substituting headlines and hysteria for facts and evidence, McCarthy has so successfully harnessed Hitler's concept of "The Big Lie" to his own purposes that many decent Americans actually believe he has exposed a Communist plot in our government and rescued the Republic from betrayal by traitors.

Many Americans who share this belief say they find McCarthy's methods repulsive, but they feel in tense times like ours we need someone to do "the dirty work" of exposing the subversives in our midst.

This widely held feeling might be more understandable if McCarthy were in fact exposing Communists and saving us from a Red plot. But fact piled relentlessly on fact shows that the evidence does not in any way support such a conclusion.

In the pitifully rare cases that he has focused his sights on what may have seemed a worthwhile target, McCarthy has so totally distorted the evidence and overplayed his hand as to render his "revelations" less than useless. In his eyes honest mistakes, misjudgments, or misunderstandings became part of a sinister pattern of conspiracy. . . .

More than four years of hit-and-run accusations have yet to produce a single conviction of a Communist in government on evidence uncovered by McCarthy.

Some Americans who know of no specific achievements in McCarthy's record of Red-baiting are still loath to criticize because they think his activities have been worthwhile in dramatizing the evils of Communism and alerting the nation to the menace. However, as Elmer Davis so crisply put it recently, "This amounts to saying that nothing brings the danger of fire more to the attention of the public than turning in false alarms all over town."

But means and methods are important to people who love liberty and cherish principles of tolerance and fair play. It is the contrast between our means and methods, and those of the totalitarians, whether Communist or Fascist, which mark one of the great gulfs between us and them. . . .

We live in a dangerous age, and surely one of the greatest dangers that confronts us is the counterfeit philosophy of Communism and its appeal to the underprivileged of humanity. But we do not begin to meet that menace by burning books, by crushing dissent, and by creating an atmosphere of hysteria. . . .

Here is the heart of our problem in this dangerous age—the challenge to oppose Communism with something better. This we can never hope to do if we abandon our most cherished democratic principles and embrace the very methods we abhor in Communism. . . . McCarthy's daily activities carry us perilously close to the Kremlin concepts that trial by jury must be replaced with trial by mere accusation; that honest, human error of judgment is equivalent to criminal offense; that dissenters are traitors, and that every friendly foreign nation must become our regimented satellite or suffer our wrath and reprisals.

The first battle in the struggle against Communism is within ourselves—to strengthen our own dedication to democracy by living its compelling principles in our daily lives.

Second Thoughts

The Verdict on Joe McCarthy

In December 1954, the Senate voted to censure McCarthy by a vote of 67 to 22. McCarthy retreated from the public forum and died from the effects of chronic alcoholism in May 1957.

Source 8　Henry Bamford Parkes, *The American Experience,* 1959

The early fifties saw a wave of anti-Communist hysteria, resulting in security regulations for all public employees and in a general pressure for conformity which did more damage both to the efficiency of the government and to America's reputation abroad than the Communists could ever have hoped to accomplish. Senator McCarthy, who succeeded in making himself the chief symbol of the hysteria, was too arrogant and brutal to acquire leadership of a major political organization; but McCarthyism, as a manifestation of certain characteristic weaknesses in the American temperament, was more significant than McCarthy. It displayed the American anti-intellectualism, the American tendency to resort to lynch law against supposed public enemies, and, above all, the American illusion of omnipotence and the resultant assumption that treachery was the only possible explanation for failure.

Source 9 Walter LaFeber, *America, Russia, and the Cold War,* 1967

Having won on issues that Republican Senator Karl Mundt neatly formulated as KCC—Korea, Communism, and Corruption—the Eisenhower Administration's foreign policy could not be impervious to McCarthy or the Cold War mentality which spawned McCarthyism. Unlike 1948, foreign policy played a central role in the 1952 campaign, and the campaign in turn left its mark on the foreign policy of the following months. In early 1953, the new Chief Counsel for McCarthy's committee, Roy M. Cohn, and a friend, David Schine, junketed throughout Europe upbraiding American diplomats supposedly soft on Communism, attacking United States Information Service libraries for exhibiting the work of such "radicals" as Mark Twain and Theodore Dreiser, and provoking the wrath of the European Press. Secretary of State Dulles did nothing to stop Cohn and Schine. . . .

Within four months after taking office, the Administration bragged that it had fired 1,456 federal employees under its "security program." The program had not, however, uncovered one proven Communist. So challenged, the Democrats replied that they had effectively fired even more "risks" under Truman's loyalty program. In the midst of the frenzy, one distinguished American Foreign Service officer who had never been tainted by any McCarthyite accusation commented, "If I had a son, I would do everything in my power to suppress any desire he might have to enter the Foreign Service of the United States."

Source 10 Senator Arthur V. Watkins, chairman of the Select Committee to Study Censure Charges, *Enough Rope,* 1969

The judgment of the years . . . is that McCarthy exploited McCarthyism as an instrument to power and personal glory. As a skilled bellringer, he . . . excited his numerous followers with variations of alarm and patriotism with a skill that has seldom been equalled by any demagogue. Yet, I cannot believe that he was a true "prophet," for it was not the cause of anti-communism which inflamed him but the "show" itself and wielding the instruments of power.

When he lost his credibility and standing, and when his showmanship techniques of derring-do (which included terror and abuse) no longer served him but actually turned increasing numbers of people from him, he collapsed like a pricked balloon. . . .

It appears to me that McCarthy hunted "communists" solely for the attention, publicity, and tumult it earned him—and for the headlines. When he lost these, he lost everything that counted.

If McCarthyism had not served its creator well, in the long run, it certainly did not contribute to the political health of the Nation. Many people observed that insecure and frightened people had frequently demonstrated their "patriotism and loyalty" by raising questions concerning the patriotism and loyalty of their fellow workers and sometime friends. This was one of the ugliest symptoms of the period. No Nation can long prosper in an atmosphere of suspicion and distrust.

We know that many Federal workers, convinced that it was their duty to report their suspicions direct to Senator McCarthy and to his Subcommittee, made allegations that frequently were not supported by even the most elemental statements of fact or proof. Oftimes, self-appointed "agents" wrote anonymously. Seldom, if ever, did a suspected person have the opportunity of facing his accusers or of testing the evidence, or indeed of even knowing that charges had been made against him.

It has been amply documented by others and, in fact, almost universally observed that the McCarthy period was noted chiefly for character assassination, slur, and suspicion.

Source 11 Robert Griffith, *The Politics of Fear*, 1970

Behind the rise of Joe McCarthy to national power lay at least five interrelated and interacting lines of causation: a fear of radicalism which sometimes bordered on the pathological; the course of America's cold war with the Soviet Union and its not-so-cold war with North Korea and China; the singular character and abilities of Joseph McCarthy; the structure of power both within the Senate and between the Senate and the Executive; and the routine operation of American party politics.

The first of these, what has been called the anti-Communist persuasion, has been a persistent theme of American history in this century. While it dictated the slogans and style used by McCarthy in his sudden rise to power, it was not in turn diminished by his equally sudden demise. The cold war furnished the concrete staples of party debate, and it was of some significance that McCarthy's rise coincided with the outbreak of hostilities in Korea while his decline came not long after the armistice.

Of greater importance was McCarthy himself. He was not the most gifted demagogue this country has ever known, but his talents in this direction were considerable. His stubborn unwillingness to underplay his hand or back down from a battle was his great strength and in the end his undoing. He also understood the cumbersome, decentralized, and individualistic nature of the Senate's internal processes, and he was a skillful manipulator of that body's institutional jealousy of the Executive.

But McCarthy's power and influence rested on more than this. His triumph was the consequence of Republican partisanship and, after 1950, of Democratic acquiescence. To many Republicans he symbolized the issues generated by more than a decade of attacks against the Democratic Administrations of Franklin Roosevelt and Harry Truman. Most Democrats feared him as a threat to personal and party fortunes. As a result, neither party acted to check McCarthy or to restrain his excessive behavior. In this sense both McCarthy and McCarthyism can be understood as products of the normal operation of American political parties.

In the end McCarthy was brought down by the Senate, although this would have never been possible had McCarthy not finally become an embarrassment to his own party and had not the Senate been forced against its will to confront him. Even then the Senate circumspectly avoided the very issues which were central to the entire McCarthy controversy. For the practical politicians who governed the Senate this was sufficient—the McCarthy interregnum was ended. For those more critical of the American party system there were two further observations—that if instrumental politics were responsible for McCarthy's defeat, they were also responsible for his rise and for the prolongation of his power, and that between 1950 and 1954 the politics of the possible were also the politics of fear.

Source 12 Thomas C. Reeves, *The Life and Times of Joe McCarthy: A Biography,* 1982

Few journalists, and even fewer historians, have ever expressed sympathy for McCarthy since his death. Not a single college textbook from a major publisher is even neutral toward him. . . . Perhaps no other figure in American history has been portrayed so consistently as the essence of evil. He is our King John. Some writers have assigned him at least partial responsibility for America's inflexible China policy, the Vietnam War, Goldwater's capture of the G.O.P. in 1964, even Watergate. . . .

Of course, there is a great deal to be said against McCarthy. He was guilty of frequent lying and slander. Untold hundreds of Americans suffered directly from his zeal to find and punish subversives. He disrupted two Administrations and impeded serious congressional activity. He lent his support to a rigid foreign policy that would haunt the nation for generations. He backed efforts to curtail academic freedom and censure unpopular ideas. Evidence strongly suggests that he lowered morale throughout the federal government. . . .

Still, Joe had many personal qualities that biographers and others have chosen to ignore. He was not the amoral, cynical, thieving, homosexual monster his critics described. . . . Nor was Joe the grave threat to the Constitution and to the nation he has seemed by some to be. He had no ideology or program of any significance. His ambition was limited. . . .

Moreover, there was more to McCarthyism than McCarthy. Joe encountered the second Red Scare somewhat late. It burned intensely for some three years after his censure. Others surely share as much, if not more, blame for the ugliness that plagued the years from 1948 to 1957.

Source 13 David M. Oshinsky, *A Conspiracy So Immense: The World of Joe McCarthy,* 1983

[T]he senator came to believe in the cause he had stumbled upon in 1950. His enemies never accepted this fact. Their Joe McCarthy was a cynic, a nihilist, a politician on the make. He believed in nothing, wrote Richard Rovere. "He could not comprehend true outrage, true indignation, true anything."

For the most part, historians have accepted this portrait of McCarthy. Some have even debunked his talents, calling him an "unimaginative opportunist" and a "second-rate politician." In doing so they have ignored the obvious questions: Why Joe McCarthy? Why did *he* dominate the era that carries his name? The answer is simple: McCarthy *was unique*. He had competitors but no equals. He was bolder than the **Mundts** and smarter than the **Welkers**. He knew how to use the media. He crafted a very effective public image. And he was adept at probing the weak spots of his opponents.

Above all, the senator provided a simple explanation for America's "decline" in the world. He spoke of a massive internal conspiracy, directed by Communists and abetted by government officials who came to include the Republican President of the United States. He provided names, documents, and statistics—in short, the *appearance* of diligent research. And he understood intuitively that force, action, and virility were essential prerequisites in the Red-hunting crusade.

Yet, for all of this, McCarthy seemed curiously self-contained. He had no desire to lead a movement, to run for higher office, or to formulate a program that went beyond the simple exposure of Communists. His political skills were keen, but his reach was limited. And his ambition was too.

He was not a would-be dictator. He did not threaten our constitutional system, but he did hurt many who lived under it. He slandered dozens of prominent citizens. . . . He played a role in chasing the China Hands out of government; as a result, he must bear some of the responsibility for America's disastrous Asian policy in later years. He terrorized witnesses who appeared before his committee. He had a devastating effect on government morale, and he made America look ridiculous— and frightening—in the eyes of much of the world. His investigations of . . . the Army Signal Corps were as destructive as any in recent memory. At his best, he produced evidence that the government's security procedures were sometimes remiss. But his critics were right: he never uncovered a Communist.

Source 14 Richard M. Fried, *Nightmare in Red: The McCarthy Era in Perspective,* 1990

There was far more to the "McCarthy era" than Senator Joseph R. McCarthy. . . . With deep roots in American culture, anti-communism flourished long before the Senator from Wisconsin adopted the issue in 1950. . . . Similarly, coverage of anti-Communism does not end with McCarthy's censure by the Senate in 1954. Though that event did contribute to anti-Communism's decline as a force in American life, the death scene was a lingering one. . . .

For many the McCarthy era stands as the grimmest time in recent memory. Beset by Cold War anxieties, Americans developed an obsession with domestic Communism that outran the actual threat and gnawed at the tissue of civil liberties. For some politicians, hunting Reds became a passport to fame—or notoriety. . . .

It is tempting to locate "McCarthyism" only in the realm of high politics—as the combined sum of national headlines, noisy rhetoric, and congressional inquiries. Yet it was more than that. The anti-Communist drive touched thousands of lesser figures: a printer in the U.S. Government Printing Office, linguists and engineers at the Voice of America overseas broadcasting service, a Seattle fireman, local public housing officials, janitors, even men's room attendants. Long before the "McCarthy era," loyalty oaths affected teachers. Lawyers, other professionals, and, in Indiana, even wrestlers had to document their loyalty. Colleges policed students' political activities. Labor leaders and unions rose or fell according to their sympathy or hostility toward Communism. Entertainers faced a "blacklist." Ordinary people responded to the anti-Communist fervor by reining in their political activities, curbing their talk, and keeping their thoughts to themselves. . . .

How deeply did anti-Communism gouge the social and political terrain of the 1950s? With dissent defined as dangerous, the range of political debate obviously was crimped. The number of times that books were labeled dangerous, thoughts were scourged as harmful, and speakers and performers were rejected as outside the pale multiplied. Anti-Communist extremism and accompanying pressures toward conformity had impact in such areas as artistic expression, the labor movement, the cause of civil rights, and the status of minorities in American life. . . .

Rampant anti-Communism narrowed the range of selection open to associations, utterances, and ideas. People were constrained by both external pressures and the inner clocks with which they reactively restricted their own affairs. Fear was manifest in delicate matters of personal choice—such as what to read and think—as well as in more public behavior. In this latter respect, the collective result was a significant slowing of the momentum of change in a number of areas of American life. . . .

Public sensitivity to civil liberties was notoriously limited in the second Red Scare. As early as the 1930s, majorities expressed support for the drastic treatment of radicals that politicians of the Cold War era would later enact. Indeed, poll respondents often advocated rougher justice than did the political elite. This low public tolerance for political deviance, along with the rhythms of party politics and the anxieties driven by events of the Cold War, has been a central theme in explaining the onset of the second Red Scare. McCarthyism was an elite phenomenon, but any explanation of it must, in some way account for the existence of consistently high levels of public support for suppression of Communists.

 ## Questioning the Past

1. "McCarthyism" entered the English language in the 1950s as a term describing, as the Random House Dictionary put it, "1. public accusation of disloyalty to one's country, esp. through pro-Communist activity, in many instances unsupported by proof, or based on slight, doubtful, or irrelevant evidence. 2. unfairness in investigative technique. 3. persistent search for, and exposure of disloyalty, esp. in government office." Based on the readings, does this definition accurately describe Joseph McCarthy's crusade and techniques?

2. Senator Joseph McCarthy is said to have used innuendo, half-truths, guilt by association, and smear tactics in attacking his opponents. Analyze the senator's attack on Drew Pearson and his questioning of General Ralph Zwicker and judge the effectiveness and the fairness of his tactics.

3. What was the impact of McCarthyism?

4. While McCarthy came to personify the era, he was only the most visible component of a crusade against political non-conformity. Why were Americans susceptible to McCarthyism? Is the America of today immune to this kind of political tactic?

Chapter 22

The Guatemala Coup

A Government Is Overthrown, *June 18, 1954*

At a time when Imperial Rome was crumbling under the assaults of barbarians and Europe was descending into what some have called its Dark
Ages, a great civilization was flourishing far to the west in a world as yet
unknown to Europeans. It was the civilization of the Maya, and its
achievements were extraordinary.

Stretching across what is now El Salvador, Honduras, Belize, Guatemala, and parts of Mexico was a nation as densely populated as modern
China; a nation whose scientific, astronomical, agricultural, and mathe-
matical knowledge was among the most advanced in the world, a nation
whose cities were marvels of engineering skill and architectural beauty.
Pyramids topped by temples rose to the height of 20-story buildings. Surrounding such structures were paved plazas and concourses, multistoried
palaces, brightly painted buildings and administrative complexes, market
places, vapor baths, athletic fields, and astronomical observatories. Res-
ervoirs trapped water for urban use, and grid patterns of canals and farm
lands—some covering thousands of square miles—produced food for distribution across the land.

For around six hundred years, the civilization of the Maya enjoyed
an unprecedented run of progress and prosperity, and then, one by one,
beginning around the year 790, the Mayan people abandoned their cities
and allowed nature to reclaim them. Hundreds of ghost cities lie buried
under a carpet of jungle vegetation today, and the Mayan people themselves, perhaps four to six million in number, still live amid the ruins of
their once great civilization.

When the Spanish conquistadors arrived in Maya lands shortly after
their conquest of Mexico, they found the remnants of the Mayan world and
subdued it. Maya lands were given by the Spanish Crown to European aristocrats. These noblemen established landed estates and virtually enslaved the
Native American population as a labor force. For almost three centuries the
Mayan people were ruled by Spain and exploited by Spanish overlords.

On September 15, 1821, the ruling families of Guatemala, inspired
by the success of their Mexican neighbors in overthrowing Spanish rule,
declared the independence of Central America. Initially, Guatemala and
the other Central American states joined the Mexican Empire. This union,
however, was shortlived. Though Chiapas—populated largely by Maya—
stayed to become a Mexican state, Guatemala, Honduras, El Salvador,

357

Nicaragua, and Costa Rica formed a federation called the United Provinces of Central America. This confederation collapsed within a generation and by 1839 Guatemala stood alone as an independent country.

Independence for Guatemala did not result in freedom for the Guatemalan people. Quite the contrary, political and economic power remained in the hands of the wealthy landed gentry and the Guatemalan government was ruled by a series of dictators. The vast majority of the population remained illiterate, impoverished and excluded from the benefits of society.

A revolution in 1931 brought General Jorge Ubico to power in Guatemala. Ubico ruled the country with an iron hand and was ruthless in his suppression of political opposition. His rigid rule led to a student revolt in 1944. So strong was the movement of the university students that Ubico was forced to resign.

The student rebellion led to a liberal constitution and democratic elections. On March 15, 1945, Dr. Juan Jose Arevalo, a university professor, was inaugurated as the first fairly elected president in Guatemala's stormy history. Arevalo and the new Guatemalan Congress moved to bring about long-overdue reforms. Labor unions were legalized and attention was given to the desperate plight of the country's large lower class. These efforts to raise wages and improve working conditions engendered resentment from Guatemala's wealthy elite and from foreign corporations long accustomed to profiting from prevailing circumstances. Twenty-four armed attempts were made by reactionary elements to overthrow the elected government, but Arevalo miraculously survived and successfully completed his term.

In the subsequent election, the voters of Guatemala elected Col. Jacobo Guzman Arbenz to succeed Arevalo. Arbenz continued the process of reform and, like his predecessor, sought to cultivate a political environment open to all viewpoints, including those of communists. In the spring of 1952, President Arbenz proposed, and the Guatemalan Congress overwhelmingly approved, a new land reform law that permitted the government to expropriate uncultivated lands and distribute them to the landless peasants of the country, most of whom were Indians. The landowners would receive long-term government bonds in compensation for the loss of their lands. It was hoped that the law would begin the breakup of the feudal landholding patterns and give the peasants an economic base. A thousand acres of Arbenz's own land went to this purpose, as did tens of thousands of acres belonging to the nation's elite and foreign companies. The most notable of these foreign firms called upon to surrender land to the peasants was the United Fruit Company, an American-owned corporation long the leading employer in much of Central America.

22.1 The United Fruit Company

The move against United Fruit marked the beginning of the end of Arbenz and democracy in Guatemala.

⚬ꝋ *First Impressions*

A Major Test of American Will

To many Guatemalans, their country was a world of its own. In fact, to many Guatemalans, the limits of their village were the limits of the world. But there was a world outside Guatemala and this larger world was in the midst of a Cold War between two great powers. These two adversaries were the poles around which global affairs revolved, and they seemed unable to think of any local event except as a skirmish in the larger battle for global supremacy.

The American secretary of state, John Foster Dulles, was convinced that Latin America would be the site chosen by the Soviet Union for a major test of American will. When he saw communists included in labor unions in Guatemala, and lands being bought from the rich and given to the poor, he saw the specter of international communism. When Guatemala attempted to buy weapons from the United States, Dulles balked because of a suspicion that these arms would be going to a potential enemy. When Guatemala then turned to the Soviet bloc for weapons, he felt his suspicion confirmed.

When the foreign ministers of the American nations met at the Tenth Inter-American Conference in Caracas, Venezuela, in March 1954, the United States pushed for passage of a resolution uniting the Americas against the Communist menace. The resolution stated that "the domination or control of the political institutions of any American state by the international communist movement . . . would constitute a threat" to the Western Hemisphere as a whole. Seventeen nations voted in favor of this resolution. Mexico and Argentina declined to vote. Only one nation voted against it. This sole dissenting vote was that of Guatemala.

22.2 Documents relating to American Foreign Policy

Was an unwillingness to oppose communism the same as support for it? Was Guatemala out of step with the values of the Americas? Many thought so.

Source 1   Paul P. Kennedy, "Revolt Launched in Guatemala: Land-Air-Sea Invasion Reported; Uprisings Under Way in Key Cities," *New York Times,* June 19, 1954

Guatemala, June 18—The battle for Guatemala is on, Foreign Minister Guillermo Toriello announced today.

Speaking from his office in the National Palace, he said that unidentified planes from an undetermined take-off point bombed the country's gasoline stores last night. He did not identify the location of these stores, but it was believed one target was San Jose, a major port on the southwestern Pacific coast.

Shortly before 10 A.M. today word reached this correspondent that shooting had broken out in Puerto Barrios, an east coast port. No details were available.

A half-hour later word came that the uprising had begun in the town of Retalhuleu about thirty miles south of the Mexican border.

Source 2   "Invaders Hold Third of Nation," Washington *Evening Star,* June 19, 1954

BULLETIN

United Nations, N.Y. (AP)—Guatemala asked today for an emergency week-end session of the U.N. Security Council to consider "aggression" against her territory, her representative to the U.N. said.

Tegucigalpa, Honduras, June 19—Two strategic Guatemala seaports were reported in the hands of invading anti-Communist "Liberation Army" forces today.

Local informants of the Liberation Army identified the two cities as Puerto Barrios on the Caribbean and San Jose on the Pacific.

The army, under command of former Guatemalan Army Lt. Col. Carlos Castillo Armas, said two important inland rail centers also may be in control of the invaders. . . .

(NBC correspondent Mac Bannell reported in a Tegucigalpa broadcast heard in New York this morning that the invaders then held a third of Guatemala. He said two planes had machine-gunned the Presidential Palace in the capital.)

The invasion was the culmination of a long-standing effort to unseat the Communist-backed government of President Jacobo Arbenz Guzman. . . .

The rebel invading force reportedly numbers about 5,000 men. The Guatemalan Army is about 6,000 strong, but many of the officers are believed disgruntled by the leftist trends of the government. United States officials have expressed fears the Arbenz regime was creating a Communist beachhead within short range of the Panama Canal. . . .

The rebel strike against Puerto Barrios apparently was at least partly a seaborne invasion. Reports said one body of heavily armed men had sailed for the port from Hog Island, off Tela on the Honduran north coast. Informants said an armed boat which pulled out of the Honduran port of La Ceiba earlier was aiming at the big East Coast shipping center.

The rebels' secret "Liberation Radio" urged Guatemalans to disobey the government's blackout orders. The broadcast, heard here, also instructed all Guatemalans opposed to the government to withdraw their money immediately from the nation's banks.

In Washington, Guatemalan Charge d'Affaires Alfredo Chocano described the uprisings as the climax of a well-laid plot. He said his government has repeatedly denounced preparations in Honduras for an attack. . . .

The conflict has been building for years but the situation became tense after the United States State Department officials denounced the Arbenz regime as Communist-influenced.

Although it has been estimated that there are not more than 1,000 actual card-carrying Communists in Guatemala, Reds control many strategic areas of public life. A declared Communist, Moscow-trained Manuel Gutierrez, heads the Guatemalan Workers Federation. A fellow traveler runs the powerful landless Farmers Union. These two groups have a combined membership of more than 100,000.

The 40-year-old president and his government have consistently denied the charges of Red domination. They insist there are no Communists in the cabinet.

Mr. Arbenz first came into prominence in 1944 as chief organizer of the army revolt that overthrew dictator Jorge Ubico that year. He was inaugurated president in 1951.

With the aid of Communists and their allies, Mr. Arbenz has pushed an ambitious program for improving the lot of the landless peasant. All but a half a million of the nation's 3,283,209 people depend on farming for their livelihood. Seventy percent of the land, however, is owned by two percent of the people.

The climax came May 17 when the State Department announced a $10 million arms shipment from Stettin, a port in Communist-ruled Poland, was being unloaded at Puerto Barrios. Mr Dulles said the shipment made Guatemala the dominant military power in Central America.

American officials expressed fears the aim was to establish a Red beachhead only 750 miles from the Panama Canal.

Source 3   United Press International, "U.S. Spurred Rebels, He Says," June 19, 1954

Mexico City, June 19 (UP)—President Arbenz called upon the Guatemalan people to help his Government's fight against the rebels.

In a twenty-seven minute speech, monitored here, Senor Arbenz attacked the United States, Honduras, and Nicaragua for encouraging the rebellion and defended his regime against the charges that it is Communist-dominated.

"Our crime is that of agrarian reform against imperialist owned companies," Senor Arbenz said. "Our crime is that we patriotically seek economic independence. Communism does not exist in these endeavors."

Source 4   Statement on Guatemala issued by the U.S. State Department, June, 19, 1954

The Department has no evidence that indicates that this is anything other than a revolt of Guatemalans against the government. . . .

The latest outbursts of violence within Guatemala confirm the previously expressed view of the United States concerning possible action by the O.A.S. (Organization of American States) on the problem of Communist intervention in Guatemala. The Department has been exchanging views with other countries of this hemisphere, who are also gravely concerned by the situation in Guatemala regarding action needed to protect the hemisphere from further encroachment by international communism.

Source 5   Paul P. Kennedy, "Anti-Reds' Invasion Progresses," *New York Times,* June 20, 1954

Guatemala City—The Guatemalan Government has announced that the invading anti-Communist rebel forces have captured the town of El Florida and have advanced about nine miles into Guatemala from the Honduras border. . . .

The capital city awakened to its second day under attack to the gunfire of hostile fighter planes and its own anti-aircraft fire.

An air raid early this morning on the city of Guatemala was the third since Foreign Minister Guillermo Toriello announced yesterday that the battle for Guatemala was on.

President Jacobo Arbenz Guzman of Guatemala, in a broadcast speech to his country at 10 P.M., Eastern daylight time, accused Honduras and Nicaragua of "open aggression" in conjunction with the United States. . . .

The Interior Ministry, in a bulletin issued this morning, said that a plane yesterday, last night and this morning had "produced a new and flagrant act of aggression." The bulletin said a fighter plane had strafed public office buildings and dropped bombs on a military establishment.

The bulletin continued: "The Government denounces before national and international public opinion these incidents, which were brought about by the enemies of Guatemala and their powerful allies."

Meanwhile, Ambassador John E. Puerifoy was called to the National Palace last night and was officially informed by Foreign Minister Toriello that the attack on Guatemala had begun and that he had requested a convocation of the United Nations Security Council to study the affair.

The Ambassador, with the French Minister and the British Charge d'affaires, were called to the Palace at 7 P.M. Other members of the diplomatic corps were called in later.

The Foreign Minister also remarked that two planes that "buzzed" the capital yesterday afternoon had been identified as of North American manufacture. Mr Peurifoy is reported to have replied that planes of North American manufacture were in all parts of the world.

The planes that "buzzed" the city were identified as P-47 Thunderbolts of post-World War II design. They roared over the downtown section at about 700 feet. They drew several bursts of anti-aircraft fire and disappeared in the southwest, gaining altitude.

Source 6   Editorial, "Guatemalan Whirlwind," Washington *Evening Star,* June 20, 1954

Guatemala today is reaping the whirlwind which the Communist-infiltrated government of President Arbenz has been sowing in recent years.

At a pace that has quickened in the past few months, the Arbenz regime has fallen more and more under the control of a hard-core group of card-carrying Communists—some of them Moscow-trained. In the course of this subversion, Guatemala's relations with the American community as a whole and with her immediate neighbors in particular have deteriorated to the point of leaving her government, though not her people, friendless in this hemisphere. And in the same period, hundreds of Guatemalans—many of them influential in the politics of the country—have gone voluntarily into exile. It is this group, rallying around the leadership of Colonel Castillo Armas—who received part of his military training in the United States—that forms the backbone of the revolutionary effort now engulfing the country.

On several occasions, Secretary of State Dulles has made clear our Government's concern with the political situation in Guatemala. And when Guatemala cast the single dissenting vote in the otherwise solid front favoring the anti-Communist Caracas resolution, Mr. Dulles' words were almost prophetic. "We shall have the task," he said, referring to the 17 American signatories, "of assuring that the enemies of freedom do not move into the breach which has been disclosed within our ranks . . . I am confident . . . this hemisphere is not good hunting ground for alien despots." Guatemalans who favor liberty over despotism are demonstrating today that Mr. Dulles' confidence had a sound foundation.

Source 7   Editorial, "Revolt in Guatemala," *New York Times*, June 20, 1954

The expected has happened in Guatemala. Elements opposed to the slow Communist infiltration of the Government have taken up arms to end it. . . .

The setting, with its great variations of climate, with its tall volcanic mountains, is melodramatic. So is the human background. This is a land of an ancient culture and race overlaid by the thin veneer of European civilization. This is not to say that the Mayas who make up most of the population of Guatemala are a truculent or unintelligent people. They are neither. They are quiet, soft-spoken, long-suffering, hampered largely by their lack of knowledge of modern technological equipment.

These toiling millions, clinging to their old traditions, cultivating their corn according to those traditions rather than to the latest findings of the agricultural experts, had nothing to say as to whether Guatemala should be Communist or not. They did have grievances that perhaps made it easy to stir them against any existing situation. They could not be expected to know that if their lot was hard now it would be infinitely worse if a new Moscow-linked tyranny were set up.

Guatemala has had ten years of uncertainty since its dictator, General Jorge Ubico, was thrown out in 1944. For a time it looked as though democratic reform might create and perpetuate a free country. But there was unrest and rivalry among the politicians and these did not express themselves freely in elections and Congressional hearings as they do here. . . .

It would be dangerously inconsistent for our Government to welcome any revolution in Latin America achieved principally by troops moving in from neighboring states. That practice, if used by reactionaries to overthrow democratic governments, would obviously seem wrong.

Source 8   James Reston, "With the Dulles Brothers in Darkest Guatemala," *New York Times*, June 20, 1954

John Foster Dulles, the Secretary of State, seldom intervenes in the internal affairs of other countries, but his brother Allen is more enterprising.

If somebody wants to start a revolution against the Communists in, say, Guatemala, it is no good talking to Foster Dulles. But Allen Dulles, head of the Central Intelligence Agency, is a more active man.

He has been watching the Guatemalan situation for a long time. . . .

The guess here is that the revolt against the Communists will succeed if the Guatemalan Army is as divided as the C.I.A. thinks it is, but the revolt will not deal with the main Latin-American problem, which is poverty and pestilence in a rich but divided continent. . . .

Latin America is not only fragmentized politically and economically, but disillusioned by the United States' emphasis on military power. The dreams of continental economic solidarity, encouraged by Washington during the last war, have not been realized, and the hopes of a post-war prosperity have been disappointed.

Politically, the United States has responded effectively over the last generation to Latin America's juridical principles. Theodore Roosevelt's corollary to the Monroe Doctrine of 1904 was revoked. The Marines were withdrawn from Nicaragua and Haiti. The Platt Amendment was repealed; Woodrow Wilson's unilateral doctrine of non-recognition was abandoned; and the good-neighbor policy established.

In the single generation between the Roosevelts the resentment against United States imperialism was very largely wiped away, but since the war the dollar surpluses built up by the sale of raw materials from 1941–45 have vanished, and the condition of the people has steadily declined.

During the first five post-war years the United States put out more than $25 billion in grants and credits to foreign countries, only $514,000,000, or 1.8 percent, went to Latin America.

During this same period the Latin American countries succeeded in attracting only about $975 million of net private direct investment capital from the United States, and much of this went not into production for domestic markets or industrial development or the fields of education, health, transportation, irrigation or reclamation but into the development of raw materials for export.

While billions were crossing the Atlantic to build strong European economies against the threat of communism, Latin America's appeals for a Marshall Plan of its own were ignored. Washington's money, it seemed, was available only to fight the Communists, and this in itself encouraged the growth of Latin American communism. . . .

Moscow is now definitely fishing in these long-troubled waters. It sees the possibility of Latin America's disillusion. It resents the strong Latin American support for the United States at the United Nations. It fears United States bases of operation near its own frontiers and is now obviously trying to establish Communist Governments near ours.

Mr Dulles (Allen, that is) can no doubt help block this objective in Guatemala but it will take John Foster Dulles and the Congress to bring about a policy change that will deal with the central economic problems of the hemisphere.

Source 9   Editorial, *The Times* of London, June 21, 1954

The world is all too familiar with the tactics and language employed when left-wing or right-wing rebels have sought to overthrow a democratic Government. Truth is the first casualty. To-day in Guatemala a movement drawing its sustenance from anti-Communist sources is trying to overthrow by force a Government with Communist sympathies which has brought its case before the United Nations. The free world has to be sure of what is happening. It should also preserve a judicial attitude.

Cool detachment may be less easy for the United States, which has great interests much more directly threatened by Communism in Guatemala, than it is for this country. The United Fruit Company has been to Guatemala what the Anglo-Iranian Oil Company has been to Persia. Since 1952 its position has been threatened, and its future will probably be affected by the outcome of the present crisis. Americans noted with anxiety the arrival of a large shipment of arms from Poland last month, and are determined to do what they can to prevent a repetition. But Americans and Communists equally have reason to wonder whether anything of lasting value can be gained just now by making a major issue of this present affair. The Russians do not usually support a sickly ally; and the United States is well aware that respect for the independence of nations is one of the western Powers' greatest moral strengths.

Source 10   "Troops Pushed Back," *The Times* of London, June 22, 1954

Guatemala City, June 21.—Government forces have engaged the anti-Communist "forces" at Gualan, near Zacapa, about 75 miles from here, a high command communique stated to-day. This was the first indication that troops loyal to President Arbenz's Government had made contact with the invading forces. It stated that the high command had "undertaken a powerful counter-offensive on all fronts invaded by the enemy," and that contact had first been made with the rebels at 11:45 p.m. yesterday. Well-equipped regular troops would use all their power "to bring about a final victory."

Rebel troops were forced to retreat after obstinate resistance in the engagement at Gualan, the communique stated. Government forces also pushed back rebel troops at the Caribbean port of Puerto Barrios after a brief skirmish yesterday. A schooner of Honduran registry carrying a cargo of arms was captured in the port and the crew taken prisoner.

Rebel aircraft had strafed military installations and railways at Zacapa City, causing slight damage. The communique added that it had been confirmed that an aircraft which had flown over Guatemala City "in the past few days" and had fired on the population was seriously damaged by anti-aircraft fire. It crossed the Mexican border and landed in the border city of Tapachula. The crew of two, both stated to be North Americans, were interned by the Mexican Government. One was seriously wounded.

Source 11   Alvarado Fuentes, Guatemalan ambassador to Mexico, statement on the origin of the invasion, June 23, 1954

The hostilities are the outcome of the refusal of the United Fruit Company to comply with the Agrarian Reform Law of 1952, which was not communistic, but nationalized uncultivated land and amply compensated owners without discrimination against foreigners. The United Fruit Company has backed the aggression, with the connivance of the United States. The rebel leaders are the ex-convict Colonel Castillo Armas, a group of politicians of the Ubico regime, and mercenaries. Guatemala has bought normal army supplies from Communist countries because the United States refused to sell them to us.

Source 12   Editorial, "Poverty and Communism," *Washington Post*, June 24, 1954

Either way the somewhat murky conflict in Guatemala turns out, as one correspondent has noted, the United States stands to get the blame. This is indicated by the vote of the Chilean Chamber of Deputies condemning the revolt and expressing to the United States its "grave preoccupation." However questionable the origin of the insurgent movement, it cannot be doubted that the Arbenz government in Guatemala has become a vehicle of Soviet imperialism. But the struggle in Guatemala is symbolic of the underlying discontent throughout Latin America, and it behooves this country in its own interest to take a closer look at some of the conditions that make Latin America such a fertile seedbed for Soviet designs.

It would be foolish to think that many of the people of Guatemala, largely Indian in background, have any sympathy with communism as such. Guatemala emerged in 1944 from long years of oppression under the dictator, Jorge Ubico. Unquestionably there was a good deal of idealism in the movement for social reform, and the Mexican Revolution of 40 years ago was held up as an example. But the revolution miscarried when the leaders found that there was no ready alternative to Guatemala's economic dependence on other countries, and they sought a scapegoat.

Many of the sins charged against the United Fruit were sins of the past: in recent years the company has paid good wages and has promoted scientific agriculture, and it has shown itself willing to share its profits fairly. It was easy enough for demagogues to play upon native anti-foreignism and to blame "foreign exploitation" for Guatemala's poverty and other ills; and it was also easy for Soviet agents, playing upon the discontent of the students and intellectuals, to bend the movement to suit Communist purposes.

The situation in Guatemala is different from other Latin American countries, but only in degree. Throughout the hemisphere there is the same sort of resentment over real or fancied economic exploitation, deriving from the fact that the production of raw materials is the primary industry. The Latin producer is somewhat in the plight of the American farmer in that he has no control over the final use of his product, but in Latin America the producer cannot generally rely on a price-support system. Hence the concern in Chile over world copper prices, the concern in Bolivia over tin markets, the recent complaint in Costa Rica that the United Fruit Co. was bigger than the government, the hypersensitivity in a number of countries to criticism of coffee prices. . . .

But the problem is not wholly economic: it also is psychological and emotional. Former Assistant Secretary of State Cabot touched on an important consideration when he pointed out that the United States cannot be placed in a position of resisting social reforms. If we hope to divert the people of Latin America from false panaceas, we must have something positive to offer in their stead. Somehow we must persuade the Latin Americans, with a lot more vigor than we have hitherto employed, that we are not dedicated to the status quo, and that we are sincerely anxious to help them better their lot. Poverty does not automatically make communism, but it is a strong ally when an international conspiracy stands ready to exploit it. That is the lesson of Guatemala.

Source 13   Paul P. Kennedy, "President of Guatemala Ousted by Anti-Communist Army Junta," *New York Times*, June 28, 1954

Guatemala, June 27—The regime of Jacobo Arbenz Guzman came to an end tonight. He agreed to step down in favor of a military junta.

The decision was forced by the Army after an all-day meeting of its chiefs. Three colonels visited the National Palace and forced the President to agree to step down. His personal safety and that of his family were guaranteed. . . .

The Army chiefs agreed that one of the junta's first acts would be to move against the Communists. . . .

The President was reported to have been extremely angry when informed that the present situation could not continue. This occurred at 4 P.M. today. Two hours later it was announced that the President would address the nation at 9 P.M.

Source 14 President Jacobo Arbenz Guzman of Guatemala, radio address to the Guatemalan people, 9:15 P.M., June 28, 1954

Workers, peasants, patriots, my friends: people of Guatemala: Guatemala is enduring a most difficult trial. For fifteen days a cruel war against Guatemala has been underway. The United Fruit Company, in collaboration with the governing circles of the United States, is responsible for what is happening to us. . . .

In whose name have they carried out these barbaric acts? What is their banner? We know very well. They have used the pretext of anti-communism. The truth is very different. The truth is to be found in the financial interests of the fruit company and the other U.S. monopolies which have invested great amounts of money in Latin America and fear that the example of Guatemala would be followed by other Latin countries. . . .

I have made a sad and cruel judgment . . . I have decided to step down and place the nation's executive power in the hands of . . . (the) chief of the armed forces of the republic. . . .

I was elected by a majority of the people of Guatemala, but I have had to fight under difficult conditions. The truth is that the sovereignty of a people cannot be maintained without the material elements to defend it. . . .

The military situation in the country is far from difficult. The enemy who commands the bands of foreign mercenaries recruited by Castillo Armas is not only weak, but completely cowardly. We have seen this in the few combat encounters we have had. The enemy was able to advance and take areas of Chiquimula only because of the attacks of mercenary aircraft. I believe that our armed forces would not have great difficulty in defeating him and expelling him from the country.

I took over the presidency with great faith in the democratic system, in liberty and in the possibility of achieving economic independence for Guatemala. I continue to believe that this program is just. I have not violated my faith in democratic liberties, in the independence of Guatemala and in all the good which is the future of humanity.

One day the obscured forces which today oppress the backward and colonial world will be defeated. I will continue to be, despite everything, a fighter for the liberty and progress of my country.

I say goodbye to you, my friends, with bitterness and pain, but remaining firm in my convictions. Remember how much it has cost. Ten years of struggle, of tears, of sacrifices and of democratic victories.

Source 15 J. A. del Vayo, "War against the U.N.," *The Nation,* 1954

United Nations, June 28

At this writing it is not certain whether the unexpected resignation of Guatemala's President, Jacobo Arbenz, will prove a victory for the United States and for the rebel forces under Castillo Armas, or merely for the military junta which forced the President out of office. It is not even clear whether the development marks the end of the tragic-comic sitzkrieg situation or the beginning of real fighting. Until Arbenz was obliged to step down, the rebel's talkative leader, despite the formidable strength attributed to him, had been able to report only one military development indisputably in his favor—the appointing of himself as a general. Therefore whatever pressures prompted the army junta to turn upon Arbenz, the fear of military defeat at the hands of the rebels was not among them.

Source 16 Washington *Evening Star,* "Guatemala Shooting Ends as Reds Flee," June 30, 1954

Guatemala, June 30.—The fighting was over today in Guatemala's 12 day civil war and the United States Embassy hailed the outcome as a victory over communism.

The new military regime called on all civilians to surrender any arms in their possession. It prepared for talks with the anti-Communist insurgents on the future course of this Central American republic.

Col. Carlos Castillo Armas' rebel forces announced that a cease-fire would remain in effect pending formal armistice negotiations.

Former President Jacobo Arbenz Guzman was reported to have taken refuge in the Mexican Embassy here, along with Communist and left-wing leaders who had supported his regime.

Col. Alfego Monzon, the leader of the new junta, called on all persons to surrender their arms or face severe punishment. . . .

Col. Monzon and Col. Castillo Armas were expected to meet today or tomorrow in neighboring El Salvador to work out details of both a new armistice and a new government.

Diplomats here in the Guatemalan capital believed the two—anti-Communists both—would join in still another new governing junta. The general feeling was that Col. Castillo Armas could dictate his own terms.

Col. Monzon's four-man junta, which took over in the capital before dawn yesterday, already had launched a roundup of Communists.

Source 17 U.S. secretary of state John Foster Dulles, text of radio address on Guatemala, June 30, 1954

Tonight I should like to talk to you about Guatemala. It is a scene of dramatic events. They expose the evil purpose of the Kremlin to destroy the inter-American system and they test the ability of the American states to maintain the peaceful integrity of the hemisphere.

For several years now international communism has been probing here and there for nesting places in the Americas. It finally chose Guatemala as a spot which it could turn into an official base from which to breed subversion which would extend to the other American republics.

The intrusion of Soviet despotism was, of course, a direct challenge to the Monroe Doctrine, the first and most fundamental of our foreign policies. . . .

In Guatemala, international communism had an initial success. It began ten years ago when a revolution occurred in Guatemala. The revolution was not without justification, but the Communists seized on it, not as an opportunity for real reforms, but as a chance to gain political power.

Communist agitators devoted themselves to infiltrating the public and private organizations of Guatemala. . . . Operating under the guise of reformers, they organized the workers and peasants under Communist leadership. And having gained control of what they call the mass organizations, they moved on to take over the official press and radio of the Guatemalan Government.

They dominated the social security organization and ran the agrarian reform program. Through the technique of the so-called popular front they dictated to the Congress and to the President . . . Arbenz, who until this week was President of Guatemala, was openly manipulated by the leaders of communism.

Guatemala is a small country, but its power of standing alone is not the threat. The master plan of international communism is to gain a solid political base in this hemisphere. A base that then can be used to extend Communist penetration to the other peoples of the American Governments.

It was not the power of the Arbenz Government that concerned us, but the power behind it.

If world communism captured any American state, however small, a new and perilous front is established which will increase the dangers of the entire free world and require even greater sacrifices from the American people.

The situation in Guatemala had become so dangerous that the American states could not ignore it. And so at Caracas last month when the American states held their tenth inter-American conference, they adopted a momentous declaration. They said that the domination or the control of the political institution of any American state by international communism would constitute a threat to the sovereignty and political independence of the American states, endangering the peace of America.

There was only one American state that voted against that resolution. That state was Guatemala.

This Caracas Declaration precipitated a dramatic and rapidly moving chain of events. From their European base, the Communist leaders moved quickly to build up the military power of their agents in Guatemala. In May, a large shipment of arms was moved from behind the Iron Curtain into Guatemala. This shipment was sought to be secreted by false manifests and false clearances. The ostensible destination of the shipment was changed three times while the shipment was en route. . . .

In the face of these events and in accordance with the spirit of the Caracas Declaration, the nations of this hemisphere laid further plans to grapple with the danger. The Arbenz Government responded with efforts to disrupt the inter-American system. And because this Guatemalan regime enjoyed the full support of Soviet Russia, which is a permanent member of the Security Council of the United Nations, Guatemala tried to bring this matter before the Security Council. It did so without first referring the matter to the American regional organization. . . .

The Foreign Minister of Guatemala openly connived in this matter with the Foreign Minister of the Soviet Union. The two were in open correspondence and ill-concealed privity. The Security Council at first voted overwhelmingly to refer this Guatemalan matter to the Organization of American States and the vote was 10 to 1, but the one negative vote was a Soviet veto. And then that encouraged the Guatemalan Government to go on and with Soviet backing it redoubled its efforts to try to supplant the American system by Security Council jurisdiction.

However, last Friday the United Nations Security Council decided not to take up the Guatemalan matter, but to leave it in the first instance to the American states themselves. That was a triumph for the system of balance between regional organization and world organization. . . .

And then the American states moved promptly to deal with the situation. Their peace commission left yesterday for Guatemala. And earlier the American states had voted overwhelmingly to call a meeting of the Foreign Ministers of the American states to consider the penetration of international communism into Guatemala and the measures required to eliminate it. Never before has there been so clear a call uttered with such a sense of urgency and strong resolve.

Throughout the period that I have outlined, the Guatemalan Government and the Communist agents throughout the world have persistently attempted to obscure the real issue, that of communist imperialism, by claiming that the United States is only interested in protecting American business. We regret that there have been disputes between the Government of Guatemala and the United Fruit Company. . . .

But this business issue is relatively unimportant. All who know the temper of the American people of the United States and the United States Government must realize that our overriding concern is that which with other American states we recorded at Caracas, namely the endangering by international communism of the peace and security of this hemisphere. . . .

Last Sunday President Arbenz of Guatemala resigned and sought asylum, and other Communists and fellow-travelers are following his example. . . .

Need for vigilance is not past. Communism is still a menace everywhere, but the people of the United States and the other American republics can tonight feel that at least one grave danger has been averted. Also an example has been set which promises increased security of the future. The ambitious and unscrupulous will be less prone to feel that communism is the wave of their future.

Source 18 President Dwight D. Eisenhower, address at the Iowa State Fair at Des Moines, August 30, 1954

Now, ladies and gentlemen, in this day and time, when our hearts are troubled about incidents that daily appear in our press, there are a thousand subjects of which I could speak briefly to you. And in doing so, I might be able to impart to you something of the urgency your Government feels in dealing with the problems that are so important to all of us.

I think I shall talk for just a few minutes about the world in which we live: about foreign things. Now, I know that primarily, and from an economic standpoint, Iowa is interested, first of all, in agriculture. All of us well know without a prosperous agriculture there is no prosperity in America. And you also know that without a prosperous America there is no prosperity for the farmer. . . .

Now, I am not going to talk about that particular phase of our foreign relations, the trade and economic phases. I merely want to talk about this: the absolute, utter necessity of every American taking thought about our relations with the world.

Why do we have friends? We are strong, and we are mighty. We are rich. With 6 percent of the world's population, we have so much of the world's resources, our industries, our agriculture is so productive, that we astonish the world.

Why, then, must we have friends? We know that today the central core of the great world problem is the aggressive intent of international communism. If the free world does not hang together, then the unity of communism, achieved by force, by the use of the police outside your door and the spy inside your home, that unity will take one nation at a time, beginning with the most exposed, and subdue it. If this process should be continued, and we made no effort to stop it, eventually the American continent, the American hemisphere—finally, possibly, North America, would be an isolated island of freedom in a sea of communism. Such a picture does not have to be long held up in front of us, before we understand that we must never let it occur.

We shall not let it occur. . . .

The first open, specific attempt of international communism to establish a beachhead on this continent has been repulsed by the majority of the people of Guatemala, and proving again that people who have tasted freedom will not willingly submit to the regimentation of the Red dictatorship.

A War of "Disinformation"

The United States organized the overthrow of the government of Guatemala. The decision to do so was made in August 1953 by the committee of the National Security Council, which supervised covert activities. President Eisenhower personally approved the project, which was code named "Operation Success," and the action was carried out jointly by the Central Intelligence Agency and the United States State Department.

The Central Intelligence Agency developed the plans for the project. The agency recruited and trained at a base in Nicaragua a mercenary force to conduct the planned invasion of Guatemala. It then recruited Carlos Castillo Armas to serve as the ostensible leader of the invasion force. The agency transported the mercenaries to bases in Honduras, just across the border from Guatemala, and brought American-supplied weapons and ammunition in American trucks to these rebel camps. But Armas and his troops never penetrated more than six miles into Guatemala and scored no meaningful military victories.

22.3 CIA Involved in the Guatemala Coup, 1954

Instead of a military operation against Arbenz, the CIA waged a successful war of "disinformation." It established a clandestine radio station that broadcast information designed to spread fear and panic among the Guatemalan people and undermine civilian and military support for the nation's elected government. The radio station, Radio Liberty, offered glowing reports of fictitious rebel military operations throughout the country, creating the impression that a large rebel army was scoring decisive victories over government troops. Journalists from the United States and other countries were duped by the CIA into presenting these fictitious military reports as fact rather than fable. Though Radio Liberty boasted that it broadcast from deep within the jungles of Guatemala, its signals in fact originated from transmitters in Nicaragua, Honduras, the Dominican Republic, and even inside the American embassy in Guatemala City.

The Central Intelligence Agency jammed the radio frequencies inside Guatemala so that the government of the country could not communicate effectively with its people. The CIA and the United States Information Agency flooded Latin America with Anti-Guatemala news reports, leaflets, cartoons, articles, much of which contained information they knew to be false.

The rebel fighter and bomber planes that flew missions over Guatemala, effectively demoralizing the populace, were actually under the direction of the CIA and flown by American pilots. At one point the CIA planes bombed a base of the Honduran Air Force inside Honduras to establish a pretext for direct U.S. military intervention should such action be necessary.

In the end, it was not the invading force of Armas that toppled the government of Guatemala, but a coup carried out by the Guatemalan military, with the encouragement of the CIA and State Department, which brought down Arbenz.

Second Thoughts

Stamping Out Communism

Carlos Armas Castillo proved to be a corrupt and ineffective ruler and was assassinated in 1957. He was merely the first in a string of repressive rulers who held power in Guatemala during the three decades that followed the covert intervention of the United States into the affairs of Guatemala.

American involvement in Guatemala did not end with the overthrow of Jacobo Arbenz, however. Successive governments in Guatemala sought to repress political opposition, At first, this repression was directed at suspected communists and a growing guerrilla movement, but after a time its victims included the Maya people and even moderates who opposed the policies of the government. The United States, in a continuing effort to stamp out communism, trained Guatemalan military and police units and provided funding for their operations. In December of 1990, following the murder of an American citizen by Guatemalan security forces, the Bush administration abruptly halted overt aid to the military and police forces of Guatemala. The CIA, however, continued to covertly channel millions of dollars to the Guatemalan armed forces until public disclosure in 1995.

More than 200,000 Guatemalans were killed during Guatemala's long civil war. Most died at the hands of their own government. Negotiations brought the conflict to an end in 1996, and in November 1999, the country held its first peaceful national election in more than four decades. Still, however, 80 percent of Guatemala's 11 million people live below the poverty line.

Source 19   Daniel James, *Red Design for the Americas: Guatemalan Prelude,* 1954

The battle of the Western Hemisphere has begun.

We enter upon a new era in our history. We face, for the first time, the prospect of continuous struggle against Communism on a hemispheric scale. We face the possibility even of war—war on our own shores of the kind hitherto characteristic of Asia. Such is the ultimate meaning of Moscow's first attempt to conquer an American country, Guatemala.

The Red beachhead which was founded on Guatemalan soil in June 1944 was washed away in the anti-Communist revolution of June 1954, but the Red design for the conquest of the Americas which was devised over the intervening decade survived. . . .

Latin America is no longer the political hinterland it was. Social Revolutionary forces have cast it into the very forefront of the global struggle between freedom and the new tyranny. Its proximity to the United States, and its ultimate historical, economic and political connections with the United States, make it of greater importance to us than even Europe or Asia. There, it is true, decisive battles are being fought—but for the United States there can be no battle more decisive than the Battle of the Western Hemisphere. We can "afford" to be defeated in China, Indo-China and even perhaps India and Western Europe; but the loss to our cause of the republics next door would be fatal, for then we should be ringed by hostile nations in our own vicinity. . . .

The Guatemalan experience has opened a new era in the Americas. It will be an era of protracted struggle against Communism which may be marked by wars and revolutions, of which the Guatemalan civil war is a foretaste. It can be, if we in the Americas will it, an era which will see the rout of the Red conquistadores. . . .

We know that Latin America hates and fears intervention, and rightly so, because our past interventions have infringed upon the sovereignty of Latin America nations. But where Communism has seized a nation, intervention is already a fact, accomplished by an alien power, and can be counteracted only by the intervention of one or more native American powers. The national sovereignty of Guatemala under Communism was a fiction which only disguised the reality of Soviet intervention. What the United States did was to *intervene against foreign intervention,* in order to restore Guatemala's national sovereignty.

There is no evidence that we supplied Castillo Armas with guns and planes. If we had, he would not have required three weeks to overthrow and replace Arbenz, but something closer to the time prescribed for Central American revolutions—48 hours.

Source 20 President Dwight D. Eisenhower, *Mandate for Change,* 1963

Things seemed to be going well for Castillo's small band until June 22. On that date Allen Dulles reported to me that Castillo had lost two of his three old bombers with which he was supporting his "invasion."

A meeting was arranged that afternoon with Foster Dulles, Allen Dulles, and Henry F. Holland, who had succeeded John Cabot as Assistant Secretary of State for Inter-American Affairs. The point at issue was whether the United States should cooperate in replacing the bombers. . . .

"What do you think Castillo's chances would be," I asked Allen Dulles, "without the aircraft?"

His answer was unequivocal: "About zero."

"Suppose we supply the aircraft. What would the chances be then?"

Again the CIA chief did not hesitate: "About 20 percent."

I considered the matter carefully. I realized full well that United States intervention in Central America and Caribbean affairs had greatly injured our standing in all of Latin America. On the other hand, it seemed to me that to refuse to cooperate in providing indirect support to a strictly anti-Communist faction in this struggle would be contrary to the letter and spirit of the Caracas resolution. I had faith in the strength of the inter-American resolve therein set forth. On the actual value of a shipment of planes, I knew from experience the important psychological impact of even a small amount of air support. In any event, our proper course of action—indeed my duty—was clear to me. We would replace the airplanes. . . .

The major factor in the successful outcome was the disaffection of the Guatemalan armed forces and the population as a whole with the tyrannical regime of Arbenz. . . . The air support gave . . . the regular armed forces an excuse to take action in their own hands to throw out Arbenz . . . Castillo Armas was later confirmed as head of the military junta and then, by a thundering majority, as President.

Source 21 U.S. Public Safety adviser John Longan, secret cable to Byron Engle, director, OPS, Department of State, January 4, 1966

In response to request from GOG (Government of Guatemala), Ambassador Mein requested a Public Safety Advisor to assist GOG law enforcement authorities on techniques and methods for combating terrorist, kidnapping and extortion tactics. After I was selected for the job, we immediately cabled the Guatemalan Ambassador requesting a meeting with him or his designee, the Chief of Station, CAS (Covert Action Section of the CIA), and Chief Public Safety Advisor prior to my making contact with any GOG officials.

This meeting was held on the afternoon of November 28 in the Deputy Chief of Mission's (DCM) home, where I was given a complete briefing and recommended the following general plan of action:

> (1) That I meet immediately with the Directors of the National Police, Judicial Police and Treasury Police to determine what progress has been made on a joint operational plan.
> (2) That we approach the problem utilizing both overt and covert means. I outlined briefly the methods we were using in Venezuela, and the Chief of Station, as well as the DCM, stated that they would like to see the same tactics used in Guatemala.
> (3) I proposed and others present agreed that I draw up immediate and long range plans, both overt and covert. Upon receiving these recommendations the Country Team or the Ambassador would pass these recommendations through appropriate channels to Col. Peralta, Chief of Government.

After several meetings held in a safe house with the Chiefs of the three previously mentioned GOG police agencies, it became obvious that because of rivalry, non-cooperation and distrust between these three agencies, there was in fact no coordinated plan of operation. I immediately informed Ambassador Mein that we would have to go to the very top government level to coordinate properly. Ambassador Mein and I met with Col. Peralta on

November 30 and discussed the problem in generalities, but at this time did not get down to specifics. At the end of the meeting, it was still agreed that I would make my recommendations to appropriate Embassy officials who would pass them to the proper GOG officials. However, two days later when I talked with the Ambassador he suggested that I go direct to the Palace and discuss the problem. This was done and Col. Peralta designated Mr. Jose Louis Aguilar de Leon, his private secretary, to coordinate all activities concerning extortions and kidnappings. At this point my plans were not yet recorded on paper. We did discuss my recommendations in detail and the Presidential Secretary made a number of notes, after which he immediately took them into Col. Peralta who issued an order that the recommendations be formulated into plans and translated into actions immediately. From this moment on I was involved in setting up plans for both the covert and overt operations. . . .

Basically, the plan was as follows:

Overt—Immediate

Combined, uniformed police raids in Guatemala City. These raids were to be coordinated at top government level and the raiding forces were not to be notified of the areas to be raided until they were on their way to the site. They were given detailed instructions on how to seal off given areas (frozen area plan diagram attached to Mr. Costello's report.) In connection with these raids, all permanent road blocks (garitas) leading from the city were to be closed and surprise road blocks were to be set up in Guatemala City. The idea behind this was to force some of the wanted communists out of hiding and into police hands, as well as to convince the Guatemalan public that the authorities were doing something to control the situation.

Overt—Long Range

To have Mr. Costello, the new Chief Public Safety Advisor, establish rapport with the various police agencies that would lead to U.S. advisors being able to influence GOG police officials and give them day-to-day operational advice. Future ability of U.S advisors to influence police operations in Guatemala is, in my opinion, a "must."

Covert—Immediate

That a safe house be immediately set up and all information concerning extortions and kidnappings be sent here. All police agencies are penetrated by the communists. A room was immediately prepared in the Palace for this purpose and as pointed out in Mr. Costello's report, Guatemalans were immediately designated to put this operation into effect. From the outset I made it clear that the overt and covert operations should be separated, with the CAS following through on the covert and the Chief Public Safety Advisor following through on the overt operation.

Covert—Long Range

This, of course, will be worked out in detail by CAS. However, before leaving Guatemala they sent some messages through their channels laying the groundwork for personnel and equipment needed to carry this phase of the program forward.

Source 22 Secret intelligence cable from Thomas L. Hughes, director of Intelligence and Research, U.S. Department of State, to the secretary of state, October 23, 1967

Subject: Guatemala: A Counter-Insurgency Running Wild?

Guatemalan counter-insurgency operations against the extreme left during the past year have been so successful that the US Embassy reports "insurgent combat involving organized guerrilla units is not a current threat to stability in any region of the country." This success has come about through a combination of overt and covert operations by the Guatemalan security forces and right wing civilian associates and auxiliaries to stamp out the insurgents. The methods employed, particularly on the covert side, have resembled those of the guerrillas themselves: kidnappings, torture, and summary executions. President Mendez Montenegro evidently gave the security forces a carte blanche in the field of internal security in exchange for military support for his administration. He may now wish to reconsider, however, as military use of such rough and ready counter-insurgency tactics is creating considerable unease in Guatemala and threatens to undermine his popular support. . . .

At the center of the Army's clandestine urban counter-terrorist apparatus is the Special Commando Unit formed in January 1967, and currently under the command of Colonel Maximo Zepeda. Composed of both military and civilian personnel, the Special Unit has carried out abductions, bombings, street assassinations, and executions of real and alleged communists, and occasionally has acted against other vaguely defined "enemies of the government."

Source 23 Secret memorandum from Viron Vaky, former U.S. deputy chief of mission in Guatemala, to Covey Oliver, assistant secretary of state for Inter-American Affairs, March 29, 1968

The Guatemalan Government's use of "counter-terror" to combat insurgency is a serious problem in three ways:

(a) the tactics are having a terribly corrosive effect on Guatemalan society and the nation's political development;
(b) they present a serious problem for the U.S. in terms of our image in Latin America and the credibility of what we say we stand for;
(c) the problem has a corrosive effect on our own judgments and conceptual values.

A. *Impact on the Country*

Counter-terror is corrosive from three points of view:

1. The counter-terror is indiscriminate, and we cannot rationalize that fact away. Looking back on its full sweep one can cite instances in which leftist but anti-Communist labor leaders were kidnapped and beaten by army units; the para-military groups armed by the Zacapa commander have operated in parts of the northeast in war-lord fashion and destroyed local PR organizations; people are killed or disappear on the basis of simple accusations. It is argued that the "excesses" of the earlier period have been corrected and now only "collaborators"

are being killed. But I question the wisdom or validity of the Guatemalan Army's criteria as to who is a collaborator or how carefully they check. Moreover, the derivative violence of right-wing vigilantes and sheer criminality made possible by the atmosphere must be laid at the door of the conceptual tactic of counter-terror. The point is that the society is being rent apart and polarized; emotions, desire for revenge and personal bitterness are being sucked in; the pure Communist issue is thus blurred; and issues of poverty and social injustice are being converted into virulent questions of outraged emotion and "tyranny." The whole cumulative impact is most unhealthy.

It is not true, in my judgment, that Guatemalans are apathetic or are not upset about the problem. Guatemalans very typically mask their feeling with outward passivity, but that does not mean they do not feel things. Guatemalans have told me they are worried, that the situation is serious and nastier than it has ever been. And I submit that we really do not know what the campesinos truly feel.

2. Counter-terror is brutal. The official squads are guilty of atrocities, interrogations are brutal, torture is used and bodies are mutilated . . . Because of the evidence of this brutality, the government is, in the eyes of many Guatemalans, a cruel government, and therefore a righteous outrage, emotion and viciousness, have been sucked into the whole political situation. . . . How fortunate for us that there is no charismatic leader around yet to spark an explosion.

3. Counter-terror has retarded modernization and institution building. The tactics have just deepened and continued the proclivity of Guatemalans to operate outside the law. It says in effect to people that the law, the constitution, the institutions mean nothing, the fastest gun counts. . . .

B. *The Image Problem*

We are associated with this tactic in the minds of many people, and whether it is right or wrong so to associate us is rapidly becoming irrelevant. In politics just as important as the way things are is the way people *think* they are. In the minds of many in Latin America, and tragically, especially in the sensitive, articulate youth, we are believed to have condoned these tactics. Therefore our image is being tarnished and the credibility of our claims to want a better and more just world are increasingly placed in doubt. . . .

C. *U.S. Values*

This leads to an aspect I personally find the most disturbing of all—that we have not been honest with ourselves. We have condoned counter-terror; we may even in effect have encouraged and blessed it. We have been so obsessed with the fear of insurgency that we have rationalized away our qualms and uneasiness. This is not only because we have concluded we cannot do anything about it, for we never really tried. Rather we suspected that maybe it is a good tactic, and that as long as Communists are being killed it is alright. Murder, torture and mutilation are alright if our side is doing it and the victims are Communists. After all hasn't man been a savage from the beginning of time so let us not be too queasy about terror. I have literally heard these arguments from our people.

Have our values been so twisted by our adversary concept of politics in the hemisphere? Is it conceivable that we are so obsessed with insurgency that we are prepared to rationalize murder as an acceptable counter-insurgency weapon? Is it possible that a nation which so reveres the principle of due process of law has so easily acquiesced in this sort of terror tactic?....

If the U.S. cannot come up with any better suggestion on how to fight insurgency in Guatemala than to condone counter-terror, we are in a bad way indeed.

Source 24 Sidney Lens, *The Forging of the American Empire,* 1971

A ... subversion of an "unfriendly" government engineered by the Dulles brothers, with Eisenhower's approval, took place in Guatemala.... The "menace" traced back to a revolution in 1944 against General Jorge Ubico, who boasted of political kinship to Adolf Hitler and claimed that "I execute first and give trial afterward." After the overthrow, a former schoolteacher named Juan Jose Arevalo was elected president by a large margin and proceeded to legalize unions, raise minimum pay (to 26 cents a day), and reclaim his country's economy from the United Fruit Company and other foreign firms. When he introduced social security reforms that cost United Fruit $200,000 a year (bananas constituted about two-fifths of the nation's exports), the company reduced its production by 80 percent, and W. R. Grace and Pan American actively discouraged the vital tourist trade. Arevalo was succeeded, after six years, by Jacobo Arbenz, who, if anything was considered by Washington to be worse. He too was no Communist, but as American pressures tightened he leaned on the Communists more and more until they became a decisive force in his regime.

Arbenz's most significant act was the introduction of an extensive land-reform act (2 percent of the population owned 70 percent of the land) which distributed tracts to 85,000 peasant families. In the process, however, the Guatemalan regime took over 234,000 uncultivated acres from United Fruit. The Company demanded $16 million for its lands, the government offered $600,000 in twenty-five-year bonds. This was the setting when—in the words of a conservative Guatemalan, Miguel Ydigoras Fuentes, as quoted in Richard J. Barnet's *Intervention and Revolution*—"a former executive of the United Fruit Company, now retired, Mr. Walter Turnbull, came to me with two gentlemen whom he introduced as agents of the CIA. They said that I was a popular figure in Guatemala and that they wanted to lend their assistance to overthrow Arbenz. When I asked their conditions for the assistance I found them unacceptable. Among other things, I was to promise to favor the United Fruit Company and the International Railways of Central America; to destroy the railroad workers labor union; ... to establish a strong-arm government, on the style of Ubico. Further, I was to pay back every cent that was involved in the undertaking."

Rebuffed by Ydigoras, the CIA fastened its hopes on Colonel Carlos Castillo Armas, who had been trained in a military school at Fort Leavenworth. Late in 1953, then, John E. (Smilin' Jack) Peurifoy, an old diplomatic hand with experience in the Greek insurgency, was dispatched as ambassador to Guatemala City for the purpose of coordinating a revolt against the government to which he was accredited. A few months later Operation el Diablo was launched. The CIA established a headquarters for Castillo at Tegucigalpa, Honduras, and not long thereafter a training camp at Mombotobito, a volcanic island belonging to Nicaragua. Meanwhile Arbenz discovered the plot through intercepted correspondence between Castillo and Ydigoras, and applied to the Soviet Union to buy $10 million of small arms. A shipment of Czech weapons aboard a Swedish ship, *Alfhem,* in mid-May brought charges from Secretary Dulles that Arbenz might be planning to attack the Panama Canal a thousand miles away, and served as a pretext for more or less open support to Castillo's invaders. On June 18 the American-inspired colonel led a band of 150 mercenaries over the border from Honduras, while four P-47 Thunderbolts, flown by U.S. pilots, bombed the Guatemalan capital. The mercenaries settled six miles across the border, waiting for the planes to wreak enough havoc for Arbenz to collapse. Unfortunately one bomber was shot full of holes and another crashed, thus hobbling the operation. But while the ambassador to the United Nations, Henry Cabot Lodge, was denying that any American planes or fliers were involved, Eisenhower made the decision to send in more. These were enough to tip the scales. Though Castillo did not get as far as the capital, he didn't have to. Arbenz, fearful of provoking a bloodbath and deserted by old friends in the army, refused to distribute arms to the unions and peasant organizations clamoring for them. To this day, Arbenz is accused in radical Guatemalan circles of having lost his nerve. While he pondered, the bombing continued and on June 27 he simply gave up.

The epilogue to this story is as interesting as the main act. United Fruit lands were promptly restored to the company and a tax on interest and dividends for foreigners abrogated, saving the company a healthy $11 million. All unions were disbanded temporarily on the grounds that they were "political," and then, after being permitted to reorganize, were harried to the point where their membership fell to 16,000. (it had been 107,000). The right to strike was abolished, and wage increases—in a nation where two-thirds of those employed earned less than $30 a month—held up. The 85,000 parcels of land distributed to the peasants were returned to the *finca* owners, some of whom went on a rampage, burning the crops of their serfs. In the next seven years the Guatemalan dictators distributed land to only 4,078 peasants—in a country where 70 percent of the rural population was landless. Upwards of 5,000 people were arrested by Castillo, and the election law was modified so that illiterates—70 percent of the population—were denied the vote. In a one-candidate election that followed, Castillo was confirmed by what Eisenhower called a "thundering majority." If there was any "improvement" in the situation it was that the annual rate of foreign—i.e., North American—investments went up dramatically, and economic aid from Washington skyrocketed as well.

Source 25   Edward J. Williams, *The Political Themes of Inter-American Relations,* 1971

The basic explanation of United States imperialistic ventures is probably what one Latin American statesman has called "defensive imperialism.". . . . The United States exercised imperialistic control because it thought that its national security was threatened. The threat was defined as the possibility of an unfriendly power gaining control of one of the weak nations near the borders. U.S. domination of Cuba, Haiti, or Nicaragua was necessary to prevent possible German, French, or Soviet control. An unfriendly Germany, France, or Soviet Union would be a threat to the lives and well-being of the American people. . . .

Control by unfriendly governments or big powers of areas close to U.S. borders dramatizes the possibility of a threat to American security. As early as 1845, the Polk Corollary established geographic propinquity as a definition of the applicability of the Monroe Doctrine. That is, an unfriendly Bolivia is less dangerous than an unfriendly Cuba. Bolivia is far away; Cuba is not. . . .

The second, and even more important, fact explaining American imperialism in that area is the Panama Canal. American control of the canal has historically been interpreted as an essential ingredient of American security. Forty years before the canal was built, President U.S. Grant was influenced in his attempt to buy Santo Domingo because of "its strategic position commanding the entrance to the Caribbean Sea and the Isthmus transit of commerce.".. .More contemporary pronouncements of American policy exemplify the same ongoing concern for the security of the canal. In 1954, the United States CIA supported Carlos Castillo Armas in overthrowing Jacobo Arbenz Guzman in Guatemala because of supposed Communist influence in the Arbenz government. The significance of Communist influence for Secretary of State John Foster Dulles and others was a possible threat to the safety of the canal. . . .

Security, not economic exploitation, primarily motivated Yankee imperialism.

Source 26 Excerpts from *Foreign and Military Intelligence,* the final report of the U.S. Senate Select Committee to Study Governmental Operations with Respect to Intelligence Activities, 1976

22.4 U.S. Policy in Guatemala, 1966–'96

With the end of the Korean conflict and as the mid-1950s approached, the intelligence community turned from the desperate concern over imminent war with the U.S.S.R. to the long-term task of containing and competing with Communism. In the "struggle for men's minds," covert action developed into a large-scale clandestine psychological and political program aimed at competing with Soviet propaganda and front organizations in international labor and student activities. Specific foreign governments considered antithetical to the United States and its allies or too receptive to the influence of the Soviet Union, such as Mosedegh in Iran in 1953 and Arbenz in Guatemala in 1954, were toppled with the help of the CIA. Anti-communist parties and groups were given aid and encouragement such as the Sumatran leaders who, in 1958, sought the overthrow of President Sukarno in Indonesia. . . .

No activity of the Central Intelligence Agency has engendered more controversy and concern than "covert action," the secret use of power and persuasion. . . . Although not a specific charter mission of the Central Intelligence Agency, covert action quickly became a primary activity. Covert action programs were first designed to counter the Soviet threat in Europe and were, at least initially, a limited and ad hoc response to an exceptional threat to American security. Covert action soon became a routine program of influencing governments and covertly exercising power—involving literally hundreds of projects each year. By 1953 there were major covert operations underway in 48 countries, consisting of propaganda, paramilitary and political action projects. By the 1960s, covert action had come to mean "any clandestine activity designed to influence foreign governments, events, organizations or persons in support of American foreign policy." Several thousand individual covert action projects have been undertaken since 1961. . . .

Given the open and democratic assumptions on which our government is based, the Committee gave serious consideration to proposing a total ban on *all* forms of covert action. The Committee has concluded, however, that the United States should maintain the option of reacting in the future to a grave, unforeseen threat to United States national security through covert means. . . .

The Committee finds that covert operations have not been an exceptional instrument used only in rare instances when the vital interests of the United States have been at risk. On the contrary, presidents and administrations have made excessive, and at times, self-defeating, use of covert action. In addition, covert action has become a routine program with a bureaucratic momentum of its own. The long-term impact, at home and abroad, of repeated disclosure of U.S covert action never appears to have been assessed. The cumulative effect of covert actions has been increasingly costly to America's interests and reputation. The Committee believes that covert action must be employed only in the most extraordinary circumstances.

Individual Views of Senator Barry Goldwater
Covert action is intended to provide the President of the U.S. and the nation with a range of actions short of war to preserve the free world and to thwart the global ambitions of Communist imperialism. Covert operations can and should be used in circumstances which might not be described as "vital" but are nevertheless necessary to prevent a crisis from occurring. One purpose of covert action is to prevent the occurrence of "most extraordinary circumstances." Those who support the above-mentioned quotation are in effect saying: "Don't put out the fire while it is small; wait until it becomes a conflagration."

Additional Views of Senator Frank Church concerning Covert Action
We live in a perilous world. Soviet submarines silently traverse the ocean floors carrying transcontinental missiles with the capacity to strike at our heartland. The nuclear arms race threatens to continue its deadly spiral toward Armageddon.

In this perilous setting, it is imperative for the United States to maintain a strong and effective intelligence service. . . . We have no choice other than to gather, analyze, and assess vital information on the intent and prowess of foreign adversaries, present or potential. . . .

What has become controversial is quite unrelated to intelligence, but has to do, instead, with the so-called covert operations of the CIA, those secret efforts to manipulate events within foreign countries in ways presumed to serve the interests of the United States. Nowhere are such activities vouchsafed in the statutory language which created the Agency in 1947. . . .

The United States came to adopt the methods and accept the value system of the "enemy." In the secret world of covert action, we threw off all restraints. Not content merely to subsidize foreign political parties, labor unions, and newspapers, the Central Intelligence Agency soon began to directly manipulate the internal politics of other countries. Spending many millions of dollars annually, the CIA filled its bag with dirty tricks—ranging from bribery and false propaganda to schemes to "alter the health" of unfriendly foreign leaders and undermine their regimes.

The United States must acquire a longer view of history.

Source 27   Morton H. Halperin, Jerry J. Berman, Robert L. Borosage, and Christine M. Marwick, *The Lawless State: The Crimes of the U.S. Intelligence Agencies,* 1976

"I don't see why we need to stand by and watch a country go communist due to the irresponsibility of its own people." So spoke Henry Kissinger at a secret June 1970 White House meeting. The topic under discussion that day was . . . covert actions the CIA should take against Salvadore Allende (the elected President of Chile), but the sentiment reflected American behavior in many countries and could have come from the lips of any of the key American foreign-policy managers of the post World War II era. These men—presidents and their chief advisors—felt that they knew best; that if other countries acted in a manner they considered irresponsible, they had a right, even a duty, to intervene with American power.

For the last thirty years, the United States has stood almost alone as the activist leader of the West, and American officials have become the arbiters of what sort of economic and political systems other nations should have. When such countries as Greece and Vietnam were threatened from the left, the United States intervened. When leftists took power in countries like Guatemala, Iran, and Chile, the United States helped to overthrow them. Stated American policy may have been that foreign countries should be free to choose their own system of government, but the reality has been that this freedom of choice applied only within American-defined limits. Successive American administrations claimed that the American objective was to spread democracy, but in fact American objectives were different and more specific.

Essentially the United States has demanded three things of foreign regimes: (1) that they support the anti-Soviet and anti-Chinese foreign policy of the United States; (2) that they allow and safeguard the investment of outside—particularly American—capital; and (3) that they maintain internal stability—which has usually translated into their repressing their own internal lefts. The intensity of American intervention has also been influenced by such other factors as the brashness or charisma of a foreign leader and a country's proximity to the United States.

With some help from its allies, the United States generally imposed its standards on other countries, particularly those of the Third World, though American intervention was not always effective. In effect the United States has served as the world's policemen. And the secret policeman—the enforcer—of this system has been the CIA.

Source 28   Stephen Schlesinger and Stephen Kinzer, *Bitter Fruit: The Untold Story of the American Coup in Guatemala,* 1982

United Fruit controlled directly or indirectly nearly 40,000 jobs in Guatemala. Its investments in the country were valued at $60 million. It functioned as a state within a state, owning Guatemala's telephone and telegraph facilities, administering its only important Atlantic harbor and monopolizing its banana export. The company's subsidiary, the International Railways of Central America (IRCA), owned 887 miles of railroad track in Guatemala, nearly every mile in the country.... United Fruit (was) by far the largest property owner in the country with about 550,000 acres on the Atlantic and Pacific.

In March 1953, the ax of land reform fell on the Company, never before the object of such a challenge. In two separate decrees, a total of 209,842 acres of uncultivated land on the Tiquisate plantation in the lush Escuinta area near the Pacific was expropriated. The *frutera* had always left large amounts of its land uncultivated (in 1953, 85 percent of its land was unused); only as many bananas were grown as could be sold abroad....

In compensation for the seized property, the government offered $627,572 in bonds, based on United Fruit's declared tax value of the land. United Fruit, like other large landowners, had historically undervalued its property in official declarations in order to reduce its already insignificant tax liability. But now that the declared value was being used to determine compensation, the company howled in protest. On April 20, 1954, a formal complaint was delivered to Guatemalan authorities, not by the Fruit Company but by the U. S. State Department, whose top officials, beginning with Secretary Dulles himself, had close ties to the Company. The note demanded $15,854,849 in compensation for the Tiquisate land, declaring that the government offer "bears not the slightest resemblance to just evaluation."...

The amount offered by Guatemala averaged about $2.99 per acre, while the State Department wanted over $75 per acre; the company had paid $1.48 per acre when it bought the land nearly twenty years earlier....

In October and February 1954, the government ordered two more expropriations of uncultivated United Fruit land—this time of the Atlantic coast—bringing the total of disputed property to 386,901 acres. Guatemala offered about $500,000 to the company for its newest takeovers. Throughout this period, Guatemalan officials were in negotiation with the State Department for an overall solution to the dispute. But at the same time, a more momentous series of meetings in Washington, called largely at the urging of United Fruit and its powerful supporters in the government, considered how to end the process which had led Guatemala to these unprecedented actions....

Indeed, the Fruit Company was at that moment working quietly but effectively to convince the American government that Arbenz was a threat to freedom and must be deposed. The company hired a corps of influential lobbyists and talented publicists to create a public and private climate in the United States favorable to Arbenz's overthrow. Working behind the scenes beginning in 1950, these men influenced and reshaped the attitudes of the American public toward Guatemala. In their hands the fate of Arbenz and his ambitious social reforms was being determined....

Without United Fruit's troubles, it seems probable that the Dulles brothers might not have paid such intense attention to the few Communists in Guatemala, since larger numbers had taken part in political activity on a greater scale during the postwar years in Brazil, Chile and Costa Rica without causing excessive concern in the U.S. government.

United Fruit could also count on an especially receptive audience in the Eisenhower administration, particularly among the main players in the Guatemalan drama. John Foster Dulles had been a senior partner of the New York law firm of Sullivan and Cromwell, which did legal work for the international financial house J. Henry Schroder Banking Corporation. Schroder Bank was the key financial advisor to the International Railways of Central America. . . . In 1936, the United Fruit Company, holding a small interest in IRCA, sought to take over the railroad company to ensure its power to set transportation rates, as well as to block the entry of any rival banana operation into Guatemala. Dulles, as general counsel to Schroder, handled the negotiations, arranging a cozy deal with United Fruit at the expense of his putative client, IRCA, and reaping a tidy profit for the Schroder Banking Corporation.

Allen Dulles also did legal work for Sullivan and Cromwell in the 1920s and 1930s, often helping his brother on Schroder Bank matters. Soon he was appointed to the board of directors of the bank. Schroder, meanwhile, maintained a share of stocks in IRCA; indeed, as late as 1954, the president of Schroder was himself on the board of the railroad company, even while it was controlled by United Fruit. The Schroder Bank was, coincidentally or not, a depository of secret CIA funds for covert operations.

Among other influential figures sympathetic to the company was John Moors Cabot, Assistant Secretary of State for Inter-American Affairs, whose family owned stock in United Fruit. His brother Thomas had served as president of the corporation in 1948. UN Ambassador Henry Cabot Lodge was a stockholder, too, and had been a vigorous public defender of United Fruit while a senator from Massachusetts. The wife of Edmund Whitman, the Fruit Company's public relations director, was Eisenhower's personal secretary, Anne Whitman. Undersecretary of State Bedell Smith was seeking an executive job with United Fruit while helping to plan the coup against Guatemala (he later was named to its board of directors). Robert Hill, ambassador to Costa Rica during the coup, was close to the Fruit Company hierarchy, having worked for Grace Shipping Lines, which had interests in Guatemala. In 1960, he also became a director of the corporation. Thus many of the significant figures behind the Guatemalan coup were intimately acquainted with high Fruit Company executives and naturally favored their views over those of a Central American government whose "Communism" they publicly abhorred and about which they knew little or nothing else.

American national security considerations were never compelling in the case of Guatemala. State Department analysts in late 1953 treated the influence of Communists as relatively trivial except insofar as they had Arbenz's ear. The much-publicized claim that Guatemala could become a base for a Soviet seizure of the Panama Canal was also difficult to sustain. Guatemala had no diplomatic or military links to Russia or any Eastern European country except for its occasional meetings with officials from Czechoslovakia, from whom Guatemala ultimately purchased a single arms shipment in cash. No serious evidence ever turned up after the coup establishing a secret tie to the Soviets. Furthermore, the country, which sits 800 miles from the Canal, at the time, maintained only a tiny, non-functional air force with a range of barely 300 miles. Guatemala had only one airport capable of handling jets, but U.S. observers could watch it at all times.

The principal evidence offered by Americans to justify fears of subversion in Guatemala was the land reform program, particularly as it affected United Fruit.

Source 29 President Ronald Reagan, "Remarks by the President Following Meeting with President Rios Montt of Guatemala," December 4, 1982

President Rios Montt and I have just had a useful exchange of ideas on the problems of the region and on our bilateral relations.

Our conversation today has done much to improve the climate of relations between our two governments. I know that President Rios Montt is a man of great integrity and commitment. His country is confronting a brutal challenge from guerrillas armed and supported by others outside Guatemala.

I have assured President Rios Montt that the United States is committed to support his efforts to restore democracy and to address the root causes of this violent insurgency. I know he wants to improve the quality of life for all Guatemalans and to promote social justice. My Administration will do all it can to support his progressive efforts.

Source 30 Rigoberta Menchú, recipient of the 1992 Nobel Peace Prize, *I, Rigoberta Menchú, An Indian Woman in Guatemala*, 1983

It was 1979, I remember, that my younger brother died, the first in my family to be tortured. He was sixteen years old. . . . The thing is that the government put about this image of us, . . . as if we were monsters, as if we were some kind of foreigners, aliens. But my father was Quiche (Maya), not Cuban. The government called us communists and accused us of being a bad influence. . . .

On 9 September 1979 my brother was kidnapped. It was Sunday, and he'd gone to another village—he worked in other villages as well as his own. He name was Petrocinio Menchú . . . . That day my brother was going to another village with a girl when they caught him. The girl and her mother followed along after him. From the first moment they tied his hands behind his back, they started to drive him along with kicks. My brother fell, he couldn't protect his face. The first part of him to begin to bleed was his face. They took him over rough ground where there were stones, fallen tree trunks. He walked about two kilometres being kicked and hit all the time. Then they started to threaten the girl and her mother. They were risking their lives by following my brother and finding out where he was being taken. Apparently, they said to them: "Do you want us to do the same to you, do you want us to rape you right here?" That's what this thug of a soldier said. And he told the senora that if she didn't go away they'd be tortured just like he was going to be because he was a communist and a subversive, and subversives deserved to be punished and to die.

It's an unbelievable story. We managed to find out how he died, what tortures were inflicted on him from start to finish. They took my brother away, bleeding from different places. When they'd done with him, he didn't look like a person any more. His whole face was disfigured from beating, from striking against the stones, the tree trunks; my brother was completely destroyed. His clothes were torn from his falling down. After that they let the women go. When he got to the camp, he was scarcely on his feet, he couldn't walk any more, they'd even forced stones into his eyes, my brother's eyes. . . . Once he arrived in the camp they inflicted terrible torture on him to make him tell where the guerrillas were and where his family was. What was he doing with the Bible, they wanted to know, why were the priests guerrillas? . . . .

So they inflicted these dreadful tortures on him. Day and night they subjected him to terrible, terrible pain. They tied him up, they tied his testicles, my brother's sexual organs, they tied them behind with string and forced him to run. Well, he couldn't stand that, my little brother, he couldn't bear that awful pain and he cried out, he asked for mercy. And they left him in a well, I don't know what it's called, a hole with water and a bit of mud in it, they left him naked there all night. There were a lot of corpses there in the hole with him and he couldn't stand the smell of all those corpses. There were other people there who'd been tortured. . . . My brother was tortured for sixteen days. They cut off his fingernails, they cut off his fingers, they cut off his skin, they burned parts of his skin. Many of the wounds, the first ones, swelled and were infected. He stayed alive. They shaved his head, just left the skin, and also they cut the skin off his head and pulled it down on either side and cut off the fleshy part of his face. My brother suffered tortures on every part of his body, but they took care not to damage the arteries or veins so that he would survive the tortures and not die. They gave him food so that he'd hold out and not die from his wounds. There were twenty men with him who had been tortured or were still undergoing torture. There was also a woman. They had raped her and then tortured her. . . .

Then, on 23 September, we heard that the military were putting out bulletins around the villages . . . (s)aying they had such and such a number of guerrillas in their power and that they were going to carry out punishment in such and such a place. . . .

So we set out at 11 in the morning on the 23rd for Chajul. We crossed long stretches of mountain country on foot . . . About 8 o'clock the next morning we were entering the village of Chajul. The soldiers had the little village surrounded. There were about five hundred of them. They'd made all the people come out of their houses, with threats that if they didn't watch the punishments they'd suffer the same punishments, the same tortures. . . .

The officer opened the meeting. I remember he started by saying that a group of guerrillas they'd caught were about to . . . suffer a little punishment. A little punishment, because there were greater punishments, he said, but you'll see the punishment they get. And that's for being communists! For being Cubans, for being subversives! And if you get mixed up with communists and subversives, you'll get the same treatment as these subversives you'll be seeing in a little while. . . .

After he'd finished talking the officer ordered the squad to take away those who'd been "punished," naked and swollen as they were. They dragged them along, they could no longer walk. Dragged them along to this place, where they lined them up all together within sight of everyone. The officer called to the worst of his criminals—the Kaibiles, who wear different clothes from other soldiers. They're the ones with the most training, the most power. Well, he called the Kaibiles and they poured petrol over each of the tortured. The captain said, "this isn't the last of their punishments, there's another one yet.

This is what we've done with all the subversives we catch, because they have to die in violence. And if this doesn't teach you a lesson, this is what'll happen to you too. The problem is that the Indians let themselves be led by the communists. Since no one's told the Indians anything, they go along with the communists." He was trying to convince the people but at the same time he was insulting them by what he said. Anyway, they lined up the tortured and poured petrol on them; and then the soldiers set fire to each of them. Many of them begged for mercy. Some of them screamed, many of them leapt but uttered no sound . . .

Well, the officer quickly gave the order for the squad to fall withdraw. They all fell back holding their weapons up and shouting slogans as if it were a celebration. They were happy! They roared with laughter and cried, "Long live the Fatherland! Long live Guatemala! Long live our President! Long live the Army, long live Lucas!" . . .

Many people hurried off for water to put out the fires, but no one fetched it in time. . . . The bodies were twitching about. Although the fire had gone out, the bodies kept twitching. It was a frightful thing for me to accept them. You know, it wasn't just my brother's life. It was many lives, and you don't think that the grief is just for yourself but for all the relatives of the others: God knows if they found relatives of theirs there or not! Anyway, they were Indians, our brothers. And what you think is that Indians are already being killed off by malnutrition, and when our parents can hardly give us enough to live on, and make such sacrifices so that we can grow up, then they burn us alive like that. Savagely. I said, this is impossible, and that was precisely the moment for me, personally, when I felt firmly convinced that if it's a sin to kill a human being, how can what the regime does to us not be a sin?

Source 31 U.S. Department of State, secret cable, December 18, 1990

Subject: Stop Delivery of Military Assistance to Guatemala.

1. This message instructs the Embassy to immediately seek an appointment with President Cerezo to inform him of the halt of delivery of military assistance. . . .

2. It has become clear that the Cerezo Administration is not going to pursue the case of the murder of U.S. citizen Divine by military personnel. The GOG intends to string the investigation out, as it has on all previous cases, until it leaves office. . . .

3. This is unacceptable. The recent massacre of 14 civilians by the Guatemalan military only reinforces the fact that the military continue to act with impunity on human rights. . . .

Source 32 Commission for Historical Clarification, *Memory of Silence,* 1999

The Commission for Historical Clarification (CEH) was established through the Accord of Oslo on 23 June 1994, in order to clarify with objectivity, equity and impartiality, the human rights violations and acts of violence connected with the armed confrontation that caused suffering among the Guatemalan people. The Commission was not established to judge—that is the function of the courts of law—but rather to clarify the history of the events of more than three decades of fratricidal war.

When we were appointed to form the CEH, each of us, through different routes and all by life's fortune, knew in general terms the outline of events. As Guatemalans, two of us had lived the entire tragedy on our native soil, and in one way or another, had suffered it. However, none of us could have imagined the full horror and magnitude of what actually happened. . . .

We received thousands of testimonies; we accompanied the survivors at such moving moments as the exhumation of their loved ones from clandestine cemeteries; we listened to former heads of State and the high command of both the Army and the guerrillas; we read thousands of pages of documents received from a full range of civil society's organizations. The Commission's Report has considered all the versions and takes into account what we have heard, seen and read regarding the many atrocities and brutalities. . . .

The main purpose of the Report is to place on record Guatemala's recent, bloody past. Although many are aware that Guatemala's armed confrontation caused death and destruction, the gravity of the abuses suffered repeatedly by its people has yet to become part of the national consciousness. The massacres that eliminated entire Maya rural communities belong to the same reality as the persecution of the urban political opposition, trade union leaders, priests and catechists. These are neither perfidious allegations, nor figments of the imagination, but an authentic chapter in Guatemala's history. . . .

With the outbreak of the internal armed confrontation in 1962, Guatemala entered a tragic and devastating stage of its history, with enormous human, material and moral cost. In the documentation of human rights violations and acts of violence connected with the armed confrontation, the Commission for Historical Clarification (CEH) registered a total of 42,275 victims, including men, women and children. Of these, 23,671 were victims of arbitrary execution and 6,159 were victims of forced disappearance. Eighty-three percent of fully identified victims were Maya and seventeen percent were Latino. Combining this data with the results of other studies of political violence in Guatemala, the CEH estimates that the number of persons killed or disappeared as a result of the fratricidal confrontation reached a total of over 200,000.

The Commission for Historical Clarification concludes that the structure and nature of economic, cultural and social relations in Guatemala are marked by profound exclusion, antagonism and conflict—a reflection of its colonial history. The proclamation of independence in 1821, an event prompted by the country's elite, saw the creation of an authoritarian State which excluded the majority of the population, was racist in its precepts and practices, and served to protect the economic interests of the privileged minority. The evidence for this, throughout Guatemala's history, but particularly so during the armed confrontation, lies in the fact that the violence was fundamentally directed by the State against the excluded, the poor and above all, the Maya people, as well as against those who fought for justice and greater social equality. . . .

The anti-democratic nature of the Guatemalan political tradition has its roots in an economic structure, which is marked by the concentration of productive wealth in the hands of a minority. This established the foundations of a system of multiple exclusions, including elements of racism, which is, in turn, the most profound manifestation of a violent and dehumanizing social system. The State gradually evolved as an instrument for the protection of this structure, guaranteeing the continuation of exclusion and injustice.

The absence of an effective state social policy, with the exception of the period from 1944 to 1954, accentuated this historical dynamic of exclusion. In many cases, more recent State policy has produced inequality, or, at the very least, endemic institutional weaknesses have accentuated it. . . .

Due to its exclusionary nature, the State was incapable of achieving social consensus around a national project able to unite the whole population. Concomitantly, it abandoned its role as mediator between divergent social and economic interests, thus creating a gulf which made direct confrontation between them more likely . . . Appropriate institutional mechanisms for channeling concerns, claims and proposals from different sectors of society were lacking. This deficit of channels for constructively directing dissent through mediation, typical of democratic systems, further consolidated a political culture of confrontation and intolerance and provoked almost uninterrupted instability, permeating the whole social order.

Thus a vicious circle was created in which social injustice led to protest and subsequently political instability, to which there were always only two responses: repression or military coups. Faced with movements proposing economic, political, social or cultural change, the State increasingly resorted to violence and terror in order to maintain social control. Political violence was thus a direct expression of structural violence. . . .

After the overthrow of the government of Colonel Jacobo Arbenz in 1954, there was a rapid reduction of the opportunity for political expression. Inspired by fundamentalist anti-communism, new legislation outlawed the extensive and diverse social movement and consolidated the restrictive and exclusionary nature of the political system. These restrictions on political participation were agreed to by the country's real powers and activated by the period's civil and political forces. In itself, this process constitutes one of the most overwhelming pieces of evidence for the close relationship between the military, the economic powers and the political parties that emerged in 1954. From 1963 onwards, in addition to the legal restrictions, growing state repression against its real or suspected opponents was another decisive factor in the closing of political options in Guatemala. . . .

The CEH recognizes that the movement of Guatemala towards polarisation, militarization and civil war was not just the result of national history. The cold war also played an important role. Whilst anti-communism, promoted by the United States within the framework of its foreign policy, received firm support from right-wing political parties and from various other powerful actors in Guatemala, the United States demonstrated that it was willing to provide support for strong military regimes in his strategic backyard. In the case of Guatemala, military assistance was directed towards reinforcing the national intelligence apparatus and for training the officer corps in counterinsurgency techniques, key factors which had significant bearing on human rights violations during the armed confrontation.

Anti-communism and the National Security Doctrine (DSN) formed part of the anti-Soviet strategy of the United States in Latin America. In Guatemala, these were first expressed as anti-reformist, then anti-democratic policies, culminating in criminal counterinsurgency. The National Security Doctrine fell on fertile ground in Guatemala where anti-communist thinking had already taken root and from the 1930s, had merged with the defence of religion, tradition and conservative values, all of which were allegedly threatened by world-wide expansion of atheistic communism. Until the 1950s, these views were strongly supported by the Catholic Church, which qualified as communist any position that contradicted its philosophy, thus contributing even further to division and confusion in Guatemalan society.

During the armed confrontation, the States's idea of the "internal enemy," intrinsic to the National Security Doctrine, became increasingly inclusive. At the same time, this doctrine became the raison d'etre of Army and State policies for several decades. Through its investigation, the CEH discovered one of the most devastating effects of this policy: state forces and related paramilitary groups were responsible for 93% of the violations documented by the CEH including 92% of the arbitrary executions and 91% of forced disappearances. Victims included men, women and children of all social strata; workers, professionals, church members, politicians, peasants, students and academics; in ethnic terms, the vast majority were Mayans. . . .

Based on its investigation, the CEH also concludes that military intelligence structures in Guatemala played a decisive role in the militarization of the country. These structures assumed functions beyond those normally assigned to intelligence systems within the framework of the democratic rule of law, namely the systematization and interpretation of information important to the country's security. Instead, the Guatemalan intelligence system became the driving force of a state policy that took advantage of the situation resulting from the armed confrontation, to control the population, the society, the State and the Army itself. . . .

The CEH has confirmed that the control exercised by military intelligence depended not only on its formal structures, but also on an extensive network of informants who infiltrated social organizations, communities and various state institutions, thus giving it access to a vast quantity of information. Thus it was able to manage other structures of the Army and to manipulate the different interests and entities of the Guatemalan State and civil society. . . .

The CEH's investigation has corroborated the involvement of military intelligence services in unconventional and irregular operations far removed from any legal order. Its illegal operations were secret, in both their preparation and execution . . . This clandestine activity was evident in the use of illegal detention centres or "clandestine prisons," which existed in nearly all Guatemalan Army facilities, in many police installations and even in homes and in other private premises. In these places, victims were not only deprived of their liberty arbitrarily, but they were almost always subjected to interrogation, accompanied by torture and cruel, inhuman or degrading treatment. In the majority of cases, the detainees were disappeared or executed.

The substantiation of the degrading contents of the training of the Army's special counterinsurgency force, known as the *Kaibiles,* has drawn the particular attention of the CEH. This training included killing animals and then eating them raw and drinking their blood in order to demonstrate courage. The extreme cruelty of these training methods, according to testimony available to the CEH, was then put into practice in a range of operations carried out by these troops, confirming one point of their decalogue: "The Kaibil is a killing machine."

The CEH concludes that the National Police and the Treasury Police, two important state security forces, also committed numerous and grave human rights violations during the armed confrontation. Beginning in the mid-1960s, these forces were subordinated to army control. . . .

The CEH confirmed that throughout the armed confrontation the Army designed and implemented a strategy to provoke terror in the population. . . . A high proportion of the human rights violations known to the CEH and committed by the Army or security forces were perpetrated publicly and with extreme brutality, especially in the Mayan communities of the country's interior. Likewise, in considering the training methods of the Armed Forces, and especially the Kaibiles, the CEH concludes that extreme cruelty was a resource used intentionally to produce and maintain a climate of terror in the population. . . .

The Army's perception of Mayan communities as natural allies of the guerrillas contributed to increasing and aggravating the human rights violations perpetrated against them, demonstrating an aggressive racist component of extreme cruelty that led to the extermination en masse, of defenseless Mayan communities purportedly linked to the guerrillas—including children, women, and the elderly—through methods whose cruelty has outraged the moral conscience of the civilised world.

These massacres and the so-called scorched earth operations, as planned by the State, resulted in the complete extermination of many Maya communities, along with their homes, cattle, crops, and other elements essential to survival. The CEH registered 626 massacres attributable to these forces. . . .

In the majority of massacres there is evidence of multiple acts of savagery, which preceded, accompanied or occurred after the deaths of the victims. Acts such as the killing of defenceless children, often by beating them against walls or throwing them alive into pits where the corpses of adults were later thrown; the amputation of limbs; the impaling of victims; the killing of persons by covering them with petrol and burning them alive; the extraction, in the presence of others, of the viscera of victims who were still alive; the confinement of people who had been mortally tortured, in agony for days; the opening of the wombs of pregnant women, and other similarly atrocious acts, were not only actions of extreme cruelty against the victims, but also morally degraded the perpetrators and those who inspired, ordered or tolerated these actions.

The CEH's investigation has demonstrated that the rape of women, during torture or before being murdered, was a common practice aimed at destroying one of the most intimate and vulnerable aspects of the individual's dignity. The majority of rape victims were Mayan women. Those who survived the crime still suffer profound trauma as a result of this aggression, and the communities themselves were deeply offended by this practice. The presence of sexual violence in the social memory of the communities has become a source of collective shame. . . .

"Death Squads" were also used; these were initially criminal groups made up of private individuals who enjoyed the tolerance and complicity of state authorities. The CEH has arrived at the well-founded presumption that, later, various actions committed by these groups were a consequence of decisions by the Army command, and that the composition of the death squads varied over time as members of the military were incorporated, until they became, in many cases, authentic clandestine military units.

Source 33 **President Bill Clinton, "Remarks of the President in Roundtable Discussion on Peace Effort," National Palace of Culture, Guatemala City, Guatemala, March 10, 1999**

Mr. President [Alvaro Arzu of Guatemala],

First, let me say how much I appreciate this opportunity that has been provided for me to meet with citizens of your country to hear about the progress of the peace process and the challenges ahead. Because of the involvement of the United States, I think it is imperative as we begin for me just to say a few words about the report of the Historical Clarification Commission.

The commission's work and the support it has received from the government shows how far Guatemala has traveled in overcoming the painful period. I have profound respect for the victims and their families who had the courage to testify, and for the courage of a nation for coming to terms with its past and moving forward.

For the United States, it is important that I state clearly that support for military forces or intelligence units which engaged in violent and widespread repression of the kind described in the report was wrong, and the United States must not repeat that mistake. We must, and we will, instead, continue to support the peace and reconciliation process in Guatemala.

 Questioning the Past

1. Why did the United States orchestrate the overthrow of the elected government of Guatemala in 1954? Was this intervention in the internal affairs of another country justified? Defend your answer.

2. Did external considerations—the Red Scare in the United States, the affairs of corporations, the world political climate—play a major or minor role in the U.S. decision to covertly affect the internal affairs of Guatemala?

3. Argue the case for the use of covert action as an instrument of the U.S. foreign policy. Present the argument against such action. Which argument is the more persuasive?

4. "The erroneous belief that the end justifies the means converted Guatemala into a country of death and sadness," the Historical Clarification Commission concluded. "It should be remembered, once and for all, that there are no values superior to the lives of human beings, and thereby superior to the existence and well-being of an entire national community. The state has no existence of its own, but rather is purely an organisational tool by which a nation addresses its vital interests." Debate the validity of this conclusion.

5. What should be the criteria for American foreign aid? Should recipient countries meet certain standards of conduct with regard to their conduct toward other countries and their treatment of their own population? Should the United States assume no right to make judgments about the conduct of other countries? Defend your view.

Chapter 23

The Sit-In Movement

Joseph McNeil Invites Some Friends to Lunch

February 1, 1960

The Constitution of the United States and the ideals of the American nation promise every citizen equal treatment. Yet a black citizen walking along the sidewalk of an American city in 1960 was likely to be confronted by signs in cafes, stores, barbershops, motels, pharmacies, and even public libraries that announced that only whites would be allowed admittance.

Though the Supreme Court of the United States had declared segregated schools to be unconstitutional and ordered integration with "all deliberate speed," many communities simply refused to comply. A child in a white public school and a child in a black public school would each begin the school day by placing hand over heart and pledging allegiance to a flag symbolizing "one nation, under God, indivisible, with liberty and justice for all," but such a characterization of the nation in which they lived divided and unequal was a boldfaced lie.

Joseph McNeil was a college freshmen at North Carolina Agricultural and Technical College, a state school for African American citizens. He visited a local variety store, F.W. Woolworth, and was distressed to find that neither he nor any other customer of his race would be permitted to sit on a stool at the store's lunch counter and enjoy food or drink. The lunch counter was open to whites only. On February 1, 1960, McNeil returned to the store with three classmates. Each sat on stools at the counter and ordered apple pie and coffee. The waitress told them that store policy forbade any lunch counter service for blacks. McNeil replied that he and his friends were prepared to wait on their stools as long as it took for the store to change its policy. Forty-five tense minutes passed, and then the store was closed. Despite taunts, insults, threats, and an attempt by the police to intimidate them, the four students did not budge from their stools. Their act took great courage. When the store opened the next day, 29 African American students seated themselves on Woolworth's stools and waited for service that never came. The following day found 63 students waiting at Woolworth's lunch counter. By week's end, there were 1,000 students joining McNeil's "sit-in."

23.1 Greensboro
Sit-Ins

☙ *First Impressions*

A Sit-Down Becomes a Standoff

For a time, southern business establishments and the media that described them clung to the notion that private owners could pick and choose the patrons they wished to serve. But like Rosa Parks, the Montgomery, Alabama, woman who in 1955 refused to give up her seat on the bus to a white passenger, young Joseph McNeil had started something big.

Source 1   "Movement by Negroes Growing," *Greensboro Daily News*, February 4, 1960

A sit-down effort started Monday by A&T College students in an attempt to obtain lunch counter service at F. W. Woolworth's store here gained momentum yesterday.

At one time, Negro students filled 63 of 68 seats at the counter. The other three were occupied by waitresses. No service was given.

More Negro students waited in the aisle to take the place of students who left. The day brought these developments:

1. A statement of policy by a Woolworth's spokesman in New York.
2. A statement from State Attorney General Malcolm Seawall in reply to a question by a *Daily News* reporter.
3. Participation by Bennet College students in what had been a movement by A&T students only.
4. Moral support of the demonstration by several Greensboro College students who said they believed other students from white colleges might back the idea.
5. The closing of a stand-up lunch bar where Negroes had been served until yesterday.

The New York spokesman for the store chain said it is the company's policy "to abide by local custom."

The spokesman said no official word of the demonstration has been received in New York.

But the spokesman said if any group succeeds in changing the custom, "We will of course go along with that."

Seawall said that as far as he could determine, North Carolina has no law which would prohibit serving members of both races at a lunch counter. But on the other hand, he said he knew of no law which would force a private business to serve anybody it did not choose to serve.

As a matter of "custom which has existed for many years," a private businessman can serve or not serve people at his discretion, Seawall noted. . . .

Both men and women students were involved in the demonstration.

Business at the luncheon counter came to a virtual standstill as waitresses ignored the Negro students.

Source 2   "Aid Given Negroes' Protest," *Greensboro Daily News*, February 5, 1960

Three Woman's College students and Negro high school students joined Negroes from A&T College in a mass sit-down protest because of failure to secure service at the F. W. Woolworth Co. lunch counter Thursday.

And for the first time since the move began Tuesday, white teen-agers and young men appeared on the scene and blocked the aisles and occupied many of the counter seats.

Near noon the Negro and white students began marching to the S. H. Kress & Co. store down the street to launch a similar sitdown.

As the day progressed more A&T students came and were joined by students from Dudley High School and Woman's College. Some estimates of the crowd ran as high as 300 persons, mostly students.

Two white youths were escorted out of the Woolworth Store by plain-clothes offices after they began yelling and swearing.

Other abusive words were yelled at the Negroes in both stores but there was no physical violence.

Some members of the white group were heard swearing at the Negroes and calling them "nigger" and "burr-head." The Negroes ignored the remarks.

The movement began Monday when Negro college students began protesting the fact that they can buy all they want standing up in the store but are refused food service when they sit down at the lunch counter. The students maintain they will continue to sit daily at the counter until served.

A spokesman for the Negro group said yesterday that no plans have been made to converge on any other lunch counter or restaurant in the city. "We represent no organization, just a group of disgruntled students, and we plan to go about this thing in an orderly and Christian way," he said.

The three Woman's College students identified themselves as Genie Seaman of Orlando, Fla., Marilyn Lott of Washington, D.C., and Ann Dearsley of London, England.

"We felt it was our moral obligation to come down here," said Genie Seaman. They said they would appear at the store daily to support the movement.

J. Melville Broughton Jr., attorney for the N.C. Assn. of Quality Restaurants, has advised member restaurants that it is "your privilege to refuse to serve anyone in your private place of business." He advised members to use a trespass complaint if persons refuse to leave after being denied service.

Harper J. Elam III, city attorney, stated that there is no city ordinance to cover the situation, and State Attorney General Malcolm Seawall has said that as far as he could determine, this state has no law which would prohibit serving members of both races at a lunch counter. But on the other hand, he said he knew of no law which would force a private business to serve anybody it did not choose to serve.

Business at both lunch counters was at a virtual standstill except for soft drinks and coffee sold to whites.

About 5:25 p.m. the Negro group filed orderly out of the stores followed by the jeering white group. Outside, both groups quickly dispersed when police patrols cars drove up.

Source 3   Editorial, "Leadership at the Five and Ten," *Greensboro Daily News,* February 5, 1960

Now that the Negro sit-down strike at the downtown Woolworth lunch counter has persisted several days, and seems to be spreading elsewhere, a time has come for community leadership by both races to assert itself.

The impasse might have solved itself in a vacuum. But no racial dispute exists in a vacuum. The incident has become nation-wide and world-wide news. Ultimately, if not solved amicably, it could erupt into something worse, and that will reflect poorly on the community, including Woolworth and the colleges involved, not to mention individuals.

An effort should be made by leaders on both sides to seek each other out and discuss ways and means of dealing with a potentially ugly situation. . . .

As Attorney General Malcolm Seawall noted, North Carolina law neither shields nor coerces the principals: The state does not prohibit serving members of both races at a lunch counter. But neither does it force a business to serve those it does not choose to serve.

Legally, Woolworth might eject the sit-downers on grounds of illegal trespass and be perfectly within its rights. But that is a course of action, we are sure, the management does not want to follow.

Negro patrons occupying seats at the lunch counter have a position which demands consideration. In downtown Greensboro there are few, if any, restaurants or cafes where they can be served. Resentment against this dearth of facilities is not without justification.

But the way to remedy such a situation is through petition and negotiation rather than through a sit-down strike. No effort has been made to contact the Woolworth management about providing such facilities. They are made available in Woolworths elsewhere. We suggest that a delegation of potential lunch counter patrons get in touch with the management and see whether something can be worked out.

The alternatives could be ugly. There could be violence. There could be outright rejection. Neither of these courses is desirable.

This is a problem for Greensboro's mayor or city manager, working on the one hand with the Woolworth management, and responsible Negro leadership on the other.

There is the proper way to handle such matters, and it ought be resorted to before something much more serious happens at the five and ten.

Source 4   "White Men Arrested at Sit-Down: Negroes Keep Up Protest Action," *Greensboro Daily News*, February 6, 1960

Three white men were arrested yesterday at Woolworth's, one for setting fire to a Negro's coat as he sat with a group of students at the store's lunch counter in protest over not being served. . . .

The protest went into its fifth day with about 250 to 300 Negroes and whites participating. A countermove by a white group of teenagers and adults partially thwarted the Negroes' move to occupy all the seats in the Woolworth and Kress Stores yesterday morning.

Several white men and women were escorted out of the Woolworth's store for using abusive language by the dozens of detectives and policemen that stood by to keep order. . . .

A spokesman for the Negro group, identifying himself as X, said that the group intends to continue the sit-down "until we are served."

X further said, "We don't expect violence, but if it comes we will meet it with passive resistance. This is a Christian movement."

George Dorsett, the Klud (chaplain) of the Greensboro Chapter of the North Carolina Ku Klux Klan, was in the Woolworth store most of the day. He said he was there to "take care of my men and to keep violence to a minimum." It could not be determined how many other Klan members were present.

The Growing Force of Protest

What began as an act of defiance by a single college freshman expanded—like the ripples from a single pebble tossed into a placid pond—across the country and through the decade until the idea that African Americans would submit to indignity indefinitely was irrevocably washed from the minds of a complacent white-dominated America. Within a few days after Joseph McNeil and his classmates began their sit-in at the Woolworth Five and Ten, the tactic spread to a second store and then to a second city, and then across the entire South. Soon segregation at stores, parks, hotels, restaurants, and lunch counters was being swept away.

23.2 Student Nonviolent Coordinating Committee

A new organization, the Student Nonviolent Coordinating Committee, established and led by college students, emerged to organize the sit-in movement. It mobilized black and white students to attack the visible barriers that blocked African Americans' access to the opportunities of American life. As the decade began, SNCC employed nonviolent resistance as its approach to gaining racial equality. Laws that were deemed immoral or that unconstitutionally infringed on liberty were openly broken, and those who defied such laws freely surrendered themselves to suffer the legal consequences of their actions. Institutions that attempted to bar blacks were challenged by sit-ins, picket lines, and boycotts. When force was used against them, the student activists replied not with an eye for an eye but by turning the other cheek. Thousands of students went to jail. Many endured physical abuse. Some went to early graves.

As the decade wore on, many of the activists in SNCC grew embittered by the struggle. Slowly they backed away from the ideal that no matter how much abuse might be inflicted upon them, they would not use force in return. By the latter part of the decade, SNCC leaders such as Stokely Carmichael and H. Rap Brown argued that violence was a legitimate tool of self-defense, and the name of the organization was changed from the Student Nonviolent Coordinating Committee to the Student National Coordinating Committee. Though the idealism of the Greensboro Woolworth sit-in had faded to cynicism by the late 1960s, legally sanctioned segregation did not survive the decade.

Source 5 Editorial, "Seating Negroes," *Dallas Morning News*, February 10, 1960

Two variety stores in Greensboro, N.C., will serve Negroes something to eat but won't let them sit down to eat it. Negro students staged a fuss. The stores closed temporarily. Demonstrations spread to Durham and Winston-Salem.

It's hard to avoid fuzzy thinking about such a situation, but these seem to be fair questions: (1) The stores are private businesses and can serve whom they please and how they please; or has the world forgotten that owners own their own property? (2) As long as the stores serve Negroes, why not give them a place to sit? But, again, it's their private business. (3) Why don't the Negroes go where they can sit if there is a place for Negro sitters in these cities?

Maybe the Supreme Court, already overworked, will decide how these private stores should run their lunch counters. Can you guess what it will decide?

Source 6   "Negroes Extend Sit-Down Protest," *New York Times,* February 10, 1960

Charlotte, N.C.—A passive resistance movement by Negro students in North Carolina against segregated lunch counters spread to Charlotte today. A young ministerial student was reported leading the protest here.

"I have no malice, no jealousy, no hatred, no envy," said Joseph Charles Jones, a Negro graduate student at Johnson C. Smith University here.

"All I want is to come in and place my order and be served and leave a tip if I feel like it."

As other Negro students had done earlier in Greensboro, Durham and Winston-Salem, the 150 demonstrators in Charlotte filed quietly into eight downtown stores and filled the lunch-counter seats.

There was no boisterousness among the well-groomed students and no protest when white waitresses ignored their presence. They sat impassively while the stores closed the lunch counters, and departed in orderly fashion when one of the stores closed its doors.

Source 7   "Group Urges Segregated Facilities," *Greensboro Daily News,* February 19, 1960

The North Carolina Defenders of States' Rights, Inc., issued a statement last night calling on merchants in the state to preserve segregated "facilities" in their stores.

In the release, it is charged that Negroes who have been staging sit-down protests at lunch counters have been breaking state law at the instigation of "agitators" from outside North Carolina.

The statement was released by Lucius M. Cheshire of Hillsboro, a director, for the board of directors. It was delivered to the Daily News by the Rev. James P. Dees of Statesville, an Episcopalian rector who is president of the organization. . . .

The statement emphasizes two points:

1. "The places of business that are being violated are privately owned and the owners have both a legal right and a personal right to serve anyone they choose, and to refuse to serve anyone they choose.
2. "The culture of the South is based on a bi-racial society, any Supreme Court decisions to the contrary notwithstanding, and a destruction of the bi-racial society will obviously result in a mongrel society."

Store owners are assured in the statement that "the people of North Carolina, with the exception of disaffected elements of our Negro brethren, will support overwhelmingly the stores concerned to preserve the practice of providing segregated facilities to the customers."

Source 8   "New Protests Are Followed by Arrests," Associated Press,
February 23, 1960

Charlotte, Feb. 23—Negro students, apparently welcoming the probability of
arrest, resumed nonviolent demonstrations against segregated lunch counters in
North Carolina today. Police in two cities arrested demonstrators.

The resumption of the passive resistance movement after a lapse of several
days in many cities followed a statewide strategy meeting in Durham of Negro
student leaders. The students voted to continue their protest by sit-down demonstrations, boycotts and picket lines until they reach their goal of desegregated
lunch counters.

Police arrested 22 demonstrators in Winston-Salem—12 Negroes and 10
whites—as they sat at a white lunch counter marked for use of F. W. Woolworth
employees and their guests. The Negro students came from Winston-Salem
Teachers College and the whites from Wake Forest College.

Negro spectators cheered as police led each of the demonstrators to patrol
cars for transportation to headquarters and booking on charges of trespass.

 ## *Second Thoughts*

A Civil Right, Not a Social Right

The lunch counter at the Woolworth's in downtown Greensboro finally
acceded to the determination of the demonstrators and integrated its food
service facilities on July 25, 1960. Civil disobedience, supplemented by
lobbying, lawsuits, and demonstrations—such as the 1963 march on
Washington where Martin Luther King delivered his "I Have a Dream"
speech—challenged segregation elsewhere. The federal Civil Rights Bill
of 1964 prohibited discrimination in public accommodations. Still, it took
the remainder of the decade of the 1960s to integrate stores, cafes, restaurants,
transportation, hotels and a myriad of other businesses that had been open
for whites but closed to blacks. The lunch counter at the Greensboro Woolworth's was purchased by the Smithsonian Institution in 1994.

Source 9   Martin Luther King Jr., "I Have a Dream," address delivered
to 250,000 people from the steps of the Lincoln Memorial,
Washington, D.C., August 28, 1963

I am happy to join with you today in what will go down in history as the
greatest demonstration for freedom in the history of our nation.

Fivescore years ago a great American, in whose symbolic shadow we stand
today, signed the Emancipation Proclamation. This momentous decree came as
a great beacon of hope to millions of Negro slaves who had been seared in the
flames of withering injustice. It came as a joyous daybreak to end the long night
of their captivity.

But one hundred years later, the Negro is still not free; one hundred years
later, the life of the Negro is still sadly crippled by the manacles of segregation
and the chains of discrimination; one hundred years later, the Negro lives on a
lonely island of poverty in the midst of a vast ocean of material prosperity; one

23.3 The
Martin Luther
King Jr. Papers
Project

hundred years later, the Negro still languishes in the corners of American society and finds himself in exile in his own land.

So we've come here today to dramatize a shameful condition. In a sense we've come to our nation's capital to cash a check. When the architects of our republic wrote the magnificent words of the Constitution and the Declaration of Independence, they were signing a promissory note to which every American was to fall heir. This note was the promise that all men, black men as well as white men, would be guaranteed the unalienable rights of life, liberty, and the pursuit of happiness.

It is obvious today that America has defaulted on this promissory note in so far as her citizens of color are concerned. Instead of honoring this sacred obligation, America has given the Negro people a bad check; a check which has come back marked "insufficient funds." We refuse to believe that there are insufficient funds in the great vaults of opportunity of this nation. And so we've come to cash this check, a check that will give us upon demand the riches of freedom and the security of justice.

We have also come to this hallowed spot to remind America of the fierce urgency of now. This is no time to engage in the luxury of cooling off or to take the tranquilizing drug of gradualism. Now is the time to make real the promises of democracy; now is the time to rise from the dark and desolate valley of segregation to the sunlit path of racial justice; now is the time to lift our nation from the quicksands of racial injustice to the solid rock of brotherhood; now is the time to make justice a reality for all of God's children. It would be fatal for the nation to overlook the urgency of the moment. This sweltering summer of the Negro's legitimate discontent will not pass until there is an invigorating autumn of freedom and equality.

Nineteen sixty-three is not an end, but a beginning. And those who hope that the Negro needed to blow off steam and will now be content, will have a rude awakening if the nation returns to business as usual.

There will be neither rest nor tranquility in America until the Negro is granted his citizenship rights. The whirlwinds of revolt will continue to shake the foundations of our nation until the bright day of justice emerges.

But there is something that I must say to my people who stand on the warm threshold which leads into the palace of justice. In the process of gaining our rightful place we must not be guilty of wrongful deeds.

Let us not seek to satisfy our thirst for freedom by drinking from the cup of bitterness and hatred. We must forever conduct our struggle on the high plane of dignity and discipline. We must not allow our creative protest to degenerate into physical violence. Again and again we must rise up to the majestic heights of meeting physical force with soul force.

The marvelous new militancy which has engulfed the Negro community must not lead us to a distrust of all white people, for many of our white brothers, as evidenced by their presence here today, have come to realize that their freedom is inextricably bound to our freedom. This offense we share, mounted to storm the battlements of injustice, must be carried forth by a biracial army. We cannot walk alone.

And as we walk, we must make the pledge that we shall always march ahead. We cannot turn back. There are those who are asking the devotees of civil rights, "When will you be satisfied?" We can never be satisfied as long as the Negro is the victim of the unspeakable horrors of police brutality.

We can never be satisfied as long as our bodies, heavy with fatigue of travel, cannot gain lodging in the motels of the highways and the hotels of the cities. We cannot be satisfied as long as the Negro's basic mobility is from a smaller ghetto to a larger one.

We can never be satisfied as long as our children are stripped of their selfhood and robbed of their dignity by signs stating "for whites only." We cannot be satisfied as long as a Negro in Mississippi cannot vote and a Negro in New York believes he has nothing for which to vote. No, we are not satisfied, and we will not be satisfied until justice rolls down like waters and righteousness like a mighty stream.

I am not unmindful that some of you come here out of excessive trials and tribulations. Some of you have come from areas where your quest for freedom left you battered by the storms of persecution and staggered by the winds of police brutality. You have been the veterans of creative suffering. Continue to work with the faith that unearned suffering is redemptive.

Go back to Mississippi; go back to Alabama; go back to South Carolina; go back to Georgia; go back to Louisiana; go back to the slums and ghettos of the northern cities, knowing that somehow this situation can, and will be changed. Let us not wallow in the valley of despair.

So I say to you, my friends, that even though we must face the difficulties of today and tomorrow, I still have a dream. It is a dream deeply rooted in the American dream that one day this nation will rise up and live out the true meaning of its creed—we hold these truths to be self-evident, that all men are created equal.

I have a dream that one day on the red hills of Georgia, sons of former slaves and sons of former slave-owners will be able to sit together at the table of brotherhood.

I have a dream that one day, even the state of Mississippi, a state sweltering with the heat of injustice, will be transformed into an oasis of freedom and justice.

I have a dream my four little children will one day live in a nation where they will not be judged by the color of their skin but by the content of their character. I have a dream today!

I have a dream that one day, down in Alabama, with its vicious racists, with its governor having his lips dripping with the words of interposition and nullification, that one day, right there in Alabama, little black boys and little black girls will be able to join hands with little white boys and white girls as sisters and brothers. I have a dream today!

I have a dream that one day every valley will be exalted, every hill and mountain shall be made low, the rough places shall be made plain, and the crooked places shall be made straight and the glory of the Lord will be revealed and all flesh shall see it together.

This is our hope. This is the faith that I go back to the South with.

With this faith we will be able to hew out of the mountain of despair a stone of hope. With this faith we will be able to transform the jangling discords of our nation into a beautiful symphony of brotherhood.

With this faith we will be able to work together, to pray together, to struggle together, to go to jail together, to stand for freedom together, knowing that we will be free one day. This will be the day when all God's children will be able to sing with a new meaning—"my country 'tis of thee, sweet land of liberty; of thee I sing;

land where my fathers died, land of the pilgrim's pride; from every mountain side, let freedom ring"—and if America is to be a great nation, this must become true.

So let freedom ring from the prodigious hilltops of New Hampshire.

Let freedom ring from the mighty mountains of New York.

Let freedom ring from the heightening Alleghenies of Pennsylvania.

Let freedom ring from the snow-capped Rockies of Colorado.

Let freedom ring from the curvaceous slopes of California.

But not only that.

Let freedom ring from Stone Mountain of Georgia.

Let freedom ring from Lookout Mountain of Tennessee.

Let freedom ring from every hill and molehill of Mississippi, from every mountainside, let freedom ring.

And when we allow freedom to ring, when we let it ring from every village and hamlet, from every state and city, we will be able to speed up that day when all of God's children—black men and white men, Jews and Gentiles, Catholics and Protestants—will be able to join hands and to sing in the words of the old Negro spiritual, "Free at last, free at last; thank God Almighty, we are free at last."

Source 10 Supreme Court justice William O. Douglas, writing a separate opinion in *Bell v. Maryland*, 1964

[In this case the high court reversed the convictions of 12 students found guilty of criminal trespass for a sit-in at a Baltimore restaurant.]

The problem in this case, and in the other sit-in cases before us, is presented as though it involved the situation of "a private operator conducting his own business on his own premises and exercising his own judgment" as to whom he will admit to the premises.

The property involved is not, however, a man's home or his yard or even his fields. Private property is involved, but it is property that is serving the public. As my Brother [Associate Justice] Goldberg says, it is a "civil" right, not a "social" right, with which we deal. Here it is a restaurant refusing service to a Negro. But so far as principle and law are concerned it might just as well be a hospital refusing admission to a sick or injured Negro . . . or a drug store refusing antibiotics to a Negro, or a bus denying transportation to a Negro, or a telephone company refusing to install a telephone in a Negro's home.

The problem with which we deal has no relation to the opening or closing of one's home. The home is of course the essence of privacy, in no way dedicated to public use, in no way extending an invitation to the public. . . .

There is no specific provision in the Constitution which protects rights of privacy and enables restaurant owners to refuse service to Negroes. . . . We, on the other hand, live under a Constitution that proclaims equal protection under the law. Why then . . . should apartheid be given constitutional sanction in the restaurant field?

Source 11 Martin Luther King Jr., *Why We Can't Wait*, 1964

Direct action is not a substitute for work in the courts and the halls of government. Bringing about the passage of a new and broad law by a city council, state legislature or the Congress, or pleading cases before the courts of the land, does not eliminate the necessity for bringing about the mass dramatization of injustice in front of a city hall. Indeed, direct action and legal action complement one another; when skillfully employed, each becomes more effective.

The chronology of the sit-ins confirms this observation. Spontaneously born, but guided by the theory of nonviolent resistance, the lunch-counter sit-ins accomplished integration in hundreds of communities at the swiftest rate of change in the civil rights movement up to that time. Yet, many communities successfully resisted lunch-counter desegregation, and pressed charges against the demonstrators. It was correct and effective that demonstrators should fill the jails; but it was necessary that these foot soldiers for freedom not be deserted to languish there or to pay excessive penalties for their devotion. Indeed, by creative use of the law, it was possible to prove that officials combating the demonstrations were using the power of the police state to deny the Negro equal protection under the law. This brought many of the cases squarely under the jurisdiction of the Fourteenth Amendment. As a consequence of combining direct and legal action, far-reaching precedents were established, which served, in turn, to extend the areas of desegregation.

Source 12 C. Vann Woodward, *The Strange Career of Jim Crow*, 1966

On 1 February of that year [1960] four Negro college boys, freshmen at the Agricultural and Technical College in Greensboro, North Carolina, asked politely for coffee at Woolworth's lunch counter and continued to sit in silent protest when refused. The "sit-in," nemesis of Jim Crow, was born. In a week it spread to six other cities of the state, and by the end of the month to seven other Southern states. The self-discipline and fortitude of the youths, who silently bore abuse and insult, touched the white South's respect for courage. A few Northern and Southern whites joined the demonstrators in parades and picket lines. In April the Student Nonviolent Coordinating Committee (S.N.C.C.) was formed—small, militant, very youthful, largely Negro, and Negro-led. The sit-in demonstrations gained momentum and power as they spread through the whole South and involved nonviolent direct action by thousands who had never protested before.

The Negro awakening of 1960 was more profound than the abortive stirring of 1867. It was deeper, surer, less contrived, more spontaneous. More than a black revolt against whites, it was in part a generational rebellion, an uprising of youth against the older generation, against the parental "Uncle Toms" and their inhibitions. It even took the N.A.A.C.P. and CORE [Congress of Racial Equality] by surprise. Negroes were in charge of their own movement now, and youth was in the vanguard. . . . One of the great uprisings of oppressed people in the twentieth century, it could have taken an ominous form had it not been for two extremely fortunate circumstances. One was the *Brown* decision of 1954 that had prepared the way for redress of grievances by constitutional means. The other was that all the major civil rights organizations, new as well as old, were committed to the philosophy of nonviolence, the doctrine preached by the most conspicuous leader in the Negro movement, Martin Luther King. "We will soon wear you down by our capacity to suffer," he told the whites, "and in winning our freedom we will so appeal to your heart and conscience that we will win you in the process." All but the most incorrigible white resistance was vulnerable to such a weapon.

The walls of segregation began to crumble under the new assault. Lunch counters yielded in more than a hundred cities within a year. The sit-in tactics were broadened to attack segregation in theaters, hotels, public parks, swimming pools, and beaches, a well as in churches, courtrooms, libraries, and art galleries.

Source 13 Civil rights activist and comedian Dick Gregory, *Write Me In!* 1968

White America's violent rebuke of the philosophy of nonviolence made Stokely Carmichael and Rap Brown what they are today. . . . You must understand what they went through when they were just kids, organizers in the South for the Student Non-violent Coordinating Committee. I'll never forget when I first met Stokely Carmichael six years ago in Greenwood, Mississippi. He insulted me. I was new to the movement and Stokely said, "If you can't be nonviolent, get the hell back up North." Many people in this country forget, or perhaps never knew, that it was Rap Brown, Stokely Carmichael and other members of SNCC who taught nonviolence. They taught nonviolence as a strategy while Martin Luther King had to fly all over the country explaining the concept to white folks. If you could have seen what those kids went through, you would understand what they are talking about now.

I used to watch them guarding their Freedom House in Greenwood, wondering when it was going to be blown up. Do you know what they were guarding it with? Nothing but a nonviolent attitude. You try that sometime. Imagine yourself waiting for someone to come with dynamite and you are sitting there with no defense but a nonviolent attitude, in a country where grown men go hunting little-bitty rabbits with shotguns.

Think what it means to be down South for six years, sleeping on the floor next to your comrades lined up in a row. And one night you notice an empty place in the line. One of your comrades has not come home that night and you know he is dead. The police have run him off the highway and then reported that he was drunk and killed in an auto accident. And you know your comrade never took a drink in his life. . . .

Or maybe you should have been with Stokely and Rap in Greenwood when they tried to integrate the schools. All during the summer months, while most Americans are on vacation, they had to canvass the black community. They had to convince poor black sharecroppers that their kids were needed to help integrate the schools. White folks were saying black folks didn't want to integrate. Even though the Supreme Court ruling says the schools must be integrated, the white folks said, the colored people won't show up.

SNCC did a good job that summer. They got twelve families to permit them to use their kids. At least they thought they had twelve when they went to bed the night before the opening day of school. The next morning only eight reported—four had copped out. Do you know what it feels like to go to a five-year-old kid's house to pick him up for school? He is all smiles and happy. And as you place his little black hand in your hand, you wonder why someone hasn't had the courage to tell him that he might be going to die.

When you pull up to the school building, you see the cops barricading it and the sheriff says, "Where you going, nigger?" And you say, "I'm going to school." The little kid looks up and says "Mornin', mister." And the sheriff snaps, "Well, you can't bring that car in here." So you park the car and get out. You tightly grip that little black hand in yours and the inside of your hand is soaking wet with sweat. Not the five-year-old kid's sweat, but your own.

About twenty-five feet from the building, where you have to turn to go up those stairs, you see something that makes you know that somebody is going to die. When you hit the steps, you know you weren't wrong. You are not only attacked by the mob, but by the sheriff and the police. The next thing you know you are lying in the gutter with that cracker's foot on your chest and a double-barreled shotgun on your throat. And you hear a voice say, "Move, nigger, and I'll blow your brains out." You're terrified but you think how ironic it is that the only time white folks will admit you have brains is when they are talking about what they are going to do to them.

It is a terrifying feeling to look up and realize for the first time that today is your day to die. And you look across the street and see the FBI taking pictures and you know damn well they will never be shown. You know also that if a black man had his foot on that cracker's chest, those pictures would be released for the "Today" show the next morning.

Then the most horrible thing happens that has ever happened to you in your life. You suddenly realize that the little black hand is not there. And you turn around to look for that little five-year-old kid. You spot him just in time to see a brick hit him right in the mouth. It just doesn't read right for some reason. You have to actually see a brick hit a five-year-old kid in the mouth, regardless of what color the kid is. Only then can you realize the depths of blind and insane hate.

You see the look in that little black child's eye. He can't even react like a five-year-old kid should react after being hurt. He can't run to the adults because they are spitting and kicking at him. You see a white mother lean over that little kid and spit on him and stomp at him. . . .

Now you have to take that bruised and bleeding little kid, whose early-morning happy smile has been pulverized and perhaps erased forever, back to his parents who entrusted him to you. And you have to try to explain what happened. You have to hope you will have their support when you are ready to try again. Your own words choke you and anything you say sounds so unconvincing.

You may never be able to justify Stokely and Rap, but when you know what they have been through, you may be able to understand them. When Stokely and Rap had faith in America, they were screaming in the dark to a nation that didn't care.

Source 14 H. Rap Brown, chairman of SNCC during 1967–1968, *Die Nigger Die,* 1969

A lot of people, Black and white, have the impression that those of us who got involved in the Movement, when it started in 1960, were fighting for integration. That's the way the white press interpreted the sit-ins and freedom rides and all that. But what they didn't understand was that none of us was concerned about sitting down next to a white man and eating a hamburger. Anybody who thinks that is reflecting white nationalism. That's that white supremacist attitude. Nothing is good unless it can be done in the company of white people. We would've been some kind of fools to get beaten up, spat on and jailed the way a lot of folks did just to sit down at a lunch counter beside a white person. Integration was never our concern. In fact, integration is impractical. You cannot legislate an attitude, and integration is based upon an attitude of mutual acceptance and respect between two racial or cultural groups in the society. A law can govern behavior, but attitudes cannot be forced or enforced, and what the Civil Rights Movement was concerned with was controlling the animalistic *behavior* of white people. I resented somebody telling me I couldn't eat at a certain place. It wasn't that I wanted to eat there. Hell no! I always knew we had the best food anyway. But as part of that constant battle waged by Black people against white america, if white folks didn't want me to eat there, in the door I went. If I had a free choice, I'd sit in the back of the bus. That's where the heater is. We weren't fighting for integration. We were letting white folks know that they could no longer legislate where we went or what we did.

Source 15   John Hope Franklin, *From Slavery to Freedom: A History of Negro Americans*, 1974

By the time the four Negro students launched the sit-in movement, the stage was already set for the beginning of the most profound, revolutionary changes in the status of black Americans that had occurred since emancipation. The road to revolution had been paved by significant shifts in the black population from rural areas to the cities and from the South to the North and West; by Supreme Court decisions on voting and school desegregation; by the Montgomery bus boycott and the emergence of Martin Luther King; by the passage of the Civil Rights Act of 1957; and by the rise of national states in Africa. The revolution would have many facets. The changes in public policy, in the way that Negroes viewed themselves and their place in American life, in the attitudes and thoughts of the larger community toward Negroes were about as far-reaching as the changes in the status of Negroes themselves. The decision of the young Negro college students to sit-in symbolized some of these changes and suggested the nature of others yet to come. In the months and years that followed, an interesting interplay of action and response developed between government and civil rights advocates. And it was this interplay that did so much to carry the revolution forward.

Source 16   William H. Chafe, *Civilities and Civil Rights: Greensboro, North Carolina, and the Black Struggle for Freedom*, 1980

In the long view of history, the Greensboro sit-ins will justifiably be seen as the catalyst that triggered a decade of revolt—one of the greatest movements in history toward self-determination and human dignity. America would never be the same once students discovered the power of direct-action protest and others followed their example. As one participant in the sit-ins declared, "That dime store . . . was the birthplace of a whirlwind." . . .

Greensboro had long boasted of being a "moderate" and progressive city. By those words whites meant a willingness to proceed, with gradualism and good manners, to discuss issues of social conflict in an attempt to find consensus and compromise. . . . A central ingredient in this style was the form of discourse that prevailed between whites and blacks. As long as the amenities were observed and Negroes conducted themselves appropriately, it was assumed by whites that an equitable solution could be found to any dilemma. Yet the boundaries set by correct behavior or the "amenities" ruled out the possibility that white leaders could hear the full depth of black disaffection. Conversely, devotion to proper social forms caused whites to reject as unrepresentative any black who failed to obey the ground rules of "correct" behavior.

From a black point of view, of course, the ground rules, or "civilities," were often just a way of delaying action. No event better crystallized the gap between form and substance than the Greensboro school board's handling of school desegregation during the late 1950's. The brazenness of the school board's arguing in court that it supported desegregation even as it transferred all white students from Caldwell School was overwhelming. Yet if good manners prevented white leaders from hearing the resounding depth of black protest, perhaps another form of communication would be necessary.

In this sense, the fundamental contribution of the sit-ins was to provide a new form through which protest could be expressed. The very act of sitting-in circumvented those forms of fraudulent communication and self-deception through which whites had historically denied black self-assertion. The sit-ins represented a new language. Moreover, the language communicated a message different from that which had been heard before. A direct connection existed between style and content. In an almost visceral way, the sit-ins expressed the dissatisfaction and anger of the black community toward white indifference. From a black point of view, the protest may have been the same as that which had been conveyed all along. But it was expressed in a manner that whites could not possibly ignore—the silence of people sitting with dignity at a lunch counter demanding their rights. Thus, from a white point of view, the message was different, because for the first time, whites could not avoid hearing it.

Source 17 "Sit-In Member Served after 25 Years," *Richmond Times-Dispatch,* **February 2, 1985**

Greensboro, N.C.—One of the four students who ordered a snack at a segregated lunch counter 25 years ago re-enacted yesterday the event that touched off civil rights demonstrations all across the South.

"The reception is quite different today," David Richmond, 43, of Greensboro, said after ordering apple pie and coffee—the same items he was refused at the downtown F. W. Woolworth counter Feb. 1, 1960. "I'm enjoying things now."

The other three former North Carolina A&T State University students who were refused service with Richmond in 1960 weren't there yesterday.

They are Franklin McCain, 43, an executive at Celanese Corp. in Charlotte; Joseph McNeil, 42, an Air Force recruiter from Bedford, N.Y.; and Jibreel Khazan, 43, who changed his name from Ezell Blair Jr. in 1970 and works with disabled adults in New Bedford, Mass.

Before sitting at the counter, Richmond embraced waitress Ima J. Edwards, who has worked there for 32 years.

"Hopefully I will be served," he joked. "I'm going to have the same thing I ordered 25 years ago. Do you remember what it was?"

Mrs. Edwards, 52, said she didn't.

"At that time it didn't seem like any big deal," she said. "I didn't think it would lead to all this."

Richmond, a nursing home employee, recalled he was "very nervous, very afraid" as he and his friends sat at the counter for 45 minutes. The store manager and the waitress, now retired, told the four they could not be served. A police officer walking behind them hit his hand with a night stick. . . .

On July 25, 1960, Woolworth integrated the lunch counter, and three black waitresses were the first to be served. Geneva Tisdale is the only one still alive.

"They said, if you don't want your picture in the paper, then get something you can eat real quick," she said. "That's what I did."

Ms. Tisdale said she had long been upset that blacks' "money was good enough to spend in the store, but we couldn't sit down to eat."

Still, she said she shook as she ate her egg salad sandwich.

"There were a lot of mean people out there—there still are," she said.

 ## Questioning the Past

1. Why was the sit-in an effective tactic to attack segregation in the South?

2. In the days when segregation was the norm, business establishments posted signs that stated: "We reserve the right to refuse service to anyone." The *Dallas Morning News* editorial asked whether the world had "forgotten that owners own their own property." Does a business that invites the public into its facilities have the right to exclude those it chooses not to serve? Argue the case for and against such a policy.

3. Compare the attitudes and objectives expressed by Martin Luther King in his "I Have a Dream" speech with those of H. Rap Brown excerpted from *Die Nigger Die*. Are these attitudes and objectives contradictory or compatible?

4. Dick Gregory has written: "The double standard in America fails to appreciate American history. White America idolizes Patrick Henry and condemns Rap Brown. But Rap Brown has only dared to become as bitter as Patrick Henry. When Patrick Henry said, 'Give me Liberty or give me Death,' he was not talking about singing freedom songs to the British. Nor was he talking about going to Boston to help them unload their tea. . . . Rap Brown said, 'Get a gun, black folks, and watch the police.' And white America went crazy. . . . Our nation's treasured Declaration of Independence clearly states that where rights and privileges are denied by a government over long periods of time it is a man's duty to abolish that government. Malcolm X did not write that document. Stokely, Rap and SNCC didn't have a thing to do with it. . . . When I read the American history book, there is one thing I just cannot believe. It says that George Washington and his ragged band . . . conquered the continent and defeated the whole British Army. And why did he do it? The history book says because of a tax on tea. . . . In 1968, most Americans don't even drink tea! Do you honestly think there is such a difference between white folks and black folks that America can give us a book bursting with pride for a Revolutionary War over a tea tax and yet not see what the black man in the ghetto is getting ready to do?" Though Gregory never advocated violence, his statement implies that African Americans were as justified in their struggle for liberty to use violence as were the Founding Fathers in their day. Debate this point.

Chapter **24**

The Cuban Missile Crisis

President Kennedy Makes an Alarming Announcement   *October 22, 1962*

It was late morning on October 16, 1962. The president of the United States had convened a special meeting of his Cabinet to hear an extraordinary briefing from the Central Intelligence Agency. With charts, maps, and photographs taken from high-flying American spy planes, officials of the CIA stunned the leaders of the American government with a startling revelation: The Soviet Union was secretly at work assembling offensive missiles only 90 miles from America's shores. When fully assembled, these missiles would be capable of raining nuclear warheads down upon America's eastern seaboard cities only minutes after launch from their bases in Communist Cuba. The moment of truth in the cold war had arrived.

In 1962, two tense worlds were uneasily coexisting on the same planet. One world was under the sway of the United States; the other was dominated by the power of the Soviet Union. These two worlds had isolated themselves from each other. Each was convinced that its own political and economic system was right for all. The movement of people, commerce, and ideas swirled within each of these two worlds but seldom between them. The lines of demarcation which divided the Western world from the communist world were marked by a series of conflict points. An ongoing state of nonmilitary warfare—a cold war—kept tension high and propelled the two superpowers and their respective allies toward an ultimate danger: each world possessed the military capability of destroying all life on the planet they precariously shared.

The introduction of Soviet nuclear weaponry at a place near the economic, military, and political core of the Western world was seen by the United States as an intolerable situation. The 13 days that began with the CIA briefing of Kennedy and his Cabinet came close to being the last for life on earth.

For six days following the revelation of October 16, the crisis was discussed in private by a committee of the president's closest and most trusted advisers. This committee finally presented President Kennedy with a list of seven options: (1) The United States could send the Soviet Union a formal note of protest over the placement of the missiles in Cuba; (2) The United States could take its complaint to the United Nations Security Council; (3) The United States could initiate some form of economic sanctions against the Soviet Union; (4) The American armed forces could be

24.1 Fourteen Days in October: The Cuban Missile Crisis

directed to form a blockade around Cuba; (5) American aircraft could conduct a surprise "surgical air strike" against the missile sites in Cuba; (6) The American military could stage an invasion of Cuba to oust Cuban prime minister Fidel Castro from power and excise the missile threat; or (7) The United States could launch a nuclear attack directly on the Soviet Union.

✂ *First Impressions*
A Step along the Road to Thermonuclear War

24.2 Archives of the New York Times: The Cuban Missile Crisis

On the evening of October 22, 1962, President Kennedy appeared on national television to give the American people their first news of the Cuban missile crisis and to tell them which option he had decided to pursue.

Source 1   President John F. Kennedy, "Radio and Television Report to the American People on the Soviet Arms Buildup in Cuba," 7 P.M., October 22, 1962

Good evening, my fellow citizens:

This Government, as promised, has maintained the closest surveillance of the Soviet military buildup on the island of Cuba. Within the past week, unmistakable evidence has established the fact that a series of offensive missile sites is now in preparation on that imprisoned island. The purpose of these bases can be none other than to provide a nuclear strike capability against the Western Hemisphere.

Upon receiving the first preliminary hard information of this nature last Tuesday morning at 9 a.m., I directed that our surveillance be stepped up. And having now confirmed and completed our evaluation of the evidence and our decision on a course of action, this Government feels obligated to report this new crisis to you in fullest detail.

The characteristics of these new missile sites indicate two distinct types of installations. Several of them include medium-range ballistic missiles, capable of carrying a nuclear warhead for a distance of more than 1,000 nautical miles. Each of these missiles, in short, is capable of striking Washington, D.C., the Panama Canal, Cape Canaveral, Mexico City, or any other city in the southeastern part of the United States, in Central America, or in the Caribbean area.

Additional sites not yet completed appear to be designed for intermediate-range ballistic missiles—capable of travelling more than twice as far—and thus capable of striking most of the major cities in the Western Hemisphere, ranging as far north as Hudson Bay, Canada, and as far south as Lima, Peru. In addition, jet bombers, capable of carrying nuclear weapons, are now being uncrated and assembled in Cuba, while the necessary bases are being prepared.

The urgent transformation of Cuba into an important strategic base—by the presence of these large, long-range, and clearly offensive weapons of sudden mass destruction—constitutes an explicit threat to the peace and security of all the Americas. . . .

Only last Thursday, as evidence of this rapid offensive buildup was already in my hand, Soviet Foreign Minister Gromyko told me in my office that he was instructed to make it clear once again, as he said his government had already done, that Soviet assistance to Cuba, and I quote, "pursued solely the purpose of contributing to the defense capabilities of Cuba," that, and I quote him, "training by Soviet specialists of Cuban nationals in handling defensive armaments was by no means offensive, and if it were otherwise," Mr. Gromyko went on, "the Soviet Government would never become involved in rendering such assistance." That statement . . . was false.

Neither the United States of America nor the world community of nations can tolerate deliberate deception and offensive threats on the part of any nation, large or small. We no longer live in a world where only the actual firing of weapons represents a sufficient challenge to a nation's security to constitute maximum peril. Nuclear weapons are so destructive and ballistic missiles are so swift, that any substantially increased possibility of their use or any sudden change in their deployment may well be regarded as a definite threat to peace.

For many years, both the Soviet Union and the United States, recognizing this fact, have deployed strategic nuclear weapons with great care, never upsetting the precarious status quo which insured that these weapons would not be used in the absence of some vital challenge. Our own strategic missiles have never been transferred to the territory ·of any other nation under a cloak of secrecy and deception; and our history—unlike that of the Soviets since the end of World War II—demonstrates that we have no desire to dominate or conquer any other nation or impose our system upon its people. Nevertheless, American citizens have become adjusted to living daily on the bull's eye of Soviet missiles located inside the Soviet Union or in submarines.

In that sense, missiles in Cuba add to an already clear and present danger—although it should be noted the nations of Latin America have never previously been subjected to a potential nuclear threat.

But this secret, swift, and extraordinary buildup of Communist missiles—in an area well known to have a special and historical relationship to the United States and the nations of the Western Hemisphere, in violation of Soviet assurances, and in defiance of American and hemispheric policy—this sudden, clandestine decision to station strategic weapons for the first time outside of Soviet soil—is a deliberatively provocative and unjustified change in the status quo which cannot be accepted by this country, if our courage and our commitments are ever to be trusted again by either friend or foe.

The 1930's taught us a clear lesson: aggressive conduct, if allowed to go unchecked and unchallenged, ultimately leads to war. . . .

Acting, therefore, in the defense of our own security and of the entire Western Hemisphere, and under the authority entrusted to me by the Constitution . . . , I have directed that the following *initial* steps be taken immediately:

First: To halt this offensive buildup, a strict quarantine on all offensive military equipment under shipment to Cuba is being initiated. All ships of any kind bound for Cuba from whatever nation or port will, if found to contain cargoes of offensive weapons, be turned back. . . .

Second: I have directed the continued and increased close surveillance of Cuba and its military buildup. . . . Should these offensive military preparations continue, thus increasing the threat to the hemisphere, further action will be justified. I have directed the Armed Forces to prepare for any eventualities; and I trust that in the interest of both the Cuban people and the Soviet technicians at the sites, the hazards to all concerned of continuing this threat will be recognized.

Third: It shall be the policy of this nation to regard any nuclear missile launched from Cuba against any nation in the Western Hemisphere as an attack by the Soviet Union on the United States, requiring a full retaliatory response upon the Soviet Union.

Fourth: As a necessary military precaution, I have reinforced our base at Guantanamo, evacuated today the dependents of our personnel there, and ordered additional units to be on a standby alert basis.

Fifth: We are calling tonight for an immediate meeting of the Organ of Consultation under the Organization of American States, to consider this threat to hemispheric security. . . .

Sixth: Under the Charter of the United Nations, we are asking tonight that an emergency meeting of the Security Council be convened without delay to take action against this latest Soviet threat to world peace. . . .

Seventh and finally: I call upon Chairman Khrushchev to halt and eliminate this clandestine, reckless, and provocative threat to world peace and stable relations between our two countries. I call upon him further to abandon this course of world domination, and to join in an historic effort to end the perilous arms race and to transform the history of man. He has an opportunity to move the world back from the abyss of destruction. . . .

My fellow citizens: let no one doubt that this is a difficult and dangerous effort on which we have set out. No one can foresee precisely what course it will take or what costs or casualties will be incurred. . . . But the greatest danger of all would be to do nothing.

The path we have chosen for the present is full of hazards, as all paths are. . . . The cost of freedom is always high—but Americans have always paid it. And one path we shall never choose, and that is the path of surrender or submission.

Our goal is not the victory of might, but the vindication of right—not peace at the expense of freedom, but both peace *and* freedom, here in this hemisphere, and we hope, around the world. God willing, that goal will be achieved.

Thank you and good night.

Source 2   CIA Director John A. McCone, "Memorandum for the File," October 22, 1962

SECRET/EYES ONLY

Subject: Meeting with the Vice President on 21 October 1962

On Sunday night, October 21 at 8:30 I briefed Vice President Lyndon Johnson at the request of the President, conveyed through McGeorge Bundy.

The briefing involved a review of photography by Lundahl paralleling briefings given to General Eisenhower and others.

We then discussed policy and details of the proposed speech by the President in considerable detail.

The thrust of the Vice President's thinking was that he favored an unannounced strike rather than the agreed plan which involved blockade and strike and invasion later if conditions warranted. He expressed displeasure at "telegraphing our punch" and also commented the blockade would be ineffective because we in effect are "locking the barn after the horse was gone."

I followed the position and the argument used in my briefing paper of 20 October. The Vice President finally agreed reluctantly but only after learning among other things the support indicated by General Eisenhower.

Source 3   Guided Missile and Astronautics Intelligence Committee, Joint Atomic Energy Intelligence Committee, and National Photographic Interpretation Center, "Joint Evaluation of Soviet Missile Threat in Cuba"

TOP SECRET

2200 Hours
23 October 1962

This supplement up-dates and amplifies previous reports. Emphasis continues to be placed on the READINESS status of the offensive missiles in Cuba. This report is based on photographic coverage through mission 3117 of 20 October 1962.

1. There are no changes in the estimates of operational readiness for the nine offensive missile sites.
2. No new missile sites have been identified.
3. The observed missile and launcher count is increasing as estimated. Three additional MRBMs and four additional MRBM launchers raise the totals to 33 missiles and 23 launchers. No IRBMs have been identified. . . .
4. One additional SAM site is now considered operational, bringing the total individually operational sites to 23 of the 24 active sites so far identified.
5. No new intelligence information has been received which modifies the nuclear storage situation since the last joint supplement.

Source 4   Response of the Soviet government to President Kennedy's announcement, October 23, 1962

President Kennedy of the United States announced last night that he had instructed the U.S. Navy to intercept all ships proceeding to Cuba, to search them and not to let pass ships carrying weapons which are defined by the U.S. authorities as offensive weapons.

Another order was issued to conduct continuous and thorough observation over Cuba. Thus, the U.S. Government, in effect, establishes a naval blockade of the Republic of Cuba. . . .

The President tries to justify these unprecedented aggressive actions by alleging that a threat to the national security of the United States emanates from Cuba.

The Soviet government has repeatedly drawn the attention of . . . world public opinion to the serious danger to the cause of peace created by the policy of the United States with regard to the Republic of Cuba.

The statement of the U.S. President shows that the U.S. imperialist circles balk at nothing in their attempts to stifle the sovereign state, a United Nations member. For this purpose, they are prepared to push the world to the abyss of a war catastrophe.

The peoples of all countries must be clearly aware that, undertaking such a gamble, the United States of America is taking a step along the road of unleashing a thermonuclear world war.

Cynically flouting international standards of conduct of states and the principles of the Charter of the U.N., the United States usurped the right . . . to attack ships of other countries on the high seas, i.e., to engage in piracy.

Imperialist quarters of the United States seek to dictate to Cuba what policy she must carry through, what domestic order ought to be established, what weapons she should have for her defense.

But who gave the United States the right to assume the role of master of the destinies of other countries and peoples? Why should the Cubans settle the internal affairs of their state not at their own discretion but so as to please the United States? Cuba belongs to the Cuban people and only they can be masters of their destiny.

In accordance with the United Nations Charter all countries, big and small, have the right to build their own life in their own way, to take such measures for insuring their security as they deem necessary, to offer rebuff to the aggressive forces which encroach on their freedom and independence. To ignore this means to undermine the foundations of the United Nations existence, to introduce jungle law into international practices, to give rise to endless conflicts and wars.

At this anxious hour, the Soviet Union regards it as its duty to issue a serious warning to the U.S. Government, warning it that by taking the measures announced by President Kennedy it . . . is recklessly playing with fire.

The leaders of the United States must, at last, understand that times have changed completely. . . . Whereas earlier the United States could regard itself as the strongest military power, it now has no foundation whatever for this.

There is another force in the world, no less powerful, which advocates that the peoples arrange their life just as they want to. Now, more than ever before, statesmen are called forth to display composure and common sense and not saber-rattling.

The Soviet government reaffirms that all weapons of the Soviet Union serve and will serve the purposes of defense against aggressors. . . . Nuclear weapons which have been created by the Soviet people . . . never will be used for the purposes of aggression. But if the aggressors touch off a war, the Soviet Union will strike a most powerful retaliatory blow. . . .

The United States Government accuses Cuba of allegedly creating a threat to the security of the United States. But who will believe that Cuba could create a threat to the United States? If one speaks of the size and resources of the two countries, of their armaments, it will not occur to any thoughtful statesman that Cuba could constitute a threat to the United States of America.

The Cubans want to safeguard their home, their independence against the threat that comes from the United States. . . .

The United States balks at nothing, including organization of armed intervention on Cuba, as it was the case in April, 1961, in order to deprive the Cuban people of the freedom and independence they have gained, to place them again under the domination of American monopolies, to make Cuba a United States puppet.

The United States demands that military equipment Cuba needs for self-defense should be removed from Cuban territory, a demand which, naturally, no state which values its independence can meet.

The Soviet Union is in favor of all foreign troops to be withdrawn from alien territories to within their own boundaries. If the United States shows real concern for . . . friendly relations with other nations and . . . durable world peace, as President Kennedy declared in his speech on Oct. 22, it should accept Soviet proposals and withdraw their troops and military equipment, close down military bases on foreign territories in different parts of the world.

However, the United States, which has flung its armed forces and armaments throughout the world, stubbornly refuses to accept this proposal. The United States is using them for interfering in the internal affairs of other states and for realizing its aggressive designs. It is American imperialism that assumed the role of international gendarme. U.S. spokesmen continually boast that American planes can attack the Soviet Union any time, drop American bombs on peaceful towns and villages and strike heavy blows. . . .

In view of these facts President Kennedy's allegation that the United States Government, in its presumptuous demands to deprive Cuba of the means of defense, is guided by the interests of peace, has a particularly false ring.

Source 5   **U.S. ambassador to the United Nations Adlai E. Stevenson's address to the UN Security Council, October 23, 1962**

I have asked for an emergency meeting of the Security Council to bring to your attention a grave threat to the Western Hemisphere and to the peace of the world.

Last night, the President of the United States reported the recent alarming military developments in Cuba. . . .

In view of this transformation of Cuba into a base for offensive weapons of sudden mass destruction, the President announced a quarantine on all offensive military weapons under shipment to Cuba. He did so because, in the view of my Government, the recent developments in Cuba—the importation of the cold war into the heart of the Americas—constitute a threat to the peace of this hemisphere, and, indeed, to the peace of the world. . . .

Chairman Khrushchev has altered many things in the Soviet Union. But there is one thing he has not altered. . . . He has not altered the basic drive to fulfill the prophesies of Marx and Lenin and make all the world Communist. . . .

I regret that people here at the United Nations seem to believe that the cold war is a private struggle between two great superpowers. It isn't a private struggle; it is a world civil war—a contest between the pluralistic world and the monolithic world. . . . Every nation that is now independent and wants to remain independent is involved, whether they know it or not. . . .

The foremost objection of the States of the Americas to the Castro regime is not because it is revolutionary, not because it is socialistic, not because it is dictatorial, not even because Dr. Castro perverted a noble revolution in the interests of a squalid totalitarianism. It is because he has aided and abetted an invasion of this hemisphere. . . .

The crucial fact is that Cuba has given the Soviet Union a bridgehead and staging area in this hemisphere—that it has invited an extracontinental, antidemocratic and expansionist power into the bosom of the American family—that it has made itself an accomplice in the Communist enterprise of world domination.

There are those who seek to equate the presence of Soviet bases in Cuba with the presence of NATO bases in parts of the world near the Soviet Union. . . .

Missiles which help a country defend its independence—which leave the political institutions of the recipient countries intact, which are not designed to subvert the territorial integrity or political independence of other states—which are installed without concealment or deceit—assistance in this form and with these purposes is consistent with the principles of the United Nations. But missiles which introduce a nuclear threat to an area now free of it—which threaten the security and independence of defenseless neighboring states—which are installed by clandestine means—which result in the most formidable nuclear base in the world outside existing treaty systems—assistance in this form and with these purposes is radically different. . . .

There is, in short, a vast difference between the long-range missile sites established years ago in Europe and the long-range missile sites established by the Soviet Union during the last three months.

There is a final significant difference . . . the principle of territorial integrity of the Western Hemisphere has been woven into the history, the life, and the thought of all the people of the Americas. In striking at that principle the Soviet Union is striking at the strongest and most enduring strain in the policy of this hemisphere. It is disrupting the convictions and aspirations of a century and a half. . . . To allow this challenge to go unanswered would be to undermine a basic and historic pillar of the security of this hemisphere. . . .

This once peaceable island is being transformed into a formidable missile and strategic air base armed with the deadliest, far-reaching modern nuclear weapons.

The statement issued by the Soviet government this morning does not deny these facts. . . . However, this same statement repeats the extraordinary claim that Soviet arms in Cuba are of a "defensive character." I should like to know what the Soviets consider "offensive" weapons. In the Soviet lexicon evidently all weapons are purely defensive, even weapons that can strike from 1,000 to 2,000 miles away. . . .

If the United States and the other nations of the Western Hemisphere should accept this new phase of aggression, we would be delinquent in our obligations to world peace. If the United States and the other nations of the Western Hemisphere should accept this basic disturbance of the world's structure of power, we would invite a new surge of Communist aggression at every point along the frontier which divides the Communist world from the democratic world. If we do not stand firm here, our adversaries may think that we will stand firm nowhere—and we guarantee a new heightening of the world civil war to new levels of intensity and danger.

Source 6   United Press International wire service report, Moscow, October 23, 1962

The Soviet Union in swift reaction to the United States blockade of Cuba today cancelled all troop leaves, ordered the entire Communist bloc to step up its military preparedness and accused the United States of "taking a step along the road to unleashing a thermonuclear world war."

The Soviet Union also postponed scheduled discharges of some rocket troops, anti-aircraft personnel and sailors of its submarine fleet. . . .

Disclosure of the military alert was made by Tass, the official Soviet news agency. Tass said the moves were made "in connection with the provocative actions of the United States Government and the aggressive intentions of the U.S. armed forces." . . .

It was understood here . . . that Premier Nikita S. Khrushchev had let it be known in Western diplomatic circles that he had issued a "go through" order to Russian ships in the event of a blockade. It was not clear whether this would prevent Soviet ships from stopping to be searched if they were so ordered.

Source 7   CIA director John A. McCone, excerpt from "Memorandum for the File," executive committee meeting on 23 October, 1962, 6 P.M.

In the prolonged discussion of report on Civil Defense problems, the President seemed particularly concerned over the situation if we should launch attacks which might result in four or five missiles being delivered on the United States. DOD spokesmen stated that the area covered by the 1100 mile missiles involved 92 million people. They felt that fall-out space was available though not equipped for about 40 million. The President asked what emergency steps could be taken. Replied that many arrangements could be made without too much publicity, such as repositioning food, actually obtaining space, putting up shelter signs, etc. I got the conclusion that not very much could be done; that whatever was done would involve a great deal of publicity and public alarm.

Source 8   "Civil Defense Shelters Being Stocked, Marked," Washington *Evening Star*, October 24, 1962

Federal Civil Defense officials stepped-up today provisioning and marking of fallout shelter areas in Government buildings. Emergency supplies—water cans, foodstuffs, medical kits and portable sanitation units—were installed in the Interstate Commerce Commission this morning in a basement shelter area.

Luminous, black and yellow "Fallout Shelter" signs and auxiliary arrow-direction signs were to be installed on and inside the building later today.

Federal and District CD officials said the program for stocking and designating all shelter areas in Washington has been accelerated. A total of 813 shelter areas in Government and private structures in the District were selected in a Federally backed survey last winter. . . .

Throughout the Capital area, CD workers told residents who asked about warning signals that the "alert" sound—indicating air raid danger but not within one hour—is a steady, non-pulsating siren tone of 3-to-5 minutes' duration. The more urgent "take cover" signal is a pulsating, rising and falling, siren tone lasting 3-to-5 minutes.

Source 9   Editorial, "Calling a Halt," *The Times* of London, October 24, 1962

In judging whether President Kennedy is right in militarily blockading Cuba, almost everything depends on the accuracy of the evidence that the Russians are in fact building missile bases on the island. Past American mistakes in coping with Cuba, the violent emotions which possess so many Americans when Fidel Castro and communism are mentioned, the wrong information which was served to the President before the [Bay of Pigs] invasion fiasco eighteen months ago, and even the President's sudden display of toughness now during a mid-election campaign in which he has been accused of softness—all these things were bound to make people in Britain extremely wary on first hearing the news. All that being said, the evidence seems to be hard. . . .

The Soviet Government may deny that the bases are there. Alternatively, it may say that the missiles are purely defensive and therefore within the terms of its assurances to the American Government. By all accepted standards, however, they are offensive. At the very least they are retaliatory or "offensive-defensive". . . . This is a development very different from moral, political, and defensive support of Castro and his revolution. President Kennedy had to make some reply. There are many grounds for assuming that the Soviet Union does not seek war. She prefers to spread her doctrine through probing, sapping, propagandizing, and pressing. Yet there is always the risk of her misjudging and going too far for recall if she meets no resistance. "The greatest danger of all would be to do nothing."

The dangers of acting are, of course, manifest. . . . Too much now depends on simply avoiding the more than usually explosive incident.

Source 10   Guided Missile and Astronautics Intelligence Committee, Joint Atomic Energy Intelligence Committee, and National Photographic Interpretation Center, "Joint Evaluation of Soviet Missile Threat in Cuba"

24.3 NSA and the Cuban Missile Crisis

TOP SECRET

0100 Hours
24 October 1962

This supplement updates and amplifies previous reports. Emphasis continues to be placed on the READINESS status of the offensive missiles in Cuba. This report is based on U-2 photographic coverage through mission 3119 of 22 October 1962. . . .

1. There are two changes in the estimated dates of full operational capability. San Cristobal MRBM Site 2 and Sagua La Grande Site 1 are now estimated to achieve this status on 25 October instead of 22 October as previously estimated.
2. No new missile sites have been identified.
3. No IRBMs per se have yet been identified.
4. Seven Soviet ships with cargo hatch openings of 75 feet or longer have now been identified as possible ballistic missile carriers. They have made 13 trips to Cuba to date, and three are currently enroute to Cuba.

Source 11 "Navy Set to Halt 25 Soviet Vessels," *Washington Post,*
October 24, 1962

The United States and Soviet Union last night edged toward a possible collision
over American attempts to impose an arms blockade on Cuba, in an atmosphere
of global anxiety and suspense.

Powerful American naval and air forces encircled the Caribbean to carry out
President Kennedy's formal order to halt, turn back, and if necessary, fire on ships
trying to carry offensive weapons to Cuba. The President's proclamation was issued
at 7:05 last night, ordering the blockade to begin at 10 A.M. (EDT) today.

While the United States prepared for the worst, it also hoped for the best.
If the Soviet Union tries to run the blockade, a shot fired across the bow of a
Soviet vessel could escalate into nuclear war. . . . About 25 Soviet bloc ships are
reported headed for Cuba.

Source 12 Attorney General Robert F. Kennedy, *Thirteen Days: A
Memoir of the Cuban Missile Crisis,* recalling October 24, 1962

The next morning, Wednesday, the quarantine went into effect, and the reports
during the early hours told of Russian ships coming steadily on toward Cuba.
I talked with the President for a few moments before we went in to our regular
meeting. He said, "It looks really mean, doesn't it? But then, really there was
no other choice. If they get this mean on this one in our part of the world,
what will they do on the next?" "I just don't think there was any choice," I
said, "and not only that, if you hadn't acted, you would have been impeached."
The President thought for a moment and said, "That's what I think—I would
have been impeached." . . .

The Wednesday morning meeting . . . seemed the most trying, the most
difficult, and the most filled with tension. The Russian ships were proceeding,
they were nearing the five-hundred-mile barrier, and we either had to intercept
them or announce we were withdrawing. I sat across the table from the President.
This was the moment we had prepared for, which we hoped would never come.
The danger and concern that we all felt hung like a cloud over us all and
particularly over the President.

The U-2s and low-flying planes had returned the previous day with their
film, and through the evening it was analyzed—by now in such volume that
the film alone was more than twenty-five miles long. The results were presented
to us at the meeting. The launching pads, the missiles, the concrete boxes, the
nuclear storage bunkers, all the components were there, by now clearly defined
and obvious. Comparisons with the pictures of a few days earlier made clear
that the work on those sites was proceeding and that within a few days several
of the launching pads would be ready for war.

It was now a few minutes after 10:00 o'clock. Secretary McNamara announced
that two Russian ships, the *Gagarin* and the *Komiles,* were within a few miles of
our quarantine barrier. The interception of both ships would probably be before
noon Washington time. Indeed, the expectation was that at least one of the vessels
would be stopped and boarded between 10:30 and 11:00 o'clock.

Then came the disturbing Navy report that a Russian submarine had moved
into position between the two ships.

It had originally been planned to have a cruiser make the first interception, but, because of the increased danger, it was decided in the past few hours to send in an aircraft carrier supported by helicopters carrying antisubmarine equipment, hovering overhead. The carrier *Essex* was to signal the submarine by sonar to surface and identify itself. If it refused, said Secretary McNamara, depth charges would be used until the submarine surfaced.

I think these few minutes were the time of gravest concern for the President. Was the world on the brink of a holocaust? Was it our error? A mistake? Was there something further that should have been done? Or not done? His hand went up to his face and covered his mouth. He opened and closed his fist. His face seemed drawn, his eyes pained, almost gray. For a few fleeting seconds, it was almost as though no one else was there and he was no longer the President.

Inexplicably, I thought of when he was ill and almost died; when he lost his child; when we learned that our oldest brother had been killed; of personal times of strain and hurt. The voices droned on but I didn't seem to hear anything until I heard the President say: "Isn't there some way we can avoid having our first exchange with a Russian submarine—almost anything but that?" "No, there's too much danger to our ships. There is no alternative," said McNamara. "Our commanders have been instructed to avoid hostilities if at all possible, but this is what we must be prepared for, and this is what we must expect."

We had come to the time of final decision. . . . I felt we were on the edge of a precipice with no way off. This time, the moment was now—not next week—not tomorrow. . . . One thousand miles away in the vast expanse of the Atlantic Ocean the final decisions were going to be made in the next few minutes. President Kennedy had initiated the course of events, but he no longer had control over them. He would have to wait—we would have to wait. The minutes in the Cabinet Room ticked slowly by. What else could we say now—what could we do?

Then it was 10:25—a messenger brought in a note to [Director of Central Intelligence] John McCone. "Mr. President we have a preliminary report which seems to indicate that some of the Russian ships have stopped dead in the water."

To the Brink . . . and Back

The Soviets had decided not to challenge the American Navy at the quarantine line. All of the Soviet vessels bound for Cuba as well as the ships of countries allied with the Soviets halted short of military confrontation. Nuclear war was, for the moment, averted.

Cuba, an impoverished island nation of eight million people, had long been an object of interest to the United States. Prior to the American Civil War, Southern statesmen had hoped the island might be acquired and added to the Union as a slave state. But attempts to purchase it from Spain failed and plans to seize it—revealed in the **Ostend Manifesto** of 1854—led only to embarrassment for the United States. In the 1890s, Americans became interested in the Cuban struggle for independence and in 1898 fought Spain to assist in the Cuban cause. Though many Americans believed an American victory over Spain justified an American annexation of Cuba, the island was granted its independence on the condition that the United States might intervene in Cuban affairs when

American leaders felt that such intervention was necessary. This option to intervene was exercised several times early in the twentieth century. By the 1950s, Cuba was controlled by the repressive dictatorship of Fulgencio Batista, a petty tyrant who enjoyed U.S. support. A guerrilla movement led by Fidel Castro overthrew the Batista regime in January 1959. Castro did not identify himself as a Communist during the revolution, but, once in power, he began to alarm the United States by moving rapidly to the left in his political views. Finally proclaiming himself a Communist, Castro sought recognition and support from the Soviet bloc. This led to American reprisals. Several attempts were made by the Central Intelligence Agency to assassinate Castro, and an ill-fated attempt was made in April 1961 to invade Cuba with a paramilitary force trained and led by the CIA. When the anticipated popular uprising against Castro did not materialize, the American-sponsored invading force was pinned down on the beach, presenting President Kennedy with the choice of withdrawing from the venture altogether or sending in regular troops to finish the job. Kennedy chose withdrawal. This failed invasion at the Bay of Pigs pushed Castro even closer to the Soviet bloc in his attempt to secure himself and his nation against American intervention. He welcomed Soviet missiles in his country as a deterrent to future United States military attempts to topple his government.

In spite of the Soviet withdrawal from Kennedy's quarantine line, the crisis was far from over. While no new missiles and military supplies were being delivered, no existing missiles were being dismantled and removed.

Moreover, American air force reconnaissance flights over Cuba showed that work on the missile bases was actually being accelerated in the hours following the confrontation at sea. It was expected that the nuclear arsenal on Cuba would shortly be operational. Notes of protest passed between the American and Soviet governments, and the crisis was debated in the forums of the United Nations, in the pages of the daily papers, and in living rooms around the world. President Kennedy continued to threaten war if the missiles were not immediately dismantled and removed. By Friday evening October 26, the expectation of world war loomed larger than ever.

On the evening of October 26, President Kennedy received a telegram from Premier Khrushchev that seemed conciliatory and offered a compromise that could ease both nations back from the brink of nuclear war. If the United States offered a guarantee not to again attempt an invasion of Cuba, the Soviet Union would withdraw its missiles from the island. But before the president had responded to this message, a second telegram arrived from the Soviet leader. Its tone was more belligerent than the first and it proposed a course of action that the Soviets knew to be unacceptable to the United States: Soviet missiles would be withdrawn from Cuba only if American missiles were pulled from Turkey. It was assumed that the second letter reflected a shift in influence among Soviet policy makers and that "hard-liners" and generals were gaining the upper hand in the Kremlin. It was possible that the hard-liners were willing to push the crisis to a nuclear showdown.

The president faced a dilemma: which message should he regard as the official position of the Soviet Union? A miscalculation of Soviet intentions could produce nuclear war. The president decided to gamble. He choose to ignore the second message and reply favorably to the first.

📖 *Second Thoughts*
"Total War Makes No Sense"

Both sides were able to claim victory by accepting the terms outlined in Kennedy's letter of October 27. Kennedy won removal of the missiles. Khrushchev removed the missiles, having won through diplomacy the security for Cuba he had claimed to seek through the missile emplacement.

Source 13   "Message to Chairman Khrushchev Calling for Removal of Soviet Missiles from Cuba," President John F. Kennedy, October 27, 1962

Dear Mr. Chairman:

I have read your letter of October 26th with great care and welcomed the statement of your desire to seek a prompt solution to the problem. The first thing that needs to be done, however, is for work to cease on offensive missile bases in Cuba and for all weapons systems in Cuba capable of offensive use to be rendered inoperable. . . .

As I read your letter, the key elements of your proposals—which seem generally acceptable as I understand them—are as follows:

1. You would agree to remove these weapons systems from Cuba under appropriate United Nations observation and supervision; and under-take, with suitable safeguards, to halt the further introduction of such weapons systems into Cuba.
2. We, on our part, would agree—-upon the establishment of adequate arrangements through the United Nations to ensure the carrying out and continuation of these commitments—(a) to remove promptly the quarantine measures now in effect and (b) to give assurances against an invasion of Cuba. . . .

I would like to say . . . that the United States is very much interested in reducing tensions and halting the arms race; and if your letter signifies that you are prepared to discuss a detente affecting NATO and the Warsaw Pact, we are quite prepared to consider with our allies any useful proposals.

But the first ingredient, let me emphasize, is the cessation of work on missile sites in Cuba. . . . The continuation of this threat, or a prolonging of this discussion concerning Cuba by linking these problems to the broader questions of European and world security, would surely lead to an intensification of the Cuban crisis and a grave risk to the peace of the world. For this reason I hope we can quickly agree along the lines outlined in this letter and in your letter of October 26th.

Source 14   President John F. Kennedy, "Commencement Address at American University," June 10, 1963

Total war makes no sense in an age when great powers can maintain large and relatively invulnerable nuclear forces and refuse to surrender without resort to those forces. It makes no sense in an age when a single nuclear weapon contains almost ten times the explosive force delivered by all of the allied air forces in the Second World War. It makes no sense in an age when the deadly poisons produced by a nuclear exchange would be carried by wind and water and soil and seed to the far corners of the globe and to generations yet unborn. . . .

It is an ironic but accurate fact that the two strongest powers are the two in the most danger of devastation. All we have built, all we have worked for, would be destroyed in the first 24 hours. And even in the cold war, which brings burdens and dangers to so many countries, . . . our two countries bear the heaviest burdens. For we are both devoting massive sums of money to weapons that could be better devoted to combating ignorance, poverty, and disease. We are both caught up in a vicious and dangerous cycle in which suspicion on the one side breeds suspicion on the other, and new weapons beget counterweapons.

Source 15 Henry M. Pachter, *Collision Course: The Cuban Missile Crisis and Coexistence,* 1963

What . . . is the real story of the conflicting notes? I suggest that we start with the description of the first telegram. Those who have seen it say that it was apparently written hastily, without the careful checking and processing that is routine in all foreign offices. Rather, it was a personal note. By contrast, the second telegram bears all the marks of having gone through the routine mill of government departments. Moreover, it reflects only a slight shift from positions on which the Soviet policy-makers stood until October 25. It takes time for such a note to be "finalized" and then processed for publication. . . .

Now, this long-winded dispatch arrived in Washington only a few hours after the other note, which, we are told, was hastily written and apparently sent precipitously after Friday's military build-up and Kennedy's "saber-rattling." There is only one possible conclusion: The note first received had been written last; the slow note of the Foreign Ministry had been overtaken by Khrushchev's panicky telegram.

Once the sequence of the notes is reversed, everything falls into place. The slow note, carefully prepared and then proceeding through channels, had fallen behind events. It opens with a reference to Kennedy's letter of October 25 to [U.N. Secretary-General] U Thant, but does not mention Kennedy's impatient gestures or the ominous events of Friday. These, I submit, produced deep apprehensions in the Kremlin and prompted Khrushchev's "hasty" note, indicating his desire to avoid a showdown at almost any price.

Source 16 Robert Ferrell, *American Diplomacy,* 1969

On October 22, Kennedy in a television "spectacular"—of a sort which no one on this earth wishes to see again—announced his policy about the missiles in a manner that not merely Khrushchev but anyone listening and watching could understand. . . . The unnerving, frightening aspect of this public message was not its content but the fact that it was public. It was a facedown. It was eyeball-to-eyeball, to use the current graphic expression. Kennedy raised up the national interest of the United States in a public showdown with the Russians.

There always is danger that the extreme publicity in such a move will produce equal intransigence on the other side. In October 1962 there could have been no recourse except Armageddon. . . .

For students who wished to learn lessons from the Cuban missile crisis, insofar as one could learn from an affair in which the full truth may never be known, a notable fact was that many well-meaning Americans had not understood that the Soviet Union had made a large aggressive move in the cold war. To a remarkable extent the Soviets were able to hoodwink people. There was a considerable feeling that Castro needed protection against the United States. . . . Some individuals also believed that, after all, the United States maintained missiles abroad, and why should not the Soviet Union have its overseas military bases? Letters appeared in newspapers asking for a mutual missile withdrawal, that the Soviet Union should take its weapons out of Cuba in exchange for removal of the squadron of fifteen American Jupiter missiles then on Turkish soil.

The Jupiter issue was a fairly complicated proposition, and public opinion easily could have misunderstood it—and of course did so, to the benefit of the Soviet Union. Here, surely, was one more evidence of how a considerable amount of American opinion can be led by the nose. In retrospect it is disquieting to see how the Soviet Union was able to exploit public ignorance during a tremendous international crisis. At one point during the 1962 crisis, Khrushchev requested an exchange of the American Jupiters in Turkey for his own country's missiles then in Cuba. The Russian leader knew what he was doing. He was putting an outrageously plausible face upon what had been a great act of aggression.

The Americans who argued for an exchange had no idea that the 1,100-mile Jupiter system was equal only in part to the Russian delivery system being established in Cuba. The United States had no missiles in Turkey or anywhere else equivalent to the intermediate-range, 2,200-mile missiles Khrushchev had shipped to Castro's island. Moreover, because of the near-certain American ability to strike the Soviet Union with atomic weapons carried from within the United States, or by submarines, and the USSR's then very weak delivery capability beyond intermediate ranges, the emplacement of Soviet missiles in Cuba was a far more important military advantage than was a comparable American base in Turkey. Also, if the Russians had wished only to force the United States into withdrawing the missiles from Turkey, there were easier ways to do that than to emplace missiles in Cuba. In previous months President Kennedy had been anxious to get the Jupiters out of Turkey, for the stationing of Polaris submarines in the Mediterranean had made the liquid-fueled, "soft"-sited Jupiters virtually useless.

Secretary of State Rusk had approached the Turkish government in the spring of 1962, but the Turks had balked about removal of the missiles. The president had instructed the state department to go ahead anyway, negotiating withdrawal of the missiles whether the Turks liked it or not. The state department made another approach. The Turks balked again. Nothing more happened, though Kennedy assumed that everything was being arranged. During the Cuban missile crisis the president then discovered to his consternation that his own government, through the state department's inefficiency, had given the Russians a plausible justification for the Cuban affair, permitting them to argue that they were only doing in Cuba what the United States had done in Turkey. The state department's failure also had given the Russians an opportunity, if the United

States had attacked Cuba, to attack Turkey and thereby challenge the whole structure of NATO (would the predominantly European NATO allies respond to an attack on the Turks?). And would the United States, with or without NATO support, thereupon fire the Jupiters at the Soviet Union? It was a complex situation, and no one who understood the Jupiter question could allow it to enter the Cuban equation.

Source 17 Graham T. Allison, *Essence of Decision,* 1971

The Cuban missile crisis was a seminal event. History offers no parallel to those thirteen days of October 1962, when the United States and the Soviet Union paused at the nuclear precipice. Never before had there been such a probability that so many lives would end suddenly. Had war come, it could have meant the death of 100 million Americans, more than 100 million Russians, as well as millions of Europeans. Beside it, the natural calamities and inhumanities of earlier history would have faded into insignificance. Given the odds on disaster—which President Kennedy estimated as "between one out of three and even"—our escape seems awesome.

Source 18 Richard J. Barnet, foreign policy analyst and State Department official in the Kennedy administration, *Roots of War,* 1972

One of the legacies of America's geographical isolation and her lack of visible enemies manning pillboxes on the frontier is that there is very little correlation between individual feelings of personal safety and the state of national security, as measured by the official criteria of the government. Only in moments of extreme crisis that are dramatized by presidential television appearances, such as the Cuban missile crisis of 1962, does the citizen make a connection between national security and personal insecurity. It is ironical that the national mood is more relaxed today than in the early postwar years when the United States was incomparably the most powerful nation on earth and the sole possessor of the atomic bomb. Yet, if we are to believe the polls, Americans, by and large, feel safer today despite the fact that the Soviet Union has three or more megaton bombs targeted on each major U.S. city. One can only conclude that ordinary people use psychological rather than rational measurements for security. The crisis atmosphere of the early 1960's, promoted by a government seeking to raise the military budget, has subsided because the government is now exploring detente with the Soviet Union and China. Yet, though the U.S.S.R. is far more formidable an adversary than twenty years ago, most people do not know what the policy of the Soviet Union is, or how strong it is. They do not even have a very clear idea of where it is.

Source 19 Howard Zinn, *Postwar America, 1945–1971,* 1973

From the end of World War II to 1970, the United States government spent a thousand billion dollars for military purposes. It trained a standing army of three million men; it built four hundred major and three thousand minor military bases in thirty countries overseas; it put seven thousand tactical nuclear weapons in Europe; it kept an undisclosed number of heavy bombers in the air constantly, carrying hydrogen bombs; and it launched forty-one submarines capable of firing more than six hundred nuclear missiles while submerged. . . .

The motivation for acquiring all this armament—offensive and defensive—was fear of aggression by the Soviet Union and Communist China against the United States. Between 1952 and 1968, the Soviet Union sent troops into neighboring Communist countries—Hungary, Czechoslovakia, Poland, East Germany—to put down rebellion. In 1959, China took military action against the border state of Tibet and against India along the frontier. Their actions were typical great-power bullying of neighboring states, not much different from American bullying of Latin America; they were quite far from constituting a threat to the United States itself. Neither the Soviet Union nor China had military bases on the borders of the United States; the United States, on the contrary, had bases, with nuclear weapons, all around the borders of both Communist countries. China had no troops stationed in other countries, while the United States had perhaps 750,000 troops and the Seventh Fleet deployed in various parts of Asia.

The one time in which the Communist countries broke through these geographic limits came in the fall of 1962, when Soviet missiles were sent to Cuba, and a serious crisis, involving the threat of nuclear war, enveloped the United States, the Soviet Union, and the world. . . .

Kennedy . . . successfully forced the Russians to pull back their missile frontier to their own borders. But the United States did no such thing, and the race between the two countries in missiles, in airplanes, in submarines, in nuclear weapons of all sorts, continued to mount in the sixties. By the spread and number of its weapons and men around the world, the United States was far more of a menace to the Soviet Union and China than those countries were to America.

Source 20 Herbert S. Dinerstein, *The Making of a Missile Crisis,* 1976

The mistake of the USSR was to believe that the United States had accepted the political consequences of augmented Soviet military strength and that, therefore, Kennedy would yield where Eisenhower had not. The American failure to follow up the indirect intervention of the Bay of Pigs with a full-scale invasion . . . confirmed the Soviet leaders in their mistaken hopes. . . .

The Soviet leaders did not know that Kennedy was silent in the face of the expanding Soviet verbal commitment to Cuba because he was unaware of it. . . . The leaders of the USSR thought that U.S. reconnaissance had detected their missiles in Cuba but maintained silence . . . in an effort to reduce the political costs of the reverse. At any rate, the effective majority assumed that the venture would come off without a hitch. When Kennedy demanded the removal of the missiles, established a quarantine, and threatened further measures, Khrushchev, like Kennedy at the Bay of Pigs, realized that he had been deceived by his own hopes and decided to cut his losses. His domestic critics argued that the Americans were bluffing and would yield in the end if the Soviet Union stood its ground. . . . In any case, the division in the Soviet Union became unmistakable only a few days later when Khrushchev's letter signaled retreat while a Presidium communication made U.S. withdrawal of its missiles from Turkey a condition of that retreat. But once the Soviet Union retired its complacent belief that the United States had already accepted the presence of the missiles, the two parties began to negotiate on the substance of the matter. . . .

Although each party to the dispute claimed that the outcome was a victory for itself and a defeat for the adversary, it was neither one nor the other. The result demonstrated what had already been theoretically apprehended. Both sides were too fearful of nuclear war to run an appreciable risk of its outbreak. Within both countries, men differed on what risks and what outcomes were acceptable before the preponderant majority on both sides reached compromise.

Source 21 John G. Stoessinger, *Nations in Darkness*, 1986

Kennedy viewed the missiles basically as a challenge to the American will. They had to be removed, not because they made America weak, but because they made her *appear* weak. And in order to get them out, Kennedy went to the brink of nuclear war. Khrushchev was able to withdraw the missiles with his ego and self-esteem substantially intact. Had he not been able to do so, had be been forced to *appear* weak, nuclear disaster might well have been the consequence. . . .

There is one final sense in which perception was perhaps decisive. Neither leader could say to the other, "Do as I say or I shall kill you"; but each was reduced to saying, "Do as I say or I shall kill us both." Force, in the crude physical sense, was no longer a predictable instrument of national policy. Each superpower could have annihilated the other, but by so doing, would have destroyed itself. To put it crassly: since everybody was somebody, nobody was anybody. Since physical force on each side was equally devastating and thus virtually cancelled out, subjective perceptions and appearances of power loomed particularly large. Psychology thus superseded hardware, and a state of mind became decisive. The missile crisis was in essence a nuclear war, but one that was fought in the minds of two men. . . . Fortunately for all of us, these two men were good men with political wisdom, moral courage, and a gift of empathy. They grasped not only with their minds but also felt deeply in their hearts both the burden and the terror of the human condition in the nuclear age.

Source 22 John A. Garraty, *The American Nation*, 1991

Critics have argued that Kennedy overreacted to the Soviet missiles. There was no evidence that the Russians were planning to attack, and in any case they already had missiles in Siberia capable of striking American targets. The Cuban missiles might be seen as a deterrent against a possible attack on the Soviet Union by United States missiles in Europe, and by demanding their withdrawal, Kennedy risked triggering a nuclear holocaust as much as Khrushchev. Yet he probably had no choice once the existence of the sites was made known to the public. (In some respects this is the most frightening aspect of the crisis.)

For better or worse, Kennedy's firmness in the missile crisis repaired the damage done to his reputation by the Bay of Pigs affair. It also led to a lessening of Soviet-America tensions. Khrushchev agreed to the installation of a telephone "hot line" between the White House and the Kremlin so that in any future crisis the leaders of the two nations could be in instant communication. Although the arms race continued unabated, in 1963 nearly 100 nations, including all the major powers except France and China, signed a treaty banning the testing of nuclear weapons in the atmosphere.

Source 23   Robert Dallek, *The Great Republic*, 1992

Days of excruciating tension marked the confrontation: the world seemed on the verge of war. We stood "eyeball to eyeball," one official later said. Both American and Soviet decision makers remembered the crisis as an agonizing moment when a misstep could have triggered the greatest catastrophe in human history. Acting responsibly, Kennedy and Krushchev reached agreement. . . .

The resolution of the Cuban missile crisis represented a turning point in world affairs generally and in Soviet-American relations in particular. Ironically, the confrontation had a positive consequence: it deepened the two superpowers' understanding of the dangers of nuclear weapons. To be sure, the Soviets partly responded to the crisis by starting their own huge military and naval buildup, which could secure them against another such humiliating political defeat. But at the same time, the missile crisis opened the way to a significant improvement in Soviet-American relations that came about principally through Kennedy's efforts. Recognizing more clearly than ever that "mankind must put an end to war or war will put an end to mankind," the president used his diplomatic victory not to humiliate the Soviets, but to advance the cause of peace. He forbade members of his administration to gloat over America's triumph and warned them against assuming that the Soviet pullback was a sign of weakness. Had Soviet national security been directly threatened in the confrontation, he said, they would have acted differently.

Source 24   Ernest R. May and Philip D. Zelikow, *The Kennedy Tapes: Inside the White House during the Cuban Missile Crisis*, 1997

Though anxiety gave way to euphoria after Khrushchev's broadcast of Sunday, October 28, the crisis was not over. Low-level reconnaissance on October 29 appeared to detect continuing construction. The Joint Chiefs suspected Khrushchev of simply trying to buy time. If Kennedy stopped aerial surveillance, as U Thant had requested, how would he know whether the Chiefs were right or wrong?

President Kennedy's position remained awkward through the last days of October. Led to believe that the crisis was essentially over, reporters expected evidence that the missiles were being pulled out. The government had no such evidence to release. Kennedy had little to go on except his own belief that Khrushchev was sincere, a belief reinforced by intelligence of Cuban and Chinese anger at what they seemed to regard as Soviet betrayal.

Questioning the Past

1. If the United States felt it acceptable to place American troops and missiles along the border of the Soviet Union, was it not equally acceptable for the Soviets to place troops and missiles in Cuba? Argue both sides of this question.

2. Should Kennedy be criticized for forcing a confrontation over the emplacement of Soviet missiles in Cuba? Did the possible consequences justify such a gamble? Could he have approached the situation in other ways?

3. Discuss the advantages and disadvantages of the seven options considered by Kennedy and his advisers before they settled on the idea of a blockade. Make a list ranking these options in order of effectiveness.

4. Winston Churchill observed in the early years of the nuclear arms race between the United States and Soviet Union that the development and stockpiling of such awesome force might actually be the best guarantor of peace. "Moralists may find it a melancholy thought that peace can find no nobler foundation than mutual terror," Churchill noted, "but for my part I shall be content if these foundations are solid. . . ." The prevailing strategy at the height of the arms race was called "mutual deterrence" or the "balance of terror." The strategy was based on the assumption that peace would be the product when the United States and the Soviet Union each possessed nuclear weapons in sufficient quantity to inflict an "unacceptable damage" on its enemy even after absorbing the strongest possible surprise attack its adversary might be able to deliver. Two conditions defined the balance of terror: 1. each country had the nuclear capability to easily destroy its enemy's population and economy; 2. Neither country could destroy its opponent's nuclear arsenal. To launch a first strike against the enemy would open a country to massive retaliation in the form of its enemy's second strike. In 1968, Robert McNamara concluded that "neither the Soviet Union nor the United States can attack the other without being destroyed in retaliation; . . . both . . . now possess an actual and credible second-strike capability against one another, and it is precisely this mutual capability that provides us both with the strongest possible motive to avoid nuclear war." Both the United States and the Soviet Union targeted their nuclear weapons against the cities of their adversary; the United States based its second strike on its "Triad" of long-range bombers, land-based missiles, and submarine-launched missiles, while the Soviets relied primarily upon land- and submarine-based missiles. Neither country had any protection for its cities against its opponent's nuclear arsenal. A critic of mutual deterrence, Richard J. Barnet, noted the irony of the strategy: "When a man with a gun threatens to shoot the passengers of an airplane unless some prisoners are released or a ransom is paid, we call that terrorism; when leaders threaten millions of deaths—and every nuclear weapon targeted on an enemy city is just such a threat—we call it strategy." Discuss the strengths and weaknesses of the strategy of mutual deterrence.

5. In his 1823 State of the Union address, President James Monroe announced that "the American continents, by the free and independent condition which they have assumed and maintain, are henceforth not to be considered as subjects for future colonization by any European powers." This, in essence, is the Monroe Doctrine. Ambassador Stevenson alluded to this doctrine in his address of October 23, 1963. What applicability, if any, did the Monroe Doctrine have to the Cuban missile crisis? What obligation, if any, would the Soviet Union or any other European nation have to respect this doctrine?

Chapter **25**

Vietnam

The *Maddox* Reports Being Attacked in the Gulf of Tonkin *August 2, 1964*

25.1 The
Vietnam War
Internet Project

"You have a row of dominoes set up," President Eisenhower explained at his press conference of April 7, 1954, "you knock over the first one, and what will happen to the last one is the certainty that it will go over very quickly." His allusion was to the spread of communist rule across Asia and beyond. Communism had toppled the government of China, and with that one move it had added one-quarter of the world's population to its dominion. The northern half of the Korean peninsula was under communist control. Vietnam now stood imperiled. If Vietnam fell to communism, surely Laos, Cambodia, Thailand, Burma, and all of South Asia would soon fall as well. Something had to be done, and it was up to the United States to do it.

The United States was then the greatest military and economic power the world had ever known. Its factories produced most of the world's manufactured goods. Its fields fed much of the world's population. Its people were prosperous and confident. Its military dominance was unprecedented. It was a superpower in every sense of the word, and its strength was still growing. Its leaders had embraced the role of champion in the global fight against communism. Few Americans could have located Vietnam on a map, but none doubted the capability of American will, ingenuity, and might to prevail anywhere on the globe, and certainly American power would find no match in some impoverished, pre-industrial land in a remote area of Asia. No more dominoes would be allowed to fall; America's leaders could be entrusted to see to that.

By the time Eisenhower left the White House, American military, political, and economic advisers were hard at work trying to shore up a pro-Western government in South Vietnam. More than $1 billion in financial aid had been poured into the effort and, with more than 1,500 Americans actively engaged in buttressing the South Vietnamese regime, the American diplomatic mission in Saigon had become the largest in the world. President Kennedy continued the American commitment, increasing financial support, military assistance, and the number of American military advisers in the area. The Central Intelligence Agency engaged in clandestine military operations in support of the effort. President Johnson likewise pursued the policies of his predecessors.

First Impressions

"An Unprovoked Attack"

By 1964, American political advisers were deeply involved in the internal politics of Vietnam and American troops were in the thick of the fighting between South Vietnam and its communist adversaries, although officially restricted to an advisory role. Still, the American effort was not enough, and the battle for South Vietnam was being lost. America could either withdraw from the struggle or escalate its involvement. The events of August 2, 1964, helped the nation make its choice.

25.2 Vietnam War

Source 1 **Murrey Marder, "U.S. Destroyer Fights off 3 PT Boats in Attack off Coast of North Viet-Nam,"** *Washington Post,* **August 3, 1964**

An attack on a United States destroyer by three North Vietnamese torpedo boats off that nation's coast yesterday was beaten off by American sea and air gunfire in what Washington treated as a limited incident.

No American casualties or damage resulted, it was announced. Officials said all three Communist boats were believed hit in the first naval engagement of its kind in the Southeast Asia crisis.

The encounter was described as an "unprovoked attack" on the *U.S.S. Maddox* in international waters off the Gulf of Tonkin, about 28 miles off the Communist North Viet-Nam coast. . . . Four Crusader jets from the *U.S.S. Ticonderoga* helped the *Maddox* drive off the PT-type boats.

Secretary of State Dean Rusk publicly stated last night that the boats were operated by the North Vietnamese. "The other side got a sting out of this," Rusk told reporters in New York, "If they do it again," he said, "they'll get another sting." . . .

The exchange of gunfire brought high diplomatic and military officials in Washington out of bed in the pre-dawn hours for conferences at the White House, State Department, and Pentagon. But there was no atmosphere of alarm or acute crisis in the city yesterday. . . . The United States will continue its naval patrols in the area, officials emphasized. There was no new talk of carrying the Viet-Nam fighting north. . . .

The text of the official announcement of the *Maddox* incident, as first issued in Honolulu yesterday and repeated by the Defense Department here, said:

"While on routine patrol at 0808 GMT (4:08 a.m. EDT) the *U.S.S. Maddox* underwent an unprovoked attack by three PT-type boats in latitude 19.40 north, longitude 106.34 east in the Tonkin Gulf. The attacking boats launched three torpedoes and used .37 millimeter gunfire.

"The *Maddox* answered with five-inch gunfire.

"Shortly thereafter four F8 aircraft from the *Ticonderoga* joined in the defense of the *Maddox*, using Zuni rockets and .20 millimeter machine guns, strafing the attackers' boats.

"The PTs were driven off with one seen to be badly damaged and not moving and the other two damaged and retiring slowly. No casualties or damage was sustained by the *Maddox* or the aircraft."

While Administration sources by late yesterday were describing the engagement as "nothing significant," Adm. Sharp, in Honolulu, told newsmen in answer to questions:

"If they are so bold as to shoot at us, it is a change."

He was referring to the overwhelming American naval might in its Seventh Fleet and other U.S. striking power in the Pacific. . . .

News of the attack reached Washington immediately after it occurred and, under standing orders, military and diplomatic officials were notified starting at 4:30 a.m. In mid-morning, President Johnson met at the White House with a number of officials. . . . All entered by side doors and the White House made no announcement of the meeting.

The United States confirmed last week that it will increase by "several thousand" the number of its more than 16,000 American servicemen now in South Viet-Nam.

Source 2   **President Lyndon Johnson's speech at Syracuse University, August 5, 1964**

On August 2, the United States destroyer *Maddox* was attacked on the high seas in the Gulf of Tonkin by hostile vessels of the government of North Viet Nam.

On August 4, that attack was repeated in those same waters against two United States destroyers. . . .

The attacks were deliberate.

The attacks were unprovoked.

The attacks have been answered.

Throughout last night and in the last 12 hours, air units of the United States 7th Fleet have sought out hostile vessels and certain of their supporting facilities. Appropriate armed action has been taken against them. . . .

The Gulf of Tonkin may be distant.

But none can be detached about what has happened there.

Aggression—deliberate, willful and systematic aggression—has unmasked its face to the entire world. The world remembers—the world must never forget—that aggression unchallenged is aggression unleashed.

We of the United States have not forgotten.

That is why we have answered this aggression.

America's course is not precipitate.

It is not without long provocation.

For 10 years, three American Presidents, President Eisenhower, President Kennedy and your present President, and the American people have been actively concerned with threats to the peace and security of the peoples of Southeast Asia from the Communist Government of North Viet Nam. . . .

Peace cannot be assured merely by assuring the safety of the United States destroyer *Maddox*—or the safety of other vessels of other flags. . . .

Peace requires that we and our friends stand firm against the present aggression of the government of North Viet Nam.

Let no friend needlessly fear—and no foe vainly hope—that this is a Nation divided in this election year. . . . There are no parties—there is no partisanship—

when our peace or the peace of the world is imperiled by aggressors in any part of the world.

We are one Nation united and indivisible. United and indivisible we shall remain.

Source 3 Editorial, "The Seventh Fleet Hits Back," Washington *Evening Star,* August 5, 1964

President Johnson's order to the Seventh Fleet to bomb North Vietnamese PT boats and the "facilities" from which they operate is fully justified. This is accurately described as a "limited" response. But it may lead nonetheless to an expansion of the war in Southeast Asia.

The motives of the North Vietnamese are hard to fathom. For they are provoking conflict with a vastly superior force in an area and under conditions which are favorable to us and highly unfavorable to them. Whatever the motives, however, there can be no doubt that the attacks were made and that they were deliberate. . . .

When the PT boats first fired their torpedoes at the *USS Maddox* there was some thought that this was an isolated incident, not part of a purposeful plan. But the second attack, occurring some 65 miles off the coast in the Gulf of Tonkin removes all doubt. This was deliberate. . . .

What counteraction if any will come from the other side remains to be seen. If they react forcibly, however, it would be logical to expect some enlargement of the war against South Vietnam. That this has been anticipated is evidenced by the report that the United States is sending "substantial" additional military elements to Southeast Asia.

Source 4 President Lyndon Johnson's message to Congress, August 5, 1964

Last night I announced to the American people that the North Vietnamese regime had conducted further deliberate attacks against U.S. naval vessels operating in international waters, and that I had therefore directed air action against gunboats and supporting facilities used in these hostile operations. This air action has now been carried out with substantial damage to the boats and facilities. Two U.S. aircraft were lost in the action.

After consultation with the leaders of both parties in the Congress, I further announced a decision to ask the Congress for a resolution expressing the unity and determination of the United States in supporting freedom and protecting peace in southeast Asia.

These latest actions of the North Vietnamese regime have given a new and grave turn to the already serious situation in southeast Asia. Our commitments in that area are well known to the Congress. They were first made in 1954 by President Eisenhower. They were further defined in the Southeast Asia Collective Defense Treaty approved by the Senate in February 1955.

This treaty with its accompanying protocol obligates the United States and other members to act in accordance with their constitutional processes to meet Communist aggression against any of the parties or protocol states.

Our policy in southeast Asia has been consistent and unchanged since 1954. I summarized it on June 2 in four simple propositions:

1. *America keeps her word.* Here as elsewhere, we must and shall honor our commitments.
2. *The issue is the future of southeast Asia as a whole.* A threat to any nation in that region is a threat to all, and a threat to us.
3. *Our purpose is peace.* We have no military, political, or territorial ambitions in the area.
4. *This is not a jungle war, but a struggle for freedom on every front of human activity.* Our military and economic assistance to South Vietnam and Laos in particular has the purpose of helping these countries to repel aggression and strengthen their independence.

The threat to the free nations of southeast Asia has long been clear. The North Vietnamese regime has constantly sought to take over South Vietnam and Laos. This Communist regime has violated the Geneva accords for Vietnam. It has systematically conducted a campaign of subversion, which includes the direction, training, and supply of personnel and arms for the conduct of guerrilla warfare in South Vietnamese territory. In Laos, the North Vietnamese regime has maintained military forces, used Laotian territory for infiltration into South Vietnam, and most recently carried out combat operations—all in direct violation of the Geneva agreements of 1962.

Source 5   "Gulf of Tonkin Resolution," joint resolution of Congress, August 7, 1964

Resolved by the Senate and House of Representatives of the United States of America in Congress assembled, That the Congress approves and supports the determination of the President, as Commander in Chief, to take all necessary measures to repel any armed attack against the forces of the United States and to prevent further aggression.

Sec. 2. The United States regards as vital to its national interest and to world peace the maintenance of international peace and security in Southeast Asia. Consonant with the Constitution of the United States and the Charter of the United Nations and in accordance with its obligations under the Southeast Asia Collective Defense Treaty, the United States is, therefore, prepared, as the President determines, to take all necessary steps, including the use of armed force, to assist any member or protocol state of the Southeast Asia Collective Defense Treaty requesting assistance in defense of its freedom.

Sec. 3. This resolution shall expire when the President shall determine that the peace and security of the area is reasonably assured by international conditions created by action of the United Nations or otherwise, except that it may be terminated earlier by concurrent resolution of the Congress.

More Anticommunist than Anti-Imperialist

With the adoption of the Gulf of Tonkin Resolution, the administration assumed it had a mandate for a deepening American role in the war for

Indochina. The following years would witness a gradual buildup of forces until an American army more than a half-million strong was deployed in Southeast Asia.

Most Americans, if they considered the mission of the American troops at all in the year of the Tonkin incident, assumed that the conflict matched good against evil. The United States was fighting to hold back the expansive forces of a massive and oppressive movement marching ever outward from the Soviet Union and its supposed ally, "Red" China. South Vietnam was a small and relatively defenseless country trying to form itself into a Western-style democracy while standing against the overwhelming might of international communism.

But the roots of conflict in Indochina were much deeper than most Americans realized in 1964. In fact, the roots went back a century into the past to the days when the great powers of Europe were competing to acquire global empires. It was the French who set the Indochinese conflict in motion. Beginning in the middle of the nineteenth century they began colonization of Southeast Asia. By the turn of the twentieth century France had claimed the right to rule what is now Vietnam, Laos, and Cambodia. Shortly after the turn of the century, a nationalist movement emerged in Indochina, hoping to drive the French out and win independence for the region. Before this movement was able to build sufficient strength to oust the French on its own, the imperial forces of Japan invaded Indochina in 1942 and established Japanese domination of Southeast Asia.

The collapse of the Japanese Empire three years later gave hope to the peoples of Indochina, and the revolutionary movement—led by a communist named Ho Chi Minh—which had organized against the French and resisted the Japanese, proclaimed Vietnam a free and independent country. The Vietnamese Declaration of Independence borrowed heavily in its wording from the American Declaration of Independence.

This declaration did not stand uncontested. Within a year of the proclamation by the Vietnamese of their independence, the French were back in force trying to reassert control over Indochina. The French effort provoked a war which raged for eight years. French forces were able to hold the major cities of Vietnam, but the Vietnamese rebels held the countryside and, more importantly, the allegiance of most of the populace. In 1954, a large French force was surrounded by the Vietnamese at a fortified location called Dienbienphu. The French position was untenable, and a negotiated withdrawal of French forces followed.

Talks among the belligerents resulted in a series of agreements called the Geneva Accords. Hostilities would be ended in Indochina and three sovereign, independent states would be recognized: Laos, Cambodia, and Vietnam. Vietnam was to be temporarily divided at the seventeenth parallel for military purposes. The forces of Ho Chi Minh would police the northern portion of Vietnam, and forces supportive of the French would police the southern part. In two years free elections would be conducted to reunify the nation under a single government of the Vietnamese people's own choosing.

The United States had been presented with a dilemma in the case of Vietnam. After declaring their nation independent in 1945, Ho Chi Minh and his new government repeatedly asked for recognition and assistance from the United States. It seemed logical that the nation that had launched the first successful war for freedom from imperial rule in 1776 would sympathize with the Vietnamese effort to do the same in 1945. But the United States had its eyes on more than its ideals: it was watching the rising influence of the Soviet Union in Europe. French support was seen as crucial to containing the growth of Soviet influence. Supporting Vietnam against France would jeopardize America's greater strategic interests. In addition, the fact that Ho Chi Minh and many of his supporters were communists blinded the American leaders to the fact that the movement Ho led was primarily nationalist.

Even before the French debacle at Dienbienphu, the United States was absorbing most of the costs of the French war to retain Indochina. When the forces in control of the portion of Vietnam south of the seventeenth parallel balked at participation in the unification elections scheduled for 1956, the United States endorsed the move to cancel the voting. Eisenhower had conceded that "possibly 80 percent of the population would have voted for the Communist Ho Chi Minh as their leader," and the United States was no more willing to see the domino fall to communism through democracy than through force.

When the July 1956 date for the unification elections passed without a national vote, Ho Chi Minh's regime in Hanoi began to train and equip rebels south of the seventeenth parallel to oppose the American-backed regime in Saigon. A guerrilla force called the Viet Cong, with a political arm known as the National Liberation Front, was founded in South Vietnam to overthrow the South Vietnamese government and drive their American advisers from the country. Later, troops from North Vietnam would join with the guerrillas of the Viet Cong in the fight for South Vietnam, and economic support would come from the Soviet Union and China. And meanwhile, as its economic and military commitment to sustain South Vietnam grew, the United States lent its support to a series of corrupt and oppressive governments in Saigon. The leaders of the Republic of South Vietnam were scarcely more inclined to embrace the democratic ideals professed by Americans than were the leaders of Hanoi against whom they fought.

With the adoption of the Gulf of Tonkin Resolution, the American role in the struggle escalated from adviser to full combatant.

25.3 The History
Net: Vietnam
Article Index

  ## *Second Thoughts*

Why Are We in Vietnam?

American troops remained in Vietnam through the years of the Johnson presidency. His successor, Richard Nixon, continued the pursuit of military victory in Indochina and even expanded both the intensity of the war and its field of battle. In 1970, he ordered an American invasion of Cambodia. Through the Johnson and Nixon years, domestic opposition to the American involvement steadily rose. Increasing discontent at home and lack of a decisive military victory abroad led Nixon to gradually withdraw American forces. During the first year of his second term in the White House, Nixon brought home the last of the American troops from Indochina. The Saigon government collapsed after two more years of war.

25.4 Vietnam:
Yesterday and Today

Source 6   President Lyndon Johnson, speech at Johns Hopkins
University, April 7, 1965

Why are we in Vietnam? We are there because we have a promise to keep. Since
1954 every American president has offered support to the people of South Vietnam.
We have helped to build, and we have helped to defend. Thus, over the years,
we have made a national pledge to help South Vietnam defend its independence.
And I intend to keep our promise.

To dishonor that pledge, to abandon this small and brave nation to its
enemy, and to the terror that must follow, would be an unforgivable wrong.

We are also there to strengthen world order. Around the globe, from Berlin
to Thailand, are people whose well-being rests, in part, on the belief that they
can count on us if they are attacked. To leave Vietnam to its fate would shake
the confidence of all those people in the value of American commitment, the
value of America's word. The result would be increased unrest and instability,
and even wider war.

We are also there because there are great stakes in the balance. Let no one
think for a moment that retreat from Vietnam would bring an end to conflict.
The battle would be renewed in one country and then another. The central
lesson of our time is that the appetite of aggression is never satisfied. To withdraw from one battlefield means only to prepare for the next. We must say in
Southeast Asia, as we did in Europe, in the words of the Bible: "Hitherto shalt
thou come but no further."

Source 7   Arthur M. Schlesinger Jr., *The Bitter Heritage:
Vietnam and American Democracy,* 1966

[A]s the number of our planes, our cannon and our ships increase, they will
inevitably be thrown into battle. Already our bombers roam over the hapless
countryside, dumping more tonnage of explosives each month than we were
dropping per month on all Europe and Africa during the Second World War—
more in a year than we dropped in the entire Pacific during the Second World
War. Just the other day our bombs killed or injured more than one hundred
civilians in a hamlet in the Mekong Delta—all on the suspicion that two Viet
Cong platoons, numbering perhaps sixty men, were there. Even if the Viet Cong
had still been around, which they weren't, would the military gain have out-
weighed the human and political loss? . . .

Our strategy in Vietnam today is rather like trying to weed a garden with
a bulldozer. We occasionally dig up some weeds, but we dig up most of the
turf, too. If we continue the pursuit of total military victory, we will leave the
tragic country gutted and devastated by bombs, burned by napalm, turned into
a wasteland by chemical defoliation, a land of ruin and wreck. This is the melancholy course to which the escalation policy commits us. The effect will be to
pulverize the political and institutional fabric which alone can give a South
Vietnamese state that hope of independent survival which is our presumed goal.
Our method, in other words, defeats our goal. . . .

Surely the United States, with all its ingenuity, could have figured out a
better way to combat guerrilla warfare than the physical obliteration of the nation
in which that warfare is taking place. If this is our best idea of "protecting" a

country against "wars of national liberation," what other country, seeing the devastation we have wrought in Vietnam, will wish American protection? What will happen to the credibility of our commitment then?

And there is a deeper question which already haunts the American conscience. Are we really carrying out this policy, as we constantly proclaim, to save the people we are methodically destroying, or are we doing it for less exalted purposes of our own? Are we treating the Vietnamese as ends in themselves, or as means to our own objectives? The war began as a struggle for the soul of Vietnam: will it end as a struggle for the soul of America?

Source 8   Senator Wayne Morse, speeches on the Senate floor, February 28 and 29, 1968

The first question to which I address myself tonight is: Was Congress and were the American people aware in August of 1964 that the *Maddox* was a ship engaged in electronic surveillance? Were they aware that one of its assigned missions was to stimulate radar and other shore installations of North Vietnam? Were they aware that the *Maddox* conducted operations as close as 4 miles off the coast of North Vietnam—a country with which we were then at peace and a country which had not engaged in any aggressive actions whatsoever against the United States?

Mr. President, the answer to each of these questions is an unequivocal "No." . . .

In the Senate, more than 35 Senators participated on August 6, 1964, in highly secret hearings with Secretary McNamara, Secretary Rusk, and General Wheeler. These were the official hearings. . . . There is not one line in those committee hearings supporting the proposition that members of those committees . . . were aware that the *Maddox* was engaged in electronic surveillance. . . .

Mr. President, there is not a word in those hearings to show that the *Maddox* proceeded to within 4 miles of the North Vietnamese shore.

What were we informed? We were told that the *Maddox* was engaged in a "routine patrol" when it was subjected to "a deliberate and unprovoked attack" while on the "high seas."

As the record of our hearings of February 20, 1968, with Mr. McNamara shows, the *Maddox* was specifically instructed, and here I quote: "to stimulate Chicom—North Vietnamese electronic reaction."

In view of the fact that we were also involved in the bombardment of the islands and of the mainland, these instructions constituted, under international law, an act of constructive aggression on the part of the Government of the United States. Not a word of this was mentioned to the two committees. The committees were not told that the *Maddox*, after being supplied with special electronic equipment in Keelung, Taiwan, was authorized to proceed to a point 9 miles off Cape Falaise, well within the territorial waters claimed by North Vietnam.

Do not forget what our Government did with this destroyer. It sent this destroyer to Taiwan before the Tonkin Gulf incident and before the bombardment, equipped it with spy ship equipment, and, for this mission, changed it from a destroyer into a spy ship. That is what the facts are in regard to the *Maddox*.

The committee was not told that on August 1, before the first attack, the *Maddox* proceeded in the direction of Hon Me and Hon Nieu, coming within 4 miles of those islands before turning southward. This patrol was, therefore, off the islands which had been attacked only 40 hours earlier by American-supplied vessels, operated by South Vietnamese. How did the North Vietnamese know whether or not our attacks were over? By what right do we assume that the North Vietnamese, having been bombarded and then having this destroyer that close to their shore, with the destroyer stimulating electronically the electronic defensive instruments in North Vietnam, how could they assume that there was not going to be additional bombardment? They had every reason to take such a course of action to protect their sovereignty. . . .

Our country supplied the South Vietnamese patrol boats. Our country equipped them. Our country trained the personnel. Officials of our Government, both military and civilian, were fully aware at all times of the aggression of the South Vietnamese against the North Vietnamese islands and shore targets. Our government helped prepare and direct the plans. . . .

Therefore, for the Secretary of Defense, military commanders, and the White House to allege that our destroyers were conducting a routine patrol on Tonkin Bay at the time of the North Vietnamese attack on the *Maddox* is simply not in accordance with the facts. . . .

The second alleged attack was on August 4. The question here is, Did this attack occur? This is important, because but for this attack the United States would not have retaliated against North Vietnam and there would presumably have been no urgent request for the Tonkin Resolution. . . .

The incident was a very confused affair. There are ample grounds to question whether North Vietnamese boats were there at all. And, if they were there, the evidence that the *Maddox* and *Turner Joy were* attacked is circumstantial. . . .

On August 4, 1964, the United States by virtue of launching an open and direct attack against North Vietnam went to war with North Vietnam. These retaliatory raids were justified to the Congress on the basis that the American ships "engaged in a routine patrol in the international waters of the Gulf of Tonkin" were the victims of a "deliberate and unprovoked" attack.

The Congress was asked to approve the "functional equivalent" of a declaration of war, to use Undersecretary of State Katzenbach's phrase, without being given the full facts as to what the American ships were doing in the Gulf of Tonkin and why they might have been attacked or harassed.

There is no such thing as a "functional declaration of war." And, under the Constitution of the United States, there has never been a declaration of war applicable to the operations of the United States in South Vietnam. Already, . . . it has cost us the lives of 18,000 American soldiers in a war that we do not dare declare.

As a consequence of the incidents in the Gulf of Tonkin, the Administration had lifted from its shoulders the very hard decision as to whether the United States should intensify its involvement in the Vietnam war. In the spring and summer of 1964, the South Vietnamese were losing the war and the United States had some very difficult decisions to make about our role in the Vietnam war. In the wake of the emotions developed during the Tonkin episodes, public and congressional debate was stilled over whether we should intensify our military role. . . .

I cannot be party to the suppression of facts that the American people are entitled to know. I do not propose to be a party to deny the American people the facts concerning the conduct and misconduct of their Government.

It was Carl Schurz who is often quoted as saying: "Our country, right or wrong"—thereby implying that mistakes once made must be compounded.

Does that statement mean we must always support the military, right or wrong? Does it mean we must never scrutinize the policies or search for the mistakes of the Executive?

My answer is "No." And that was the answer of Carl Schurz, also.

I close with the full quotation from Carl Schurz: "Our country, right or wrong. When right, to be kept right; when wrong, to be put right."

The time has come to put a wrong right in this country. The time has come to stop the slaughtering of American boys in Southeast Asia, in an undeclared war, in a wrong war. That is why I consider it my duty to make this historic record today for future generations.

We were wrong in the Gulf of Tonkin. We were a provocateur in the Gulf of Tonkin.

Source 9   Democratic National Convention, transcript of debate on platform plank on Vietnam, August 28, 1968

Philip Burton, Congressman, California: . . . I am opposed to the current course of the war in Vietnam.

I view this war as an effort to resolve by military means problems that are essentially political, social, and economic. I view this conflict as essentially an indigenous one, where the people of Vietnam are just seeking to have the opportunity and the right to carve out their own destiny without the oppression or the dictation of the Japanese, as they did in the 1940's, without the oppression or dictation of the French, as they did in the 1950's. And I am certain they view our effort in that area no differently than the other two countries that had prevented them, in my view, from arranging and determining the course of events as they saw fit.

I submit, if we continue our effort in Vietnam, we are going to wander more and more into the jungle mists of Asia. I fear that more and more Vietnamese will be killed, many more brave Americans will perish, many mothers and fathers will weep, and this nation will be cast over by a shadow that only the passage of time will dispel. . . .

Mr. Chairman, as the war in Vietnam continues, and we find ourselves committed to more money expended in any given month to destroy the countryside some 10,000 miles away than we spend in a full year on our war on poverty at home, I would think that this is not acceptable.

And as we find, and we know that education is a desperate problem in this land, that we spend more money in two weeks in destruction in Vietnam than we spend under the Federal Elementary and Secondary Act to educate the youth of our land, then I think that any nation whose resources are spent in a way where we spend so much more on destruction than we do on reconstruction and reconciliation at home must re-order its priorities.

So I say, Is it not time to say "let us disengage"? Is it not time to act in a way as to de-escalate the conflict? How much more of the life blood of this nation must be shed? How many more needs of our people must go unmet and promises of a better living unfulfilled? How long must we wait before we heed the voices of men and women of good will who, across this land, call for peace?

Gale McGee, Senator, Wyoming: . . . We stand here today in this convention nearly a quarter of a century after we committed to assist and to shield the newly independent governments of Southeast Asia in achieving a measure of dignity through independence.

A whole generation of new leaders, a whole generation of new governments, a whole generation of new economic and social programs in all of those lands have been undertaken in the expectation that the United States would assist in trying to achieve some semblance of orderly change in the area. That is what is at stake now.

It behooves us to ask ourselves what happens if we withdraw so rapidly without any measure of the consequences elsewhere?

What happens to Laos when we leave? They are gone. What happens to Cambodia? What happens to the neighboring nations? Singapore has reminded us that if we recede before their own infrastructure of security can be realized that their days are numbered.

The ruler of Malaysia when he was here reminded us of the same grim note.

If Southeast Asia comes unraveled, who then can vouch for the capabilities of preventing the unhinging of Korea and all that that portends?

You see, so much hangs on this tiny little place on the globe. . . . The world has become a matter of massive concern to us because of our role of leadership into which the history of our time has cast us.

Jack Gilligan, Congressman, Ohio: . . . We must now consider not only what this long and tragic conflict in Viet Nam has done to that tortured nation, but what it has done to America, to our plans, to our ideals, to our image of ourself as a people.

We have not only devastated Viet Nam, but we have distorted the vision of America.

We went to Viet Nam to help, but now we remain to destroy.

We did not intend it so, but as someone once said, 'they have created a desert and called it peace.'

We wanted the people of Viet Nam to live in freedom. Now our concern is that they be able to live at all.

We went there to preserve freedom. Now there is no freedom in Viet Nam, North or South.

We wanted to save the children of Viet Nam from tyranny. Now we want to save them from death.

And what of ourselves, and what of our people, and what of our sons?

We have lost 25,000 young American lives in Viet Nam, lives and talents which this nation desperately needs for the solution of our problems at home?

We have spent $100 billion, money and resources which again are needed for the repair of the ravages in our own society. Scripture says, "What fathers, if asked by their sons for bread, would give them a stone?"

Our young men have asked for a chance to build and develop, and we have sent them over the seas to destroy and to kill.

Our young black people have asked to be trained for a job, and we have trained them for warfare.

We are told we cannot afford to rebuild our cities because the necessary funds are diverted to this destruction of the villages of Viet Nam.

John Conyers, Congressman, Michigan: . . . Because of my conviction that we have misplaced our emphasis in Viet Nam, I must tell you that I have voted against supplemental appropriations every time they have come up every year, and will continue to do so as long as my district sends me to the Congress.

And I would like to remind you that it was in this spirit that the late, beloved Dr. Martin Luther King began to acquaint me with the deeper, more philosophical meanings of nonviolence, because he asked me how I could be nonviolent as a person, and not help lead the greatest nation in the world to the nonviolent philosophy.

I couldn't answer him. And that is why I stand here, urging black and white Americans to join us in making this great issue have an honest and deep conviction to all of us everywhere.

I cannot continue to tell those in the ghettoes and slums across America that we can't produce the domestic programs, an America of opportunity to all, when every time I present a program, my own party leaders tell me the war in Viet Nam prevents it.

Wayne Hays, Congressman, Ohio: . . . When I was a boy in high school, I walked into my first history class one day in September and the teacher . . . had written on the blackboard the following definition of history: "History is a record of the past, a guide to the present, and a forecast of the future."

And I hope that this great party of ours is not trying to turn the clock back to 1938 to seek another Chamberlain to go to another Munich to surrender to the people who last week managed the rape of Czechoslovakia. That word hasn't been mentioned today—Czechoslovakia, but it is on my mind and it is on the minds of the American people. And there are 200,000 Soviet troops in that unhappy land today.

Source 10 John Galloway, *The Gulf of Tonkin Resolution*, 1970

There is no direct evidence to suggest that President Johnson had decided upon a *major escalation* prior to the Tonkin Affair in August, but by mid-July he had a prototype of the Tonkin Resolution in his possession ready to introduce at the appropriate moment. It is unlikely, however, that he viewed the resolution primarily as a means of laying the legal groundwork for future escalations. Rather it appears that he considered the resolution and the bombing not only good politics, but an opportunity to impress Hanoi with his determination to persevere in Vietnam. . . .

The August incidents in the Gulf of Tonkin occurred at a propitious moment insofar as the resolution was concerned. But more important, they gave President Johnson, who was attempting to be all things to all people, an opportunity to exhibit what most saw as both strength and restraint. As a White

House aide later said, one of his purposes was "to win Republicans and conservatives with a responsible show of force. He already had the Left." It was, as
Chalmers M. Roberts wrote at the time in *The Washington Post,* "a classic case
where what looked like good statesmanship and good politics combined for the
President." Not for long, however, for not only did the resolution fail to impress
Hanoi, but as the truth about Tonkin began to unfold, the resolution, which
was not needed in the first place, did further damage to the President's reputation
and as such came to symbolize the stealthful ways of the nation's 36th President.

Source 11 "Report of the Department of the Army Review of the
Preliminary Investigations into the My Lai Incident,"
March 14, 1970

THE SON MY INCIDENT

During the period 16–19 March 1968, a tactical operation was conducted into
Son My Village, Son Tinh District, Quang Ngai province, Republic of Vietnam,
by Task Force (TF) Barker, a battalion-sized unit of the American Division. . . .
The Task Force was composed of a rifle company from each of the 11th Brigade's
three organic infantry battalions—A/3-1 Inf, B/4-3 Inf, C/1-20 Inf. The commander was LTC Frank A. Barker.

The plans for the operation were never reduced to writing but it was
reportedly aimed at destroying the 48th VC Local Force (LF) Battalion, thought
to be located in Son My Village. . . .

On the morning of 16 March 1968, the operation began as planned. A/3-1
was reported in blocking positions at 0725 hours. At about that same time the
artillery preparation and fires of supporting helicopter gunship were placed on
the C/1-20 Inf LZ (Landing Zone) and a part of **My Lai (4).** LTC Barker controlled the artillery preparation and combat assault from his helicopter. . . .

At 0750 hours all elements of C/1-20 Inf were on the ground. Before
entering My Lai (4), they killed several Vietnamese fleeing the area in the rice
paddies around the subhamlet and along Route 521 to the south of the subhamlet. No resistance was encountered at this time or later in the day.

The infantry assault on My Lai (4) began a few minutes before 0800 hours.
During the 1st Platoon's movement through the southern half of the subhamlet,
its members were involved in widespread killing of Vietnamese civilians—comprised almost exclusively of old men, women, and children—and also in property
destruction. Most of the inhabitants who were not killed immediately were
rounded up into two groups. The first group, consisting of about 70-80 Vietnamese, was taken to a large ditch east of My Lai (4) and later shot. A second
group, consisting of about 20–50 Vietnamese was taken south of the hamlet and
shot there on a trail. Similar killings of smaller groups took place within the
subhamlet.

Members of the 2d Platoon killed at least 60-70 Vietnamese men, women,
and children, as they swept through the northern half of My Lai (4) and through
Binh Tay, a small subhamlet about 400 meters north of My Lai (4). They also
committed several rapes.

The 3d Platoon, having secured the LZ, followed behind the 1st and 2d and burned and destroyed what remained of the houses in My Lai (4) and killed most of the remaining livestock. Its members also rounded up and killed a group of 7-12 women and children. . . .

By the time C/1-20 Inf departed My Lai (4) in the early afternoon, . . . its members had killed at least 175-200 Vietnamese men, women, and children. Casualty figures . . . were developed by this inquiry solely on the basis of statements and testimony of US personnel. Separate estimates by the Criminal Investigation Division (CID) agency, together with other evidence, indicates the number of Vietnamese killed in the overall area of Son My Village may have exceeded 400. The evidence indicates that only 3 or 4 were confirmed as Viet Cong. . . .

On the evening of 16 March 1968, after C/1-20 Inf and B/4-3 Inf had linked up in a night defensive position, a Viet Cong suspect was apparently tortured and maimed by a US officer. He was subsequently killed along with some additional suspects by Vietnamese National Police in the presence of US personnel.

During the period 17–19 March 1968 both C/1-20 Inf and B/4-3 Inf were involved in additional burning and destruction of dwellings, and in the mistreatment of Vietnamese detainees. . . .

SUMMARY OF FINDINGS

During the period of 16–19 March 1968, troops of Task Force Barker massacred a large number of Vietnamese nationals in the village of Son My.

Knowledge as to the extent of the incident existed at company level, at least among key staff officers and commanders at the Task Force Barker level, and at the 11th Brigade command level. . . .

The commander of the 11th Brigade, upon learning that a war crime had probably been committed, deliberately set out to conceal the fact from proper authority. . . .

Efforts were made at every level of command from company to division to withhold and suppress information concerning the Son My incident.

Source 12 Ralph Stavins, *Washington Plans an Aggressive War*, 1971

Was Congress deceived by the Executive when it passed the Gulf of Tonkin Resolution? . . . Congress was not advised of the extensive preparation for war, or appraised of the Administration's view that once it obtained a joint resolution, the light would shift from amber to green. Congress was simply told that the Executive needed the power to be flexible. . . . Congress was seduced into supporting the preordained decision of the Executive to wage an aggressive war against North Vietnam. Indeed, the Executive needed a Congressional resolution precisely because it was planning to wage an aggressive war. The Executive wanted Congress in its hip pocket to lend an aura of legitimacy to that aggressive war. In sum, the Executive deceived Congress into believing that the Administration had done nothing to incur the attack and that the resolution might or might not be employed in the future.

Source 13   Guenter Lewy, *America in Vietnam*, 1978

Many of America's military leaders argue to this day that their ability to conduct a winning strategy was hamstrung not only by overly restrictive rules of engagement, designed to protect civilian life and property, but also by geographical constraints imposed on them for fear of a collision with Communist China and the Soviet Union. This argument is less than persuasive, for the war, in the final analysis, had to be won in South Vietnam. Military action in Laos and Cambodia at an early stage of the war, seeking to block the Ho Chi Minh Trail, would have made the North Vietnamese supply effort far more difficult, but basically an expansion of the conflict would not have achieved the American task. Certainly, an invasion of North Vietnam would only have magnified the difficulties faced.

The war not only had to be won in South Vietnam, but it had to be won by the South Vietnamese. Unfortunately, to the end South Vietnamese performance remained the Achilles' heel of the allied effort. A totalitarian state like North Vietnam, possessing a monopoly of indoctrination and social control, was bound to display greater military morale and unity than a fragmented and barely authoritarian country like South Vietnam. . . . The ignominious collapse of ARVN [the South Vietnamese military] in 1975 . . . was due not only to ARVN's inferiority in heavy weapons and the shortage of ammunition but in considerable measure was also the result of lack of will and morale. . . .

Both critics and defenders of American policy in Vietnam can agree that, as [U.S. secretary of state Henry] Kissinger put it in 1975, "outside effort can only supplement, but not create, local efforts and local will to resist. . . . And there is no question that popular will and social justice are, in the last analysis, the essential underpinnings of resistance to subversion and external challenge." To bolster local ability, effort, and will to resist was, of course, the basic purpose of the American policy of Vietnamization. The fact that South Vietnam, abandoned by its ally, finally succumbed to a powerful and ruthless antagonist does not prove that this policy could not have had a less tragic ending. Neither does it vitiate the moral impulse which played a significant part in the original decision to help protect the independence of South Vietnam.

Source 14   George C. Herring, *America's Longest War*, 1986

The ongoing debate over U.S. involvement in Vietnam leaves many questions unanswered. Whether a more decisive use of military power could have brought a more satisfactory conclusion to the war without causing even more disastrous consequences remains highly doubtful. Whether the adoption of a more vigorous and imaginative counterinsurgency program at an earlier stage could have wrested control of the countryside from the Vietcong can never be known, and the ability of the United States to develop such a program in an alien environment is dubious. That the United States exaggerated the importance of Vietnam, as the liberals suggest, seems clear. . . .

The United States intervened in Vietnam to block the apparent march of a Soviet-directed Communism across Asia, enlarged its commitment to halt a presumably expansionist Communist China, and eventually made Vietnam a test of its determination to uphold world order. By wrongly attributing the Vietnamese conflict to external sources, the United States drastically misjudged its internal dynamics. By intervening in what was essentially a local struggle, it placed itself at the mercy of local forces, a weak client, and a determined adversary. It elevated into a major international conflict what might have remained a localized struggle. By raising the stakes into a test of its own credibility, it perilously narrowed its options. A policy so flawed in its premises cannot help but fail, and in this case the results were disastrous.

Vietnam made clear the inherent unworkability of a policy of global containment. In the 1940s the world seemed dangerous but manageable. The United States enjoyed a position of unprecedented power and influence, and achieved some notable early successes in Europe. Much of America's power derived from the weakness of other nations rather than from its own intrinsic strength, however, and Vietnam demonstrated conclusively that its power, however great, had limits.

Source 15   John G. Stoessinger, *Why Nations Go to War*, 1993

The American involvement in Indochina began almost imperceptibly, rather like a mild toothache. At the end, it ran through Vietnam and America like a pestilence. Each president based his policies on exaggerated fears and, later, on exaggerated hopes. Consequently each president left the problem to his successor in worse shape than he had found it.

The United States dropped more than 7 million tons of bombs on Indochina. This is eighty times the amount that was dropped on Britain during World War II and equal to more than three hundred of the atomic bombs that fell on Japan in 1945. The bombs left 20 million craters that ranged from 20 to 50 feet wide and 5 to 20 feet deep. After the bombardments much of Vietnam looked like a moonscape. Nothing will grow there for generations.

America too was in anguish over the war. Her leadership lost the respect of an entire generation, universities were disrupted, careers blighted, and the economy bloated by war inflation. The metal caskets in which 55,000 Americans returned from Vietnam became the symbol of the war's ultimate and only meaning.

In historical perspective, the great unanswered question about Vietnam will probably be: Which would have been less costly, an earlier Communist victory or the agony of this war? One cannot help but wonder what might have happened if not one American soldier had reached Indochina. Since history does not present alternatives, one cannot know where this road not taken might have led. Vietnam might well have gone Communist much earlier. But its form of Communism would probably have been of the Titoist variety, combining a strong dose of nationalism with a fierce tradition of independence vis-a-vis both Moscow and Peking. The United States could certainly have lived with that outcome. Its postponement was hardly worth the sacrifice of more than 55,000 American lives, hundreds of thousands of Vietnamese lives, and $150 billion. . . .

The end of this story was not without irony. In 1978 Vietnam, now a Communist nation backed by the Soviet Union, invaded and virtually dismembered Cambodia, which was receiving the support of China. The genocide of the Cambodian Khmer Rouge (which murdered at least one million of its own citizens) thus was ended not through the moral pressures brought to bear by an outraged humanity, but through the power interests of the Sino-Soviet conflict. Very soon after the American withdrawal from Vietnam the only wars in Asia were fought by Communists against other Communists. And by 1990, Communism the world over was in full retreat. Even Communist Vietnam was once again on speaking terms with the United States. When considered in this perspective, the awesome truth about Vietnam is clear: it was in vain that combatants and civilians had suffered, the land had been devastated, and the dead had died.

Source 16 **Former secretary of defense Robert S. McNamara,**
In Retrospect: The Tragedy and Lessons of Vietnam, **1995**

Let me be simple and direct—I want to be clearly understood: the United States of America fought in Vietnam for eight years for what it believed to be good and honest reasons. By such action, administrations of both parties sought to protect our security, prevent the spread of totalitarian Communism, and promote individual freedom and political democracy. The Kennedy, Johnson, and Nixon administrations made their decisions and by those decisions demanded sacrifices and, yes, inflicted terrible suffering in light of those goals and values.

Their hindsight was better than their foresight. The adage echoes down the corridors of time, applying to many individuals, in many situations, in many ages. People are human; they are fallible. I concede with painful candor and a heavy heart that the adage applies to me and my generation of American leadership regarding Vietnam. Although we sought to do the right thing—and believed we were doing the right thing—in my judgment, hindsight proves us wrong. We both overestimated the effect of South Vietnam's loss on the security of the West and failed to adhere to the fundamental principle that, in the final analysis, if the South Vietnamese were to be saved, they had to win the war themselves. Straying from this central truth, we built a progressively more massive effort on an inherently unstable foundation. External military force cannot substitute for the political order and stability that must be forged by a people *for* themselves.

 Questioning the Past

1. Compare the description of the incidents in the Gulf of Tonkin offered at the time by President Johnson with those offered in 1968 by Senator Morse.

2. The Gulf of Tonkin Resolution was repealed in May 1970, though American troops remained in Vietnam for three more years. Was the resolution the "functional equivalent" of a declaration of war? If it was not, by what authority did the American government conduct the war in Indochina? If it was, by what constitutional authority was the war in Indochina conducted by the American government after its repeal?

3. Argue the case for and against the American involvement in the Vietnam War. Which argument is the more persuasive?

4. John G. Stoessinger argues that America's involvement in Indochina was in vain. Present arguments for and against this conclusion.

Chapter 26

The Moon Landing

Neil Armstrong Steps onto the Moon *July 20, 1969*

On December 17, 1903, Orville Wright climbed into the pilot's position on a biplane he and his brother Wilbur had designed at their North Carolina bicycle shop. While Wilbur steadied the wing, the four-cylinder gasoline engine pulled the plane along a rail and lifted it off the ground for the first flight of a heavier-than-air, motor-driven aircraft. The flight lasted 12 seconds and covered a distance of 120 feet. Who could have imagined that such humble beginnings would lead humans to the moon only 66 years later—well within the life span of a person born on that historic day?

✎ *First Impressions*

The Race for Space

26.1 Apollo to the Moon

A hotly contested race for the moon between the Americans and the Soviets began in 1957 with the successful launching of an artificial satellite in earth orbit by the Soviet Union. Since the Soviets jumped out into an early lead, the United States chased Soviet successes for almost a decade before the moon race reached its finish line in July of 1969. The United States' manned space program began with suborbital and, later, orbital flights of the one-person *Mercury* capsule. The Gemini program, involving a two-person craft, followed. The Apollo series was designed to accommodate three people for the trek to the moon.

Source 1   **Associated Press wire service dispatch from Moscow,
October 5, 1957**

The Soviet Union announced today it has launched the earth's first man-made satellite 560 miles out in space and it now is circling the globe at tremendous speed.

The dramatic claim that Russia had beaten the United States in the satellite race came in an announcement saying the artificial moon was launched yesterday by multiple-stage rockets. The site of the launching was not given....

The instrument-laden globe was described as 23 inches in diameter and weighing 185 pounds. The announced weight is about nine times that of a projected 22-inch United States earth satellite....

The announcement by Tass was spread over the front pages of Pravda and Izvestia without comment.

No comment was necessary, however, to tell the Soviet people that their leaders had carried off a feat whose propaganda value may far outweigh its contributions to IGY (International Geophysical Year) studies.

Source 2   Soviet jet propulsion scientist Dr. K. P. Stanyukovich's statement broadcast over Radio Moscow, October 5, 1957

It can now be said with confidence that in a few years flights to the moon . . . will become as much a reality as the launching of the first artificial satellite.

In the near future, new artificial satellites will be equipped with special instruments which will make it possible to study the more precise properties of the uppermost layers of the atmosphere and cosmic space.

The launching of the artificial satellite is not only a tremendous scientific event in the life of mankind but it is also the necessary first stage in the conquering of interplanetary space—it is the necessary first stage in the flight to the moon.

26.2 Red Star:
The Soviet
Moon Program

Source 3   Editorial, " 'Moon' over the World," Washington *Evening Star,* October 6, 1957

We know that above us, some 560 miles up, a Soviet-made and Soviet-launched artificial moon is at this very moment looping around the earth at a speed of 18,000 miles an hour. . . . [T]here can be no doubt that this history-making event constitutes a major triumph for the Kremlin in terms of enhancing its prestige and giving a powerful boost to its propaganda throughout the world. . . .

More than that, it would be sheer blindness on our part if we failed to recognize this Russian achievement as a singularly convincing confirmation of Moscow's past claims about its success in developing an intercontinental ballistic missile. . . . [A]ny country that can make a vehicle ride far out in space, 560 miles above the earth, is a country very well advanced in the art of rocketry, and we can pooh-pooh that only at our peril.

All of which raises the question whether we are really doing as much as we can, as fast as we can, in the missile field. The advent of Russia's artificial moon, several months before ours is scheduled to go up, suggests that we have been just a bit too sluggish, and perhaps just a bit too complacent, in our approach to the whole fantastic business. Certainly, if that is the case, we had better wake up and redouble our efforts. Otherwise we may live to regret our mistakes as we have never regretted anything else before.

Source 4   Editorial, *Aviation Week,* October 14, 1957

We believe the people of this country have a right to know the facts about the relative position of the U.S. and the Soviet Union in this technological race which is perhaps the most significant single event of our times. They have the right to find out why a nation with our vastly superior scientific, economic and military potential is being at the very least equalled and perhaps being surpassed by a country that less than two decades ago couldn't even play in the same scientific ball park.

They also have a right to make the decisions as to whether they want their government to maintain our current leadership of the free world regardless of the cost in dollars and sweat or whether they wish to supinely abdicate this position, in favor of enjoying a few more years of the hedonistic prosperity that now enfolds our country.

Source 5   B. J. Cutler, "Soviet Launches a Half-Ton Satellite: Dog on Board Reported Alive, Well," *Washington Post*, November 4, 1957

Russia launched today its second earth satellite. It is a monster projectile weighing half a ton and carrying history's first space passenger—a small dog.

There was no immediate official statement whether the dog was expected to return safely to earth or how this could be accomplished. But a spokesman for the Moscow Planetarium hinted today that the satellite contained a device that, at a prearranged time, which he would not disclose, could eject the container with the dog out of the rocket nose. . . .

Instruments aboard the satellite were checking the dog's heartbeat, blood pressure and breathing. This data was being radioed to earth together with observations of cosmic rays and other phenomena of the upper atmosphere.

The satellite weighed 1120 pounds. . . . An official announcement placed the satellite 1056 miles out in space. . . . It was ripping along at a speed of 17,840 miles an hour.

Source 6   Nate Haseltine, "Vanguard Fails, Burns in Test Firing," *Washington Post*, December 7, 1957

The Nation's first real try to launch a test satellite into outer space died yesterday in a roar of flames. The 72-foot rocket that was to carry a 3 3/4-pound sphere into a possible orbit around the earth barely rose clear of its launching platform at Cape Canaveral, Fla., settled back as its power failed, teetered forward off the stand, and then was largely consumed in its own flaming fuels.

There was no explosion in the blast sense of the word, and no one was hurt physically. The official version was that "lack of thrust" caused the misfiring. Just what caused the "lack of thrust," however, was still a mystery last night.

John P. Hagan, Director of Project Vanguard, the program set up to put an American satellite into space, said later that another try would be made "as soon as possible." . . . Appearing for a belated news conference at Vanguard's Information Center, Naval Research Laboratory here, Hagan said everyone was "tremendously disappointed" over the failure.

Source 7   Milton Bracker, "Army Launches U.S. Satellite into Orbit," *New York Times*, February 1, 1958

Cape Canaveral, Fla., Jan. 31—The United States' first earth satellite was borne spaceward tonight on a tremendous golden jet that roared its way across the sky from the base of the Army's Jupiter-C rocket. At 10:48 p.m., after an agonizing fifteen and three-quarter seconds between the actual firing command and the lift-off, the giant rocket lit up the night with a seething burst of flame and gradually accelerated directly upward from the pad.

As the Jupiter-C gained speed, it emitted a violent roar that filled the entire area. Never wavering on its course, the rocket rose faster and faster, cut through a layer of overcast and reappeared as a steadily diminishing spark burning its way out of sight. . . .

[T]he Jupiter-C was about 68.8 feet long, and the pointed cylindrical satellite case containing the scientific instruments was 80 inches long and 5 inches in diameter. . . . The weight of the satellite proper was 18.13 pounds.

Source 8   President John F. Kennedy, "Message to Chairman Khrushchev concerning the Flight of the Soviet Astronaut," April 12, 1961

[Major Yuri Gagarin had successfully orbited the Earth in 1 hour and 48 minutes.]

The people of the United States share with the people of the Soviet Union their satisfaction for the safe flight of the astronaut in man's first venture into space. We congratulate you and the Soviet scientists and engineers who made this feat possible. It is my sincere desire that in the continuing quest for knowledge of outer space our nations can work together to obtain the greatest benefit to mankind.

Source 9   Editorial, "Beautiful Sight," *Washington Post,* May 6, 1961

The words of the country's first astronaut, radioed from 115 miles out in space, form an appropriate commentary upon the achievement. What a beautiful sight, indeed! Americans needed a reason to look up, and Lt. Cmdr. Alan B. Shepard, Jr. gave it to them.

Everywhere in the country the feeling will be one of exultation, first that Commander Shepard completed his mission safely, and second that the United States succeeded in an effort that has so much bearing upon scientific accomplishment and national prestige. . . .

Let us not delude ourselves, however, that this feat overcomes the Soviet lead. Major Gagarin will forever hold the honor of having been the first man in space. His craft orbited the earth, an achievement which this country has not yet paralleled. . . .

Moreover, the rockets which propelled the Soviet craft developed vastly more thrust than any the United States has yet perfected. . . .

The first American to sample the reaches of space owes his success not only to his own discipline and bravery but also to the devoted work of thousands of persons. The accomplishment is only the beginning of a costly and illimitable endeavor; it is no more a cause for the United States to rest on its laurels than the voyage of Columbus was a signal for the complacent conclusion that all was discovered. But for the moment Americans can share proudly if vicariously in the zest of exploration of the unknown.

Source 10   President John F. Kennedy, "Special Message to the Congress on Urgent National Needs," May 25, 1961

[I]f we are to win the battle that is now going on around the world between freedom and tyranny, the dramatic achievements in space which occurred in recent weeks should have made clear to us all, as did the Sputnik in 1957, the impact of this adventure on the minds of men everywhere, who are attempting to make a determination of which road they should take. Since early in my term, our efforts in space have been under review. With the advice of the Vice President, who is Chairman of the National Space Council, we have examined where we are strong and where we are not, where we may succeed and where we may not. Now it is time to take longer strides—time for a great new American enterprise—time for this nation to take a clearly leading role in space achievement, which in many ways may hold the key to our future on earth.

I believe we possess all the resources and talents necessary. But the facts of the matter are that we have never made the national decisions or marshalled the national resources required for such leadership. We have never specified long-range goals on an urgent time schedule, or managed our resources and our time so as to insure their fulfillment.

Recognizing the head start obtained by the Soviets with their large rocket engines, which gives them many months of lead-time, and recognizing the likelihood that they will exploit this lead for some time to come in still more impressive successes, we nevertheless are required to make new efforts on our own. For while we cannot guarantee that we shall one day be first, we can guarantee that any failure to make this effort will make us last. We take an additional risk by making it in full view of the world, but as shown by the feat of astronaut Shepard, this very risk enhances our stature when we are successful. But this is not merely a race. Space is open to us now; and our eagerness to share its meaning is not governed by the efforts of others. We go into space because whatever mankind must undertake, free men must fully share. . . .

I believe that this nation should commit itself to achieving the goal, before the decade is out, of landing a man on the moon and returning him safely to the earth. No single space project in this period will be more impressive to mankind, or more important for the long-range exploration of space; and none will be so difficult or expensive to accomplish. We propose to accelerate the development of the appropriate lunar space craft. We propose to develop alternate liquid and solid fuel boosters, much larger than any now being developed, until certain which is superior. We propose additional funds for other engine development and for unmanned explorations—explorations which are particularly important for one purpose which this nation will never overlook: the survival of the man who first makes this daring flight. But in a very real sense, it will not be one man going to the moon—if we make this judgment affirmatively, it will be an entire nation. For all of us must work to put him there.

Source 11   John G. Norris, "Glenn Lands Safely after Three Orbits," *Washington Post*, February 21, 1962

Cape Canaveral, Fla., Feb. 20—Astronaut John H. Glenn whipped three times around the world today in just under five hours to reestablish America as a strong contender in the space race. After what Glenn himself called a real "fireball" reentry into the earth's atmosphere, the astronaut's capsule descended by parachute into the Atlantic 166 statute miles due east of Grand Turk Island in the Bahamas. His Friendship 7 capsule was fished out of the ocean by the destroyer *Noa* within 21 minutes after coming down at 2:43 p.m. with the astronaut reporting he was in "good condition." . . .

Officials announced that the American space man flew about 81,000 miles during his 4-hour-and-56-minute flight. He was weightless about 4 3/4 hours, and experienced a maximum of 8 "Gs."

Source 12 William Hines, "Three Apollo Astronauts Killed by Flash Fire in Crash on Pad," January 28, 1967

The three-man crew of the first Project Apollo mission was killed last night in the worst accident in the history of the American manned space flight effort. Astronauts Virgil I. Grissom, Edward H. White II and Roger B. Chaffee perished, apparently almost simultaneously as a sheet of flame fanned by pure oxygen swept through their spacecraft while they were going through a dress rehearsal. . . .

A space agency official said today that one of the three astronauts trapped aboard the spacecraft was able to report the fire in an instant before the three men perished. . . .

The exact effect on the United States' $23 billion moon program could not be ascertained immediately, but the accident was bound to result in a delay of several months. . . . Engineers believe a spark somewhere in the complex electrical system caused the flash fire, but it is not known which of a multitude of connections was at fault.

Source 13 "Apollo Astronauts on Way after Flawless Liftoff," *Boston Globe,* July 17, 1969

After one million years confined to his own Earth, man is within 77 hours of landing on another planet.

By noon today America's three Apollo astronauts will be almost halfway to the moon. They are scheduled to land Sunday afternoon.

Mankind's greatest adventure began at 9:32 a.m., Wednesday, July 16, at Cape Kennedy, when the giant Apollo 11 lifted slowly but powerfully from the pad, watched by 1 million people on the site and half a billion around the world.

British writer Arthur C. Clark said it for everyone: "It's the last day of the old world."

The departure was a symphony of perfection from countdown to flawless liftoff to the critical maneuvers that put the spacecraft on a path to the moon.

"For that particular moment and second," said Rev. Ralph Abernathy, "I really forgot the fact that we have so many hungry people in the United States of America." The leader of a Poor People's demonstration at Cape Kennedy, Rev. Mr. Abernathy added that the launch made him feel "one of the proudest Americans." . . .

26.3 Project Apollo

"Courageous people" was the way the Soviet news agency Tass hailed the astronauts. News media in the USSR reported the launch with unusual speed and in greater detail than usual. The Soviet Union's unmanned Luna 15 space-craft, which has presumably been trying to upstage the Apollo mission since its launching Sunday, added a mystery to yesterday's events. It produced two sudden bursts of signals, the last only four minutes before the Cape Kennedy liftoff. . . .

Source 14 "Soviet Luna Remains a Mystery," Associated Press wire service dispatch from Jodrell Bank, England, July 17, 1969

The 250-foot radio telescope at Jodrell Bank tracked the Soviet Luna 15 three-quarters of the way to the moon yesterday. Sir Bernard Lovell, director of the observatory, said the observatory received signals from Luna 15 until a few min-utes before the Apollo 11 liftoff from Florida. . . .

With Luna 15 nearing the moon, Sir Bernard said the unmanned Soviet probe was as much a puzzle as ever. "We simply do not know what Luna 15 is going to do," he said. "But I have no doubt it is the beginning of a series to bring back lunar soil." . . .

Lovell said another puzzling feature of Luna 15 was its launching on Sunday in the face of a new moon. He said he thought that if the Russians were going to land the spacecraft on the moon they would have wanted to watch it through television cameras—and this would be more feasible if the moon were full.

Lovell's aide said Luna 15 would reach the vicinity of the moon today between 10 a.m. and noon (5 a.m. and 7 a.m., EDT). He said the spacecraft was taking 100 hours to reach the moon, instead of 80 as on previous Soviet moon shots, and was also sending a new kind of signal that "we cannot interpret."

Source 15 Associated Press dispatch from Jodrell Bank, England, July 18, 1969

Luna 15 circled the moon every two hours yesterday while Moscow left the world wondering whether the unmanned probe was a decoy or a real bid to steal the show from America's Apollo 11. Soviet authorities, uncommunicative as usual about their space efforts, said only that Luna 15 had become a satellite of the moon. This led Moscow observers to speculate that its mission was completed.

But at Jodrell Bank, observatory director Sir Bernard Lovell said he judged it likely that Luna 15 would try to land on the moon and scoop up some soil this morning.

The U.S. Space Agency would, if absolutely necessary, ask the Soviet Union to take action to prevent the unmanned Luna 15 from endangering the lives of Apollo 11 moon landing astronauts, an official told Reuters yesterday.

Source 16 Fred Farrar, "Apollo in Grasp of Moon," *Chicago Tribune,* July 19, 1969

The Apollo 11 astronauts closed in on the moon early today, ready to blast themselves into lunar orbit and start two days of great human experience.

Apollo 11 is scheduled to fire its rocket to swing into lunar orbit at 12:26 p.m. (Chicago time) today when the astronauts are behind the moon and out of radio contact.

The world will not know whether the engine ignited properly until Apollo 11 reappears around the edge of the moon 26 minutes later.

Last night the astronauts started to pick up speed as they escaped the earth's gravity and entered the moon's. When they hit the dividing line, 211,000 miles from earth, they were traveling at 2,070 miles per hour. They will continue to gain speed until going into orbit around the moon. Their highest speed before going into moon orbit will be 3,643 miles per hour.

Source 17 Fred Farrar, "Go for Moon Drop Today," *Chicago Tribune,*
July 20, 1969

Houston, July 19—The Apollo 11 astronauts went into orbit around the moon shortly after noon Chicago time today, setting the stage for man's first landing and walk on the moon.

Less than three hours later they turned their color television camera on the surface of the moon and traced the path that Astronauts Neil A. Armstrong and Edwin E. Aldrin Jr. will fly to their landing.

The historic landing is now scheduled for approximately 3:15 p.m. tomorrow, and the moon walk is set for shortly after 1 a.m. Monday. It could come four hours earlier if Armstrong, Aldrin, and the space agency agree. . . .

Early tonight, Aldrin crawled from the command ship into the small lunar lander called Eagle to test the equipment that must work if he and Armstrong are to land on the moon and return.

The air force colonel powered up the moon cab for the first time since it was rocketed away from Cape Kennedy four days and 250,000 miles ago. He also tested the communications systems that will carry every word and picture of man's first step on another celestial body.

Source 18 Dialogue among NASA Mission Control, the lunar lander
Eagle, and the mother ship *Columbia,* July 20, 1969

Columbia: Eagle, this is Columbia—they just gave you a "go" for powered descent. . . .

MC: Current altitude about 46,000 feet . . . Everything's looking good here.

Eagle: Our position check downrange shows us to be a little off.

MC: You are to continue your descent. It's looking good. Everything's looking good here, over.

Eagle: Copy.

MC: Two minutes 20 seconds, everything looking good.

Eagle: I'm getting a little fluctuation in—

MC: Looking good.

Eagle: —Shows us to be a little long.

MC: You're go to continue power descent, you're go to continue power descent. You're looking good.

Eagle: Altitude lights out. Got the earth right out our front window.

MC: You're looking great, Eagle, you're looking great. You're go for landing.

Eagle: Roger, understand. Go for landing, 3,000 feet . . . 2,000 feet. . . . OK, looks like it's holding.

MC: Roger. We've got good data. You're looking great at 8 minutes. . . . Eagle looking great, you're go. . . .

Eagle: 540 feet . . . 400 feet . . . coming down nicely . . . 200 feet . . . 100 . . . 75 feet, still looking good. Drifting to the right a little. O.K. Engines stopped.

MC: We copy you down, Eagle.

Eagle: Houston, uh, Tranquility base here. The Eagle has landed.

MC: Roger, Tranquility. We copy you on the ground. You got a bunch of guys about to turn blue. We're breathing again. Thanks a lot. . . .

Eagle [Armstrong]: Thank you . . . that may have seemed like a very long phase. The auto targeting was taking us right into a football-field-size, uh, football-field-size crater. There's a large number of big boulders and rocks for about one or two crater diameters around it. And it required us to plunk down in P66 non-automatic flight and fly in manually over the rock field to find a reasonably good area. We'll get to the details of what's around us here but it looks like a collection of just about every variety of shape, angularity, granularity, and every variety of rock you could find. The colors, well, it varies pretty much depending on how you're looking relative to the . . . there doesn't appear to be too much of a general color at all. . . .

Eagle [Aldrin]: It's pretty much without color. It's gray, and it's very white, chalky gray as you look into the zero phase line and it's considerably darker gray, more like ash, ashen gray as you look out 90 degrees to the sun.

Source 19   "Apollo Fever Hits Japan: Half-Holidays Expected,"
    Japan Times of Tokyo, July 20, 1969

Japan has been seized with the "Apollo fever," with TV stations blaring round-the-clock Apollo programs, and government officials are expected to turn the day into a half-day holiday.

NHK and commercial TV stations started all-night programs after midnight. Each station has been staffed with about 100 Apollo experts.

About 120 scholars and other authorities were virtually confined to such stations overnight.

TV coverage will continue this afternoon with a two-hour-40-minute spectacular entitled "First Step on the Moon."

The Sony Building in Ginza kept its first floor open overnight and provided 10 color television sets for Ginza night owls.

According to Tokyo Electric Power Co., power consumption rose by 500,000 kilowatts at blast-off time Wednesday evening. This far exceeded the jump of 200,000 kilowatts recorded at the time of the opening ceremony of the 1964 Tokyo Olympics.

With these figures in mind, the power company predicted an increase of 700,000 to 800,000 kilowatts this morning and afternoon.

Meanwhile, color TV sets enjoyed brisk sales Sunday. A department store in Ikebukure which set up a special corner for color TV at its first-floor entrance said 41 sets—this year's high—were sold yesterday alone.

Source 20 **Astronaut Neil Armstrong's communications to Mission Control as he descended the ladder to the moon's surface, July 20, 1969**

Eagle [Armstrong]: This is Tranquility base. We are beginning our EVA prep.

Eagle: At the foot of the ladder the left foot pads are only depressed in the surface about one or two inches although the surface appears to be very fine grained as you get closer to it. It's almost like a powder.

Eagle: Going to step off the Lem now.

Eagle: That's one small step for man, one giant leap for mankind. The surface is fine and powdery. I can pick it up loosely with my toe. It does adhere in fine layers like powdered charcoal to the sole and inside of my boots. I only go in a small fraction of an inch—an eighth of an inch—but I can see the footprints of my boots and the treads in the fine sandy particles.

Source 21 **Wire service dispatch from Manchester, England, *Boston Globe*, extra edition, July 21, 1969**

The unmanned Russian spacecraft Luna 15 landed today on the Moon's Sea of Crisis, 500 miles from the Apollo 11 Lunar module and its two American astronauts, Jodrell Bank Observatory reported. Western scientists speculated the Russian ship is on a robot rock-collecting mission to the moon and will be brought back to Earth.

But before landing, it baffled the world by circling the Moon for more than five days—and letting pass the chance of landing before the Apollo 11 touched down last night. . . .

Space scientist Sir Bernard Lovell, director of he observatory, said the Russian spacecraft stopped signaling in a manner "appropriate to that of landing." He added that Jodrell Bank scientists were "slightly bothered" by one factor: records indicate Luna's radio transmitting device had been traveling at 300 m.p.h. when the signals stopped and "it is unlikely that anything could have survived such an impact."

But he said this did not necessarily indicate a complete crash landing, that it was possible the radio transmitter had been switched off at some point prior to touchdown or that "something was ejected that would continue operating." Asked if it was a hard or soft landing, he said, "We shall have to wait and see if we get more signals to see if it lifts off again."

Source 22   Editorial, "Wonder of the World," *The Times* of London, July 21, 1969

Most of the world was able to share the drama of the moon landing, a drama which obviously could have ended in disaster and indeed there are still more hazards to come. As the television clock showed the last twenty minutes ticking away, second by second, and we heard the matter-of-fact voices of the American astronauts, any family with a television set was present at one of the most exciting moments of man's history. July 20, 1969, will be remembered when little children who were brought down half asleep are grandparents. It is the first event of such historic significance to be shared so widely and known so immediately.

Yet what does it mean? Obviously it is an epic of human bravery, similar to the conquest of Everest or the great voyages of discovery. Obviously it is a great feat of scientific and professional skill. . . . Obviously, also, it is a reproach; the nation which personifies this and other advances is unable to solve social problems which should perhaps be simpler but are more difficult. Obviously, also, it is a symbolic act, man reaching out beyond his previous confines, an astonishing demonstration of the capacity of the most ridiculous of animals.

This celebrated event is also most mysterious in its consequences. It may be little more than a brilliantly lit blind alley, a successful act of scientific curiosity, but also an intrusion into an atmosphere so alien that it will remain of as little use to man as the much more convenient polar regions. It could therefore be a step that leads little further than itself or it could lead to a whole series of further explorations, to a new way of life for man and not merely to the satisfaction of his curiosity or the extension of his psychological boundaries.

For the present we have the fact itself, and the fact is so remarkable that it is enough. The American astronauts have landed on the moon and we have heard their conversation from the moon and seen their progress. Their achievement will always be one of the wonders of the world.

Source 23   William L. Ryan, "Why Did Russians Lose to Americans in Race for Moon?" Associated Press, July 21, 1969

The Russians once looked like the winners in the race to put a man on the moon. Then they seemed resigned to surrendering the honor to Americans. Why?

There is reason to believe that the Soviet military decided that the moon could wait.

As long as six or seven years ago there seemed to be differences of opinion among Soviet military leaders—and between military men and civilian politicians—about the advisability of a full-speed drive to put a Russian on the moon.

Possibly the Russians took a long, careful look at the cost. Politicians would grieve at the loss of the enormous world propaganda impact of a manned expedition. But the generals seemed to argue that continued unmanned probes would be cheaper. That would leave a more generous share of the science budget for projects promising quicker military dividends. . . .

When Sputnik I, the first artificial satellite, was lofted in October 1957, it caused near-panic in some Western circles aware of the meaning in terms of Soviet rocket power.

On April 12, 1961, Maj. Yuri Gagarin became the first man to orbit the earth. Pravda gloated that it showed the might of a Communist nation. . . .

Orbiting satellites could carry nuclear weapons. Now a new dimension—the human element—was added. The United States' reaction was predictable: an urge to step up the American program.

Khrushchev delighted in taunting the Americans about Soviet moon probes. By 1963, after four unmanned moon shots, Soviet scientists already were striving for a soft landing, necessary if a man were to be placed on the moon.

Then vague Soviet doubts began to surface, notably among the military. . . . The space exploration cost had been huge and was increasing constantly. Was the moons race worth it? To military men, was it worth cutting into other sections of the arms budget?

Khrushchev worried publicly about devoting more Soviet resources to mending the consumer economy, a suggestion that the costs of space exploration, on top of a huge military investment, were becoming painful. . . .

In 1965, four attempts failed to achieve a soft landing of an unmanned craft. The next year, the Russians brought it off, with Luna 9. The first such American attempt would take place a few months later.

It was still a race. The Russians seemed well ahead. It was widely expected that thereafter they would make swift strides. But things went sour.

Experiments failed to accomplish goals. For two years the Russians did not put a man into space. Then, in April 1967, Cosmonaut Vladimir N. Komarov was killed trying to land from his returning craft, Soyuz I. That put a crimp in the moon program and revived the moon race debate.

It seemed likely that 1967 was a target date for a Russian on the moon. It would be the 50th anniversary of the Bolshevik Revolution. Failure in so important a year would be intolerable to political and military leaders alike. . . .

Probably in 1967 the moon program was cut back. . . . The weight of the military men may have been thrown into the balance at that time. The Russians seemed to be considering manned space stations, which would have huge military meaning. For the moon, they appeared to think in terms of an unmanned vehicle. . . .

It had cost the Americans 24 billion dollars to get ready to put men on the moon. Subsequent steps would cost tens of billions more. Perhaps Russian resources were severely strained by the space race. The question in Moscow may have been: which sort of program—a man on the moon or other space efforts—might pay the best dividends?

📖 *Second Thoughts*
A Giant Leap for Mankind?

The race to place a human on the moon was won by the United States. Though the Soviets announced at one point that Russian cosmonauts would land on the lunar surface sometime in the early 1970s, this objective is still unrealized. Instead, the Soviets shifted their focus toward the construction of a space station in Earth's orbit and have succeeded in keeping cosmonauts in residence aboard such a craft for months on end. The United States succeeded in carrying out five more manned expeditions to the moon before shifting the emphasis of the American manned space program toward the development of the space shuttle.

Still, of the six visits made to date by humans to their nearest celestial neighbor, none had the impact or the drama of the first. With television projecting the adventure live into the homes of billions of people, it was almost as if the entire human race were descending the ladder and taking the giant step with Astronaut Armstrong. *Apollo 11* made the journey to the moon in 109 hours, 8 minutes, and 5 seconds. It landed on the moon's surface at 4:17:45 E.D.T., Sunday morning, July 20, 1969. Whether that moment will be recorded as a great turning point in human history is still to be determined.

Source 24 John M. Logsdon, director of policy studies in science and technology at George Washington University, *The Decision to Go to the Moon: Project Apollo and the National Interest,* 1970

That man can do whatever he chooses, given only the will to do it and the techniques required, is a belief that reflects motivations and characteristics basic to Western and especially to American civilization—a will to action, confidence in man's mastery over nature, a sense of mission. . . . The "Apollo approach" to the achievement of social objectives can only be adopted in a society where this belief is held both by the general population and by the society's leadership. It may turn out that this approach can in fact only be used in the United States, where both confidence in our ability to attack and solve major problems and a preference for technological, "engineering" means to achieve our objectives are deeply ingrained. . . . But this potential for achievement carries with it the danger of subverting the democratic principles upon which American society is based.

The essence of the "Apollo approach" is concentration of effort and a corresponding concentration of control. There is a constant tension between this concentration of control, which seems required if objectives of the scope of the lunar landing are to be chosen and implemented successfully, and the democratic ethic, which distrusts such a concentration of control and power. The final lesson of Apollo may be that such a tension can be maintained without either destroying democratic values or making government efforts impossible. . . .

The purpose of government is to do things for a society which cannot be done by individual or combined private efforts. Sending men to the moon was one such thing. There are many others which are worth doing. But the organized energy which government can command must be applied in the interests of the whole society and ultimately of each individual in it. . . . The experience of

Project Apollo shows it is indeed possible to organize other "great American enterprises," intended to achieve objectives equal or greater in human significance than landing on the moon. It is up to us as citizens of this country to make sure that such enterprises do not in seeking their objectives destroy or diminish the values or beliefs they are intended to foster.

Source 25 Kathleen Teltsch, "Pact on Moon's Riches Reached," *New York Times,* July 4, 1979

[The "Agreement Governing the Activities of States on the Moon and Other Celestial Bodies" was ultimately ratified on July 11, 1984.]

UNITED NATIONS, N.Y., July 3—After seven year's labor, an international treaty on the exploitation of the moon's resources was approved by the 47-member Committee on Outer Space today.

The agreement seeks to insure that smaller powers lacking the ability to explore space will have a stake in the mineral wealth of the moon and other celestial bodies by proclaiming these resources to be the "common heritage of mankind." Any commercial exploitation, however, is regarded as decades away. . . .

Agreement on the new treaty was stalled for years because the Soviet Union was unwilling to accept the concept that the moon's resources should be a common heritage. The third world countries had been pressing for a commitment from the space powers similar to the one they have sought on the mining of seabed minerals. They will be continuing their campaign to have ocean minerals declared a common heritage at the next session of the Conference on the Law of the Sea, which begins here on July 19.

The text of the moon treaty, which the committee approved without a formal vote, now has to be accepted by the General Assembly, which is scheduled to meet here in September. The pact will come into force after five governments complete ratification.

The controversial article designating the moon and its resources a common heritage stipulates that neither the surface nor subsurface shall become the property of any country. The treaty commits countries to establish an international regime to see that the benefits of lunar exploitation are shared equitably once commercial exploitation "is to become feasible." An international conference would be called to draft a detailed treaty on the development and management of lunar resources.

Source 26 Charles Murray and Catherine Bly Cox, *Apollo: The Race to the Moon,* 1989

Looking back twenty years after the first landing, many of the people of Apollo agree with John Aaron's sentiment—it was a little like gulping good wine. Few had the time to step outside of events and assess what was going on until later. "It was funny," Rod Rose reminisces, "Just a little while ago, when I retired, people asked me to look back, and all that. And it wasn't until then that it came to me—'My God, I've been involved in the first quarter of a century of manned space flight!' " Another veteran notes that when his children come to visit and look through his memorabilia, they ask him why he doesn't have autographs of the astronauts and presidents and celebrities who came to watch him at work. "You were right there!" they say. But he was always so busy, he tells them, he just didn't pay attention. "We knew we were doing something, but nobody really felt the impact of what was really going on." The job was too consuming for that—"almost a crusade," said another veteran, nothing like any other job he ever had.

Some are unhappy that the rest of the country has never truly comprehended the historic nature of our first journey to another world. Many people think of Apollo as just another episode in the tumultuous sixties, secondary to the Vietnam War and America's social upheaval, not as something that will still figure large in the history books when Vietnam and John Kennedy and Lyndon Johnson are consigned to footnotes.

Source 27   Robert A. Divine, *The Sputnik Challenge*, 1993

As the Cold War passes from the realm of current events into history, Sputnik remains one of its most enduring landmarks. The Soviet launch of the world's first artificial satellite created a crisis in confidence for the American people. How could a backward Communist nation beat the United States into space? Many citizens reacted by questioning the validity of an entire way of life, expressing concern that Sputnik signalled the weakness of American science, the failure of American schools, and the complacency of American political leadership. Worst of all, they feared that the Soviet Union had gained a lead in developing long-range missiles, thereby threatening the very security of the United States in the nuclear age.

The panicky response to Sputnik had long-lasting effects on American life. It opened a debate over the state of education, science, space exploration, and national security that lasted well into the 1960s. The Sputnik furor contributed significantly to the election of John F. Kennedy in 1960, to the passage of massive federal aid-to-education measures under Lyndon Johnson, and to the decision to send American astronauts to the moon. In a sense, the anxiety raised by Sputnik did not end until Neil Armstrong and Buzz Aldrin took their historic steps in July 1969.

Dwight D. Eisenhower was one of the few Americans who was not impressed by the Russian feat. Contemporaries saw his calm reaction as proof of his complacency, if not senility, and condemned him for a lack of leadership. The passage of time has confirmed the wisdom of the president's response. He believed that American science and American education were much sounder than critics charged, and, above all, he was confident that the United States held a commanding lead over the Soviet Union in strategic striking power. His refusal to support hasty or extreme measures in the wake of Sputnik proved fully justified.

Yet Eisenhower, for all his prudence and restraint, failed to meet one of the crucial tests of presidential leadership: convincing the American people that all was well in the world. His inability to understand the profound uneasiness and sense of impending doom that gripped the American public as a result of

Sputnik was a political failure of the first order. He simply could not comprehend why the nation refused to accept his reassurances; he finally was forced to go against his deeply ingrained fiscal conservatism and approve defense expenditures he did not believe were really needed.

Source 28 George Lardner Jr., and Walter Pincus, "Military Had Plan to Blame Cuba if Glenn's Space Mission Failed," *Washington Post*, November 19, 1997

When John Glenn lifted off into space in a Mercury capsule on Feb. 20, 1962, military planners at the Pentagon were thinking of blaming Fidel Castro if the astronaut failed to come down again.

The proposal was called Operation Dirty Trick and, according to long-secret documents made public yesterday, the idea was "to provide irrevocable proof that, should the MERCURY manned orbit flight fail, the fault lies with Communists et al. Cuba."

That could be accomplished, the planners suggested in a Feb. 2, 1962, memo, "by manufacturing various pieces of evidence which would prove electronic interference on the part of the Cubans."

Glenn, of course, returned safely after becoming the first American to orbit Earth. But the memo, addressed to Air Force Brig. Gen. Edward G. Lansdale, head of Operation Mongoose, an elaborate scheme aimed at promoting revolt in Cuba, was full of other suggestions, some quite zany. There was, for instance, Operation Good Time, which would have fabricated a photograph of "an obese Castro with two beauties in any situation desired" near "a table brimming over with the most delectable Cuban food," accompanied by the caption, "My ration is different."

"This should put even a Commie dictator in the proper perspective with the underlying masses," the memo said.

The covert action proposals were among 1,500 pages of previously classified records made public yesterday by the Assassination Records Review Board, a small agency overseeing the release of records related to the 1963 assassination of President John F. Kennedy.

 ## Questioning the Past

1. What was the significance, if any, of the landing on the moon of an American spacecraft on July 20, 1969?

2. Did the moon landing represent "a giant leap for mankind"? Debate the point.

3. In its editorial of July 21, 1969, *The Times* of London wondered whether history would view the moon expedition as "a brilliantly lit blind alley." What was meant by this? Is this a valid description of the Apollo missions? Explain.

4. Who should control the moon and for what purposes? Should it be claimed as a whole by the United States as the first country to reach it? Should countries be able to stake claims to parts they explore? Should the moon be, as international law now proclaims it, the "common heritage of mankind"? Should the moon be exploited at

all? Should its mineral wealth be brought back for national or corporate gain? Should it be protected and preserved as it is, as an "international park"?

5. On February 3, 1994, the American space shuttle Discovery blasted off from Cape Canaveral with a crew that included Sergei Krikalev, a Russian cosmonaut. It was the first time that Americans and Russians were part of the same crew, and it marked the beginning of what was planned to be a new era of cooperative effort in space. The head of the Russian Space Agency, Yuri Koptev, said, "I'm very glad to say that the time we have been rivals in space . . . is over." Would space exploration have proceeded further and faster had America and Russia cooperated all along, or does competition rather than cooperation spur advancement?

6. "We choose to go to the moon in this decade and do other things [in space], not because they are easy, but because they are hard, because that goal will serve to organize and measure the best of our energies and skills." So spoke President Kennedy in Houston in 1962. Did Apollo 11 show that the American people, if challenged, could overcome all obstacles to achieve the difficult? If not, what did it show? If so, why do America's leaders not challenge the nation to undertake great national goals more often?

Chapter 27

Watergate

Five Burglars Are Arrested in Washington

June 17, 1972

At one o'clock in the morning on June 17, 1972, a security guard was in the midst of routine rounds in a Washington office building when he discovered a piece of tape on a door in the building's basement. This tape had been placed on the door to keep the latch from locking when the door was shut. But it held together more than that. When the guard pulled it off, the biggest political conspiracy in modern American history began to fall apart.

The guard was a young man named Frank Wills. The building was a part of the exclusive Watergate complex, the most expensive piece of privately owned real estate in the nation's capital. Wills was not troubled by the presence of the tape at the moment he removed it. He assumed he was all alone in the massive building and that the tape must have been placed there much earlier, during the building's business hours. Continuing his rounds, Wills found nothing else amiss. But a few minutes later, returning to the same door, he saw something startling. The tape was back.

Wills called for back-up. A short time later, five burglars were arrested in one of the offices on an upper floor of the building. Burglary arrests are not unusual in Washington. But there was something out of the ordinary about this one. The five were not arrested in some corporate office cracking open a safe. They were apprehended while photographing files and installing listening devices in the offices of the National Committee of the Democratic Party.

In the days that followed, another curious thing emerged regarding the burglars: they had interesting connections. Four of the five had ties to the Central Intelligence Agency and had been involved in the CIA's ill-fated invasion of Cuba at the Bay of Pigs. One, James McCord Jr., was chief of security for the Committee to Reelect the President. Another had listed in his address book the telephone number of E. Howard Hunt. Hunt was an aide to Charles Colson. Colson worked in the White House as special counsel to the president of the United States.

27.1 All Politics:
Watergate

🕶️ *First Impressions*

Double Dealing and Dirty Tricks

It took more than two years to reveal enough of the truth about Watergate to judge who had been responsible for the break-in. During this time, the president continued to assure the American people that he had played no role in the matter.

27.2
WashingtonPost.
com:Watergate

Source 1 Alfred E. Lewis, *Washington Post,* June 18, 1972

5 HELD IN PLOT TO BUG DEMOCRATS' OFFICE HERE

Five men, one of whom said he is a former employee of the Central Intelligence Agency, were arrested at 2:30 a.m. yesterday in what authorities described as an elaborate plot to bug the offices of the Democratic National Committee here.

Three of the men were native-born Cubans and another was said to have trained Cuban exiles for guerrilla activity after the 1961 Bay of Pigs invasion.

They were arrested at gunpoint by three plainclothes officers of the metropolitan police department in a sixth-floor office at the plush Watergate . . . where the Democratic National Committee occupies the entire floor.

There was no immediate explanation as to why the five suspects would want to bug the Democratic National Committee offices or whether or not they were working for any other individuals or organizations. . . .

All wearing rubber surgical gloves, the five suspects were captured inside a small office within the committee's headquarters suite.

Police said the men had with them at least two sophisticated devices capable of picking up and transmitting all talk, including telephone conversations. In addition, police found lock-picks and door jimmies, almost $2,300 in cash, most of it in $100 bills with the serial numbers in sequence.

The men also had with them one walkie-talkie, a short wave receiver that could pick up police calls, 40 rolls of unexposed film, two 35 millimeter cameras and three pen-sized tear gas guns. . . .

According to police and a desk clerk at the Watergate, four of the five suspects—all using fictitious names—rented two rooms, number 214 and 314 at the Watergate Hotel, around noon on Friday. They were said to have dined together on lobsters at the Watergate Restaurant on Friday night.

Yesterday afternoon, the U.S. Attorney's office obtained warrants to search the hotel rooms rented by the suspects. They found another $4,200 in $100 bills of the same serial number sequence as the money taken from the suspects, more burglary tools and electronic bugging equipment stashed in six suitcases.

Source 2 President Richard Nixon, press conference, June 22, 1972

Q. Mr. O'Brien [Democratic Party Chairman] has said that the people who bugged his headquarters had a direct link to the White House. Have you had any sort of investigation made to determine whether this is true?

A. Mr. Ziegler [presidential press secretary] and also Mr. Mitchell [Attorney General], speaking for the campaign committee, have responded to questions on this in great detail. They have stated my position and have also stated the facts accurately.

This kind of activity, as Mr. Ziegler has indicated, has no place whatever in our electoral process, or in our governmental process. And, as Mr. Ziegler has stated, the White House has had no involvement whatever in this particular incident.

Source 3 **President Richard Nixon's statement, May 22, 1973**

The burglary and bugging of the Democratic National Committee headquarters came as a complete surprise to me. I had no inkling that any such illegal activities had been planned by persons associated with my campaign; if I had known, I would not have permitted it. My immediate reaction was that those guilty should be brought to justice and, with the five burglars themselves already in custody, I assumed that they would be.

Within a few days, however, I was advised that there was a possibility of CIA involvement in some way.

It did seem to me possible that, because of the involvement of former CIA personnel, and because of some of their apparent associations, the investigation could lead to the uncovering of covert CIA operations totally unrelated to the Watergate break-in.

In addition, by this time, the name of Mr. Hunt had surfaced in connection with Watergate, and I was alerted to the fact that he had previously been a member of the special investigations unit in the White House. Therefore, I was also concerned that the Watergate investigation might well lead to an inquiry of the special investigations unit itself. . . .

I wanted justice done with regard to Watergate; but in the scale of national priorities with which I had to deal—and not at that time having any idea of the extent of political abuse which Watergate reflected—I also had to be deeply concerned with insuring that neither the covert operations of the CIA nor the special investigations unit should be compromised. Therefore, I instructed Mr. Haldeman and Mr. Ehrlichman to insure that the investigation of the break-in not expose either an unrelated covert operation of the CIA or the activities of the White House investigations unit. . . .

It now appears that later, through whatever complex of individual motives and possible misunderstandings, there were apparently wide-ranging efforts to limit the investigation or to conceal the possible involvement of members of the Administration and the campaign committee.

I was not aware of any such efforts at the time.

Source 4 **President Richard Nixon, "State of the Union Address,"**
January 30, 1974

Mr. Speaker and Mr. Vice President and my distinguished colleagues and our guests:

. . . I would like to add a personal word with regard to an issue that has been of great concern to all Americans over the past year. I refer, of course, to the investigations of the so-called Watergate affair.

As you know, I have provided to the special prosecutor voluntarily a great deal of material that he needs to conclude his investigations and to proceed to prosecute the guilty and to clear the innocent.

I believe the time has come to bring that investigation to an end. One year of Watergate is enough. . . .

Like every member of the House and Senate assembled here tonight, I was elected to the office that I hold. And like every member of the House and Senate, when I was elected to that office, I knew that I was elected for the purpose of doing a job and doing it as well as I possibly can. And I want you to know that I have no intention whatever of walking away from the job that the people elected me to do for the people of the United States.

"I Am Not a Crook"

In January of 1973, two months after President Nixon had won reelection by a landslide, the five burglars finally came to trial. All but McCord pleaded guilty and kept their silence about the break-in at the Watergate. McCord pleaded not guilty but was nevertheless convicted. Before sentence was pronounced, however, McCord wrote a letter to the judge in his case, John J. Sirica, on March 19, 1973. His letter made two points: high government officials had ordered the break-in, and the burglars had been paid to remain silent.

Owing to the tenacity of Judge Sirica, the persistence of a Senate Committee chaired by Senator Sam Ervin, and particularly the perseverance of two reporters for the *Washington Post,* aided by a mysterious contact known only by the code name "Deep Throat," the Watergate story slowly unfolded to reveal a broader conspiracy against the integrity of the American political process. The president's reelection committee had a department of "dirty tricks." Its mission was to destroy the reputations of political opponents of the president. The campaign staffs of opposition candidates were infiltrated by Republican partisans who stole copies of campaign plans, copied mail and mailing lists, sabotaged campaign events. Nixon's backers did such underhanded deeds as printing a letter on the stationery of Democratic presidential-hopeful Edmund Muskie accusing his fellow Democrats Senators Hubert Humphrey and Henry Jackson of sexual misconduct. The Republicans paid people to make late-night calls to the homes of white voters in New Hampshire, identifying themselves as members of the Harlem for Muskie Committee. They used Democratic Party stationery to cancel campaign events or to invite voters and engage entertainers to attend events that never happened. Such clandestine activities helped to winnow out the candidates who might oppose the president until Nixon could face the one he thought he could most readily defeat: George McGovern.

Beyond the efforts to manipulate the outcome of the election, Nixon was found to have created a special White House unit called the "Plumbers," whose task was to plug information leaks in the administration. This group engaged in numerous clandestine activities at White House behest that violated the Bill of Rights. Moreover, Nixon spent $10 million in public funds for improvements to his two homes, and he backdated a gift of his personal papers to the National Archives and took a $576,000 tax deduction. He defied Congress and the courts and tried to keep secret from the American people his ordering of American troops into Cambodia, a neutral country. His administration solicited large political donations from corporations and granted favors to them in return.

The Watergate break-in was but the tip of an iceberg. But it ripped open the Nixon administration and sank the president's chances to complete his second term. One by one, the associates of the president were implicated in acts of political subversion. The chairman of the Committee to Reelect the President admitted his involvement in the Watergate conspiracy and was arrested. John Ehrlichman, assistant to the president for Domestic Affairs, and H. R. Haldeman, White House chief of staff, were indicted and convicted. Attorney General John Mitchell and the secretary of Commerce were sent to prison. The vice president pleaded no contest to charges of tax evasion and receiving kick-backs from developers and resigned. But all of the president's advisers insisted that the president had played no role in either the break-in or the conspiracy to cover it up. And Nixon himself publicly maintained to the end that he had not been involved in an attempt to obstruct justice.

The president's supporters in Congress said they would believe the president capable of criminal activity only if they saw him standing over the body of a victim with a smoking gun in his hand. It appeared such proof would never be discovered, and, had it not been for a revelation made by a minor witness before the Senate Committee, Nixon probably would have finished out his term. The revelation involved tape-recording devices that the president had installed in his own office. After much drama and heated confrontation between the legislative and judicial branches of government on the one side and the executive branch on the other, the president finally agreed to release the tapes. One tape, which recorded conversations in the Oval Office only hours after the break-in, had a suspicious 18-minute gap, caused by erasure. Others were indeed incriminating, and one, recorded five days after the break-in, became known as the "Smoking Gun." It contradicted President Nixon's assertion on May 22, 1973, that "At no time did I attempt, nor did I authorize others to attempt, to implicate the CIA in the Watergate matter."

The storm of outrage over the Smoking Gun tape led a committee of the House of Representatives to adopt articles of impeachment against President Nixon, who resigned on August 9, 1974.

Source 5   The Smoking Gun tape, recorded at the White House, June 23, 1972

Haldeman: Now, on the investigation, you know the Democratic break-in thing, we're back in the problem area because the FBI is not under control, because [FBI Director] Gray doesn't exactly know how to control it . . . because they've been able to trace the money . . . through the bank sources—the banker. And, it goes in some directions we don't want it to go. Ah, also there have been some things—like an informant came in off the street in Miami who was a photographer or has a friend who is a photographer who developed some films through this guy [Watergate burglar Bernard] Barker and the films had pictures of Democratic National Committee letterhead documents and things. So it's things like that that are filtering in. Mitchell came up with yesterday, and John Dean analyzed very carefully last night and concludes, concurs now with Mitchell's recommendation that the only way to solve this, and we're set up beautifully to do it, oh, . . . the only network that paid any attention to it last night was NBC—they did a massive story on the Cuban thing.

President: That's right.

Haldeman: That the way to handle this now is for us to have [CIA Deputy Director Vernon] Waters call Pat Gray and just say, "Stay the hell out of this—this is ah, business here, we don't want you to go any further on it." That's not an unusual development, and ah, that would take care of it.

President: What about Pat Gray—you mean Pat Gray doesn't want to?

Haldeman: Pat does want to. He doesn't know how to, and he doesn't have . . . any basis for doing it. Given this, he will then have the basis. He'll call [FBI Deputy Associate Director] Mark Felt in, and the two of them—and Mark Felt wants to cooperate because he's ambitious.

President: Yeah.

Haldeman: He'll call him in and say, "We've got the signal from across the river [CIA headquarters on the Virginia side of the Potomac] to put the hold on this." And that will fit rather well because the FBI agents who are working on the case, at this point, feel that's what it is.

President: This is CIA? They've traced the money? Who'd they trace it to?

Haldeman: Well, they've traced it to a name, but they haven't gotten to the guy yet.

President: Would it be somebody here?

Haldeman: Ken Dahlberg.

President: Who the hell is Ken Dahlberg?

Haldeman: He gave $25,000 in Minnesota [to the Committee to Reelect the President], and ah, the check went directly to his guy, Barker.

President: It isn't from the committee, though, from [CRP Finance Chairman] Stans?

Haldeman: Yeah, it is. It's directly traceable and there's some more through some Texas people that went to the Mexican bank which can be traced to the Mexican bank—they'll get their names today. . . .

President: Well, I mean, there's no way—I'm just thinking if they don't cooperate, what do they say? That they were approached by the Cubans. That's what Dahlberg has to say, the Texans, too, that they . . .

Haldeman: Well, if they will. But then we're relying on more and more people all the time. That's the problem, and they'll stop if we could take this other route.

President: All right.

Haldeman: And you seem to think the thing to do is to get them [the FBI] to stop?

President: Right, fine.

Haldeman: They say the only way to do that is from White House instructions. And it's got to be to [CIA Director] Helms and to—ah, what's his name—Walters.

President: Walters.

Haldeman: And the proposal would be that Ehrlichman and I call them in, and say, ah . . .

President: All right, fine. How do you call him in—I mean you just—well, we protected Helms from one hell of a lot of things.

Haldeman: That's what Ehrlichman says.

President: Of course, this Hunt, that will uncover a lot of things. You open that scab, there's a hell of a lot of hanky-panky that we have nothing to do with ourselves. Well, what the hell, did Mitchell know about this?

Haldeman: I think so. I don't think he knew the details, but I think he knew.

President: He didn't know how it was going to be handled though—with Dahlberg and the Texans and so forth? Well, who was the asshole that did? Is it [CRP Finance Counsel G. Gordon] Liddy? Is that the fellow? He must be a little nuts!

Haldeman: He is.

President: I mean he just isn't well screwed on is he? Is that the problem?

Haldeman: No, but he was under pressure, apparently, to get more information, and as he got more pressure, he pushed the people harder to move harder.

President: Pressure from Mitchell?

Haldeman: Apparently. . . .

President: All right, fine, I understand it all. We won't second-guess Mitchell and the rest. Thank God it wasn't [Special Counsel to the President Charles] Colson.

Haldeman: The FBI interviewed Colson yesterday. . . . [T]he FBI guys working the case concluded that there were one or two possibilities—one, that this was a White House—they don't think that there is anything at the Election Committee—they think it was either a White House operation and they had some obscure reasons for it—non-political, or it was a Cuban and the CIA. And after their interrogation of Colson yesterday, they concluded it was not the White House, but are now convinced it is a CIA thing, so the CIA turnoff would . . .

President: Well, [if they're] not sure of their analysis, I'm not going to get that involved. . . .

Haldeman: No, sir, we don't want you to.

President: You call them in.

Haldeman: Good deal.

President: Play it tough. That's the way they play it and that's the way we're going to play it.

Haldeman: O.K. . . .

President: When you get in—when you get in (unintelligible) people, say, "Look, the problem is that this will open the whole Bay of Pigs thing, and the President just feels that ah, without going into the details—don't, don't lie to them to the extent to say there is no involvement, but just say this is a comedy of errors, without getting into it, the President believes that it is going to open the whole Bay of Pigs thing up again. And, ah, because these people are plugging for (unintelligible) and that they should call the FBI in and (unintelligible) don't go any further into this case period!

Second Thoughts
A Fascinating and Enigmatic Episode

27.3 Illusion
and Delusion:
The Watergate
Decade

The most succinct explanation for Watergate was offered by Senator Sam Ervin: "Richard M. Nixon was narrowly defeated for the presidency by John Kennedy in 1960, and narrowly won the presidency over Hubert H. Humphrey in 1968. The motivation for Watergate had its origins in these events. President Nixon and his aides who participated in the planning of his reelection campaign were determined that the presidential election of 1972 should not be a cliff-hanger." The meaning of Watergate, however, is not so easily explained, as the sources that follow indicate.

Source 6   Henry Steele Commager, *The Defeat of America: Presidential Power and the National Character,* 1974

It was the Cold War, the transfer of that war from the foreign to the domestic arena and then the war in Laos, Vietnam and Cambodia that led inexorably to the follies, illegalities and immoralities of the Nixon Administration. What was new in all this was not so much the trickery and duplicity. What was new was the overt attack on the Constitution and the Bill of Rights, the unashamed subversion of those political processes which Americans had developed to enable the constitutional provisions to work. What was new was the usurpation of a war power constitutionally assigned to the Congress, and the full-throated attack upon the principle of the separation of powers; the contemptuous resort to secrecy to prevent either the Congress or the people from exercising their constitutional right and obligation to participate in the making of political decisions. What was new was the presumptuous claim that the President was above the law.

It is in all likelihood this feature of the constitutional crisis that future historians will regard as the most threatening and the most significant. For had Mr. Nixon succeeded in his pretensions and his ambitions, the character of the American Presidency would have been decisively and irrevocably altered, and with it the character of the American constitutional system. Such a shift in the center of political and constitutional gravity would have logically led to totalitarianism, for the power to commit a nation to war (something the other branches cannot do by themselves) is in its very nature arbitrary and autocratic. Mr. Nixon and his sycophantic camp followers have tried desperately to give the impression that Watergate, and all that it symbolized of the aggrandizement of political power, was really much ado about nothing: an unfortunate administrative blunder, an error of judgment, something regrettable but without any deep significance. This is, of course, merely another . . . example of that duplicity which has characterized Mr. Nixon throughout his public career. Watergate—if we include in that symbolic term not only domestic crimes but crimes in the conduct of foreign relations—was the major crisis of the Constitution since Appomattox. . . .

[B]ut the Constitution survived. . . . [O]nce again, . . . the Constitution and the political processes that it nourished proved themselves tough and enduring. Without disorder, confusion or even bitterness, we have quietly forced Mr. Nixon out of office and quietly installed Mr. Ford. This is a revolution. In most countries of the globe it would be a violent revolution, but in the United States it is peaceful and legal. It is indeed constitutional revolution, for just as the Founding Fathers invented the constitutional convention as a legal method of altering or abolishing government and instituting a new one, they and their successors also devised the complex process of impeachment, resignation, and succession as a constitutional method of removing a head of state and installing his successor.

Thus at every stage of Watergate and the "Grand Inquest" that followed, we have a vindication of the Constitution and of the political habits that have grown up under it. . . .

Some questions that should have been settled remain, to be sure, unsettled: the question of presidential war-making, for example, or the reach of presidential privileges and immunities, or of the balance (if any) between the claims of national security and the guarantees of the Bill of Rights. It is by no means clear, however, that impeachment would have settled these questions; but it is highly probable that for all practical purposes they have been answered by public opinion. It is wildly improbable that President Ford or his successors in the foreseeable future will wage war on a neutral country, impound congressional appropriations, interfere with the processes of justice, openly flout the guarantees of freedom of speech and of the press or seek to establish a police state—all of which Mr. Nixon did. . . .

The expulsion of Richard Nixon and the repudiation of his impudent claims to privilege, prerogatives and power will have a restorative effect on the whole body politic. It will go far to reestablish that equality and balance of the three departments of government so central to the thinking of the Founding Fathers.

Source 7   Russell Baker, "It Didn't Work," *New York Times,* August 14, 1974

So many people have announced that "the system worked" in the recent Presidential affair that we are in danger of believing it.

Survivors' euphoria probably accounts for the rosy judgments, but when the giddiness has subsided it will probably be seen that the system, in fact, failed almost completely from beginning to end. If things have ended happily, . . . we can thank fate for a felicitous whim, for the system constantly nudged us toward increasingly grotesque outcomes from which we were saved by sheerest luck.

Even with the luck, the outcome produced by the system is a political absurdity in a nation boastful of its democracy. What do we have as the logical, legal product of the system's working? A President who has never run for national office and who, when his party last worried about going to the people, was not even considered a useful candidate for the dim office of Vice President.

The system left the choosing of this new President to his predecessor, a man driven from office by bipartisan suspicion of felonious conduct, a man whose previous selection at the Vice President shop had earlier been driven from office for taking cash under the desk and cheating on his income tax. . . .

The system's failures do not begin and end with the exotic transition. If they did, solution would be easy. We could provide for interim national elections on occasions such as this and give democratic legitimacy to governments like Mr. Ford's.

But the system doesn't work much better in elections either. It creaked dismally in 1972. The system made it possible for the White House to manipulate the democratic choice of Presidential candidate, and then, thanks to the system's way of conducting elections, gave us a stacked-deck choice between Mr. Nixon and the man he most wanted to run against.

The system's informational machinery failed to communicate any idea of Nixon the man. How else explain the fact that after a quarter-century of full exposure to the American public, he was the nation's overwhelming favorite in 1972, yet had a popular majority willing to see him impeached less than two years later? Something somewhere didn't get itself communicated.

Courts and Congress worked beautifully, we are told. This is arguable, too. What really worked beautifully were the White House tape recorders.

No one believes that without the tapes Congress or courts would have had any systemic machinery for defenestrating the President and the tapes were most definitely not a part of the system. Everything about them was pure luck.

Under the system we have been cheated in a Presidential election, submitted to nearly two years of government by men of criminal proclivity, and encouraged to feel delighted with the prospect of government by men we have not elected.

If your car worked as well as the system, you would have had it in the shop ages ago, if not on the used car lot.

Source 8   John A. Garraty, *The American Nation*, 1975

The meaning of "Watergate" became immediately the subject of much speculation and shall no doubt so remain for many years. Whether Nixon's crude efforts to dominate Congress, crush or inhibit dissent, and subvert the electoral process would have permanently altered the American political system if they had succeeded is probably unanswerable, although the orderly way in which these efforts were checked suggests that the system would have survived in any case. Whether the long trend toward ever-increasing presidential authority was eroded and reversed by Nixon's disgrace, the future will reveal.

Nixon's own drama is and must remain one of the most fascinating and enigmatic episodes in our history, but despite his fall from the heights because of personal flaws, his was not a tragedy in the Greek sense. Even when he finally yielded power he seemed without either remorse or real awareness of his transgressions. Although he enjoyed the pomp and circumstance attendant upon his high office and trumpeted his achievements to all the world, he was also devoid of the classic hero's pride. Did he really intend to smash all opposition and rule like a tyrant, or was he driven by a lack of confidence in himself? His stubborn aggressiveness and his overblown view of executive privilege may have reflected a need for constant reassurance that he was a mighty leader, that the nation accepted his right to exercise authority. One element in his downfall, preserved for posterity in videotapes of his television appearances, was that he did not look like the victim of the machinations of over-zealous supporters even when he was assuring the country of his innocence most vehemently. Perhaps at some profound level he did not want to be believed. And why, the immorality of his clandestine tapes aside, did he allow them to run on while he discussed the embarrassments attending Watergate with his closest advisors?

Source 9   Michael Parenti, *Democracy for the Few,* 1980

Not long after Nixon retired with his presidential pardon and a yearly $55,000 pension, many opinion makers were announcing with satisfaction that the "system worked." Apparently they believed the tapes would be there again next time. But how did the system work? It was not only Nixon and his aides who attempted to limit the Watergate crisis to save their necks; Congress and even the press, which is credited with exposing the scandal, played a part in downplaying Watergate, first by not making any investigation for half a year after the break-in, then by emphasizing Nixon's personal role and defining the events in narrow ways. The press and Congress focused on Nixon's failure to pay his income taxes, his personal corruption in appropriating funds for his estate; his use of illegal campaign funds and his attempt at cover-up. Little attention was given to the president's repeated violations of the Constitution, his unlawful and genocidal bombing of Cambodia, his role in the assassination of foreign leaders, his unlawful campaign to destroy radical groups, his use of political sabotage and denial of civil rights to leftists and others, and the unlawful cover-up role played by the entire intelligence community, including the FBI and CIA.

In addition, Congress and the press used Watergate to legitimate the system by treating it as a unique and unprecedented instance of government lawlessness. In fact, for more than half a century the same illegal and clandestine tactics have been and continue to be employed against political heretics. What shocked the establishment politicians was that in this instance the crimes were committed against a segment of the establishment itself—specifically, the Democratic party and mass-media newsmen.

Source 10   Stanley I. Kutler, *The Wars of Watergate,* 1990

Watergate became a permanent part of American political language after 1972. . . . It also elevated moral considerations in the judgment of public officers and in the conduct of public business. Whether involving limitations on campaign funds, ethical standards for elected and appointed officials, governmental intervention in the private sphere, or the conduct of foreign policy, a national consciousness of the need of checks on powerholders was sparked by Watergate. That concern has remained vital in the years since, prompting and rationalizing both legislation and criticism that reflected some standards for the proper conduct of political leaders and governmental officials. However excessive, faulty, or even misguided the character of the responses to Watergate, they reflected an understanding that public officials must themselves adhere to the same rule of law they so piously demand that the governed obey. Richard Nixon's most ardent and passionate defenders, those who most readily assail his persecutors, must either agree, or defend the alien proposition that a president is above the law.

Source 11   Robert Dallek, *The Great Republic,* 1992

Never conscionable about his political practices, as demonstrated by his vicious attacks on Alger Hiss and Helen Gahagan Douglas (his opponent in the 1950 Senate race), and by his behavior during the Eisenhower years, Nixon had an affinity for dirty tricks and a disregard for the law that put his actions in the Watergate affair in line with much that he had done before. . . .

Nixon's political demise, although he never acknowledged it, was self-inflicted. Greedy for an unprecedented mandate, or at least one large enough to allow him close to a free hand in dealing with domestic and foreign affairs during a second term, Nixon overreached himself. Having succeeded repeatedly in past campaigns with the sort of underhanded tactics used in 1972, he was blind to the possibility that he might be brought down for his actions. His failure to destroy the tapes when they became public knowledge is a good case in point: he believed that the prestige and might of the presidency would insulate him from an effective congressional or judicial investigation of his misdeeds. . . .

The Watergate scandal and its outcome greatly undermined the prestige of the "imperial presidency," and it meant a considerable—although temporary—resurgence of congressional power. . . . Congress, however, was to prove generally ineffectual in exercising its revived authority. Despite the blow to the presidency inflicted by Nixon's resignation, more than forty years of expansive executive authority coupled with a reliance on presidents to ensure the national security in a dangerous world made it impossible for the legislative and judicial branches of government substantially to rein in the White House.

Questioning the Past

1. What crimes, if any, did Nixon commit? Had he not resigned, should he have been impeached? Why or why not?

2. Did the system perform well or poorly in the events surrounding the Watergate affair? Argue both sides of the question.

3. While the burglars and many of those under Nixon in the White House chain of command were sentenced to prison terms, Nixon was given a full pardon by Gerald Ford, the man Nixon had personally nominated to replace him. On September 8, 1974, President Ford granted "a full, free, and absolute pardon unto Richard Nixon for all offenses against the United States which he, Richard Nixon, has committed, or may have committed, or taken part in" during his presidency. Ford said he believed that Nixon had suffered enough and that he wished to spare the nation and Nixon the agonies and the spectacle of a prolonged judicial proceeding. He hoped his pardon of Nixon would allow the nation to put an end to the Watergate controversy and move forward on other matters. Present arguments in support of such a pardon. Present arguments against it. Which arguments are the more compelling?

4. In what ways, if any, does the Smoking Gun tape incriminate the president? Does it indicate that he had any foreknowledge of the Watergate break-in? Does it indicate his involvement in a plot to obstruct justice?

5. In a television interview with David Frost on May 19, 1977, Richard Nixon stated: "When the president does it, that means it is not illegal." Argue this point.

Chapter 28

The Exxon Valdez

An Oil Tanker Runs Aground   *March 24, 1989*

Oil made the twentieth century unlike any era that preceded it. Petroleum products powered and lubricated machinery that became essential to the way of life of most of the six billion people who inhabited the planet by century's end. But oil is finite and the demand for it seemingly infinite. This led, and continues to lead, to an almost frantic drive to find new sources of petroleum.

In 1968, the Atlantic Richfield Company discovered a large field of oil under the North Slope of Alaska. The retrieval of this oil, however, posed a problem. How could oil be transported from well inside the Arctic Circle to refineries in the lower 48 states? Where was there to be found a port that was ice free so far north, or a channel through the Arctic Ocean free of icebergs?

The Atlantic Richfield Company proposed an ambitious solution to the problem: an oil pipeline to cross the entire state of Alaska from north to south and terminate at an ice-free port on Prince William Sound, east of Anchorage. The petroleum industry backed the proposal. Environmentalists opposed it.

Defenders of the environment raised concerns about the effects of spills on the delicate terrain of the Alaskan wilderness, the impact of the pipeline and its construction on animal life, and the implications of the oil boom for the indigenous peoples of the north. Challenges to the project were filed in state and federal courts. In April 1973, the United States Supreme Court upheld a lower court decision forbidding the Interior Department to issue permits for construction of the pipeline until the environmental issues could be addressed.

But the need for oil was pressing and President Richard Nixon pushed for the issuance of the construction permits "without any further delay." The president cited the growing dependence of the nation upon foreign sources of oil and the troubling outflow of capital from the United States that was the result of importing from abroad items of greater value than were being exported. The two million barrels of oil per day which could come from the North Slope would alleviate both problems.

Many in Congress shared the president's views, and a motion was introduced by Alaska's two senators to declare that all requirements of the National Environmental Protection Act had been satisfied and that no more challenges from environmentalists could be brought to the courts. On July 17, 1973, this motion was adopted by the United States Senate on a vote of 49 to 48, with three senators not voting. A motion to reconsider—a parliamentary tactic by the majority to seal its victory— was immediately introduced by the sponsors of the legislation. As the vote was being taken, however, Senator Cranston of California, one of the senators not present for the first vote, entered the Senate Chamber and cast his vote with the opponents, producing a 49 to 49 tie. Under the rules of the Senate, the vice president of the United States may vote to make or break a tie. Spiro T. Agnew did not hesitate in casting the deciding vote in favor of the motion to bar further legal challenges to the Alaska pipeline project.

The House of Representatives subsequently approved the motion as well, and the decision of the Arab states to impose an embargo on foreign oil supplies to the United States in October 1973, assured that the bill would become law.

A consortium of oil companies created the Alyeska Pipeline Service Company and announced that oil would be flowing through the pipeline to awaiting tanker ships at the port of Valdez, Alaska, by 1977.

✤ *First Impressions*

A Pipeline Is Built

28.1 Trans-Alaska Pipeline System

Twenty-one thousand laborers spent the next four years building the Trans-Alaska Pipeline. Working under difficult conditions, surviving two unusually bitter winters, overcoming an endless series of engineering obstacles, the laborers pressed on. They elevated the forty-eight-inch diameter pipeline above ground in long stretches to prevent the warm oil it would carry from thawing the permanently frozen subsoil of the far north. They ran their pipeline up and over the Endicott Mountains at an altitude of 2,800 feet above sea level. They crossed the Alaska Range at 3,300 feet and the glacier-covered Chugach Mountains. They went over or under more than 120 rivers. The pipeline they built traversed 800 miles of Alaska, much of which had not previously known human construction. The terminus for the pipeline was at Valdez, where rows of green holding tanks and a lattice of gray pipes were to contain the oil pending its transfer to ocean-going vessels. The Trans-Alaska Pipeline was the largest private peacetime construction project ever attempted. It cost $9.2 billion.

On June 20, 1977, a valve was opened at the origin of the pipeline at Prudhoe Bay to send the first oil toward Valdez. On July 8, there was an explosion at Pumping Station Number 8, southeast of Fairbanks. One worker was killed, five injured, and several thousand gallons of oil escaped into the Alaskan countryside. But the damage was quickly contained, repairs made, and oil resumed its southward flow. On July 28, 1977, the oil reached Valdez and has continued to flow ever since.

Environmentalists remained skeptical of the venture, but the Alyeska Pipeline Supply Company assured the public that elaborate precautions would be taken to keep the Trans-Alaska Pipeline safe and secure and that the company would respond immediately and decisively in the unlikely event that some catastrophe should occur.

Source 1   Edward Wenk, *Tradeoffs: Imperatives of Choice in a High-Tech World,* 1986

In contemporary society, the most powerful engines of change are human invention, innovation, and applications of scientific knowledge. Collectively, we call these functions "technology."

Technology has always been a source of cultural transformation. The artifacts left by our predecessors have become treasures of insight as to how people coped with their strenuous, hostile, and capricious natural environment. Indeed, we define these cultures by their tools and their material achievements. Technology was the springboard for change, from hunting and gathering to agriculture, from use of fire and the arrow to the intercontinental, nuclear-tipped missile. Once, the wheel was high-tech. Interactions between culture and technology are so powerful that we are spontaneously but wrongly inclined to equate technology with civilization. . . .

We began to glorify technology over a century ago, with its cascade of inventions: the steam engine, electric lights, farm machinery, the sewing machine, even running water. Then came the automobile, the telephone, radio, television, jet aircraft, modern medicine, and nuclear energy. Along with these inventions came a manufacturing and marketing infrastructure, soft technology to foster penetration into all of society.

In World War II, technology became the great equalizer, helping purchase victory with a minimum loss of life by superiority in industrial production and sophisticated weapons. The heyday of science as an endless frontier was further excited by the 1957 Soviet space surprise. We entered the competition with gusto. We adopted technology as our chosen vehicle to global superiority in the race for people's minds, as well as to domestic progress.

Today we are hooked on technology. It underpins every aspect of life: national security; the energy supply; industrial productivity; food production; health care delivery; urban habitation and infrastructure; education, entertainment, and telecommunications. We refer to ourselves as the information society, a condition made feasible only by new advances in computer virtuosity.

Yet, we are not comfortable with all the changes wrought by technology. Every technology introduced for its intended benefits carries inadvertent side effects, direct and indirect. The direct by-products may be benign, or they may be harmful; or they may be both, but to different people. They are all the more bewildering because they are usually hidden, and may hibernate only to burst on the scene unexpectedly, endangering life, health, property, or the environment. Pesticides to improve agricultural productivity are poisonous; nuclear power plants generate both power and dangerous waste; swift jet aircraft create objectionable aircraft noise; computers invade privacy. The list of side effects is endless, literally endless, because *every* technology plays Jekyll and Hyde. To these chronic disabilities must be added the risk of catastrophic accident involving hazardous materials in routine transit, chemical plant leakage, or nuclear plant meltdown.

A Catastrophic Occurrence

Between July of 1977 and the end of March of 1989, more than 286 billion gallons of oil passed through the Trans-Alaska Pipeline. Eight thousand-eight tanker loads of oil left the Port of Valdez. The process of moving the petroleum from the North Slope had become routine.

The Alyeska Pipeline Supply Company maintained a 250-page contingency plan to chart its response to any spilling of oil that might occur in the delicate waters of Prince William Sound, the waterway that lay between the Port of Valdez and the open sea. Moreover, Alyeska initially established an emergency response team that was ready twenty-four hours a day to rush to any disaster and take appropriate corrective action. The team was equipped with a barge loaded with 7,000 feet of containment boom designed to surround and control an oil spill. It had enough chemical dispersant at Valdez to clean up a spill of up to 6,500 barrels.

These preparations were considered by Alyeska to be far more than adequate. In fact, so confident was the company that in 1981 it disbanded its round-the-clock response team as a cost saving measure.

In early March 1989, the boom-deployment barge was damaged by a storm. Its containment booms were unloaded from the vessel and stored temporarily on a dock. Meanwhile, a replacement barge was ordered from a firm in Texas. This replacement barge was larger and better equipped than its damaged predecessor but had to be moved from Texas to Valdez by way of the Panama Canal. By March 23, the barge had progressed as far as Seattle, 1,200 miles from Valdez.

At 9:30 P.M., on March 23, 1989, the *Exxon Valdez,* one of the largest tankers ever built, sailed from the port of Valdez with a load of 1.26 million barrels of oil (a barrel contains 42 gallons). As the *Exxon Valdez* left port, its captain, Joseph Hazelwood, was on deck and in command. At 11:30 P.M., the ship requested permission from the Coast Guard tracking station to alter its course to avoid chunks of ice floating in the outbound channel of Prince William Sound. Permission was granted and the *Exxon Valdez* changed course, crossing the inbound shipping lanes. The shipping channel in Prince William Sound is wide and anywhere from 900 to 100 feet deep. But just beyond the shipping lanes is Bligh Reef, that can be as little as 13 feet below the surface of the Sound. The course change taken by the *Exxon Valdez* sent the vessel toward Bligh Reef.

Source 2   Maura Dolan and Ronald Taylor, "Alaska Oil Spill May Be Largest in U.S. Waters," *Los Angeles Times,* March 25, 1989

A Long Beach-bound Exxon oil tanker ran aground on a reef Friday and spilled up to 12 million gallons of crude oil into Alaska's Prince William Sound, a pristine Pacific waterway rich in wildlife, fisheries and tourist attractions. It was shaping up as the nation's largest spill ever.

The *Exxon Valdez,* a 987-foot tanker owned by Exxon Shipping Co., rammed the Bligh Reef about 25 miles from the city of Valdez, the northernmost ice-free port in the United States at 12:30 A.M.

Exxon spokesman Tom Cirigliano acknowledged that the "ship (was) not where it would normally have been. . . . He (the captain) was trying to avoid the ice" from the nearby Columbia Glacier. The captain "had received permission to maneuver around some ice. We're still trying to assess why it ended up where it did."

Cirigliano said Exxon's spill estimates ranged from 170,000 to 300,000 barrels worth—a barrel holds 42 gallons—from a ship that carried 1.3 million barrels of crude. The Coast Guard was estimating that more than a quarter-million barrels had spilled into the sound.

A representative of the U.S. Fish and Wildlife Service said the tanker had been spilling at a rate of 10,000 barrels an hour, but the Coast Guard said the leak had become a mere trickle by 2:30 P.M. Alaska time.

"This is the largest oil spill in U.S. history, and it unfortunately took place in an enclosed water body with numerous islands, channels, bays and fiords," Richard Golob, publisher of the *Golob Oil Pollution Bulletin,* told the Associated Press. . . .

"We've had no report of any wildlife hurt at this time," U.S. Coast Guard Petty Officer John Gonzales said. But environmentalists feared that if the oil reached the shore, marine birds would be threatened. Herring hatch at this time of year and attract up to 20,000 sea birds for the feast. Environmentalists also expressed concern about whales, sea lions and other wildlife.

Twenty people were aboard the ship but there were no immediate reports of injuries, said Dave Parish, a spokesman for Exxon USA, in a telephone interview from Anchorage. He said three planes from British Columbia, California and England had been dispatched to the scene for aerial spraying to dilute the oil.

Another Exxon tanker was attempting to pump the oil out of the crippled vessel, and two Coast Guard investigators were on board the *Exxon Valdez,* he said.

Aerial spraying of oil dispersants was to begin by first light today, Cirigliano said, and containment booms and skimming devices would also be used.

Jon Nelson, a deputy regional director of the U.S. Fish and Wildlife Service in Anchorage, said the reef ripped a 150-foot gash in the vessel, and there was a fear that the tanker could break apart further.

"If it breaks up on the rocks, then anything could happen," he said in a telephone interview. The seas were calm Friday, and the forecast was for continued calm until Sunday.

Infuriated local residents and environmentalists complained about the slow pace of the cleanup.

"Where was the crackerjack response team that was supposed to be out there? They are moving way too slowly," said University of Alaska professor Richard Steiner, who flew over the slick Friday. "There (was) no oil (cleanup equipment) out there, and it's been 14 hours since it happened.

"It is huge, literally huge," he said in a telephone interview from Cordova. "It looks devastating. The slick is probably five miles long by three miles wide. Fortunately, there is no wind. . . . We saw six sea lions inside the slick, swimming, trying to avoid it, and they had no idea which way to go."

Cindy Lowry, Alaska regional director for Greenpeace, also complained about the pace of the cleanup. "It is more than 12 hours later and there is no (cleanup) boom, no sweepers. They are bringing equipment from as far away as England. It is just absurd that the equipment is not here already. . . . This will affect everything in the food chain, from crab larvae to orca whales."

At a late-night town-hall style meeting with worried Valdez residents, Exxon officials "assured everyone we will. . . . assume full responsibility for the cleanup and any impact mitigation."

Exxon's Parish said everything possible was being done. "It takes time to get activated," he said. The immediate response to the spill was handled by crews from the terminal at Valdez.

Gonzales, the Coast Guard spokesman, said the terminal has cleanup equipment on site for minor spills. He said employees of the Alyeska Pipeline Service Co., which operates the Alaska pipeline for a consortium of oil companies, were getting floating oil booms in place by late afternoon.

Prince William Sound, home to orcas, sea otters, and fur seals, is important to both the fishing and recreation industries.

"It's a gorgeous marine environment and ecosystem, with lots of little islands and inlets and bays," said Emily Barneet, Alaska issues specialist for the Sierra Club in Anchorage. "It's also a pretty well-established tourist attraction, with sailing and glacier viewing trips. Prince William is a gem."

The spill is expected to add fuel to a campaign by environmentalists to prevent further oil development in Alaska, particularly in the Arctic National Wildlife Refuge. "It's of concern for two reasons: one is the size of the spill and that this is such a sensitive, very productive area," said Lisa Speer, senior staff scientist with the Natural Resources Defense Council in New York. "This is a consequence of North Slope oil development that is rarely mentioned."

Valdez City Manager Doug Griffen told the Associated Press that the 800-mile trans-Alaska pipeline, which carries oil from Prudhoe Bay to Valdez and the marine terminal, has a good environmental record.

"But this could be a catastrophic occurrence, so we're concerned," he said. "Living in Valdez, we've always worried that sometime something like this could happen."

Source 3   Tamara Jones and Michael Parrish, "Oil Spill Cleanup Effort in Alaska Drawing Fire," *Los Angeles Times,* March 26, 1989

28.2 The *Exxon Valdez* Oil Spill Restoration Site

Valdez, Alaska—Sluggish cleanup efforts came under fire Saturday as killer whales and sea lions swam in the purplish muck of the worst oil spill in U.S. history, which threatened the rich resources of Prince William Sound.

Initial investigations pointed toward human error as the most likely cause of the grounding of the Long Beach-bound tanker *Exxon Valdez,* and authorities tested crew members for alcohol and drug use. Results of these tests were not released.

Plying the pristine waters of the sound under ideal conditions at 12:30 A.M. Friday, the 2-year-old tanker, owned by Exxon Shipping Co., rammed the clearly charted Bligh Reef and hemorrhaged about 11 million gallons—or 240,000 barrels—of Alaska crude into the environmentally sensitive area. . . .

Another 1 million barrels of oil remained aboard the grounded, 987-foot vessel Saturday and tentative attempts to transfer the cargo were halted for fear of unleashing a new spill.

By late Saturday, attempts to corral the main slick with booms appeared minuscule and a handful of skimmers made little progress in vacuuming the oil from the sea's surface. The Coast Guard said the slick spread out 50 square miles and of that an area of 10 to 12 square miles was almost completely covered with oil.

Divers discovered six to eight gouges "big enough for a human being to swim through" in eight of the tanker's 13 cargo tanks, said Frank Iarossi, president of Exxon Shipping Co.

Experts from as far away as Europe converged on the tiny pipeline village to offer advice, while Valdez residents complained that their offers of help were rebuffed.

As many as 14 hours after the ship ran aground, "there wasn't even a Kleenex in the water" to sop up the oil, said Doug Fleming, a 23-year-old Valdez fisherman.

Source 4   Richard Mauer, "Unlicensed Mate Was in Charge of Ship
That Hit Reef, Exxon Says," *New York Times,* March 27, 1989

Valdez, Alaska, March 26—An uncertified officer was in command when the *Exxon Valdez* hit an undersea reef and began spilling 250,000 barrels of oil into Prince William Sound, a company official said today.

The official, Frank Iorossi, president of the Exxon Shipping Company, disclosed that the *Valdez* struck a first reef and sustained serious damage to her starboard tanks and hull about two miles before coming aground on a second rocky reef.

Mr. Iorossi said he did not know why Capt. Joseph Hazelwood of Huntington, L.I., had left the bridge shortly after midnight Friday morning, just before the crash, or why the third mate, Gregory Cousins' of Tampa, Fla., was left in command.

Mr. Cousins was not licensed by the Coast Guard to pilot a tanker through Prince William Sound, so his being in command violated both Federal regulations and company policy, Mr. Iorossi said.

The 987-foot tanker strayed from the normal shipping channels under Mr. Cousins command and into an area of charted treacherous reefs.

The first strike was noted in the ship's log, Mr. Iorossi said. But he did not know whether Captain Hazelwood had returned to the bridge between the first and second strikes or whether the first collision was immediately reported to the Coast Guard by radio. He said the ship's speed was about eight nautical miles an hour, meaning there would have been about 15 minutes between the two impacts. . . .

While Mr. Cousins has a Coast Guard certificate to command the ship on most waters, he does not have a special certificate that is required for Prince William Sound. The island-dotted Sound supports a $90 million fishery, is a habitat for a wealth of marine mammals and sea birds and supports a growing tourist and charter boat industry.

Source 5   Timothy Egan, "High Winds Hamper Oil Spill Cleanup off
Alaska," *New York Times,* March 28, 1989

Valdez, Alaska, March 27—The cumbrous attempt to clean up the biggest oil spill from a tanker in North American waters, already slowed for three days by organizational snafus and lack of proper equipment, was further hampered today by winds in excess of 70 miles an hour. . . .

Fingers of oil spill spread today into inlets and smaller coves in this part of Alaska, where glacial mountains meet the sea. Dead birds, frozen after their plumage became fouled with oil, have washed up on several beaches that dot the sound.

Nearly 900,000 barrels of oil remain in the tanker. Mr. Iorossi said it would take three to four days for all the oil to be pumped into a companion ship. Pumping is being done at a rate of 3,600 barrels an hour. A barrel is 42 gallons.

The high winds moved the grounded *Exxon Valdez* 12 degrees overnight, and there was the possibility it could break up and release the rest of its cargo into the sound.

The wind also blew the oil slick onto several beaches today and ripped apart booms that were supposed to contain some of the spill. The wind was so fierce that it tore off a roof on the Valdez Airport and nearly blew away several grounded Exxon helicopters.

Source 6   James Bone, "Environmentalists Launch Attack," *The Times* of London, March 29, 1989

Environmentalists went on the offensive yesterday as Exxon, owner of the supertanker that ran aground off Alaska, conceded that its attempt to clean up the worst oil spill in American history had run into difficulty.

High winds halted clean-up efforts on Monday and blew the oil ashore on several islands in the wildlife-rich Prince William Sound, where the *Exxon Valdez* went aground on Friday, spilling 10.1 million gallons of crude.

"What happened was our worst fears and that was that very high winds gusting up to 73 mph essentially stampeded that slick out of the centre of the sound," said Mr. Frank Iorossi president of Exxon Shipping Company.

Yesterday, it emerged that the captain of the wrecked tanker had a history of drinking, including two convictions for drink-driving offences in the last five years. Captain Joseph Hazelwood had left the ship in command of a third mate unqualified to pilot the treacherous sound and was in his cabin at the time of the accident. Captain Hazelwood, the third mate and the helmsman have all given blood samples for alcohol testing.

The bad weather prevented aerial spraying of chemical dispersants to break up the slick, and scuppered plans to burn off some of the oil on the surface. The winds, which whipped up eight-foot waves, shifted the grounded super-tanker through 12 degrees, raising fears that it could break up and release the millions of gallons of oil still on board.

The storm also blew away the containment boom placed around the vessel.

Environmentalist groups seized on the disaster to support their campaign against further oil development in the Arctic.

Source 7   Timothy Egan, "Fishermen and State Take Charge of Efforts to Control Alaska Spill," *New York Times*, March 29, 1989

Valdez, Alaska, March 28—Frustrated fishermen and Alaska state officials today took charge of the attempt to stop the spread of a fast-moving oil slick in Prince William Sound, choosing to defend some of the hundreds of islands that dot one of North America's prime salmon nurseries.

In the five days since the 978-foot *Exxon Valdez* ran aground on a shallow reef 25 miles southwest of here, its owner, the Exxon Shipping Company, has been able to scoop up less than 4,000 of the 240,000 barrels that spilled and now admits it has lost its best chance to contain the spill.

Denny Kelso, Alaska's Environmental Conservation Commissioner, said: "Frankly, we are past the opportunity to recover much oil. We have a spill that's on the move and we're looking at defensive measures to save what we can.". . . .

Two days of good weather have been followed by two days of high winds, and the company, which is charged by law with cleaning up oil spills it has caused, abandoned efforts today to use a chemical cleaning agent on the oil. On Monday, high winds blew away booms the company had placed around part of the slick and pushed its frothy edges, likened to chocolate mousse, into further reaches of the sound.

"It's unbelievable—that slick is moving like it's on a superhighway," said Frank Iorossi, president of Exxon Shipping.

As the wind slackened somewhat today, fishermen, who had been waiting on the sidelines while Exxon tried to clean up the slick, moved boats and booms to several islands about 50 miles southwest of the accident site, trying to save three crucial salmon hatcheries. The oil is approaching those islands at the same time that several hundred million young salmon are being released into the sound to begin their adult cycle at sea. . . .

Beaches of wilderness islands to the southwest, a favorite destination of kayakers and sightseers, were covered with the froth of crude oil today, and the air was fouled by the odor. . . .

The fishermen are trying to protect the hatcheries' entrance to Prince William Sound to save the pink salmon that produce about half of the 25 million that return to Prince William Sound each year. The salmon harvest here is worth $75 million a year.

"We felt like we had to take things into our own hands," said Jack Lamb, president of a Prince William Sound fishermen's organization.

Don Corbett, the coordinator of Exxon Shipping's Alaska operations, said it was impossible to contain the slick "with the equipment we have available today."

"The big opportunity was missed Sunday, when that oil was sitting there just as calm as could be." He said the company did not have adequate equipment to gather the oil, nor did it have permission to begin burning.

The admission of failure in the cleanup drew an angry response from John Devens, the Mayor of Valdez. "Over the years, they have promised they would do everything to clean up a spill and to maintain our quality of life," he said. "I think it's quite clear right now that our area is faced with destruction of our entire way of life."

Source 8 Timothy Egan, "Exxon Concedes It Can't Contain Most of Oil Spill," *New York Times,* March 30, 1989

Valdez, Alaska, March 29—Officials of the Exxon Shipping Company acknowledged today that they had effectively lost the opportunity to control most of the 240,000 barrels of fast-spreading crude oil that spilled after the tanker *Exxon Valdez* ran aground Friday.

"This spill has pretty much blown into Prince William Sound," said Don Corbett, Exxon's coordinator in Alaska. "We will never get back those 240,000 barrels, but we will continue to try, even if it takes months."

Oil company officials acknowledged that they did not begin putting out cleanup booms until 10 hours after the accident—twice the amount of time called for in the cleanup plan they are required to maintain. The contingency plan also says chemical dispersants should be the chief method of breaking up the oil in such a large spill. But by Tuesday, Exxon officials said it was too late to use the chemicals.

The currents and wind have spread the oil more than 50 miles from the stricken tanker, blackening pristine island beaches, coating plant and marine life and endangering one of the world's biggest salmon runs.

Source 9   Editorial, "Oil on the Water, Oil in the Ground," *New York Times,* March 30, 1989

Does the Exxon tanker spill show that Arctic oil shipping is being mismanaged? Should the industry have been better prepared to cope with the accident? Should the spill deflect President Bush from his plan to open more of Alaska to oil exploration?

Six days after the *Exxon Valdez* dumped 240,000 barrels of crude into the frigid waters of Prince William Sound, questions come more easily than answers. But it is not too early to distinguish between the issue of regulation and the broader question of exploiting energy resources in the Arctic. The accident shouldn't change one truth: Alaskan oil is too valuable to leave in the ground.

Exxon has much to explain. The tanker captain has a history of alcohol abuse. The officer in charge of the vessel at the time of the spill was not certified to navigate in the sound. The Company's cleanup efforts have been woefully ineffective. Local industries, notably fishing, face potentially disastrous consequences, and the Government needs to hold the company to its promise to pay. More important, Washington has an obligation to impose and enforce rules strict enough to reduce the risks of another spill.

That said, it's worth putting the event in perspective. Before last Friday, tens of thousands of tanker runs from Valdez had been completed without a serious mishap. Alaska now pumps two million barrels through the pipeline each day. And it would be almost unthinkable to restrict access to one-fourth of the nation's total oil production.

The far tougher question is whether the accident is sufficient reason to slow exploration for additional oil in the Arctic. The single most promising source of oil in America lies on the north coast of Alaska, a few hundred miles east of the big fields at Prudhoe Bay. But this remote tundra is part of the Arctic National Wildlife Refuge, and since 1980 Congress has been trying to decide whether to allow exploratory drilling.

Environmental organizations have long opposed such exploration, arguing that the ecology of the refuge is both unusual and fragile. This week they used the occasion of the tanker spill to call for further delays while the damage from the *Exxon Valdez* spill is assessed.

More information is always better than less. But long delay would have a cost, too: Prudhoe Bay production will begin to tail off in the mid-1990s. If exploration is permitted in the refuge and little oil is found, development will never take place and damage to the environment will be insignificant. If development does prove worthwhile, the process will undoubtedly degrade the environment. But the compensation will be a lot of badly needed fuel.

Environmentalists consider that, at most, the refuge will add one year's supply to America's reserves. They are right, but one year of oil is a lot of oil. The 3.2 billion barrels, if found, would be worth about $60 billion at today's prices, enough to generate at least $10 billion in royalties for Alaska and the Federal Government. By denying access to it, Congress would be saying implicitly that the absolute purity of the environment was worth at least as much as the forgone $10 billion.

Put it another way. Suppose the royalties were dedicated to buying and maintaining parkland in the rest of the nation—a not unthinkable legislative option. Would Americans really want to pass by, say, $10 billion worth of land in order to prevent oil companies from covering a few thousand acres of the Arctic with roads, drilling pads and pipelines?

Washington can't afford to assume that the *Exxon Valdez* accident was a freak that will never happen again. But neither can it afford to treat the accident as a reason for fencing off what may be the last great oilfield in the nation.

Source 10 Philip Shabecoff, "Captain of Tanker Had Been Drinking, Blood Tests Show," *New York Times,* March 31, 1989

Valdez, Alaska, March 30—The Coast Guard today opened formal legal proceedings against the captain of the tanker that ran aground here last week after the head of an investigating team reported that the captain had unacceptably high levels of alcohol in his blood nine hours after the accident.

The Coast Guard said the investigation could result in the loss of the captain's license if he is found to have operated the ship while intoxicated. The Exxon Shipping Company, which owns the tanker, immediately dismissed the captain, Joseph J. Hazelwood. . . .

William R. Woody, who is heading the investigation for the National Transportation Safety Board, said today that blood tests on Captain Hazelwood taken last Friday showed an alcohol content of 0.061 percent. The Coast Guard, under Federal law, has set a maximum permissible level of 0.040, percent for operating a commercial vessel, he said. . . .

Mr. Woody said that tests on the crewmen who were on the bridge at the time of the accident, the largest tanker spill in United States history, did not find evidence of alcohol in their systems. . . .

The testing of Captain Hazelwood did not begin until between 9:30 and 11:00 A.M., at least nine hours after the accident, which dumped about 240,000 barrels of oil into the sound. Alcohol is eliminated from the system at about 0.015 percentage points per hour; the longer the delay in giving such a test, the lower the blood alcohol reading.

Source 11   "Officials Make Report," *New York Times*, March 31, 1989

President Bush today called the Alaska oil spill "a major tragedy," but Administration officials said the Government would not take over the cleanup.

Admiral Paul Yost, the Coast Guard Commandant, bristled when asked if the service had to share the blame when its radar did not warn the ship about the reef and when the crew was not tested "in a timely manner" for alcohol.

"Remember, we've got 10 miles of open water there, and for that vessel to have come over and hit a reef is almost unbelievable," he said. "This was not a treacherous area, as you people in the press have called it. It is not treacherous in the area they went aground. It's 10 miles wide. Your children could drive a tanker up through it."

Source 12   Keith Schneider, "Under Oil's Powerful Spell, Alaska Was Off Guard," *New York Times*, April 2, 1989

Valdez, Alaska, April 1—All through this decade, while earning billions from petroleum, Alaskans have allowed the oil industry to save money by curtailing preparations for an environmental emergency like the one that has now fouled Prince William Sound.

One dramatic example was an industry decision to disband a 20-member emergency team prepared for round-the-clock response to oil spills in Valdez Harbor and the sound.

The reaction from Alaskan officials was modest. Town leaders dropped their complaints quickly after the industry consortium that owns the Trans-Alaska Pipeline told them "a full-time team wasn't necessary and would be a waste," Lieut. Gov. Stephen McAlpine, who was Mayor of Valdez at the time, said in an interview.

Besides disbanding the team, the oil consortium allowed maintenance to lapse on equipment critical to dealing with a spill. And it spurned an offer from the town to store cleanup equipment, Mr. McAlpine said, saying it was unnecessary.

So when the *Exxon Valdez* ran aground in the sound on March 24, it took more than a day for emergency work to start.

Curtailing the means to fight a spill had seemed justified, state leaders said, by their strong and ultimately unrealistic belief that an emergency of the magnitude that occurred was virtually impossible.

This view is also a reflection of the strong bonds Alaska has developed with big oil. Oil has enriched the state and its people, affording a sense of economic strength. But the price seems to have been a dependence on the benefactor that led the state to abide decisions now being regretted.

Periodic proposals to increase the number of inspectors and safety experts, particularly in the State Department of Environmental Conservation, the principal regulatory agency for Alaska's oil industry, were stymied by the industry's political strength, its popularity among Alaskans and the belief that enough safeguards were in place to prevent an accident. . . .

Residents here said they are heart-sick over the accident that has stained hundreds of square miles of Prince William Sound to the color of dark tea. Yet they also realize that in many ways they must share part of the blame for the spill, a disaster many now say seemed almost inevitable.

Many of this town's 3,000 residents were among the thousands of people lured from the lower 48 states to build the $8 billion Trans-Alaska Pipeline. . . . Oil wealth built Valdez's modern town hall, its efficient and well-stocked library, schools and handsome cedar homes.

Oil money did the same thing across much of southern Alaska. This fiscal year, 85 percent of Alaska's $2.3 billion budget is supported by oil sales and taxes collected from oil companies.

Source 13 Ken Wells and Charles McCoy, "Out of Control: How Unpreparedness Turned the Alaska Spill into Ecological Debacle," *Wall Street Journal*, April 3, 1989

Valdez, Alaska—It is the afternoon of March 27, four days after the *Exxon Valdez* spewed 10 million gallons of oil into Prince William Sound. After several false starts, Exxon is at last spraying the huge slick with chemical dispersants. A C-130 plane, chartered by Exxon for the task, is roaring across the sound and is supposed to stop spraying more than a mile from the stricken tanker. But to the horror of the Coast Guard crew aboard the vessel, the plane inexplicably keeps on coming, unleashing some of its load from an ear-splitting altitude of 50 feet, directly on the men.

"My guys are up on the deck; they're oily, they're cold," says Coast Guard Commander Steven McCall. "And then they get slimed."

Nothing much has gone right for Exxon from the very moment the *Exxon Valdez* went aground early in the morning of March 24, causing the largest oil spill ever in North America and an environmental disaster covering 1,300 square miles. Nor for Alyeska Pipeline Service Co., the eight-company consortium that operates the Valdez oil terminal and that was supposed to mount the initial defense against the spill.

It took the companies 35 hours to fully encircle the stricken tanker with barrier booms that were supposed to restrict the spill. By then oil was floating miles from the ship. It took much longer to mount an air attack with the dispersants that were supposed to dissolve the oil. Both tactics were too little, too late.

The delays have sparked heated criticism of Exxon and Alyeska, compounded by a finding Thursday that the tanker's captain was intoxicated under Coast Guard rules nine hours after the accident. Exxon also admitted that it knew the captain had gone through an alcohol detoxification program, but still put him in command of its largest tanker. Federal and state criminal investigations are under way, and four lawsuits have been filed, and are expected to seek punitive damages. The Coast Guard is also trying to explain its own shortcomings during the affair.

Whatever conclusions are reached about the cause of this particular wreck, the disaster has exposed a much deeper problem: the seeming inability of the oil industry to fight major oil spills. In response to the deluge of criticism, Exxon Chairman Lawrence Rawl said last week that his company was getting a "bad rap" for the alleged delays. . . .

But a chronology of the first four days after the spill—assembled from state and Coast Guard official reports and dozens of interviews with company spokesmen, fishermen and others—sharply contradicts many of the oil companies' assertions. Among other things, it shows:

- Not only was Alyeska's only containment barge stripped for repairs, but when it was finally loaded, it was with equipment meant to take oil off the tanker, rather than barrier booms to fight the spill. It had to be reloaded, taking hours.
- Neither Alyeska nor Exxon had enough booms or dispersants.
- The oil companies weren't ready to test for dispersants for 18 hours, and they then did so by ineffectively tossing buckets of chemicals out of the door of a helicopter.
- The skimmer boats' equipment used to scoop oil out of the sea was so old it kept breaking down and clogging.
- Both Alyeska and Exxon failed, despite pleas from fishermen, to mobilize squads of private boats poised to rush to the scene.

The oil companies' lack of preparedness makes a mockery of a 250-page containment plan, approved by the state, for fighting spills in Prince William Sound. The plan, for example, required encirclement of a spill or tanker within five hours. *The Exxon Valdez* wasn't encircled for 35 hours.

Source 14 Malcolm W. Browne, "Radar Could Have Tracked Tanker," *New York Times*, April 5, 1989

Valdez, Alaska, April 4—Coast Guard officials acknowledged today that contrary to their earlier statements, their radar station here could have detected the supertanker *Exxon Valdez* heading for a reef on March 24 if operators had followed the ship on her journey out of Prince William Sound.

But a spokesman said that the ship had sailed farther south than the point at which Coast Guard radar normally stops tracking vessels. As a result, the *Exxon Valdez* was reliant on the ship's own navigational aids and on light buoys when the tanker went aground on Bligh Reef. . . .

In the days after the accident, Coast Guard officials said repeatedly that the Exxon Valdez was beyond the range of their radar. But fishermen in the area contradicted this, saying coastguardsmen in Valdez had often warned them away from the same reef by radio. . . .

Commander Steven McCall, a senior officer of the Coast Guard station at Valdez, said the limit of coverage by the Potato Point radar station is about 15 nautical miles, depending on atmospheric conditions, and that Bligh reef, about 1½ miles from the shipping lane, is about 13 nautical miles from Potato Point; the tanker had left the safe shipping lane about 4 nautical miles to the north, or about 9 miles from Potato Point. . . .

Whatever role the crew played in the accident, it has begun to appear that other factors contributed to the accident.

"The Coast Guard bears a good share of the blame in this," a supertanker captain said.

The captain, who works for another oil company and requested anonymity, said, "The Coast Guard could easily have kept track of the *Exxon Valdez* and given it a warning when they saw it stray off course. Just what are we paying those guys to do, anyway?"

The Coast Guard replied that the major share of all decision making must be left to the master of a ship once she has sailed south of Rocky Point into wider water in the main body of Prince William Sound, where there are fewer hazards to navigation.

The Next Retelling of History

Each step toward civilization has left an indelible footprint. For a million or more years our ancestors lived as hunters and gatherers, wanderers in search of wild animals and plants. But about ten thousand years ago—a mere instant within the entirety of human existence—a great change took place: humans began to take control of their surroundings. They gained control of their food sources by domesticating plants and animals. Where before they had largely adapted themselves to their environment they now began to adapt the environment to themselves. As farmers and herdsmen, they abandoned nomadic ways and literally planted the roots of civilization.

Controlling their food supply meant an end to wandering and want. An agricultural surplus freed people from the constant search for sustenance that attends a hand-to-mouth existence and permitted specialization of tasks followed by urbanization and civilization. But with domestication of animals and plants, humans also took the first of many steps toward the breakdown of the world in which they lived. Deforestation and plowing led to erosion and climate changes. The cross-breeding of plants to create heartier and more abundant crops and the selective breeding of livestock to create new, more useful lines of domesticated animals altered the course of nature. As village dwellers, our ancestors began to live amid their own wastes and the wastes of the animals they gathered around them. Bacteria feeding upon these wastes evolved alongside human civilization producing an evolving string of plague and disease. As our ancestors entered the age of metals, they scarred the earth and began the contamination of the land and water around them with new pollutants.

But only in the last two hundred years has the pace of environmental destruction begun to threaten the civilization that created it. Urbanization on an unprecedented scale and industrialization have begun to sacrifice the wealth giver. Nonrenewable resources—fixtures on the planet for millions, perhaps billions of years—have been tapped and brought to depletion within but a few human generations. The supply of fresh water has been victim of steady contamination, and the oceans have been overfished and polluted to the point that "dead areas" within them no longer support any forms of life. The diversity of living things, both plant and animal, has dwindled as a consequence of the human resculpting of nature. Each day witnesses more extinctions. Pollution increasingly threatens land, water, and sky and all things dependent upon them.

This sure and steady destruction of the environment resulting from the chronic and catastrophic consequences of civilization has gone largely unnoticed in the telling of human history. It has not attracted the attention of historians to the same extent as say, the building of the Great Pyramids

28.3 Survivors of the *Exxon Valdez* Oil Spill

of Giza or the Wall of China, or the exploits of Genghis Khan or Julius Caesar, or the empires of Napoleon or Hitler, but its impact on the long run of history may turn out to be more consequential.

It is possible that historians twenty or thirty years into the future, faced with the immediacy of a human-induced warming of the planet that brought ocean water from melting polar caps into the streets of the world's coastal cities and upset the delicacy of the reproductive cycles of plant and animal life, will be forced to rewrite each chapter of human development to show its environmental impact. They may tell the tales of pyramids, walls, and empires with an acknowledgement that each had an environmental side-effect. Their need to rewrite the story of the past will be driven by their need to explain their present. Looking back from their place farther along the continuum of time, they will see the trends of our day from a more distant vantage point. They will seek to explain our time and the time of our ancestors—just as has every generation of historians preceding them—in a way that helps them make sense of their own time.

Second Thoughts

"Were We Fully Prepared for This Eventuality?"

For thirteen days the *Exxon Valdez* remained grounded upon Bligh Reef. The initial fear was that the damaged tanker, still holding a million barrels of oil in its punctured cargo tanks, would likely capsize if it slipped off the rocky ledge that pierced its hull.

Forty-six hours after the ship ran aground, Exxon began to pump oil from the *Exxon Valdez* into the tanks of other vessels. By April 4, all but 20,761 barrels of oil had been removed from the stricken vessel. At 10:30 A.M., on April 5, 1989, the *Exxon Valdez* was successfully refloated. Though the ship was saved, the sea around it was not as fortunate.

Exxon spent millions of dollars in an effort to repair what had been done to Prince William Sound in the early minutes of March 24, 1989. Its efforts won mixed marks. The company was also fined $5 billion dollars. By the tenth anniversary of the grounding of the *Exxon Valdez*, however, this fine remained unpaid.

28.4 Response to the *Exxon Valdez* Spill

Source 15 Philip Shabecoff, "U.S. Said to Censor Memo on Oil Risks," *New York Times*, April 6, 1989

Washington, April 5—Reagan Administration documents show that the Interior Department suppressed warnings last year about the risks of offshore drilling and about the adequacy of technology for cleaning up oil spills, several members of Congress said today.

Warnings from the staffs of the Interior Department's Fish and Wildlife Service were either expunged from the Department's final recommendations for a sale of drilling leases or simply not made public, members of California's Congressional delegation said.

The lawmakers, including Bill Lowery, a Republican, wrote to President Bush today asking him to cancel the sale of leases for drilling in sensitive areas off the California coast in light of the apparent suppression of Federal assessments of the possibility of a major accident off their state.

Disputed offshore oil leases off the East and West Coasts are being held in abeyance while their environmental consequences are assessed by a Federal study group appointed by President Bush.

Representative Mel Levine, a California Democrat who obtained the documents under the Freedom of Information Act, said at a news conference today that the Reagan Administration's willingness to play down the dangers of oil spills and the lack of adequate means to deal with such an emergency contributed to the disaster caused by the tanker accident in Alaska's Prince William Sound.

"The Federal Government refused to plan for a worst-case scenario in Alaska and the result is one of the nation's worst environmental disasters," Mr. Levine said.

Source 16 Excerpts from testimony before the U.S. House of Representatives Subcommittee on Coast Guard and Navigation regarding the Exxon Valdez Oil Spill, April 6, 1989

Mr. Tauzin. The Subcommittee will come to order. . . . I am authorized to say that the Full Committee Chairman, Chairman Jones, will be here later, and he has an opening statement which, without objection, will be included as a part of the record.

Statement of Hon. Walter B. Jones
The unthinkable has happened, a major oil spill off our shores. The question we must all ask ourselves is "Were we fully prepared for this eventuality?" Regrettably, I am afraid we must answer "No."

Since 1976, the United States Congress has approached the need for comprehensive oil spill legislation with varying degrees of interest and success. We in this Committee can be proud of our staunch support for such legislation. A long held belief has been that it would take a disaster to get others to realize the necessity of such legislation. Well, the disaster has occurred and while some would be tempted to gloat, I feel only sadness. The spill once again exposes the uncertainties in the crazy-quilt system of laws and plans currently in place to deal with disasters such as the Exxon accident. I no longer fear sounding like Chicken Little with idle threats that the sky is falling; instead, for the people and the wildlife of Alaska, the sky has fallen and all will suffer as a result of our unpreparedness. . . .

Statement of Hon. Helen Delich Bentley

Clearly, this incident has demonstrated that no one, in particular the oil industry, is properly equipped to adequately respond to an oil spill disaster of this magnitude.

The question this Subcommittee needs to ask is: Why not? Is this a case where the industry, and Exxon in particular, maintains minimal resources, rather than resources sufficient to handle a worst case scenario?

Well, Mr. Chairman, we are dealing with the worst case scenario in Prince William Sound. . . .

There are those, I am sure, who will exploit the Exxon Valdez accident and call for a prohibition to energy exploration and development in environmentally sensitive areas, such as the Arctic National Wildlife Refuge. That . . . would be wrong.

We must resist any exploitation of this incident to thwart future development of our energy resources.

The United States is becoming more and more dependent on foreign sources for its energy needs. From a strategic perspective, this is dangerous. . . .

Overall, the oil industry, admittedly with prodding and encouragement from environmental groups, has an excellent record in Prudhoe Bay, Alaska.

This unfortunate accident, which is the apparent result of irresponsible human behavior on the part of one person and the inexperience of another, will, for the time being, overshadow that good record. . . .

Opening Statement of Hon. Claudine Schneider

Miss Schneider . . . I am very distressed, in that for 20 years now, we have heard from many people warning us about the potential of such an accident. This accident, covering a 1,300 square mile area, which is larger than my own State of Rhode Island, is really awesome to comprehend, and the supposed "environmental dooms-dayers" have been warning about such a catastrophe for nearly 20 years now, but the Congress and the American public have been assured by the oil industry that there was nothing to be concerned about.

I would like to share with you a quote that I think all of the Members should be sensitive to in the future when we hear such assurances.

This is a quote from a British Petroleum official back in 1971. He said: "From my own experience, and the studies of many other workers in the pollution field, I am satisfied that tanker traffic to and from Port Valdez, and the operation of an oil port there will not cause any significant damage to the marine environment or to fisheries' interests."

Well, it appears that that opinion was incorrect, and the $13 million annual herring roe fishery has already been cancelled for this year. . . .

Opening Statement of Hon. Nita M. Lowey

Mrs. Lowey . . . I am having an especially difficult time understanding how Captain Joseph Hazelwood could have been in charge of piloting a 1,000-foot oil tanker when his New York driver's license had been revoked three times.

In fact he has not been allowed to drive a car in New York State since last November, yet he is fully certified to pilot an oil tanker carrying 53 million gallons of crude oil. Does that make sense?

Bringing Captain Hazelwood to justice will not erase the damage that has been done to the pristine environment of Prince William Sound, but it can, and should, deter other ship pilots from committing the same infractions.

Statement of Admiral Paul A. Yost, Jr., Commandant, U.S. Coast Guard

Admiral Yost . . . I am satisfied that this country's national response organization is working well, considering the severity of the spill and the remoteness of the area. . . .

Mr. Tauzin . . . News reports this morning indicate that the Governor of Alaska has concluded, in his opinion, that Exxon is just too big and bureaucratic to handle this cleanup effort, and is now making another request that the Coast Guard take over management of the cleanup since it has military command capabilities.

Are you prepared to respond to that request, and, if so, what is your response?

Admiral Yost. Well, I think the Governor and I have come to the same basic conclusion. . . .

My district commander is now taking on more of the guidance of the spill cleanup than we have heretofore. . . . Frankly, we want to take full advantage of Exxon's willingness to open their checkbook and fund this cleanup.

Mr. Tauzin. Admiral, I know, because I was with you when this incident began to break, that you responded before being requested to respond by Exxon, in sending equipment to aid in this cleanup. . . . And I am aware, of course, that you have exercised extraordinary concern on behalf of the Coast Guard and its responsibilities here.

But the question that this Committee will be interested in as we pursue this tragedy to its conclusion is the ability of the Coast Guard, and in fact our Federal system, to respond, if in fact we made the choice to federalize this cleanup.

Is it a fact that Exxon has more money and more resources than our U.S. Coast Guard?

Is it a fact that our oil spill liability fund is so small, so weak, and that you were not really faced with the right kinds of options here, and that you had to rely on Exxon to clean up this mess?

Admiral Yost. Well, some of that is perhaps true. The oil liability fund, the 311(k) fund, is now down to some $3 million or $4 million. We are looking at a $100 million-$200 million spill. We are looking at a corporate giant who has been a good corporate citizen in their response so far, willing to open their checkbook, put no limits on it.

I would be very reluctant to federalize this spill with $4 million in my pockets when I know that we are spending over $100 million a day to—by "we," Exxon is. So some of what you said is certainly true.

Also, I am well aware the Coast Guard is a military organization, a very responsive organization, an operational organization. We need to provide the guidance and direction to Exxon as we move forward on this thing.

Another thing of interest is the massive contracting problem that the Federal Goverment—to wit, the Coast Guard—would have, were we to federalize the cleanup.

I estimated yesterday that it would take something over 20 or 30 contracting officers alone to go to Alaska to start to supervise these contracts.

Now, a corporate entity does not have the Federal procurement rules, the regulations, all of the problems that you have in the Federal Government of taking bids, being sure that everybody has a shot at it.

You cannot just go out and begin to write checks, as Exxon can.

So I think we need to be very careful as we move towards a full federalization, and it would be much better if we could manage this spill using Exxon as the checkbook. I think we will do much better at that.

By the way, in 1988, we had some 1,600 spills cleaned up. Fourteen hundred of them were by private people. Less than 200 did we federalize and manage ourselves. This spill is mammoth compared to anything we have seen so far.

Mr. Tauzin. Admiral, recognizing that, indeed, Exxon is spending—I think about $1 million a day—in the cleanup right now, and that—

Admiral Yost. Yes, a million.

Mr. Tauzin. Yes. And that with the oil spill liability fund at about $3 million, if you were to federalize you would last three days out there. . . .

Mr. Clement. Admiral Yost, I understand that the shipping lanes into and out of Prince William Sound are well marked for oil-carrying vessels. Since the opening of the oil terminal at Valdez, how many incidents have there been of tankers straying without authorization out of those shipping lanes?

Admiral Yost. Well, I am not aware of any. . . .

Mr. Clement. So you really have not had a problem in that area?

Admiral Yost. There have been no groundings, and there have been 8,700 tanker trips through there—no groundings of any kind, no collisions. It has been a very safe operation. . . .

Mr. Coble. . . . Much attention, Admiral, has been directed to the skipper, Captain Hazelwood. I want to focus, for the moment on the third mate who presumably was in command at the time of the grounding.

If you will, Admiral, tell us—if you know—if the third mate was in fact qualified to discharge the duties that he presumably was performing in the wheelhouse at the time of the tragedy.

Admiral Yost. I do not have personal knowledge, but I am convinced that any third mate of a tanker of that size, having taken the Coast Guard license, and having been hired by a company like Exxon, a big corporation, was in fact a competent mariner.

This was a competent mariner who just did not happen to have pilotage for that stretch of water. Now pilotage requires a certain number of round trips. He did not happen to have that number of round trips.

But here we have a licensed, presumably competent mariner of a major ship, one of the major ships of the world, hired by one of the major corporations in the world. I think, until proven otherwise, we have got to assume we had a competent mariner on the bridge.

There was some kind of an awful lapse on that bridge. We do not know what it was. It is almost unbelievable, that there could be a lapse of a competent mariner of that type, who would run that ship right up on a rock in an area that is 8 to 10 miles wide, when he should have been heading just past Hinchinbrook to sea.

It is inconceivable to me.

Source 17 Art Davidson, *In the Wake of the Exxon Valdez: The Devastating Impact of the Alaska Oil Spill,* 1990

What is the extent of Exxon's responsibility in the perpetration of the spill? Judging Exxon's performance is no easy matter, partly because so many people in so many different arenas were involved. Yes, the captain of the vessel had a well-known drinking problem. Yes, crew fatigue and policy violations could have played a part. Yes, the Coast Guard was negligent in its vessel-tracking responsibilities. Yes, the state's laissez-faire attitude toward tanker operations fostered neglect. Still, the inescapable fact remains that the chain of command traces up to the company's policy- and decision-makers. In both practical and moral terms, Exxon is responsible for the grounding of its tanker.

As for Exxon's performance in response to the events, though unprepared for a spill of this magnitude, the company responded faster than any government agency and marshaled enormous resources to fight the oil. Lightering 40 million gallons of oil from the stricken tanker was a major accomplishment. Moreover, Exxon mounted its response amidst the confusion of state and federal officials trying to determine their roles, their responsibilities, and the extent of their authority.

In the future, companies causing large spills may not match Exxon's effort. A case in point is the mid-December 1989 explosion aboard the Iranian tanker *Khark 5,* which spilled some 30 million gallons of crude into the Atlantic Ocean. Following the explosion, a 200-mile-long oil slick drifted toward the coast of Morocco for *thirteen days* before any response was mounted. While the ship's owners haggled over salvage rights, they made no attempt to contain the spilled oil or lighter the remaining 53 million gallons, which a French observer called "a floating bomb."

Also to Exxon's credit, the company promptly established a claims process, which no law required. In one year, Exxon spent close to $2 billion as a result of the *Exxon Valdez* wreck, making this the most costly oil spill in history by more than a billion dollars. Exxon, with profits of $5.3 billion in 1988, is one of the few companies in the world capable of actually paying the costs of the spill, which could reach $4 billion by the time all the lawyers and claims are factored in.

However, for all its efforts, Exxon, according to government surveys, recovered only 3 to 13 percent of the spilled oil. Regardless of all the efforts to divert, contain, disperse, and recover it, the massive slick inexorably ran its course.

The fact, that Exxon did mount an extensive response makes the wreck of the *Exxon Valdez* a highly instructive case study. Experts and lay observers worldwide learned that no amount of money could get the spilled oil back in the ship and that the farther the oil spread from Bligh Reef the less benefit Exxon got for each dollar spent. The billions of dollars Exxon threw willy-nilly at the spill brought to mind a well-known scenario: all the king's horses and all the king's men—and, above all, all the king's money—couldn't put Humpty together again.

Source 18   John Keeble, *Out of the Channel, the Exxon Valdez Oil Spill in Prince William Sound,* 1991

The American consumer, as we have allowed ourselves to be called, makes up the most dangerous influence in the country—dangerous in the sense that our insatiable appetite for raw materials causes continuous and destructive change in the world. We seem unable to attend to the effects of our habits. Our heedlessness has become systemic. . . . There are statistics to confirm our role in the world—the fact that we use two and a half times more energy per capita than citizens of Japan and western Europe, or that we use almost 40 times as much energy per capita as do citizens of, say, Nigeria and India, or that in little over ten years since the OPEC embargo and the shortage scare, and despite efficiency measures, we have allowed our consumption of petroleum products to creep back nearly to the record 1978 levels. These, and even more troubling statistics that tell of our part in the worldwide effects of pollution, are rolled out for public viewing regularly, but we seem unable to come to grips with them. While opinion polls suggest that we want environmental measures to be taken, we seem to lean toward action only fleetingly, when faced with an industrial or ecological calamity. Then, as the incident in Prince William Sound would seem to suggest, the nation flagellates itself, the press and broadcast news feed our frenzy with half-assimilated information, and we fasten on symbols in order to allay our disturbing sense of ignorance and guilt.

In this case one symbol was Exxon, what many came to regard as an evil empire, though it is, in fact, us.

Source 19   Edward Tenner, *Why Things Bite Back: Technology and the Revenge of Unintended Consequences,* 1996

Why are the lines at automatic cash dispensers longer in the evening than those at tellers' windows used to be during banking hours? Why do helmets and other protective gear help make football more dangerous than rugby? Why do filter-tip cigarettes usually fail to reduce nicotine intake? Why has yesterday's miracle vine become today's weed from hell? And why have today's paperback prices overtaken yesterday's clothbound prices? Why has the leisure society gone the way of the leisure suit?

The real revenge is not what we do intentionally against one another. It is the tendency of the world around us to get even, to twist our cleverness against us. Or it is our own unconscious twisting against ourselves. Either way, wherever we turn we face the unintended consequences of mechanical, chemical, biological, and medical ingenuity—revenge effects, they might be called. . . .

A revenge effect is not the same thing as a side effect. If a cancer chemotherapy treatment causes baldness, that is not a revenge effect: but if it induces another equally lethal cancer, that is a revenge effect. If an experimental hair-growing drug were shown to raise the likelihood of cancer, it would be banned; but its risk would be a side effect rather than a revenge effect. On the other hand, if it turned out to accelerate hair loss under certain conditions, that would be a revenge effect. A revenge effect also is not just a trade-off. If legally required safety features raise airline fares, that is a trade-off. But suppose, say, requiring separate seats (with child restraints) for infants, and charging a child's fare for them, would lead many families to drive rather than fly. More children could in principle die from transportation accidents than if the airlines had continued to permit parents to hold babies on their laps. This outcome would be a revenge effect.

Security is another window on revenge effects. Power lock doors, now standard on most cars, increase the sense of safety. But they have helped triple or quadruple the number of drivers locked out over the last two decades—costing $400 million a year and exposing stranded drivers to the very criminals the locks were supposed to defeat. Advanced alarm systems also are now standard equipment on many luxury cars and popular options on even moderately priced models. It is true that most owners don't mind occasional incidents. . . . But squirrel explorations and other transient events spook the systems so easily that the rest of us assume sirens to be screaming wolf. In cities where alarms appear most needed, hotheaded neighbors silence malfunctioning systems by trashing cars. Then the damages are a revenge effect. If legislatures, manufacturers, and insurance companies encourage installation of the alarms and frustrated automobile thieves turn to armed carjacking, there is not just an individual but a social revenge effect. At home, too, cheaper security systems are flooding police with false alarms, half of them caused by user errors. In Philadelphia, only 3,000 of 157,000 calls from automatic security systems over three years were real; by diverting the full-time equivalent of fifty-eight police officers for useless calls, the systems may have promoted crime elsewhere. . . .

When the *Exxon Valdez* hit Bligh Reef off the Alaska coast in 1989, the murky discharge of 35,000 tons of crude oil was an ethical Rorschach test. To some it was simply another example of human failure—resulting from flaws of character and responsibility, and of course from drinking on the job. To others it expressed the heedlessness of corporate capitalism at its worst, the inevitable outcome of putting profits above safe operation. And to still others, the real fault was neither the captain's nor the corporation's but the consumer's: an inexorable price of the industrial world's insatiable hunger for energy. In fact, . . . great oil spills threaten species diversity far less than some other consequences of shipping do. They may not even be the ugliest fruits of marine traffic. One report in 1986 estimated that ships and drilling rigs were dumping hundreds of thousands of tons of plastic debris into the world's oceans each year, the U.S. Navy alone accounting for sixty tons a day. Plastics strangle birds and seals, poison turtles, and fatally ensnarl whales. But litter, excepting medical waste, isn't newsworthy. Television spreads the more spectacular ugliness of spills electronically around the world, and it would take a very stony-hearted policy analyst to argue that shippers and governments are already spending too much money to prevent them.

Decades of megaspills from the world's growing supertanker fleet before the *Valdez* affair suggest that the problem is indeed structural. The even larger wrecks of the *Torrey Canyon* in 1967 and the *Amaco Cadiz* in 1978 had already shown it was worldwide. Europe's coasts have suffered much more than America's. And the U.S. National Research Council and others have pointed to a potential technological revenge effect. Computerized design lets naval architects model the result of stresses on larger and larger ships; the *Seawise Giant* of 1980 has a deadweight of 565,000 tons. . . . Far from making shipping safer, new design technology—like Humphrey Davy's mining lamp, which initially resulted in deeper shafts and more accidents—encouraged owners to push the limits of risk. They specified lighter, high-tensile steel which saved fuel but could rupture when repeated stresses began to produce small but potentially deadly cracks. Stronger steel is less ductile and more likely to break under some circumstances (in the early 1980s, wings fell off airplanes, storage tanks exploded, and hip implants cracked). It is harder to weld properly, and shipbuilders don't always provide a suitable internal framework. . . .

When treaties in the 1970s forbade ballast water in empty petroleum tanks, they slashed the steady pollution of seas and harbors from the flushed water. Unfortunately, oil in the higher-riding ships with separate ballast tanks has ever since been under greater pressure from the sea. If a hull is ruptured, more oil pours out. The most popular recommendation for tanker safety, adding a second hull about a meter or more from the ship's exterior, might let petroleum vapors seep into the space between hulls and explode. Safety inspections, already covering twelve hundred kilometers of welded seam on the vast single hulls, could be so daunting that more sources of leaks could be missed. Keeping tanks partly empty to reduce pressure relative to the sea might retain most oil within tanks in small accidents, but it could increase dangerous stresses in high waves. Pumps to maintain negative pressure after accidents could also promote explosions. And owners argue that larger numbers of smaller, safer ships might actually result in more accidents and more oil spillage than conventional supertankers do now. (They also warn of a social revenge effect: if liability under the U.S. Oil Pollution Act is too risky, serving the U.S. market will be left to doubtful operators.) . . .

Once a spill does happen, it is ugly. There is a grandeur in natural hazards, even when they devastate natural habitats, as the eruption of Mount St. Helens did in Washington State and Hurricane Andrew did in the Southeast. The horrific images of an oil slick, the struggles of oil-coated seabirds and mammals, the contaminated shorelines—all assault cameras and consciences. They call for technologies to repair what technology has wrought. Unfortunately the record of cleanup technology has so far been filled with revenge effects of its own. England experienced some of these problems as early as 1967, when napalm failed to burn off the oil from the *Torrey Canyon* and shores and harbors were treated to ten thousand tons of chemical dispersants. These turned out to kill many of the remaining crustaceans and other animal and plants that the oil spill itself had spared. Even in the 1990s, dispersants have potential revenge effects. By breaking down petroleum into minute globules that will mix with water and sink below the surface, they relieve some of the unsightly signs of a leak. They also keep blobs of oil from washing up onto the shoreline and from contaminating sediments. But as the petroleum is free to sink below the water's surface, it is more likely to harm the reproduction of organisms on the seafloor, from fish eggs to lobsters.

Tidying up an oil spill mechanically can have even more serious revenge effects. The $2 billion cleanup of the *Exxon Valdez* disaster relied heavily on hot water applied to the shoreline through high-velocity pumps—Exxon's response to outrage. A later independent report for the Hazardous Materials Response unit of the National Oceanic and Atmospheric Administration (NOAA) showed just how unexpected the consequences of purification could be. David Kennedy of NOAA's Seattle office explained: "The treatment scalded the beach, killing many organisms that had survived the oil, including some that were little affected by it. It also blasted off barnacles and limpets. And it drove a mixture of sediment and oil down the beach face, depositing them in a subtidal area richer in many forms of marine life—one where there hadn't been much oil." A report commissioned by NOAA suggested that the high-pressure cleanup had disrupted rock-surface ecology by destroying mussel and rockweed populations, "relatively tolerant" to petroleum, making surfaces more vulnerable to waves and predators. Fewer mollusks also encouraged opportunistic algae to preempt surfaces from rockweed and red algae. The oil flushed from the surface killed hard-shelled clams and crustaceans in intertidal and subtidal zones. It apparently also reduced the productivity of the eelgrass that shelters young fish and shrimp. The water pressure itself was even more damaging. At up to one hundred pounds per square inch it disrupted the natural sediments of beaches, both gravel and sand, smothering clams and worms.

Rescuing animals from spills may also result in revenge effects. Of the 357 sea otters saved from the spill and treated by veterinarians and volunteers, 200 returned to the sea. A number of biologists now believe, though, that these spread a herpes virus to otters in eastern Prince William Sound that had avoided the spill itself. The transplanted otters also died in unusual numbers. While some form of the virus appears to be endemic in the waters off Alaska, the treated otters had lesions that could have transmitted the disease, or a more virulent form of it. Stressed animals are potentially dangerous, and some biologists and veterinarians now favor keeping them in captivity. They also point out that the efforts to save the most seriously injured otters may only have made them suffer longer.

The *Torrey Canyon* and especially the *Exxon Valdez* disasters show the perils of purification. Contamination anywhere in the world can become so unbearably visible that it seems to cry out for equally televisable remedies. Exxon officials still defend cleanup methods even though most scientists now believe a less costly strategy—for Exxon too—would have been more effective. This does not mean that cleanup never works. It should not discourage us from reducing and correcting our degradation of nature—whether chronic or acute. But the big marine spills underscore how complex natural systems are, and how creative and flexible human management of them has to be. It is fortunate for us that crude petroleum seeps into the ocean on its own, since natural selection has already engineered bacteria that thrive on it. In fact, the existence of natural pollution of Prince William Sound sped its recovery; local spruce trees produce hydrocarbons related to those in the Prudhoe Bay crude spilled by the *Exxon Valdez*. (Refined products are less likely to find preadapted bacteria.) Recovery rates have varied from one site to another, but a study by the Congressional Research Service specialist James E. Mielke underscored the ability of marine ecosystems to recover from even severe impacts. Fishing and hunting have a far greater impact than oil spills do on those species that are harvested; most species recolonize polluted areas quickly.

The closer we look at marine oil pollution, the less catastrophic and the more chronic it turns out to be. During the 1980s, global oil pollution from sea and land disasters like spills, shipwrecks, and fires declined from 328 million gallons to between 8 and 16 percent of that figure annually. In 1985, tanker accidents accounted for only 12.5 percent of oil pollution—not much more than natural marine seeps and sediment erosion. In spite of the ban on ballast water in tanks, routine bilge and fuel oil pollution from tankers was almost as bad a problem as tanker accidents, and other "normal" tanker operations caused as much pollution as the last two combined. Municipal and industrial sources put nearly three times as much oil pollution in the sea as all tanker accidents combined.

On land, too, it is smaller leaks, seepage, and waste-oil storage—not catastrophe—that pose the most dangerous threats to both wildlife and human health. The U.S. Fish and Wildlife Service has estimated that more than twice as many migratory birds died after landing in open ponds and containers of waste oil in five Southwestern states alone in one year as were lost in the *Exxon Valdez* spill. Tank farms and pipelines on a Brooklyn site have been slowly leaking over one and a half times the spill of the *Exxon Valdez*. Another tank farm in Indiana is being forced to remedy leaks that could have been three times as large. Rusting pipes, bad welding, leaking valves, and sloppy maintenance account for most of the loss. Leak detectors are so unreliable that in January 1990, 567,000 gallons of heating oil were discharged from an Exxon facility in New Jersey where warnings had been ignored after twelve years of false alarms. And the problem extends to the retail level. Richard Golob, publisher of an oil pollution newsletter, has calculated that at any given time, 100,000 of America's 1.5 million underground fuel storage tanks are leaking or starting to leak; the safer tanks that local service stations are required to put in their place may leak anyway after careless, cut-rate installation. In fact, the chronic leakage can turn into a catastrophic risk of explosion if the electrical conduits needed by the new systems are not sealed expertly.

Source 20   William Booth, "Spill's Residue Still Sticks in Alaska's Craw: 10 Years after Tanker Crash, Recovery Is Elusive," *Washington Post,* March 23, 1999

Researchers now suspect that much of the most costly clean-up in history, the summers spent scrubbing individual beach stones and "rehabilitating" otters, did little, if anything, to restore Prince William Sound—and may have hurt.

Once oil reaches a shore or coats an animal, it is now thought, the damage is mostly irreversible. Exxon spent millions of dollars steam-cleaning the beaches, but almost all the oil from the spill would have degraded over time.

The presence of hundreds of workers cleaning rocks probably also damaged the beaches and intertidal zones.

It did make humans feel better, however, and it did make a handful of the displaced fishermen and women who chartered their boats for cleanup for thousands of dollars a day "spillionaires." Exxon spent $113 million dollars in Cordova alone, a town of 2,500 souls, including $80 million for cleanup and $26 million compensating its citizens for lost income. But most of the boat captains and their crews have little to show for the windfall today.

What undeniably helped the ecosystem was the $900 million settlement that Exxon paid to the state and federal governments. The money not only bought an unprecedented wealth of scientific study, a volume of research that never would have been supported otherwise, but also allowed for the purchase of some 650,000 acres of wilderness, preserving for generations hundreds of miles of shoreline and spawning streams, protecting the waters from mining, logging and development.

In the aftermath of the spill, too, new measures were put into place to protect the Sound. Harbor pilots now accompany outgoing tankers from the oil pipeline terminus in Valdez beyond the Bligh Reef, serving as temporary captains to ensure the ships pass safely. Powerful tractor tugs will now be tethered to the tankers, making sure they stay in the shipping lanes. And fishing boats and emergency crews are on constant standby, ready to assist if or when another tanker runs afoul.

 ## Questioning the Past

1. What factors led to the grounding of the *Exxon Valdez* and the ecological disaster that followed? Who, or what is to blame for the incident?

2. Are chronic and catastrophic environmental degradation an inevitable and acceptable consequence of technology?

3. What, if anything, could have been done to prevent the grounding of the *Exxon Valdez*? What actions, if any, could have better contained the effects of the spill?

Chapter 29

Impeachment

The House of Representatives Impeaches President Clinton, *December 19, 1998*

When Bill Clinton launched his campaign to win the White House in 1992, many Americans might well have minimized his chances of success. He was young—a whole generation younger than the incumbent he sought to replace. He was little known outside of his home state of Arkansas, a state that has traditionally played little role in presidential politics. He had to run not only against a popular incumbent, George Bush, but also against the memory of Bush's even more popular predecessor, Ronald Reagan. But Bill Clinton was not without political skills. And when the economy took a turn for the worse, he seized the issue and rode it to the presidency.

As president, Clinton stumbled briefly as he learned his way around on the national scene but then seemed to hit his stride. The economy turned around, the budget was brought into balance, inflation rates dropped, interest rates declined, the stock market soared, and economic growth brought full employment. Clinton charted a centrist course and the polls indicated his presidency enjoyed popular support. As the electorate voted his party out of power in the Congress in 1996 it returned Bill Clinton to the White House.

✎ *First Impressions*

A Presidential Indiscretion

29.1 *Washington Post* Special Report: Clinton Accused

But despite his obvious appeal and ability, many sensed a basic character flaw. Rumors of extramarital affairs continued to surface. In May of 1994, a former state employee of the Arkansas government, Paula Corbin Jones, filed a civil suit against President Clinton alleging sexual harassment. She claimed that Clinton, while Governor of Arkansas, had made improper sexual advances to her in a Little Rock hotel room. President Clinton professed his innocence of the charge. In an effort to prove that the allegation was credible by documenting a pattern of such behavior, attorneys for Jones asked the president for the names of all women employed by either the state of Arkansas or the U.S. government with whom he had had sexual relations since 1986. The president responded that there had been "None." Meanwhile, the attorneys for Jones had acquired from other sources a list of women who might have had a sexual relationship with Clinton and sent each of them a subpoena requesting information. One of these women was Monica Lewinsky.

Source 1   Monica Lewinsky, excerpts from an affidavit in the Paula Jones lawsuit, January 7, 1998

I am 24 years old. . . .

I worked at the White House in the summer of 1995 as a White House intern. Beginning in December 1995, I worked in the Office of Legislative Affairs as a staff assistant for correspondence. In April 1996, I accepted a job as assistant secretary for public affairs at the U.S. Department of Defense. I maintained that job until Dec. 26, 1997. I am currently unemployed but seeking a new job.

In the course of my employment at the White House, I met President Clinton several times. I also saw the president at a number of social functions held at the White House. When I worked as an intern, he appeared at occasional functions attended by me and several other interns. The correspondence I drafted while I worked at the Office of Legislative Affairs was seen and edited by supervisors who either had the President's signature affixed by mechanism or, I believe, had the president sign the correspondence himself.

I have the utmost respect for the president, who has always behaved appropriately in my presence.

I have never had a sexual relationship with the president, he did not propose that we have a sexual relationship, he did not offer me employment or other benefits in exchange for a sexual relationship, he did not deny me employment or other benefits for rejecting a sexual relationship.

I do not know of any other person who had a sexual relationship with the president, was offered employment or other benefits in exchange for a sexual relationship, or was denied employment or other benefits for rejecting a sexual relationship.

The occasions that I saw the president after I left my employment at the White House in April 1996 were official receptions, formal functions or events related to the U. S. Department of Defense, where I was working at the time. There were other people present on those occasions . . .

I declare under the penalty of perjury that the foregoing is true and correct.

Monica Lewinsky

Source 2   President Bill Clinton, excerpts from a deposition given in the case of *Jones v. Clinton*, January 17, 1998

Judge Wright: Do you swear or affirm . . . that the testimony you are about to give in the matter before the court is the truth, the whole truth, and nothing but the truth, so help you God?

The President: I do.

Question from counsel for Paula Jones: And your testimony is subject to the penalty of perjury; do you understand that, Sir?

Answer from the President: I do.

Q. Now do you know a woman named Monica Lewinsky?

A. I do.

Q. How do you know her?

A. She worked in the White House for a while, first as an intern, and then in, as the, in the legislative affairs office. . . .

Q. Is it true that when she worked at the White House she met with you several times?

A. I don't know about several times. There was a period when the Republican Congress shut the Government down that the whole White House was being run by interns, and she was assigned to work back in the chief of staff's office, and we were all working there, and so I saw her on two or three occasions then, and then when she worked at the White House, I think there was one or two other times when she brought some documents to me. . . .

Q. At any time were you and Monica alone together in the Oval Office?

A. I don't recall, but as I said, when she worked at the legislative affairs office, they always had somebody there on the weekends. I typically worked some on the weekends. Sometimes they'd bring me things on the weekends. She—it seems to me she brought things to me once or twice on the weekends. In that case, whatever time she would be in there, drop it off, exchange a few words and go, she was there. I don't have any specific recollections of what the issues were, what was going on, but when the Congress is there, we're working all the time, and typically I would do some work on one of the days of the weekend in the afternoon.

Q. So I understand, your testimony is that it was possible, then, that you were alone with her, but you have no specific recollections of that ever happening?

A. Yes, that's correct. It's possible that she, in, while she was working there, brought something to me and that at the time she brought it to me, she was the only person there. That's possible. . . .

Q. Do you recall ever walking with Lewinsky down the hallway from the Oval Office to your private kitchen there in the White House?

A. Well, let me describe the facts first, because you keep talking about this private kitchen. . . . My recollection is that, that at some point during the government shutdown, when Ms. Lewinsky was still an intern but was working the chief-of-staff's office because all the employees had to go home, that she was back there with a pizza that she brought to me and to others. I do not believe she was there alone, however, I don't think she was. And my recollection is that on a couple of occasions after that she was there but my secretary, Betty Currie, was there with her. . . .

Q. Have you ever met with Monica Lewinsky in the White House between the hours of midnight and 6 A.M.?

A. I certainly don't think so. . . . Now let me just say, when she was working there, during, there may have been a time when we were all—we were up working late. There are lots of, on any given night, when the Congress is in session, there are always several people around until late in the night, but I don't have any memory of that. I just can't say that there could have been a time when that occurred, I just—but I don't remember it.

Q. Certainly if it happened, nothing remarkable would have occurred?

A. No, nothing remarkable. I don't remember it. . . .

Q. When was the last time you spoke with Monica Lewinsky?

A. I'm trying to remember. Probably some time before Christmas. She came by to see Betty sometime before Christmas. And she was there talking to her, and I stuck my head out, said hello to her. . . .

Q. Did she tell you she had been served with a subpoena in this case?

A. No, I don't know if she had been.

Q. Did anyone other than your attorneys ever tell you that Monica Lewinsky had been served with a subpoena in this case?

A. I don't think so.

Q. Did you ever talk with Monica Lewinsky about the possibility that she might be asked to testify in this case?

A. Bruce Lindsey, I think Bruce Lindsey told me that she was, I think maybe that's the first person told me she was. I want to be as accurate as I can.

Q. Did you talk to Mr. Lindsey about what action, if any, should be taken as a result of her being served with a subpoena?

A. No.

Q. Have you ever talked to Monica Lewinsky about the possibility that she might be asked to testify in this lawsuit?

A. I'm not sure, and let me tell you why I'm not sure. It seems to me the, the, the—I want to be as accurate as I can here. Seems to me that last time she was there to see Betty before Christmas we were joking about how you-all, with the help of the Rutherford Institute, were going to call every woman I'd ever talked to, and I said, you know—And I said that you-all might call every woman I ever talked to and ask them that, and so I said you would qualify, or something like that. I don't, I don't think we ever had more of a conversation than that about it, but I might have mentioned something to her about it, because when I saw how long the witness list was, or I heard about it, before I saw, but actually by the time I saw it her name was in it, but I think that was after all this had happened. I might have said something like that, so I don't want to say for sure I didn't, because I might have said something like that. . . .

Q. Well, have you ever given any gifts to Monica Lewinsky?

A. I don't recall. Do you know what they were?

Q. A hat pin?

A. I don't, I don't remember. But I certainly, I could have.

Q. A book about Walt Whitman?

A. I give—Let me just say, I give people a lot of gifts, and when people are around I give a lot of things I have at the White House away, so I could have given her a gift, but I don't remember a specific gift . . .

Q. Has Monica Lewinsky ever given you any gifts?

A. Once or twice. I think she's given me a book or two.

Q. Did she give you a silver cigar box?

A. No.

Q. Did she give you a tie?

A. Yes, she had given me a tie before. I believe that's right . . .

Q. Did you have an extramarital sexual affair with Monica Lewinsky?

A. No.

Q. If she told someone that she had a sexual affair with you beginning in November of 1995, would that be a lie?

A. It's certainly not the truth. It would not be the truth.

Q. I think I used the term "sexual affair." And so the record is completely clear, have you ever had sexual relations with Monica Lewinsky, as that term is defined in Deposition Exhibit 1, as modified by the Court. . . . [for the purposes of this deposition, a person engages in "sexual relations" when the person knowingly engages in or causes . . . contact with the genitalia, anus, groin, breast, inner thigh, or buttocks of any person with an intent to arouse or gratify the sexual desire of any person. . . . "Contact" means intentional touching, either directly or through clothing.]

A. I have never had sexual relations with Monica Lewinsky. I've never had an affair with her.

The Independent Counsel: "Unaccountable, Uncontrollable, and Unavoidably Expensive"

The Paula Jones inquiry was not the only investigation of the President's conduct underway. Since January of 1994, an independent counsel had been conducting an investigation of the President's possible involvement in a fraudulent real estate deal in Arkansas called "Whitewater." This effort, led by Independent Counsel Kenneth Starr, had by the midpoint of 1998 spent $39 million, and, while it had proven wrongdoing on the part of several of the president's former business associates, no evidence had been found to indicate any illegal conduct on the part of Bill Clinton or his wife, Hillary Rodham Clinton. On January 16, 1998, the day before President Clinton was deposed in the Paula Jones case, the Office of the Independent Counsel asked for and was granted authority to investigate whether Monica Lewinsky and others had "suborned perjury, obstructed justice, intimidated witnesses, or otherwise violated federal law" in the civil suit filed by Paula Jones.

In 1978, Congress enacted the Ethics in Government Act. This law provided for an independent counsel to be appointed to assure an impartial investigation into any allegations of wrongdoing by high government officials. Following the attempt by President Richard Nixon and his attorney-general John Mitchell to use the powers of government to thwart rather than pursue justice in the Watergate investigation, the public was uneasy about the prospects of future corrupt leaders being responsible for investigating themselves. An independent counsel would be appointed in such instances, with budget and powers not dependent upon the established agencies, to take an investigation wherever the facts might lead. Fifteen different investigations were launched between 1978 and 1998 under this statute, some leading to convictions, others finding no cause.

Still, there were critics of the concept of an independent counsel. Many argued that the independent counsel had powers too broad for a democratic society. There were no checks and balances to guarantee that the powers of the counsel were themselves not abused. Indeed, Kenneth Starr aggressively pursued his investigations, pressuring witnesses through a variety of legal strong-arm tactics. To some critics, Starr seemed overzealous in both his pursuit of evidence and his pursuit of the president. He even subpoenaed bookstores and video stores to find information on reading and viewing habits of witnesses. Critics argued that the position of independent counsel permitted a partisan attack on an officeholder by a prosecutor whose actions were "unaccountable, uncontrollable, and unavoidably expensive."

Source 3   Susan Schmidt, Peter Baker, and Toni Locy, "Clinton Accused of Urging Aide to Lie," *Washington Post*, January 21, 1998

Independent Counsel Kenneth W. Starr has expanded his investigation of President Clinton to examine whether Clinton and his close friend Vernon E. Jordan Jr. encouraged a 24-year-old former White House intern to lie to lawyers for Paula Jones about whether the intern had an affair with the president, sources close to the investigation said yesterday.

A three-judge appeals court panel on Friday authorized Starr to examine allegations of suborning perjury, false statements and obstruction of justice involving the president, the sources said. A Justice Department official confirmed that Attorney General Janet Reno had forwarded Starr's request to the panel that oversees independent counsels after Starr had asked her for "expeditious" consideration of his request.

The expansion of the investigation was prompted by information brought to Starr within the past few weeks by a former White House aide who surreptitiously made tape recordings of conversations she had with the former White House intern describing a relationship with Clinton.

The former intern, Monica Lewinsky, began work in the White House in 1995 at age 21 and later moved to a political job at the Pentagon, where she worked with Linda R. Tripp, who had moved there from an administrative job at the White House.

Sources said Tripp provided Starr with audiotapes of more than 10 conversations she had with Lewinsky over recent months in which Lewinsky graphically recounted details of a year-and-a-half-long affair she had with Clinton. In some of the conversations—including one in recent days—Lewinsky described

Clinton and Jordan directing her to testify falsely in the Paula Jones sexual harassment case against the president.

Lewinsky gave an affidavit in connection with the Jones case Jan. 7 and sources who have seen the sworn statement said she denied having an affair with Clinton. . . . In his own deposition in the Jones case Saturday, Clinton was asked about Lewinsky and denied under oath having a sexual relationship with her, according to a source familiar with the testimony.

White House officials said they were unaware of the expansion of Starr's investigation and referred calls to Robert S. Bennett, the president's lawyer in the Jones case.

"The president adamantly denies he ever had a relationship with Ms. Lewinsky and she has confirmed the truth of that," Bennett said.

Source 4   Televised remarks by President Clinton at the White House Education News Conference, Monday, January 26, 1998, 10 A.M.

I want to say one thing to the American people. I want you to listen to me. I'm going to say this again: I did not have sexual relations with that woman, Miss Lewinsky. I never told anybody to lie, not a single time. Never. These allegations are false.

Source 5   Roger Simon, "Clinton Vehemently Denies the Charges." *Chicago Tribune,* January 27, 1998

Washington—A defiant President Clinton wagged his finger at the cameras and thumped the lectern Monday as he insisted he did not have sex with a young White House intern or ask her to deny it under oath. With Hillary Rodham Clinton nodding her approval at his side in the Roosevelt Room of the White House, only a few yards away from where the alleged liaisons were supposed to have taken place, a stern-faced Clinton addressed the American people. . . .

Monica Lewinsky, 24, has signed a sworn statement denying she had a relationship with Clinton, but her lawyer, William Ginsburg, has indicated she might change her story if she is granted immunity from prosecution. . . .

One of the president's biggest cheerleaders, Vice President Al Gore, traveled to Capitol Hill on Monday to speak with some House Democrats and to tell them he believed Clinton's denial. Rep. Tomothy Roemer said, "The vice president was very confident and very upbeat."

"Upbeat" was the official mood of the day at the White House, with (Press Secretary Mike) McCurry dismissing Clinton's drop in the polls as a meaningless "snapshot" and said it "is probably going to take a while for the American people to understand and digest" these events.

"What will clear the air," McCurry said, "is people basing their opinion on the facts and not on speculation and allegations and leaks."

Source 6   Televised address of President Clinton, August 18, 1998, from the White House

Good evening.

This afternoon in this room, from this chair, I testified before the Office of the Independent Counsel and the grand jury.

I answered their questions truthfully, including questions about my private life, questions no American citizen would ever want to answer.

Still, I must take complete responsibility for all my actions, both public and private. And that is why I am speaking to you tonight.

As you know, in a deposition in January, I was asked questions about my relationship with Monica Lewinsky. While my answers were legally accurate, I did not volunteer information.

Indeed, I did have a relationship with Ms. Lewinsky that was not appropriate. In fact, it was wrong. It constituted a critical lapse in judgment and a personal failure on my part for which I am solely and completely responsible.

But I told the grand jury today and I say to you now that at no time did I ask anyone to lie, to hide or destroy evidence or take any other unlawful action.

I know that my public comments and my silence about this matter gave a false impression. I misled people, including my own wife. I deeply regret that.

I can only tell you I was motivated by many factors. First, by a desire to protect myself from the embarrassment of my own conduct.

I was also very concerned about protecting my family. The fact that these questions were being asked in a politically inspired lawsuit, which has since been dismissed, was a consideration, too.

In addition, I had real and serious concerns about an independent counsel investigation that began with private business dealings 20 years ago, dealings, I might add, about which an independent federal agency found no evidence of wrongdoing by me or my wife over two years ago.

The independent counsel investigation moved on to my staff and friends, then into my private life. And now the investigation itself is under investigation.

This has gone on too long, cost too much and hurt too many innocent people.

Now, this matter is between me, the two people I love most—my wife and our daughter—and our God. I must put it right, and I am prepared to do whatever it takes to do so.

Nothing is more important to me personally. But it is private, and I intend to reclaim my family life for my family. It's nobody's business but ours.

Even presidents have private lives. It is time to stop the pursuit of personal destruction and the prying into private lives and get on with our national life.

Our country has been distracted by this matter for too long, and I take my responsibility for my part in all of this. That is all I can do.

Now is the time—in fact, it is past time—to move on.

We have important work to do—real opportunities to seize, real problems to solve, real security matters to face.

And so tonight, I ask you to turn away from the spectacle of the past seven months, to repair the fabric of our national discourse, and to return our attention to all the challenges and all the promise of the next American century.

Thank you for watching. And good night.

***Source* 7** Excerpts from the Official Report of the Independent
Counsel's Investigation of the President, September 11, 1998

Introduction

As required by Section 595 (c) of Title 28 of the United States Code, the Office
of the Independent Counsel ("OIC" or "Office") hereby submits substantial and
credible information that President William Jefferson Clinton committed acts
that may constitute grounds for impeachment.

> The information reveals that President Clinton:
>
> lied under oath at a civil deposition while he was a defendant in a
> sexual harassment lawsuit;
>
> lied under oath to a grand jury;
>
> attempted to influence the testimony of a potential witness who had
> direct knowledge of facts that would reveal the falsity of his depo-
> sition testimony;
>
> attempted to obstruct justice by facilitating a witness's plan to refuse
> to comply with a subpoena;
>
> attempted to obstruct justice by encouraging a witness to file an
> affidavit that the President knew would be false, and then by making
> use of that false affidavit at his own deposition;
>
> lied to potential grand jury witnesses, knowing that they would re-
> peat those lies before the grand jury; and
>
> engaged in a pattern of conduct that was inconsistent with his con-
> stitutional duty to faithfully execute the laws.

The evidence shows that these acts, and others, were part of a pattern that
began as an effort to prevent disclosure of information about the President's
relationship with a former White House intern and employee, Monica S. Lewinsky, and continued as an effort to prevent the information from being disclosed
in an ongoing criminal investigation . . .

The Significance of the Evidence of Wrongdoing

From the beginning, this phase of the OIC's investigation has been criticized as
an improper inquiry into the President's personal behavior; indeed, the President
himself suggested that specific inquiries into his conduct were part of an effort
to "criminalize my private life." The regrettable fact that the investigation has
often required witnesses to discuss sensitive personal matters has fueled this
perception.

All Americans, including the President, are entitled to enjoy a private family life, free from public or governmental scrutiny. But the privacy concerns
raised in this case are subject to limits, three of which are briefly set forth here.

First. The first limit was imposed when the President was sued in federal
court for alleged sexual harassment. The evidence in such litigation is often
personal. At times, that evidence is highly embarrassing for both plaintiff and

defendant. As Judge Wright noted at the President's January deposition, "I have never had a sexual harassment case where there was not some embarrassment." Nevertheless, Congress and the Supreme Court have concluded that embarrassment-related concerns must give way to the greater interest in allowing aggrieved parties to pursue their claims. Courts have long recognized the difficulties of proving sexual harassment in the workplace, inasmuch as improper or unlawful behavior often takes place in private. To excuse a party who lied or concealed evidence on the ground that the evidence covered only "personal" or "private" behavior would frustrate the goals that Congress and the Courts sought to achieve in enacting and interpreting the Nation's sexual harassment laws. That is particularly true when the conduct that is being concealed—sexual relations in the workplace between a high official and a young subordinate employee— itself conflicts with these goals.

Second. The second limit was imposed when Judge Wright required disclosure of the precise information that is in part the subject of this referral. A federal judge specifically ordered the President, on more than one occasion, to provide the requested information about relationships with other women, including Monica Lewinsky. The fact that Judge Wright later determined that the evidence would not be admissible at trial, and still later granted judgment in the President's favor, does not change the President's legal duty at the time he testified. Like every litigant, the President was entitled to object to the discovery questions, and to seek guidance from the court if he thought those questions were improper. But having failed to convince the court that his objections were well founded, the President was duty bound to testify truthfully and fully. Perjury and attempts to obstruct the gathering of evidence can never be an acceptable response to a court order, regardless of the eventual course or outcome of the litigation.

The Supreme Court has spoken forcefully about perjury and other forms of obstruction of justice:

In this constitutional process of securing a witness' testimony, perjury simply has no place whatever. Perjured testimony is an obvious and flagrant affront to the basic concepts of judicial proceedings. Effective restraints against this type of egregious offense are therefore imperative.

The insidious effects of perjury occur whether the case is civil or criminal. Only a few years ago, the Supreme Court considered a false statement made in a civil administrative proceeding: "False testimony in a formal proceeding is intolerable. We must neither reward nor condone such a 'flagrant affront' to the truth-seeking functions of adversary proceedings. . . . Perjury should be severely sanctioned in appropriate cases." Stated more simply, "(p)erjury is an obstruction of justice."

Third. The third limit is unique to the President. "The Presidency is more than an executive responsibility. It is the inspiring symbol of all that is highest in American purpose and ideals." When he took the Oath of Office in 1993 and again in 1997, President Clinton swore that he would "faithfully execute the Office of the President." As head of the Executive Branch, the President has the constitutional duty to "take Care that the Laws be faithfully executed." The President gave his testimony in the *Jones* case under oath and in the presence of a federal judge, a member of a co-equal branch of government; he then testified before a federal grand jury, a body of citizens who had themselves taken an oath to seek the truth. In view of the enormous trust and responsibility attendant to his high Office, the President has a manifest duty to ensure that all his conduct at all times complies with the law of the land. As Justice Robert Jackson warned: "no other personality in public life can begin to compete with (the President) in access to the public mind through modern methods of communications. By his prestige as head of state and his influence upon public opinion he exerts a leverage upon those who are supposed to check and balance his power which often cancels their effectiveness."

In sum, perjury and acts that obstruct justice by any citizen—whether in a criminal case, a grand jury investigation, a congressional hearing, a civil case, or civil discovery—are profoundly serious matters. When such acts are committed by the President of the United States, we believe those acts "may constitute grounds for an impeachment."

Evidence That President Clinton Lied under Oath during the Civil Case Summary

The detailed testimony of Ms. Lewinsky, her corroborating prior consistent statements to her friends, family members, and counselors, and the evidence of the President's semen on Ms. Lewinsky's dress establish that Ms. Lewinsky and the President engaged in substantial sexual activity between November 15, 1995, and December 28, 1997. . . .

The President and Ms. Lewinsky had ten sexual encounters that included direct contact with the genitalia of at least one party, and two other encounters that included kissing. On nine of the ten occasions, Ms. Lewinsky performed oral sex on the president. On nine occasions the President touched and kissed Ms. Lewinsky's bare breast. On four occasions, the President also touched her genitalia. On one occasion, the President inserted a cigar into her vagina to stimulate her. The President and Ms. Lewinsky also had phone sex on at least fifteen occasions. . . .

The President, however, testified under oath in the civil case—both in his deposition and in a written answer to an interrogatory—that he did not have a "sexual relationship" or a "sexual affair" or "sexual relations" with Ms. Lewinsky. In addition, he denied engaging in activity covered by a more specific definition of "sexual relations" used at the deposition. . . .

The President's denials—semantic and factual—do not withstand scrutiny. . . .

Concerning oral sex, the President's sole answer to the charge that he lied under oath at the deposition focused on his interpretation of "any person" in the definition. Ms. Lewinsky testified that she performed oral sex on the President on nine occasions. The President said that by receiving oral sex, he would not "engage in" or "cause" contact with the genitalia, anus, groin, breast, inner thigh, or buttocks of "any person" because "any person" really means "any other person." The President further testified before the grand jury: "(I)f the deponent is the person who has oral sex performed on him, then the contact is with—not with anything on that list, but with the lips of another person."

The President's linguistic parsing is unreasonable. Under the President's interpretation (which he says he followed at his deposition), in an oral sex encounter, one person is engaged in sexual relations, but the other person is not engaged in sexual relations. . . .

At the time of his civil deposition, the President also could have presumed that he could lie under oath without risk because—as he knew—Ms. Lewinsky had already filed a false affidavit denying a sexual relationship with the President. Indeed, they had an understanding that each would lie under oath. So the President might have expected that he could lie without consequence on the belief that no one would ever successfully challenge his denial of a sexual relationship with her.

In sum, based on all of the evidence and considering the President's various responses, there is substantial and credible information that the President lied under oath in his civil deposition and his interrogatory answer in denying a sexual relationship, a sexual affair, or sexual relations with Ms. Lewinsky.

Source 8   Editorial, *Philadelphia Inquirer,* September 12, 1998

Bill Clinton should resign. He should resign because his repeated, reckless deceits have dishonored his presidency beyond repair. He should resign because the impeachment anguish that his lies have invited will paralyze his Administration, at a time when an anxious world looks to the White House for sure-footed leadership.

He should resign because, if he does not, his once-glittering agenda of centrist change faces a devastating setback in November's Congressional elections. And those results will reflect not the view of the American majority of the issues—they are with him there—but only a weary, tragic turning away from a politics turned sordid.

Source 9   Editorial, *Charlotte Observer,* September 12, 1998

The nation is not endangered by having Bill Clinton in the White House. Our economy is not collapsing, and we're not under attack, there's no threat of a coup. Surely the worst that can be said of him has been said. He continues to exercise the powers of office, and did so rather well in Ireland and Russia. There is ample time for Congress to consider Starr's report and to receive a detailed reply from Clinton, then decide what course to pursue.

Removal of a President from office, by the impeachment process or by forced resignation, is a grave action. The notion that presidents should be removed or resign because of public outrage or unpopularity is foreign to our system.

Source 10   Editorial, "Go, You Despicable Man, Go, and Be Gone," *Washington Times,* September 13, 1998

President Clinton is a liar. That much was established beyond a doubt in August, when the man admitted he had "misled" people about his "inappropriate" relationship with Monica Lewinsky. But now that the Starr report is out, far more has been established, specifically, that the president lied under oath in a federal civil suit, lied before a federal grand jury, and at every turn attempted to get others to lie as well. Mr. Clinton has committed perjury. Mr. Clinton has tampered with witnesses. Mr. Clinton has obstructed justice. Mr. Clinton has abused his office. Of these things there is now abundant proof. . . .

Mr. Clinton's pathetic lies are not only violations of law, they are an ongoing insult to the American people. When the president appeared before the grand jury in August, he defended his lies as "legally accurate" evasions. He did not have sexual relations with Miss Lewinsky because he was only the recipient of oral sex. Mr. Clinton then repeated that whopper to the nation in his infamous non-apology speech. Even if it were true that Mr. Clinton was merely the passive beneficiary of Miss Lewinsky's generosity, Mr. Clinton had sex. To claim otherwise does violence to the English language and to common sense. Trying to pass such sophistry off on the grand jury and the American public is an insult to both, and no small indication of the contempt Mr. Clinton has for the law. . . .

For all the practiced hang-dog contrition, for all the moving rhetoric of repentance, the president continues to lie. It is an insult. It is brazen. And all people of conscience should now be demanding that he resign—and once for all take his leave of the sewer he has made out of public life.

Source 11   Editorial, "Low Crimes and Misdemeanors," *Washington Post,* September 13, 1998

Kenneth Starr's report to Congress on evidence of possibly impeachable conduct by President Clinton paints a devastating portrait of Mr. Clinton's behavior, honor, candor and respect for the obligations and dignity of his office. The compilation is such that Congress has no choice but to initiate an impeachment inquiry exploring seriously both the allegations themselves and the threshold standard for the impeachment and removal of a president. . . .

Unfortunately, however, Mr. Starr did not satisfy himself with making allegations that the evidence unambiguously supports, nor did he act in the restrained manner we would have hoped. Despite the report's repeated protestations that the president's testimony necessitated describing the affair in lurid detail, a clear demonstration that Mr. Clinton's conduct constituted "sexual relations" under the definition could have been accomplished by discreet citations to grand jury transcripts and exhibits. The decision to write the report in a form that resembles a steamy paperback smacks of an effort to embarrass the president. . . .

Even more arrogant is the aggressive advocacy for impeachment in Mr. Starr's document. To be sure, this advocacy is always couched in language sufficiently respectful of the constitutional fact that Congress—not any prosecutor—has the power to impeach the president. Yet the willingness of the prosecutors to draw inferences and make judgments plainly designed to color Congress's judgment is unmistakable and sharply in contrast to the restraint shown by the special prosecutor during Watergate.

Mr. Starr's errors, however, do not save Mr. Clinton. For even when the excesses are stripped away, the case he has presented is serious, while Mr. Clinton's current defense is contemptible. . . .

The question that Congress now faces is whether the president's public conduct warrants impeachment and removal. It is not an easy question, and it goes to the heart of what does and does not constitute "high crimes and misdemeanors." On the one hand, the crimes alleged are serious ones and the evidence is quite strong; on the other hand, this misconduct took place in the context of a subsequently dismissed civil case and would probably not, in other circumstances, have been deemed worthy of investigation or prosecution. Mr. Clinton's behavior is at the margins of impeachability—straddling the line that separates disqualifying crimes from conduct that merely mars indelibly the presidential office and the man who holds it.

Source 12 Editorial, "Starr's Report, Clinton's Rebuttal," *Chicago Tribune,* September 13, 1998

For eight months the American people have watched and listened with a mixture of embarrassment, bemusement, anger and indifference as bits and pieces of the Clinton-Lewinsky scandal leaked out.

On Friday the dam broke and the leaks became a torrent. With a click of a computer mouse, the whole sordid tale—or at least Independent Counsel Kenneth Starr's rendition of it—suddenly was on the record and available to all. It soon was followed by a rebuttal from President Clinton's legal team.

None of the documents paint an edifying picture. Indeed, as many people have noted during the Starr investigation, the details of the Clinton-Lewinsky liaison are so lurid and tawdry that parents would not let their children listen to news reports about them.

Turning one's head and covering one's ears may be acceptable for children but not for adults in a democratic republic. Not for citizens when our elected representatives must make one of the gravest decisions they are charged with: whether to set aside the results of a popular election and remove from office the president of the United States.

Source 13 Peter Baker and Juliet Eilperin, "Clinton Impeached," *Washington Post,* December 20, 1998

The House of Representatives impeached the president of the United States yesterday for only the second time in American history, charging William Jefferson Clinton with "high crimes and misdemeanors"—for lying under oath and obstructing justice to cover up an Oval Office affair with a young intern.

29.2 The Impeachment of William Jefferson Clinton

At 1:25 P.M. on a day of constitutional drama and personal trauma, the Republican-led House voted 228 to 206 largely along party lines to approve the first article of impeachment accusing the Democratic president of perjury before a grand jury. Within the hour, lawmakers went on to pass another article alleging he tampered with witnesses and helped hide evidence, but rejected two other articles on perjury and abuse of power.

A solemn, all-Republican delegation led by Judiciary Chairman Henry Hyde then marched across the Capitol to formally deliver the articles of impeachment to the secretary of the Senate, triggering what promises to be a trial like no other to determine whether the 42nd president will be removed from office. At the same time, scores of restive House Democrats piled into buses to drive up Pennsylvania Avenue and rally around their embattled leader at the White House.

Emerging from the Oval Office with first lady Hillary Rodham Clinton on his arm and Vice President Gore at his side, the president stood with his Democratic defenders and decried the partisan vote against him. Brushing aside calls for resignation, Clinton vowed to serve "until the last hour of the last day of my term."

The historic votes in the grand chamber at the Capitol came just hours after the newly anointed House speaker, Bob Livingston, called on Clinton to resign and then, abruptly and unexpectedly, took his own advice. "I must set the example that I hope President Clinton will follow," Livingston said, announcing he will step down because of the extramarital affairs he had reluctantly revealed on the eve of the impeachment debate.

Rarely has the capital been so whipsawed by events, as the nation's top leadership was left in disarray at the same time U.S. military forces mounted a fourth and final day of bombing runs against Iraq. . . . "This is all so overwhelming," said Rep. Michael N. Castle, one of the moderates who tried unsuccessfully to find a bipartisan compromise to impeachment but ultimately supported one of the articles calling for Clinton's removal. "There have been so many bombshells you can hardly turn your back."

Livingston's abdication may have chastened some lawmakers into restraining their rhetoric on the floor, but it also robbed much of import from the House vote.

"What's happened has just squeezed the life out of what will be the most important vote anyone here will ever cast. There's no drama," said Rep. Earl Blumenauer. "It's like another nerve gas, a pathogen in this medicine chest of toxic politics. . . . It continues a pattern here that this is all smaller than life: war, impeachment, the second speaker biting the dust, but I don't think you see the grand moment."

"High Crimes and Misdemeanors"

ARTICLE I, Section 2 of the Constitution provides that the House of Representatives "shall have the sole Power of Impeachment." Impeachment is the formal charge that the president, vice president, or some other civil officer of the federal government has committed an act of "Treason, Bribery, or other High Crimes and Misdemeanors." When such a charge is leveled at an official, the Senate sits as a court and hears the case. If the President is the accused, the Chief Justice of the Supreme Court presides over the Senate trial. The remedy—the only remedy—available to the Senate, should it find the charges valid, is to remove the accused from office.

The Office of the Independent Counsel submitted its report alleging impeachable offenses had been committed by President Clinton to the House of Representatives on September 9, 1998. The House Committee on the Judiciary began hearings on the charges on November 19th, and by December 12th was ready to present its findings. The Committee voted to recommend that the full House impeach the president on four counts stemming from his attempts to prevent disclosure of his affair with Monica Lewinsky from being revealed as part of the Paula Jones suit. The House of Representatives approved two of the four proposed articles of impeachment on December 19th, and referred the matter to the Senate.

At one o'clock on the afternoon of January 7, 1999, the Senate convened a trial that would last a little over five weeks. The case for impeachment was presented by a team of House Managers consisting of the Republican membership of the House Committee on the Judiciary. The president was represented by private counsel. A vote by a two-thirds majority in the Senate—67 or more of the 100 senators—to approve either of the two articles of impeachment would have resulted in the removal of Bill Clinton from office and the elevation of Al Gore to the presidency.

If the framers of the Constitution had expected an open and objective consideration by Congress of the facts and issues raised in such a proceeding, the impeachment and trial of President Clinton would have disappointed them. All the votes from beginning to end were highly partisan.

Source 14 Alison Mitchell, "Clinton Acquitted Decisively, No Majority for Either Charge," *New York Times*, February, 13, 1999

Washington, Feb. 12—The Senate today acquitted President Clinton on two articles of impeachment, falling short of even a majority vote on either of the charges against him: perjury and obstruction of justice.

29.3 The Clinton Crisis Front Page

After a harrowing year of scandal and investigation, the five-week-long Senate trial of the President—only the second in the 210-year history of the Republic—culminated shortly after noon when roll calls began that would determine Mr. Clinton's fate.

"Is respondent William Jefferson Clinton guilty or not guilty?" asked Chief Justice William H. Rehnquist in his gold-striped black robe. In a hushed chamber, with senators standing one by one to pronounce Mr. Clinton "guilty" or "not guilty," the Senate rejected the charge of perjury, 55 to 45, with 10 Republicans voting against conviction.

It then split 50-50 on a second article accusing Mr. Clinton of obstruction of justice in concealing his affair with Monica S. Lewinsky. Five Republicans broke ranks on the obstruction-of-justice charge. No Democrats voted to convict on either charge, and it would have taken a dozen of them, and all 55 Republicans, to reach the two-thirds majority of 67 senators required for conviction.

Chief Justice Rehnquist announced the acquittal of the nation's 42nd President at 12:39 P.M. "It is therefore ordered and adjudged that the said William Jefferson Clinton be, and he hereby is, acquitted of the charges in the said articles," he said. Almost immediately, the mood in the Senate lightened.

Source 15 President Clinton, statement to reporters, February 12, 1999

Now that the Senate has fulfilled its constitutional responsibility, bringing this process to a conclusion, I want to say again to the American people how profoundly sorry I am for what I said and did to trigger these events and the great burden they have imposed on the Congress and on the American people.

I am humbled and very grateful for the support and the prayers I have received from millions of Americans over the past year.

Now I ask all Americans, and I hope all Americans here in Washington and throughout our land, will rededicate ourselves to the work of serving our nation and building our future together. This can be a time of reconciliation and renewal for America.

Thank you very much.

Q. In your heart, sir, can you forgive and forget?

President Clinton. I believe any person who asks for forgiveness has to be prepared to give it.

📖 *Second Thoughts*
A Turning Point of History
or an Obscure Footnote?

The conduct of President Clinton was held on display before the American people and the world for over a year. There seemed for a time no topic more important or more widely aired. The ethics of the president's conduct in the courtroom was debated. The morality of the president's behavior in the bedroom was discussed. Matters once considered unmentionable were suddenly visible as topics on the evening news. Newspapers offered seemingly daily revelations, some true, some wild stretches of imagination. Cable news channels that boasted of being "All News" were derisively rechristened as "All Monica" networks. The "All Monica, all the time" format seemed also to infect the nation's tabloids and many of its leading newspapers. From the pulpit, in the classrooms, over the airways, and in the press, accusers and defenders held forth on the issue. In the end, the Congress judged the president and left him at his post. The judgment of history is yet to be rendered.

Source 16 **Editorial, "Congratulations, Mr. President,"** *Washington Times,* **February 13, 1999**

They bought it. They really bought it. Apparently the members of the World's Greatest Deliberative Body actually believed Mr. Clinton was just trying to refresh his memory when he made statements to Betty Currie that he knew were false. Monica the stalker came on to him, right?

They believed Vernon Jordan just happened to draft the Fortune 500 to get her a job. They believed it was only coincidence Ms. Currie stashed the gifts he gave to Ms. Lewinsky under Ms. Currie's own bed.

It all made so much sense that the Senate failed to muster majorities for either of the House articles of impeachment in Friday's vote. To a person, Democrats denounced the president for his despicable, heinous, appalling, indefensible conduct. And to a person they voted to condone it by keeping him in office.

Source 17 **Editorial, "Constitutional Justice,"** *New York Times,* **February 13, 1999**

In a season of frailty, the Constitution has prevailed once again.

It remains the great anchor rock of the Republic, enduring through partisan storms in the Congress, immune in the end to even so large and unpredicted a betrayal as the president's dereliction of duty.

If history were written on the same principles that govern news articles, that would be the lead of the sad story of William Jefferson Clinton and how he was spared to finish his second term. Neither the cheapness of Mr. Clinton's liaison with Monica Lewinsky nor the zealotry of some of his opponents should cause us to overlook the grandeur and symmetry of the constitutional template that yesterday produced the acquittal of the President on two articles of impeachment. . . .

As the curtain fell in windy Washington, it seemed more than ever a drama of tragical lineament. That is to say, the conflict that swirled all round the stage originated from the conflict within the protagonist's mind. Mr. Clinton and his constituency must look there for even a partial understanding of the hash he has made of his one and only one Presidency. Given what has been wasted, it is understandable that Mr. Clinton would be drawn to blame a conspiracy rather than his own addiction to reckless and bad advice.

Yet in the end, we still believe that Mr. Clinton's tragedy is a personal rather than a general one. With respect, we disagree with Arthur Schlesinger Jr.'s conclusion that because America has had a weak President it now has a weakened Presidency. The people stepping forward from both parties to compete for the office look capable of treating it with honor. And Congress has just demonstrated that an impeachment based solely on partisanship cannot succeed under a process that, like the Presidency itself, is founded on so steadfast a rock.

Source 18 Representative Henry Hyde, chairman of the House Committee on the Judiciary, "An Issue of Principles, Not Politics," *Chicago Tribune,* February 18, 1999

The impeachment of President Clinton was not a political struggle . . . but a historic constitutional test. A bedrock principle of democracy, first formulated by our Anglo-Saxon legal tradition in the Magna Carta, was at stake: the principle that no person is above the law. Birth, wealth and social position do not put someone above the law. Neither does public office. That, and nothing less than that, is what was at stake here. This was not a political struggle between Republicans and Democrats, conservatives and liberals, the World War II generation and the Baby Boom generation. This was a constitutional test of whether the United States government remains a government of laws, not of men.

That the gravity of this test is not recognized by some of my colleagues in the Congress is a cause for serious and ongoing concern. That no member of the Cabinet felt obliged to resign after the President had lied to them is a cause for concern. That many members of the Senate were unfamiliar with the facts of the case despite months of hearings in the House and Senate and extensive media coverage is a cause for concern.

That not a single Senate Democrat, in a group of strong, independent-minded individuals, was prepared to say publicly, at the trial's outset, that this was a matter of the gravest constitutional import and that he or she would step back and look at the facts with an unbiased eye and then render a judgment solely on those facts irrespective of party considerations is cause for concern. . . .

That the Senate Democrats treated this as a party-line vote is a matter for concern. . . .

What I cannot understand, frankly, is why not a single Senate Democrat, including those who condemned the President in language even harsher than their House colleagues proposed, called upon the President to resign.

The members of the House who voted to impeach a President for actions many members of his own party concede were felonious have nothing to apologize for. We did our duty.

If you choose to define this debate as just a squabble over "lying about sex," then I agree, impeachment might be overkill. But we understood this to be about lying under oath to a federal grand jury and obstructing justice by one bound faithfully to execute the laws—matters the independent counsel law placed squarely in our Judiciary Committee's jurisdiction. We sought a constitutional remedy to a constitutional issue.

Historians will judge how well we marshaled the evidence and argued the case. History also will judge the partisanship that led far too many senators to treat this as simply a political matter, much like any other vote. . . .

It never occurred to me as leader of the House managers, to think of this as a question in which there are winners and losers, as those terms are usually understood in politics. At issue was the Constitution and the rule of law. The Constitution and the rule of law would win, or they would lose.

The President has won his acquittal. It remains to be seen whether the Constitution and the rule of law have lost in the process.

Source 19   Jonathan Schell, "Coming to Judgment," *The Nation*, March 1, 1999

As this article goes to press the Senate is engaged in secret deliberations to render judgment on the conduct of William Jefferson Clinton. (When impeaching Presidents, it turns out, the middle name of the accused must always be used—as if, were it left out, some part of the President might wiggle free of condemnation.) Although attention is on the Senate, citizens also have to make up their minds. Since a political commentator, as I see it, is not as much an expert of any kind as merely a fairly well-informed citizen with a pen in his hand, and since I've been commenting regularly on impeachment for this magazine, it seems in order to say how I would have voted in the Senate (there's no mystery here—I'd acquit) and why.

One senator said the House managers did a "tremendous job of connecting the dots" of the case. Manager Bill McCollum told the senators, "The big picture is what you need to keep in mind." The details bearing on the question of Clinton's innocence or guilt were indeed displayed in abundance to the Senate. That question, however, is only one of those raised by the crisis, and perhaps not the most significant one. It may, in a sense, even be a distraction from the more important issues. For, from the start, the battle for the presidency of Bill Clinton, which began with the investigations of the Whitewater affair four and a half years ago, has combined two stories of official misconduct and abuse of power. One is Bill Clinton's conduct; the other is the conduct of his Republican accusers. Only the former tale of misconduct has been placed before the Senate. But both must be weighed. Both must be judged. What makes the task more difficult is that neither can be judged independently of the other. If we judge Clinton leniently, we must judge the Republicans harshly, and vice versa. If Clinton has committed serious crimes, then the Republicans are saving the constitutional order from great danger. But if Clinton's misdeeds are trivial, then the Republicans are on a rampage, and it is they who endanger the Constitution.

Consider, for example, the dots that must be connected by any reasonable person to form a "big picture" of the events on January 16 and January 17, 1998.

Until the 17th, Clinton had not committed any crimes, large or small. His reputation had withstood the longest and most relentless investigations ever made of a President—not only by the special prosecutor but by the Paula Jones lawyers—and he had emerged untouched.

It was on January 16 that Linda Tripp, equipped with a wire by the special prosecutor's team, surreptitiously taped Monica Lewinsky at the Ritz-Carlton Hotel. That evening, Tripp raced to meet with the Jones lawyers, with whom she had already been in contact, to tell them what she had learned from Lewinsky, in order to prepare them to ask questions of the President, whose deposition was scheduled for the next day. The importance of this timing is very striking. If Tripp had not talked to the Jones lawyers then, they would not have been able to ask the President the detailed questions about Lewinsky that launched him on his prevarications. Only further investigation will reveal the extent of contact between Tripp, Starr and the Jones lawyers, and whether illegal conduct occurred. It could be, for instance, that the Jones lawyers already knew about Lewinsky from Tripp, and needed the meeting that night in order to be able to justify their knowledge. However that might be, it is plain to the ordinary person that on January 17 Clinton walked into a trap—a trap prepared by the outlandish combination of a treacherous friend, who had been a holdover from the Bush Administration and was in search of a book deal; a runaway special prosecutor; and a legal team in a worthless sexual harassment suit fueled by the President's most dedicated enemies. Such are some of the "dots"—none of them presented for consideration by the Senate—that the citizens must connect when weighing the real big picture of the impeachment proceedings.

Justice that is not equal is not justice. The justice meted out to Clinton over four years had been so unequal as to amount to persecution. His life had been subjected to unparalleled investigation. Even then, the investigation discovered no misconduct; it produced misconduct, which subsequent investigation, itself marked by further abuses of power, then uncovered.

These facts—these "dots"—do not bear on the technical questions of whether Clinton committed perjury or obstructed justice, but they hugely influence my judgment not only of his conduct but of the case as a whole. I do not think I should know about Clinton's, or anyone else's, affairs. (I won't deny, though, having the average, chronic, low-grade and seemingly inexpungeable reflex of human curiosity about such matters.) The means by which I was made to know of the affair strike me as dangerous and, to use a term much applied to Clinton, "reprehensible." I fear them a hundred times more than I fear Clinton's deceptions. I do not think Linda Tripp should have secretly taped Monica Lewinsky. I do not think anyone should ever be forced to reveal in court to an entire class of people with whom they may have had sexual relations. I do not think Starr should have adopted the case when it was brought to him. I don't think anyone else should have adopted it, either. Faced with the unwelcome intrusion of this information into my life, I feel like a juror in a trial at one of those moments when a lawyer blurts out some forbidden piece of information, and the judge orders it stricken from the record and tells the jury it must disregard what it has learned. Like those jurors, who are required somehow to subtract from their judgments information that they cannot, after all, literally eject from their minds, I seek to refrain from judging Clinton on the basis of this information. . . .

Can my position—involving a sort of willed disregard of known facts—be justified? For of course the story goes on—the dots that need connecting keep appearing. That brings us to the charges against Clinton in the articles of impeachment. A trap may have been laid, but then Clinton did unquestionably put his foot in it. Who can deny that he lied in the Paula Jones lawsuit, for instance, when he said he had never been "alone" with Lewinsky? There is another lie that, although it also is omitted from the articles, constitutes for me the worst thing Clinton did—his declaration to the whole world, "I did not have sexual relations with that woman, Miss Lewinsky." The most offensive part of the lie was the "I want you to listen to me" with which he prefaced it. If Clinton, as he said this, maintained the mental reservation that oral sex did not constitute sexual relations, then I can only answer with William Blake: "A truth that's told with bad intent/Beats all the lies you can invent."

But did he commit the offenses named in the articles of impeachment? Regarding the perjury charge, it seems to me that what Clinton said before the grand jury about the Jones testimony—that he sought to walk through it as if it were a "minefield" without technically telling lies—though false about the Jones testimony, was true of his grand jury testimony. Clinton's challenge was to testify blurrily enough to say things that, while true, did not directly contradict the lies he'd told in the previous deposition. If he succeeded in this—as, arguably, he did (that is, it's not beyond a reasonable doubt that he didn't)—the performance is a tribute to his evasive skills, not his honesty. Much the same can be said of the obstruction of justice charge. Both Clinton and Vernon Jordan are experienced lawyers who certainly would go to great pains not to step over the technical line that would implicate them in obstruction of justice. If they did keep on the safe side of the line, then the reason may be the one Jordan gave when asked whether he'd told Lewinsky to get rid of her notes to the President: "I am not a fool." But if I apply not the "beyond a reasonable doubt" test, or even the less demanding "preponderance of the evidence" test, but only the ordinary person's "Whad-dya think?" test, I'd say it looks as if Clinton was doing all he possibly could, perhaps short of obvious lawbreaking, to keep Monica well disposed, in the hope—well justified, as it turned out—that in her deposition in the Jones case she would lie her head off.

It's been a notable fact that throughout the crisis, the ordinary citizen has believed the President guilty of such misconduct or worse, yet has not wished him impeached or removed from office. One reason may be that citizens—including citizen-commentators—are freer to give rein to their common sense than senators, who, as juror-judges, are quite properly constrained by the technical requirements of their role. . . .

Many people may indeed frankly wish that Clinton and Lewinsky had succeeded in concealing their relationship from the Jones lawyers, ending the scandal then and there—especially in view of the dismissal of the case shortly thereafter. The President's lawyers were hardly going to say to the Senate, "Clinton's lies in the deposition, backing up the lies Lewinsky had already told, were not such a bad idea, because he had good reason to think he could get away with them, sparing himself and the country a pointless ordeal—and anyway, who really expected Clinton, a known philanderer, to regale the country with a recitation of his sexual encounters with government employees?" . . .

There remains, then, an egregious disproportion between Clinton's misconduct and the legal and constitutional arsenal deployed against him. If I were to put a numerical value on this disproportion, I'd say that 20 percent of the impeachment crisis has been due to Clinton's misdeeds and about 80 percent to the extremism of the Republican Party. Impeachment has been more dangerous to the country by far than the behavior it condemns. By using the impeachment clause of the Constitution to prosecute minor offenses, the Republican Party has shown itself unworthy of the immense power placed at its disposal by the voters when they gave it control of both houses of Congress.

Source 20   Lisa Jardine, "Object of Oppression," *New Statesman*, April 2, 1999

When the Starr report was published in September 1998, the first instinct of many people who read it, or who cringed at the sexually explicit extracts conveniently made available by the media, was to deny that its contents could possibly be true. Here was a right-wing Republican conspiracy to blacken the name of a popular Democratic president.

It was the Harvard professor Stephen Greenblatt, in an op-ed piece for the *New York Times,* who alerted us to something fundamentally unsettling about the tone of the report. He compared it to the depositions in the 17th-century Salem witch trials: "The only other texts in which I have encountered comparable details—cold accounts of humans stripped of all the protective covering with which we contrive to cloak our nakedness—are the legal documents of the witchcraft trials in the Middle Ages and Renaissance, trials that extended in our own land well into the 17th century."

Greenblatt was referring to now-infamous matter-of-fact testimony starting with phrases such as, "According to Ms. Lewinsky, she performed oral sex on the president on nine occasions," and proceeding gratuitously to itemise the precise details of these encounters, as if performed in a morally neutral environment by robots. With such inventories of "wickedness" shared with the testimony of outraged inhabitants of 17th-century Salem against an unfortunate collection of vulnerable women, in Greenblatt's view, was the absolute, obsessive certainty of the prosecuting counsel that the conduct of the "accused" threatened to undermine the very foundations of civilized America. "Prosecutors and judges were so certain that the alleged crimes were a monstrous threat to the fabric of society, so convinced that the accused were absolutely evil, so determined to achieve the public finality of conviction and execution that they proceeded (legally for the most part) to violate every principle of equity, respect, ordinary common sense and decency. After all, the enemy was Satan and in the struggle against Satan all measures were justified."

Violating every principle of decency, Greenblatt concluded, Kenneth Starr and his team had demonised Monica Lewinsky and the president, translating their possibly innocuous conduct into grotesque perversions of human relations. Now, however, we have *Monica's Story,* the ghosted autobiography in which Monica herself attests to her own "culpability." Whereas six months ago the sub-pornographic details documented in the Starr report seemed altogether too lurid to believe, now Monica "'fesses up to all." Yes, it's true, on their very first encounter inside the White House in 1995 she "put her hands on her hips and with her thumbs lifted the back of her jacket, allowing (the president) a fleeting glimpse of her thong underwear."

Contriving another meeting, just hours later that same evening, the encounter indeed became "a good deal more intimate, their clothing unbuttoned, their hands exploring each other." And, oh yes, on Sunday, 31 March 1996 Monica "moistened one of the president's cigars in a most intimate fashion" and "realised that she had fallen in love."

But in *Monica's Story,* as told to Andrew Morton, Princess Diana's unauthorised biographer, as indeed in Monica's televised interviews with Barbara Walters and Jon Snow, these are not shameful incidents, guiltily or reluctantly recounted. Rather, she emerges as a determined, if insecure, young woman who knew what she wanted and how to get it. She embarked on a flirtation with a president with a reputation for his wandering eye, pursued the sexual liaison as far as she could, and persisted with the relationship even after the president panicked and tried to end it. In her Barbara Walters interview for prime-time American TV, under considerable emotional pressure from Walters, Lewinsky neither broke down nor backed down. She refused categorically to say she regretted the affair, and suggested she would do the same again. "I'm a sensual person," she said. Sex (including phone sex) was fun, intercourse an intrinsic part of a relationship, even outside marriage, even with a married man.

Monica Lewinsky is utterly misguided in her belief that she was in any sense in charge of events as they unfolded. There is something troubling about the way she represents herself as on the brink of being totally in control of her life. Her description of "pulling" the president of the United States reads as if she, rather than he, were making the running. Her response to his attempts to break off the relationship is to doubt that he means it, and contrive ingenious ways to gain access to him and win him back with her erotic charms. Just as disturbing is Andrew Morton's complicity in producing a narrative which is, spuriously, driven by Monica.

She would have been in control, she explains, except . . . over and over again in *Monica's Story* comes a single refrain. Everything would have been all right, she could have controlled everything, she could have controlled her president, outwitted Starr, and had her revenge on Linda Tripp. She could have had all this if only she hadn't had a weight problem. If she could only have kept herself slim, nothing dreadful would have happened to her. Morton, as onlooker and occasional commentator, agrees, regularly emphasising the fluctuations in Monica's weight, her diets and exercising, her counseling and the "fat camps" she goes to.

The historian Lyndal Roper has shown us how, heartbreakingly, women accused of witchcraft in the 16th-century produced vivid confessions, in graphic detail, of sex with the devil, of exhuming and eating their dead babies, of damaging crops and hurting their neighbor's children. Admitting their guilt, glorifying the damage they had supposedly done, gave them a kind of power in the midst of their helplessness. Abused, insulted and ultimately put to death, they sustained themselves for a brief commanding moment by becoming the absolute incarnation of evil in female form their male accusers were looking for.

Witch and prosecutor enter into an unholy alliance. The witch confesses, the prosecutor persuades her that her "powers" have deserted her, she is guilty and despicable. That is exactly what Starr and his team did to Lewinsky. Here,

I think we have the obscene heart of the "Lewinsky affair"; its obscenity is that of unmitigated oppression of women and it troublingly recalls the Salem witch trials. Hounded by viciously determined, unscrupulous prosecutors, held in isolation in contravention of her civil liberties, threatened, cajoled into confession, terrified into submission, Lewinsky, like the victims of the witch trials, entered into the belief-world of her enemies. Misogynists to a man, they passed the blame for everything they regarded as rotten in Bill Clinton's Democratic administration to the vulnerable, self-deprecating woman with an eating disorder.

Morton's biography bears witness to the hypnotic power of such persecution to persuade the victims to become, paradoxically, the desired object of their oppressors.

Source 21 Michael G. Gartner, "How the Monica Story Played in Mid-America," *Columbia Journalism Review,* May 1999

It is true, as critics note, that the scandal shoved other important news off the front pages and off the evening news. But were those stories more important than impeachment and the events leading up to it? Probably not. Campaign finance, Social Security, even East Timor and Uganda will still be in the news next month and next year, and you can always get back to them. But impeachment was the story of the year.

The output was prodigious. The Washington bureau of the Associated Press moved 4,109 stories on the scandal in the one year after it broke on January 21, 1998. It had twenty-five reporters working regularly on the story. The *New York Times* had a dozen Washington reporters on it, with another handful working on it in other cities.

Was all of this coverage—as some charge—a "feeding frenzy" by an over-eager press pushed by Washington bureau chiefs who delight in seeing big politicians tumble? In my view it's outrageous even to make such a charge. This was the greatest human, moral, political, and constitutional drama in our country since the end of the Civil War. It threatened to bring down a government and, perhaps more significantly, turn the country into a parliamentary democracy. It will reverberate forever. This was not just a lurid story like that of O. J. Simpson or JonBenet Ramsey. It was a drama about democracy.

The impeachment of a president comes along only "once every 130 years," says AP Washington bureau chief Sandy Johnson. "Lord knows that (a big story that comes) once a century is the story of any journalist, the story of his or her career." Who could fault this argument? Well, historian Arthur Schlesinger for one. He likened the press's performance to the yellow journalism of the old Hearst and Pulitzer days. And, he said at a *Columbia Journalism Review* forum on the eve of the impeachment vote: "I've never seen a greater disjunction between the media and the electorate than as we see at this moment."

Schlesinger was only half right. But the mainstream press went out of its way to avoid yellow journalism. Alan Murray, Washington bureau chief of the *Wall Street Journal,* said it was "a race to be last" in printing sex news about the president. Joseph Lelyveld, executive editor of the *New York Times,* told his staff: "This is the only area of news where I can't imagine wanting to be first. I need not just an excuse to do it. I need to be deprived of my last excuse not to do it." . . .

When mainstream newspapers did publish steamy and seamy news, it was usually only after it became general knowledge through the news media—the Internet and the all-news cable networks—and only after it had been verified and deemed relevant.

Still, there was a disjunction. The three traditional networks devoted 1,931 minutes to the Clinton scandal on their evening news shows in 1998—more than the next seven most-aired subjects combined. Those seven were the year's news from Iraq, Serbia, and the Mideast, the Wall Street gyrations, El Niño, tornadoes, and the embassy bombings in Africa. . . .

Yet the Pew Research Center for the People and the Press reports the Monica Lewinsky/Bill Clinton investigation barely made the top ten among the stories that Americans said they were "following very closely" in 1998. The top three stories they were interested in, according to a Pew poll of 805 adults interviewed December 19 to 21, were the school shootings in Jonesboro, in Oregon, and at the Capitol. Wars, elections, and the weather also were of more interest than the scandal. The impeachment vote itself "was a non-starter to the American public," the Pew Center reported. More people watched the CBS telecast of the New York Jets-Buffalo Bills football game on the Saturday of the impeachment vote in the House than watched the actual vote on ABC and NBC. . . .

The fact that the public wasn't very interested in the story is immaterial. This was a huge story, swirling in a new atmosphere, but it was the old media using the old rules that carried the day.

Source 22 Joanne Barkan, "Democratic Questions," *Dissent*, Spring 1999

The end of Bill Clinton's impeachment trial was a signal to the nation's varsity pundits—time to begin overall evaluations of the l'affaire Monica. The award for "most lugubrious wrap-up" goes to David Gergen. Speaking on a panel aired by C-SPAN, Gergen explained oh-so-gravely that the American people remain "deeply troubled" by Bill Clinton's lying; they crave "closure," but the system failed to provide it. For Gergen, Watergate gets a higher rating for closure: Richard Nixon resigned, Gerald Ford pardoned him, people felt the system worked.

Gergen misses the mark on both the 1974 pardon and this year's ordeal. We got grade-A closure as soon as William Rehnquist, presiding over the Senate trial, proclaimed the not-guilty verdict and banged the gavel. In fact, the one benefit of the protracted trial was a common sense of closure when it finally ended. Are the American people—that mythic whole—deeply troubled? No, two-thirds of them applauded the verdict; they continue to separate Clinton's lying about a sexual liaison from his responsibilities as president. And the other one-third of Americans? Angry frustration, not profound angst, probably describes their feelings. Their representatives fought hard to get rid of Clinton and lost. . . .

I don't minimize the threat to Constitution and political institutions posed by Ken Starr and the Republicans in Congress. Pie-eyed with their own moralizing, junked-out on personal antipathy toward Clinton, they trampled legal protections, twisted precedents, and would have gladly demolished the separation of powers. We counted all along on the Senate's sixty-seven-vote threshold to stop them. A handful of votes seems like flimsy armor for democratic institutions. Yet everything that protects a democracy—freedom of the press, independent judiciary, reasonable public opinion, engaged citizenry—is fragile. They all require endless cultivation.

Source 23 Richard John Neuhaus, "Bill Clinton and the American Character," *First Things: A Monthly Journal of Religion and Public Life,* June 1999

The political philosopher Leo Strauss liked to say that the American system was built on foundations that are low and solid. The Clinton presidency was built on foundations that are low and sordid. For all his successes in life, it seems that Bill Clinton as a person never rose above his origins. That is a difficult subject not untouched by the delicate question of class, but the fact is that Clinton plays to the pit. Maureen Dowd of the *Times,* who nonetheless opposed the impeachment, writes: "He campaigned and governed using lowbrow forums of popular entertainment . . . and now the lowbrow culture he cultivated has engulfed his presidency and, most likely, his legacy. Just as movie and television comedy is permeated with the ill-mannered, self-indulgent mentality of adolescent boys, Mr. Clinton has reversed the usual pattern of the presidency, switching from a paternal model to an adolescent model. He expects us to clean up, ignore, or forgive his messes . . . You might call it a vast gross-out conspiracy."

Lowbrow. As in lower class. It is a term deemed dangerously incorrect today, but it is a reality that cannot be denied. Here it means not the economically poor but the morally impoverished. In the past we were a lot more candid about the fact that a large number of people in any society, including this one, are moral slobs . . . Once upon a time there were "our kind of people" and other kind of people. The better kind of people felt an obligation to help uplift the lesser breeds. Today the lesser breeds are victims and the better kind of people are the victimizers—or at least so our academic and media elites would convince us. . . .

Like none who have held office before him, the MTV President has exulted in playing to the pit in a populism not of policy but of appetite. In an orchestrated slander against a woman on whom Clinton tried to force himself, and with whom he later settled out of court for a huge sum, a Clinton media lackey spoke of the trash that turns up when you trawl money through a trailer park. It is a fitting image of this presidency, and the trailer park is not just Arkansas, for every state and every community has a sub-culture that wallows in being pandered to, even as the panderer wallows in their gratitude for his being one of them. Ronald Reagan started out in Hollywood and lived it down by living up to the presidency. Bill Clinton's achievement is to be accepted by a Hollywood responsible for a meretricious popular culture to which he has defined down the presidency. With a wink and a nudge, the media and politics junkies went along with it for a long time, declaring him a political genius. Until it became evident that he viewed them, too, as trash to be trawled—and casually discarded when they no longer play the game.

Over the year, . . . puzzlement was regularly expressed at Clinton's high ratings in the opinion polls. Playing low can keep the ratings high. A majority was agreeing with Senator Harkin that Clinton is a failed human being but a good President—or at least that he is not so bad a President that he should be removed, or at least that he should not be removed for an adolescent sexual indulgence, or at the very least that he should not be forced out of office by those whom the nightly news portray as vicious partisans out to get him.

Moreover, put together the numbers: feminists and those intimidated by them, for whom the only issue is abortion; die-hard liberal Democrats and leftists on the commanding heights of culture for whom conservatism is pure evil; big labor, especially in education and other parts of the pubic sector, for whom the alternative to Clinton is catastrophe; and blacks who are publicly grateful for the assurance that Master feels their pain. Add in the very large number of sensible Americans who found the whole thing repugnant and just wanted it to go away, and you ended up with those high "approval" ratings. . . .

What happened beginning in January 1998 does not tell us much worth knowing about "the American people." The fact is that nothing like this has happened to us before. If it is allowed to happen again any time soon, we might have to reconsider the dark ponderings about the American character that have gained such currency. The most hopeful thought is that enough Americans have learned from this experience never again to entrust the presidency to a person of such reckless habits and suspect character. But that hope comes with no guarantee.

Meanwhile, we have a President who is guilty of perjury, witness tampering, the obstruction of justice, and sexual predation, including, it seems, at least one rape. Very likely there will be further charges, and possibly further crimes, in the months to come. . . . Until somebody comes up with a better idea, the course of wisdom is to pray for the nation while averting our eyes as much as public duty permits from the sorry spectacle of a man stumbling through the rubble of what remains of a ruined presidency.

Source 24   Roberto Suro, "Clinton Is Sanctioned in Jones Lawsuit, *Washington Post*, July 30, 1999

A federal judge yesterday ordered President Clinton to pay nearly $90,000 to Paula Jones's legal team for giving false testimony about his relationship with Monica Lewinsky, marking the first time a sitting president has been punished for contempt of court.

In a 19-page order, U.S. District Court Judge Susan Webber Wright of Arkansas said, "sanctions must be imposed to redress the President's misconduct and to deter others who might consider emulating the President's misconduct." The payment—to compensate Jones' lawyers for extra time and expense they incurred because of Clinton's false statements—is far less than the sum sought by the Jones lawyers but almost triple what Clinton had suggested . . .

Wright says she "takes no pleasure in imposing contempt sanctions against this Nation's President, and no doubt like many others grows weary of this matter."

However, she said, "The Court has determined that the president deliberately violated this Court's discovery orders, thereby undermining the integrity of the judicial system."

In a statement, Clinton attorney Robert S. Bennett said, "We accept the order and will comply with it." . . .

Jones claimed in the original lawsuit that Clinton had made unwanted sexual advances toward her in 1991, when she was a state employee and he was governor of Arkansas. Clinton settled the lawsuit for $850,000 in November, just as Congress began impeachment proceedings against him.

 ## Questioning the Past

1. Should President Clinton, or any other person, be compelled to reveal details of a consensual sexual relationship in court?

2. Did the offenses committed by President Clinton justify his removal from office? Defend your answer.

3. Was the struggle over impeachment, as Henry Hyde argued, an "issue of the Constitution and the rule of law"? Or, was it a highly partisan political confrontation founded in fundamental differences of political philosophy? Or was it merely a "squabble over lying about sex." Present evidence in support of each of these contentions. Which view is the more persuasive?

4. The report by Office of the Independent Counsel asserted that the president should be held to an even higher standard than that of other citizens because the presidency "is the inspiring symbol of all that is highest in American purpose and ideals." Debate this assertion.

5. It seems clear that the president did not tell the truth when testifying under oath. Did this set a precedent that could adversely affect the behavior of other citizens and jeopardize the effectiveness of the judicial process?

6. Is there a need to appoint an independent counsel to investigate the conduct of high government officials or is it sufficient to rely on the established investigative agencies? Defend your answer.

Glossary

barbette an armored structure protecting a gun turret on a warship 5

barrage balloons sausage-shaped balloons whose tethering cables would destroy fighter planes flying low enough to target their bombs accurately 315

battery group of warship guns 4

Black Kettle leader of a band of Cheyenne camped at Sand Creek, Colorado, that was attacked by state militiamen and federal troops on November 29, 1864, despite the fact that the Cheyenne were at peace with the U.S. government and Black Kettle flew an American flag over his tipi. Black Kettle escaped, but some 450 Cheyenne were killed in what a congressional investigation termed a "barbarity of the most revolting character." Four years later, Black Kettle's camp was again attacked without provocation, this time by Custer and his 7th Cavalry. Black Kettle was killed. 84

boodlers bribers 229

braggadocio cockiness, or empty boasting 132

buncombe humbug or empty talk, from the North Carolina congressman of 1819–21 who continually felt compelled to "make a speech for Buncombe," his home county; sometimes spelled bunkum 264

captiousness a highly critical or carping mood 218

Cloaca Maxima an underground passageway built beneath the Roman Forum to carry away sewage. Built in the third century B.C., it is still in use. 344

communes Carl Browne's term for the units of the workers' army 110

condign deserved, appropriate 59

Corregidor a 2-square-mile island at the entrance to Manila Bay 145

debauch an orgy 232

Donnelly, Ignatius a Populist politician from Minnesota at the turn of the century, who was a persuasive speaker, using humor and a commanding array of facts and figures to win audiences over to reform 118

flambeaux of Chautauqua the torches used to light activities at a popular New York State camp on Chautauqua Lake that presented lectures and concerts in the late nineteenth and early twentieth centuries 264

fusillade many shots fired simultaneously or in rapid succession 94

Gabriel Gabriel Prosser, who led 1,000 slaves in rebellion in Richmond in 1800 129

Gatling guns machine guns with a revolving cluster of barrels, named after their inventor, Richard J. Gatling 87

General Slocum a wooden paddle steamer that caught fire on the East River in New York City on June 15, 1904, while carrying 640 adults and 740 children on a Sunday School outing. The captain and crew had no training in firefighting, the ship's firefighting equipment didn't function, the lifeboats had not been inspected in 13 years, and the captain continued sailing into the wind, which caused the fire to burn back onto the passengers. More than 1,000 children perished in the disaster, and the captain was sentenced to 10 years in prison for his negligence. 183

gibbetted executed by hanging, from an upright post with a projecting arm designed for public display to deter crime 97

habeas corpus A writ issued by a judge if the court finds that a prisoner was illegally incarcerated. The prisoner must then be released. This is a right guaranteed under Article I Section 9 of the U.S. Constitution. 35

hinds an archaic meaning of this word was rustic people 265

Hotchkiss guns weapons made in Paris, France, in a factory founded by Benjamin Hotchkiss, an American. This type of weapon was probably light artillery that was suitable for use in the mountains, since it could be broken down and carried by mules. 84

Hottentots a pastoral people of southern Africa, or generally any primitive group 268

iron clads warships with metal armor; previously naval vessels were made of wood 18

Issei Japanese term for people born in Japan who emigrated to the United States. These immigrants were ineligible for U.S. citizenship on racial grounds. 316

Kibei Japanese term for the grandchildren of Japanese immigrants, the second generation to be born in the United States 316

Jim Crow a stereotype of a black male character in a nineteenth-century song and dance act 125

lex talionis a Latin phrase literally meaning law of the claw; retaliatory law, such as "an eye for an eye, a tooth for a tooth" 98

Maidanek a notorious Nazi death camp in Poland, where an estimated 1.4 million Jews were executed during World War II 330

milieu environment, setting, or background 69

Mundt, Karl a conservative U.S. senator who was a contemporary of Joseph McCarthy 355

My Lai (4) a subhamlet so designated on United States military maps, but called Thuan Yen by the Vietnamese. U.S. maps noted six My Lai subhamlets, located on the coast of the South China Sea some five miles northeast of Quang Ngai City in Quang Ngai Province. 443

Nesei often spelled Nisei, the Japanese term for the first generation of children born in the United States to immigrant parents 306

Ostend Manifesto a confidential diplomatic dispatch drafted in 1854 by three United States ambassadors: James Buchanan (Great Britain), John Y. Mason (France), and Pierre Soule (Spain) during a meeting in Ostend, Belgium. President Pierce had directed Soule to offer Spain $130 million for Cuba, and the ambassadors suggested in the manifesto that if Spain refused to sell, the United States should take Cuba by force under the "great Law of self-preservation." When the dispatch was leaked to the public, it led to a political scandal among Northerners who interpreted it as part of a Southern conspiracy to expand slavery into Cuba. 420

padrone from the Italian word for patron, the inside contractor who hired factory workers 188

Piegan member of a tribe that was part of the Blackfeet Nation. On January 23, 1870, troops acting on orders from Philip Sheridan attacked a Piegan village and massacred some 200 men, women, and children, many of whom were ill with smallpox contracted from white settlers. 80

pot-valiant Falstaff describing someone made brave or foolhardy by alcohol; derived from the fat, roguish Shakespearean character in the plays *Merry Wives of Windsor* and *Henry IV* 116

quiddities quibbles or trifling points 100

rams warships designed to pierce the sides of wooden warships below the waterline. Confederate rams were used to resist the blockade of Southern ports by the Union navy. 18

saturnalian resembling an orgy or unrestrained celebration, from the ancient Roman festival of Saturn 97

shibboleth originally a Hebrew word for stream, different pronunciations of which betrayed people's regional origins; now a word or saying used by adherents of a party or cause, which opponents usually regard as empty of real meaning 286

Simpson, Sockless Jerry a Populist politician and orator in Kansas at the turn of the century, who criticized a Republican opponent's aristocratic appearance by dubbing him a "Prince Hal" in silk stockings. Simpson got his nickname from a scornful newspaper story that termed him a country bumpkin who wore no socks. 118

six-shooter term originating in 1844 for a six-chambered revolver; later called a six-gun 65

square deal concept that originated with President Theodore Roosevelt, who said in a 1903 speech, "A man who is good enough to shed his blood for his country is good enough to be given a square deal afterwards." In his 1913 autobiography he wrote, "We demand that big business give the people a square deal; in return we must insist that when anyone engaged in big business honestly endeavors to do right he shall himself be given a square deal." 69

superforts short for superfortresses, a common nickname for B-29 bombers 324

tatterdemalion a ragamuffin, or person in ragged clothes 265

Tillman, Pitchfork Ben a conservative southern Congressman at the turn of the century 118

tipsin an edible root 85

Toussaint the Saviour Toussaint-L'Ouverture, leader of a successful slave rebellion in the 1790s in Haiti and the Dominican Republic. Considered a brilliant administrator, he established a republic of freed slaves. 129

Turner Nat Turner, leader of a slave rebellion in Virginia in 1831 (see chapter 19 of Volume I, *Historical Moments*) 129

Vesey Denmark Vesey, who planned and led a potential slave rebellion in Charleston in 1822; the rebels abandoned their quest because of stormy weather. 129

volley simultaneous discharge of a battery of weapons 5

Weaver, James a politician, attorney, successful orator, and Union veteran of the Civil War who toured the country supporting various reform movements. He was the Greenback Party candidate for president in 1880 and the People's Party candidate in 1892. 118

Welker, Herman a conservative U.S. senator who was a contemporary of Joseph McCarthy 355

Sources

Chapter 1: Civil War

Source 1: Gideon Welles, *Diary of Gideon Welles* (Boston: Houghton Mifflin, 1911), pp. 3–4.

Source 2: *Alexandria Gazette and Virginia Advertiser.*

Source 3: Mary Boykin Chesnut, *A Diary From Dixie* (Boston: Houghton Mifflin, 1949), p. 36.

Source 4: *Alexandria Gazette and Virginia Advertiser,* April 15, 1861.

Source 5: Frank Moore, ed., *The Rebellion Record,* vol. 1 (New York: G. P. Putnam, 1861), pp. 166–175.

Source 6: James D. Richardson, ed., *Messages and Papers of the Presidents,* vol. 6 (Washington, DC: U.S. Government Printing Office, 1897), pp. 20–31.

Source 7: Henry Wilson, "Speech on Bill to Confiscate the Property and Free the Slaves of Rebels," Mayo W. Hazeltine, ed., *Masterpieces of Eloquence: Famous Orations of Great World Leaders from Early Greece to the Present Time,* vol. XVII (New York: P. F. Collier & Son, 1905), pp. 7224–7226.

Source 8: Clement L. Vallandigham, "Speech on the War and Its Conduct," Mayo W. Hazeltine, ed., *Masterpieces of Eloquence: Famous Orations of Great World Leaders from Early Greece to the Present Time,"* vol. XIX (New York; P. F. Collier & Son, 1905), pp. 8138–8139.

Source 9: Edward Pollard, *The Lost Cause: A New Southern History of the War of the Confederates* (New York: E. B. Treat, 1866), pp. 46–51.

Source 10: Alexander H. Stephens, *A Constitutional View of the Late War between the States,* vol. 1 (Philadelphia: National Publishing Company, 1868), pp. 9–10.

Source 11: Henry Wilson, *The History of the Rise and Fall of Slavepower in America* (Boston: Osgood & Company, 1877), pp. 127–128.

Source 12: James Ford Rhodes, *Lectures on the American Civil War* (New York: The Macmillan Company, 1913), pp. 2, 6.

Source 13: Charles and Mary Beard, *The Rise of American Civilization* (New York: Macmillan Company, 1933), vol. 1, pp. 632–633, vol. 2, pp. 53–54. Copyright © 1933 by Macmillan Publish-ing Company, Inc., renewed 1961 by William Beard and Miriam B. Vagts. Reprinted by permission of Prentice-Hall, Inc., Upper Saddle River, NJ.

Source 14: Allan Nevins, *The Emergence of Lincoln,* vol. 2, (New York: Charles Scribner's Sons, 1950), p. 468.

Source 15: David Donald, *Lincoln Reconsidered: Essays on the Civil War Era* (New York: Vintage Books, 1961), pp. 215, 217, 226–228, 233–235. Copyright © 1947, 1950, 1951, 1956 by David Donald. Reprinted by permission of Alfred A. Knopf, Inc.

Source 16: Eugene Genovese, *The Political Economy of Slavery: Studies in the Economy and Society of the Slave South* (New York: Vintage Books, 1967), p. 8.

Source 17: Howard Zinn, *A People's History of the United States* (New York: Harper & Row, 1980), p. 184. Copyright © 1980 by Howard Zinn. Reprinted by permission of HarperCollins Publishers, Inc.

Chapter 2: One Nation, Indivisible

Source 1: *Alexandria Gazette,* April 10, 1865.

Source 2: "The Rebellion," *New York Times,* April 11, 1865.

Source 3: "Lee Surrenders!", *New York Tribune,* April 15, 1865.

Source 4: *Alexandria Gazette,* April 12, 1865.

Source 5: "Magnanimity in Triumph," *New York Tribune,* April 15, 1865.

Source 6: Walter L. Fleming, *Documentary History of Reconstruction: Political, Military, Social, Religious, Educational & Industrial, 1865 to the Present Time,* vol. I, (Cleveland, Ohio: The Arthur H. Clark Company, 1906), p. 137.

Source 7: Fleming, vol. I, p. 116.

Source 8: *"New York Times,* May 5, 1865.

Source 9: Fleming, vol. I, pp. 1281–1130.

Source 10: Fleming, vol. I, p. 247.

Source 11: Fleming, vol. I, p. 117.

Source 12: Fleming, vol. I, pp. 251–253.

Source 13: Fleming, vol. I, p. 117.

Source 14: Fleming, vol I, pp. 147–149.

Source 15: Constitution of the United States.

Source 16: Ignatius Donnelly, "Reconstruction," Mayo W. Hazeltine, ed., *Masters of Eloquence: Famous Orations of Great World Leaders from Early Greece to the Present Time,* vol. XXII (New York: P. F. Collier & Son, 1905), pp. 9423–9427.

Source 17: Olive Perry Morton, "On the Issues of 1868," Mayo W. Hazeltine, ed., *Masters of Eloquence: Famous Orations of Great World Leaders from Early Greece to the Present Time,* vol. XX (New York: P. F. Collier & Son, 1905), pp. 8486–8487, 8491–8492.

Source 18: Donald Brice Johnson, *National Party Platforms: 1840–1956,* vol. I (Urbana: University of Illinois Press, 1978), pp. 37–38.

Source 19: Constitution of the United States.

Source 20: Constitution of the United States.

Source 21: Walter L. Fleming, *Documentary History of Reconstruction: Political, Military, Social, Religious, Educational & Industrial, 1865 to the Present Time,* vol. II, (Cleveland, Ohio: The Arthur H. Clark Company, 1906), p. 295.

Source 22: Hilary A. Herbert, *et al., Why, the Solid South? Or, Reconstruction and Its Results* (Baltimore: R. H. Woodward & Company, 1890), pp. 430, 437–438, 440.

Source 23: John W. Burgess, *Reconstruction and the Constitution, 1866–1876* (New York: Charles Scribner's Sons, 1902), pp. 297–298.

Source 24: James Ford Rhodes, *The History of the United States, from the Compromise of 1850 to the Final Restoration of Home Rule at the South in 1877,* vol. VII (New York: The Macmillan Company, 1906), pp. 170–171.

Source 25: William Archibald Dunning, *Reconstruction: Political and Economic, 1865–1877* (New York: Harper & Brothers, 1907), pp. 205, 208–209, 213–214.

Source 26: Fleming, vol. II, pp. 381–383.

Source 27: W. E. B. Du Bois, *Black Reconstruction: An Essay toward a History of the Part Black Folk Played in the Attempt to Reconstruct Democracy in America, 1860–1880* (New York: S. A. Russell Company, 1935), pp. 712, 723, 725–726.

Source 28: Carl N. Degler, *Out of Our Past: The Forces That Shaped Modern America* (New York: Harper & Row, 1970), pp. 208–210. Copyright © 1959, 1970 by Carl N. Degler. Reprinted by permission of HarperCollins Publishers, Inc.

Source 29: Barbara Jeanne Fields, *Slavery and Freedom on the Middle Ground: Maryland during the Nineteenth Century* (New Haven:Yale University Press, 1985), pp. 167, 192–193. Copyright © 1985 by the Yale University Press. Reprinted by permission of Yale University Press.

Source 30: Eric Foner, *Reconstruction: America's Unfinished Revolution, 1863–1877* (New York: Harper & Row, 1988), pp. xxvii, 603.

Source 31: Robert A. Divine, T. H. Breen, George M. Fredrickson, R. Hal Williams, *America: Past and Present,* vol. II (New York: Longman, 1998), p. 496–497. Copyright © 1999 by Addison Wesley Educational Publishers, Inc.

Chapter 3: The Assassination

Source 1: Washington *Evening Star,* April 15, 1865; (Washington) *National Intelligencer,* April 15, 1865.

Source 2: *Evening Star,* April 15, 1865.

Source 3: *National Intelligencer,* April 15, 1865.

Source 4: *Evening Star,* April 15, 1865.

Source 5: Ibid.

Source 6: Ibid., April 18, 1865.

Source 7: Ibid.

Source 8: Ibid., April 21, 1865.

Source 9: Ibid., April 22, 1865.

Source 10: Ibid., April 25, 1865; April 27, 1865; April 28, 1865.

Source 11: Louis Untermeyer, ed., *A Treasury of Great Poems English and American* (New York: Simon & Schuster, 1955), pp. 904–905.

Source 12: James D. Richardson, ed., *Messages and Papers of the Presidents, 1787–1897,* vol. 6 (Washington, DC: U.S. Government Bureau of National Art and Literature, 1900), pp. 307–308.

Source 13: *New York Times,*. May 5, 1865.

Source 14: Horace Greeley, *The American Conflict: A History of the Great Rebellion in the United States, 1860–65,* vol. 2 (Hartford: O. D. Case, 1976), pp. 748–750.

Source 15: *Evening Star,* December 7, 1870.

Source 16: Paul M. Angle, ed., *Herndon's Life of Lincoln* (New York: Albert & Charles Boni, 1936), p. 460.

Source 17: John G. Nicolay and John Hay, *Abraham Lincoln: A History* (New York: Century, 1909), p. 431.

Source 18: William Archibald Dunning, *Reconstruction: Political & Economic* (New York: Harper Torchbook, 1962), pp. 20–21.

Source 19: W. E. B. Du Bois, *Black Reconstruction in America* (New York: Russell & Russell, 1963), p. 165.

Source 20: Kenneth M. Stampp, *The Era of Reconstruction, 1865–1877* (New York: Alfred A. Knopf, 1965), pp. 27, 36, 48–49.

Chapter 4: The Wild West

Source 1: *The Life of John Wesley Hardin, as Written by Himself* (Norman: University of Oklahoma Press, 1961), pp. 88–95.

Source 2: Ibid., pp. 124–125.

Source 3: *El Paso Daily Herald,* August 20, 1895.

Source 4: Walter Prescott Webb, *The Great Plains* (New York: Grosset & Dunlap, 1931), pp. 496–498, 500. Copyright © 1931 by Walter Prescott Webb.

Source 5: E. C. Abbott and Helena Huntington Smith, *We Pointed Them North: Recollections of a Cowpuncher* (Norman: University of Oklahoma Press, 1971), pp. 23–25.

Source 6: C. L. Sonnichsen, *I'll Die before I'll Run: The Story of the Great Texas Feuds* (New York: Harper & Brothers, 1951), pp. 46–47.

Source 7: Lewis Nordyke, *John Wesley Hardin: Texas Gunman* (New York: William Morrow, 1957), pp. 268, Foreword, 268–269.

Source 8: Ramon F. Adams, "Cowboys and Horses of the American West," in *The Book of the American West,* Jay Monaghan, ed. (New York: Julian Messner and Bonanza Books, 1963), p. 333.

Source 9: Bill O'Neal, *Encyclopedia of Western Gunfighters* (Norman: University of Oklahoma Press, 1979), pp. 3–5.

Source 10: John Spanier, *Games Nations Play* (Washington, DC: Congressional Quarterly Press, 1993), pp. 549–550.

Chapter 5: Little Bighorn

Source 1: Frederick W. Turner III, ed., *The Portable North American Indian Reader* (New York: Penguin Books, 1980), p. 255.

Source 2: "Letter from One of Terry's Staff," *New York Times,* July 9, 1876.

Source 3: "Uncle Sam's Crook: Will He Straighten the Sinuous Sioux of the Yellowstone?" *Chicago Times,* July 1, 1876.

Source 4: *Evening Star* (Washington, DC), July 7, 1876.

Source 5: "Massacre of Our Troops," *New York Times,* July 6, 1876.

Source 6: "Massacre by the Indians," *Morning News* (Savannah, GA) July 7, 1876.

Source 7: "Gen. Custer," *New York Times,* July 9, 1876.

Source 8: "Custer's Last Battle," *Evening Star,* July 7, 1876.

Source 9: "An Indian Victory," *New York Times,* July 7, 1876.

Source 10: "The Little Horn Massacre," *Morning News* (Savannah), July 7, 1976.

Source 11: "Dispatches from Gen. Sheridan," *New York Times,* July 9, 1876.

Source 12: "What Is Thought in Washington," *New York Times,* July 8, 1876.

Source 13: "Gen. Terry's Official Report," *New York Times,* July 9, 1876.

Source 14: *Evening Star* (Washington), July 10, 1876.

Source 15: John F. Finerty, *War-Path and Bivouac: The Big Horn and Yellowstone Expedition* (Lincoln: University of Nebraska Press, 1955), pp. 203–204.

Source 16: Stanley Vestal, *Sitting Bull: Champion of the Sioux* (Norman: University of Oklahoma Press, 1989), pp. 160–167.

Source 17: George Armstrong Custer, *My Life on the Plains,* Milo Milton Quaife, ed. (Lincoln: University of Nebraska Press, 1966), p. ix.

Source 18: Mari Sandoz, *The Battle of the Little Big Horn* (Philadelphia: J. B. Lippincott, 1966), pp. 176–177.

Source 19: Vine Deloria Jr., *Custer Died for Your Sins: An Indian Manifesto* (New York: Avon Books, 1970), pp. 150–152. Copyright © 1969, renewed 1997 by Vine Deloria Jr. Reprinted by permission of Scribner, a division of Simon & Schuster, Inc.

Source 20: Robert M. Utley, *Cavalier in Buckskin: George Armstrong Custer and the Western Military Frontier* (Norman: University of Oklahoma Press, 1988), pp. 194–197. Reprinted by permission of the publishers.

Chapter 6: The Haymarket Affair

Source 1: August Spies, "The Revenge Circular," May 3, 1886.

Source 2: Handbill circulated in Chicago, May 4, 1886.

Source 3: "Now It Is Blood!" *Inter Ocean* (Chicago), May 5, 1886.

Source 4: Dyer D. Lum, *The Great Trial of the Chicago Anarchists* (New York: Arno Press & the New York Times, 1969), pp. 26–29.

Source 5: "The Chicago Murders," *New York Times,* May 6, 1886.

Source 6: Lum, pp. 29–30.

Source 7: Henry David, *The History of the Haymarket Affair: A Study of the American Social-Revolutionary and Labor Movements* (New York: Farrar & Rinehart, 1936), p. 322.

Source 8: *The Accused and the Accusers: The Famous Speeches of the Eight Chicago Anarchists in Court* (New York: Arno Press & the *New York Times*, 1969), pp. 176–177.

Source 9: Ibid., pp. 182–183.

Source 10: Lum, p. 174.

Source 11: "The Executions," *New York Times*, November 12, 1887.

Source 12: U.S. Supreme Court, *Schenck v. U.S.*, 249 U.S. 47 (1919).

Source 13: James Ford Rhodes, *History of the United States, from the Compromise of 1850 to the McKinley-Bryan Campaign of 1896*, vol. 8 (New York: Macmillan, 1920), pp. 278–279, 283–284.

Source 14: Philip Taft and John A. Sessions, eds., *Seventy Years of Labor: An Autobiography by Samuel Gompers* (New York: E. P. Dutton, 1957), pp. 237–239.

Source 15: Alexander Berkman, *What is Communist Anarchism? [Now and After: The ABC of Communist Anarchism]* (New York: Dover Publications, 1972), pp. xxv–xxvi, 49, 57–60, 173–174, 178–181.

Source 16: Matthew Josephson, *The Robber Barons: The Great American Capitalists, 1861–1901* (New York: Harcourt, Brace & World, 1962), pp. 365–367.

Source 17: David, p. 528.

Source 18: Foster Rhea Dulles, *Labor in America* (New York: Thomas Y. Crowell, 1960), pp. 124–125, 146.

Source 19: Joseph G. Rayback, *A History of American Labor* (New York: Free Press, 1966), pp. 167–168.

Source 20: Paul Avrich, *The Haymarket Tragedy* (Princeton, NJ: Princeton University Press, 1984), pp. 454, 456.

Chapter 7: Coxey's Army

Source 1: "Coxey Declares He Will Speak If He Goes to Jail for It," *Washington Post*, May 1, 1894.

Source 2: "Leaving the Camp," *Evening Star* (Washington), May 1, 1894.

Source 3: "The March on the Capitol: A Spectacle Unlike Anything Ever Before Witnessed in Washington," *Washington Post*, May 2, 1894.

Source 4: "Exciting Scene at the Capitol," *Evening Star* (Washington), Extra Edition, May 1, 1894.

Source 5: "Coxey Silenced by Police," *New York Times*, May 2, 1894.

Source 6: "Mr. Coxey's Protest," *Evening Star*, May 1, 1894; "The Protest Coxey Didn't Read," *New York Times*, May 2, 1894.

Source 7: Oliver Otis Howard, "The Menace of Coxeyism: Significance and Aims of the Movement," *North American Review*, CCCCLI (June 1894), pp. 687–688.

Source 8: Thomas Byrnes, "The Menace of Coxeyism: Character and Methods of the Men," *North American Review*, CCCCLI (June 1894), p. 697.

Source 9: Alvah H. Doty, "The Menace of Coxeyism: The Danger to the Public Health," *North American Review*, CCCCLI (June, 1894), pp. 701, 704.

Source 10: Henry Vincent, *The Story of the Commonweal: Complete and Graphic Narrative of the Origin and Growth of the Movement* (Chicago: W. B. Conkey, 1894), p. 164.

Source 11: Ibid., pp. 16–17.

Source 12: W. T. Stead, "Coxeyism: A Character Sketch," *American Review of Reviews*, vol. 10, July 1894, p. 47.

Source 13: Donald L. McMurry, *Coxey's Army: The Story of the Industrial Army Movement* (New York: AMS Press, 1970), pp. 261–262, 277–278. Copyright © 1929 by Donald L. McMurry.

Source 14: Russel B. Nye, *A Baker's Dozen* (East Lansing: Michigan State University Press, 1956), pp. 229–230.

Source 15: Richard Hofstadter, William Miller, Daniel Aaron, Winthrop D. Jordan, and Leonard F. Litwack, *The United States* (Englewood Cliffs, NJ: Prentice Hall, 1976), p. 401.

Source 16: Carlos A. Schwantes, *Coxey's Army: An American Odyssey* (Lincoln: University of Nebraska Press, 1985), pp. ix, 274–278. Copyright © 1985 by the University of Nebraska Press. Reprinted by permission of the University of Nebraska Press.

Source 17: John A. Garraty and Robert A. McCaughey, *The American Nation: A History of the United States* (New York: Harper & Row, 1987), pp. 617–618.

Source 18: John L. Thomas, *The Great Republic: A History of the American People* (Lexington, MA: D. C. Heath, 1992), pp. 170–171.

Chapter 8: The Race Question

Source 1: Booker T. Washington, *Up from Slavery: An Autobiography* (Boston: Houghton Mifflin, 1901), pp. 218–225.

Source 2: U.S. Supreme Court, *Plessy v. Ferguson*, 163 U.S. 537 (1896).

Source 3: Ibid.

Source 4: W. E. B. Du Bois, *The Souls of Black Folks* (New York: Washington Square Press, 1970), pp. 34–35, 41–44, 47–48.

Source 5: *Congressional Record,* 59th Cong., 2nd sess. (Washington, DC: U.S. Government Printing Office, January 21, 1907), pp. 1440–1444.

Source 6: William English Walling, "The Race War in the North," *Independent* (September 3, 1908), 529–534.

Source 7: *Congressional Record,* 63rd Cong., 2nd sess. (Washington, DC: U.S. Government Printing Office, February 6, 1914), p. 3040.

Source 8: W. E. B. Du Bois, "The Immediate Program of the American Negro," *The Crisis,* IX (April 1915), pp. 310–312.

Source 9: Robert A. Hill, ed., *The Marcus Garvey and Universal Negro Improvement Association Papers,* vol. 4 (University of California Press, 1985), pp. 34–35.

Source 10: U.S. Supreme Court, *Brown v. Board of Education of Topeka,* 347 U.S. 483 (1954).

Source 11: Martin Luther King Jr., *Why We Can't Wait* (New York: Signet Books, 1964), pp. 32–37. Copyright © 1963 by Martin Luther King Jr., renewed 1991 by Coretta Scott King. Reprinted by arrangement with The Heirs to the Estate of Martin Luther King Jr., c/o Writer's House., Inc. as agent for the proprietor.

Source 12: C. Vann Woodward, *The Strange Career of Jim Crow* (New York: Oxford University Press, 1966), pp. 81–82. Copyright © 1966, 1974 by Oxford University Press, Inc. Reprinted by permission of the publisher.

Source 13: John Hope Franklin, *From Slavery to Freedom: A History of Negro Americans* (New York: Alfred A. Knopf, 1974), pp. 288–290. Copyright © 1974 by Alfred A. Knopf, Inc. Reprinted by permission of the publisher.

Chapter 9: The Philippine Question

Source 1: William McKinley, *Message from the President of the United States to the Two Houses of Congress at the Beginning of the Fifty-fifth Congress* (Washington, DC: U.S. Government Printing Office, 1899), vol. 4, p. 68.

Source 2: Ibid., p. 68.

Source 3: Ibid., p. 68.

Source 4: Ibid., p. 69.

Source 5: Charles S. Olcott, *William McKinley* (Boston: Houghton Mifflin, 1916), vol. 2, pp. 166–168.

Source 6: Ibid., pp. 110–111.

Source 7: Albert J. Beveridge, "The March of the Flag," Mayo W. Hazeltine, ed., *Masterpieces of Eloquence: Famous Orations of Great World Leaders from Early Greece to the Present Time,* vol. XXV (New York: P. F. Collier & Son, 1905), pp. 10979–10980, 10988–10993.

Source 8: John Barrett, "The Problem of the Philippines," *North American Review* (September 1898), vol. 167, no. 3, pp. 259–261.

Source 9: P. H. Colomb, "The United States Navy under the New Conditions of National Life." *North American Review* (October 1898), vol. 167, no. 4, p. 435.

Source 10: Thomas B. Reed, ed., *Modern Eloquence,* vol. 1 (Chicago: Geo. L. Shuman, 1900), pp. 94–97.

Source 11: Theodore Roosevelt, *The Strenuous Life: Essays and Addresses* (New York: Century, 1902), pp. 4, 6–8.

Source 12: Carl Schurz, "Address to the Anti-Imperialistic Conference in Chicago, October 17, 1899," Mayo W. Hazeltine, ed., *Masterpieces of Eloquence: Famous Orations of Great World Leaders from Early Greece to the Present Time,* vol. XXI (New York: P. F. Collier & Son, 1905), pp. 9088–9089, 9095.

Source 13: Mark Twain, *New York Herald,* October 16, 1900.

Source 14: Donald Bruce Johnson, ed., *National Party Platforms,* vol. 1 (Urbana: University of Illinois Press, 1978), p. 113.

Source 15: Ibid., p. 124.

Source 16: Mark Twain, "To the Person Sitting in Darkness," *North American Review,* vol. 172, no. 2 (February 1901), pp. 171–173.

Source 17: *Argonaut* (San Francisco), May 26, 1902.

Source 18: Olcott, pp. 187–189, 190–191.

Source 19: Thomas A. Bailey, *A Diplomatic History of the American People* (New York: F. S. Crofts, 1946), p. 524.

Source 20: George F. Kennan, *American Diplomacy, 1900–1950* (Chicago: University of Chicago Press, 1951), pp. 16–21. Reprinted by permission.

Source 21: Samuel Flagg Bemis, *The United States As a World Power: A Diplomatic History, 1900–1955* (New York: Henry Holt, 1955), pp. 30–31.

Source 22: Robert H. Ferrell, *American Diplomacy: A History* (W. W. Norton, 1969), p. 393.

Source 23: Samuel Eliot Morison, *The Oxford History of the American People,* vol. 3 (New York: Mentor Books, 1972), pp. 123–124.

Chapter 10: The Tin Lizzie

Source 1: John B. Rae, ed., *Henry Ford* (Englewood Cliffs, NJ: Prentice Hall, 1969), pp. 18–19.

Source 2. *New York Times,* June 5, 1910.

Source 3: "Gives $10,000,000 to 26,000 Employees," *New York Times,* January 6, 1914.

Source 4: *New York Times,* January 4, 1914.

Source 5: Rae, pp. 27–28.

Source 6: *New York Times,* May 3, 1925.

Source 7: Henry Ford, *My Philosophy of Industry (An Authorized Interview by Fay Leone Faurote)* (New York: Coward-McCann, 1929), pp. 92–94.

Source 8: Charles Merz, *And Then Came Ford* (New York: Doubleday, Doran, 1929), pp. 111, 113–117, 205, 265–67. Copyright © 1929 by Doubleday.

Source 9: Upton Sinclair, *The Flivver King: A Story of Ford-America* (Pasadena, CA: Upton Sinclair, 1937), pp. 63–66.

Source 10: Keith Sward, *The Legend of Henry Ford* (New York: Rinehart, 1948), pp. 50–52.

Source 11: Frederick Lewis Allen, *The Big Change: America Transforms Itself, 1900–1950* (New York: Harper & Brothers, 1952), pp. 111–113.

Source 12: Merrill Denison, *The Power to Go* (Garden City, NY: Doubleday, 1956), pp. 127–128.

Source 13: Allan Nevins and Frank Ernest Hill, *Ford: Expansion and Challenge, 1915–1933* (New York: Charles Scribner's Sons, 1957), pp. 432–436. Copyright © 1957 by Allan Nevins; renewed 1985 by Meredith Nevins Moyar and Anne Nevins Loftos.

Source 14: John B. Rae, *The American Automobile: A Brief History* (Chicago: University of Chicago Press, 1965), p. 1.

Source 15: John Jerome, *The Death of the Automobile: The Fatal Effects of the Golden Era, 1955–1970* (New York: W. W. Norton, 1972), pp. 233–235. Copyright © 1972 by John Jerome. reprinted by permission of W. W. Norton & Company, Inc.

Source 16: Andrew Rolle, *Los Angeles: From Pueblo to City of the Future* (San Francisco: Boyd & Fraser, 1981), pp. 53, 85–86.

Source 17: John B. Rae, *The American Automobile Industry* (Boston: Twayne, 1984), pp. 34, 37–38.

Source 18: Robert Lacey, *Ford: The Men and the Machines* (Boston: Little, Brown, 1986), pp. 96, 97–98.

Source 19: Michael Renner, "Rethinking Transportation," Lester R. Brown *et al.,* eds., *State of the World, 1989: A World Watch Institute Report on Progress toward a Sustainable Society* (New York: W. W. Norton, 1989), pp. 97, 106–107. Copyright © 1989 by the Worldwatch Institute. Reprinted by permission of W. W. Norton & Company, Inc.

Source 20: Deborah Gordon, *Steering a New Course: Transportation, Energy, and the Environment* (Washington, DC: Island Press, 1991), pp. 3–4, 207. Copyright © 1991 by Island Press, Covelo, CA. Reprinted by permission of the publisher.

Source 21: Odil Tunali, "A Billion Cars: The Road Ahead," *World Watch,* vol. 9, no. 1, January/February 1996, pp. 24–26. Reprinted by permission of the Worldwatch Institute.

Chapter 11: The Triangle Shirtwaist Factory Fire

Source 1: "154 Killed in Skyscraper Factory Fire," *New York World,* March 26, 1911.

Source 2: James Cooper, "World Reporter Passing When Fire Started; Saw Girls Jump to Death," *New York World,* March 26, 1911.

Source 3: "Law Students Save Twenty," *New York World,* March 26, 1911.

Source 4: Ibid.

Source 5: Cooper, March 26, 1911.

Source 6: "Fire Traps There Are Here," *New York Times,* March 27, 1911.

Source 7: "Murdered by Incompetent Government," *New York World,* March 27, 1911.

Source 8: Leon Stein, *The Triangle Fire* (Philadelphia: J. B. Lippincott, 1962), pp. 210–211. Copyright © 1962 by Leon Stein.

Source 9: "Triangle Fire Anniversary," *New York Times,* March 25, 1961.

Source 10: Stein, pp. 211–212.

Source 11: Stein, pp. 159–162.

Source 12: Joseph G. Rayback, *A History of American Labor* (New York: Free Press, 1966), pp. 263–264.

Source 13: Allen Weinstein and R. Jackson Wilson, *Freedom and Crisis* (New York: Random House, 1974), pp. 557–558. Reprinted by permission of The McGraw-Hill Companies.

Chapter 12: Margaret Sanger

Source 1: Anthony Comstock, *Traps for the Young,* Robert Bremmer, ed. (Cambridge, MA: Belknap Press of Harvard University Press, 1967), pp. 132–133, 158–159. Copyright © 1967 by the President and Fellows of Harvard College.

Source 2: Margaret Sanger, *My Fight for Birth Control* (New York: Farrar & Rinehart, 1931), p. 155.

Source 3: Margaret Sanger, *An Autobiography* (New York: W. W. Norton, 1938), pp. 216–221.

Source 4: *New York Times,* January 30, 1917.

Source 5: Heywood Broun and Margaret Leech, *Anthony Comstock: Roundsman of the Lord* (New York: Albert & Charles Boni, 1927), pp. 249–250.

Source 6: Sanger, *My Fight for Birth Control,* pp. 44–45.

Source 7: J. Gordon Melton, ed., *The Churches Speak On: Sex and Family Life* (Detroit: Gale Research Inc., 1991), pp. 9–10. Copyright © 1991 by Gale Research Inc.

Source 8: Emily Taft Douglas, *Margaret Sanger: Pioneer of the Future* (New York: Holt, Rinehart & Winston, 1970), pp. 1–3.

Source 9: David M. Kennedy, *Birth Control in America: The Career of Margaret Sanger* (New Haven: Yale University Press, 1970), pp. vii, ix, 271.

Source 10: Ellen Chesler, *Woman of Valor: Margaret Sanger and the Birth Control Movement in America* (New York: Simon & Schuster, 1992), pp. 11–12, 14. Copyright © 1992 by Ellen Chesler. Reprinted by permission of ICM, Inc.

Source 11: Timothy Wirth, U.S. Department of State, Daily Press Briefing, Tuesday, January 11, 1994, pp. 2, 11.

Chapter 13: World War I

Source 1: *The Messages and Papers of Woodrow Wilson* (New York: Review of Reviews Corporation, 1924), pp. 217–219.

Source 2: Ibid., pp. 223–224.

Source 3: Ibid, pp. 220–222.

Source 4: *New York Times,* May 1, 1915.

Source 5: *New York Times,* May 8, 1915.

Source 6: Ibid.

Source 7: Ibid.

Source 8: Ibid.

Source 9: Louis Synder, *Historic Documents of World War I* (Princeton, NJ: D. Van Nostrand Company, 1958), p. 150.

Source 10: Walter Lippmann, "The Defense of the Atlantic World," *New Republic,* vol. 10, no. 120 (February 17, 1917), pp. 59–60.

Source 11: *Washington Post,* April 1, 1917.

Source 12: Ibid.

Source 13: *Washington Post,* April 3, 1917.

Source 14: *Washington Post,* April 4, 1917.

Source 15: Eugene V. Debs, *The Canton Speech, with Statements to the Jury and the Court* (New York: Oriole Chapbooks, 1918) pp. 3, 6–7, 11.

Source 16: Harry Elmer Barnes, *The Genesis of the World War: An Introduction to the Problem of War Guilt* (New York: Alfred A. Knopf, 1929), pp. 598–599, 618, 619, 646, 647. Copyright © 1926, 1927 by Alfred A. Knopf, Inc., and renewed 1954, 1955 by Harry Elmer Barnes. Reprinted by permission of the publisher.

Source 17: James Duane Squires, *British Propaganda at Home and in the United States from 1914 to 1917* (Cambridge, MA: Harvard University Press, 1935), pp. 67, 81.

Source 18: Charles Seymour, *American Diplomacy during the World War* (Baltimore: Johns Hopkins University Press, 1934), pp. 207–208, 209–210.

Source 19: Newton D. Baker, *Why We Went to War* (New York: Harper & Brothers, 1936), pp. 156–157.

Source 20: Charles Beard, *The Devil Theory of War: An Inquiry into the Nature of History and the Possibility of Keeping Out of War* (New York: Vanguard Press, 1936), pp. 23–29. Copyright © 1936 by Arlene Beard and Detlev Vagts.

Source 21: Thomas A. Bailey, *A Diplomatic History of the American People* (New York: F. S. Crofts, 1946), pp. 645–646.

Source 22: Edward H. Buehrig, *Woodrow Wilson and the Balance of Power* (Bloomington: University of Indiana Press, 1955), pp. vii–ix, 103. Reprinted by permission of Indiana University Press.

Source 23: H. Stuart Hughes, *Contemporary Europe: A History* (Englewood Cliffs, NJ: Prentice Hall, 1961), pp. 75–76. Reprinted by permission of the publisher.

Source 24: Barbara W. Tuchman, *The Zimmermann Telegram* (New York: Macmillan, 1966), p. 200.

Source 25: Robert H. Ferrell, *American Diplomacy: A History* (New York: W. W. Norton, 1969), p. 517.

Chapter 14: Prohibition

Source 1: Yandell Henderson, *A New Deal in Liquor: A Plea for Dilution* (New York: Doubleday, Doran, 1934), pp. 189–194.

Source 2: Barbara M. Cross, ed., *The Autobiography of Lyman Beecher* (Cambridge, MA: Harvard University Press, 1961), pp. 23–25.

Source 3: Donald Bruce Johnson and Kirk H. Porter, *National Party Platforms, 1840–1972* (Urbana: University of Illinois Press, 1975), p. 45.

Source 4: Anna A. Gordon, *The Beautiful Life of Frances E. Willard* (Chicago: Women's Temperance Publishing Association, 1898), pp. 99–100.

Source 5: Emmet G. Coleman, *The Temperance Songbook: A Peerless Collection of Temperance Songs and Hymns* (New York: American Heritage Press, 1971), p. 17.

Source 6: Andrew Sinclair, *Era of Excess: A Social History of the Prohibition Movement* (New York: Harper Colophon Books, 1964), p. 51.

Source 7: William T. Ellis, *Billy Sunday: The Man and His Message* (Chicago: Moody Press, 1959), pp. 173–174.

Source 8: Amendment XVIII, Constitution of the United States.

Source 9: "Prospect and Retrospect," *Washington Post,* January 17, 1920.

Source 10: *Dispatch from His Majesty's Ambassador at Washington Enclosing a Memorandum on the Effects of Prohibition in the United States* (London: His Majesty's Stationery Office, 1923), pp. 2–4.

Source 11: Paul Goodman and Frank Otto Gatell, *America in the Twenties: The Beginnings of Contemporary America* (New York: Holt, Rinehart & Winston, 1972), pp. 150–151, 152–153, 156–157. Copyright © 1972 by Holt, Rinehart & Winston, Inc.

Source 12: Henry Ford, *My Philosophy of Industry* (New York: Coward-McCann, 1929), pp. 14–16.

Source 13: "U.S. Prohibition Ends Today through Presidential Edict; Nation's Rum Flows at 3 P.M.," *Washington Post,* December 5, 1933.

Source 14: "Today's Meaning," *Washington Post,* December 5, 1933.

Source 15: Amendment XXI, Constitution of the United States.

Source 16: Charles A. Beard and Mary R. Beard, *The Rise of American Civilization,* New York: Macmillan, 1949), pp. 763–765. Copyright © 1927, 1930, 1933 by Macmillan College Publishing Company, renewed 1955, 1958 by Mary R. Beard, 1961 by William Beard Vagts.

Source 17: Richard Hofstadter, *The Age of Reform: From Bryan to FDR* (New York: Vintage Books, 1955), pp. 288–290. Copyright © 1955 by Richard Hofstadter. Reprinted by permission of Alfred A. Knopf, Inc.

Source 18: Sinclair, p. 5.

Source 19: Goodman and Gatell, pp. 143–144. Copyright © 1972 by Holt, Rinehart & Winston, Inc. Reprinted by permission of the publisher.

Source 20: Bernard Bailyn, Robert Dallek, David Brion Davis, David Herbert Donald, John L. Thomas, Gordon S. Wood, *The Great Republic: A History of the American People* (Lexington, MA: D. C. Heath, 1992), pp. 340–341. Copyright © 1992 by D. C. Heath & Company. Reprinted by permission of Houghton Mifflin Company.

Chapter 15: Women's Suffrage

Source 1: "Suffrage Crusaders in Thrilling Pageant Take City by Storm," *Evening Star* (Washington), March 3, 1913.

Source 2: "Woman's Beauty, Grace, and Art Bewilder the Capital," *Washington Post,* March 4, 1913.

Source 3: "Score the Police for Inefficiency," *Evening Star,* March 4, 1913.

Source 4: "Row in the House," *Washington Post,* March 4, 1913.

Source 5: "The Women's Parade," *Evening Star,* March 4, 1913.

Source 6: Inez Haynes Irwin, *The Story of the Woman's Party* (New York: Harcourt, Brace, 1921), p. 42.

Source 7: Ibid., pp. 49–50.

Source 8: Ibid., pp. 64–65.

Source 9: Eleanor Flexner, *Century of Struggle: The Women's Rights Movement in the United States* (Cambridge: Belknap Press of Harvard University Press, 1975), pp. 286–287.

Source 10: Ida Husted Harper, *The History of Woman Suffrage,* vol. 5 (New York: J. J. Little & Ives, 1922), pp. 586–588.

Source 11: *Congressional Record,* September 27, 1918, p. 10853.

Source 12: *Congressional Record,* September 27–30, 1918, pp. 10842–10845, 10848–10849, 10851–10852, 10856, 10893, 10894, 10898, 10925.

Source 13: *Congressional Record,* September 30, 1918, pp. 10928–10929.

Source 14: Amendment XIX, Constitution of the United States.

Source 15: Irwin, pp. 28–29, 31.

Source 16: Harper, pp. xix–xx.

Source 17: Charles A. Beard and Mary R. Beard, *The Rise of American Civilization* (New York: Macmillan, 1949), pp. 562–564. Copyright 1927, 1930, 1933 by Macmillan College Publishing Company, renewed 1955, 1958 by Mary R. Beard, 1961 by William Beard Vagts.

Source 18: Flexner, pp. 297–298.

Source 19: Nancy Woloch, *Women and the American Experience* (New York: Alfred A. Knopf, 1984), pp. 350–353. Copyright © 1984 by Alfred A. Knopf. Reproduced by permission of The McGraw-Hill Companies.

Source 20: Linda G. Ford, *Iron-Jawed Angels: The Suffrage Militancy of the National Woman's Party, 1912–1920* (Lanham, MD: University Press of America, 1991), pp. 244–245.

Chapter 16: The Scopes Trial

Source 1: John T. Scopes, *World's Most Famous Court Trial* (Cincinnati: National Book Company, 1925), pp. 284–289, 291, 298–302.

Source 2: *New York Times,* July 22, 1925. Copyright © 1925 by The New York Times Company.

Source 3: *Evening Star* (Washington, DC), July 21, 1925.

Source 4: *The Times* (London, England), July 22, 1925.

Source 5: *Washington Post,* July 22, 1925.

Source 6: *New York Times,* July 22, 1925.

Source 7: Sheldon Norman Grebstein, *Monkey Trial: The State of Tennessee vs. John T. Scopes* (Boston: Houghton Mifflin, 1960), pp. 198–199.

Source 8: H. L. Mencken, editorial, *The American Mercury* (October 1925), vol. 6, no. 22, pp. 158–159.

Source 9: Clarence Darrow, *The Story of My Life* (New York: Charles Scribner's Sons, 1932), pp. 244–245, 266–267.

Source 10: W. J. Cash, *The Mind of the South* (New York: Vintage Books, 1941), pp. 299, 300, 301, 346–347, 349–350. Copyright © 1941 by Alfred A. Knopf, Inc., and renewed 1969 by Mary R. Maury. Reprinted by permission of the publisher.

Source 11: Richard Hofstadter, *The American Political Tradition: And the Men Who Made It* (New York: Vintage Books, 1948), pp. 204–205.

Source 12: William E. Leuchtenburg, *The Perils of Prosperity, 1914–1932* (Chicago: University of Chicago Press, 1958), p. 221.

Source 13: Ray Ginger, *Six Days or Forever? Tennessee v. John Thomas Scopes* (New York: Oxford University Press, 1974), pp. 231–233.

Source 14: Grebstein, pp. ix–x.

Source 15: Winthrop S. Hudson, *Religion in America: An Historical Account of the Development of American Religious Life* (New York: Charles Scribner's Sons, 1973), pp. 369–371. Copyright © 1973. Reprinted by permission of Prentice-Hall, Inc., Upper Saddle River, NJ.

Chapter 17: The New Deal

Source 1: *The State Papers and Other Public Writings of Herbert Hoover,* vol. 1 (Garden City, NY: Doubleday, Doran, 1934), pp. 496–497.

Source 2: *The Public Papers and Addresses of Franklin D. Roosevelt,* vol. 1 (New York: Random House, 1938), pp. 647–649, 657–659.

Source 3: Ibid., vol. 2, pp. 11–16.

Source 4: Bryan B. Sterling and Frances N. Sterling, eds., *A Will Rogers Treasury: Reflections and Observations* (New York: Crown Publishers, 1982), pp. 211–222.

Source 5: Donald Bruce Johnson and Kirk H. Porter, *National Party Platforms, 1840–1972* (Urbana: University of Illinois Press, 1975), pp. 364–366. Copyright © 1978 by the Board of Trustees of the University of Illinois.

Source 6: Ibid., pp. 356–359.

Source 7: *Roosevelt,* vol. 2, pp. 4–5.

Source 8: Charles A. Beard and Mary R. Beard, *America at Midpassage* (New York: Macmillan Company, 1939), pp. 247–250. Copyright © 1939 by Arlene Beard and Detlev Vagts.

Source 9: John T. Flynn, *The Roosevelt Myth* (New York: Devin-Adair, 1948), pp. 413–414. Copyright © 1948 by Devin-Adair Publishers, Inc., Old Greenwich, CT, 06870.

Source 10: Eric F. Goldman, *Rendezvous with Destiny: A History of Modern American Reform* (New York: Alfred A. Knopf, 1952), pp. 371–372.

Source 11: David M. Potter, *People of Plenty: Economic Abundance and the American Character* (Chicago: University of Chicago Press, 1954), pp. 120–121.

Source 12: Dean Acheson, *A Democrat Looks at His Party* (New York: Harper & Brothers, 1955), pp. 48–50. Copyright © 1955 by Dean Acheson, renewed 1983 by Alice S. Acheson. Reprinted by permission of HarperCollins Publishers, Inc.

Source 13: Arthur M. Schlesinger Jr., *The Politics of Upheaval* (Boston: Houghton Mifflin, 1960), pp. 347–349. Copyright © 1960 by Arthur M. Schlesinger Jr.

Source 14: Barry Goldwater, *The Conscience of a Conservative* (New York: MacFadden Books, 1961), pp. 15–16. Copyright © 1961 by Regnery Gateway, Inc.

Source 15: V. O. Key Jr., *Politics, Parties, and Pressure Groups,* 5th ed. (New York: Thomas Y. Crowell, 1964), pp. 523–524, 531–532. Copyright © 1942, 1947, 1952, 1958, 1964 by The Thomas Y. Crowell Company. Reprinted by permission of HarperCollins Publishers, Inc.

Source 16: Carl N. Degler, *Out of Our Past: The Forces That Shaped Modern America* (New York: Harper Colophon Books, 1970), pp. 379, 384, 413. Copyright © 1959, 1970 by Carl N. Degler. Reprinted by permission of HarperCollins Publishers, Inc.

Source 17: Ira Katznelson and Mark Kesselman, *The Politics of Power: A Critical Introduction to American Government* (New York: Harcourt Brace Jovanovich, 1975), pp. 200–201.

Source 18: Howard Zinn, *A People's History of the United States* (New York: Harper & Row, 1980), p. 394.

Source 19: John A. Garraty and Robert A. McCaughey, *The American Nation: A History of the United States* (New York: Harper & Row, 1987), p. 784.

Source 20: Michael Parenti, *Democracy for the Few* (New York: St. Martin's Press, 1980), pp. 77–80. Copyright © 1980 by St. Marti's Press, Inc. Reprinted by permission of Bedford/St. Martin's Press, Inc.

Chapter 18: Pearl Harbor

Source 1: *Washington Post*, December 8, 1941.

Source 2: *The New York Times*, December 8, 1941.

Source 3: *The Times* (London), December 8, 1941.

Source 4: *Washington Post*, December 8, 1941. © 1941 by The Washington Post. Reprinted with permission.

Source 5: *Mainichi* (Osaka), December 9, 1941.

Source 6: Samuel I. Rosenman, ed., *The Public Papers and Addresses of Franklin D. Roosevelt, 1941* (New York: Harper & Brothers, 1950), pp. 514–515.

Source 7: *Nippon Times*, December 9, 1941.

Source 8: *Mainichi*, December 9, 1941.

Source 9: *Nippon Times* (Tokyo), December 9, 1941.

Source 10: *Nippon Times*, December 9, 1941.

Source 11: *Mainichi*, December 12, 1941.

Source 12: Thomas A. Bailey, *A Diplomatic History of the American People* (New York: F. S. Crofts, 1946), pp. 796–798, 807.

Source 13: Henry L. Stimson and McGeorge Bundy, *On Active Service in Peace and War* (Harper & Brothers, 1948), pp. 391, 392–394. Copyright © 1948 by Henry L. Stimson and McGeorge Bundy. Copyright renewed 1976 by McGeorge Bundy. Reprinted by permission of HarperCollins Publishers, Inc.

Source 14: John T. Flynn, *The Roosevelt Myth: A Critical Account of the New Deal* (New York: Devin-Adair, 1948), pp. 297, 303–304.

Source 15: Harry Elmer Barnes, *Perpetual War for Perpetual Peace* (Caldwell, ID: Caxton Printers, 1953), p. 651.

Source 16: Robert A. Divine, *The Reluctant Belligerent: American Entry into World War II* (New York: John Wiley & Sons, 1965), p. 158.

Source 17: Robert H. Ferrell, *American Diplomacy: A History*, 2nd ed. (New York: W. W. Norton, 1969), pp. 630–632. Copyright © 1959, 1969 by W. W. Norton & Company, Inc. Reprinted by permission of W. W. Norton & Company, Inc.

Source 18: Robert Dallek, *Franklin D. Roosevelt and American Foreign Policy, 1932–1945: With a New Afterword* (New York: Oxford University Press, 1979), pp. 312–313. Copyright © 1979, 1995 by Oxford University Press. Reprinted by permission of Oxford University Press, Inc.

Source 19: Haynes Johnson, "The Day Washington Found Its Future," *Washington Post*, December 7, 1991.

Source 20: United States Congress, *Congressional Record*, May 24, 1999, p. S5819.

Source 21: *Ibid.*, pp. S5818–5819.

Chapter 19: Internment

Source 1: "Death Sentence of a Mad Dog," editorial, *Los Angeles Times*, December 8, 1941.

Source 2: "Japanese Aliens Roundup Starts," *Los Angeles Times*, December 8, 1941.

Source 3: " 'Lincoln Would Intern Japs,' " *Los Angeles Times*, February 13, 1942.

Source 4: Kyle Palmer, "Rapid Evacuation of Japanese Urged," *Los Angeles Times*, February 14, 1942.

Source 5: Commission on the Wartime Relocation and Internment of Civilians, *Personal Justice Denied*, Part 1 (Washington, DC: U.S. Government Printing Office, 1982), p. 6.

Source 6: "Scores of Farmers Seek Land Evacuated by Jap Aliens," *Los Angeles Times*, February 19, 1942.

Source 7: "Indian Lands Urged For Japs," *Los Angeles Times*, February 20, 1942.

Source 8: Roger Daniels, *Prisoners without Trial: Japanese Americans in World War II* (New York: Hill & Wang, 1993), pp. 129–130.

Source 9: *Personal Justice Denied*, Part 1, p. 135.

Source 10: Ibid., p. 136.

Source 11: Ibid.

Source 12: Ibid., 151.

Source 13: Ibid.

Source 14: Ibid., p. 160.

Source 15: Michi Weglyn, *Years of Infamy: The Untold Story of America's Concentration Camps* (New York: William Morrow, 1976), pp. 190–191. Copyright © 1976 by Michi Weglyn, 1999 by Dr. B. Suzuki, California State Polytechnic University, Pomona. Reprinted by permission of Si Spiegel, executor of the estate of Michi Weglyn and Dr. B. Suzuki.

Source 16: U.S. Supreme Court, *Fred Toyosaburo Korematsu v. United States of America* (323 U.S. 214–248).

Source 17: Ibid.

Source 18: Weglyn, p. 82.

Source 19: T. Harry Williams, Richard N. Current, and Frank Freidel, *A History of the United States* (New York: Alfred A. Knopf, 1961).

Source 20: James MacGregor Burns, *Roosevelt: The Soldier of Freedom* (New York: Harcourt Brace Jovanovich, 1970), pp. 213, 215–216.

Source 21: Harry H. L. Kitano, *Race Relations* (Englewood Cliffs, NJ: Prentice Hall, 1974), pp. 216–217. Copyright © 1974. Reprinted by permission of Prentice-Hall, Inc., Upper Saddle River, NJ.

Source 22: *Public Papers of the Presidents of the United States: Gerald R. Ford,* Book 1 (Washington, DC: U.S. Government Printing Office, 1979), p. 366.

Source 23: Weglyn, pp. 54–55.

Source 24: *Personal Justice Denied,* Part 1, pp. 2–3, 12–13, 15, 18.

Source 25: "Final Payments for Japanese Internees," *New York Times,* April 26, 1988. Copyright ©1988 The New York Times Company. Reprinted by permission of the New York Times.

Source 26: U.S. Public Law 100-383, "An Act To Implement Recommendations of the Commission on Wartime Relocation and Internment of Civilians" (100th Cong., 2d sess., 102 Stat. 903, August 10, 1988).

Source 27: John Hersey, "Behind Barbed Wire," *New York Times Magazine,* September 11, 1988, pp. 58–59, 73. From Peter Wright and John C. Armor, P.A., *Manzanar.* Copyright © 1989 1989 by Peter Wright and John C. Armor, P.A. "A Mistake of Terrifically Horrible Proportions," Copyright © 1989 by John Hersey. Reprinted by permission of Times Books, a division of Random House.

Source 28: Daniels, pp. 1, 47–48. Copyright © 1993 by Roger Daniels.

Chapter 20: Hiroshima

Source 1: *Nippon Times* (Tokyo), August 12, 1945.

Source 2: *Nippon Times,* August 11, 1945.

Source 3: Allen Weinstein and R. Jackson Wilson, *An American History: Freedom and Crisis* (New York: Random House, 1974), p. 726.

Source 4: *Public Papers of the Presidents of the United States: Harry S. Truman, Containing the Public Messages, Speeches, and Statements of the President, April 12 to December 31, 1945* (Washington, DC: U.S. Government Printing Office, 1961), pp. 197–199.

Source 5: *The Times* of London, August 8, 1945.

Source 6: *Public Papers,* p. 200.

Source 7: Ibid., p. 212.

Source 8: *Nippon Times,* August 10, 1945.

Source 9: *Mainichi,* August 12, 1945.

Source 10: *Nippon Times,* August 14, 1945.

Source 11: *Nippon Times,* August 12, 1945.

Source 12: *Nippon Times,* August 15, 1945.

Source 13: Barton J. Bernstein, *The Atomic Bomb: The Critical Issues* (Boston: Little, Brown, 1976), pp. 144–145.

Source 14: Herbert Feis, *The Atomic Bomb and the End of World War II* (Princeton: Princeton University Press, 1966), p. 191. Copyright © 1966 by Princeton University Press. Reprinted by permission of the publisher.

Source 15: James F. Byrnes, *Speaking Frankly* (New York: Harper & Brothers, 1947), pp. 164–165.

Source 16: Henry L. Stimson and McGeorge Bundy, *On Active Service in Peace and War* (New York: Harper & Brothers, 1948), pp. 631–633. Copyright © 1948 by Henry L. Stimson and McGeorge Bundy, renewed 1976 by McGeorge Bundy. Reprinted by permission of HarperCollins.

Source 17: Stimson and Bundy, p. 629.

Source 18: Howard Zinn, *Postwar America: 1945–1971* (Indianapolis: Bobbs-Merrill Company, 1973), pp. 17, 18. Copyright © 1973 by Howard Zinn. Reprinted by permission of Howard Zinn.

Source 19: Bernstein, pp. 34–36, 39.

Source 20: "Was A-Bomb on Japan A Mistake?" *U.S. News & World Report,* August 15, 1960, pp. 65–66.

Source 21: Ibid., pp. 68, 70.

Source 22: Gar Alperovitz, *Atomic Diplomacy* (New York: Viking Penguin, 1965), pp. 285, 288, 289–290. Gar Alperovitz is Lionel R. Bauman Professor of Political Economy, Department of Government and Politics, University of Maryland, College Park. Reprinted by permission.

Source 23: Feis, pp. 189, 191–193, 200.

Source 24: William Appleman Williams, *The Tragedy of American Diplomacy* (New York: Dell Publishing, 1972), p. 253.

Source 25: Zinn, pp. 16, 17.

Source 26: Sheila K. Johnson, *American Attitudes toward Japan, 1941–1975* (Washington, DC: American Enterprise Institute for Public Policy Research, 1975), pp. 17–18.

Source 27: Bernard Bailyn, et al., *The Great Republic: A History of the American People* (Lexington, MA: D. C. Heath, 1992), p. 435. Copyright © 1992 by D. C. Heath & Company. Reprinted by permission of Houghton Mifflin Company.

Chapter 21: McCarthyism

Source 1: Joe McCarthy, *Major Speeches and Debates of Senator Joe McCarthy, Delivered in the United States Senate, 1950–1951* (Washington, DC: U.S. Government Printing Office, ca. 1952), pp. 7–14.

Source 2: Ibid., pp. 161, 171–174.

Source 3: Ibid. pp. 1–3.

Source 4: Donald Bruce Johnson and Kirk H. Porter, *National Party Platforms, 1840–1972* (Urbana: University of Illinois Press, 1975), p. 500.

Source 5: Democratic National Committee, *Campaign Handbook: How to Win in 1952* (Washington, DC: Democratic National Committee, 1952), p. 147.

Source 6: *Report of the Select Committee to Study Censure Charges* (83rd Cong., 2nd sess., Senate Report 2508, November 8, 1954, pursuant to Senate Resolution 301) (U.S. Government Printing Office, 1954), pp. 51–54.

Source 7: "The Big Truth," *The Progressive* (April 1954), vol. 18, no. 4, pp. 91–92.

Source 8: Henry Bamford Parkes, *The American Experience: An Interpretation of the History and Civilization of the American People* (New York: Vintage Books, 1959), p. 348.

Source 9: Walter LaFeber, *America, Russia, and the Cold War, 1945–1966* (New York: John Wiley & Sons, 1967), pp. 137–138.

Source 10: Arthur V. Watkins, *Enough Rope,* (Englewood Cliffs, NJ: Prentice Hall, 1969), pp. 198–199.

Source 11: Robert Griffith, *The Politics of Fear: Joseph R. McCarthy and the Senate,* 2nd ed. (Amherst: The University of Massachusetts Press, 1987), pp. 319–320. Copyright © 1970 by Robert Griffith and Introduction to the Second Edition copyright © 1987 by Robert Griffith. Reprinted by permission of the publisher.

Source 12: Thomas C. Reeves. *The Life and Times of Joe McCarthy: A Biography* (Lanham, MD: Madison Book, 1982). Reprinted by permission of the publisher.

Source 13: David Oshinsky, *A Conspiracy So Immense: The World of Joe McCarthy* (New York: Free Press, 1983), pp. 506–507. Copyright © 1983 by The Free Press. Reprinted by permission of The Free Press, a division of Macmillan, Inc.

Source 14: Richard M. Fried, *Nightmare in Red: The McCarthy Era in Perspective* (New York: Oxford University Press, 1990), pp. vii–viii, 3–4, 161, 164, 201.

Chapter 22: The Guatemala Coup

Source 1: Paul Kennedy, "Revolt Launched in Guatemala: Land-Air-Sea Invasion Reported; Uprisings Under Way in Key Cities," *New York Times,* June 19, 1954.

Source 2: "Invaders Hold Third of Nation," Washington *Evening Star,* June 19, 1954. Copyright © 1954 by The Washington Post. Reprinted by permission.

Source 3: United Press International, "U.S. Spurred Rebels, He Says," *New York Times,* June 19, 1954.

Source 4: "War Is Family Row, U.S. Says: Text of a Statement Issued Yesterday by the State Department," Washington *Evening Star,* June 20, 1954.

Source 5: Paul P. Kennedy, "Anti-Reds' Invasion Progresses," *New York Times,* June 20, 1954. Copyright © 1954 by the New York Times Company. Reprinted by permission.

Source 6: "Guatemalan Whirlwind," Washington *Evening Star,* June 20, 1954. Copyright © 1954 by the Washington Post. Reprinted by permission

Source 7: *New York Times,* "Revolt in Guatemala," June 20, 1954. Copyright © 1954 by the New York Times Company. Reprinted by permission.

Source 8: James Reston, "With the Dulles Brothers in Darkest Guatemala," *New York Times,* June 20, 1954. Copyright © 1954 by the New York Times Company. Reprinted by permission.

Source 9: *The Times* of London, June 21, 1954.

Source 10: "Troops Pushed Back," *The Times* of London, June 22, 1954.

Source 11: "Reasons for the Rising: Ambassador's Statement," *The Times* of London, June 24, 1954.

Source 12: "Poverty and Communism," *Washington Post,* June 24, 1954. Copyright © 1954 by The Washington Post. Reprinted by permission.

Source 13: Paul P. Kennedy, ""President of Guatemala Ousted by Anti-Communist Army Junta," *New York Times,* June 28, 1954.

Source 14: Stephen Schlesinger and Stephen Kinzer, *Bitter Fruit: The Untold Story of the American Coup in Guatemala* (Garden City, New York: Doubleday, 1982), pp. 199–200. Reprinted by permission.

Source 15: J. A. Del Vayo, "War against the U.N.," *The Nation,* July 3, 1954, pp. 2–4.

Source 16: Washington *Evening Star,* "Guatemalan Shooting Ends as Reds Flee; Rebels Map New Rule," June 30, 1954.

Source 17: "The Text of Dulles' Speech on Guatemalan Upset." *New York Times,* July 1, 1954. Copyright © 1954 by the New York Times Company. Reprinted by permission of the New York Times.

Source 18: Dwight D. Eisenhower, *Public Papers of the President of the United States, Containing the Public Messages, Speeches, and Statements of the President, 1954* (Washington, D.C.: U.S. Government Printing Office, 1960), pp. 787–789.

Source 19: Daniel James, *Red Design for the Americas: Guatemalan Prelude* (New York: John Day Company, 1954), pp. 11, 26, 315–316.

Source 20: Dwight D. Eisenhower, *Mandate for Change, 1953–1956* (Garden City, New York: Doubleday, 1963), pp. 425–426. Copyright © 1963 by Dwight D. Eisenhower. Reprinted by permission of Doubleday, a division of Random House, Inc.

Source 21: John P. Longan, Cable to Byron Engels, "TDY Guatemala, November 27 through December 7, 1965," U.S. State Department, January 4, 1966.

Source 22: Thomas L. Hughes, Intelligence Note #843, "Guatemala: A Counter-Insurgency Running Wild?" United States State Department, Bureau of Intelligence and Research, October 23, 1967.

Source 23: Viron Vaky, Memorandum, "Guatemala and Counter-terror," to Covey Oliver, United States State Department, Policy Planning Council, March 29, 1968.

Source 24: Sidney Lens, *The Forging of the American Empire* (New York: Thomas Y. Crowell, 1971), pp. 389–391. Reprinted by permission.

Source 25: Edward J. Williams, *The Political Themes of Inter-American Relations* (Belmont, California: Duxbury Press, 1971), pp. 21–22.

Source 26: U.S. Senate, "Final Report of the Select Committee to Study Government Operations with Respect to Intelligence Activities," *Foreign and Military Intelligence,* Book 1 (Washington: Government Printing Office, 1976), pp. 24, 141, 153, 159, 586, 563–564.

Source 27: Morton H. Halperin, Jerry J. Berman, Robert L. Borosage, and Christine M. Marwick, *The Lawless State: The Crimes of the U.S. Intelligence Agencies* (New York: Penguin Books, 1976), pp. 30–31.

Source 28: Stephen Schlesinger and Stephen Kinzer, *Bitter Fruit: The Untold Story of the American Coup in Guatemala* (Garden City, New York: Doubleday, 1982), pp. 75–77, 106. Reprinted by permission.

Source 29: Ronald Reagan, "Remarks the President Following Meeting With President Rios Montt of Guatemala," White House: Office of the Press Secretary, December 4, 1982.

Source 30: Rigoberta Menchú, *I, Rigoberta Menchú, An Indian Woman in Guatemala,* trans. Ann Wright, Elisabeth Burgos-Debray, ed. (New York: Verso, 1984), pp. 172–180. Reprinted by permission.

Source 31: U.S. Department of State, "Stop Delivery of Military Assistance to Guatemala," December 18, 1990.

Source 32: Guatemalan Commission for Historical Clarification, *Guatemala: Memory of Silence: Report of the Commission for Historical Clarification, Conclusions and Recommendations,* (New York: UN Secretariat, by authority of the Government of Guatemala and the Unidad Revolucionaria Nacional Guatemalteca, 1999), paragraphs 1–9, 13–15, 31–32, 38–46, 85–87, 91, 93–97.

Source 33: William Jefferson Clinton, "Remarks by the President in Roundtable Discussion on Peace Efforts," National Palace of Culture, Guatemala City, Guatemala, The White House: Office of the Press Secretary, March 10, 1999.

Chapter 23: The Sit-In Movement

Source 1: "Movement by Negroes Growing," *Greensboro Daily News,* February 4, 1960.

Source 2: "Aid Given Negroes' Protest," *Greensboro Daily News,* February 5, 1960.

Source 3: "Leadership at the Five and Ten," *Greensboro Daily News,* February 5, 1960.

Source 4: "White Men Arrested at Sitdown: Negroes Keep Up Protest Action," *Greensboro Daily News,* February 6, 1960.

Source 5: "Seating Negroes," *Dallas Morning News,* February 10, 1960.

Source 6: "Negroes Extend Sitdown Protest," *New York Times,* February 10, 1960.

Source 7: "Group Urges Segregated Facilities," *Greensboro Daily News,* February 19, 1960.

Source 8: "New Protests Are Followed by Arrests," *Greensboro Daily News,* February 24, 1960.

Source 9: Martin Luther King Jr., *I Have a Dream: Writings and Speeches That Changed the World* (New York: HarperCollins, 1992), pp. 101–106. Copyright ©1963 by Martin Luther King Jr., renewed 1991 by Coretta Scott King. Reprinted by arrangement with The Heirs to the Estate of Martin Luther King Jr., c/o Writers House, Inc. as agent for the proprietor.

Source 10: U.S. Supreme Court, *Bell v. Maryland,* 378 U.S. 226 (1964).

Source 11: Martin Luther King Jr., *Why We Can't Wait* (New York: Signet Books, 1964), pp. 42–43. Copyright © 1963 by Martin Luther King Jr., renewed 1991 by Coretta Scott King. Reprinted by arrangement with The Heirs to the Estate of Martin Luther King, Jr., c/o Writers House as agent for the proprietor.

Source 12: C. Vann Woodward, *The Strange Career of Jim Crow,* Third Revised Edition (New York: Oxford University Press, 1974). Copyright © 1974 by Oxford University Press, Inc. Reprinted by permission of Oxford University Press, Inc.

Source 13: Dick Gregory, *Write Me In!* (New York: Bantam Books, 1968), pp. 44–45, 46–48. Copyright © 1968 by Dick Gregory. Reprinted by permission of Bantam Books, a division of Bantam Doubleday Dell Publishing Group, Inc.

Source 14: H. Rap Brown, *Die Nigger Die* (New York: Dial Press, 1969), pp. 55–56. Copyright © 1969 by Lynne Brown. Used by permission of Doubleday, a division of Random House, Inc.

Source 15: John Hope Franklin, *From Slavery to Freedom: A History of Negro Americans* (New York: Alfred A. Knopf, 1974), pp. 476–477. Copyright © 1974 by Alfred A. Knopf. Reprinted by permission of McGraw-Hill.

Source 16: William H. Chafe, *Civilities and Civil Rights: Greensboro, North Carolina, and the Black Struggle for Freedom* (New York: Oxford University Press, 1980), pp. 137–139. Copyright © 1980 by Oxford University Press, Inc. Reprinted by permission of Oxford University Press, Inc.

Source 17: "Sit-in Member Served After 25 Years," *Richmond Times-Dispatch,* February 2, 1985. Reprinted by permission of Associated Press.

Chapter 24: The Cuban Missile Crisis

Source 1: *Public Papers of the Presidents of the United States: John Kennedy, Containing the Public Messages, Speeches, and Statements of the President, January 1 to December 31, 1962* (Washington, DC: U.S. Government Printing Office, 1963), pp. 806–809.

Source 2: John A. McCone, "Memorandum for the File," in Mary S. McAuliffe, ed., *CIA Documents on the Cuban Missile Crisis* (Washington, D.C.: History Staff, Central Intelligence Agency, October 1992), p. 245.

Source 3: Guided Missile and Astronautics Intelligence Committee, Joint Atomic Energy Intelligence Committee, and National Photographic Interpretation Center, "Joint Evaluation of Soviet Missile Threat in Cuba," October 22, 1962, in Mary S. McAuliffe, ed., *CIA Documents on the Cuban Missile Crisis* (Washington, D.C.: History Staff, Central Intelligence Agency, October 1992), p. 281–282.

Source 4: "Text of Statement Released by Government of Soviet Union," *Washington Post,* October 24, 1962.

Source 5: "Stevenson at U.N. States Case on Cuba," *Evening Star* (Washington), October 24, 1962.

Source 6: "Red Bloc on Alert," *Washington Post,* October 24, 1962.

Source 7: John A. McCone, "Memorandum for the File," in Mary S. McAuliffe, ed., *CIA Documents on the Cuban Missile Crisis* (Washington, D.C.: History Staff, Central Intelligence Agency, October 1992), p. 291–292.

Source 8: "Civil Defense Shelters Being Stocked, Marked," *Evening Star,* October 24, 1962.

Source 9: "Calling A Halt," editorial, *The Times* (London), October 24, 1962.

Source 10: Guided Missile and Astronautics Intelligence Committee, Joint Atomic Energy Intelligence Committee, and National Photographic Interpretation Center, "Joint Evaluation of Soviet Missile Threat in Cuba," October 24, 1962, in Mary S. McAuliffe, ed., *CIA Documents on the Cuban Missile Crisis* (Washington, D.C.: History Staff, Central Intelligence Agency, October 1992), p. 293–294.

Source 11: "Navy Set to Halt 25 Soviet Vessels," *Washington Post,* October 24, 1962.

Source 12: Robert F. Kennedy, *Thirteen Days: A Memoir of the Cuban Missile Crisis* (New York: W. W. Norton, 1969), pp. 67–71.

Source 13: *Public Papers of John F. Kennedy,* pp. 813–814.

Source 14: *Public Papers of John F. Kennedy, January 1 to November 22, 1963* (Washington, DC: U.S. Government Printing Office, 1964), pp. 460–462.

Source 15: Henry M. Pachter, *Collision Course: The Cuban Missile Crisis and Coexistence* (New York: Frederick A. Praeger, 1963), pp. 67–68.

Source 16: Robert H. Ferrell, *American Diplomacy: A History,* 3rd ed. (New York: W. W. Norton, 1969), pp. 837, 839–841. Copyright © 1959, 1969, 1975 by W. W. Norton & Company, Inc., renewed © 1987 by Robert H. Ferrell. Reprinted by the permission of W. W. Norton & Company, Inc.

Source 17: Graham T. Allison, *Essence of Decision: Explaining the Cuban Missile Crisis* (Boston: Little, Brown, 1971), p. 1.

Source 18: Richard J. Barnet, *Roots of War: The Men and Institutions behind U.S. Foreign Policy* (Baltimore: Penguin Books, 1972), p. 253.

Source 19: Howard Zinn, *Postwar America, 1945–1971* (Indianapolis: Bobbs-Merrill, 1973), pp. 73–75. Reprinted by permission of Howard Zinn.

Source 20: Herbert S. Dinerstein, *The Making of a Missile Crisis: October 1962* (Baltimore/London: The Johns Hopkins University Press, 1976), pp. 235–236. Reprinted by permission of the Johns Hopkins University Press.

Source 21: John G. Stoessinger, *Nations in Darkness: China, Russia, and America* (New York: Random House, 1986), p. 207.

Source 22: John A. Garraty, *The American Nation: A History of the United States,* vol. 2, 5th ed. (New York: HarperCollins, 1991), pp. 848–849. Copyright © 1966, 1971, 1975, 1979, 1983 by John A. Garraty. Illustrations, maps, captions, graphs, and related text copyright © 1966, 1971, 1975, 1978 by Harper & Row, Publishers Inc. Reprinted by permission of HarperCollins Publishers, Inc.

Source 23: Bernard Bailyn *et al., The Great Republic: A History of the American People,* vol. 2, 4th ed. (Lexington, MA: D. C. Heath, 1992), pp. 529–530. Copyright © 1992 by D. C. Heath & Company. Reprinted by permission of Houghton Mifflin Company.

Source 24: Ernest R. May and Philip D. Zelikow, *The Kennedy Tapes: Inside the White House during the Cuban Missile Crisis,* (Cambridge: The Belknap Press of Harvard University Press, 1997), p. 663.

Chapter 25: Vietnam

Source 1: Murrey Marder, "U.S. Destroyer Fights off 3 PT Boats in Attack off Coast of North Viet-Nam," *Washington Post,* August 3, 1964. Copyright © 1964 by the Washington Post Writers Group. Reprinted by permission.

Source 2: "President's New Report," *Evening Star* (Washington), August 5, 1964.

Source 3: "The Seventh Fleet Hits Back," *Evening Star,* August 5, 1964.

Source 4: Department of State Bulletin, August 24, 1964.

Source 5: Ibid.

Source 6: Department of State Bulletin, April 26, 1965.

Source 7: Arthur M. Schlesinger Jr., *The Bitter Heritage: Vietnam and American Democracy, 1941–1966* (Boston: Houghton Mifflin, 1966), pp.

46–49. Copyright © 1966 by Houghton Mifflin Company. Reprinted by permission of Houghton Mifflin Company. All rights reserved.

Source 8: John Galloway, *The Gulf of Tonkin Resolution* (Rutherford, NJ: Fairleigh Dickinson University Press, 1970), pp. 444–446, 456, 478–479, 481–482.

Source 9: *Transcript of Proceedings: The 35th Quadrennial Convention, Democratic National Convention,* August 28, 1968 (Washington, DC: Alderson Reporting Company, 1968), pp. 360–362, 364–365, 376–377, 380–381, 408. Reprinted by permission of Alderson Reporting Company, Inc.

Source 10: Galloway, pp. 161–162.

Source 11: *Report of the Department of Army Review of the Preliminary Investigations into the My Lai Incident,* vol. 1 (Washington, DC: U.S. Government Printing Office, March 14, 1970), pp. 2–1 through 2–4, 2–12 through 2–13.

Source 12: Ralph Stavins, Richard J. Barnet, and Marcus G. Raskin, *Washington Plans an Aggressive War* (New York: Vintage Books, 1971), pp. 124–126.

Source 13: Guenter Lewy, *America in Vietnam* (New York: Oxford University Press, 1978), pp. 438–439, 441. Copyright © 1978 by Guenter Lewy. Reprinted by permission of Oxford University Press, Inc.

Source 14: George C. Herring, *America's Longest War: The United States and Vietnam, 1950–1975* (New York: Alfred A. Knopf, 1986), pp. 279–280. Copyright © 1986 by Alfred A. Knopf. Reprinted by permission of McGraw-Hill.

Source 15: John G. Stoessinger, *Why Nations Go to War* (New York: St. Martin's Press, 1993), pp. 107–108. Copyright © 1993 by St. Martin's Press, Inc. Reprinted by permission of Bedford/St. Martin's Press, Inc.

Source 16: Robert S. McNamara, with Brian VanDeMark *In Retrospect: The Tragedy and Lessons of Vietnam* (New York: Times Books, 1995), p. 333. Copyright © 1995 by Robert S. McNamara. Reprinted by permission of Times Books, a division of Random House, Inc.

Chapter 26: The Moon Landing

Source 1: "185-lb. Sphere 560 Miles Up, Moscow Says," *Evening Star* (Washington), October 5, 1957.

Source 2: "Red Predicts Flight to Moon," *Evening Star,* October 5, 1957.

Source 3: " 'Moon' Over the World," *Evening Star,* October 6, 1957.

Source 4: "Sputnik in the Sky," *Aviation Week,* October 14, 1957.

Source 5: B. J. Cutler, "Soviet Launches a Half-Ton Satellite; Dog Aboard Reported Alive, Well," *Washington Post,* November 4, 1957.

Source 6: Nate Haseltine, "Vanguard Fails, Burns in Test Firing," *Washington Post,* December 7, 1957.

Source 7: Milton Bracker, "Army Launches U.S. Satellite into Orbit," *New York Times,* February 1, 1958. Copyright © 1958 by The New York Times Company.

Source 8: *Public Papers of the Presidents of the United States: John F. Kennedy, Containing the Public Messages, Speeches, and Statements of the President, January 20 to December 31, 1961* (Washington, DC: U.S. Government Printing Office, 1962), pp. 403–404.

Source 9: "Beautiful Sight," *Washington Post,* May 6, 1961.

Source 10: *Public Papers of John F. Kennedy,* p. 257.

Source 11: John G. Norris, "Glen Lands Safely after Three Orbits," *Washington Post,* February 21, 1962.

Source 12: William Hines, "3 Apollo Astronauts Killed by Flash Fire," *Evening Star,* January 28, 1967.

Source 13: "Apollo Astronauts on Way after Flawless Liftoff," *Boston Globe,* July 17, 1969.

Source 14: "Soviet Luna Remains a Mystery," *Boston Globe,* July 17, 1969.

Source 15: "U.S. Would Ask Soviets' Help Should Luna 15 Pose Threat," *Boston Globe,* July 18, 1969.

Source 16: Fred Farrar, "Apollo in Grasp of Moon," *Chicago Tribune,* July 19, 1969.

Source 17: Fred Farrar, "Go for Moon Drop Today," *Chicago Tribune,* July 20, 1969.

Source 18: "Voices in Space as an Eagle Lands," *Chicago Tribune,* July 21, 1969.

Source 19: "Apollo Fever Hits Japan; Half-Holidays Expected," *Japan Times* (Tokyo), July 21, 1969.

Source 20: "Voices in Space as an Eagle Lands," *Chicago Tribune,* July 21, 1969.

Source 21: *Boston Globe,* Extra Edition, July 21, 1969.

Source 22: "Wonder of the World," *The Times* (London), July 21, 1969. Copyright © Times Newspapers Limited, 1969.

Source 23: William L. Ryan, "Why Did Russia Lose to Americans in Race for Moon?" *Chicago Tribune,* July 21, 1969. Reprinted by permission of Associated Press.

Source 24: John M. Logsdon, *The Decision to Go to the Moon: Project Apollo and the National Interest* (Cambridge, MA: MIT Press, 1970), pp. 3, 181–182.

Source 25: Kathleen Teltsch, "Pact on Moon's Riches Approved," *New York Times,* July 4, 1979. Copyright © 1979 by The New York Times Company. Reprinted by permission of the new York Times.

Source 26: Charles Murray and Catherine Bly Cox, *Apollo: The Race to the Moon* (New York: Simon & Schuster, 1989), pp. 459–460.

Source 27: Robert A. Divine, *The Sputnik Challenge: Eisenhower's Response* (New York: Oxford University Press, 1993), pp. vii–viii. Copyright © 1993 by Robert A. Divine. Reprinted by permission of Oxford University Press, Inc.

Source 28: George Lardner, Jr., and Walter Pincus, "Military Had Plan to Blame Cuba if Glenn's Space Mission Failed," *Washington Post,* November 19, 1997, p. A2. Copyright © 1997 by The Washington Post. Reprinted by permission.

Chapter 27: Watergate

Source 1: *Washington Post,* June 18, 1972. Copyright © 1972 by The Washington Post. Reprinted by permission.

Source 2: *New York Times,* June 23, 1972.

Source 3: Richard Nixon's Presidential Statement, *New York* Times, May 23, 1973. Copyright © 1973 by The New York Times Company. Reprinted by permission of the New York Times.

Source 4: *Washington Post,* January 31, 1974.

Source 5: Sam J. Ervin Jr., *The Whole Truth: The Watergate Conspiracy* (New York: Random House, 1980), pp. 285–287. Copyright © 1980 by Sam J. Ervin Jr. Reprinted by permission of Random House, Inc.

Source 6: Henry Steele Commager, *The Defeat of America: Presidential Power and the National Character* (New York: Simon & Schuster, 1974), pp. 15–16, 159–161. Copyright © 1968, 1971, 1972, 1973, 1974 by Henry Steele Commager. Reprinted by permission of Simon & Schuster, Inc.

Source 7: Russell Baker, "It Didn't Work," *New York Times,* August 17, 1974. Copyright © 1974 by The New York Times Company. Reprinted by permission of the New York Times.

Source 8: John A. Garraty, *The American Nation: A History of the United States,* 5th ed. (New York: Harper & Row, 1975), pp. 875–876. Copyright © 1966, 1971, 1975, 1983 by John A. Garraty. Illustrations, maps, captions, graphs, and related text copyright © 1966, 1971, 1975, 1978 by Harper & Row Publishers, Inc. Reprinted by permission of HarperCollins Publishers, Inc.

Source 9: Michael Parenti, *Democracy for the Few* (New York: St. Martin's Press, 1980), pp. 157–158. Copyright © 1980 by St. Martin's Press, Inc. Reprinted by permission of Bedford/St.Martin's Press, Inc.

Source 10: Stanley I. Kutler, *The Wars of Watergate: The Last Crisis of Richard Nixon* (New York: Alfred A. Knopf, 1990), p. 610.

Source 11: Bernard Bailyn, Robert Dallek, David Brion Davis, David Herbert Donald, John L. Thomas, and Gordon S. Wood, *The Great Republic: A History of the American People,* 4th ed. (Lexington: MA: D. C. Heath, 1992), pp. 588, 590–591. Copyright © 1992 by D. C. Heath & Company. Reprinted by permission of Houghton Mifflin Company.

Chapter 28: The Exxon Valdez

Source 1: Edward Wenk, Jr., *Tradeoffs: Imperatives of Choice in a High-Tech World.* (Baltimore: Johns Hopkins University Press, 1986), pp. 6–8. Reprinted by permission of Johns Hopkins University Press.

Source 2: Maura Dolan and Ronald Taylor, "Alaska Oil Spill May Be Largest in U.S. Waters: *Los Angeles Times,* March 25, 1989, pp. 1, 15. Reprinted by permission of the Los Angeles Times.

Source 3: Tamara Jones and Michael Parrish, "Oil Spill Cleanup Effort in Alaska Drawing Fire," *Los Angeles Times*, March 26, 1989, pp. 1, 12. Reprinted by permission of the Los Angeles Times.

Source 4: Richard Mauer, "Unlicensed Mate Was in Charge of Ship That Hit Reef, Exxon Says," *New York Times*, March 27, 1989. Copyright © 1989 by the New York Times Company. Reprinted by permission of the New York Times.

Source 5: Timothy Egan, "High Winds Hamper Oil Spill Cleanup Off Alaska," *New York Times,* March 28, 1989.

Source 6: James Bone, "Environmentalists Launch Attack," *The Times* of London, March 29, 1989, p. 8. Copyright © 1989 by the Times Newspapers Limited. Reprinted by permission.

Source 7: Timothy Egan, "Fishermen and State Take Charge of Efforts to Control Alaska Spill," *New York Times,* March 29, 1989. Copyright © 1989 by the New York Times Company. Reprinted by permission of the New York Times.

Source 8: Timothy Egan, "Exxon Concedes It Can't Contain Most of Oil Spill," *New York Times,* March 30, 1989.

Source 9: "Oil on the Water, Oil in the Ground," *New York Times,* March 30, 1989. Copyright © 1989 by the New York Times Company. Reprinted by permission of the New York Times.

Source 10: Philip Shabecoff, "Captain of Tanker Had Been Drinking, Blood Tests Show," *New York Times,* March 31, 1989. Copyright © 1989 by the New York Times Company. Reprinted by permission of the New York Times.

Source 11: "Officials Make Report," *New York Times,* March 31, 1989, A12.

Source 12: Keith Schneider, "Under Oil's Powerful Spell, Alaska Was Off Guard," *New York Times,* April 2, 1989. Copyright © by the New York Times Company. Reprinted by permission of the New York Times.

Source 13: Ken Wells and Charles McCoy, "Out of Control: How Unpreparedness Turned the Alaska Spill into Ecological Debacle," *Wall Street Journal,* April 3, 1989, p. 1. Reprinted by permission.

Source 14: Malcolm W. Browne, "Radar Could Have Tracked Tanker," *New York Times,* April 5, 1989. Copyright © 1989 by the New York Times Company. Reprinted by permission of the New York Times.

Source 15: Philip Shabecoff, "U.S. Said to Censor Memo on Oil Risks," *New York Times,* April 6, 1989.

Source 16: United States, House of Representatives, "*Exxon Valdez* Oil Spill," Hearing before the Subcommittee on Coast Guard and Navigation of the Committee on Merchant Marine and Fisheries, Serial No. 101–9 (Washington, D.C.: U.S. Government Printing Office, 1989), pp. 1–3, 6–7, 14, 19–23, 30–31, 37–38.

Source 17: Art Davidson, *In the Wake of the Exxon Valdez: The Devastating Impact of the Alaska Oil Spill* (San Francisco: Sierra Club Books, 1990), pp. 295–297. Copyright © 1990 by Art Davidson. Reprinted by permission of the New York Times.

Source 18: John Keeble, *Out of the Channel: The Exxon Valdez Oil Spill in Prince William Sound* (New York: HarperCollins, 1991) p. 262. Copyright © 1991, 1999 by John Keeble. Reprinted by permission.

Source 19: Edward Tenner, *Why Things Bite Back: Technology and the Revenge of Unintended Consequences* (New York: Alfred A. Knopf, 1996), pp. 5–7, 88–92. Copyright © 1996 by Edward Tenner. Reprinted by permission of Alfred A. Knopf.

Source 20: William Booth, "Spill's Residue Still Sticks in Alaska's Craw," *Washington Post,* March

23, 1999, A3. Copyright © 1999 by the Washington Post. Reprinted by permission.

Chapter 29 Impeachment

Source 1: "Lewinsky's Affidavit in Jones Lawsuit," The *New York Times* on the Web, http://www.nytimes.com/library/politics/031498clinton-lewinsky-text.html. Copyright © 1998 by the New York Times Company. Reprinted by permission of the New York Times.

Source 2: The Starr Report: The Official Report of the Independent Counsel's Investigation of the President (Rocklin, California: Prima Publishing, 1998), pp. 314–316; "Excerpts from a Deposition Given By Clinton in January," The *New York Times* on the Web, http://www.nytimes.com/library/politics/072998clinton-testimony.html/

Source 3: Susan Schmidt, Peter Baker, and Toni Locy, "Clinton Accused of Urging Aide to Lie," *Washington Post,* January 21, 1998. Copyright © 1998 by the Washington Post. Reprinted by permission.

Source 4: The Starr Report: The Official Report of the Independent Counsel's Investigation of the President (Rocklin, Ca: Prima Publishing, 1998), pp. 209, 309.

Source 5: Roger Simon, "Clinton Vehemently Denies the Charges," *Chicago Tribune,* January 27, 1998. Copyright © 1998 by the Chicago Tribune Company. Reprinted by permission of the Chicago Tribune.

Source 6: "Text of Clinton's Address to the Nation," *New York Times* on the Web, http://www.nytimes.com/library/politics/081898clinton-text.html. Copyright © 1999 by the New York Times Company. Reprinted by permission of the New York Times.

Source 7: The Starr Report: The Official Report of the Independent Counsel's Investigation of the President, pp. 35–36, 41–44, 327, 442, 327Z–330, 332.

Source 8: "A Sampling of Viewpoints from Nation's Newspapers," *New York Times* on the Web, http://www.nytimes.com/library/politics/091498clinton-editorial.html

Source 9: Ibid.

Source 10: "Go, You Despicable Man, Go, and Be Gone," *Washington Times,* September 13, 1998. Copyright © 1998 by News World Communications, Inc. Reprinted by permission.

Source 11: "Low Crimes and Misdemeanors," *Washington Post,* September 13, 1998. Copyright © 1998 by the Washington Post. Reprinted by permission.

Source 12: "Starr's Report: Clinton's Rebuttal," *Chicago Tribune,* September 13, 1998.

Source 13: Peter Baker and Juliet Eilferin, "Clinton Impeached," *Washington Post,* December 20, 1998. Copyright © 1998 by the Washington Post. Reprinted by permission.

Source 14: Alison Mitchell, "Clinton Acquitted Decisively, No Majority for Either Charge," *New York Times,* February 13, 1999. Copyright © 1999 by the New York Times Company. Reprinted by permission of the New York Times.

Source 15: "Clinton Statement," *New York Times,* February 13, 1999. Copyright © 1999 by the New York Times Company. Reprinted by permission of the New York Times.

Source 16: "Congratulations, Mr. President," *Washington Times,* February 13, 1999.

Source 17: "Constitutional Justice," *New York Times,* February 13, 1999. Copyright © 1999 by the New York Times Company. Reprinted by permission of the New York Times.

Source 18: Henry Hyde, "An Issue of Principles, Not Politics," *Chicago Tribune,* February 18, 1999. Reprinted by permission of Henry J. Hyde.

Source 19: Jonathan Schell, "Coming to Judgment," *The Nation,* March 1, 1999, vol. 268, no. 8, p. 8. Reprinted by permission of The Nation.

Source 20: Lisa Jardine, "Object of Oppression," *New Statesman,* April 2, 1999, p. 46. Copyright © 1999 by New Statesman. Reprinted by permission.

Source 21: Michael G. Gartner, "How the Monica Story Played in Mid-America," *Columbia Journalism Review,* May 1999, vol. 38, Issue 1, p. 34. Copyright © 1999 by Columbia Journalism Review. Reprinted by permission.

Source 22: Joanne Barkan, "Democratic Questions," *Dissent,* vol. 46, no. 2, Spring 1999, pp. 10–11. Copyright © 1999 by Dissent. Reprinted by permission of Dissent.

Source 23: Richard John Neuhaus, "Bill Clinton and the American Character," *First Things: A Monthly Journal of Religion and Public Life,* June 1999, p. 63. Reprinted by permission. *First Things* is a monthly journal published in New York City by the Institute on Religion and Public Life.

Source 24: Roberto Suro, "Clinton Is Sanctioned in Jones Lawsuit," *Washington Post,* July 30, 1999.